D1062032

The Church of Ireland
Ecclesiastical Reform and Revolution, 1800–1885

The Church of Ireland

Ecclesiastical Reform and Revolution, 1800–1885

by Donald Harman Akenson

New Haven and London : Yale University Press

1971

Designed by John O. C. McCrillis
and set in Times Roman type.
Printed in the United States of America by
The Colonial Press Inc., Clinton, Massachusetts.

Distributed in Great Britain, Europe, and Africa by
Yale University Press, Ltd., London; in Canada by
McGill-Queen's University Press, Montreal; in Mexico
by Centro Interamericano de Libros Académicos,
Mexico City; in Central and South America by Kaiman
& Polon, Inc., New York City; in Australasia by
Australia and New Zealand Book Co., Pty., Ltd.,
Artarmon, New South Wales; in India by UBS Publishers'
Distributors Pvt., Ltd., Delhi; in Japan by John
Weatherhill, Inc., Tokyo.

In memory of
MAUDE KENYON HARMAN
and
EDWARD WILLIAM HARMAN

Contents

Preface

I fully realize that to begin a preface with a warning to the reader, and in the first person at that, breaks at least two rules of scholarly writing, but fair warning is due: although this book is the story of a religious organization during a portion of its history, the book has everything to do with men and nothing to do with God. This is not to draw a simplistic (and false) philosophic distinction between thought and action. The distinction is practical, not philosophic. In a study of this length covering a long period of time one must focus on a relatively narrow band of events if one is to be rigorous and analytic. To give equal attention to the theological development of the Church of Ireland and to its organizational development in a book this length would be to treat each inadequately. Instead of investigating what Irish churchmen preached and wrote on theology, I have studied how they acted in church affairs. This means, for example, that when the evangelicals are mentioned, it is neither their origin nor their salvationist mien which bears notice, but the extent to which they affected the efficient operation of the Church of Ireland as an institution.

Similarly, I have not given much emphasis to canon law. This may at first seem surprising, but in the Church of Ireland the canon law was parallel to the church's moral theology: an idealized expression of how people should act, not a description of how they did act. Despite the elaborate set of canons prescribing clerical behavior and the baroque intricacies of the ecclesiastical court system, clerical behavior was a function primarily of customary law. In other words, clerical behavior was determined more by social usage than by ecclesiastical statutes. (The residency crisis of the late eighteenth and early nineteenth centuries conclusively demonstrates this point.) Further, although canon law may have been of some use to the church in dealing with odd cases of liturgical eccentricity or theological deviance, it was of little import during the major reforms of the nineteenth century when the entire church structure was being reshaped.

Another warning: except as the activities of individual men were typical of the activities of a larger group of persons, or influential upon the destiny of the entire church, I have not described individual activities in detail. The focus of this book is the Church of Ireland as an organization. Because the patterns of an organization transcend the activities of any one individual, the church is approached as a social system, and the approach adopted (though, I hope, not the syntax) is that of the social sciences. Inevitably this means that numbers are employed a good deal and that statistics are often used as adjectives and adverbs. By using numbers whenever appropriate I have hoped to avoid one of the characteristics that flaws so much religious historiography, namely, the tendency to make impressionistic overgeneralizations based on small samples of religious behavior. Whenever possible, the entire range of behavior or structures in the Church of Ireland is surveyed, because only by performing the tedious task of tallying activities and arrangements parish by parish, and clergyman by clergyman, can one simultaneously arrive at justifiable generalizations and at an appreciation of the range of divergence within the church.

Throughout the years here under study the activities of the Church of Ireland intersected the Irish political and social system at many points, but in describing such interconnections I have focused only on the effects the political and social determinants had upon the organization and activities of the church. The reasons that reform demands emanated from the larger society are important to the social and political historian who must account for their origin, but for our purposes it is sufficient to analyze in detail the results of these demands. It is assumed that the reader is familiar with the general outlines of English and of Irish history and that he does not need to be told who Joseph Hume was or what Catholic emancipation meant.

Although comparisons are made between the Church of Ireland and the Church of England, no comparisons are made to other churches. There are no others sufficiently similar to the Irish church to allow legitimate comparisons, and if one begins comparing the Church of Ireland to, say, the Roman Catholic Church in France, one will soon be coursing hares throughout Christendom. The Church of Ireland has an organizational integrity and historical legitimacy of its own, and no apologies are needed for giving it nearly all of our attention. This study, then, is the biography of an Irish organization.

The decision to focus on the organizational history of the church implies a point worth underscoring; namely, that in this study I have assumed that the primary purpose of the Church of Ireland was a religious purpose, to wit, the delivery of pastoral services to the Irish Anglican community. Admittedly, the church had numerous peripheral functions, but to emphasize the church's political or social role at the expense of the religious would be to replace the central with the peripheral as the focus of our attention. Given the assumption that the purpose of the church was to deliver pastoral services to the Anglican constituency, the criterion for judging whether or not a given practice or activity was functional or dysfunctional to the organization is whether the practice implemented or impeded the delivery of these pastoral services.

I have described the Church of Ireland in the first chapter as if the reader were totally unfamiliar with it; this is not an intentional insult to those already acquainted with the Church of Ireland and its history. Also, readers acquainted with the elaborate nomenclature of ecclesiastical titles will note that I have usually contented myself with "the Reverend" or simply a full name in referring to men of the cloth, and have not become enmeshed in elaborate distinctions between "venerable," "very Reverend," "most Reverend," and so on. No disrespect is intended.

Religion being the most contentious topic a historian of Ireland can deal with, I must emphasize that no theological judgments are implied in my use of certain words. "Catholic" is used as a synonym for "Roman Catholic." By so doing, I do not mean to indicate any denial of the Church of Ireland's connection with the Holy Catholic Church. Similarly, I use the word "priest" as a synonym for minister or clergyman. This is an operational word and carries no theological overtones. For convenience, the word "Anglican" is employed throughout this study, even though the word was not in common use by contemporaries during part of the period under study.

The following persons in Ireland, England, and America were of assistance in a variety of ways: Professors J. C. Beckett, John V. Kelleher, Standish Meacham, T. W. Moody, Frederick Pottle; The Very Reverend T. N. D. C. Salmon; Mr. Nicholas Wheeler Robinson. Professor Emmet Larkin read an earlier version of this study; I am very grateful for his sharp and always constructive criticism.

The librarians and staffs of the following institutions were helpful and hospitable: the British Museum; the County Record Office, Stafford; the Dublin City Library; the National Library of Ireland; the Public Record Office of Northern Ireland; the Public Record Office of the Republic of Ireland; Queen's University, Belfast; Trinity College, Dublin; Sterling Library, Yale University; and Widener Library, Harvard University.

I wish especially to thank the librarians and keepers of the library of the Representative Church Body, Dublin, and of the Armagh Public Library, for their extraordinary patience and graciousness in guiding me through the extensive material in their collections.

I am indebted for research assistance and clerical aid to my secretary, Nancy Di Benedetto, and for assistance and cogent criticism to my wife, Mary E. R. Akenson.

D. H. A.

Davenport College
Yale University
May 1970

1 The Eighteenth-Century Church as an Administrative System

INTRODUCTION

The problem which immediately greets anyone interested in religious history is to find words to describe the subject about which he is writing. The word "church" obscures more than it describes, for it has several meanings and bears highly emotional connotations. The church as a Christian theological concept is a useful, if controversial, word describing a body founded by Christ and receiving inspiration from him and the Holy Ghost. As such it is not simply a voluntary assemblage of individuals, but a group with a corporate spirit transcending the character of its individual members. Theologians have battled about whether this church is an invisible body to which all Christians are joined by their acts of faith, or whether it is a visible body with publicly defined orders and levels of membership. Useful as these theological discussions of the nature of the church may be for devotional purposes, they are of no value for the present study.

Most emphatically, "church" as used herein is not a theological, but an organizational term. It is used to describe a system of human relationships. Specifically we are dealing with a set of relationships existing in Ireland during the eighteenth and nineteenth centuries. The sum of these relationships is the Anglican Church in Ireland, or alternatively the Church of Ireland.[1] Equally important, in this study the human relationships covered by the rubric "church" will be treated as in no way unique. Whatever the reality behind the church's religious beliefs, as an organization it differs in form, but not in substance, from the organizations of the secular world. Admittedly, the system of relationships in a large religious institution is apt to be more complex than those in most business firms and government agencies (if for no other reason than that the persons in religious bodies are usually more complex), but the fact remains that the church as an organization is amenable to the same method of structural analysis that is used to investigate secular organizations.

Now, if we are analyzing the church in the same way administrative scientists approach secular bodies, then we must define membership in the church in the same way that membership in a secular body is defined, namely operationally. For our purposes anyone who was generally accepted as a member of the Church of Ireland by his co-religionists is regarded as being a full member. Participation, not salvation, is the proof of membership.

In analyzing the structure of the Anglican Church in Ireland it is most useful if we treat it as an administrative system. Having decided this, however,

1

there is no reason to seize immediately upon one of the theoretical models of administrative systems developed by social scientists and to apply the model, as if by force, to the history of the Anglican Church in Ireland. Such uncritical social scientism would be folly, for there is no theoretical model which even comes close to approximating the complicated realities of the church in the eighteenth and nineteenth centuries. We will, therefore, use concepts from the major schools of administrative theory which will help illuminate Irish church history, but at no time will we attempt to force the data into theoretical schemata.

One approach to social organizations whose tenets are often useful when applied to the church is that of classical bureaucratic theory. The "ideal type" of classical bureaucratic theory portrays a network of a large number of participants who are rationally related to each other by function. Each individual in such a network performs a highly specialized task. This specialization creates a need for a system of coordination. Therefore, a hierarchy of authority develops to direct these specialized activities. In an ideal bureaucracy a system of rules is framed to insure similar behavior from those holding similar jobs. Both the hierarchy of authority and the system of rules dictate that the bureaucracy will be relatively impersonal and that relationships between participants will depend more upon their function in the organization than upon their personalities.[2] Obviously the key concepts from classical bureaucratic theory—specialization, hierarchy of authority, a system of rules, and impersonality—cannot be indiscriminately applied to the eighteenth-century church. Specialization in the church was only partial (all priests performed essentially the same job) and relationships between members were more apt to be personal than impersonal. We will, however, wish to pay considerable attention to the system of hierarchy to which bureaucratic theory calls our attention, for in theory the church consisted of one vast chain of command, from the Almighty to the monarch to the archbishops to the suffragan bishops to the cathedral and parish clergy to the laity. Theoretically, a rigid code of behavior bound the life of those in the church, especially the professional religious.

If bureaucratic theory implies a highly formal organizational structure, empirical researchers have found that "informal systems" often arise. Whatever the rules governing human relations that an organization may attempt to enforce, human beings find ways to circumvent them. Individuals in an organization form social groups which in turn give rise to norms for behavior that have little in common with the printed rule established by the groups' overseers. Power in large organizations is supposed to follow the lines of hierarchy drawn on the formal organization chart, but actual power is often distributed on an entirely different pattern. For example, despite the formal lines of power, a low level employee who has close friends or relatives in the upper echelons often is almost totally free from the control of the man who is intended to be his immediate superior. The idea of an informal system existing within a formal system of organization is especially useful when dealing with the eighteenth-century Anglican Church. In that church, matters such as family connections, place of education, and political affiliations created informal subsystems which were often stronger than the formal organizational shell of the church.[3]

Recent attempts to provide a unified approach to human behavior in organizations have focused on the need to redefine concepts of how individual behavior in the institution is determined. Authority, these attempts note, is but one of several forms of social influence. Persuasion, consultation, and discussion are employed more often than naked authority. An individual responds perfectly to the imposition of authority only when he is completely dependent for his position upon the person in charge. As a person becomes less dependent, the imposition of authority becomes less sure.[4] The idea that dependency relationships are crucial to understanding the relationship of any individual to his superior, and to the organization of which he is a member, is clearly applicable to Irish church history. For instance, we will find that in the eighteenth century the relative independence of well-born and relatively wealthy vicars allowed them to do almost whatever they pleased about residing or not residing in their parishes, with little fear of the bishop's invoking sanctions against them. Strikingly, after disestablishment when the dependency relationship shifted radically, making the clergy dependent on their congregations for financial support, the clergy were universally in residence. The change came not from an invoking of authority, but from a change in the dependency relationship.

THE MINIMUM HISTORICAL BACKGROUND

The Church of Ireland traces its origin to the fifth century, to Saint Patrick and beyond.[5] Saint Patrick's mission and its successors were triumphant, producing a Christian nation and blotting out all but the most indistinct traces of the pagan antecedents. For a time, before the Viking invasions of the eighth and ninth centuries, the Irish church was among the most vigorous and the most sophisticated in Christendom. Although originally patterned on the continental model, the Celtic one soon became organizationally eccentric. Instead of being organized on traditional diocesan lines, the Celtic church system was a network of monastic houses. Irish bishops did indeed exist but they were usually of much less consequence than the abbots. This curious system was reformed in the twelfth century and replaced by a diocesan system of organization. The first major reform was taken in 1110 at the Synod of Rathbreasil (County Tipperary) in which the outlines of twenty-four dioceses, plus the archepiscopal See of Armagh, were firmly drawn. The number of dioceses changed during the subsequent centuries, but the basic diocesan nature of the church became permanent.

Reform efforts continued, most notably under the generalship of Malachy, Archbishop of Armagh. His efforts had the posthumous result of stimulating the Pope to send a legate to Ireland in 1152 to complete the reforms. The legate consecrated four archbishops, namely, Armagh, Cashel, Dublin, and Tuam—ranks which were to be preserved unchanged in the Church of Ireland until the nineteenth century. The Church of Ireland, therefore, assumed and preserved as its most basic characteristic as an organization a hierarchical diocesan structure similar to that prevailing throughout the western Catholic church.

The Reformation of the sixteenth century fixed certain other features of the church's organization. One of these was that the church became a national state church. Although the Reformation in Ireland had nowhere near the level of popular support it commanded in England, it was inevitable that if England broke away from Rome, so too would Ireland. Impelling and obvious reasons of statecraft dictated that the King of England, who was also King of Ireland, could not officially countenance such a deep religious division in his realm. Admittedly, the English monarch had exercised a great deal of influence on appointments and activities of the pre-Reformation church. The break with Rome was nevertheless crucial, for it now precluded interference in religious affairs of the Church of Ireland by papal emissaries, and the control over the church which pre-Reformation monarchs had exercised in practice was now confirmed both in law and theology.

Simultaneously with the legal ratification and theological sanctification of the monarch as head of the Church of Ireland, there occurred a subtle shift in the church's position vis-à-vis the civil state. The church now became not only an established church, but an established national church. The Church of Ireland was no longer the Irish branch of the western Christian church but the state church of Ireland, owing temporal and spiritual allegiance to the king and to no one outside his realm.

The position of the Church of Ireland as the established national church provided security and prominence denied voluntary religious groups. Monarchs and politicians, however, realized that money and perquisites are mediums of exchange, and in return for its favored position the Church of Ireland accepted a role as a department of the state. Although it survived intact the religious wars of the seventeenth century, the Church of Ireland hailed the reign of William and Mary in tattered and breathless condition. The church was in no position to resist government pressures even had its leaders been so inclined. The eighteenth-century Anglican Church in Ireland, therefore, was a supinely Erastian body. Its chief offices were appointed by politicians, advancement depended upon political patronage, and the policies of the church were in every way manipulated to serve the ends of the state.

An obvious implication of the break with Rome was that the Church of Ireland in some sense became Protestant. One must say "in some sense" because the Reformation in Ireland (as in England) was at first chiefly a change in administrative arrangements at the top echelons. In Ireland there was at first very little of the extreme Protestant emphasis upon the Scripture as the sole source of religious authority, and little inclination to deny the validity of the church as an institution with its hierarchy, priests' orders, and rules of discipline.[6] Only in the seventeenth century, with the influx of pre-ponderantly Puritan influences, did the church become manifestly Protes-tant. This influence was chiefly an inpouring of Calvinist clergy to the Church of Ireland. Yet, however Protestant the church became, it clung to the hierarchical pattern inherited from the ancient church, rather than emu-lating the congregational structure of the Dissenting denominations.

Because the great majority of the Irish people remained devotedly Roman Catholic, only a minority were affiliated with the Church of Ireland. Three further conditions, moreover, guaranteed that the bulk of the population would not be merely unaffiliated, but bitterly alienated from the church. The first of these was that the church was not only a tool of the state, but a tool of the English state. England ruled Ireland during the eighteenth cen-tury with the same imperious disregard for the indigenous population as it later evinced in the crown colonies. The worst sort of English political hacks were foisted upon Ireland, and the church received more than its share of sycophants and place-hunters from beyond the sea. Second, the Church of Ireland was maintained in the eighteenth century not only by its positive assertion of rights as the state church, but through legislative attempts to destroy all other forms of religion. Admittedly, the penal laws against the Roman Catholic faith never were enforced fully, but the fact remains that the Anglican Church in Ireland was associated with an attempt by a religious minority to hobble the religious expression and destroy the economic posi-tion of the majority of Ireland's people. Third, the Church of Ireland was identified with the Irish landlord class. The Irish landlord was notoriously less conscientious than his English counterpart and, whether resident in Ireland or not, was well known for mulcting the tenantry for every possible farthing. The all-too-visible partnership of landlord and bishop, and of estate agent and vicar, made the church an accessory to the economic op-pression of the peasantry. The fact that most of the landed property which had been in Catholic hands in the early seventeenth century was, by the mid-eighteenth century, in Anglican hands (either through transfer of land from Catholics to Anglicans or through Catholic landowners conforming under pressure to the Established Church) greatly reinforced the Catholics' bitterness.

Finally, we should note that in comparison to its insecurity in the seven-teenth century, the church was a stable, secure institution. During the eighteenth century no major changes in the church's organization, theology, or constituency took place. Thus, the Church of Ireland in the mid-

eighteenth century was distinguished by these chief features: It was a hierarchical organization divided into diocesan units. The church was established
by law and was a national church completely subservient to the state. The
church was Protestant and, though a national church, was not the native one,
for the bulk of the population was Roman Catholic. As an organization,
the church in the mid-eighteenth century was stable and predictable. Upon
closer inspection we will find that this structure veiled an admixture of inefficiency and confusion.

A FORMAL ORGANIZATIONAL OUTLINE

Throughout the eighteenth century the diocesan structure of the Church
of Ireland remained constant at four archbishops and eighteen suffragan
bishops.[7] (See the accompanying map.) From 1752 to 1800 the diocesan
structure was arranged as indicated in table 1.[8]

We now turn from the largest unit of ecclesiastical administration, the
diocese, to the smallest, the parish. Each diocese was divided into parish
units over which the bishop of the diocese had administrative jurisdiction.[9]
The boundaries of the Church of Ireland parishes had remained remarkably
stable for centuries, and the parishes of the eighteenth century corresponded
closely to the medieval parishes.[10] In 1787 the Reverend Daniel Augustus
Beaufuort[11] compiled a survey of the parochial structure of Ireland which
he published in 1792 under the title *Memoir of a Map of Ireland*. This was
the first thorough survey of Irish ecclesiastical conditions. From Beaufort's
information we can establish the outlines of the parish structure shown in
table 2.

What intermediate links were there which coordinated activities on the
diocesan and the parish levels? There were none. In England archdeacons
served as an intermediate rank between the bishop of a diocese and his
clergy. Their duties were usually a general disciplinary supervision over the
clergy, and often with special authority for the care of ecclesiastical property. In eighteenth-century Ireland, although there were thirty-four arch-
deaconries, the holders of these offices did not have a visitorial jurisdiction
over the clergy in their respective dioceses. In the nineteenth century the
office was to become a functional one, but during the eighteenth most archdeacons were merely accessories to cathedral chapters, and in some instances did not even have a stall in the chapter.

A second way in which the gap between the diocesan and the parish authorities could have been bridged was through the employment of rural
deans; that is, beneficed clergymen of the diocese who served as a channel
of communication between the bishop and the parish clergy. Normally the
diocese would be broken into several rural deaneries, each served by a
rural dean chosen from the clergy of the deanery. The office in Ireland, however, had almost completely died out, and it was not until the end of the

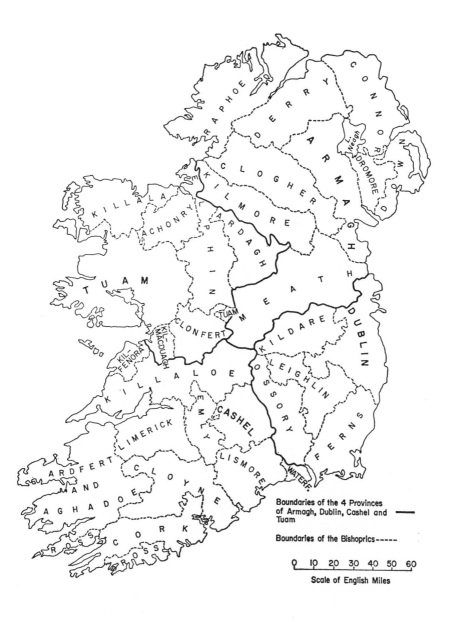

Boundaries of the 4 Provinces of Armagh, Dublin, Cashel and Tuam ———

Boundaries of the Bishoprics - - - - -

0 10 20 30 40 50 60
Scale of English Miles

The provinces and dioceses of Ireland. This map is based on a reduced version of Daniel A. Beaufort's *Memoir of a Map of Ireland*, as found in Richard Mant, *History of the Church of Ireland*, 2:xxix.

TABLE 1
IRISH DIOCESAN ORGANIZATION

Province of Armagh

Metropolitan: Archbishop of Armagh
Dioceses: Armagh (archdiocese)
                 Clogher
                 Derry
                 Down & Connor
                 Dromore
                 Kilmore
                 Meath
                 Raphoe

Province of Dublin

Metropolitan: Archbishop of Dublin
Dioceses: Dublin (archdiocese)
                 Kildare
                 Ferns & Leighlin
                 Ossory

Province of Cashel

Metropolitan: Archbishop of Cashel
Dioceses: Cashel (archdiocese) & Emly
                 Cloyne
                 Cork & Ross
                 Killaloe & Kilfenora
                 Limerick, Ardfert & Aghadoe
                 Waterford & Lismore

Province of Tuam

Metropolitan: Archbishop of Tuam
Dioceses: Tuam (archdiocese) & Ardagh
                 Clonfert & Kilmacduagh
                 Elphin
                 Killala & Achonry

eighteenth century that a significant attempt was made to revive it. The absence of rural deaneries and the failure of the archdeaconries as intermediate offices meant there was no direct channel of communication between the diocesan and his clergy; and no general method of supervising the clergy except through the ordinary's annual visitation.

But, it might be argued, the cathedral chapters served as intermediaries between the bishops and the parish clergy. At first examination this suggestion is plausible because the cathedral chapters comprised clerics intermediate in prestige and stature between the bishops and the average

TABLE 2
LATE EIGHTEENTH-CENTURY PARISH STRUCTURE

Diocese	Parishes	Parishes in united diocese
Province of Armagh		
Armagh	103	
Clogher	41	
Derry	48	
Down	38 ⎱	114
Connor	76 ⎰	
Dromore	26	
Kilmore	39	
Meath	224	
Raphoe	31	
Provincial total	626	
Province of Dublin		
Dublin	209	
Kildare	81	
Ferns	143 ⎱	232
Leighlin	89 ⎰	
Ossory	136	
Provincial total	658	
Province of Cashel		
Cashel	97 ⎱	155
Emly	58 ⎰	
Cloyne	137	
Cork	94 ⎱	127
Ross	33 ⎰	
Killaloe	119 ⎱	138
Kilfenora	19 ⎰	
Limerick	88 ⎱	176
Ardfert & Aghadoe	88 ⎰	
Waterford	33 ⎱	106
Lismore	73 ⎰	
Provincial total	839	
Province of Tuam		
Tuam	89	
Ardagh	37	
Clonfert	40 ⎱	60
Kilmacduagh	20 ⎰	
Elphin	75	
Killala	25 ⎱	52
Achonry	27 ⎰	
Provincial total	313	
National total	2436	

Note: A large number of the parishes were held in union with other parishes by a single incumbent. Nevertheless, the parish remained the basic administrative unit and in the case of unions the identity of the individual parishes composing the union was maintained.

Source: Beaufort, pp. 107–37.

clergymen. The cathedral chapters will be discussed in greater detail later, but suffice it to say that they normally consisted of a dean, precentor, chancellor, treasurer, and a number of prebendaries and canons. The incomes of several parishes often went to support each of these officeholders. The income of the dignities was often large, and the offices were consequently much in demand. However, to conclude from these facts that the cathedral officers served as intermediate links is to confuse status with function. Cathedral officers were intermediate in status between ordinary clergymen and the hierarchy, but they had no responsibility for liaison between the two levels. Moreover, the cathedral chapter did not exercise supervisory jurisdiction over anyone outside its own body, a fact which precluded the cathedral from exercising general supervisory power over the lower clergy.

Viewing the formal outlines of the Church of Ireland as a whole, therefore, we are led to conclude that it possessed a well-defined and clearly articulated structure on the diocese and the parish levels, but to suspect that communication between the two levels was sporadic and their relations a potential source of argument and inefficiency.

THE UPPER ECHELON

Becoming a Bishop

In order to understand the manner in which the highest echelons of the church were filled it is helpful to remember that the Anglican Church as an organization was an "open" system; that is, a system constantly open to external influences. At no point was the openness to outside influence more obvious than in the appointment of bishops. In the following pages it will become clear that the appointment of Irish bishops was a function of eighteenth-century factional politics. Having described this phenomenon, one next has to make an interpretative judgment. There are two major alternatives. One can simply note that patronage and factionalism was the way in which eighteenth-century Irish politics operated and stop there. This interpretation has a fashionable Namieresque ring, but is of little aid in understanding the Church of Ireland. Instead of interpreting the appointment process in this manner we will invoke the criterion of organizational efficiency. It is assumed that the primary purpose of a religious organization is to deliver pastoral services to its constituency. Whether or not a given practice is functional or dysfunctional to the organization will be judged by whether it furthers or impedes the delivery of these pastoral services.

In examining the episcopal appointment process, one should first recall the church-state relationship which impinged on the selection process. In Anglican civil and ecclesiastical theory there was no clear line between the civil order and the ecclesiastical order. The church and state were, respectively, spiritual and temporal aspects of the same commonwealth. In order to avoid secularizing the church, Anglican theologians had, therefore, to sanctify the head of the religio-politico commonwealth, the king: the king of England and of Ireland was head of the Churches of England and of Ireland. (The title "head of the Church" was used only by Henry VIII and Edward VI, not by subsequent monarchs; but this technical fact did not impinge upon the basic theology of the church.) The monarch, either personally or at the behest of his chief ministers, had considerable influence over the church. He could investigate any aspect of the ecclesiastical establishment through a royal visitation by commissioners appointed by the Crown. Crown influence, however, was exercised chiefly through the Crown's possession of the sole right of nomination (meaning right of appointment) to vacant bishoprics, to most deaneries, to certain prebends and to a number of parish livings. Actually, the monarch himself did not dabble often in Irish ecclesiastical affairs and the appointments under royal jurisdiction were made by the Lord Lieutenant of Ireland in consultation with his English political colleagues. In the case of appointment below the episcopal level, the archbishop or bishop of the diocese involved could refuse to ordain a royal nominee, but such instances were extremely rare. Because the Irish government during most of the eighteenth century was politically subservient to the English government, this in term meant that the Irish church was subservient to the wishes of English politicians and that appointments and activities of the church were manipulated to serve English purposes.[12]

English politicians used the church for a number of purposes. Irish church offices became part of the English patronage network and were used as payment for English political and social debts. For much of the eighteenth century the Irish church establishment was charged, as was the English church, with the duty of keeping the Whigs in office. More important, in Ireland the politicians expected the church to bulwark the position of the Protestant ascendancy, and in particular the position of the Protestant landlord class. In fulfilling this latter role the church was of course expected to help maintain civil order, even to the extent of liturgically memorializing the authorities' seventeenth-century victory over a band of Irish rebels! [13]

In fairness to the church it should be emphasized that its position vis-à-vis the state was only partially one of subservience. It was also one of alliance. The following statement was made about the eighteenth-century English church but it holds true for Ireland as well:

"The ancient partnership of Church and State secured advantages to each: the State got the influence of religion in support of Government and was on the whole freed from clerical hostility; the Church, in return for an Erastian surrender of independence, received a public endowment for the clergy, a significant voice in the House of Lords, coercive authority for its courts, and finally, the earthly comforts of the Test Acts." [14]

Accepting then, that a symbiotic relation existed between church and state, it is obvious that both branches would exercise their influence to maintain the alliance while bending it as much as possible to their own advantage. In the case of episcopal appointments, to which we now turn in detail, it is only reasonable to expect, given the structure of eighteenth-century politics, that the politicians who controlled the nomination process would manipulate that process to meet their own purposes.

The first question we must answer in dealing with eighteenth-century political appointments is, Of what nationality was the Church of Ireland bishop apt to be—English or Irish? (We are ignoring for the moment the fact that a bishop's political affiliation was often of more importance than his nationality.) Summarized below are the national origins of all ecclesiastics who sat on the Irish bench of bishops at any time from the beginning of the year 1750 to the close of the year 1800.[15]

National origin	Number
English	39
Irish	34
Scottish	2
	75

If we exclude those of the above number appointed before 1750 and tabulate the national origins of those eighteenth-century bishops who were appointed in the year 1750 or thereafter, the results are as follows:[16]

National origin	Number
English	27
Irish	24
Scottish	2
	53

A slight majority of the Church of Ireland bishops, therefore, were Englishmen. This was not a new phenomenon, nor was it one fated to disappear quickly. Of the 310 appointments made to Irish sees between 1690 and 1840, 153 were Irishmen.[17]

Eighteenth-century explanations of why so many Englishmen held the highest offices in the Irish church varied. One explanation was that Englishmen made better bishops because the Roman Catholic peasantry naturally preferred the moderate principles of an Englishman to the Protestant bigotry of a Scotsman or an Irishman.[18] Hugh Boulter, Archbishop of Armagh (1724–42) and a Lord Justice of Ireland, wrote to the Duke of Newcastle about appointments to the ecclesiastical bench:

> It was purely in obedience to his Majesty's pleasure that I came hither; and, now I am here, the only thing that can make me uneasy is, if I

should not be enabled to carry on his Majesty's service here, the prospect of which is the greatest comfort in my present station. But, if the bishopricks here are to be disposed of elsewhere, without leaving me room for anything more than, as it may happen, objecting against a person, who may be sent over to the best promotions here, when I have done so; and if I be not allowed to form proper dependencies here, to break the present Dublin faction on the bench, it will be impossible for me to serve his Majesty further than in my single capacity.[19]

The result was that of the twenty-three bishops appointed or translated during Boulter's hegemony, thirteen were English.[20]

A second question naturally arises about the group of bishops: What was the path by which they came to their office? Although the entire ladder of ecclesiastical preferment climbed by each is much too complicated to analyze, a study of the appointment held previous to each man's elevation

TABLE 3

PREVIOUS APPOINTMENT OF MEN RAISED TO BISHOPRICS
IN IRELAND ANY TIME BETWEEN 1750 AND 1800, INCLUSIVE

Appointment	Englishmen	Irishmen	Scotsmen	Total
English bishopric	1	–	–	1
Viceregal chaplain or chaplain to a lord justice	24	3	2	29
Dean of an Irish cathedral	6	19	–	25
Dean of an English cathedral	2	–	–	2
Nondecanal Irish cathedral rank	1	2	–	3
Nondecanal English cathedral rank	2	1	–	3
Chaplain of Irish House of Commons	–	1	–	1
Fellow of Trinity College, Dublin	–	2	–	2
Fellow of an English university college	1	–	–	1
Irish parish clergyman	–	3	–	3
English parish clergyman	1	–	–	1
Undetermined	1	3	–	4
Total	39	34	2	75

Note: In cases where another office was held in plurality with the viceregal chaplaincy, the man is tallied under the chaplaincy only. When two or more ranks are mentioned, the highest is used in the tabulation. The only significant distortion induced by the latter method is that in addition to the one Irishman indicated as chaplain to the Irish House of Commons, two others held the chaplaincy simultaneously with deanships of cathedrals.

Source: Mant, 2: 781–91.

to a bishopric is revealing. The last previous appointment before first ascending to the bench, for all those who held a bishopric between the beginning of the year 1750 and the close of the year 1800, is given in table 3.

From these figures it is obvious that the most common route for an Englishman to an Irish bishopric was through a viceregal chaplaincy. Significantly, this route to the bench was much more apt to be the path of elevation for Englishmen (twenty-four of thirty-nine cases) and for Scots (two of two cases), than for Irishmen (only three of thirty-four cases). In contrast, the second most common route to a bishopric, the achievement of decanal rank in an Irish cathedral, was the path most often followed by Irishmen. Whereas only six of the nineteen Englishmen upon the bench had possessed Irish deanships as their primary previous rank, nineteen of the thirty-four Irishmen raised to the bench in this period were deans in the Irish church at the time of their elevation. Revealed here is a curiously bifurcated system of promotion in which the influx of English bishops was through the essentially political position of chaplaincy to the Lord Lieutenant, while the Irishmen were promoted through essentially religious channels, namely, cathedral offices. Certainly it would be a mistake to overread these figures and make a simplistic statement that Irishmen were promoted according to religious merit, while Englishmen were named to the bench for political service; there were men of religious ability in both groups, and both groups were chosen from among men thought to be politically trustworthy. The fact remains, however, that from an administrative point of view the Irish church was a dangerously divided system. Any time one finds two forms of advancement, each of which seems largely restricted to one social or national group, there is a considerable chance that a two-caste arrangement will develop within the organization. Almost inevitably friction will develop between the groups and the efficiency of the organization will be impaired. This friction was evident in the Irish church from the early eighteenth century. Irish prelates developed a sensitivity to national distinctions on the bench considerably before the "garrison nationalism" of the Irish Protestant population began to emerge in the 1760s.

Recognizing the disparities in mode of entry between Irishmen and Englishmen into the episcopate of the Church of Ireland, it is logical to ask whether or not there was discrimination as to the point of entry. Specifically, to what sees was a man apt to be promoted as his first diocese? Table 4 indicates the first appointment to the bench of men appointed from mid-February 1752 to the end of December 1800.

The conclusions dictated by this table are clear. Entry into the Irish hierarchy was made at certain well-defined points and made irrespective of national origin. These points were certain sees which we can call "beginning bishoprics": Dromore, Ferns and Leighlin, Ossory, Cloyne, Cork and Ross, Killaloe and Kilfenora, Clonfert and Kilmacduagh, and Killala and Achonry. To a lesser extent, Down and Connor, Kilmore and Limerick, Ardfert and Aghadoe served as first sees. With only one exception newcomers to the Irish hierarchy were barred by practice from immediately assuming an archbishopric. That one exception was the Honorable William Stuart who was appointed Archbishop of Armagh in 1800. Previous to his Irish appoint-

TABLE 4

FIRST APPOINTMENT OF MEN APPOINTED TO BISHOPRICS, 1752–1800, INCLUSIVE

See to which first appointment made	Englishmen	Irishmen	Scotsmen	Total
Province of Armagh				
Armagh	1	–	–	1
Clogher	–	–	–	–
Derry	–	–	–	–
Down & Connor	–	1	1	2
Dromore	3	3	–	6
Kilmore	2	–	–	2
Meath	–	–	–	–
Raphoe	–	–	–	–
Provincial Total	6	4	1	11
Province of Dublin				
Dublin	–	–	–	–
Kildare	–	–	–	–
Ferns & Leighlin	3	1	–	4
Ossory	3	2	–	5
Provincial Total	6	3	–	9
Province of Cashel				
Cashel & Emly	–	–	–	–
Cloyne	2	3	–	5
Cork & Ross	4	2	–	6
Killaloe & Kilfenora	2	1	–	3
Limerick, Ardfert & Aghadoe	–	2	–	2
Waterford & Lismore	–	–	–	–
Provincial Total	8	8	–	16
Province of Tuam				
Tuam & Ardagh	–	–	–	–
Clonfert & Kilmacduagh	4	5	1	10
Elphin	–	–	–	–
Killala & Achonry	2	3	–	5
Provincial Total	6	8	1	15
National Totals	26	23	2	51

Note: The table begins with February 1752 because in that year the diocesan arrangement of the Church of Ireland became fixed in a pattern from which it did not vary for the remainder of the century.

Source: Powicke and Fryde, pp. 352–79.

ment, however, he had received his initial episcopal experience as Bishop of Saint Davids, Wales. Therefore, even though there were clearly separate systems of promotion to the hierarchy for English and Irishmen, it appears that entry into the hierarchy was roughly identical for each group. It is still possible, however, that although discrimination between national groups

was not practiced at point of entry, discrimination could have taken place
internally; that is, with regard to which members already on the bench
received desirable translation to other sees. Examination of that possibility
is undertaken in a later section.

To close the discussion on how the bench was filled we must return to
the subject which began the section, namely, how and by whom the appointment was obtained. Earlier we discussed the appointment within the
context of Anglican theology. Now the question can also be treated at a
practical level by asking, How did any given individual become a bishop
of the Church of Ireland? The first step, clearly, was that normally he
had to be well born. The next step for an aspirant to the episcopate was
to obtain the backing of one or more influential men. The patron was often
a temporal peer. On other occasions he was a ranking member of the
episcopate, such as the Archbishop of Armagh or Dublin. (Even the highest of the religious professionals were given to job-hunting for their clients,
as when Robert Fowler, Archbishop of Dublin, wrote that the recent death
of the Bishop of Cloyne "very fortunately makes room on our bench for
Dr. Woodward," the Dean of Clogher, whom Fowler was sponsoring for
promotion.)[21]

Most often, an aspirant to a bishopric found his most influential sponsor
in a political personage. Ranking politicians lobbied continually with the
Lord Lieutenant and with the chief members of the English government
for the promotion of their favorites. Dr. Johnson's comment on the English
church, although a trifle exaggerated, might well have been applied to the
Irish: "No man can now be made a bishop for his learning and piety, his
only chance for promotion is his being connected with somebody who has
parliamentary interest."[22] Among English politicians, Walpole and Newcastle were especially needful of patronage and the Irish church necessarily
became part of the English political ambit.[23] Newcastle was a master of
juggling episcopal appointments, as the following extract from a letter to
the Duke of Dorset, the Lord Lieutenant, indicates:

> The Attorney General makes a strong application that his friend
> and relation [the Bishop of Down] may succeed to the Archbishopric
> of Tuam if the Bishop of Meath, to whom it has been offered, will not
> accept the translation. I earnestly hope you will in that case do it for
> him.[24]

Occasionally the politicians would make a great hash of the appointments,
and the Lord Lieutenant sometimes faced obloquy rather than gratitude
for his apparent distribution of favors:

> Tho' it has generally been thought in England that the favours of
> the Lord Lieutenant have been withheld from the old friends of Gov-

ernment, it is the contrary conduct which has contributed to produce the present difficulty. The appointing Mr. Carlton Solicitor-General, at the recommendation of the Attorney-General, the engaging the deanery of Derry to the Speaker's brother, and the next vacant bishop-rick to Mr. Beresford, has in my opinion determined the case of all the late proceedings.[25]

In certain cases the politician sponsored his client for a bishopric not merely to repay a past debt or to carry out a family duty, but to assure his own political future. Such was the case of Sir Thomas Butler who pressed for the appointment to the Bishopric of Ferns and Leighlin a man who would overcome the tendency of the local clergy to oppose Sir Thomas's electoral interests.[26]

Recalling now our basic criterion that the episcopal selection process should be judged according to its contribution to the church's main pur-pose—namely, to delivery of pastoral services to the Anglican population—it becomes clear that we are dealing with a selection system which was largely irrational. The successful candidates for the bench were those who had the proper combination of birth, patronage, and good fortune. Indi-viduals were elevated to the hierarchy not according to religious merit or competence in managing ecclesiastical organizations but according to their political and family ties. In an institution at least theoretically devoted to the promotion of religious practice among its constituents, such practices were an anomaly. Even if we admit that some of the responsibilities of a bishop were political, this was hardly the bishop's entire duty. Moreover, appointments made even for political reasons were usually made to pay political debts that had little to do with the individual aspirant to the bench. A man was rarely raised to the bench for his own political achievement, but instead was raised because of a political debt owed to his patron. Of course one can simply conclude that these were the workings of eighteenth-century politics, but such a conclusion is meaningless. The significant con-clusion is that the intersecting of the Church of Ireland with the existing political system was dysfunctional from the standpoint of the church's primary purpose as an organization. Indeed, given the method of choosing the church's leaders it can only have seemed to many that the survival of the Church of Ireland was in itself an evidence of the continuing power of the Almighty to work miracles.

Lordly Mobility: The Mechanics of Translation

Because entry to the hierarchy came only at certain limited points, it was inevitable that there would be a good deal of mobility within the episcopate as bishops jockeyed for the more desirable sees. Table 5 provides an indi-cation of the tenure of the average bishop and of the mobility of the bishops. The striking point about these figures is that they indicate an impressive

TABLE 5
TENURE OF IRISH BISHOPS

		English and Scots	*Irish*	*Combined*
A.	Average number of years on the bench for all who were first nominated after mid-February 1752 and who had begun to serve before 1 Jan. 1801	22.0	17.7	20.0
B.	Average number of years on the bench for all who served at any time between 1 Jan. 1750 and 1 Jan. 1801	23.2	20.5	22.0
C.	Average number of sees in career of bishops nominated after mid-Feb. 1752 and beginning service before 1 Jan. 1801	2.0	1.9	2.0
D.	Average number of sees in career of bishops who served at any time between 1 Jan. 1750 and 1 Jan. 1801	2.2	2.1	2.2

Note: The rather awkward definition of the categories is necessary because of the diocesan arrangements of February 1752.
Source: Powicke and Fryde, pp. 352–79.

degree of stability on the bench. The popular conception of the Irish bishop as continually playing ecclesiastical leapfrog is clearly unfounded. The typical bishop had only two sees in his career on the bench and spent an average of ten years in each diocese. This can hardly be described as an unnecessary amount of flux. Clearly there was no excuse for a bishop's not coming to know his diocese well. Any conscientious bishop was apt to be in his diocese long enough to have full opportunity to effect reforms and reorganization if he so desired. If we assume that the life expectancy for a member of the bench was somewhere between sixty and seventy years, the bishops, at first appointment, must usually have been in their forties. Even in his second see, probably reached during his fifties, a bishop should have been in full vigor and at the height of his powers. As far as stability of organization and age of the leading personnel were concerned, the nomination and translation procedures were not dysfunctional. Of course averages veil eccentric cases. Table 6 is presented to indicate the range of mobility-frequencies. Even while indicating the extremes of episcopal mobility, these data confirm the conclusion that in general there was not excessive mobility among members of the bench.

Just as the calculation of averages hides the behavior of atypical individuals, so the averages obscure the situation in any given diocese. As

TABLE 6

NUMBER OF SEES HELD IN THE CAREER OF ALL WHO SERVED
ON THE BENCH AT ANY TIME BETWEEN 1 JANUARY 1750
AND 1 JANUARY 1801

Frequency	English and Scots	Irish	Total
One diocese in career	10	10	20
Two dioceses in career	19	14	33
Three dioceses in career	7	6	13
Four dioceses in career	5	3	8
Five dioceses in career	–	1	1
Total	41	34	75

Source: Powicke and Fryde, pp. 352–79.

table 7 indicates, some dioceses fared much better than others in the matter of continuity among their ecclesiastical pastors.

Predictably, the dioceses which were earlier found to be "beginning bishoprics," that is, the ones to which first episcopal appointments were most often made, had the greatest turnover. Each of them—Dromore, Ferns and Leighlin, Ossory, Cloyne, Cork and Ross, Killaloe and Kilfenora, Clonfert and Kilmacduagh, and Killala and Achonry—had an average episcopal term of office less than the national average (9.9 years for the group as defined in the table). In the cases of Ferns and Leighlin, and Clonfert and Kilmacduagh, the stay of the average bishop was so short that one suspects that the administration of the diocese must have suffered as a result. At the other extreme one finds that of the four archbishoprics, three had an average term of office significantly longer than the average— this in spite of the fact that archbishops tended to be older when assuming their positions than the average diocesan. At the archepiscopal level, there-fore, the church personnel was remarkably stable. The statistics for the other dioceses are self-explanatory, with the See of Derry being the most noteworthy. Clearly, one left the stewardship of that most lucrative post only when called to account for the stewardship thereof.

Given that men did move about during their careers, what patterns can we see in their movement? Table 8 summarizes all of the movements within the hierarchy made during their entire career by men who first came to the bench between February 1752 (when the diocesan structure was stabilized) and the end of December 1800. The chart should be read with the con-sciousness that the careers of men who began on the bench during the sec-ond half of the eighteenth century often extended well into the nineteenth.

We are now at the stage where it would be helpful to determine the peck order of the dioceses as far as their desirability as bishoprics was concerned.

TABLE 7
AVERAGE NUMBER OF YEARS
FOR WHICH EACH SEE WAS HELD,
CALCULATED FOR ALL MEN APPOINTED
TO RESPECTIVE SEES BETWEEN MID-FEBRUARY 1752
AND 1 JANUARY 1801

Province of Armagh
Armagh	19
Clogher	15.25
Derry	35
Down & Connor	13
Dromore	6.9
Kilmore	8.8
Meath	13
Raphoe	18.3

Province of Dublin
Dublin	9
Kildare	14.3
Ferns & Leighlin	5.7
Ossory	6.3

Province of Cashel
Cashel & Emly	16.3
Cloyne	9.6
Cork & Ross	6.6
Killaloe & Kilfenora	8
Limerick, Ardfert & Aghadoe	10.2
Waterford & Lismore	11.5

Province of Tuam
Tuam & Ardagh	16.75
Clonfert & Kilmacduagh	4.4
Elphin	12
Killala & Achonry	8.5

Source: Powicke and Fryde, pp. 352–79.

There are two ways to frame the list, the lazy method and the proper one. Under the former approach one could, with relatively little effort, state that the desirability of a bishopric was determined by the income of the see, modified to some extent by geography. One would then list the income of each bishopric and note how far it was from a major population center, most especially Dublin. This method is here rejected because it forces the twentieth-century observer to make assumptions about the preferences of eighteenth-century ecclesiastics as far as the trade-off of money and geography was concerned. Instead of using the lazy approach we will focus on the behavior of the bishops themselves as they moved from one diocese to

TABLE 8

PATTERN OF TRANSLATION

Translation made from:	First app't	Translation made to:																					
		A	C	D	D&C	D	K	M	R	D	K	F&L	O	C&E	C	C&R	K&K	L	W&L	T&A	C&K	E	K&A
Armagh	1	*	—	—	—	—	—	—	—	—	—	—	—	—	—	—	—	—	—	—	—	—	—
Clogher	—	—	*	—	—	—	—	—	—	—	—	—	—	—	—	—	—	—	—	—	—	—	—
Derry	—	—	—	*	—	—	—	—	—	—	—	—	—	—	—	—	—	—	—	—	—	—	—
Down & Connor	2	—	—	—	*	—	—	—	—	—	—	—	—	—	—	—	—	—	—	—	—	—	—
Dromore	6	—	—	—	1	*	1	—	—	1	2	1	—	—	—	—	—	—	—	—	—	—	—
Kilmore	2	—	1	—	—	—	*	—	—	2	—	—	—	—	—	—	—	—	—	—	—	—	—
Meath	—	—	—	—	—	—	—	*	*	—	—	—	—	—	—	—	—	—	—	—	—	—	—
Raphoe	—	—	—	—	—	—	—	*	*	—	—	—	—	—	—	—	—	—	—	—	—	—	—
Dublin	—	—	—	—	—	—	—	*	—	—	—	—	—	—	—	—	—	—	—	—	—	—	—
Kildare	—	1	1	—	—	—	—	—	*	—	—	*	—	—	—	—	—	—	—	—	—	—	—
Ferns & Leighlin	4	1	1	—	—	1	—	1	—	1	—	*	—	—	—	—	—	—	1	1	—	—	1
Ossory	5	1	1	—	—	—	—	2	—	1	*	—	—	—	—	—	—	—	1	1	—	1	—
Cashel & Emly	—	—	—	—	—	—	—	—	—	1	—	—	*	1	—	—	—	—	—	*	—	—	—
Cloyne	5	1	1	—	—	—	—	—	—	1	—	—	1	*	1	1	—	—	—	—	—	—	—
Cork & Ross	6	1	1	—	—	—	—	—	—	1	—	—	1	—	*	—	—	—	—	—	—	—	—
Killaloe & Kilfenora	3	—	—	—	—	1	—	—	—	—	—	1	—	—	—	—	*	1	*	—	—	—	—
Limerick, etc.	2	1	—	—	—	—	—	—	—	—	—	—	—	—	—	—	—	*	—	—	—	—	—
Waterford & Lismore	—	1	—	—	—	—	—	—	—	—	—	—	—	—	—	—	—	—	*	—	—	—	—
Tuam & Ardagh	—	—	—	—	—	—	—	—	—	—	—	—	—	—	—	—	—	—	—	*	—	—	—
Clonfert & Kilmacduagh	10	—	—	1	1	—	—	—	—	—	2	2	—	—	—	—	—	—	—	—	*	1	1
Elphin	—	—	—	—	—	—	—	—	—	—	—	1	1	—	—	1	—	1	—	—	—	*	—
Killala & Achonry	5	*	—	—	—	—	—	—	—	—	—	1	—	—	—	—	—	—	1	*	1	1	*

Note: Column 1 represents the number of first appointments as bishop. The remaining columns list the sees, by initial, in the order given in the stub column.

Source: Powicke and Fryde, pp. 352–79.

TABLE 9
RELATIVE DESIRABILITY OF IRISH BISHOPRICS

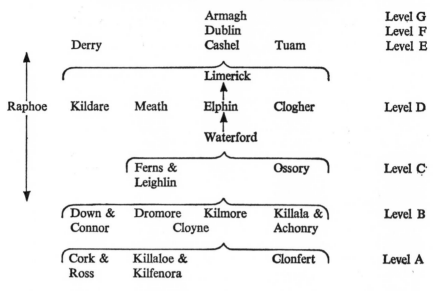

			Armagh		Level G
			Dublin		Level F
Derry			Cashel	Tuam	Level E

| Raphoe | Kildare | Meath | Limerick / Elphin / Waterford | Clogher | Level D |

| | Ferns & Leighlin | | Ossory | | Level C |

| Down & Connor | Dromore | Kilmore / Cloyne | Killala & Achonry | | Level B |

| Cork & Ross | Killaloe & Kilfenora | | Clonfert | | Level A |

Note: Level A consists solely of dioceses which were "beginning sees," and to which no member of the hierarchy was translated during the period under study; it is safe to assume that they were the least desirable sees. Level B comprises dioceses whose possessors were usually men serving their first bishopric, though on at least one occasion a man was translated to this level from level A. Level C is made up of two bishoprics usually filled by new members of the bench but occasionally filled by translation of men previously holding sees on levels A and B. Level D is the most difficult to deal with because of the limited information at our disposal. Kildare, Elphin, Meath, Waterford, and Clogher each took translations from level C, thus establishing themselves on a higher level than C. In 1810 a bishop of Waterford and Lismore (not covered in the chart because of the chart's cutoff date) chose to move from Waterford to Elphin, thereby establishing the peck order of those two sees. Since our chart covers the case of mobility from Elphin to Limerick, it is possible to place the three sees of Limerick, Elphin, and Waterford, in ordinal position. This does not, however, reveal to us precisely where they stood in relation to Clogher, Meath, and Kildare except that they were of roughly comparable rank. Raphoe is presented as being either level C or D because the translations made during the eighteenth and early nineteenth century allow one to determine that it was above level B, but not to determine if it should be on level C or D.

Cashel and Tuam are placed on level E because of their rank as the minor archbishoprics and also because each was filled at least once by a bishop who had previously served at level D. In the case of Tuam the validation of its position above level D is found in the translation of the Bishop of Elphin to Tuam in 1775, a case not covered in the chart because the bishop involved had been first elevated to the Irish bench before 1752. Derry is placed on the same level as Cashel and Tuam because it was filled in 1727 by the translation of the Bishop of Meath (a case also not covered by table 8). Level F, the Archbishopric of Dublin, is placed alone above the minor archbishoprics because of its having been filled once by the Archbishop of Cashel. Although there is no decisive indication that Meath and Tuam were not its equal in desirability (no man was translated from either of the sees to Dublin during

TABLE 9 (Continued)

the eighteenth or early nineteenth century) the fact that Dublin was second in precedence in the Irish hierarchy and implied attendance in the capital city, dictates that it should be listed alone. Armagh is listed above Dublin, in level G, not only because of its episcopal primacy, but because once in the eighteenth and once in the nineteenth century it was filled by the translation of the Archbishop of Dublin (both events being outside the time lines of our basic table).

Finally, it remains to be added that the peck order derived from charting the behavior of individual bishops is necessarily based on an extremely limited number of cases (translations were not everyday occurrences) and therefore while accurate for providing an approximation of the relative desirability of the sees, it remains a somewhat crude index, indicating relative positions, but not the precise degree of difference between any two dioceses.

another. The information in table 8 allows us to determine the relative desirability of the bishoprics by observing eighteenth-century behavior, rather than employing twentieth-century assumptions.

Table 9 is an approximation of the hierarchy of sees. If, within a defined time span two men moved, one, for example, from Clonfert to Dromore and the other from Clonfert to Kilmore, we can conclude that the sees of Dromore and of Kilmore are more desirable than Clonfert. But merely because they are each more desirable than Clonfert does not mean that each is equally desirable. Only when we know to what dioceses Bishops of Dromore and Kilmore move can we place them accurately within the hierarchy of desirability. Special cases of ambiguous relationships are discussed in the note to the table.

With this background on the general ranking of the sees we can ask how high the average bishop was apt to rise in his career. We can also examine the crucial issue of discrimination between Irishmen and Englishmen on the bench by tabulating where those of each nationality ended their ecclesiastical careers; that is, what was the highest see they held. The results are given in table 10. As far as career probabilities can be indicated by such a chart, it appears that the average bishop could reasonably expect to reach one of the more desirable bishoprics by the close of his ecclesiastical career. Almost one of three men (twenty-four of seventy-five covered by the table) reached the sees of level D by the conclusion of their careers. Balancing these relatively successful bishops were the sixteen members of the hierarchy whose careers never extended above the bishoprics of level B, sees which were usually reserved for new appointees to the bench. Significantly, if we group levels E, F, and G together, we discover that the chances were nearly one in three (twenty-three of seventy-five) that a man who entered the hierarchy would rise to an archbishopric or to the See of Derry. This, one can conjecture, represented a high enough chance of promotion to be a significant factor in motivating the behavior of the individual bishop. Indeed the probabilities were slightly better than one in seven (eleven of

TABLE 10
BISHOPRICS HELD AT END OF CAREER OF ALL WHO SAT ON THE BENCH
ANYTIME BETWEEN 1 JANUARY 1750 AND 1 JANUARY 1801

Dioceses	English & Scots	Irish	Total
Level G: Armagh	4	–	4
Level F: Dublin	5	2	7
Level E: Cashel	1	3	4
Tuam	1	4	5
Derry	2	1	3
Level D: Limerick	2	4	6
Elphin	2	1	3
Waterford & Lismore	1	2	3
Kildare	3	–	3
Clogher	4	1	5
Meath	1	3	4
Level C or D: Raphoe	3	1	4
Level C: Ferns & Leighlin	3	1	4
Ossory	–	2	2
Level B: Cloyne	2	4	6
Down & Connor	1	1	2
Dromore	2	–	2
Killala & Achonry	1	1	2
Kilmore	1	1	2
Level A: Clonfert & Kilmacduagh	–	1	1
Cork & Ross	2	–	2
Killaloe & Kilfenora	–	1	1
Total	41	34	75

Source: Powicke and Fryde, pp. 352–79.

seventy-five) that a man would rise to either the Archbishopric of Armagh or of Dublin. Therefore, in regard to probabilities of appointment or translation to a desirable see, the Church of Ireland in the eighteenth and early nineteenth century presented excellent prospects to the ambitious ecclesiastic.

If we compare the probabilities of Irishmen or Scotsmen and Englishmen reaching any given level, the differences between the groups appear insignificant, except at the three highest levels. Granted, if we amalgamate the two lowest levels it is clear that the chances for an Irishman being marooned at either of those levels (nine of thirty-four) were slightly greater than those of a Britisher (nine of forty-one). But at the middle levels of C and D the career opportunities were almost identical (nineteen of forty-one for Britishers and fifteen of thirty-four for Irishmen). Indeed, the differences of the two groups are hidden even when we consider the three highest levels together; for ten of the thirty-four Irishmen rose to that level, a figure comparable to the thirteen of forty-one British who made the ascent.

Only when we distinguish events at the three highest levels does the difference between the position of Irish and British churchmen become clear. During this period no Irishman could reasonably hope to rise to the Primacy of All Ireland, Armagh; and the probabilities of his being appointed to the Archbishopric of Dublin were considerably less than those of his British counterparts on the bench. On the other hand, the Archbishoprics of Tuam and Cashel were generally reserved for Irish bishops. In general, therefore, the probabilities of an Irish bishop's remaining on the lowest rungs of the ladder were slightly greater than for a British bishop of the Church of Ireland, while the chances of the Irishman's rising to the highest two ranks in the church were considerably less than the Britisher's.

Another way of illuminating the same question is to focus not on the bishops themselves but upon the sees. Table 11 gives the national origin of the men who held each see, from February 1752 to the close of the year 1800. Like the previous table, these figures tend to indicate that internal discrimination was occurring within the higher ranks of the church and that this discrimination was at least partially on national lines. It is clear that the very highest positions on the bench went chiefly to Englishmen. No Irishman held the primacy of all Ireland during this period. Indeed, from 1702 until 1822 the highest rank in the Church of Ireland was held by Englishmen. The church's second highest rank, the Archbishopric of Dublin, was bestowed upon an Irishman only one of four times the appointment was made between 1752 and 1800. Further, the wealthiest bishopric, Derry (whose revenues were reputed to be higher than those of the Archdiocese of Dublin), was held continuously by Englishmen during the second half of the eighteenth century. Similarly, the Diocese of Kildare, considered to be a prize because it was held simultaneously with the Deanship of Christ Church Cathedral, Dublin, and allowed uninterrupted residence in Dublin, was invariably filled with Englishmen. In general, appointments in the Protestant areas of the country (the Province of Armagh), and in the areas closest to Dublin, the political and cultural capital (the Province of Dublin), went to Englishmen. On the other hand, appointments in the Provinces of Cashel and of Tuam, generally the poorest parts of the country and also the parts with the lowest proportion of Protestants in the population, were dominated by the Irish-born prelates. Through the latter half of the century both the Archbishoprics of Cashel and of Tuam were held by men of Irish birth. In absolute numbers of appointments, Irishmen dominated in the two latter provinces, a fact made more significant by their being in a numerical minority on the bench. A blurred but perceptible pattern emerges: the Irish church was divided into two overlapping subsystems as far as episcopal appointments were concerned: one system dominated by Englishmen, the other characterized chiefly by the appointment of Irishmen.

TABLE 11
NATIONAL ORIGIN OF BISHOPS OF EACH DIOCESE, MID-FEBRUARY 1752
TO 1 JANUARY 1801

Diocese	Englishmen	Irishmen	Scotsmen	Total
Province of Armagh				
Armagh	4	–	–	4
Clogher	3	1	–	4
Derry	2	–	–	2
Down & Connor	1	2	1	4
Dromore	5	3	–	8
Kilmore	4	1	–	5
Meath	1	4	1	6
Raphoe	3	1	–	4
Province of Dublin				
Dublin	3	1	1	5
Kildare	4	–	–	4
Ferns & Leighlin	8	2	1	11
Ossory	3	5	–	9
Province of Cashel				
Cashel & Emly	–	4	–	4
Cloyne	4	5	–	9
Cork & Ross	4	2	–	6
Killaloe & Kilfenora	2	3	–	5
Limerick, Ardfert & Aghadoe	2	4	–	6
Waterford & Lismore	2	1	–	3
Province of Tuam				
Tuam & Ardagh	–	4	–	4
Clonfert & Kilmacduagh	4	7	1	12
Elphin	2	3	–	5
Killala & Achonry	4	3	–	7

Source: Mant, 2: 781–91, with refinement of dating from Powicke and Fryde, pp. 352–79.

To maintain proper perspective, three comments are required: first, these subsystems were not absolutely demarcated. Irishmen were often found in Armagh and in Dublin, and Englishmen were not strangers to the Provinces of Cashel or Tuam. The figures indicate certain tendencies which hold over a large number of cases, and should not be taken to indicate an absolute rule for any individual instance. Second, we are dealing here with patterns of ecclesiastical appointment. This is not a synonym for ecclesiastical power. By noting that the appointment of Englishmen predominated in one place and Irishmen in the other, we are not saying that Englishmen controlled the church in the Provinces of Armagh and Dublin, and the Irish in Cashel and Tuam. The church was an overarching body which enveloped both of these subsystems and forced them to interact with one another. Third, it should be reiterated that the discrimination in appointments which prevented Irishmen from reaching the very most desirable positions came after they had been in the hierarchy for a time and were being translated to more desirable benefices. The differentiation between the Irishmen and Englishmen on the bench can only have been detrimental to the church's effectiveness. That the very highest ranks were open only to the English must have been painfully obvious to anyone. By appointing only Englishmen to the most desirable sees the church squandered one device for controlling the behavior of its Irish bishops, namely the hope of promotion to the very highest episcopal levels.

Let us turn from describing statistically the patterns of episcopal mobility in the Church of Ireland and ask how, in practice, a man might secure a translation for himself. The answer is that he had to have influential friends, and it helped if he were alert to medical symptoms among his colleagues. As soon as a member of the bench began looking pale, or was reputed to have anything beyond the most trifling illness, letters were drafted, asking to be appointed to his see upon his demise. For example, Jemmett Browne, the Bishop of Cork and Ross, cheerily wrote the Lord Lieutenant, "If there is not actually a vacancy in the See of Dublin, most probably there will be in a few hours. I need not inform your excellency how happy I should be to succeed him, and to owe my doing so to you." [27] (Actually Browne was prematurely sepulchral by almost two years, and when the see became vacant, it did not go to him.) [28] Of course bishops seeking their own advantage were not the only ones to play vultures to the bench. Politicians made plans contingent upon a convenient ecclesiastical demise. "The Bishop of Meath is very ill," wrote the Duke of Newcastle to the Duke of Dorset. "If he should not recover, Ryder may then have Meath." [29]

Upon reflection, the means and patterns by which men were moved about from bishopric to bishopric seems at once absurd and reasonable. Absurd, from the viewpoint of the church's major purpose, the delivery of pastoral services, because men were translated chiefly through patronage and primarily for reasons other than their usefulness as ecclesiastical administrators or religious statesmen. Reasonable, because the patterns of mobility were not chaotic or disruptive to the organization. Since most bishops stayed on the bench twenty-plus years and usually held only two sees in their career, the hierarchy was a stable body whose membership changed with evolutionary slowness rather than with revolutionary swiftness. (Admittedly, a few dioceses, notably Clonfert and Kilmacduagh, Cloyne, and Ferns and Leighlin, may have suffered somewhat from the brevity of episcopal tenures therein, but this represents only a minority of cases.) Further, there was a reasonable opportunity of a bishop's being translated to one of the more desirable sees and a chance of his becoming an archbishop. The great irrationality in the system was the implicit arrangement whereby the two highest posts, Armagh and Dublin, usually went to Britishers, with Tuam and Cashel being the highest appointments that normally went to Irish prelates.

The Bishops' Work

The manifest purpose of the Church of Ireland was the provision of pastoral services for the Anglican population, and, in theory at least, the primary duty of a bishop was to act as spiritual overseer of his diocese. The bishop remained a priest, of course, and could be expected to perform his priestly role, but this was secondary to his duty to oversee the activities of his clergy and the manners and morals of his people. The standard division of a bishop's duties into three parts which was formulated for England [30] can be applied as well to Ireland. The three duties were the ordination of new clergy, the visitation of the clergy in the parishes, and the confirmation of the laity. These duties the bishop himself was solely responsible for, there being no coadjutor bishops in the Church of Ireland at this time (indeed, when a coadjutor bishop was appointed for the Archdiocese of Dublin in 1811, the move was so completely unprecedented that the Lord Chancellor was entirely ignorant of the power of such an office and could not find it defined in any law book).[31]

The ordination and confirmation roles are self-explanatory, but because we are focusing in this study upon the administrative aspects of the church, the right of visitation merits further attention. Unlike England, where visitation was rarely annual, the policy for bishops in Ireland was to inspect the local parishes at yearly intervals.[32] This policy could be honored both in its fulfillment and in the breach, but the more conscientious bishops not only honored it, but made special visits to parishes whose circumstances warranted particular attention.[33] Possessing the right to visit or inspect every part of his diocese at pleasure, the bishop also possessed in theory the right to censure and to suspend clergy where cause existed. In practice, however, the right to suspend or to censure was so hedged about with restrictions and procedural complications that penalties were invoked only in the most outrageous cases. As an extension of his right to inspect his diocese, the bishop had power to unite and consolidate parishes so long as such unions were not perpetual. He had the right to erect new churches or chapels as desired to serve a given parish, although his financial powers for this task were undefined. In large parishes a bishop could cause a chapel of ease to be built and endow it with tithes for the officiating curate.[34]

In coordinating the work of their dioceses, the bishops could, if they wished, have recourse to annual synods of their clergy. How general such a practice was, is difficult to determine. By the early nineteenth century the practice appears to have been nearly universal, these annual convocations of the clergy rendering unnecessary an actual physical visitation by the bishop of each benefice.[35]

In theory there existed on the national level a similar device for coordinating episcopal administration, namely convocation. Convocation in principle was a clerical equivalent of parliament, through which the clergy dealt with church matters and voted their own taxation and subsidies to the Crown. Like parliament it was a bicameral structure: the upper house comprising the prelates, the lower house the representatives of the other clergy. The history of convocation following the Restoration was not an auspicious one. It met in 1661 and appears to have sat until 1666. Thereafter it was not again called until 1704, from which time it continued its sessions until 1711. Then, for no specific reason, convocation as an operative body disappeared. Since the body was assembled solely by force of royal writ, the government determined whether or not it would meet. Although assembling convocation was contemplated in 1713, and again in 1728, nothing came of the suggestions, and from 1711 until the disestablishment of the church in the nineteenth century the body did not meet.[36] The result of the government's refusal to permit convocation's assembly was that the Church of Ireland lost the use of an important appendage, one which would have permitted communication across dioceses and perhaps permitted an improvement in the administration of the Church.

Significantly, during the eighteenth century it was never made clear who, if anybody, could make certain that the bishops performed their religious duties. Within scandalously wide limits the bishop could do as he pleased religiously without fear of punishment or deprivation of his post. Granted, the Crown had a right in theory to appoint a royal visitation to inquire into any matter of the establishment,[37] but the use of royal commissions for reform and disciplinary purposes did not become a standard practice until the next century. Granted, also, the archbishop of each province had certain supervisory powers, for in theory he was responsible for the standard of religious practice throughout his entire province. Therefore, just as a suffragan bishop made visitation to his clergy, the metropolitan made a visitation of his suffragans. Previous to his visitation, the metropolitan usually issued an inhibition, the effect of which was to suspend all episcopal powers of the suffragan except confirmation and ordination. After the visitation was successfully completed, the suffragan's powers were restored. This procedure certainly sounds rigorous, but its severity was noticeably undercut by the practice of conducting archepiscopal visitation only once every three years. Admittedly, the archbishop had the power to censure a suffragan and on notorious causes to bring proceedings to deprive him of his office, but the threat was of value only in the most scandalous cases.

For minor lapses, such as simple neglect of ecclesiastical duties, the archbishops had no remedy.[38]

How nearly impossible it was to enforce high standards of ecclesiastical
conduct on the part of the prelates is indicated by the problem of episcopal
residency in the eighteenth century. This is not the kind of point which
the evidence allows us to describe statistically, but Dr. Milne's statement is
an excellent summation: "While a great deal is heard of the damage done
to Ireland by the absentee landlords of the eighteenth and nineteenth centuries, from the point of view of the Church of Ireland the absentee bishops
were equally disastrous." [39] At one point in the eighteenth century there
were only two bishops living permanently in the Province of Armagh.[40]
Neither Down and Connor nor Kildare possessed palaces for the bishops,[41]
thus making residence nearly impossible. The correspondence of eighteenth-
century Irish bishops leaves one with the impression that they spent more
time in Dublin, London, Oxford, or Cambridge, than in their dioceses.
Small wonder that we find the newly appointed Bishop of Clogher casually
reporting, "I mentioned my having been lately on an expedition. It was to
Clogher. I took advantage of our present parliamentary recess to run down
and see what sort of a thing I had gotten." [42] The great problem as far
as ecclesiastical efficiency was concerned was that no one had the power
to compel a bishop to make such expeditions any more often than the
bishop's individual inclinations led him to do so.

If the archbishops lacked effective authority for producing efficient day-
to-day performance of religious duties among their suffragans, did the
suffragans in turn lack adequate controls over their subordinates? Each
diocese possessed a registry and consistorial court. The technical matters
under the courts' purview were those relating to marriage and to testamentary affairs. It also had ordinary jurisdiction in inquiring into ecclesiastical causes. The court was held under the bishop's jurisdiction, but the
bishop was prohibited from personally presiding. His jurisdiction, therefore, was delegated to a person, lay or clerical, who in most cases had
earned the secular degree of doctor of laws and who bore the title of vicar-
general. The position of vicar-general differed from most ecclesiastical
offices, since it was a specialized one, filled by an individual specially
trained for his duties. Thus, in matrimonial suits and in the testamentary
matters with which these courts dealt the bishops were able to exercise
adequate control through the direction of their legal offices, men armed
with expert knowledge. A person not satisfied with the judgment of the
diocesan consistorial court could appeal to the metropolitan court of the
provincial archbishop. The courts also adjudicated petty squabbles between
clergymen on such subjects as dilapidations, suits for tithes, and fees of
various sorts.[43] As will be discussed in the next chapter, the problem
of control was particularly acute in regard to clerical nonresidency, there

being almost nothing a bishop could do to force a footloose clergyman to reside in his parish and perform personally his parish duties.[44]

Up to this point we have been discussing the bishops' manifest function, the superintending of pastoral matters. In reality, the eighteenth-century Anglican bishops had heavy extrareligious duties as well, which often interfered with their pastoral tasks. The most important nonreligious duty was political. Of course various bishops served their political masters with varying degrees of fidelity, but few ignored their political duties altogether. It was the duty of the bishops to support the government in the House of Lords. In the first third of the eighteenth century, the smallness of the Irish temporal peerage meant that the bishops' leverage was considerable and that the government had to depend upon them to ensure control of the upper house. The importance of the bishops to the government seems to have been greatest relatively early in the eighteenth century. In the first session of George II's Irish parliament, the average attendance in the House of Lords was twenty, and on thirty-seven of the session's fifty-three sittings the bishops formed a majority of those in attendance. Later in George II's reign, the importance of the bishops diminished somewhat, for a number of new temporal peers were created. Thus, in the 1739 session, the bishops formed a majority of those present on only eighteen of the sixty-seven sittings. This trend continued. By the 1751 session the bishops were in a majority at only two of sixty-two meetings (even though average attendance in the House of Lords had actually declined). In the 1760 session, the bishops constituted a majority at only seven of sixty sittings, again in spite of a decline in average attendance.[45] This is not to say that the bishops were politically impotent in the latter half of the century, but their importance in controlling the Lords did decline. To note that the average attendance in the Lords dropped (an indication of its diminishing political importance) while simultaneously noting that the proportion of times in which the bishops were in a majority also declined, is to say that as the century passed, the average bishop spent less and less time in the House of Lords. And the cynic might add that even an Irish bishop, with time on his hands, might turn to ecclesiastical matters if all other pursuits failed.

How loyal politically to the government of the day were the bishops? To answer this question for the entire last fifty years of the century would be to immerse ourselves unnecessarily in Irish factional politics, but it is useful to examine the situation in the middle decade of that period. Lord Harcourt, Viceroy from November 1772 to January 1777, prepared in his last month of office a list of the political dispositions of the Irish bishops, presumably for the edification of his successor. Significantly, of the twenty-two bishops, Harcourt was confident that eighteen were in the government's control politically. Only one bishop was categorized as opposed to the government, with the remaining three being so much absent from Ireland as to be political ciphers.[46]

How did Dublin Castle authorities ensure such loyalty from the bishops? First, they carefully selected men whom they trusted politically. Certainly a few went astray over the years but the percentage was remarkably small. Second, most bishops supported the government politically because they knew that departing therefrom would destroy their chances of future promotion. Significantly, in controlling the bishops' political behavior, the government lacked negative sanctions. If a bishop decided to go his own way, there was almost nothing the politicians could do about it. The bishop held appointment for life, except in the cases of grossest misbehavior. Therefore, as long as a bishop was willing to forgo chances of translation and minor political favors, there was nothing the politician could do to bully the bishop into line.

This point is sharply illustrated by the activities of Frederick Augustus Hervey (Earl of Bristol, 1779), Bishop of Cloyne (1767–68), and Bishop of Derry (1768–1803). One outraged historian of the period has reported: "The family of which he was the head was noted for eccentricity; and it used to be said that all the eccentricity of the race was concentrated in him." [47] Immensely wealthy, possessed of the richest nonmetropolitan post in the hierarchy, and willfully erratic in his personal behavior, Hervey was beyond the touch of discipline. Some of his actions were merely personal foibles grown large, such as his habit of riding about Rome (where he spent a good deal of his time) in red plush breeches and a broad-brimmed white or straw hat, a costume which gave a most glamorous impression of Irish ecclesiastical dress.[48] He was willing to spread his immense wealth about the compass, subscribing to Roman Catholic, Anglican, and Presbyterian churches with equal readiness. He was reputed to be profane, worldly, and a thorough libertine.[49] To the Dublin authorities, all this eccentricity was forgivable, if somewhat frowned upon, but what the authorities could not abide was the bishop's unpredictable political enthusiasms. During the early 1780s, Hervey assumed two radical political viewpoints, namely that the House of Commons needed sweeping reform and that the Roman Catholics should be granted the franchise. Neither of these was a position apt to endear him to the government, but the unforgivable sin was his announcement in 1782 that he intended to join the company of the Londonderry Volunteers. His great wealth and enormous energies soon brought him to the fore of the Volunteer movement. The high point of his paramilitary career came in November 1783 when he paraded from the north to the convention in Dublin attended by a troop of dragoons from his diocese. The earl-bishop himself was dressed entirely in purple and entered Dublin in an open landau drawn by six horses accessoried in purple trappings. With characteristic unpredictability, Hervey gave up politics altogether when the Volunteer movement declined, and near the close of his career was found recording his vote for the Act of Union.[50]

The crucial point about Hervey's situation is that the Dublin administration could do nothing to curb his activities during the hectic days of 1782–83. Those conversant with Irish affairs may have felt that he had "thoughts of becoming a Right Reverend O. Cromwell, and if his cassock was to be searched possibly breviare similar to that of Cardinal de Retz might be found," [51] but verbal sniping was all they could do.

If a bishop had political duties on the national level, he also had duties, both political and social, on a more local scale. A bishop, if he chose to exercise his powers and exert his influence, had much the same position as, and responsibilities of, a territorial magnate. His territorial political powers could be quite extensive, for the basic unit of Irish local government was the county, a unit similar in extent to the diocese. This contrasts with the English situation in which the chief local administrative unit, the parish, was not sufficiently powerful for a man of bishop's stature to pay much attention to its function. If an Irish bishop wished, therefore, he could without loss of stature join with the handful of leading Protestant landowners to control the county grand jury. The only impediment to such participation was the tendency of many bishops to spend a large portion of each year living outside their dioceses. Naturally those bishops who spent a significant portion of the year in their dioceses were often closely involved with electoral politics at the county level. In addition, four of the Irish bishops controlled boroughs[52] and in so doing not only became involved as local political figures but often came to control membership in the local ruling body. The Bishop of Ferns and Leighlin, for example, in 1835–36, stated that by immemorial custom the burgesses of Old Leighlin were admitted to the respective offices upon the sole nomination and appointment of the Bishop of Ferns and Leighlin. Indeed, the bishop had followed the practice of appointing his clergy as burgesses.[53]

The most curious local civic responsibility exercised by an eighteenth-century bishop was the Archbishop of Dublin's hegemony over the liberty of Saint Sepulchre's in the City of Dublin. This was one of four medieval liberties surviving in Dublin. The archbishop's seneschal exercised the primate's jurisdiction. In addition, the archbishop appointed a marshal, coroner, weighmaster, clerk of the market, and a grand jury. The archbishop's liberty had three courts—a court of record for personal pleas, a court of criminal jurisdiction (the latter fell into disuse during the eighteenth century), and a court leet at which the constables and the grand jury were sworn. Moreover, the archbishop was vested with the regulation of police in the liberty. The liberty had its own prison for debtors, but other prisoners were lodged in the county jail. As their titles imply, the clerk and weighmaster of the market had important economic functions. Although various ad hoc bodies were beginning to encroach upon the independence of the liberty, during the eighteenth century the Archbishop of Dublin was chief governor of a city within a city.[54]

Although no other bishop governed a medieval fief of his own, each of the bishops acted in time-honored ways as territorial figures. Thus, for example, one finds the Bishop of Dromore apprehending a quarrel between Roman Catholics and Dissenters on market day, and applying for a small party of soldiers from Newry whose presence maintained the peace inviolate.[55] Similarly, it was an implicit duty of the bishops to dispense local charity. And when they were not providing their own funds, they often served as intermediaries, promoting the cases of those under their charge. We observe, therefore, James Leslie, Bishop of Limerick, importuning the Lord Lieutenant's benevolence for a late barracks master, "Ye poor unfortunate lunatick Timothy Enraghty," [56] and the Bishop of Raphoe seeking funds from the Lord Lieutenant to support the widow and three children of a Captain George Innes, who had served forty-five years in the Royal Foot Regiment.[57] These examples could be multiplied by the score, for both in their local political and social functions the bishops performed the same duties as did other powerful landed gentlemen throughout the British Isles.

If one surveys the entire range of the prelates' responsibilities, both religious and secular, one cannot help but speculate that on many occasions the prelates' diverse responsibilities were self-contradictory. For example, there must have been many instances when the spiritual good of a diocese clashed with the government's demand that certain parishes be used as part of the government's patronage system. Although consecrated as spiritual leaders, the bishops were expected to be political servants of the government as well. In all probability confusion in these roles must often have occurred, since religious duties and political imperative are potentially at odds. Thus, the very men who were expected to command the church probably often felt themselves in an ambiguous and uneasy position vis-à-vis their own duties. This is conjecture, but the speculation is certainly a reasonable one.

Another flaw in the church's episcopal organization was that the relationship of superior and subordinate was not close or controllable. This was because the dependency relationships were curiously one-sided. Both local clerics and members of the bench depended upon their superiors for appointment to desirable benefices, but there the dependence ended. Within very broad limits a man, above curate's level, held his office for life and was therefore almost totally independent of his superior for continuation of his appointment. Because the superiors lacked the right to impose negative sanctions to any significant degree, any subordinate who was willing to give up his chances for promotion was almost totally independent of his superior's control. This held on the episcopal level, where it was impossible for the government to press the Bishop of Derry into its political crew, and where an archbishop had only limited powers to compel a bishop to reside in his diocese. It held true on the parish level where a suffragan bishop could do little to make his clergy reside in their parishes and perform their offices.

The obvious remedies for these flaws were for the bishops of the church to be freed from political responsibility, and for those in positions of religious authority to be given sanctions whereby they could guarantee that their subordinates performed their ecclesiastical duties satisfactorily. To the Church of Ireland's great benefit in the early nineteenth century, these failings were largely remedied.

The Bishops' Rewards

In assessing just how well the Irish bishops were rewarded for their labors, we are faced with the problem that eighteenth-century accounting procedures were somewhat less precise than those of our own time. Therefore, in the income tables which will follow, the reader is warned that those reporting the figures did not specify whether they were in English currency or in Irish currency. Further, when they reported that a see was "worth" a certain amount they did not specify whether they meant gross income or income after deductions had been made for necessary episcopal expenses, obligatory charity contributions, and the like. Also, it is clear that the figures do not include implicit or "invisible" income (such as lodgings). For example, each diocese with the exception of Kildare and of Down and Connor provided the bishops with a diocesan palace, this residence certainly being of some value and thus an implicit addition to the prelate's income.

This warning having been given, a few eighteenth-century figures are presented to establish the general range of episcopal incomes. In Lord Primate Boulter's time (1724–42), the See of Kilmore was reported to be worth somewhat more than £2,000 a year, and Derry over £2,200. Kildare, with Christ Church Cathedral's deanship attached, was worth £1,600 as was Ferns and Leighlin. The Bishopric of Clonfert was valued between approximately £1,200 and £1,500, and Killala at £1,100, per annum.[58] In 1782 the newly appointed Bishop of Clogher reported that his see was valued at £4,000 a year.[59] In 1794 the Lord Lieutenant stated that the value of Cloyne was £4,300 per anum.[60] These figures establish the general range of episcopal incomes, and also indicate the inflation that probably occurred during the eighteenth century. Much more comprehensive was the valuation made by Arthur Young between 1776 and 1779. This information, arranged in descending order of income, is presented below:[61]

Armagh	£8,000
Derry	7,000
Dublin	5,000
Cashel and Emly	4,000
Tuam and Ardagh	4,000
Clogher	4,000
Elphin	3,700
Limerick, Ardfert and Aghadoe	3,500
Meath	3,400
Killala and Achonry	2,900
Cork and Ross	2,700
Kilmore	2,600
Raphoe	2,600
Kildare	2,600
Waterford and Lismore	2,500
Cloyne	2,500
Clonfert and Kilmacduagh	2,400
Down and Connor	2,300
Killaloe and Kilfenora	2,300
Ferns and Leighlin	2,200
Ossory	2,000
Dromore	2,000

Young's figures should be compared with those compiled for Lord Harcourt, apparently done shortly before the end of his lord lieutenancy in late 1776:[62]

Armagh	Not available
Derry	£7,000
Dublin	£5,000
Cashel and Emly	Not available
Tuam and Ardagh	Not available
Clogher	£4,000
Killala and Achonry	"full £4,000"
Meath	"near £4,000"
Elphin	£3,800
Limerick, Ardfert and Aghadoe	£3,500
Kildare	"about £3,400"
Cork	"full £3,000"
Raphoe	£3,000
Cloyne	£2,300
Kilmore	£2,800

Ferns and Leighlin	£2,600
Killaloe and Kilfenora	£2,500
Ossory	£2,500
Down and Connor	£2,300
Waterford and Lismore	£2,200
Dromore	£2,200
Clonfert and Kilmacduagh	£2,200

Given that we are dealing with highly imprecise estimates, the similarity between the two tables is striking, and suggests that we are viewing reasonably reliable estimates. The greatest variation occurs in the figures for Killala and Achonry, Meath, Kildare, and Ossory, in which the variation is £500 or greater (that there is some variation between the tables indicates that each estimate was made independently of the other). A comparison of either of these tables with table 9 on the peck order of dioceses makes it clear that there is a strong positive correlation between the desirability of the sees and the annual revenue of the dioceses, but that this correlation should not be mistaken for identity. Other factors, such as location and the condition of the episcopal palaces, often overcame mere financial considerations in the mind of a bishop who was pressing for a translation.

Precise comparisons with financial rewards for English bishops is almost impossible because of the question of currency and the impossibility of knowing whether income was defined identically in each country. According to a list drawn up for George III during the early years of his reign, the English bishoprics yielded revenue as follows: Canterbury, £7,000; York, £4,500; Durham, £6,000; London, £4,000; Winchester, £5,000; Ely, £3,400; Salisbury, £3,000; Worcester, £3,000; Lincoln, Chichester, Exeter, Hereford, and Lichfield, between £1,000 and £1,400; Rochester, £600; Llandaff, £550; Oxford, £500; Bristol, £450.[63] By any reasonable standard, the Irish bishops were well paid for their services. A man on the Irish bench could live well and die rich. The achievement of Archbishop Smyth of Dublin in amassing property worth £50,000 during his career was impressive but not unprecedented.[64] Well might a member of the bench repeat the reported words of an archbishop of the first half of the eighteenth century: "I conclude, that a good bishop has nothing more to do than to eat, drink, grow fat, rich, and die; which laudable example I propose for the remainder of my life to follow." [65]

The Irish bishops, like all men of power, were rewarded not only with direct money payments, but indirectly as well. The very real if intangible reward of simply having power and immense prestige, of being a member of the House of Lords, of moving in the upper levels of Irish society—these must have been most satisfying to the men of the bench. There were other non-money rewards that were much less psychic in nature, namely the favors provided the bishops by the Dublin authorities. Rather than multiply random examples, table 12 presents a systematic statement of the

TABLE 12

NON-MONEY PAYMENTS TO IRISH BISHOPS

Armagh	"Lord Townshend obtained a Bishp^{rk} for his Friend Dean Cope. Lord Harcourt has given to his Grace's Recommendation the office of Distributor of Stamps for the County of Armagh."
Dublin	"Lord Townshend obtained a Company to his Son in Law, Mr. Hamilton. Lord Harcourt procured him a Troop, which he has since been allowed to sell. And is now aid de Camp and Comm. of Barracks . . . Lord Harcourt gave to his Rec^{dn} a Hearth Money Collection."
Cashel	——
Tuam	——
Clogher	——
Derry	"Lord Harcourt obtained an Ensigncy for one friend, and a Company for another. He made His Lordship a Trustee of the Linen Board.
Down & Connor	——
Dromore	"Ld. Harcourt at the desire of Lord North and His Excy. gave him a ^{s}y. Tidewaiter."
Kilmore	"His Lp. got a Clerkship in the P. Office for a young man he recom^{d} [name illegible].
Meath	——
Raphoe	——
Kildare	——
Ferns & Leighlin	——
Ossory	——
Cloyne	——
Cork & Ross	"Lord Harcourt made his Nephew Dist^{r} of Stamps for Cork."
Killaloe & Kilfenora	——
Limerick, Ardfert & Aghadoe	"Lord Harcourt obtained an Ensigncy to his Recommendation."
Waterford & Lismore	——
Clonfert & Kilmacduagh	——
Elphin	——
Killala & Achonry	——

Note: A dash indicates no mention of a non-money payment.
Source: DCL, Gilbert Collection, MS. 94, pp. 321–59.

non-money payments made by the Lord Lieutenant to the Bishops. The material is derived from the records of Lord Harcourt, Viceroy from 1772 to late 1775. The non-money payments to the bishops were listed in the same entry as the annual value of their see, the strong implication being that the government looked upon them as part of the bishops' remuneration.

Not everything the bishops received was unencumbered. The expenses of the office were considerable, and, like the temporal nobility, a bishop could not live below his station. Indeed, there is some indication that Irishmen of gentlemanly rank lived considerably more lavishly than their English counterparts and that the social obligations of a Church of Ireland bishop were heavy and expensive.[66] Further, there were considerable hidden expenses. For instance, if one may use an early nineteenth-century example: Joseph Stock, Bishop of Killala and Achonry from 1798 to 1810 found that his translation to Waterford and Lismore was a temporary but severe strain on his finances. The various expenses of translation cost him £500. He had to reimburse the new holder of Killala for dilapidations to the episcopal palace and grounds, a process that dragged through litigation because the parties were more than £400 apart in their estimate of how much was owed. Additional moneys had to be paid the Board of First Fruits. Pressed by these expenses, Bishop Stock wondered anxiously if his sucessor at Killala would buy the furniture of the Killala Palace, thus providing him with cash and saving the expense of moving the articles.[67]

Similarly, the civil patronage granted to the bishops by the government was often encumbered by pressure for reciprocal grants of a certain amount of the normal episcopal patronage. The bishops possessed both religious and lay patronage of the sort useful to the government for paying small political and social debts. The most useful of the lay posts was the position of agent to a bishop. Letters to Lord Townshend from two of his bishops make it clear that he pressed them to appoint his nominees to the agency and that they were far from enthusiastic about so doing.[68] It is equally clear that the government pressed the bishops to appoint governmental favorites to livings under episcopal patronage. The bishops were less than enthusiastic about giving up portions of their patronage to the government, for by so doing they were being taxed on their non-money income, and they could be expected to resist just as they would a tax on their money income. Therefore the usual response to a request by the Lord Lieutenant that one of his choices be appointed to a living was a respectful, evasive, and negative letter.[69]

THE CATHEDRAL "SYSTEM"

Earlier, when viewing the formal outlines of the Church of Ireland, we discovered that there was no functioning middle rank between the bishops and the parish clergy. The office of rural dean was not fully revived until the nineteenth century. Irish archdeacons, in contrast to those in England, did not exercise general supervision over the clergy. The only functioning members of the middle ranks were the vicars-general who headed the consistorial courts. Since, however, their jurisdiction was limited to exceptional matters of clerical misbehavior, they alone could not serve as a continuing liaison between the bench and the parish. Therefore, we are left to deal with the middle level of the ecclesiastical army; namely, the cathedral dignitaries, who were intermediate in status between the levels of bishop and parish clergyman, but who were not specifically charged with coordinating the two levels. Collectively, the Irish cathedral chapters bear the label "system" only as a courtesy title; in practice they were eccentric, unsystematic, and independent.

One would expect the cathedral system to parallel closely the diocesan system, but, as in so many Irish church matters, the situation was somewhat more confusing than it might at first appear. Certain dioceses possessed deans, but no chapters. Other dioceses had deans and chapters, but no cathedrals. The situation is summarized in table 13.

If one considers solely the dioceses as united, there was a dean and cathedral chapter in all except Kilmore and Meath. In many of the united dioceses there were two deans and two chapters, remnants of the days before the union of the sees. The Bishops of Kilmore and of Meath were the bishops not having a building under their charge designated as a cathedral. Kilmore and Ardagh each possessed a dean, but neither possessed a cathedral nor a chapter. The same held for Clonmacnoise, a portion of the modern diocese of Meath; the position of dean (without chapter) kept alive the memory of Clonmacnoise as a formerly independent diocese. Both Connor and Kilmacduagh were in the position of having a dean and chapter, but no cathedral.

A cathedral is, of course, the church of the bishop of the diocese.[70] In the Church of Ireland the relation of bishop to his cathedral and to the cathedral chapter was extremely close, and in this respect contrasted with the situation in the Church of England. Bishops were often benefactors of the cathedrals, and some bishops, such as the Archbishop of Cashel and the Bishop of Limerick, held ranks within their cathedral as well as being the ordinary of the diocese. At Armagh the archbishop was not only in theory, but in practice as well, the directing authority in cathedral matters. And, unlike the situation in England, most stalls in the chapter were under the patronage of the diocesan bishop. Although it is dangerous to infer eighteenth-century practice from nineteenth-century rulings, the 1846 decision of Dr. Radcliff, Vicar-General of the Consistorial Court of Dublin, is worth attention. In that decision Radcliff concluded that in all Irish cathedrals (except Saint Patrick's, which was a special case) the bishop was the "principal head" of the chapter, as distinct from the dean who

TABLE 13
IRISH CATHEDRAL SYSTEM IN THE EIGHTEENTH CENTURY

Diocese	Dean	Chapter	Cathedral
Armagh	+	+	+
Clogher	+	+	+
Derry	+	+	+
Down	+	+	+
Connor	+	+	0[a]
Dromore	+	+	+
Kilmore	+	0	0
Meath[b]	0	0	0
Raphoe	+	+	+
Dublin:			
St. Patrick's	+	+	+
Christ Church	+	+	+
Kildare	+	+	+
Ferns	+	+	+
Leighlin	+	+	+
Ossory	+	+	+
Cashel	+	+	+
Emly	+	+	+
Cloyne	+	+	+
Cork	+	+	+
Ross	+	+	+
Killaloe	+	+	+
Kilfenora	+	+	+
Limerick	+	+	+
Ardfert & Aghadoe	+	+	+
Waterford	+	+	+
Lismore	+	+	+
Tuam	+	+	+
Ardagh	+	0	0
Clonfert	+	+	+
Kilmacduagh	+	+	0
Elphin	+	+	+
Killala	+	+	+
Achonry	+	+	+

Note: A plus sign indicates the existence of a dean, a chapter, or a cathedral; a zero indicates the absence. The number of cathedrals is somewhat problematical because a large parish church was on occasion designated a cathedral, and in many instances the cathedral and the parish church were one.

[a] The cathedral church of Connor was in ruins, but the parish church at Lisburn was constituted a cathedral for use of the chapters of Down and of Connor.

[b] There was a Dean of Clonmacnoise but no chapter or cathedral.

Source: Beaufort, pp. 105–36. In a few instances, additional information from other sources has been used.

was the "numeral head." Radcliff's judgment indicated that if the bishop wished, he could force his way into almost every detail of cathedral life simply from his position as ordinary of the diocese. But neither in the nineteenth nor in the eighteenth century did the bishop intervene a great deal in everyday affairs, an abstinence which should probably be perceived as a wise avoidance of petty squabbles rather than any dereliction of duty.[71]

As the mother church of the diocese, the cathedral was expected to be the venue of regular worship services. The Irish canons laid down that in each cathedral Holy Communion should be administered at least once a month. Side by side with this minimum standard was the strong recommendation by many ranking divines that the Eucharist be celebrated at least weekly. This latter standard, however, appears not to have been generally reached in cathedral practice, partially, one can conjecture, because of the strong Puritan element in Irish Anglican tradition.

In Dublin during much of the eighteenth century, the Dean and Chapter of Saint Patrick's cathedral held weekly Communion, but in Christ Church it was celebrated only monthly. Saint Finbarre's in Cork held Communion only monthly. Although the evidence is spotty, it appears that weekly celebration was the exception rather than the rule.[72] At least two services, morning and evening prayer, were held in each cathedral on Sundays. The evidence as to whether or not the two services were conducted on each of the other days of the week in most Irish cathedrals is not decisive. Certainly the provision of daily choral services was exceptional rather than regular practice, for only about one-third of the cathedrals had choral foundations of any sort. Even in those with such foundations daily choral service was not always observed. On the other hand, the eighteenth-century practice in Christ Church, Dublin, was to conduct three services daily, and two services were held each day in Saint Patrick's, Dublin.[73]

Before proceeding to a discussion of the structure of the Irish cathedrals, we should add a cautionary note on the differences between Irish and English cathedral practice and should underline the obvious point that it is dangerous to draw conclusions about Irish practice from English precedents. Earlier it was mentioned that the relationship of the bishop to his cathedral was much closer in Ireland than in England, and that the bishop possessed considerably more power over the chapter and patronage in the chapter than in England. A second difference: the Irish cathedrals were generally less well endowed, both in revenue and in fabric than their English counterparts. A common complaint of travelers in Ireland was that the cathedrals often appeared little more impressive than English parish churches. Third, the smallness of Irish endowments meant that deans and chapters were never resident to the same degree they were in England. Further, the chapters tended to be much smaller in Ireland than England.[74]

The structures of the Irish cathedral chapters varied, but a general pattern prevailed. At the head of each was a dean; in a full chapter there would typically also be a precentor, chancellor, treasurer, and archdeacon, with a number of prebendaries. The dean always headed the body, but the rank order of the other dignitaries varied from chapter to chapter. Each cathedral office had its corps, a parish or union of parishes, most of whose revenue went to the cathedral officer. In some cases the chapter member performed duty in the parishes, in others the duties were carried on by a vicar or curate. The structure of individual Irish cathedral chapters during the late eighteenth century is presented in table 14. (Minor canons and vicars choral are not included.)

The chief duties of a dean were precisely what one would expect them to be, namely the superintendence of the cathedral. In subordination to the bishop, the dean had inspecting and presiding power over the chapter of the cathedral. He gave possession of stalls and benefices to the members and inspected them in the discharge of their duties. He was required to preach not only in the cathedral but in other churches of the same diocese from which he received any income. The dean convened chapter meetings and presided over the chapter's transaction of business. In theory, he was to visit all churches within his jurisdiction at least once every three years. In addition the dean was responsible directly for the spiritual welfare of the parishes which composed the corps of the deanery.[75]

Certain of the deaneries had no cure of souls attached and were total sinecures. The deaneries of Dromore and of Ross, and those of Christ Church, Dublin, and Saint Patrick's, Dublin, had fully endowed vicarages, thereby relieving their deans of all parish responsibilities.[76] In the idiosyncratic case of the Dean of Lismore one finds that this dignitary possessed an extensive and unique jurisdiction beyond that of most deans. He exercised complete ecclesiastical jurisdiction and discipline (as distinct from being responsible for the cures of souls therein) over four large parishes of the dioceses. The jurisdiction lasted for eleven months each year, with the normal episcopal jurisdiction being exercised by the bishop only in the month of November. The Dean of Lismore had his own consistorial court and seal, issued marriage licenses, probated wills, and performed other functions normally reserved for the bishop's court.[77]

Deans, like bishops, were rewarded for their work by prestige and by money. To deans and provosts was extended the designation "very reverend." The reported incomes of the various deans in the years 1776–79 are given in table 15. In viewing the table, cautions about the reliability of eighteenth-century figures of incomes should be recalled.

Obviously the salary of some of the deaneries was nominal. Almost equally obvious, the duties of such posts must have been nominal. Residence or nonresidence in most instances appears to have been a matter of personal inclination or convenience. Even the most lucrative of the deaneries did

TABLE 14

STAFFING OF IRISH CATHEDRAL CHAPTERS

Cathedral	Dean	Prov- ost	Pre- centor	Chan- cellor	Treas- urer	Arch- deacon	Prebend- aries	Total
Armagh	1	–	1	1	1	1	4	9
Clogher	1	–	1	1	–	1	5	9
Derry	1	–	–	–	–	1	3	5
Down	1	–	1	1	–	1	2	6
Connor	1	–	1	1	–	1	4	8
Dromore	1	–	1	1	1	1	1	6
Kilmore[a]	1	–	–	–	–	–	–	1
Clonmacnoise (Meath)[a]	1	–	–	–	–	–	–	1
Raphoe	1	–	–	–	–	1	4	6
Dublin:								
St. Patrick's	1	–	1	1	1	2	19	25
Christ Church	1	–	1	1	1	1	3	8
Kildare	1	–	1	1	1	1	4	9
Ferns	1	–	1	1	1	1	10	15
Leighlin	1	–	1	1	1	1	4	9
Ossory	1	–	1	1	1	1	7	12
Cashel	1	–	1	1	1	1	4	9
Emly	1	–	1	1	–	1	4	8
Cloyne	1	–	1	1	1	1	14	19
Cork	1	–	1	1	1	1	12	17
Ross	1	–	1	1	1	1	5	10
Killaloe	1	–	1	1	1	1	5	10
Kilfenora	1	–	1	1	1	1	–	5
Limerick	1	–	1	1	1	1	11	16
Ardfert & Aghadoe	1	–	1	1	1	1	–	5
Waterford[b]	1	–	1	1	1	–	–	4
Lismore	1	–	1	1	1	1	10	15
Tuam	1	1	–	–	–	1	8	11
Ardagh[a]	1	–	–	–	–	–	–	1
Clonfert[c]	1	–	–	–	–	1	8	11
Kilmacduagh	1	1	–	1	–	1	2	6
Elphin	1	–	1	–	–	1	8	11
Killala	1	–	1	–	–	1	5	8
Achonry	1	–	1	–	–	1	3	6

[a] No chapter, but an archdeaconry existed without corporate cathedral attachments.

[b] Archdeaconry extant, but holder not a chapter member.

[c] A sacrist member of chapter.

Source: Beaufort, pp. 107–36.

TABLE 15
ANNUAL VALUE OF IRISH DEANERIES
(In pounds)

Down	1,700
Derry	1,600
Raphoe	1,600
St. Patrick's	800
Clogher	800
Kilmore	600
Ossory	600
Limerick	600
Waterford	400
Cork	400
Dromore	400
Tuam	300
Ferns	300
Lismore	300
Elphin	250
Cloyne	220
Kilfenora	210
Christ Church	200
Cashel	200
Ardagh	200
Connor	200
Armagh	150
Killala	150
Killaloe	140
Kildare	120
Kilmacduagh	120
Emly	100
Achonry	100
Leighlin	80
Ardfert	60
Ross	20
Clonfert	20

Note: The Dean of Clonmacnoise is not
mentioned.
Source: Mant, 2: 659–70.

not prove sufficient inducement for its possessor to perform his duties: one
newly appointed mid-eighteenth-century Dean of Down learned to his dis-
may that his predecessor had spent only two days in the deanery in his six
years in office. Still this conscientious new divine, Dean Delany, kept a
promise he made to his wife to spend every third year in England.[78]

In most cathedrals the second ranking dignitary was the precentor.
Twenty-five men held precentorships in the various Irish cathedrals in the

late eighteenth century. This rank (and those that follow) was a more than purely honorific position, but the duties were minimal. Historically, the precentor was responsible for the direction of the choral services. In reality these duties were generally nonexistent since the majority of Irish cathedrals did not have vicars choral or similar bodies. Even in those with choral bodies the duties were usually nominal or at least nonmusical. The precentor's cathedral duties were more often than not held in addition to responsibilities as a parish priest.

The chancellor usually ranked next in order of precedence. Essentially he served as secretary of the chapter, a not onerous responsibility. Unlike English practice, under which the office of chancellor and vicar-general were usually united, the two offices remained separate in Ireland, with all matters of ecclesiastical jurisdiction being executed by the vicar-general.[79] The chancellor normally served as a parish priest. Twenty-three chancellor-ships were found in Church of Ireland chapters in the late eighteenth century.

The fourth pillar of the typical chapter was the treasurer into whose custody the cathedral plate and valuables were entrusted. He also served as bursar of the chapter and received all rents and revenue. Most treasurers, like most men holding any cathedral dignity, did parish duty as well as cathedral duty. Eighteen men held the rank of treasurer.

Although not historically ranked with the preceding four dignitaries, who formed the "four pillars" of a classically composed cathedral chapter, the archdeacon in the Church of Ireland was often a man of considerable importance, who, in some instances, held precedence over the others save the dean. An archdeacon was not by right a member of a chapter, although in Ireland he ordinarily was a member, and the office of archdeacon did not depend on there being a cathedral chapter in the diocese. One finds, therefore, that the office existed in the Diocese of Waterford, but that the holder had no stall in the cathedral. And in the cases of Kilmore, Meath, and Ardagh, there was no chapter, but the rank of archdeacon was preserved. Of the thirty-four men who held the title of archdeacon in the church in the late eighteenth century, twenty-nine were cathedral dignitaries. Although in most cases the other dignitaries took precedence, in the Chapters of Connor, Down, Dromore, and Clogher, the archdeacons ranked next to the dean.[80] More than for any other member of the chapter, the archdeacon's duties varied from diocese to diocese. In some he served as an active aid to the bishop in diocesan affairs. In others, the rank was purely titular. Unlike the archdeacons of the English church, those of the Irish did not possess visitorial jurisdiction over the parish clergy. In the nineteenth century the archdeacons were to become fully functional administrative officers, but in the eighteenth their duties remained ill-defined and irregular.

In the Chapters of Tuam and of Kilmacduagh the ancient rank of provost survived. The provost ranked next to the dean in those cathedrals. Neither the provostship of Tuam nor that of Kilmacduagh possessed a cure of souls, and although the Provost of Tuam at least preached in turn in the cathedral, the Provost of Kilmacdaugh had no cathedral duties of any sort.[81]

An equally eccentric office was that of sacrist, a position found only in the Chapter of Clonfert. The sacrist's duties in the Clonfert chapter are unclear; it appears that he probably served in the role of precentor.

After the dignitaries came the prebendaries. The prebendaries were of two sorts, those who had cure of souls and those who did not. The former category was the most common, most prebendaries being assigned certain parishes which were historically tied to their stall. Often the prebend carried a geographic name, corresponding to its parishes. One hundred and sixty-nine prebendaries held office in the eighteenth century. The office was a desirable one since it rarely required cathedral residence except when preaching in rotation and often was tied to a lucrative benefice.

At this point a brief parenthesis on terminology is necessary. In general religious practice it is common for "prebendary" to be used synonymously with "canon." In the Church of England during the nineteenth century, "canon" replaced "prebendary" as the normal appellation. Actually, there is some difference, for "canon" is chiefly a spiritual title referring to the spiritual right obtained by being received into a chapter. (It also referred to a right to share in the common fund, but in Irish practice this right was not important.) A prebendary, on the other hand, by virtue of his office held certain parishes, the title thus being one of maintenance. In actual practice in the Irish church, all those having prebends were automatically canons as well. During the eighteenth and nineteenth centuries the general usage of the Church of Ireland, in contrast to the Church of England, favored the term "prebendary" rather than "canon." For this reason, and for the additional reason that "canon" in the Irish church often referred to minor canons (i.e. vicars-choral), the word "prebendary" is employed in referring to pre-disestablishment chapters. After disestablishment our terminology will have to change because financial pressures forced an operational distinction to be made in the two offices.[82] That, however, is in the future.

Most cathedral officers had the dual responsibility of supervising a parish as well as performing cathedral duties. The latter was not difficult, being the keeping of a regular number of services. With few exceptions (which will be mentioned later) cathedral personnel were not expected to be residential. But, in regard to their parish duties, how active were most cathedral officers? Unhappily, adequate information from the eighteenth century is not available. Therefore, it is necessary to use information gathered in the early 1830s to answer this question. Because cathedral chapters changed only slowly, and because the data were gathered before the reforms of the 1830s, this information will give us a reasonably accurate general idea for the eighteenth century. Nine of the thirty-three deans did not have benefices with the cure of souls annexed to them: Armagh, Clonmacnoise, Dromore, Christ Church (Dublin), Saint Patrick's (Dublin), Lismore, Ross, Tuam, and Clonfert. The same held true for nine of the twenty-five precentorships, for five of the twenty-three chancellorships, for five of the eighteen treasurerships, and for eleven of the thirty-four arch-deaconries. Of the two provosts, neither held a benefice with cure of souls, nor did the the the one sacrist. Fifty-two of the 169 prebendaries had no parish responsibility of cure of souls.[83] A reasonable estimate, therefore, is that about 31 percent (94 of the 305 men who held offices) did not have parish duties annexed to their post. Although it would be a mistake to adjudge all those who held cathedral offices without cure of souls as ecclesiastical drones—some may have paid assiduous attention to cathedral activities, and others may have held parishes with cure not connected with the chapter—the fact remains that the Irish cathedral system was open to abuse. If a cleric wished to be indolent, inefficient, or was merely incompetent, there was wide range for the exercise of those propensities.

It is logical to turn from discussing the cathedral system in terms of indi-vidual functionaries, to discussing its corporate aspects. Significantly we find that corporate matters were of surprisingly little importance. Histor-ically, the chapters had served as advisers to the bishops and had elected the bishop. These duties were totally lost by the eighteenth century.[84] The most important corporate functions, therefore, were not spiritual, but tem-poral; specifically, the holding of property and the management of revenue. About half of the cathedrals (the number was reported to be sixteen in 1834) possessed economy estates; that is, lands and property whose income was specifically reserved for the sustenation of cathedral fabric and the maintenance of officers and servants of the cathedral. The total incomes from all such estates in the early 1830s was slightly over £11,000 a year. At that time the sum was reported to be inadequate in many cases for necessary repairs; there is no reason to doubt that the same held true in the eighteenth century.

The idea that the chapters possessed a common fund which could be divided among the officers at will is a misconception. Only the Deans and Chapters of Kildare and of Waterford had the right to divide their common fund between themselves if they wished, and the Dean and Chapter of Lismore took nine-tenths of each renewal fine for their individual pos-session, but these were the exceptions. In all but these three chapters, cor-porate revenues were tied to maintenance of fabric and service and the corporations were limited to a narrow band of choices in deciding how they were to be used.[85]

If the corporate decision of how common funds should be spent was a constricted one, the problem of managing investments was nevertheless an important communal activity. The revenues were of two sorts, each of which demanded careful superintendence. The chief of these was the corporate lands. These lands were usually leased for twenty-one years, but occasionally for forty years or longer, with most of the income being derived from renewal fines. The other form of corporate revenue, much less common, was the receipt of the greater part of the tithes (the rectorial tithes) from certain parishes. This was a major form of income at Cork, Cloyne, Ross, Cashel, Killaloe, Lismore, Leighlin, and Tuam.[86] Granting that the management of corporation investments and the expenditure of funds must have involved a certain amount of time and attention from the chapter, the fact remains that in only about half the chapters was there any such common fund to administer.

But, it might be argued, there were other corporate duties, such as the administration of patronage vested in the chapter, which must have demanded attention. Again, we are dealing with a misconception, for we find that only six chapters possessed any corporate patronage. These were Christ Church, Dublin (three prebends, six vicar choralships, four benefices, and, an alternate turn of presentation, to one benefice and a fourth turn of presentation to another), Saint Patrick's, Dublin (four benefices), Leighlin (one benefice), Ossory (five benefices), Cork (one perpetual cure and one chapelry), Killaloe (three benefices).[87] The conclusion dictated by surveying the temporal and spiritual duties of the deans and chapters as corporate bodies is that the corporate aspects of the Irish cathedral system were relatively unimportant. Instead of being composed of small, unified bodies of clergymen, as is usually supposed, the cathedral system can more accurately be depicted as a sprinkling of church buildings, through whose doors at infrequent and uncoordinated intervals passed various clerics.

For the sake of completeness we should note that a number of cathedrals had subsidiary corporations: the minor canons or vicars-choral, men who were deputized for the prebendaries for choral purposes. The formation of such bodies may be looked upon as a desirable degree of professionalization, or specialization, which undoubtedly raised the standard of cathedral services. As corporations, these minor bodies were headed by the dean, who most often appointed the vicars-choral or minor canons, although in some cases he shared rights of patronage with other dignitaries. Like the cathedral chapters, these minor bodies possessed full corporate characteristics, had a common seal, could hold lands and endowments, and could be sued or sue at law.[88] Regularity not being a characteristic of the Church of Ireland, one finds such bodies in only about one-third of the cathedrals. There were eleven corporations of vicars-choral, one found in each of the following cathedrals: Armagh, Christ Church (Dublin), Saint Patrick's

(Dublin), Ossory, Limerick, Cashel, Lismore, Cork, Ross, Cloyne, and Tuam. Minor canonries were found at Ardfert, Saint Patrick's (Dublin), and Kildare. The distribution of these foundations is noteworthy: even a rapid glance indicates that the provinces of Armagh, Dublin, and Tuam were scantily served in comparison to Cashel, which had more choral foundations than the other provinces put together.[89]

Merely possessing choral foundations and actually having effective foundations were two entirely different things. Although in most cases the corporations still consisted of several persons, by the early 1830s the corporations of Tuam, Ross, and Ardfert had each dwindled down to a single person. In none of these three cases did the officeholder perform any duty, being satisfied simply to collect the emoluments attached to the office.[90] In other cases the effectiveness of the choral foundation was undercut by its revenues being small. In still others, the vicars choral were nonresident, taking emoluments for performing no duty. The clerical members of these corporations usually held parishes as well as their vicar choralships. Inevitably, a conflict arose between cathedral and parish duties. Added to this was the temptation to treat the clerical vicars-choral as cathedral drones, making them take inconvenient services and perform miscellaneous duties having nothing to do with their choral posts.[91]

Three cathedrals deserve individual attention: Kildare, Christ Church (Dublin), and Saint Patrick's (Dublin). The first is noteworthy because, like Christ Church, it possessed a residential chapter in the manner of the English cathedrals. In addition to the four dignitaries, the archdeacon, and four prebendaries, the chapter contained four canons who, together with the dean, were charged with residing and reading services. The canons possessed their own endowment which amounted in the early 1830s to somewhat more than £10,000. The canons in many ways were analogous to vicars-choral, for they were endowed to perform divine service, but unlike vicars-choral they served as full members of the chapter.[92]

Like the canons of Kildare, the prebendaries of Christ Church, Dublin, were residential, being charged with daily attendance, in turn, at the cathedral's morning and evening services. The Deanship of Christ Church was unusual, for it was combined with a bishopric, that of Kildare. It can be inferred that the decanal duties received greater attention than the episcopal ones in this relationship, because the holder of the joint offices resided in Dublin, having no residence in the Kildare Diocese.[93] During the early eighteenth century, Christ Church had been the focus of prolonged dispute between the Archbishop of Dublin and the Dean and Chapter of Christ Church. The issue was whether or not the archbishop held general jurisdiction over the chapter and the right of visitation thereof, and whether or not the Archdeacon of Dublin held a right to a seat in the chapter. The chapter maintained the negative, the archbishop the affirmative position. The matter first came to public legal hearing in 1704, but dragged on without solution for nearly twenty years. Finally, in 1724, the English House of Lords concluded the controversy by deciding in the archbishop's favor. The feud died at once and for the remainder of the century relations between the archbishop and the Dean and Chapter of Christ Church were amicable.[94]

The third noteworthy cathedral chapter, that of Saint Patrick's, Dublin, was the largest in Ireland, having nineteen prebendaries, two archdeacons, and a total of twenty-five members. Its most unusual characteristic (which it shared only with Kildare) was that its deanship was filled by election by the chapter.[95] Because of Saint Patrick's size and importance, this opened the way to bitterness in a contested election. Fortunately for the peace of the cathedral, the Deanship of Saint Patrick's usually became vacant through the incumbent dean being appointed to the bench, thereby giving the Crown the right of presentation to the deanery.[96] In 1817, however, a bitter conflict followed a contested election. The contest was between John Pomeroy, a prebendary, and Richard Ponsonby, the chancellor, Pomeroy was declared elected by a majority of one. Unhappily, his majority was based on proxy votes; the majority actually present voted for Ponsonby. Thus, the issue hinged on whether proxies were admissible. The ecclesiastical court ruled that they were not and thereby reversed the results that had been previously declared official.[97] Such adventures in ecclesiastical democracy can only have divided the chapter and embittered those on the losing side.

Both Saint Patrick's and Christ Church were also unusual in maintaining vestigial feudal jurisdictions in the city of Dublin. Control of the Liberty of Saint Sepulchre's by the Archbishop of Dublin has already been discussed. The Liberty of Saint Patrick's and that of Christ Church were essentially the same, being independent civil jurisdictions. The Liberty of Christ Church lay partially in Dublin City and partially within the jurisdiction of Dublin County, not City. The Liberty of Saint Patrick's lay totally within Dublin City, and indeed, totally within the boundaries of the Liberty of Saint Sepulchre's, from which, however, it claimed complete administrative independence. In such a situation the chance for a conflict between the Archbishop of Dublin, under whose charge came the Liberty of Saint Sepulchre's, and the Dean and Chapter of Saint Patrick's was great. Tempers flared in 1753 when Archbishop Cobbe had his seneschal draw up a statement claiming that the chapter's jurisdiction was concurrent with, and not exclusive of, that of the archbishop. In support of the argument, the seneschal maintained that the archbishop's coroner and weighmaster had continually exercised their office in Saint Patrick's Liberty, and that within living memory the archbishop's clerk of market had operated therein. Friction increased, and in 1757 the seneschal of Saint Sepulchre's was resisted when he attempted to exercise his alleged jurisdiction over the markets of Saint Patrick's. The archbishop was thereby successfully blocked, and although he never conceded the matter, public practice, court decisions, and further legislation served to bulwark the claims of dean and chapter.[98]

Having discussed the constitution and activities of cathedral chapters and members, we must conclude by asking who held the patronage of the various offices. At the decanal level the answer is simple. With three exceptions the patronage was in Crown hands as represented by Irish and English political leaders. The exceptions were Kildare and Saint Patrick's, Dublin, in which the deans were elected by the chapter, and the Deanship of Clonmacnoise which was collative by the Bishop of Meath. As far as the appointment of dignitaries and prebendaries was concerned, the Irish bishops usually held patronage. This is in contrast to the situation prevailing in England where the bishops' patronage was relatively limited and where conflicting rights of patronage often snarled the election of dignitaries and prebendaries. The exceptions to the patronage of bishops in cathedral matters were minor. As enumerated in 1834 they were as follows: The Crown appointed the four nondecanal dignitaries of Christ Church, Dublin. The precentorship of Clogher was in the patronage of the University of Dublin. A total of only fourteen prebends were filled by others than the bishop of the diocese, namely, four prebends of Kildare (two in lay patronage, one in alternate presentation of Crown and bishop, and one in which the lay patron had two turns to the bishop's one); three prebends in Christ Church, Dublin (lay patronage); two prebends in Saint Patrick's, Dublin (lay patronage); two prebends in Limerick (lay patronage); one prebend in Cork (Crown patronage) and two prebends in Killaloe (lay patronage).[99]

THE PARISH BASE

Parish Function and Parish Structure

The parish was both a religious and a civil unit. In each parish or group of parishes four major religious observances were conducted. The first of these was the celebration of Holy Communion. Monthly Communion was the usual practice in Ireland, and there is no evidence that any parish church began conducting weekly Communion before the nineteenth century. Morning and evening prayer constituted the second major religious observance at the parish level. Such services were conducted at least weekly, and in many cases during the week. Eighteenth-century evidence for provincial parishes is too scant to permit generalization, but in Dublin daily prayers seem to have been a regular practice. In 1703 Archbishop

King, having been recently translated from Derry to Dublin, noted that daily prayers were provided in the Dublin churches, and in the 1720s the organists of at least four Dublin churches were required to serve morning and evening prayer daily. By 1821 it was reported that service was held in every church in Dublin at least once a day. The third and fourth important ceremonies held in each parish were self-explanatory, namely marriage and the burial of the dead.[100]

The civil functions of the parish were those of a minor local government. The Church of Ireland parish had fewer responsibilities and powers than did its English counterpart. The Protestant population in Ireland was in most places scattered too thinly to allow the Anglican vestry to be as effective an organization of control as was the case in England. Therefore, Irish local government was conducted chiefly on a county level and administered by grand juries. These juries were composed of twenty-three large landholders nominated by the sheriff of the county. Nevertheless, the smallest unit of government, the local parish vestry, did have certain powers; the most important of which was the right to levy small taxes and to spend these revenues on church repairs and on minor public works such as roads, the regulation of beggars, the hiring of constables, and the reduction of vagrancy.[101]

The Irish vestries worked on a dual level. The "select vestry," composed of rate-paying Protestants, laid certain small taxes for the physical maintenance of the Established Church and for the payment of minor church officers such as the sexton. (In most cases, the greater part of local religious revenues came from tithes which were usually the property of the incumbent or a local landlord, and were not under effective control of the vestry.) There was also a "general vestry" which, after the abolition of the penal laws, included all rate payers regardless of religious affiliation. The general vestry voted sums for minor local services such as roads, constables, and the like. Despite the inclusion of non-Protestants in the general vestry, minority control over local government was guaranteed by the provision that all officers were required to be members of the Established Church. This stipulation was sometimes ignored in practice, but was doubtless irksome to the Catholic and Presbyterian populations.[102]

The key vestry officers were the two churchwardens, elected annually, whose duty was to protect the church and serve as its legal representatives. To aid the wardens, the select vestry often appointed other officers: such as a sexton, who was charged with maintenance duties; and a parish clerk, who often served as parish schoolmaster. The general vestry frequently added constables to the list of parish officers. Local health officers and local assessors were also appointed in some parishes. The actual civil activities of any parish were unpredictable. In some areas the civil duties of the parish were almost totally ignored, while in others the vestries became comprehensive bodies which fed and buried the indigent, repaired roads and public buildings, governed civil celebrations, and provided elementary sanitary services. Illegal though it was, in some areas the vestry became a truly ecumenical unit by allocating some of its funds for the construction of Roman Catholic chapels and Presbyterian meeting houses. The great unpredictables in any parish were the attitudes of the local squire, whose cooperation was needed for the parish to function effectively in civil matters, and the Church of Ireland minister who, although in theory excluded from the operation of the vestry itself, was often a predominant influence in its decisions.[103]

Two examples—one from rural Ireland, the other from Dublin City—will suffice to illustrate the wide range of parish function and organization. The first is the Parish of Derriaghy, a rural Ulster parish. Derriaghy was an active parish unit both ecclesiastically and civilly. The parish was divided into three constablewicks, each in the charge of parish constables, of unreported number. There were two churchwardens and two sidesmen, also a parish clerk and a sexton. In 1729 the parish also appointed a director of the highway, for road construction and maintenance, and the director had under him six surveyors, two for each constablewick. Later in 1753 or 1754 (the precise date is uncertain), the parish appointed eight overseers of roads. The parish vestry levied and applied the cess which was used to pay the salaries of the sexton, parish clerk, and director of the highway, plus church repairs and the maintenance of the poor and of orphans. The salaries paid were small: two pounds for the directors; about ten pounds for the parish clerk; and one pound, ten shillings per year for the sexton. In this parish the vestry also levied the tithes and seems to have taken a major portion of the responsibility for their collection. A compact and self-contained unit, the Parish of Derriaghy was an example—although an atypical one—of the Irish parish system at its best.[104]

The second example is the Parish of Saint Michan's in the City of Dublin. During the first half of the eighteenth century, the parish was well off; indeed, so well off that the church wardens could afford to buy stocks for those who caused a disturbance during divine service and still have enough on hand to provide a fire engine and attending officer for the use of the parish. The churchwardens had a good deal of responsibility. Each year they perambulated the parish, valuing each house therein. They were responsible for providing basic municipal services such as sewers. They hired scavengers who undertook to remove the rubbish and filth from the streets. The churchwardens were responsible for law and order, paying for the maintenance of the watch. In 1784, in response to serious riots in the city, the wardens hired special police officers to patrol the street each evening from seven to nine; this proved unsatisfactory and a central police force for the city was established. The parish vestry paid for the new police system out of the cess, an expense of more than £1,100 in the year 1790. Additionally, the parish, as represented by the churchwardens, supported the poor and registered beggars. They maintained persons in the workhouse, where expenses in 1730 came to above £500.[105]

The churchwardens and those overseeing the parish vestry were essentially amateurs. The professionals in the parish system were the clergy whose lives were given over, full time, to parish duties. Parish clergy were basically of two sorts, those holding effectively permanent appointments and those holding temporary posts. The former group was divided into three further categories: to wit, rectors, vicars and perpetual curates. These three had similar duties, each being in sole charge of a parish or group of parishes under the general supervision of the diocesan bishop. Whether a clergyman was a rector or a vicar had nothing to do with his clerical duties, but rather was determined by the condition of the tithes in his benefice. If all the tithes in the benefice were payable to him, then he was known as a rector. If, in contrast, a portion belonged to someone other than the incumbent, then he was termed a vicar (the technicalities of the tithe system will be discussed in the next chapter).

Perpetual curates were those holding permanent appointment to parishes in which the whole tithe was paid to someone other than the priest, without any endowment being made for a vicar. In many instances, these were parishes to which the pre-Reformation tithes were paid to a monastery which then provided the parish with a temporary curate. After the Reformation the tithes passed into lay hands with the layman obtaining thereby the right to nominate the parson (and often paying a large portion of his salary personally). Once nominated, the perpetual curate could not be removed by the lay patron, but only by the bishop himself, as in the case of rectors and vicars. (Here, the reader is forewarned. In practice, perpetual curates were often called vicars, and eighteenth- and nineteenth-century writers often used the words "rector" and "vicar" interchangeably.) At the very bottom of the ecclesiastical ladder were found the temporary curates who served as assistants to the beneficed clergy. These men, insecure in their appointment and borderline in social position, waited forlornly for promotion to benefices of their own.[106]

If, in the abstract, the basic unit of ecclesiastical government was the parish, in practice it was the benefice. (A benefice refers to a religious office rather than to a geographic unit.) Often a clergyman held a single parish as his benefice, but in many two or more parishes were formally united and held by a single clergyman, the combined parishes constituting his benefice. In the dioceses of the Church of Ireland which served few

TABLE 16
IRISH PARISH STRUCTURE, LATE EIGHTEENTH CENTURY

Diocese	Parishes	Benefices	Churches
Province of Armagh			
Armagh	103	69	69
Clogher	41	40	49
Derry	48	43	51
Down & Connor	114	65	76
Dromore	26	24	27
Kilmore	39	30	36
Meath	224	99	77
Raphoe	31	25	32
Provincial Total	626	395	417
Province of Dublin			
Dublin	209	86	82
Kildare	81	31	28
Ferns & Leighlin	232	79	71
Ossory	136	56	36
Provincial Total	658	252	217
Province of Cashel			
Cashel & Emly	155	47	35
Cloyne	137	69	51
Cork & Ross	127	64	53
Killaloe & Kilfenora	138	50	38
Limerick, Ardfert & Aghadoe	176	88	47
Waterford & Lismore	106	44	30
Provincial Total	839	362	254
Province of Tuam			
Tuam & Ardagh	126	47	53
Clonfert & Kilmacduagh	60	15	14
Elphin	75	29	26
Killala & Achonry	52	20	20
Provincial Total	313	111	113
National Total	2,436	1,120	1,001

Source: Beaufort, p. 137, with arithmetical corrections.

Protestants or in which tithe revenues were scant, one finds that several parishes had to be united in this form. The late eighteenth-century situation is shown in table 16.

Flaws in the Webbing

Even a cursory examination of table 16 indicates a serious flaw in the parish system: the provision of churches was uneven. But spotty though church provision may have been late in the century, it probably was considerably better than at mid-century. The following tabulation was made of selected dioceses in the years 1746–56.[107]

Dioceses	Churches in repair	Churches in ruins
Waterford	9	22
Lismore	14	49
Cork	30	46
Ross	11	21
Cloyne	47	22
Ardfert and Aghadoe	15	54

Now, using table 16 to compare the number of benefices to the number of churches, it is clear that not every benefice (which usually consisted of at least two parishes) had a church: there were 1,120 benefices and 1,001 churches. The result was the existence in Ireland of a species of ecclesiastical appointments known as "non-cures." This was a benefice in which the incumbent, having been instituted for the ostensible purpose of the cure of souls but having no church and no place of residence, was allowed to abandon his clerical responsibilities altogether;[108] at the same time he collected whatever tithes were attached to the benefice.

Early in the eighteenth century it became obvious that the provision of churches was insufficient to allow every member of the Church of Ireland convenient access to a place of worship. An early Hanoverian statute (6 George I, c. 13) therefore provided that in parishes where there was a considerable number of parishioners more than six (Irish) miles from a church, one or two chapels of ease might be erected and curates hired for their service.[109] The evidence from the latter years of the century indicate clearly that the act was far from an effective solution to the problem.

Just as distressing to devout churchmen as the shortage of churches, was the union of parishes into overlarge benefices. As mentioned earlier, the average benefice in Ireland consisted of approximately two parishes, with considerable regional variation. While one must recognize that the parish network was thin in many places, the excuse for this situation is worth noting. The explanation is financial, not spiritual: unions between parishes occurred chiefly in areas in which the tithes were too small to support a clergyman. In the usual cases, this occurred in districts in which the tithes were wholly or largely impropriated to laymen. Paradoxically, parish unions abounded in the parts of Ireland where one would not expect them to be— the areas of fertile tillage land—which often had considerable Protestant populations. For example, Meath, Kildare, Dublin, Ossory, Cashel and Emly, and Ferns and Leighlin all had extensive unions. The reason was that the monks and monasteries of Ireland had settled in the best parts of the country and had absorbed most of the tithes, and during the Reformation the tithes passed largely into lay hands. In such areas, therefore, unions were necessary to raise revenue to support even a single church and clergyman.[110] At the other end of the scale, in the areas of poor land such as Tuam, Clonfert and Kilmacduagh, Elphin, also Limerick, Ardfert and Aghadoe, unions were necessary to raise enough revenue to support clergymen, even when tithes were not impropriated.

What were the procedures for making unions, and the restrictions thereon? If any patron of a clergyman desired a union of parishes, he and all other interested parties had to petition the Irish privy council. In their petition they were to include certificates of approbation from the archbishop of their province and from the bishop of the diocese—certifying, among other things, the value of the livings involved and indicating how the union would better accommodate the parishioners. Special attention was to be paid to the distance of the most remote part of the parish from the united church. Consent of the patrons and incumbents of the parishes involved was demanded, under seal. Equally elaborate requirements had to be fulfilled for the moving of a parish church.[111] The interesting point is that the decision was made ultimately by political appointees —the members of the privy council—and not by episcopal authorities. The bishops had a veto right over permanent unions, but no power of their own to sanction them. In addition to these procedures for creating permanent unions, the bishop of any diocese had the right to create temporary unions which expired on the death of the incumbent.[112]

To the credit of the church leaders, in the third decade of the eighteenth century they promoted a bill which would have given the Lord Lieutenant and a committee of six privy councillors the right to divide overly large benefices; that is, providing the diocesan agreed, but without requiring the consent of the incumbent. The bill, introduced into the House of Lords in 1732, passed by a large majority but was thrown out by the Commons. Any hope of reducing the number of unions disappeared in 1735 when the Irish House of Commons deprived the clergy of the tithes on pasturage for dry and barren cattle. Financially, therefore, unions were more necessary than ever.[113]

Not surprisingly, government officials occasionally worried about the effect upon the population of too few clergy. Thus, in 1788, one finds the Lord Lieutenant, the Marquis of Buckingham, writing to the Archbishop of Dublin a long letter voicing his concern about the "paucity of resident Ministers of the Gospel." He therefore suggested that whenever a union became vacant an inquiry should be made by the privy council to ascertain whether the union was still justified. The decision was to be made by the privy council, with prior investigation and recommendation by the ordinary of the diocese.[114] Unfortunately for the administrative health of the Church of Ireland, the number of unions was not significantly reduced until the nineteenth century.

The problem of the proliferation of unions was snarled further by the prevalence of pluralities, a practice on which there are unfortunately no reliable statistics for the eighteenth century. Shocking cases of pluralism are easy enough to find, but it is difficult to tell how representative they were of the church as a whole. For example, in 1782 Charles Agar, Archdeacon of Emly and Vicar of Tipperary, decided to reside in the latter benefice where he would be assisted by a curate. To take care of the few souls under his charge in the corps of the archdeaconry, he hired a Reverend Garrett Wall as curate for £4 a year and another curate, a Reverend A. Armstrong, at £3 a year. But Wall and Armstrong were not downtrodden clerical serfs, for they themselves were pluralists. Wall was vicar of a comfortable living that adjoined the corps of the archdeaconry, while Armstrong was simultaneously Vicar of Emly and Prebendary of Killardry.[115]

What the actual practice was, concerning regulation of pluralities, is somewhat cloudy. From 1666 onwards, it had been illegal for anyone to hold benefices simultaneously in England and in Ireland. Within Ireland the holding of more than one benefice was allowed, without requiring episcopal approval if the benefices were "compatible." Compatibility meant that only one of the two (or several) benefices involved the cure of souls. If more than one cure with souls was involved, a dispensation, or faculty, had to be obtained. This faculty was obtained from the Lord Primate of All Ireland. Previous to Primate Boulter's administration, it had apparently been common to evade the requirement of the Lord Primate's license. Boulter zealously reestablished the rights of his office.

The archbishop appears to have had a great deal of latitude in deciding on pluralities, but in 1788 we find Lord Rokeby, Archbishop of Armagh, conscientiously limiting pluralities according to the practice of the Church of England. This practice was to permit pluralities only when the benefices were within thirty miles of each other. English precedents were not binding. The Lord Lieutenant was clearly worried that Rokeby's successor might be less rigorous, and pressed for making English practice compulsory in Ireland, with the English thirty-mile limit, however, being extended to fifty miles because of Irish conditions. But nothing was done, and, as in so many matters, a flaw in the church found in the eighteenth century was not to be mended until well into the nineteenth.[116]

The inadequate number of churches in relation to the number of benefices and the existence of pluralities, when combined with the reluctance of many clergy to live in rural areas, merged into one macroproblem plaguing the Church of Ireland: namely, the nonresidence of the parochial clergy. It is easy to see that in benefices lacking churches, and in the cases of incumbents holding more than one cure, nonresidence was probable, if not inevitable. To this was added the vexing point that the Church of Ireland was painfully short of residences for its parish clergy. In 1787 there were only 354 glebe houses in all of Ireland: 212 in the province of Armagh, 64 in Dublin, 61 in Cashel, and 17 in Tuam.[117] The reasons for this shortage will be discussed in the next chapter; the crucial point here is that ministers without a manse could scarcely be expected to reside in their parishes. Admittedly, some of them managed to find suitable lodgings near their benefices, but for many this was impossible. Even in places with a church manse and no pluralities, the parish clergy was often nonresident. Many of the bishops freely granted dispensations for nonresidence, for reasons ranging from ill-health of the incumbent to dampness in the parish rectory. Statistics are hard to find, but Archbishop King's estimate for Clonfert has the stamp of his knowledgeability: it showed that about half of the beneficed clergy of that diocese were nonresident.[118] In fairness one should add that Clonfert, because of its location, probably suffered more from nonresidence than most dioceses.

The most baffling part of the nonresidence problem was that even a conscientious bishop could not force his clergy to reside. For although the clergy were canonically required to do so, the bishop had no sanction available, short of deprivation, and this weapon was too drastic and too complicated to invoke in such cases. In the 1780s the Marquis of Buckingham analyzed the situation and concluded that the only solution was a statute under which nonresident clergy would face pecuniary fines. The Lord Lieutenant suggested that the Board of First Fruits should have the power of prosecution—such actions being taken in civil rather than in ecclesiastical courts. That such a suggestion was necessary is good indication of the impotence of ecclesiastical courts and canon law in this matter.[119] Only in the very closing years of the eighteenth century was a concerted effort begun to impose clergy residency, a movement whose history really belongs to the subsequent century.

The superior-subordinate relationship was further confused by the existence of an unofficial superior over most benefices: the local landlord, if he were resident. Granted, even in livings of which he was the patron, the landlord, or magnate, did not possess the power of removing an incumbent once instituted and inducted; but his local authority made him a man to placate, if not obey. The landlord, for example, had a great deal of influence over whether or not the local peasantry paid their tithes, the tithes being the chief source of income for a parish minister. The case of the Reverend Dr. Pelissier, of Newton Stewart, near Omagh, County Tyrone, is instructive in this regard. Upon arriving at his parish, he wrote to the local magnate, the Earl of Abercorn, noting:

> When a clergyman first comes to a parish he is bound not only in duty, but also in point of prudence to lay a solid foundation for a lasting peace and good will with his parishioners.
>
> Upon this principle I am resolved to give them all a reasonable offer of their tithes.
>
> To prevent their refusing such an offer and their entering combinations to distress the Rector is in your Lordship's power.
>
> Might I flatter myself that you will be so kind as to lend such instructions to your agents, as may at all events secure my property without disturbing that of your tenants.[120]

Similarly, the approval of the same landlord was sought by another clergyman who wished to move the local church. Implicit in the request was an admission that the landlord had veto power over any such move.[121] That such precautions were not merely courtesies was indicated by the way the earl's agent handled the defense of eight of the earl's tenants who had been cited by the consistorial court of the Diocese of Raphoe for nonpayment of tithes.[122] Clearly, the local landlord had a good deal of power over a clergyman. Indeed, in some ways his power exceeded a bishop's, for the landlord had the power to impose a fine of sorts if the clergyman incurred his displeasure—simply through encouraging the tenants to refuse to pay tithes.

What kind of rewards could a parish clergyman expect for his doing, or ignoring, as the case might be, his parish work? Above the level of temporary curate he could expect lifetime security and, of course, money. In 1787 Richard Woodward, Bishop of Cloyne, attempted to find out exactly how much money. Because of the difficulties in gathering complete information, he was able to make estimates only for some of the better-paying dioceses. The bishop added together all the income of all parishes and cathedral offices, and divided this by the number of clergymen. He thereupon arrived at the following figures for the annual income per head of the Irish clergy:

Raphoe	£250
Clogher	187
Cloyne	180
Cork and Ross	150
Waterford and Lismore	125
Killaloe and Kilfenora	120
Dublin	115
Clonfert and Kilmacduagh	116
Killala and Achonry	90

The bishop then added the diocesan average incomes together, divided by the number of dioceses and concluded that the general average income was

£ 148 2s. 2½d. He estimated that it cost about 5 percent for a clergyman to have his dues collected by tithe proctors, therefore leaving the average net sum at £ 133 16s. for each clergyman. Upon his personal knowledge, the bishop testified the incomes in the rest of the country did not exceed these figures.[123] In contrast to the position of the ambitious clergyman, who had prospects of earning several hundred pounds a year, during most of the eighteenth century temporary curates could not expect to earn £ 100 annually. The statute 6 George I, c. 13, allowed the bishops under certain circumstances to stipulate the salary a curate should receive, within the limits of a £ 20 a year minimum and a £ 50 maximum. Near the end of George II's reign the maximum figure was raised and the Trustees of the First Fruits were empowered to augment the maintenance of all clergy having cure of souls who received less than £ 60 a year (29 George II, c. 18). In the nineteenth century, this figure was raised to £ 75 (40 George III, c. 27).[124]

Considered as a means of motivating the clergy, the financial structure of the parish system seems half-rational, half-senseless. On the one hand, within any given parish the arrangements were unresponsive to an individual clergyman's exertion. A clergyman received the same income from his benefice whether or not he was conscientious in performing his duties. Whether his tithes were paid depended chiefly on his relations with the local landlord and upon the efficiency of his tithe proctor and not upon how well the clergyman did his pastoral work. Therefore, within the context of any given benefice, the financial arrangements provided no incentive whatsoever for the incumbent in his religious duty. On the other hand, the great range of value of the benefices of the Irish church meant that an incumbent could look forward to promotion to a more valuable living if he was politically and socially astute and moderately responsible in caring for his parish. In this regard, therefore, the financial arrangements of the parish system were responsive to individual exertion, and one can assume that they were an incentive to the clergy.

As a final point of discussion it is well to ask how a man might come to hold a benefice in the Church of Ireland. The answer is that he applied to whoever held patronage over the living he desired. In the emphasis on patronage rather than on merit as the mode of entry and the allocation of appointments, the eighteenth-century Church of Ireland was no different from other departments of the eighteenth-century English and Irish civil service. The important question, therefore, is who controlled the patronage? Table 17 gives the answer, as of the late 1780s.

The table reveals three important characteristics of the Church of Ireland. First, in contrast to the situation in England, the bishops of the Irish church controlled most of the patronage. This meant that in parish matters the power of an Irish bishop was apt to be greater than that of his English counterpart. Given majority control over the patronage of his diocese, a conscientious bishop had a reasonable chance over a few years time of filling the vacancies in his see with men of high qualifications and standards. In point of fact, this episcopal strength would become the church's saving grace in the nineteenth century when a group of conscientious bishops were able to transform the standards of parochial worship and clerical conduct. Second, the Crown possessed very little patronage on the parish level. The Crown controlled well under 15 percent of the parish livings. Third, laymen in the Irish church played a much smaller role in determining who held parish livings than was the case in England. Laymen, especially resident magnates, had a great deal of influence in local church affairs, but the extent of their patronage was much less than it was usually believed to be.

It was accepted practice in the eighteenth century for a bishop to use his patronage to take care of his family, relations, and friends. Occasionally such appointments were so ludicrous as to be outrageous. In 1784 one observer reported of the Bishop of Derry:

> Lord Bristol has outdone his own doings; . . . He has ordained his nephew Fitzgerald, the Fitzgerald who for years had been a nuisance to Society here, and when England was grown too hot to hold him he went over to Ireland, seized his own father, confined him, set the whole civil power of the country at defiance, and was the cause of a great deal of bloodshed. He has fought one duel even since he has been in orders. Church preferments to the amount of £2,000 a year are given to him or intended for him. I think this to be much the most indecent thing, not to say the greatest outrage to Society, that has happened in my time.[125]

Patrons of livings were constantly under pressure from all sides. Lord George Germain successfully pressured the Archbishop of Dublin into appointing a young client to a living;[126] the Earl of Abercorn was importuned for a living under his patronage by a fallen member of the nobility who was desperately short of funds;[127] Lord Townshend, when Lord Lieutenant, immediately gave way to Lord Chief Baron Forster's request that his son, whom Townshend had already granted a living, be granted a dignity as well;[128] Townshend was petitioned by an Irish member of Parliament for a relative whose chief qualification seems to have been that he had "many children and no provision in the Church, but a small curacy." [129] The Bishop of Saint David's pressed for the appointment of one of his friends on the grounds that the benefice was "in the midst of all his mother's relations." [130] Perhaps most curious of all was the request of a Roman Catholic landowner that a certain clergyman be appointed to a living to which his father owned the right of advowson, but which the Crown had assumed because of his father's being a Roman Catholic.[131] None of these

TABLE 17

PATRONAGE OF IRISH PARISHES, LATE EIGHTEENTH CENTURY

Dioceses	Par- ishes	Bishop of diocese	TCD	Cathe- dral chap- ters	Crown	Lay- men	Other	Unde- ter- mined
Province of Armagh								
Armagh	103	60	5	3	13	22	–	–
Clogher	41	33	4	–	1	2	–	1
Derry	48	33	3	–	3	9	–	–
Down & Connor	114	53	–	–	12	36	3[a]	10
Dromore	26	23	–	–	–	2	1[a]	–
Kilmore	39	33	1	–	3	2	–	–
Meath	224	69	–	–	81	37	2[a]	35
Raphoe	31	15	7	–	6	3	–	–
Provincial Total	626	319	20	3	119	113	6	46
Province of Dublin								
Dublin	209	144	–	32	15	16	2[b]	–
Kildare	81	30	–	–	27	24	–	–
Ferns & Leighlin	232	171	1	–	18	37	–	5
Ossory	136	76	–	4	26	30	–	–
Provincial Total	658	421	1	36	86	107	2	5
Province of Cashel								
Cashel & Emly	155	–	–	–	–	–	–	155
Cloyne	137	106	–	–	10	7	11[c]	3
Cork & Ross	127	94	–	–	8	14	11[c]	–
Killaloe & Kilfenora	138	–	–	–	–	–	–	138[d]
Limerick, Ardfert & Aghadoe	176	84	13	–	27	52	–	–
Waterford & Lismore	106	43	–	–	24	30	9[e]	–
Provincial Total	839	327	13	0	69	103	31	296
Province of Tuam								
Tuam & Ardagh	126	109	–	–	1	6	10[e]	–
Clonfert & Kilmacduagh	60	43	–	–	3	14	–	–
Elphin	75	72	–	–	2	1	–	–
Killala & Achonry	52	48	–	–	2	–	–	2
Provincial Total	313	272	0	0	8	21	10	2
National Total	2,436	1,339	34	39	282	344	49	349

TABLE 17 (Continued)

Note: The situation in England and Wales in 1830 was as follows: Crown, 952; archbishops and bishops, 1,248; deans and chapters as corporations aggregate, 787; dignitaries as corporations sole, 1,851; universities, hospitals, etc., 721; laymen, 5,096; municipal corporations, 53. See Coolidge, "The Finances of the Church of England, 1830–1880," pp. 219–20.

ᵃ Archbishop of Armagh.

ᵇ Lord Chancellor, and Chief Justices with Archbishop of Dublin.

ᶜ Wholly impropriate.

ᵈ Designated as undetermined because Beaufort did not calculate the patronage of that united diocese on the same principle he used in calculating the others.

ᵉ Wardenship of Galway.

Source: Beaufort, pp. 107–36.

cases will deflect anyone from the conclusion that in view of the church's primary purpose—the provision of pastoral services—the parish system of the Church of Ireland was irrational and unpredictable.

THE LAITY

It is hard to know exactly how and where to include the laity in an examination of the administrative structure of the eighteenth-century Church of Ireland. The laity, unlike the bishops, deans, and parish clergy, were amateurs in the sense that they did not make their livelihood in religious activities. They cannot, therefore, be fitted into an administrative hierarchy in the same way the religious professionals can. One traditional way of describing the laity is to depict them as the foot troops of the Christian army. However useful such an analogy may be theologically, it is far from accurate operationally. The laity, for one thing, could drop out of the army any time they pleased without endangering their temporal livelihood. They were not, therefore, under the same limitations and obligations as the professionally religious. Further, certain of the laity possessed the right to appoint the professional men to their posts. This lay power, which was exercised by patrons of livings and by politicians who appointed deans and bishops, was hardly compatible with the military analogy, for no infantryman appoints his sergeants, colonels, or generals. Clearly the position of the laity was a complex and sometimes paradoxical one.

The laity of the Church of Ireland was both powerful and sparse. They were powerful because they possessed most of the land in the country, had a monopoly of political power, and, for most of the century, filled almost all of the desirable civil and military offices. But they were few in number relative to the total population of Ireland. Precise indications of the membership of the Church of Ireland are impossible to obtain for the eighteenth century. The Irish House of Lords, in 1766, instituted a church census, but unhappily most of the returns were burned in the Four Courts fire of 1922.[132] An accurate decennial census did not become a regular event in Ireland until well into the nineteenth century. The following figures from the hearth tax returns of the 1730s give the situation as accurately as it can be determined.[133]

Province	Protestants	Catholics	Proportion of Protestants to Catholics
Ulster	62,624	38,459	3 to 2
Leinster	25,241	92,434	1 to 3.6
Munster	13,337	106,407	1 to 8
Connaught	4,299	44,101	1 to 10

In reading these figures it is well to remember that both Anglicans and Dissenters were lumped together as Protestants, and that the Church of Ireland proportions of the total population would be even smaller than the Protestant proportion. The leaders of the Church of Ireland did well, therefore, to emphasize the power of their members rather than the actual membership. The number was small, and in the nineteenth century both friendly reformers and bitter opponents of the church would seize upon the absurdity of such a small membership being served by such a large ecclesiastical establishment.

Equally important for understanding the position of the Church of Ireland in the eighteenth century is a recognition of the attitude of those outside the church—the laity of other denominations. The Presbyterians and the Roman Catholics were not merely outside the Church of Ireland; they were most bitterly alienated from it. The Church of Ireland was not simply a minority church, it was one surrounded by a sea of hatred.

The Presbyterians had a great many grievances, for they were former allies who were not only excluded from the spoils of victory but were penalized as well.[134] The Presbyterians had unhesitatingly joined the Anglicans in supporting the revolution of William III of Orange, and one would reasonably have expected the Anglican-dominated government to be generous to them. Unhappily for the Presbyterians, there was really no need for the government to treat them well, because they could always be counted on to aid the Anglicans in putting down any Roman Catholic insurgency, no matter how the Presbyterians themselves were treated. Their position in the years after the revolution was a curious one. Legally, they did not have a right to exist, since no toleration act was passed. On the other hand, the king and the English parliament underwrote some of their religious expenses (through the royal grant, the *Regium donum*), and through the abrogation of the Act of Supremacy in 1691 they were allowed to enter the public service. In the later years of the seventeenth century the Presbyterian grievances were twofold: the absence of a toleration act and the government's refusal to admit the legal validity of Presbyterian marriages.

Far from cooperating with the Presbyterians in their quest for toleration, the members and officials of the Anglican Church by and large tried to thwart them. Indeed, the Anglicans were able to undercut the Presbyterians' position seriously when, in 1703, an act "To prevent the further growth of popery" was passed by the Irish parliament. The measure was sent to England where the English government added a test clause that applied to Presbyterians as well as Roman Catholics. Thus, in 1704 a test was required whereby any person holding a civil or military post under the Crown had to take Communion according to the usage of the Church of Ireland within three months of his taking office and to produce a certificate that he had done so. A conscientious Presbyterian, therefore, was excluded from public office, at least so long as the act was rigorously enforced.

Nearly as objectionable to some Presbyterians was the extension by the English parliament of the Oath of Abjuration to Ireland, in 1703. The oath had to be taken by all Presbyterian ministers, the majority of whom probably would have taken it without much hesitation. Three or four ministers, however, managed to read the oath as implying that they were obliged to defend the existing church establishment and, therefore, refused to take it. Local authorities began to harry the men, and only with the Hanoverian accession did the government finally stop the harassments.

During the Hanoverian years the position of the Presbyterians was gradually ameliorated, although the Anglican Church militant was still powerful enough to prevent the penal statutes from being revoked. Over the opposition of the Anglican bishops—most notably Archbishop King— a Toleration Act was passed in 1719, giving the Presbyterians the legal right to exist, if not excusing them from the implications of the Test Act. Also, in 1719 the first of a long series of Indemnity Acts was passed, indemnifying those who had failed to take either the required oaths or the sacrament. Presbyterians could now enter the public service if they desired. Nevertheless, during the middle years of the eighteenth century, the Presbyterians continued as second-class citizens, a position which they naturally resented. Finally, in 1778 a clause providing for the repeal of the sacramental test was added to a Roman Catholic relief bill. The clause was removed by the English government, but a bill to repeal the test was introduced the following year by the Irish government and became a law in March 1780. The measure was passed under the implicit pressure of the international uncertainties and of the formation of the volunteer companies, and was acceded to grudgingly by the official class over the opposition of the Anglican ecclesiastical leaders. Small wonder, therefore, that Presbyterians looked upon the Anglican Church with bitterness.

But the alienation of the Presbyterians was nothing as compared to that of the Roman Catholics; for the Presbyterians were merely inconvenienced while the Catholics were actively persecuted. The Irish penal code, which was written and enforced by Anglicans, is too well known to need detailed reproduction here.[135] In point of fact, the "code" was not a code at all, but a heterogeneous collection of overlapping statutes. These laws are usually divided into three categories. The first consisted of statutes directed at inhibiting the practice of the Roman Catholic religion. All Roman Catholic archbishops, bishops, vicar generals, deans, and all regular clergy were banished from Ireland. Any one of these who returned was guilty of high treason and was to suffer accordingly. If no archbishops or bishops remained in Ireland, ordination of priests would be impossible; and to reinforce the effects of the banishments, foreign-trained clergy were also banned. All secular priests were required to register with the government. Rewards were offered for the apprehension of clergy illegally in the country, and a noxious profession of priest-hunting was born.

The second category of laws disabled the Roman Catholic from participating in trades and in the professions. Oaths abjuring the temporal authority of the Pope and renouncing transubstantiation were required for entrance into trade guilds, civil offices, and franchises. The Test Act made the taking of Holy Communion according to Anglican practice a condition of entering the professions, the corporations, and government positions. Since very few Catholics would take either the oaths or the test, the great majority of the Irish population were excluded from the most desirable positions and from participation in the government of their homeland.

A third sort of penal statute was especially vicious; for it was punitive in nature, penalizing the Roman Catholic laity simply because it was Catholic, even if Catholic laymen did not try to enter the restricted Protestant corporations or franchises. Roman Catholics were forbidden the practice of primogeniture, a prohibition which meant that Catholic landholdings were fragmented. The amount of land a Catholic could hold was severely limited. If the child of a Roman Catholic turned Protestant, his parents became tenants for life upon the family estate, with title passing immediately to the heir. If a Roman Catholic landowner died, the child did not become the ward of a Catholic but was handed over to the nearest Protestant relative.

How fully enforced the penal code actually was is still undetermined.[136] For our purposes the crucial point is that the code permanently alienated the Roman Catholics who formed the bulk of the population from the Established Church. Recollection of the penal days was seared into the folk memory and it would be generations before a Catholic layman could regard the Anglican Church with anything beside hatred and contempt.

The repeal of the penal measures gained the Anglican Church scant praise, for most of its leaders opposed repeal.

REPRISE

This chapter has described the eighteenth century Church of Ireland as an administrative unit, thus establishing a base line by which we can evaluate later changes in the church. It is hard to avoid the conclusion that the church was remarkably inefficient in pursuing its primary task: the provision of pastoral service to the Irish Anglican community. (This is not to say that the church was "corrupt," for that is a term of moral judgment rather than one of administrative evaluation.) Its remarkable inefficiency was partially a result of the interposition at all levels of politicians, land-lords, and others who controlled many positions in the church and used this control for their own advantage. The manifest purpose of the church, to promote Christ's religion in Ireland, was often incompatible with the criteria under which men were selected for service therein. That is, men were often appointed to religious posts for political and social reasons— reasons opposed to the apparent purpose of a religious institution. Because of the imposition of state authority at all levels, and especially at the highest, the Church of Ireland was constantly at odds with itself. The chances of internal friction were greatly increased by the potential cleavage on the bench between the Irishmen and the Englishmen, the latter being appointed from abroad to the most desirable Irish sees.

A second reason for the church's inefficiency, one which permeated all ranks, was the absence of strong superior-subordinate relationships. At all levels of clerical life above that of temporary curate, the appointee was a lifetime officeholder and could be removed only with difficulty. Superiors in this situation, be they Crown representatives over the bishops or bishops over parish clergy, had few effective negative sanctions at their disposal. The result was that anyone in the system who was willing to give up his chance of promotion could do just about what he pleased within very broad boundaries. It was, for example, impossible to compel bishops to reside in their dioceses and nearly as difficult to force a parish minister to live in his parish.

At the base of the pyramid, the local parish, the situation was espe-cially shaky. Most parishes were grouped into unions. These unions, un-fortunately, did not all possess churches. In many instances, a clergyman held two or more benefices in plurality. Further, the absence of glebe houses in most benefices meant that a large proportion of the clergymen would not reside.

Finally, in regard to the laity, the church was in a ludicrous and painful position. The Church of Ireland population was small. The majority of the country was Roman Catholic, with a strong Presbyterian representation in Ulster. These groups were not merely non-members of the Church of Ireland, but were actively hostile to it. Representing a narrow constituency, surrounded by a hostile majority, controlling great endowments, uncertain of its priorities, inefficient in its administration, the Church of Ireland was ripe for either reform or revolution.

In the nineteenth century it experienced both.

2 The Era of Graceful Reform, 1800–1830

THE EFFECTS OF THE UNION

A great deal changed in the Established Church in the first three decades of the nineteenth century, but the process was relatively painless, at least in view of the jolting reforms the church was to undergo a little later. During these first three decades the church was united, in name at least, to the Church of England; it was animated by a more conscientious bench and an evangelical inspired laity; its administration was improved; the number of churches increased; clerical residence became more uniform; and church finance was regularized. It was a period of tension, but also one of optimism. The mood of quiet confidence was typified by Charles Brodrick, Archbishop of Cashel, in a letter to the Bishop of Cloyne:

> The unfortunate circumstances of the Country in former Days imposed a necessity on the Legislature of uniting many Livings. . . .
> The times are now changed and in the place of the general poverty
> . . . by which the country was distinguished and which poverty
> operated so severely against the Established Church by causing the
> reduction of the numbers of the clergy so far below the necessities of
> the Country, we see plenty and riches on all sides, the population of
> the Country rapidly increasing and the Clergy happily partaking in
> the general prosperity and increased wealth. This then seems to be the
> critical period . . . to restore the church to its originally intended
> strength in point of numbers.[1]

The single most visible change in the church's position came through the Act of Union which united the Churches of England and of Ireland as well as the kingdoms of England and Ireland.[2] The chronicle of the parliamentary stages of the Union is too well known to need rehearsing here.[3] The act took effect on 1 January 1801. The following article of the Act of Union formed the central arch of the new church:

> That it be the Fifth Article of Union, That the Churches of England
> and Ireland, as now by law established, be united into one Protestant
> Episcopal Church, to be called the United Church of England and
> Ireland; and that the doctrine, worship, discipline, and government of
> the said United Church shall be and shall remain in full force for ever,
> as the same are now by law established for the Church of England;
> and that the continuance and preservation of the said United Church,
> as the Established Church of England and Ireland, shall be deemed
> and taken to be an essential and fundamental part of the Union; and
> that in like manner the doctrine, worship, discipline, and government

of the Church of Scotland shall remain and be preserved as the same
are now established by law, and by the Acts for the Union of the two
Kingdoms of England and Scotland.[4]

This article was more significant for what it omitted than for what it included. The Church of Ireland became part of the United Church of
England and Ireland in name but in little else. The change was more verbal
than structural, for the Irish church remained intact and distinct as an
administrative system. The hierarchies and clergy of the two churches were
not amalgamated. Only in matters of religious formularies did a merger
occur; in this case, the Church of Ireland lost its right to define and enforce
its own religious formularies.[5]

The fourth article of the Act of Union provided "that Four Lords
Spiritual of Ireland by rotation of Sessions . . . shall be the number to sit
and vote on the part of Ireland in the House of Lords of the Parliament
of the United Kingdom." Article eight regulated the rotation of the spiritual
lords:

> . . . the Primate of all Ireland for the time being shall sit in the first
> Session of the Parliament of the United Kingdom, the Archbishop of
> Dublin for the time being in the second, the Archbishop of Cashel for
> the time being in the third, the Archbishop of Tuam for the time
> being in the fourth, and so by rotation of sessions for ever, such rota-
> tion to proceed regularly and without interruption from session to
> session, notwithstanding any dissolution or expiration of Parliament:
> That three suffragan bishops shall in like manner sit according to rota-
> tion of their sees, from session to session, in the following order: the
> Lord Bishop of Meath, the Lord Bishop of Kildare, the Lord Bishop
> of Derry, in the first Session of the Parliament of the United Kingdom;
> the Lord Bishop of Raphoe, the Lord Bishop of Limerick, Ardfert
> and Aghadoe, the Lord Bishop of Dromore, in the second Session of
> the Parliament of the United Kingdom; the Lord Bishop of Elphin,
> the Lord Bishop of Down and Connor, the Lord Bishop of Waterford
> and Lismore, in the third Session of the Parliament of the United
> Kingdom; the Lord Bishop of Leighlin and Ferns, the Lord Bishop of
> Cloyne, the Lord Bishop of Cork and Ross, in the fourth Session of
> the Parliament of the United Kingdom; the Lord Bishop of Killaloe
> and Kilfenora, the Lord Bishop of Kilmore, the Lord Bishop of
> Clogher, in the fifth Session of the Parliament of the United Kingdom;
> the Lord Bishop of Ossory, the Lord Bishop of Killala and Achonry,
> the Lord Bishop of Clonfert and Kilmacduagh, in the sixth Session of
> the Parliament of the United Kingdom.

These then were the ecclesiastical provisions of the Act of Union affecting the Church of Ireland: the Churches of England and Ireland were

united, the Church of Ireland conformed completely to the formularies of the Church of England, and the Irish bishops lost a good deal of their political power.[6] None of these provisions in their explicit form had a great impact upon the administration of the Church of Ireland. The two churches were united in name only: the formularies of the Church of Ireland were already nearly identical with those of the Church of England, and the bishops' political powers had been gradually eroding since the mid-eighteenth century anyway.

Therefore, to understand the effects of the Act of Union upon the administration of the Church of Ireland we must look not upon the Union's explicit provisions, but upon the way it indirectly affected the church. First, the provision that only a portion of the Irish bishops could sit in the Lords at any one session meant that the time taken up by empty political routine was considerably reduced. A conscientious man, therefore, had greater time to spend upon ecclesiastical administration. Second, the importance to the government of the Irish bishops' political votes in the Lords declined greatly. The rank of bishop continued to be a useful patronage plum to be distributed by the government; but direct political considerations were less relevant when appointing a bishop, since the English House of Lords was at peace with the government during most of the first three decades of the century. Third, to some extent the union of the two churches seems to have given Irish churchmen greater confidence, since they now felt that they were not merely a minority church but part of the United Church of England and Ireland. Fourth, this union, nominal though it was, was potentially troublesome to the Irish church, for it opened the church to the criticism of the British radicals. Whereas the Irish parliament had been notoriously supine, the English parliament was destined to have its share of abuse-hunters, and few institutions were more justly open to criticism than the Church of Ireland.

The most immediate effect of the Union, however, was none of those mentioned above. Rather, it was the sudden pressure which developed for appointments to bishoprics. The government owed a considerable number of debts to secular politicians who had promoted the Union, and the currency of payment for some was the appointment of members of their families to the bench. Further, only two members of the Irish bench had voted against the Union with England and the government therefore owed favors to many bishops, among which were promises for translation to more desirable sees. Because a large proportion of these political debts was owed to Irishmen a side effect of the so-called "Union engagements" was that the church became more Irish at the episcopal level; but this was accidental, not a conscious piece of reconstruction.

Indeed, in the half-decade immediately following the Union it appeared that only two episcopal appointments were made which are not easily identifiable as political payments. The first of these was crucial, for it was to the Archbishopric of Armagh. Lord Rokeby died on 11 January 1800, and the vacant see seemed a boon to a government which desperately needed patronage. In this case, however, the king himself resisted the ministerial demands that the Lord Primacy of All Ireland be used for political ends, with the result that the man nominated in October 1800, the Honorable William Stuart, was outside the ring of Irish political debts. The youngest son of the Earl of Bute, Stuart was a man of personal courage and independence who had previously served as Bishop of Saint David's in Wales. As will be indicated later, Stuart was vigorously opposed to the manipulation of the church for secular ends, and did what he could to inhibit the practice.[7]

The second exception was Charles Brodrick whose translation from Kilmore to the Archbishopric of Cashel came in late 1801. Although at first glance this translation appears to be a Union engagement, the evidence indicates otherwise. Brodrick's name did not appear on any of the Lord Lieutenant's lists of Union engagements, and Brodrick himself explicitly stated that he was not promoted for political reasons. The translation was a wise one, for Brodrick became one of the most effective reformers within the Irish church.[8]

But these men were exceptions, and most appointments in the years following the Union were political payments. Presiding over the great patronage scramble was the Lord Lieutenant, the Earl of Hardwicke. Fortunately for historians, Hardwicke kept meticulous lists of those on his patronage rolls. The promises made by Dublin officials affecting the bench may be summarized as follows (more than three times this number of engagements was made for lower ecclesiastical appointments):

1. The Archbishop of Cashel to succeed to Dublin.
2. The Reverend Dr. Alexander to be raised to the bench.
3. The Bishop of Killaloe (William Knox) to be translated, although precisely where was unspecified.
4. The Reverend Mr. Trench to be raised to the bench.
5. Dean Warburton to be raised to the bench after the other Union engagements had been fulfilled.[9]

In addition to these specific promises, Hardwicke had to meet the pressure for places from the dozens who had received generalized promises of advancement for themselves or their relatives.

The first of the debts to be paid was that owed Charles Agar (Viscount Somerton), Archbishop of Cashel. Robert Fowler, previously Archbishop of Dublin, died in October 1801, conveniently leaving the government free to fulfill its promise to Agar. The latter was a strikingly avaricious member of the bench who had made a considerable fortune in church lands. He had originally bargained for the Archbishopric of Armagh, but the king found that appointment unacceptable. Agar therefore agreed to accept the See of Dublin and a promise of an earldom. The latter promise was redeemed in 1806 when he became the Earl of Normantown.[10]

The next piece of business, the filling of Kilmore, was less easily dealt with, for the Union engagements did not precisely cover the case. When Agar was appointed to Dublin, Cashel became vacant and was filled by Brodrick, leaving Kilmore open. The Lord Lieutenant's immediate instinct was to fill Kilmore with the Reverend Dr. Alexander, thus discharging that obligation.[11] This seemed reasonable enough, and late in October Hardwicke confidently basked in the knowledge that the king approved of Alexander's elevation.[12] The affair became more complicated, however, when John Beresford, representative of the most powerful family in Irish politics, wrote to Hardwicke suggesting that George de la Poer Beresford, who had been nominated to the See of Clonfert and Kilmacduagh less than a year previously, be promoted to the more lucrative Bishopric of Kilmore. Beresford ascribed the lateness of his interest to his own earlier assumption that the Bishop of Killaloe (William Knox) was to be promoted to Cashel and therefore had not bothered the government. Now that Kilmore was open, he wanted that plum for his family.[13] Hardwicke was sufficiently nimble on his political feet to recognize that Beresford claims took precedence and therefore wrote Lord Pelham (the Home Secretary) proposing that the Beresford wish be gratified and rationalized that Alexander had merely been promised a bishopric—but not any particular one—so that faith with him was not being broken. To this, the Home Secretary agreed.[14]

Now, at this point, we must recall that William Stuart had become Archbishop of Armagh less than a year previously, and that he took his episcopal duties seriously. One can imagine the consternation in the British cabinet, therefore, when the Prime Minister received the following communication from him about the contemplated Beresford translation:

> It is with great reluctance that I trouble you even with a few lines, but a report prevails in this country that you have promised to recommend Mr. Beresford to his Majesty to succeed the Bishop of Kilmore; and, as I firmly believe no measure can be more decidedly fatal to the Established Church, I trust you will excuse the liberty I now take of expressing the grounds of that opinion.
>
> Mr. Beresford is reported to be one of the most profligate men in Europe. His language and his manners have given universal offence. Indeed, such is his character that were His Majesty's Ministers to give him a living in my diocese to hold *in commendam*, I should be wanting in my duty if I did not refuse him institution. . . .
>
> Even if every tale told to the discredit of Mr. Beresford were false,

it would scarcely mend the matter, as most undoubtedly his reputation is bad, and these tales are universally credited.[15]

One can, of course, speculate on Stuart's motives in writing such a letter. Doubtless, he was sincerely concerned about the moral tone of the suffragans in his province. One should also note, however, that the appointment was decided upon without consulting the archbishop despite the fact that it took place in his province.[16]

Prime Minister Addington moved slowly and it was only in mid-December that he wrote the Lord Lieutenant on the subject. He asked for information as to the accuracy of the archbishop's charge and said that the appointment was to be suspended until the matter could be clarified.[17] Lord Hardwicke replied that although the archbishop's charges were entitled to their weight, no such information unfavorable to Beresford's character had come to his own ears. Hardwicke argued that to refuse to carry out a translation that was already settled would fix a stigma on Beresford that would reflect unfairly both on him and upon the government which originally raised him to the bench.[18] Obviously at that point Hardwicke's task was to placate the archbishop while pressing the Beresford appointment upon the English ministry. He therefore deputized the Chief Secretary for Ireland, Charles Abbot, to deal with the archbishop. Accordingly, Abbot wrote the archbishop, explaining the government's reason for pressing Beresford's promotion over Alexander's and suggesting a meeting in Dublin.[19] The Lord Primate's long reply was restrained but firm. First, he noted that the Chief Secretary had earlier informed him in writing that Dr. Alexander was to receive Kilmore. This new turn of events was clearly a case of the Prime Minister's overruling the Lord Lieutenant of Ireland. Second, he maintained his stance that the promotion of Beresford was "decisive as to the fate of the Church." Third, he threatened:

> I sincerely wish to retire, and entertain hope that his Majesty will be graciously pleased to allow me to resign a situation which he compelled me to assume, and which I can no longer hold with advantage to the country, or honour to myself. If his Majesty should reject this request, I shall confine my attention solely to the business of this diocese. With the province I can have little concern. It would be absurd to inspect the conduct of such a man as Beresford, for the same interest which places him at Kilmore will most assuredly be exerted to protect him.[20]

Lord Hardwicke was in an unpleasant situation. Awkwardly and anxiously he tried to explain the problem to the Prime Minister,[21] and then, almost desperately, he wrote directly to the archbishop. In his letter, Hardwicke proposed to send his own brother-in-law and private secretary, Dr. Lindsay, to wait upon his Grace.[22] The proposal to send Lindsay earned Hardwicke approval from the Prime Minister[23] and another request to be allowed to resign from the Lord Primate.[24] Unhappily, the peace mission failed, and Stuart repeated his appeal to be allowed to resign, a desire which the exasperated Hardwicke was now inclined to gratify.[25] In the end, the government ignored the archbishop and translated George de la Poer Beresford to Kilmore where he served until his death in 1841, a vigorous reformer and guardian of the church's interests.

While the Beresford matter had been taking the government's time, other debts remained unpaid. Fortunately for Hardwicke, the translation of Beresford from Clonfert to Kilmore left Clonfert vacant. In early 1802 Hardwicke raised Nathaniel Alexander to Clonfert, thus fulfilling the Union engagement to that cleric.[26]

The convenient death of Richard Marlay, Bishop of Waterford and Lismore, gave Hardwicke the opportunity to redeem another governmental pledge—in this case the promise to raise Power Le Poer Trench to the bishopric. Trench was the son of Lord Kilconnel; his elder brother, Richard Trench, had been a member of Parliament in the Irish House of Commons for County Galway. Richard Trench had voted against the Union in the 1799 session, but voted for it in 1800. The head of the family, Lord Kilconnel, supported the Union in the Lords and was raised to the title of Viscount Dunlo in December 1800 and to the Earldom of Clancarty in 1803. The family was also promised a bishopric for the younger son. Accordingly, Power Le Poer Trench was consecrated Bishop of Waterford and Lismore on 21 November 1802.[27]

Meanwhile, Dublin Castle still had not discharged its formally acknowledged debt to William Knox, Bishop of Killaloe, whose services to the Union had earned him a promise of a more lucrative see. In July 1803 the death of the Bishop of Derry opened that great ecclesiastical prize. Accordingly, after some hesitation on the part of the British ministers, Hardwicke was able to have Knox translated to Derry, where he remained until his death in 1831.[28]

Outside of the implied obligation to promote Dean Warburton to the bench at some undetermined point in the future, the formal Union engagements made by Irish officials were now met. Having translated Knox from Killaloe to Derry, Hardwicke felt sufficiently free to appoint his own brother-in-law, the Reverend Dr. Lindsay, to the vacant See of Killaloe.[29]

Now, although Hardwicke had met the Union engagements made by the Lord Lieutenant and Chief Secretary of Ireland to gain the Union's passage, he still had one major debt to discharge, a debt which was not Irish in origin. For supporting the Union, the Earl of Ely had been promised a marquisate in the Irish peerage and a baronetcy in the peerage of the United Kingdom, the sinecure job of Postmaster-General for Ireland, a post in the treasury for his son Lord Loftus, and a bishopric for his youngest son, Lord Robert Ponsonby Loftus. This price may seem high, but Ely had controlled six boroughs which returned eight members to the Irish House of Commons.[30] The promise of the bishopric for the younger son had been made by the Duke of Portland, Home Secretary, and did not find a place on the list of engagements which Cornwallis supplied to Hardwicke. Therefore it was not until early 1803 that Dublin Castle became aware of the debt as a consequence of Lord Loftus's informing the Prime Minister of his obligation.[31]

Late in 1803 the Bishop of Raphoe, James Hawkins, fell ill, and the occasion seemed propitious for Lord Ely's claim to be satisfied. But two other claimants entered the lists. One of these was the Dean of Waterford, the Reverend Dr. Butson, who was a friend of Addington and who was reported to be boasting that he had been promised the next episcopal vacancy.[32] The other was a member of the Beresford clan, Lord John Beresford who was urged for promotion by Lord Waterford.[33] After a good deal of dickering, the Lord Lieutenant decided that the first vacancy on the bench should go to Dr. Butson, that the next should go to the Beresfords, and that Lord Ely had already been sufficiently rewarded for his services.[34]

Ironically, the Bishop of Raphoe, who had been reported seriously ill, upset everyone's calculations by recovering and living three and a half years more. An opening in the episcopacy was created, however, with the death of the Bishop of Kildare in April 1804. The Reverend Dr. Lindsay, Lord Hardwicke's brother-in-law, was translated from Killaloe to Kildare. The Reverend Dr. Alexander was translated from Clonfert to Killaloe. A three-way contest for Clonfert then evolved between Dean Butson, the Loftus family, and the Beresford interests. Lord Hardwicke threw his weight behind the first of these, sending the official recommendation to Whitehall for Butson's appointment.[35] The Beresford faction temporarily dropped from the scene, deciding to forgo immediate satisfaction for long-range security. Lord Waterford obtained this by allowing the Butson and Loftus interests to struggle against each other while receiving the assurance of Hardwicke that the new Prime Minister, Pitt, would appoint Lord John Beresford to the first bishopric to become vacant after Clonfert.[36] This left the Butson and Loftus forces battling each other for Clonfert. Hardwicke, as already noted, preferred Butson. Lord Ely, however, circumvented the Lord Lieutenant by having his elder son meet personally with the Duke of Portland and Prime Minister Addington.[37] Addington sided with the Loftus claim only reluctantly, for he was infuriated that the Duke of Portland in his capacity as Home Secretary had promised, with royal approval but without consulting his colleagues, a bishopric to Lord Ely's family.[38] However, before the matter could be finally settled, William Pitt became Prime Minister and Lord Hawkesbury Home Secretary. Hawkesbury took up the line of the previous administration and favored Loftus's appointment to Clonfert.[39] The matter might have ended there, except that Lord Hardwicke balked. He opposed the appointment of Loftus with vigor and finally threatened to resign if his candidate, the Reverend Dr. Butson, was not appointed Bishop of Clonfert.[40] Thereupon, the new ministry, still unsure of itself in Irish matters, gave in to the Lord Lieutenant. Dr. Butson became Bishop of Clonfert.

The Irish administration was still faced by the demands of two factions: the Loftus and the Beresford interests. The Marquis of Waterford had been promised the first vacant bishopric for Lord John Beresford, and the Earl of Ely presented claims that were now formally recognized by the Westminster authorities. When the See of Down became vacant in September 1804, Hardwicke decided, despite the promise to Waterford, that the Loftus family had first call, and he therefore asked Archbishop Stuart if he would accept Lord Robert Ponsonby Loftus as Bishop of Down.[41] Ever rigorous in his standards, the archbishop replied that he would prefer other persons, since Loftus had never previously performed any clerical duties.[42] This dilemma was solved by translating the Bishop of Killaloe, Nathaniel Alexander, to Down and promoting Loftus to Killaloe.[43]

The Beresfords did not have long to wait before their claims for Lord John were satisfied. In January 1805 the Bishop of Cork and Ross died. Although Lord John would have liked to wait for the richer See of Raphoe to become vacant, he decided to accept Cork and Ross. He was translated to Raphoe in 1807, Clogher in 1819, Dublin in 1820, and finally Armagh in 1822, where he served until his death in 1862.[44]

Dean Warburton remained the only person who had any claim to be promoted to the bench on the basis of Union engagements, and this engagement was understood to be of the lowest priority. Warburton, a former Roman Catholic, had remained at his post in Ardagh during the rebellion of 1798, when most of the clergy fled, and had thereby recommended himself to the government. Despite the displeasure of the king, who maintained that Warburton was the son of an Irish harper, he became Bishop of Limerick in 1806.[45]

As a result of the Union, the bench of bishops had received an infusion of new members. Whether these newly appointed bishops would be an improvement on their predecessors remained to be seen.

FINANCIAL REFORM

The Church's Financial Structure

The Church of Ireland required large sums of money to support its activities, but as a corporate institution it possessed almost no financial resources. The revenues of the Church were almost entirely attached to specific offices rather than to the church as an abstract corporate entity. This is to say, that the revenue of each archbishop, bishop, dean, and lower cleric was provided by certain endowments and revenues that were paid to him directly by virtue of his holding a specific office. The church itself did not pay its functionaries. Rather, each officeholder or functionary was responsible for the management and collection of the revenues that were his due, without the organization's acting as an intermediary. As a result, the Irish church's financial system was chaotic, for, in legalistic terminology, each office was a "corporation sole." Whether or not a bishop was able to live up to his station depended not only on the theoretical value of his see, but on how well his agent managed the episcopal estates; and whether a local vicar was able to ride with the local gentry often depended on his ability to find an efficient local agent to collect his tithes. Within the broadest of limits (chiefly those on the permanent disposal of church property) each man was his own broker; and practices on rental of church property, the valuation of episcopal estates, and the collection of tithes varied radically from diocese to diocese and from parish to parish.

Most of the church's revenue came from land. Admittedly, there was some income from parliamentary grants and some from the local church cess, but these amounts were relatively small. The income of the lower clergy came chiefly from the tithe, a tax on agricultural produce. The income of the higher clergy came both from tithes and from the rent of agricultural land. In a few instances collegiate corporations had investments in nonagricultural speculations, but these examples were so infrequent as to be inconsequential. Because of the dependence on land revenue, the income of the Church of Ireland was extremely variable. A series of bad harvests would not only directly reduce church income by reducing agricultural yields, but would indirectly reduce it through heightening agrarian agitation, such agitation being detrimental to the collection of tithes.

The above points all dictate that statistics on Irish church revenues should be approached with considerable caution, for we are dealing with a financial structure given to wide variability and considerable eccentricity. The material to be presented later was compiled during the 1830s, and within the limits of contemporary methods is accurate.

The revenue of the bishops came from two major sources: land rents and tithes.[46] As far as episcopal property was concerned, the bishop was a tenant for life, controlling the property as long as he held office but forbidden to alienate the property permanently. The greater part of the bishop's income came from leases on land. In Ireland three forms of leases prevailed: those for twenty-one years, those for forty years, and those for one or more lives. Under the latter rubric it was generally customary to lease the land for three lives. These three lives were most often members of the family of the lessee but also could be important persons not involved in the transaction at all. The bishop received a renewal fine upon the death of any one of the three lives in the lease. This fine was computed by taking into account three factors: the annual value of the land, the probable length

TABLE 18
EPISCOPAL LAND HOLDINGS, 1831

Diocese	Total acres *(statute measure)*	"Profitable acres" *(statute measure)*
Armagh	100,563	87,809
Clogher	22,591	18,851
Derry	77,102	39,621
Down	6,411	6,411
Connor	23,833	23,833
Dromore	18,422	18,422
Kilmore	28,531	28,531
Meath	29,269	20,266
Raphoe	1,392	1,392
Dublin	34,040	23,926
Kildare	911	911
Christ Church Deanery (held with Kildare)	4,163	4,163
Ferns	13,370	13,370
Leighlin	12,924	12,924
Ossory	21,730	21,730
Cashel & Emly	20,046	20,046
Cloyne	12,482	12,482
Cork	3,306	3,298
Ross	8,179	8,179
Killaloe	7,528	6,795
Limerick, Ardfert & Aghadoe	12,985	4,171
Waterford & Lismore	13,189	13,189
Tuam	64,683	26,337
Ardagh	22,216	13,194
Clonfert	7,794	3,844
Kilmacduagh	3,950	1,673
Elphin	42,843	29,235
Killala	33,668	10,176
Achonry	11,874	8,391
Total	669,247	485,532

Note: Fractions of acres are not included in the individual diocesan figures; therefore, the totals are slightly higher than the column sums.

Source: First Report of His Majesty's Commissioners on Ecclesiastical Revenue and Patronage, Ireland, pp. 212–13.

of life of the next lessee and the rate of interest to be given the lessee. These calculations were, of course, open to considerable bargaining and the lessee always had the option of refusing the renewal; but in land-hungry Ireland, the upper hand in the bargaining was clearly with the bishop's agent. Obviously the setting of leases for lives had its drawback. For one thing, the income from such an arrangement was most unstable, for renewal fines came only after the demise of someone on whom the lives were set—an unpredictable event at best. Moreover, the method of leasing was open to abuse, for a bishop hard-pressed for funds was tempted to beggar his successor by substituting young lives for old on such leases in return for an immediate payment by the tenant.

Another form of episcopal lease was for twenty-one years. This form had the advantage of predictability which the lease for lives did not possess. In Ireland, twenty-one year leases could be extended by the tenant annually, thus providing the tenant with security while ensuring regularity of episcopal income through renewal fines. This contrasts with the situation in England where the twenty-one year leases were renewed and fines paid only at seven year intervals.[47] The third arrangement was the forty year lease, a plan much less rigid than the twenty-one year lease; in some cases the forty year leases were renewed annually thus providing regular revenue; in others they were renewed at longer intervals.[48] Below, as of the early 1830s, are the frequencies of the various leaseholds:[49]

Leases for lives: 80
Leases for forty years: 405
Leases for twenty-one years: 1,198

The total amount of land held by the Irish bishops is indicated in table 18. The total episcopal revenue is found in table 19.

To keep these revenue figures in perspective they should be related to those for the gross annual income of English and Welsh bishoprics given below for the year 1830:[50]

York	£23,518
Durham	21,499
Canterbury	20,110
Ely	19,583
London	14,599
Winchester	10,924
Worcester	7,781
St. Asaph	7,269
Bangor	7,164
Norwich	6,606
Bath & Wells	6,482
Lincoln	4,350

Lichfield	4,280
Peterborough	3,664
St. David's	3,360
Chichester	3,342
Hereford	3,168
Salisbury	2,812
Exeter	2,581
Oxford	2,451
Gloucester	1,938
Chester	1,682
Bristol	1,674
Carlisle	1,598
Rochester	962
Llandaff	Not Available

A comparison of the English and the Irish figures reveals that the Irish bishops' gross revenues were nearly on a par with those of their English colleagues. The average gross revenues for the English and Welsh bishoprics on which we have information was less than £500 above the average gross revenue of the Irish bishoprics. Further, it should be noted that the Irish bench of bishops was not significantly smaller in number than the English and Welsh bench; and as a result, the total amount of revenues controlled by the Irish bishops was only about one-sixth smaller than the aggregate controlled by the English and Welsh bishops. This near-parity of the Irish bishops with the English and Welsh bench is especially noteworthy in view of the fact that the Irish bishops had only a fraction of parishioners their English and Welsh counterparts had. The conclusion that members of parliament were to draw during the 1830s from this and related information was that too large a portion of the available Irish resources was being allocated to the bishops of the Church of Ireland.

Such, then, was the financial situation of the top level of the Irish church: the episcopal bench. The second level was that of the cathedral corporations and their associated dignitaries. The matter of cathedral income is somewhat difficult to deal with, for income was of three sorts: revenues from collegiate property, appropriate tithes, and revenue from annexed benefices with cure of souls. Most collegiate revenues came from leases of collegiate lands. The revenues of individual dignitaries came chiefly from tithes.[51] Of the tithe revenue received by individuals more money came from the attached corps, which were benefices with the cure of souls, than from appropriate tithes without cure. In order to avoid double-counting, however, the income from benefices with cure of souls constituting the corps of dignities and prebends are not included as part of collegiate revenues. (They will be included later in the calculations of parochial

TABLE 19
EPISCOPAL REVENUES, 1831
(In pounds)

Diocese	Gross revenues	Net revenues
Armagh	17,669	14,494
Clogher	10,371	8,668
Derry	14,193	12,159
Down & Connor	5,896	4,204
Dromore	4,813	4,216
Kilmore	7,477	6,225
Meath	5,220	4,068
Raphoe	5,787	5,052
Dublin	9,320	7,786
Kildare	6,451	6,061
Ferns & Leighlin	6,550	5,730
Ossory	3,859	3,322
Cashel & Emly	7,354	6,308
Cloyne	5,008	4,091
Cork & Ross	4,345	3,901
Killaloe & Kilfenora	4,532	3,966
Limerick, Ardfert & Aghadoe	5,368	4,973
Waterford & Lismore	4,323	3,933
Tuam & Ardagh	8,206	6,996
Clonfert & Kilmacduagh	3,260	2,970
Elphin	7,034	6,263
Killala & Achonry	4,081	3,410
Total	151,127	128,808
Average per Bishop	6,869	5,855

Note: Amounts less than £1 are ignored. Expenses charged against gross income to determine net income include expenses of employing diocesan schoolmasters, rates, cesses, and various taxes, but not administrative expenses, such as hiring agents to manage the property. The episcopal revenues were chiefly from land rents, although in some cases the bishops received tithes from dignities and other preferments attached to their sees. The proportion of tithes was small, and at this period of time not determinable.

Source: First Report of His Majesty's Commissioners on Ecclesiastical Revenue and Patronage, Ireland, pp. 40–43.

revenues.) Table 20 indicates that the revenues unique to collegiate corporation were of four varieties: those of the deans and chapters; those specifically assigned to economy estates; those of minor corporations of minor canons or vicars-choral; and the incomes paid directly to dignitaries and prebendaries, exclusive of their income from the corps attached to their office. The most striking implication of this table is that the revenues of

TABLE 20
REVENUES ATTACHED TO CATHEDRAL CHAPTERS, 1832
(In pounds)

Category	Gross annual income	Net annual income
Corporations of deans and chapters	1,042	928
Economy estates of cathedral churches	11,055	10,660
Minor ecclesiastical corporations	10,525	8,581
Income of dignities exclusive of benefices with cure of souls	31,329	29,575
Income of prebends exclusive of benefices with cure of souls	8,993	8,019
Subtotal	62,947	57,763
Corrected total[a]	57,105	52,541

Note: Amounts less than £1 are ignored.

[a] Deduct £5,841 for gross and £5,221 for net amounts of dignities and prebends attached to episcopal dignities and included in the report for those bishoprics: Deanery of Christ Church, Dublin; Prebend of Glankeen, Diocese of Cashel; Prebend of Isertlaurence, Diocese of Emly; Prebend of Athnett, Diocese of Limerick.

Source: Second Report of His Majesty's Commissioners on Ecclesiastical Revenue and Patronage, Ireland, p. 296.

the deans and chapters were very small. Once again it becomes clear that resources of the Irish church were attached to specific offices rather than to corporations aggregate or other abstract groupings of the religious.

In contrast to the bishops and to the cathedral corporations, the great bulk of the income of the lower clergy came from tithes. In some instances, the rental of glebe lands augmented tithe revenues; but almost never were glebe rents the major source of a clergyman's livelihood. The lower clergy also augmented their income by small fees for performing marriages and funerals, registering births and deaths, and similar services. Table 21 indicates the gross and net incomes (not including miscellaneous fees) attached to benefices in the respective dioceses. Of course, aggregate figures do not indicate the economic position of individual clergymen. Information on the distribution of clerical incomes, both gross and net, is provided in table 22 with a column of relevant comparative information on the income of churchmen in England. The fact that the incomes of the holders of Irish benefices approximated those of their English counterparts was

TABLE 21
INCOME OF IRISH PAROCHIAL BENEFICES, 1832
(In pounds)

Diocese	Gross income	Net income
Armagh	53,252	44,310
Clogher	28,087	24,334
Derry	41,072	35,315
Down	14,085	11,715
Connor	19,568	16,691
Dromore	10,196	8,466
Kilmore	22,797	19,343
Meath	36,480	30,291
Raphoe	16,803	13,955
Dublin	34,939	29,406
Kildare	12,872	10,873
Ferns	25,498	21,494
Leighlin	21,299	18,422
Ossory	27,248	22,987
Cashel	22,279	19,186
Emly	8,927	7,631
Cloyne	44,443	38,514
Cork	29,714	25,747
Ross	8,362	7,157
Killaloe	22,366	10,012
Kilfenora	1,804	1,666
Limerick	19,135	16,292
Ardfert & Aghadoe	15,616	13,580
Waterford	3,293	2,743
Lismore	13,739	11,814
Tuam	17,637	15,296
Ardagh	14,028	12,213
Clonfert	4,134	3,581
Kilmacduagh	2,062	1,853
Elphin	9,433	7,931
Killala	5,041	4,349
Achonry	4,429	3,879
Total	610,653	520,063

Note: Amounts less than £1 are ignored.

Sources: Third Report of His Majesty's Commissioners on Ecclesiastical Revenue and Patronage in Ireland, pp. 97, 147, 243, 283, 331, 355, 407, 437, 475, 503, 537, 561, 591, 613, 617; *Fourth Report of His Majesty's Commissioners on Ecclesiastical Revenue and Patronage in Ireland*, pp. 101, 141, 187, 235, 281, 317, 335, 347, 383, 431, 469, 517, 539, 605, 659, 669, 673.

TABLE 22

INCOME DISTRIBUTION OF IRISH BENEFICES, 1832

	Annual gross income, Ireland	Annual net income, Ireland	Annual gross income, England
Under £100	157	237	1,926
£100–£200	262	251	2,956
£200–£300	190	216	1,979
£300–£400	158	174	1,326
£400–£500	153	154	830
£500–£700	239	206	843
£700–£1,000	133	99	434
£1,000–£1,500	72	45	134
£1,500–£2,000	20	12	32
£2,000 and up	10	3	18

Sources: As in table 21; *Third Report*, p. 616, *Fourth Report*, p. 672.

significant, and when this fact became public knowledge, it was an invitation to political intervention in the church's financial affairs.

The Tithe System

During the first quarter of the nineteenth century, most of the church's financial arrangements were not matters of public concern. Tithes, however, were a different matter. Because so much controversy—much of it unintelligent and nearly unintelligible—surrounded nineteenth-century discussions of tithes, it is best to explain at once what tithes were. They were simply an agricultural tax, similar in form and application to any impost on agricultural production. We should, therefore, rid ourselves of the emotional overtones surrounding the word and deal with tithes as we would any other tax. Now, tithes as a tax seem to have been almost perfectly designed to be highly unpopular. Why? First, because a tax is felt to be "painful" by a population in direct relation to how visible it is. The Irish tithes were almost maximally visible. In most cases the clergyman, or other owner of the tithes, did not collect them himself; rather, he hired an intermediary, a tithe proctor or tithe farmer to collect them for him. Usually the proctor paid the clergyman a set amount and was allowed to keep whatever he collected in excess of this payment. Hence, the tithe farmer had an interest in collecting as much money as possible, for each marginal pound went entirely into his own pocket.

Second, tithes inevitably were unpopular because responsibility for making the payments rested upon the peasantry rather than upon the landlord. This is not to say that the landlords did not pay indirectly for part of the tithes through having to charge lower rents than otherwise would have been the case (indeed, landlord agitation against the tithe in the eighteenth century clearly indicates that a portion of tithe expenses was being passed on to the landlords). But such an arrangement guaranteed that the tax would seem more unjust than it actually was. A tax paid in the first instance by the poor seems more oppressive than a tax paid in the first instance by the rich, even though in the final analysis both groups might share the same burden under either plan. Third, and most important, tithes were certain to be an unpopular tax because the social benefits of tithe taxation were far from obvious to the bulk of the population. Most people will bear even highly visible and apparently inequitable taxes with resignation if it is clear that the tax revenue is being spent on necessary social services or on national defense requirements, but will object to even small taxes which seem to have no purpose. However, tithes in Ireland were associated with the support of a church which most Irishmen believed to be heretical. Thus, purely from the standpoint of economic analysis and uncluttered by religious rhetoric, the tithe as a tax on agricultural produce was an ill-conceived instrument, almost inevitably destined to engender strong resistance among the Irish peasantry.

Under the tithe system the usual procedure was for the proctor and his assistant to view the crops during the month of July, noting the yield and its potential value. They again visited shortly before the harvest and at that time made a bargain with the occupier as to how much tithe should be paid. If no bargain was agreed upon, the matter was reported to the tithe owner for his action. Most payments of tithes were made in cash rather than in produce. This was advantageous to both parties since the collection and disposal of produce was a serious inconvenience to the proctor; therefore, if a man paid cash his tithes were estimated lower than if he paid in produce. Payments for tithes usually lagged a year to a year and a half behind their determination. Long-term debtors of forty shillings and more could be summoned before two magistrates who were empowered to give decrees enforcing the assessment. For sums above ten pounds the tenant could be hailed into a bishop's court[52] (although it will be recalled the powers of the bishops' courts were too limited to be very effective). Obviously such a system of tax collection was highly provocative. The more money the collecting agent, or tithe proctor, made, the more arbitrary and despotic he became; nothing approaching equality of bargaining power existed between the two parties to the transaction; there were no adequate checks on the rapacity of the proctors and the courts served to reinforce their claims rather than guard the interests of the tenantry. The only effective method available to the peasantry of checking the tithe proctor was combining to commit violence or at least to threaten him.

It is impossible to determine the precise level of tithes in early nineteenth-century Ireland, but fragmentary reports can be pieced together into a reasonably coherent picture. In dealing with the tithe assessment it is crucial to realize that Ireland did not possess a national system of tithe assessment. Practices varied from diocese to diocese and even from parish to parish. In theory tithes were levied at the rate of 10 percent on all agricultural produce, but the practice was far different. In Ireland most of the small tithes—those on orchards, on the young of swine, and on fish, rabbits, eggs, fruit, bees, and milk—were not collected. Only in Munster was the tithe on potatoes collected with regularity. It was not collected at all in Ulster or Connaught, and so rarely in Leinster that most people assumed there was no collection. These exemptions meant, therefore, that large portions of Irish land were not subject to tithes of any sort. Further, far from being the theoretical 10 percent, Irish tithes were estimated to be less than a thirtieth of the produce of the land.[53] Given below are the tithes paid in County Cork for the year 1786 (per Irish acre):[54]

Potatoes	8s. 0d.	to	16s. 0d.
Wheat	6 4		16 0
Barley	6 4		11 2
Oats	1 7		6 4
Meadow	0 0		6 4

In the nineteenth century, the speeches of Sir Henry Parnell in the House of Commons contained useful data. In 1809 Parnell reported that there were no small tithes in Ireland, or tithes on cattle. An acre of wheat, estimated to produce a crop of eight barrels, was usually charged at the rate of 10 shillings—5 percent of its market value. An acre of barley, producing an average crop of thirteen barrels, would be taxed for 9s. 6d. in tithes, one-tenth of the market value being 19s. 6d. An acre of oats, producing an average crop of twelve barrels, would yield a tithe of 7 shillings, 10 percent charge being 16 shillings. An acre of meadow brought about 6 shillings in tithes, a 10 percent charge being 12s. 6d., and in places where potatoes were taxed, an acre of potatoes, producing an average crop of seventy barrels, paid a tithe of 8 shillings; a 10 percent tithe would have been 28 shillings.[55]

Much the most useful data on tithe rates is found in a manuscript notebook of tithe rates for various Irish dioceses presented by the Reverend Canon Leslie to the Public Record Office, Belfast.[56] Table 23 summarizes that information.

Not all tithes collected were turned over to Anglican clergymen. To understand this situation a brief definitional parenthesis is required. Three sets of terms were used in the early nineteenth century to describe tithes; the first two are useless as analytic categories, but are often found in the contemporary literature and therefore deserve attention; the third is of central importance to our analysis. Ancient usage divided the tithes into

TABLE 23

AVERAGE TITHE RATES, PER ACRE, IN ENGLISH CURRENCY AND ENGLISH LAND MEASURE, 1817–21

	Wheat	Barley	Oats	Hay	Flax	Potatoes	Sheep	Lambs	Meadow	Rape
Ardagh	7s. 6d.	6s. 7d.	4s. 0d.	2s. 11d.	7s. 7½d.	6s. 11d.	5d.	0s. 6d.	4s. 6½d.	4s. 6½d.
Cashel	6 11	5 11½	5 9		6 11		6	1		
Clogher	6 11	5 8½	4							
Clonfert	6 4½	5 11½	4 6½				4½	4½		
Cloyne	6 7	6 2½	4	4		6 11			2 11	
Dublin	6 11	4 1½	5 2							
Elphin	6 11	4 6½	4 6		7 5				3	
Kildare	5 9	6 11	4						3	
Killala	8		5 9	3 10	5 9					6 7
Killaloe & Kilfenora	5 2	4 10	4			5 2			3 6½	5 2
Kilmore	6 11	5 3	4	2 11½	2 7				2 7	
Meath	6 3	3	3 8½		6 3					6 4½
Ossory	5 9	4 6½	3 5			5 9			3 8½	5 9
Raphoe	6 5	6 5	4 10			6 5			3 5	5
Tuam	5 8	5 8½	5 2		7 7½	6 3	5½	5½		
Waterford	6 3	5 2							4	

Source: PROB, D. 175.

three sorts: praedial, personal, and mixed. The first were tithes on the fruits of the ground; the second on the profits on labor; and the third on the produce resulting from a combination of the first two forms of endeavor. In the first category were tithes on grains, legumes, and fruits; in the second, tithes on domestic industry; and in the third, tithes on lambs, colts, and calves. A second set of definitions divided the tithes into great tithes and small tithes. The former were tithes on major crops, such as wheat and oats; the latter, tithes on minor produce such as lambs, chickens, and small animals.[57]

Neither of these sets of categories was operationally important; but the third, which divided tithes into rectorial and vicarial, was. Rectorial tithes (roughly corresponding to the great tithes) and the vicarial tithes (roughly corresponding to the small tithes) were separable; that is, they could be assigned to different individuals. This meant that in many instances a parish clergyman did not necessarily receive all the tithes of his benefice, or, for that matter, any of them. It was not at all uncommon for the rectorial portion (in some cases all the tithes) to be annexed to a cathedral chapter or to a dignity. This was an inheritance from the Middle Ages when portions of tithes were permanently annexed to monasteries as part of their endowments. Tithes payable to ecclesiastics other than the parish priest were referred to as being "appropriate." Just as tithes could be assigned to clergy, so could they be assigned to laymen. This arrangement was common because at the Reformation monastic tithes often passed into lay hands. In such cases the assigned tithes were "impropriate." In the case of parishes in which all the tithes, both rectorial and vicarial, were paid to external religious figures (bishops, cathedral dignitaries, etc.), the parish tithes were "wholly appropriate"; while in the analogous cases of parish tithes owned completely by laymen, these levies were "wholly impropriate." [58] In the case of either a wholly appropriate or wholly impropriate parish, the parish clergyman faced the unhappy situation of being assigned a parish with almost no revenue, one probably unable to support either the church therein or a resident clergyman.

This confusing and unhealthy situation was first documented, insofar as impropriations were concerned, by the Reverend Dr. Beaufort in his 1787 survey, which was published in 1792. In viewing the results from that survey, presented in table 24, one should note especially the dioceses with relatively high percentages of impropriations. In most cases these were dioceses in which there had been large monastic appropriations before the Protestant Reformation.[59]

If we wish now to deal with actual amounts of money it is necessary to turn to the material generated by the investigations of the early 1830s. These data are tabulated in table 25.

It goes almost without saying that if the more than £108,000 a year

TABLE 24
TITHE IMPROPRIATIONS, LATE EIGHTEENTH CENTURY

Diocese	No. of parishes	Parishes with rectorial tithes impropriate	Percentage of total	Parishes wholly impropriate	Percentage of total
Armagh	103	12	11.6%	9	8.7%
Clogher	41	5	12.2	–	–
Derry	48	1	2.4	–	–
Down & Connor	114	17	14.9	15	13.2
Dromore	26	3	11.5	–	–
Kilmore	39	10	25.6	–	–
Meath	224	64	28.6	35	15.6
Raphoe	31	3	9.7	–	–
Provincial Total	626	115	18.4	59	9.4
Dublin	209	24	11.5	1	.5
Kildare	81	31	38.3	1	1.2
Ferns & Leighlin	232	66	28.4	13	5.6
Ossory	136	37	27.2	1	.7
Provincial Total	658	158	24.0	16	2.4
Cashel & Emly	155	28	18.1	3	1.9
Cloyne	137	30	21.9	14	10.2
Cork & Ross	127	24	18.9	11	8.7
Killaloe & Kilfenora	138	24	17.4	7	5.1
Limerick, Ardfert & Aghadoe	176	52	29.5	3	1.7
Waterford & Lismore	106	41	38.7	3	2.8
Provincial Total	839	199	23.7	41	4.9

Tuam & Ardagh	126	20	15.9	1	.8
Clonfert & Kilmacduagh	60	–	–	–	1.3
Elphin	75	46	61.3	1	–
Killala & Achonry	52	24	46.2	2	.6
Provincial Total	313	90	28.8		
National Total	2,436	562	23.1	118	.5

Note: Beaufort did not tally the cases in which the vicarial tithes were held by laymen, but in which the rectorial were not. This omission is unimportant because in almost all cases in which laymen held the vicarial they held the rectorial as well. The episcopal revenues were chiefly from land rents, although in some cases the bishops received tithes from dignities and other preferments attached to their sees. The proportion of tithes was small, and at this period of time not determinable.

Source: Beaufort, p. 137.

TABLE 25
TITHE APPROPRIATIONS AND IMPROPRIATIONS, 1832
(In pounds)

Diocese	Gross parochial income	Amount of rectorial tithes appropriate	Amount of rectorial tithes impropriate
Armagh	53,252	432	2,801
Clogher	28,087	525	1,592
Derry	41,072	nil	nil
Down	14,085	1,848	2,064
Connor	19,568	546	4,033
Dromore	10,196	2,977	514
Kilmore	22,797	682	2,567
Meath	36,480	4,727	12,076
Raphoe	16,803	nil	399
Dublin	34,939	8,270	3,186
Kildare	12,872	725	2,583
Ferns	25,498	1,382	5,850
Leighlin	21,299	1,970	4,931
Ossory	27,248	2,871	5,850
Cashel	22,279	789	3,078
Emly	8,927	392	2,323
Cloyne	44,443	1,396	11,435
Cork	29,714	1,178	4,539
Ross	8,362	1,268	2,867
Killaloe	22,366	1,895	3,976
Kilfenora	1,804	559	nil
Limerick	19,135	1,475	4,969
Ardfert & Aghadoe	15,616	295	5,248
Waterford	3,293	705	385
Lismore	13,739	3,103	8,696
Tuam	17,637	1,777	713
Ardagh	14,028	185	3,723
Clonfert	4,134	2,020	nil
Kilmacduagh	2,062	1,033	23
Elphin	9,433	836	4,168
Killala	5,041	2,012	1,487
Achonry	4,429	147	2,791
Total	610,653	48,034	108,879

Note: The reader will note that the investigators did not determine what the value of the vicarial tithes payable to appropriators or impropriators was. The amount was probably relatively small for two reasons: first, the number of parishes wholly appropriate or impropriate was relatively small (and the cases of vicarial tithes alone being impropriate or appropriate were rare) and second, the vicarial tithes in Ireland were of small value com-

TABLE 25   (Continued)

pared to the rectorial. Therefore the data, though incomplete, stand as a fair guide to the allocation of tithe revenues between parochial clergymen, clerical appropriators, and laymen. One further caution: the total parochial revenue figures include other forms of income beside tithes, of which glebe rents were the most significant. Tithes, however, formed all but a very small proportion of parochial income. With these cautions, the nineteenth century data are of considerable value.

Amounts less than £1 are ignored. For additional information on specific cases, see the comments in the pages referred to in the source note.

Source: Third Report of His Majesty's Commissioners on Ecclesiastical Revenue and Patronage in Ireland, pp. 97, 147, 243, 283, 331, 355, 407, 437, 475, 503, 537, 561, 591, 613, 617; Fourth Report of His Majesty's Commissioners on Ecclesiastical Revenue and Patronage in Ireland, pp. 101, 141, 187, 235, 281, 317, 335, 347, 383, 431, 469, 517, 539, 605, 659, 669, 673.

which were paid to laymen had been paid to local incumbents, the church would have been greatly strengthened at the very point where it was weakest—namely, the parish level. The ratio of parochial revenues to lay impropriations was roughly six to one. A one-sixth increase in parochial incomes would have greatly changed the pattern of organization by making extensive unions unnecessary, and thereby improving the efficiency of the Irish church. Unlike the impropriations it is difficult to know how harmful the appropriations were. On the one hand, it may be argued that the cathedral chapters and dignitaries which benefited by appropriations were an important part of the church and deserved support; on the other, the appropriations can only have lowered the standard of parish ministry in the countryside.

Eighteenth-Century Tithe Legislation

Anyone viewing the Irish tithe system with a candid eye could see that it desperately needed reform. From an economic viewpoint it was the most obnoxious of taxes. From the viewpoint of the Irish peasant it was coercive in the extreme. To a member of the Roman Catholic faith it was a form of religious persecution. To a landlord it was clearly a levy on his profits. And to a clergyman it was often an inadequate and inefficient source of parochial revenue. Obvious as the need for change was, the proper mode of alteration was far from obvious, and generations of Irishmen fought over reforming the tithe system, often neutralizing each other's efforts.

The first important "reform" of the eighteenth century benefited the peasantry slightly, the landlords considerably, but hurt the clergy financially. The issue in question was the tithe of agistment, the tithe on pasturage for dry and barren cattle. This was regularly collected in the north, but not in the remainder of the country. With the increase in pasturage in Irish agriculture in the early eighteenth century the tithe became a potentially great income source. Therefore, a test case in 1707 brought matters to a head when a clergyman obtained a Court of King's Bench judgment in Dublin, which was later upheld in London, affirming his right to such tithes. Landlord resistance intensified. In 1722 the Court of Exchequer of Ireland at the behest of Archdeacon Neale of Leighlin again upheld the clergy's claim—a claim that was reaffirmed upon appeal to London.[60] But lay resistance led by influential landlords continued. In December 1735 a petition was introduced into the Irish House of Commons praying for relief against suits of tithes of agistment, and claiming these tithes had never been paid or demanded until recent years.[61] The petition was followed by a second from another group of landowners on behalf of themselves and other Irish landowners, claiming that the clergy were instituting a new tithe on pasturage for dry and barren cattle, and that this practice should be forbidden. A committee of the Irish House of Commons investigated the matter and reported on 18 March 1735.[62] The committee concluded that the petitioners had proved their case, with which the House agreed. The Commons then passed a motion "that the commencing suit upon these new demands must impair the Protestant interest, by driving many useful hands out of this kingdom; must disable those that remain to support his Majesty's establishment, and occasion popery and infidelity to gain ground, by the contest that must necessarily arise between the laity and clergy." The Commons concluded by resolving "that all legal ways and means ought to be made use of, to oppose all attempts that shall hereafter be framed to carry demands of tithe agistment into execution, until a proper remedy can be provided by legislature." These resolutions, although not having the effect of law, effectively hamstrung the tithe owners in collecting the tithe agistment. Irish landlords formed themselves into associations to resist the tithe of agistment, funds were raised and a treasurer chosen to support those who were sued by the clergy. The House of Commons quietly threatened to appoint a committee to investigate the behavior of bishops and clergy in their pastoral duties. The churchmen were thoroughly intimidated and the tithe of agistment passed from their hands into the landlords' pockets.[63] Years later the situation was formalized by Act 40, George III, c. 23, which legally abolished the tithe of agistment.[64]

Tithes again became the focus of national attention in the 1780s, but this time it was the peasantry not the landlords who were fighting the system. By the mid-1780s, peasant opposition to tithes, which took the form of sporadic agrarian violence and of combinations to resist payment, was financially strangling the parish clergy. In May 1786 the Lord Lieutenant wrote to the Chief Secretary for Ireland, "The state of the province of Munster, as far as relates to the clergy, is very alarming. Not a guinea will be received from any living. The combinations increase. The Whiteboys still are rising." [65] The clergy were terrified of violence. The Bishop of Cloyne reported that Dr. Atterbury, a dignitary in his cathedral and a cleric constantly resident in his parish, had been surrounded by a band of, roughly, two hundred men who forced him at gun point to promise to accept a tithe composition of about one-third the usual rate.[66] Reports of this sort swirled about the country, frightening the clergy and greatly reinforcing the effectiveness of the peasant agitation.

In the face of the tithe agitation, the government had two options: to shore-up the tithe system by compensating the clergy for their losses or to reform the system itself. The government chose the former course while the parliamentary opposition favored the latter. By June 1786 Thomas Orde, the Chief Secretary, had become convinced that tithes would inevitably be a subject of discussion in the next session of the Irish parliament. Therefore he suggested that the Lord Lieutenant contact the Archbishop of Armagh and the Archbishop of Cashel as to the course to follow. Above all else, Orde counseled the Lord Lieutenant to be certain the churchmen were agreed to any plan set forward by the government.[67] Not surprisingly, when the subject of tithes was mentioned in the speech from the throne opening the parliament of 1787, it was clear that the Established church was to be buttressed, not criticized: "Your uniform regard for the rights of your fellow subjects," the Lord Lieutenant's message to the Commons read, "and your zealous attachment to the religious and civil constitutions of your country, will stimulate your attention to their inseparable interests, and will ensure your especial support of the Established Church, and the respectable situation of its ministers." [68] Significantly, in 1787, in contrast to 1735, the major landowners rallied to the church, rather than attacking it. Their defense of the church in the face of the agrarian agitation was a result of the conviction that their own position was tied to that of the church; for, if one form of agrarian property could be destroyed by the peasantry, so could others. Most landowners came to agree with Lord Tyrone, an expert at viewing with alarm: "Now comes the Church. Agencies and the letting of land will be the next, if the country exist so long." [69]

The results of collaboration between the government and the landowners in the hope of protecting the church were two acts designed to make life safer and more profitable for the parish clergy. The first act (27 George III, c. 15) was designed to prevent risings and to more effectively punish illegal combinations and those perpetrating agrarian outrage. Much of this act was of a general nature, but two clauses were designed to deal specifically with the tithe agitation. The fifth clause of the act declared it a felony to burn or pull down an Anglican church; and to prevent or obstruct, by force or by threat, a Church of Ireland clergyman from performing divine service. The eleventh clause of the act detailed fines, imprisonment, or corporal punishment for persons convicted of unlawful combination to defraud either a lay impropriator or a clergyman of his tithes. Obstructing a tithe-owner from viewing, setting, selling or collecting his tithes was in violation of the act.[70]

A second measure (27 George III, c. 36) was passed to give the clergy compensation for lost tithes, the bill being drafted by John Hely Hutchinson and the Irish Attorney General.[71] This act applied to the counties of Limerick, Kerry, Cork, Tipperary, Waterford, Clare and Kilkenny, the areas of greatest tithe agitation. Under the measure, a clergyman who had been deprived of his tithes through violence or threats in the year 1786 could sue in secular courts, rather than ecclesiastical, for tithes up to the average of the last seven years' value. The measure was renewed the following year and then dropped when the agitation died down.[72]

Much more interesting than the government's policy of bulwarking the church were the attacks upon the tithe system by the opposition, most notably by Henry Grattan. As early as 1780 Grattan envisaged a tithe reform under which the tithes should be levied like any other county tax; namely, by the chief constable and other county authorities.[73] Grattan did not, however, campaign vigorously until the tithe distress of 1787. On 13 March, Grattan called the Commons' attention to the distress of the lower orders caused by the Irish tithe system. With biting words he detailed the vices of the system of tithes proctors, the oppressiveness of ecclesiastical courts, and the irresponsibility of landlords and clergy. He concluded his speech by moving that an inquiry be made into the Irish tithe system, with the view to finding some more desirable method of supporting the Anglican clergy. Naturally the government opposed such an inquiry and it was smothered without a division.[74] Grattan kept trying, however, and the next year he moved for a committee to inquire whether there was "any just cause" in the Munster districts on account of tithes or tithe collections. Once again, the government and the landlords rallied and the motion was defeated 121 to 49.[75] In 1789 Grattan attempted for the third time to introduce a bill to investigate the tithe system and to frame tithe reforms, but the bill failed on its first reading without a division being necessary.[76] At the beginning of the nineteenth century, therefore, the Irish tithe system was as inefficient and as frustrating as ever.[77]

Tithe Reforms, 1800–1820

There were three general categories under which a tenant could have his tithe burden reduced or relieved altogether. The first of these consisted of instances in which it could be shown that from time immemorial some practice other than normal tithe procedures was binding. For example, there were a few parishes in which no tithes whatsoever were demanded. This was known as a custom *de non decimando;* the practice could hold for specific geographic regions or for individuals. The king by immemorial custom paid no tithes, and neither did a vicar pay tithes to the owner of the rectorial tithes, or vice versa. Besides those cases in which custom provided freedom from all tithes, there were many more instances in which tithes were paid by immemorial practice on terms different from those usually prevailing. This custom was known as *a modus decimandi* (usually called a *modus*) and under it a peculiar set of local practices prevailed: such as a fixed pecuniary compensation for the tithe; or a compensation by work-payment other than money.

The second major category of special tithe arrangement was more important to the individual tenant. It comprised those cases in which the tithe owner and the tenant came to a mutually agreeable "real composition." Under this arrangement the tenant's or landowner's holdings were discharged from tithe by virtue of the parson's receiving some land or other real compensation (often a fixed annual payment). Because early Protestant clergy were often profligate in their alienation of church property, an act of 13 Elizabeth I, c. 10, prohibited parsons from making such agreements for longer than three lives or twenty-one years.[78]

Third, a tithe-payer's burden might be reduced by special parliamentary legislation dealing with all of Ireland or at least a large portion of the country. This legislation usually bore the name "tithe composition" or "tithe commutation," the terms being used without great precision. In practice, most tithe-reform acts, whatever they were called, reduced the amount of tithes payable and usually fixed the annual payment over a considerable period in lieu of the fluctuating tithe payment. It was this third category, legislative reform, that was to dominate the public and popular thinking on the tithe question in the early years of the nineteenth century.

As a concomitant of the Union, Castlereagh had contemplated a plan which would have augmented the income of the lower Anglican clergy, increased the grants to the Presbyterians, and made some financial provision for the Roman Catholic clergy; but the measure did not have direct tithe implications.[79] Pitt, however, was reported to have favored the commutation of Irish tithes by compensating the clergyman with land, but the precise nature of his plan and its date are unknown.[80] That British politicians were concerned about matters of finance in the Irish church is evidenced by Castlereagh's writing Grenville in September 1800 and indicating that, in compliance with Grenville's request, he had thought seriously about the practicability of a proportional commutation between tithe and rent.[81] Castlereagh thereupon worked out his own views upon the tithe question[82] and his opinion was four-fold. First, he believed that tithes discouraged the improvement of land by tenants more than did money rents. Second, tithes seemed to him to be deficient as a source of income for the clergy because they were difficult to collect and unpredictable in yield. The natural propensity of the clergy to hire tithe proctors to do the collecting brought the church into odium without enriching its ministers. Third, the local tenants' method of thwarting the clergyman—through their right to force him to collect the tithe in kind rather than in money—often led to undesirable combinations among the tenants. Fourth, Castlereagh believed the tithes fell most heavily upon the tenants of the tillage areas of the country and relatively lightly upon the rich grazers, a situation of which he disapproved because of its inequity.

As a remedy, Castlereagh proposed that instead of allowing tithes to be settled in kind, only money payments be allowed. These payments would be for a fixed amount for each species of produce and would be fixed for a considerable period of time, twenty-one years being Castlereagh's suggestion. At the end of such period if either the incumbent or three-quarters of the parishioners wished a reevaluation, the justices of the quarter session were to recalculate the tithe rates—based upon the general price average in Ireland for the commodity—and adjust the rate accordingly. Castlereagh added specific and complicated details which need not detain us here. The central point is that he proposed to overcome the uncertainty of tithes as clerical revenue, reduce their inequities, and encourage the tenant to do intelligent long-range planning through commuting his tithe to a predictable annual fee similar to land rents.

While the Chief Secretary was writing to Grenville about tithe reform, the Marquis of Buckingham was propounding his own views for Grenville. Buckingham demanded attention, both as a former Lord Lieutenant of Ireland and as the ranking member of the Grenville clan. Buckingham quite frankly despaired of successfully tinkering with the existing system. He saw no possible way to equalize the tithe where it was collected; or of giving compensation to the clergy in instances, such as agistment, when it was not collected. Therefore, he proposed a plan of tithe commutation whose specific details were muddled but whose foundation was the substitution of a tax based on the price of corn for the existing arrangements. The impost would be levied in the same manner as were the county rates, and presumably would do away with the need for clergymen to hire tithe proctors. The levy would fluctuate with the price of corn; commissioners would set it at the average value of tithes for the preceding seven years and the average number of barrels of wheat which the titheable land had produced over the same period of time. Presumably, the abolition of the post of tithe proctor, combined with the lessening of annual fluctuations through the averaging process, would allow both the clergy and the peasantry to plan more accurately, while removing some of the unpleasant aspects of the tithe-proctor system.[83]

For the moment nothing came of either of these plans, Buckingham was in no position to press his, and Castlereagh soon left Ireland. Grenville, who had been Chief Secretary for Ireland from 1782 to 1783, remained keen on Irish affairs, and when he became Prime Minister in the Ministry of All the Talents in February 1806, the chances for Irish tithe reform rose considerably. At the same time renewed agrarian agitation focused political attention on the Irish tithe question. Buckingham reported to Grenville that matters in Ireland were in a most serious state. The tenants on his County Longford estate, the same men who had stood untainted in the last rebellion even though the whole country was in an uproar, were refusing to pay tithes; they had taken an oath to pay only four shillings tithe per acre and were convinced that they were doing no wrong. The government's policy in Ireland was so pusillanimously conciliatory that many tenants were convinced that the government condoned the proceedings—or at least so Buckingham reported. Buckingham's remedy, predictably enough, was to advise calling out the troops.[84]

Grenville was more constructive in his approach and had the Lord Lieutenant, the Duke of Bedford, make a detailed investigation and provide recommendations. In his initial report to the Prime Minister, the Lord Lieutenant recognized that the Prime Minister had himself suggested three possible reform schemes (the conversion of tithes to long leases, the exemption of small cottagers operating subsistence farms from tithes, and the conversion of tithes into land annuities). Bedford concluded that a preferable procedure would be to establish a fair valuation of tithes which would be set for a considerable period of time: perhaps seven, ten, or fourteen years. This valuation would be determined by commissioners appointed by parliament especially for this purpose, or by mutual agreement of the payer and the receiver, subject to the approbation of two magistrates sitting in quarter session. This system would be most efficient, Bedford said, if the payment of tithe was charged solely to the proprietor of the land, not to the occupier, and then recovered in the rent charge.[85] Later, however, Bedford came to prefer the idea of commuting the tithes for land, in spite of the obvious danger of turning the parish clergy into men more concerned with farming than with religion.[86] In any event, the Prime Minister was convinced that the chances of getting a tithe bill through parliament were small due to the awakened "spirit of bigotry" on such matters,[87] and before any purposive action could be taken, the Grenville ministry was swept from office.

Succeeding administrations did little in the way of concrete action or even thought on the Irish tithe problem; as the tithe agitation died down after 1807, officials were not pressed to face the issue. The focus of activity on tithe matters therefore shifted from the government to private members of parliament. Of these members, Sir Henry Parnell, M.P. for the Queen's County, was the most insistent. In April 1808 he called the Commons' attention to Irish tithes by moving successfully for a return of the civil bills for tithe matters which had been tried in Ireland during the preceding year. This call was made because litigation was common and was rapidly becoming endemic.[88] The next year Parnell moved from peripheral issues to the question of the expediency of maintaining the tithe system. Parnell professed to do this with some reluctance; for in the preceding year he had called privately on the Chancellor of the Exchequer, Spencer Perceval, who said the matter was under the ministry's consideration and that a relief measure was in the offing. The bill outlined by Perceval was to enable incumbents to make leases of tithes to their parishioners for twenty-one years, a measure of which Parnell approved. During the 1809 session, however, it became clear that the government was not planning to actually bring in a tithe-leasing measure. Parnell, therefore, moved to bring in a twenty-one-year leasing bill as the first installment of a more general plan of tithe reform. The government forces rallied smoothly and Parnell was crushed by 137 to 62.[89]

Greatly to his credit, Parnell pressed on. In the session of 1810 he again raised the tithe problem, and in so doing provided the English-dominated House of Commons with a first-rate lecture on the difference between the Irish and the English tithe system. In the first place, he called parliament's attention to the obvious fact that in Ireland, unlike England, the religion of the people dictated that they regard as odious the tithe system because it provided income for the clergy of the Established Church. Second, in Ireland the tithes bore more heavily on the lowest agricultural classes. In England the demand for farm labor was so great and so constant that the agricultural laboring class could depend upon daily wages to provide for their subsistence. In Ireland, however, the surplus of labor meant that it was necessary for the poorer classes to have a piece of land to produce their own food, since they stood scant chance in the glutted labor market of earning enough to buy food. Therefore, since the lowest of the English agricultural classes—the day-laborers—escaped paying tithes, even the poorest agricultural Irishman paid them. Third, the Irish laws for tithe collection were much more severe than those in England. Finally, in the specific case of the flax tithe, the amount was limited by law to five shillings an acre in England whereas no such regulation existed in Ireland.

These observations, Parnell felt, made it obvious that the peculiar circumstances of the Irish tithe situation demanded parliamentary investigation, and he therefore moved to appoint a select committee. Parnell, by now long experienced in parliamentary frustration, could hardly have been surprised when the Commons rejected his motion this time by a vote of 69 to 48.[90] The small size of the vote indicated how uninterested parliament was in the Irish tithe issue. And if that point were not well-enough made by the British legislators, their vote in the following year—54 to 49 against Parnell's motion to consider Irish tithes in the next session—underlined it with insulting indifference.[91]

Under Irish ecclesiastical law, the ecclesiastical courts could punish for a misdemeanor tenants who, in groups of four or five or more, simultaneously informed the clergyman that he had to collect his tithes from them in kind. In such cases it was usually impossible for the clergyman or his proctor to collect the produce before it became over-ripe and spoiled, and the clergyman was thereupon forced to settle with the tenants for a money payment well below the crop value. The ecclesiastical courts had power to punish conspiracies in such instances, but it was believed that they punished tenants who gave notices simultaneously even when no evidence of conspiracy was available. The Earl of Kingston, therefore, introduced a bill into the Lords in May 1816 to clarify the conspiracy matter, an intention which frightened the leaders of the Irish church. They perceived the bill as a dangerous one partly because it represented a secular encroachment on ecclesiastical rights and partly because the Earl of Kingston was believed to be an enemy of the church.[92] For an alleged enemy, Kingston proved nearly supine in debate, and accepted the assurances of the Lord Chancellor and of the Archbishop of Cashel that the ecclesiastical courts were not moving unless there was sound evidence of conspiracy. Thereupon, Kingston expressed satisfaction and withdrew his bill.[93] Here (aside from one more attempt by Sir Henry Parnell at passing a long-leasing tithe measure)[94] matters rested twenty years after the Union. A great variety of reforms had been contemplated but none had been completed.

Tithe Composition Acts

Discomfort and misfortune being the root of most reforms in Ireland, it is not surprising that effective tithe reforms occurred only when the peasantry were so seriously pressed economically that they either refused or were unable to pay their tithes, and the tithe owners were themselves inconvenienced. The agitation of 1806–08 had dwindled with the rise in agricultural prices, but the resulting agricultural prosperity did not last long and from 1817 onwards farm prices slid continually downward.[95] The peasantry by 1821 were hard pressed and began withholding their tithes. In the three southern provinces, withholding became general. The result was that during the years from 1821 to 1823 the parish clergy were in tight financial straits. The case of the Reverend Thomas Clarke, rector of Inishmacsaint Parish in County Fermanagh, is typical. One feels some sympathy for the man upon hearing that much of his tithes of 1819, 1820, and 1822 remained unpaid, as no one would undertake their collection. But one then finds that he was an absentee rector, and that his agent was going to the extreme of having levy warrants signed for the seizure of peasant property. But the agent reported the process was tedious because "the magistrates feel so much for the distress of the poor" that they allow months "from the convictions . . . before signing the levy warrants." [96] And when attempted, seizures were useless: "The lower part of the middle division appear determined to pay none and will rescue any seizure which the collectors would succeed in [making]." [97] So powerful and united were the peasantry that the collectors claimed they dared not execute the levy warrants for fear of their own lives.

By early 1822 the combined problems of agrarian disorder and clerical impoverishment had overcome governmental inertia. The government transmitted the heads of a proposed bill to Archbishop Stuart and the other Irish archbishops. The Prime Minister, Lord Liverpool, explained didactically to Archbishop Stuart that as far as tithes were concerned the government was confronted with three different situations: in some places all the parties involved were satisfied with the existing system; in others, all parties were desirous of commutation; and elsewhere, one party was desirous of commutation but the others objected to it. Now, with the first and second categories no one would wish to interfere; but in the case of the third something had to be done and that was to introduce (but only after a two-year grace period) the principle of compulsory commutation. There was, Liverpool said, ample precedent for compulsion in the enclosure acts of earlier years. The important desideratum in any compulsory composition was to be certain that the commutation was a just one. To assure this, Lord Liverpool suggested that the man who paid the tithe should appoint one arbiter and the tithe owner another; if these two disagreed, a third decisive arbiter should be appointed by the Irish administration. Arrangements made under the proposed act would be for twenty-one years.[98]

Although Lord Liverpool contemplated an element of compulsion, Henry Goulburn, the Irish Chief Secretary who was drafting the actual bill, was moving with much less confidence. His first draft of a bill in April was timid, providing for the abolition of tithes on potatoes, with compensation to the clergy, and very little more.[99]

Ultimately, Goulburn's bill, when finally introduced, had little to do with either Liverpool's or his own planning but rather reflected the thinking of the Lord Lieutenant, the Marquis of Wellesley.[100] As introduced by Goulburn in mid-June 1822, the proposed measure was merely a long-term tithe-leasing proposal. Goulburn's rambling introductory speech was more preamble than substance, and that preamble was a long invocation of the inviolability of property designed to reassure both landowners and churchmen that he was no revolutionary. Because tithes were an ancient form of clerical property, Goulburn intoned, the government approached the issue with great delicacy. The bill he presented was one which would allow the incumbent to enter into a lease for tithes for twenty-one years with the owner—not with the occupier of the soil. Presumably the owner would then pass the tithes on to the tenant as a portion of the rent charge. Such a measure would be attractive to the tithe owner because it would regularize his income over a long period of time. Because the bill specially provided that such agreements, unlike existing tithe leases, would be binding for the full lease even in case of the death of the incumbent, the financial position of a new vicar or rector would be quickly regularized and the transition from new to old incumbent facilitated. In order to keep the incumbent from making a lease detrimental to future incumbents Goulburn decided that the lease would have to be approved by the bishop of the diocese, and by the patron in benefices under lay patronage. Presumably the government believed that this plan would reduce peasant agitation against tithes by disguising them as rent payments made to the landlord. Goulburn did not explain why the Irish landlords should accept the duty of collecting tithes; one can assume that the only reason an Irish landlord would enter into the leasing arrangement would be if he could collect more from the tenantry than he had to pay the clergyman. In any case, Goulburn was given leave to bring in his mild measure, but nothing came of it before the session ended.[101]

Finally, in 1823, Goulburn and the government came to realize that significant state intervention in the Irish tithes system was no longer avoidable. Almost inevitably, that intervention would require some form of compulsory reduction of tithes. Specifically, Goulburn contemplated a measure of conversion of tithes into a fixed tax ("composition" was Goulburn's term for the process) if either the incumbent or the parish tithe-payers so demanded. The Chief Secretary, therefore, realized that surrender of the doctrine of sanctity of ecclesiastical property was the price to be paid for agrarian peace. Goulburn feared the reaction of Irish churchmen, and therefore took the precaution of having the bill approved by various cabinet ministers before submitting it to the Irish prelates.[102]

Goulburn was correct in fearing the churchmen's ire. Lord John George Beresford, recently raised to the Archbishopric of Armagh, wrote to the Lord Lieutenant upon reading the draft bill:

> I declare that this bill is in principle unjust and unconstitutional and in operation would be irritating, vexatious, impracticable; That it is built on [illeg.] fallacious principles totally inapplicable to the real circumstances of this Country; that it sets at nought the rights and interests of the Clergy . . . and if enforced will invoke many parishes in Ireland in tumult and insurrection.[103]

Not content to stop with the Lord Lieutenant, Beresford launched a salvo in the general direction of the Prime Minister. To Liverpool he repeated much of what he had written Wellesley, and added, "My Lord, so far from thinking these expressions too strong, they do not strongly enough describe the Evils which would most certainly flow from this Bill. From your Lordship's known attachment to the Established Church, I conclude that you have not considered this Measure, but depended on the Irish Government." [104] As concerned as he was about the substance of the bill, Beresford seemed equally concerned about matters of professional courtesy. He believed the government was ignoring him. In his letter to Liverpool he complained that he had been snubbed as an adviser on the tithe leasing bill of the previous year[105] and not consulted on the present measure. He embroidered on the theme of neglect in writing to the Archbishop of Canterbury. The Lord Lieutenant, he said, had requested his opinion on the subject of composition but before he had time to answer, the government had committed itself. In high dudgeon, Beresford fumed that the government had submitted the bill to him only a week before its announcement in the House of Commons, and (most insulting of all, we can conjecture) Beresford reported that it was placed in the hands of one of the other archbishops before being shown to himself, the Lord Primate of All Ireland.[106]

Whatever the precise sequence in which the information was received by the Irish hierarchy, and whatever Beresford's actual motives, the four Irish archbishops learned of the substance of the bill at approximately the same time, and Beresford almost instantly requested that they meet with him in Dublin near the end of February. At that meeting (which had to be postponed, thus precluding the Archbishop of Cashel's attending) a memorial was drafted to the Lord Lieutenant condemning the bill. Unanimity among the archbishops, however, was more apparent than actual, for the Archbishop of Cashel, Richard Laurence, warmly supported the measure.[107] The majority of the hierarchy, however, enrolled in the ranks of the opposition and signed the protesting memorial that was presented to Wellesley on the sixth of March. The memorialists repeated the refrain that heretofore church property had been subject to the same law as private property. By the compulsory provisions of the bill, however, church property would now become less sacrosanct than property in private hands. Almost as a footnote, the bishops added that since the measure applied only to the Irish branch of the Church of England and Ireland, the "fundamental unity" of the two churches would be endangered.[108]

As if the Irish bishops were not sufficiently worried, on 4 March 1823 (two days before the government formally introduced its measure) the radical Joseph Hume frightened them by attacking the church in the House of Commons. In the course of a caustic and incisive speech, Hume stated that his object was gradually to reduce the members of the Irish bench to one archbishop and four bishops, to abolish the cathedral ranks through leaving the posts unfilled as they became vacant, and to set the income of parish clergymen between £150 and £500 a year in place of the existing great disparity of remuneration. Hume therefore moved four resolutions. The first of these declared that the property of the Church of Ireland in the possession of the bishops, deans, and chapters, was public property and was at the disposal of the legislature for the support of religion in whatever manner parliament deemed beneficial to the community. Second, it was expedient to inquire into whether the present church establishment could not be reduced in size and income. The third resolution stated that the best interest of Ireland would be served by a commutation of all tithes, with compensation to the present owners. Fourth, Hume moved the appointment of a select committee to consider in what way these resolutions might best be carried into effect. Of course, Hume's resolutions stood little chance of passage, but they were frightening to churchmen and a harbinger of the criticisms the church would face in the 1830s. In the course of events, Hume's first, third and fourth resolutions were negatived without a division, the second resolution being lost by a vote of 107 to 62.[109]

Goulburn's immediate reaction to Hume's foray was to conjecture that it might render the government's task more difficult because the Irish bishops would be more adverse to the tithe bill. On the other hand, he consoled himself that the Bishops of Derry and Cloyne as well as the Archbishop of Cashel acquiesced in the measure, and both Cashel and Derry were now in rotation as representatives of the Irish church in the House of Lords.[110] In point of fact, two bills were finally introduced on 6 March 1823 by the Irish Chief Secretary. One bill was facilitative and non-controversial, the other central and controversial. The first measure was long, detailed, but simple in its basic outlines.[111] First, it proposed a body to be known as "The Commissioners for the Commutation of Tithes in Ireland." This body was to consist of the Lord Chancellor, the four Irish archbishops, the Irish Chief Justices and the Chief Secretary for Ireland, together with three persons to be appointed by the Lord Lieutenant. Second, when any composition was made under any act to be passed in the 1823 session of parliament, the incumbent was to have the right to petition the commissioners for land instead of money as tithe composition. In such a case, the commissioners were empowered to contract for lands where income was commensurate with the value of tithes in the process of being extinguished. Similar provisos were to be made for lay impropriators or other tithe owners who preferred lands to tithe compositions. Having accepted the lands, the tithe owner's right to tithes naturally ceased. Third, in parishes where no composition was made, the Lord Lieutenant upon application of the tithe owner (either lay or clerical), would be empowered to appoint a commissioner to evaluate the matter and assign lands in place of tithes. Fourth, in cases where tithes were extinguished in return for the government's providing lands, they were to become a permanent tax upon the parish, payable and collected by the government in the same manner as any other tax. Presumably, the advantages of the proposed arrangements were that the maximum freedom would be given to the clergy, since they could choose either composition or lands. At the same time the tenantry was given the boon either of reduced tithes, or of tithes becoming invisible through conversion into a governmental tax. Surprisingly, this facilitating measure never garnered much enthusiasm. It received its second reading on 24 April and nothing more was heard of it, the committee stage being continually deferred until the session was over.[112]

The actual composition scheme, therefore, became the heart of the tithe reform issue. The bill, as introduced by Goulburn on 6 March 1823, was hardly the revolutionary gesture the churchmen thought it to be. It simply gave everyone involved deeply in the matter a chance to replace existing tithe arrangements with a tithe composition. Upon application of the incumbent, of the lay impropriator, or of five landowners occupying lands worth twenty pounds a year each, the Lord Lieutenant could create a "special vestry" in each parish for the purpose of carrying out the composition act. The special vestry would be composed of those paying the largest amount of tithes in each parish (in the course of passage the number was set at fifteen to twenty persons), and elaborate precautions were made that the list would be subject to public scrutiny and review in case of protest. Complicated provisions were made for parishes totally impropriate. In any case, those paying the highest tithes were to assemble in special vestry and vote (by an elaborate system of multiple voting dependent on how much tithe each individual paid), whether or not they desired a tithe composition. If so, then they and the incumbent each appointed one representative as commissioner to determine an amount designating composition for all tithes. These two commissioners were empowered to fix a composition which would replace all scattered tithe payments, and be at least equal to the amounts paid for the last seven years. (A longer time could, if desired, be used for purposes of calculation.) The composition was not to exceed one-third above the average payment. It would be set for twenty-one years, subject to triennial revision. In cases of disagreement between the two commissioners, the Irish government was to appoint an umpire.[113]

All this was rather complex and hardly revolutionary. Under the terms of the bill the incumbent would receive a minimum of his average tithe over the last seven years (admittedly from 1820–23 tithe revenues were very low) and could receive up to one-third more. The compositions effected by the select vestries were to be made by the agrarian middle orders—substantial tithe payers, rather than agitated lower peasantry. The bill's chief merit was that it simplified the tithe system by substituting a single money payment for the myriad small calculations on each type of produce. Further, it made the tithe both as a tax and as a source of revenue more predictable. At the same time the three year re-evaluation provision meant that the tithe revenue would be reasonably reflective of the national economic condition.

Goulburn, finally allowing himself to be optimistic about the measure, reported to the Lord Lieutenant that the bill was very favorably received and that many compliments were paid by the opposition. Cautiously he added, "Compliments from political opponents usually foretell a coming storm." [114] Actually, Goulburn need not have worried, for the "storm" when it came was surprisingly light. As expected, the radicals attacked the bill as a mere trifle when thorough-going reform was necessary. Attack from the other side—from the churchmen and conservative landowners—was effectively forestalled by the government's gracefully surrendering the principle of compulsion, thus removing the major bone of contention. This surrender, which many felt cut the heart from the measure, made passage easy and on 19 July it received the royal assent.[115]

Within its own limitations the 1823 tithe measure was reasonably successful. By March 1824 there had been 1,002 applications for special vestries under the act. The only drawback was that the measure was not compulsory. If either the vestry or the incumbent refused to accept the principle of composition, the whole matter had to be dropped. Thus, in 369 of the 1,002 cases, the parties had been unable to agree on the principle of composition and the vestry had to be adjourned *sine die*.[116] To remedy this flaw, the government successfully introduced an amending measure in the 1824 session of parliament which provided for compulsion in a form palatable to the church and the landowners. Under the tithe composition amending act the Lord Lieutenant assumed the power, in cases where the special vestry and the incumbent could not agree to mutually accept the principle of composition, to compel both parties to appoint composition commissioners anyway. This meant that either the incumbent, or the tithe owners assembled in special vestry, could force tithe composition to take place, if the Lord Lieutenant was willing to apply vice-regal coercion to the situation.[117]

Taken together, the 1823 and 1824 tithe composition statutes were a considerable success, rationalizing tithe payments and making them slightly less irritating to the peasantry. By early 1832 a composition of tithes had been effected in over half of the parishes of Ireland. The state of tithe composition in February 1832 is given in table 26.

Our survey of the financial structure of the church is now completed.[118] Several conclusions bear underlining. The first is that in comparison to its rival, the Irish Roman Catholic Church, the Church of Ireland was immensely wealthy in relation to the constituency it served. In the 1830s, the Anglican Church paid an annual net income to holders of religious offices of rather more than £701,000 (funds earmarked for the maintenance of cathedral fabric, etc., are included in this calculation). The expenditure of the Roman Catholic Church during the same period for maintenance of the clergy has been estimated at approximately £500,000 per annum.[119] Ireland in 1834 was 81 percent Roman Catholic and only 11 percent Anglican (see tables 34 and 36). Another way of indicating the

TABLE 26
IRISH TITHE COMPOSITIONS, 1832

Diocese	No. of parishes	No. under composition acts	Total amount of composition	Average comp. per parish
Armagh	115	54	£21,736	£403
Clogher	46	30	14,563	486
Derry	55	42	22,968	547
Down & Connor	119	53	18,625	351
Dromore	26	10	4,445	444
Kilmore	44	30	5,692	284
Meath	214	162	38,152	228
Raphoe	37	16	8,167	510
Dublin	185	107	22,207	208
Kildare	73	39	10,153	260
Ferns & Leighlin	224	116	37,478	323
Ossory	138	70	20,215	289
Cashel & Emly	152	118	30,125	255
Cloyne	137	69	28,608	415
Cork & Ross	130	71	31,861	449
Killaloe & Kilfenora	130	129	27,843	216
Limerick, Ardfert & Aghadoe	175	146	34,180	234
Waterford & Lismore	108	61	18,559	304
Tuam & Ardagh	141	94	24,320	259
Clonfert & Kilmacduagh	61	59	8,868	150
Elphin	78	58	9,961	172
Killala & Achonry	52	15	3,696	246
Totals	2,450	1,539	£442,419	£287 9s. 6d.

Note: Given the average amount of composition for those parishes which compounded, and multiplying it by the number of parishes in Ireland, one derives the sum £704,313 as an approximation of the actual amount of tithes due in Ireland. This number fits very well with the sum of £610,653 which was the amount of gross income of the Irish benefices as estimated as of 1832 by the Royal Commissioners on the Irish church. We can expect tithes due to be somewhat greater than parochial revenues since some of the tithes were paid to members of the bench and dignitaries without cure and to lay impropriators whose income was not included in the calculation of parochial incomes.

Source: SCRO, D.260/M/OI #1879.

wealth of the Church of Ireland is to note that the annual income of its personnel was approximately 1.7 percent of Irish national income.[120]

A second point: In the years 1800 to 1830, the financial position of those members of the church depending on tithes (chiefly parish clergy) was regularized through the tithe composition measures. The process was an anxiety-producing one for the churchmen, but its end results were indisputably beneficial to the parish clergymen. Third, as much "because of" as "in spite of" the Church of Ireland's wealth, it was in a precarious position. It remained a wealthy church amid a non-Protestant population and was a constant goad to the nationalist and radical agitators. Moreover, the tithe legislation of the 1820s, while beneficial to the parish clergy, set a precedent: church property could be redistributed or reorganized for the general good. Following the tithe composition acts, the tithes were more predictable and less open to petty litigation and misunderstandings, but they remained a grievance for the Roman Catholic population. In 1830 the church was stronger and more rationally organized financially than it had been in 1800; but it was also coming closer to the religious revolution of the 1830s.

INTERNAL RENOVATIONS

Glebes, Parish Churches, and the Board of First Fruits

Part of the Church of Ireland's inheritance from the eighteenth century was a snarl of related problems, each of which impaired the church's efficiency at the parochial level. These flaws in the administrative webbing were the inadequacy of glebe house provisions for the parish clergy, extensive clerical nonresidence, the absence of a church in many parishes, overly large unions of parishes, and the holding of pluralities by parish clergymen. Each of these faults had to be corrected if the church was to function effectively at the local level. The process by which the problems were solved was sometimes tense but generally graceful. As the following pages will indicate, the church was fortunate in having Archbishops Stuart and Brodrick at the head of the reforming party, for these men combined a sense of ecclesiastical probity with an ability to deal with politicians. Their political acumen was absolutely essential: for each time a measure for church improvement came near the House of Commons, there was the danger that the radicals would use the opportunity to mount a full-scale attack upon the church—an attack which might have been justified but which would certainly have interfered with the quiet reconstruction which the church was undergoing.

In order to allow us to reach firm conclusions about the improvement in the church's administration in the years under study, we must first establish a set of measures by which we may judge later developments. With this purpose in mind, table 27 is presented as an indication of the availability of church facilities at the parish level.

From this information it is clear where the greatest improvements had to be made: in the province of Cashel and in the Dioceses of Ossory and of Meath. In these areas, roughly one quarter of the beneficed clergy were without parish churches—an open invitation to clerical non-residence and neglect of all parochial duties. With the exception of the Diocese of Meath,

TABLE 27
IRISH CHURCH FACILITIES, 1787

Diocese	No. of churches	No. of churches as % of no. of parishes	No. of churches as % of no. of benefices
Armagh	69	67.0%	100.0%
Clogher	49	119.5	122.5
Derry	51	106.2	118.6
Down & Connor	76	66.7	116.9
Dromore	27	103.8	112.5
Kilmore	36	92.3	120.0
Meath	77	34.4	77.8
Raphoe	32	103.2	128.0
Provincial Total	417	66.6	105.6
Dublin	82	39.2	95.3
Kildare	28	34.6	90.3
Ferns & Leighlin	71	30.6	89.9
Ossory	36	26.5	64.3
Provincial Total	217	33.0	86.1
Cashel & Emly	35	22.6	74.5
Cloyne	51	37.2	73.9
Cork & Ross	53	41.7	82.8
Killaloe & Kilfenora	38	27.5	76.0
Limerick, Ardfert & Aghadoe	47	26.7	53.4
Waterfore & Lismore	30	28.3	68.2
Provincial Total	254	30.3	70.2
Tuam & Ardagh	53	52.1	112.8
Clonfert & Kilmacduagh	14	23.3	93.3
Elphin	26	34.7	89.7
Killala & Achonry	20	38.5	100.0
Provincial Total	113	36.1	101.8
National Total	1,001	41.1	89.4

Source: Beaufort, p. 137. See table 16 for the raw figures.

the Province of Armagh was well supplied with places of worship. In the Province of Tuam the great majority of beneficed clergymen held livings with churches, although the thinness of the Protestant population and the extensive unions of parishes meant that only about a third of the individual parishes actually had churches within their bounds. The situation in the Province of Dublin was similar to that in the Province of Tuam, with the exception of Ossory which was notoriously ill-served in facilities for public worship.

The second standard by which we will assess administrative improvement in the Church of Ireland is the provision of clergy residences. In Irish ecclesiastical usage these residences were called glebe houses. The houses were located on glebe lands, which in addition to being homesites, often encompassed quite extensive and scattered agricultural holdings. Irish benefices were most irregularly provided for; some had both house and glebe lands (possession of the former automatically implied possession of at least a small amount of the latter); other benefices had glebe lands attached but no houses, and still others had neither glebe lands nor residences. Acreage of the glebe lands varied from a tiny plot barely large enough for a homesite to (in rare instances) six or seven hundred acres. In the majority of cases, glebe lands were well under one hundred acres.[121] Glebe houses and glebe lands were important because the existence of a habitable glebe house was probably the single greatest inducement to clerical residence, and the glebe lands represented a source of income undisturbed by the uncertainties and fluctuations of the tithe system. Table 28, which deals with the glebe situation in the later years of the eighteenth century, indicates that the provision of glebe houses was at best inadequate and at worst disgracefully sparse. Less than a third of the benefices were provided with glebe houses. As was the case in the matter of church provision, the Province of Cashel was relatively the least endowed, with 17 percent of the benefices having clerical residences. The provinces of Dublin and of Tuam were only slightly better off, approximately 25 percent of their benefices being equipped with glebe houses. Only in the Province of Armagh was there even one glebe house for every two incumbents. And only one diocese in all of Ireland, Derry, possessed glebe house provision for as many as 75 percent of the benefices.

At first glance it may seem strange to place church provision and glebe provision side-by-side as indicators of developments in religious administration, and in logic there is no reason for doing so. Yet the problems of scarcity of churches and glebe houses were attacked by the same agency, the Board of First Fruits. Therefore, by the accidents of history, if not by the dictates of logic, the two problems belong together.

Turning, then, to the Board of First Fruits, its early history is undistinguished. First fruits (also called annates) represented the first year's revenue of a benefice, dignity, or bishopric. Before the Reformation this tax was remitted to Rome. In 1534, Henry VIII's Annates Statute transferred payment to the English Crown (25 Henry VIII, c. 20). An Irish statute (28 Henry VIII, c. 8), gave Irish authorities power to determine the true value of the first fruits and to arrange for their payment. Between the original enactment and the first year of Charles I's reign, there were five separate valuations for annates; but none of them came close to taking in the entire country, and the amount paid was never more than a fraction of the actual first year's income of the benefices involved.[122]

When in 1704 Queen Anne remitted the payment of first fruits in England, it was inevitable that the Irish churchmen would push for a similar

TABLE 28
IRISH GLEBES, 1787

Diocese	No. of benefices	No. without glebe houses or land	No. with glebe lands only	Glebe houses	Percentage of benefices with glebe houses
Armagh	69	14	4	51	73.9%
Clogher	40	–	14	26	65.0
Derry	43	1	9	33	76.7
Down & Connor	65	26	16	23	35.4
Dromore	24	8	2	14	58.3
Kilmore	30	–	21	9	30.0
Meath	99	32	38	29	29.3
Raphoe	25	–	8	17	68.0
Provincial Total	395	81	112	202	51.1
Dublin	86	29	22	35	40.7
Kildare	31	21	2	8	25.8
Ferns & Leighlin	79	38	35	6	7.6
Ossory	56	13	28	15	26.8
Provincial Total	252	101	87	64	25.4
Cashel & Emly	47	14	17	16	34.0
Cloyne	69	25	39	5	7.2
Cork & Ross	64	18	32	14	21.9
Killaloe & Kilfenora	50	16	30	4	8.0
Limerick, Ardfert & Aghadoe	88	51	23	14	15.9
Waterford & Lismore	44	14	22	8	18.2
Provincial Total	362	138	163	61	16.8
Tuam & Ardagh	47	20	15	12	25.5
Clonfert & Kilmacduagh	15	1	12	2	13.3
Elphin	29	19	5	5	17.2
Killala & Achonry	20	6	6	8	40.0
Provincial Total	111	46	38	27	24.3
National Total	1,120	366	400	354	31.6

Source: Beaufort, p. 137.

concession, plus a remission of the twentieth parts (a tax of twelve pence on the pound payable annually from all benefices as they were valued at the Reformation). The lobbying for Irish interests was begun by the Bishop of Cloyne, Charles Crow, and was continued by Dean Swift, who acted as representatives of the Irish bishops in the matter. Although the attempts to exact concessions from the Whigs failed, the Tory ministry of 1710 was headed by Robert Harley who held the chancellorship of the exchequer and was predisposed to innovations. He appears to have been largely responsible for the decision in 1711 to forgive entirely the twentieth parts and to use the first fruits for the buying up of impropriations by a board established for that purpose. As actually incorporated, the Board of First Fruits (composed chiefly of members of the hierarchy) was empowered to use its revenue not only to buy impropriations, but to aid the building and repairing of parish churches and to aid in the purchase of glebes and the building of glebe houses. The purpose of each of these types of grant was to help poor incumbents establish themselves in areas with few religious facilities. The activities of the Board of First Fruits were hindered from the beginning by the smallness of its revenue, and on occasion the board had recourse to seeking voluntary contributions. By 1780, the board had purchased glebe lands for sixteen benefices at the cost of £3,543; had assisted the building of forty-five glebe houses by gifts of £4,080; and had bought impropriate tithes for fourteen incumbents at a cost of £5,855—a useful, but not extensive, philanthropy.[123]

Then, to the great advantage of the Church of Ireland, the Irish parliament voted in the session of 1777–78 a grant to the Board of First Fruits. Thereafter, this was awarded annually; and since the parliamentary grants were considerably greater than the actual income from the annates the Board of First Fruits, despite its name, became in reality an agency for the distribution of government funds. The parliamentary votes and the amounts actually received are given below from their inception to the Union.[124]

Year	Parliamentary Vote
1777–78	£6,000
1779–80	1,500
1781–82	6,000
1783–84	3,000
1785	5,000
1786	5,000
1787	5,000
1788	5,000
1789	5,000
1790	5,000
1791	5,000
1792	5,000
1793	5,000
1794	5,000
1795	5,000
1796	5,000
1797	5,000
1798	5,000
1799	5,000
1800	5,000

The board was now able to move meaningfully, if not lavishly, in pursuit of its purposes. In practice, it concentrated on church building and the provision of glebe houses and the provision of churches. From 1791 to 1803, the Board of First Fruits granted the sum of £500—the standard amount—for the building of churches in 88 cases, representing an expenditure of £44,000. During the same period the board made its customary grant of £100 towards each of the 116 glebe houses, an expense of £11,600.[125]

Despite this relative prosperity, the board was forced to be austere in its financial regulations; for, in Ireland, opportunities for parochial reform far outstripped resources. Thus, the £100 paid towards each new glebe house was payable only after the clergyman himself had built a house equal in cost to two years of his own salary. The clergyman received £100 from the Board of First Fruits and the whole sum spent on house and improvements eventually was recovered from his immediate successor in the benefice; the successor receiving three-fourths from his successor, the next one-half, and the next one-fourth. These arrangements, while reasonable enough in the long run, left the newly promoted parish clergyman to raise the money for his glebe house by his own means. In the case of a man promoted to a living from a curacy, it was extremely difficult for him to raise the required sum of money. A second restriction was necessary to keep the demand for funds to build churches in line with resources. This was the requirement that the benefices must have been bereft of churches for at least twenty years before the Board of First Fruits would make the £500 grant for building a new church. Obviously, in a parish where the Anglican church had been in ruins for twenty years, many of the parishioners would have abandoned the Anglican communion altogether.[126]

If the Board of First Fruits could obtain more money, it could remove these restrictive regulations and begin a large-scale program of church building and glebe-house construction. Alert to the need, the leaders of the hierarchy, notably Stuart and Brodrick, remembered that the government had yet to compensate the church for the loss of the clerical boroughs through the Act of Union. Because laymen had been well compensated for the loss of their political property, the churchmen felt they too should be recompensed. Archbishop Brodrick undertook negotiations with the government on behalf of the bishops, and was notably successful.[127] For the loss of the three ecclesiastical boroughs of Clogher, St. Canice, and Old Leighlin, the church received the total of £46,863. This money was invested in 5 percent government debentures and was kept in a separate Borough Compensation Fund, the yield on investment being used by the Board of First Fruits. In 1808 the fund ceased to be a separate accounting entity and was merged with the board's other funds.[128]

Churchmen fell to considering how to spend their windfall. Although there were several plans advanced by the various prelates, there was general agreement that the money—or at least the interest on it—should be used to provide interest-free loans to clergymen wishing to build glebe houses.[129] Simultaneously, Stuart and Brodrick were negotiating with the government for additional governmental funds beyond the borough compensation money. The result of the two forces—the pressure to spend the borough compensation money and the petitions for additional parliamentary funds —was the passage of two parliamentary acts. These acts (43 George III, c. 106 and 43 George III, c. 158) gave the Board of First Fruits the power to lend money for glebe construction, not merely to provide grants upon house completion as it had in the past. These loans were to be made interest-free to the incumbents. Further, the Irish Treasury was given the power to lend up to £50,000 interest-free to the Board of First Fruits for the purpose of increasing the number of glebe loans. Ironically, after all the attention the matter was given, the board continued its old policy of grants rather than loans, approving only eight glebe house loans by the year 1808.[130]

In 1808 the Board of First Fruits finally came into its own. An act of that year (48 George III, c. 65) consolidated all the board's funds into a single account and removed most of the restrictions on its freedom of operation. The board was now allowed to lend money or give grants in amounts, at its own discretion, for either church building or glebe construction. Further, it could now spend its funds on parish churches without having to wait for twenty years for them to be in ruins. In the years following the passage of this act, the board utilized a good deal of its resources not only upon construction of new churches but upon renovation of old. Equally important, the parliament of the United Kingdom began increasing its grants to the board. Moneys voted by parliament from the Union to the cessation of grants in 1823 are given below.[131]

Year	Parliamentary grants
1801	£ 5,000
1802	5,000
1803	5,000
1804	5,000
1805	5,000
1806	5,000
1807	5,000
1808	10,000
1809	10,000
1810	60,000
1811	60,000
1812	60,000
1813	60,000

Year	Parliamentary grants
1814	60,000
1815	60,000
1816	60,000
1817	30,000
1818	30,000
1819	30,000
1820	30,000
1821	30,000
1822	10,000
1823	10,000

Significantly, the money was given to the Board of First Fruits with effectively no restrictions, save that it be used to encourage church building and glebe construction. The Board of First Fruits, therefore, was able to inaugurate a major program of gifts and loans for religious improvement.

TABLE 29

GIFTS AND LOANS FOR PERPETUAL CURATES, VICARS, AND CURATES,
AS ADOPTED BY THE BOARD OF FIRST FRUITS, CA. 1811
(In pounds)

Benefices, yearly value	Loan for houses	Gift for houses	Gift for glebe lands
—	50	450	450
0–100	2 yrs. income	450	450
100–200	2 yrs. income	400	400
200–250	450	350	350
250–300	500	300	300
300–350	550	250	250
350–400	600	200	200
400–450	675	100	200
450–500	750	100	200
500–550	825	100	200
550–600	900	100	200
600–650	975	100	200
650–700	1,050	100	200
700–750	1,125	100	200
750–800	1,200	100	200
800–850	1,275	100	200
850–900	1,350	100	200
900–950	1,425	100	200
1,000+	1,500	100	200

Source: Orders and Regulations agreed upon by the Trustees and Commissioners of the First Fruits Payable out of Ecclesiastical Benefices in Ireland, p. 2. Printed document, NLI N5297/P5406, place of origin and publisher unspecified, printed in 1811.

On matters of purchase of glebe lands and building of glebe houses, the board framed a sensible schedule for gifts and loans based on the principle of providing the greatest amount of non-repayable grants to those clergymen with the lowest incomes. The schedule was as shown in table 29. The board was also able to be much more generous in its policy toward church construction. No longer did the board wait for a church to lie in ruins for twenty years before providing aid. Money was now used for renovation and improvement as well as new construction. Further, whereas in the past the board had limited its activities to the £500 grants, it now provided grants of considerably larger sums, in one case the amount of £3,075. Further, the board began lending money to local vestries for church construction, the largest single loan being £3,500.[132] Even after the parliamentary grants ceased, the board could afford to be generous, for it received a goodly amount each year in interest on its holdings of government debentures and repayments on loans which ranged from £3,000 to roughly £16,000 a year, in addition to the nominal sum of a few hundred pounds each year from the first fruits themselves.[133]

The more than one million pounds that passed through the hands of the Board of First Fruits between the Union and the end of the year 1822 was allocated as follows:[134]

Gifts for churches	£149,269
Loans for churches	281,148
Loans for glebe houses	211,638
Gifts for glebe houses	110,532
Gifts for glebe lands	54,761
Gifts for tithes	6,450
"Contingencies"	21,273
Debentures and stock	143,510
Balance unspent	42,070
	£1,020,653

When one surveys the activities of the Board of First Fruits up to 1829, one finds that the board granted gifts and loans for building 550 glebe houses; for building, rebuilding or enlarging 697 churches; and for the purchase of 193 pieces of glebe land, representing 1,440 instances of intervention in the Irish parish structure.[135]

Through the board's activity, a large number of flaws in the administrative structure of the church at the local level were mended. The grants for parish churches and clerical residences made possible a considerable increase in the number of Irish benefices. The number of benefices, rather than the number of parishes, is, for us, the key number for gauging the effectiveness of the church at the local level; the parish is a theoretical unit, whereas the benefice is an operational one. The existence of a benefice always implied the assignment of at least one clergyman to a given area and usually implied the presence of a parish church. By increasing the number of churches, augmenting the number of glebe houses, and buying tithes and glebe lands for Irish clergymen, the Board of First Fruits made it possible for the countryside to support more livings for Church of Ireland clergymen. Table 30 indicates that the increase in the number of benefices in Ireland, between the late eighteenth century and the close of the first third of the nineteenth century, was considerable. Between the years 1787 and 1832, every diocese in Ireland except Clonfert and Kilmacduagh experienced an increase in the number of benefices within its boundaries.

TABLE 30
IRISH BENEFICES, 1787 AND 1832

	1787	1832
Province of Armagh	395	474
Armagh	69	88
Clogher	40	45
Derry	43	57
Down & Connor	65	83
Dromore	24	25
Kilmore	30	39
Meath	99	103
Raphoe	25	34
Province of Dublin	252	326
Dublin	86	102
Kildare	31	47
Ferns & Leighlin	79	118
Ossory	56	59
Province of Cashel	362	467
Cashel & Emly	47	60
Cloyne	69	89
Cork & Ross	64	85
Killaloe & Kilfenora	50	73
Limerick, Ardfert & Aghadoe	88	106
Waterford & Lismore	44	54
Province of Tuam	111	128
Tuam	47	59
Clonfert & Kilmacduagh	15	15
Elphin	29	32
Killala & Achonry	20	22
National Total	1,120	1,395

Sources: Beaufort, p. 137; *Third Report of His Majesty's Commissioners on Ecclesiastical Revenue and Patronage in Ireland*, p. 4; *Fourth Report of His Majesty's Commissioners on Ecclesiastical Revenue and Patronage in Ireland*, p. 3.

Nationally, the increase was almost 25 percent, an increment that considerably improved the church's efficiency at the lowest level of the ecclesiastical pyramid.

The increment in the number of benefices was partially the result of the increase in the number of churches in Ireland. Through the efforts of the Board of First Fruits the number of churches had grown considerably. In 1787, there were 1,001 Anglican churches in Ireland. In 1832, there were 1,293 churches,[136] an increase of nearly 30 percent. Moreover, the number of churches grew as a percentage of the number of benefices, even though the absolute number of benefices was rising at the same time. Whereas the number of churches in 1787 was 89.4 percent of the number of benefices, by 1832 the figure had risen to 92.6 percent.

Equally important in facilitating the increase in the number of benefices was the increment in the number of glebe houses. The number increased from 354 in 1787 to 829 in 1832. Significantly, the percentage of benefices with glebe houses grew, even, as stated above, while the number of benefices was rising. These developments are detailed in table 31.

A further effect of the Board of First Fruits' activities needs mention here only briefly, for it was one in which the board was contributory but not determinative. This was the increasing propensity of Irish clergy to reside in their benefices. As glebe houses became the rule rather than the exception, the traditional excuse for nonresidence among the parish clergy was removed. When ordered by his bishop to reside, a clergyman had no choice but to obey or face the consequences. And during the first three decades of the nineteenth century, the consequences—for those who chose the path of nonresidence in intentional defiance of their ordinary—changed radically. The bishops came to be armed with effective methods of enforcing residency; and these methods, when combined with the improvement in glebe house provision, forced the clerical gentleman who wished to spend his winters in Bath either to reform his ways or resign his living. To the development of the clergy residency question, we now turn.

Nonresidency Attacked

"The Reformed Church must be extinguished here, in half a century at furthest," the Bishop of Kildare wrote in 1805 to the Lord Lieutenant, "unless there be a provision made for a greater number of Clergy in the King's and Queen's counties, being in the Diocese of Kildare. In the former there are no more than eight resident clergymen including the Curates— in the latter five." [137] The Archbishop of Armagh, elaborating on the problem of nonresidence in 1806 in a letter to the Archbishop of Cashel, stated emphatically that the bishops were not to blame for nonresidence of the parish clergy. "They are utterly destitute of power to enforce it, there being no statute law to compel the residence of clergymen and the Ecclesiastical

TABLE 31
GLEBE HOUSE PROVISIONS, 1787 AND 1832

	1787				*1832*		
Diocese	*Glebe houses*	*Percentage of benefices with glebe houses*	*Parishes*	*Benefices*	*Glebe houses*	*Percentage of benefices with glebe houses*	*Percentage increase glebe houses 1787–1832*
Armagh	51	73.9%	118	88	73	83.0%	43.1%
Clogher	26	65.0	46	45	35	77.8	34.6
Derry	33	76.7	58	57	43	75.4	30.3
Down & Connor	23	35.4	115	83	53	63.9	130.4
Dromore	14	58.3	27	25	21	84.0	50.0
Kilmore	9	30.0	45	39	30	76.9	233.3
Meath	29	29.3	206	103	87	84.4	200.0
Raphoe	17	68.0	35	34	27	79.4	58.8
Provincial Total	202	51.1	650	474	369	77.8	82.7
Dublin	35	40.7	181	102	45	44.1	28.6
Kildare	8	25.8	78	47	19	40.4	137.5
Ferns & Leighlin	6	7.6	222	118	54	45.8	800.0
Ossory	15	26.8	128	59	38	64.4	153.3
Provincial Total	64	25.4	609	326	156	47.9	143.8
Cashel & Emly	16	34.0	136	60	36	60.0	131.2
Cloyne	5	7.2	119	89	25	28.1	400.0
Cork & Ross	14	21.9	122	85	38	44.7	171.4
Killaloe & Kilfenora	4	8.0	126	73	43	58.9	975.0
Limerick, Ardfert & Aghadoe	14	15.9	166	106	47	44.3	235.7
Waterford & Lismore	8	18.2	103	54	18	33.3	125.0
Provincial Total	61	16.8	772	467	207	44.3	239.3
Tuam & Ardagh	12	25.5	129	59	43	72.9	258.3
Clonfert & Kilmacduagh	2	13.3	59	15	13	86.7	550.0
Elphin	5	17.2	76	32	23	71.9	360.0
Killala & Achonry	8	40.0	52	22	18	81.9	125.0
Provincial Total	27	24.3	316	128	97	75.8	322.2
National Total	354	31.6	2,347	1,395	829	59.4	134.2

TABLE 31 (Continued)

Note: The reader will notice that the number of parishes in each diocese varies slightly from source to source. Although theoretically unchanging, the fact is that some divergence in reports is inevitable, for two reasons. First, in the less populous areas of the country, where extensive unions were commonplace, ancient parish names simply dropped out of use and were forgotten, and on other occasions parishes which everyone had long since forgotten were rediscovered by an industrious diocesan registrar or parliamentary commissioner. Second, the thoroughness and competence of various investigators and reporters varied considerably. Neither of these sources of variation can be controlled, and lacking the raw data from which the nineteenth century investigators worked no "true" enumeration can be provided. The divergences, however, as presented below, are not so large as to provide any great obstacle to our depiction of the Church of Ireland's administrative structure. Column A indicates Beaufort's enumeration of parishes as of 1787, column B (from table 26 on tithe composition) is taken from information compiled for Dublin Castle in 1832, and column C is the enumeration of the parliamentary investigators for the royal commission of the 1830s.

Province	A	B	C
Armagh	626	656	650
Dublin	658	620	609
Cashel	839	832	[772
Tuam	313	332	316
	2,436	2,450	2,347

Source: Beaufort, p. 137; *Third Report of His Majesty's Commissioners on Ecclesiastical Revenue and Patronage in Ireland*, pp. 96–97, 146–47.

Law being so ridiculed and ill understood by Judges and Masters in Chancery upon whom the decision ultimately depends, that no Bishop will in time to come venture to institute a suit against a clergyman who is able to contend." [138] He described a law case of the Bishop of Ferns against a nonresident clergyman that took four years to settle at an expense of £300. Stuart later made much the same statement to the Chief Secretary and pointed to two other cases: one in which progress through the courts had taken seven years, the other five years at the expense of £500 to the bishop. "Here then," said the archbishop, "is the end of canon law for any practical purpose." [139]

Canon law being unenforceable, secular law was required. This meant dealing with the parliament of the United Kingdom. From the bishops' viewpoint, the danger of approaching parliament was that once the latter's attention was fixed upon the Established Church, it might well focus entirely upon the church's flaws and forget altogether about the remedies— or prescribe a more drastic cure for the church's ills than the churchmen would find palatable. In 1805, Sir John Newport, M.P. for Waterford and a critic of the Irish church, had led the Commons in a demand for preliminary returns on the state of the church.[140] These returns—which had to do with clerical residence, church attendance, clerical incomes, and similar topics—were so fragmentary as to be almost useless, but the possibility of a sweeping investigation was obvious. In response to Newport's implied attack upon the church Dr. Patrick Duigenan, M.P. for the city of Armagh and a well-meaning but bumbling supporter of the church, brought in a clergy residence bill.[141] The bill was not well received by the Commons. Henry Grattan, in particular, scorned the measure as ill-fitted to Ireland, being based upon English precedents.[142] During the course of discussion Duigenan stated that the bill was brought forward at the request of the Board of First Fruits.[143] This unfortunate fumble had the twin liabilities of implicating the Board of First Fruits in Duigenan's hastily conceived measure and of being untrue. Although several of the bishops were greatly offended at this more than poetic liberty on Duigenan's part, the Archbishop of Armagh counseled wisely that it would do no good to expose Duigenan since he was the "only friend we have in the House of Commons"; and that the best course would be to convince him to withdraw the bill.[144] Lord Grenville, the Prime Minister, thought the residence bill premature and, in the face of combined governmental and episcopal opinion, Dr. Duigenan consented to withdraw the measure.[145]

The damage had been done, however, for the government now had its attention drawn to the Irish church. Even before Duigenan withdrew his bill, the Prime Minister had tentatively decided to move for a royal commission to inquire into the state of the Church of Ireland.[146] Before moving, however, he asked the Lord Lieutenant to report what the Archbishop of Armagh and other church leaders thought of such an idea.[147] In private, there was no doubt about what the archbishop thought of the proposal ("I have always considered a Royal visitation as a great evil. . . ."[148]). When writing to the Lord Lieutenant, he pointed out that a royal commission was not a good idea because most of the bishops and clergy would be suspicious and would consider it a measure calculated to reflect unfavorably upon the discipline and conduct of the church. This suspicion would make it impossible for the commissioners to obtain accurate information, and as a result, the matter might lead to public reaction beyond the government's control. The archbishop claimed to share the government's judgment: that the returns consequent upon Sir John Newport's 1805 motion were incomplete and unsatisfactory and should be supplemented by accurate information. Given this need and the inexpediency of a royal commission, what could be done? The archbishop's answer was for the government to work through the four archbishops of the Church of Ireland. Because they were in much closer contact with their suffragans than were the English bishops, it would be possible for the government to draw up a list of queries which it wished answered and to direct those queries to the archbishops who would then obtain the information from their suffragans. In this manner, accurate information would be provided without endangering the church with a royal visitation.[149] Bedford transmitted a copy of the archbishop's letter to Grenville,[150] and the Prime Minister agreed to Stuart's suggestions.[151] For the moment, the danger was passed. When the returns were published in 1807, they were lacking summary tabulations, save for the province of Armagh. This made it inconvenient for critics of the church to use the information effectively.[152]

Once again the redoubtable Dr. Duigenan stepped forward, with plans now for a reintroduction of his 1806 residence bill.[153] This time, the government had a measure of its own in preparation which passed parliament and received the royal assent on 18 June 1808, as 48 George III, c. 66. For the first time, the bishops were provided with effective sanctions to enforce clerical residence. Under the terms of the act, any incumbent who did not reside in his benefice at least nine months in the year was liable to receive a "monition" from his diocesan. This monition was a formal notice to mend the ecclesiastical misbehavior of nonresidence and to return to the benefice. If the bishop desired, he could require the cleric's return to be certified under oath. If a return was not made by the absent clergyman, the bishop could sequester the profits of the benefice (profits being the income after a curate had been paid). If the absent incumbent returned to his benefice in response to a monition but left it again within six months, the bishop was empowered to sequester the benefice without further monition. If sequestration continued for three years, the benefice was declared vacant and a new incumbent appointed. Holders of sinecure livings as well as bishops and archbishops were exempted from the residence requirements. Although this civil statute did not preclude recourse to canonical punishments for nonresidents, it was clear that in practice it substituted civil law for ecclesiastical law. Bishops were not required to employ the sanctions recommended by the act; and most of them could be expected to make exceptions in the case of men assigned impecunious livings, in poor health, or with other valid excuses for nonresidence. The important point is that, for the first time, the bishops had a set of workable sanctions through which they could greatly raise the standard of clerical conduct in the country.

Useful as these sometimes were, it became clear after a while that the bishops needed still greater power to reduce clerical nonresidence; and in 1824 Henry Goulburn, Irish Chief Secretary, introduced another bill on clerical residence in Ireland. The measure as passed (5 George IV, c. 91), added to the instruments of enforcement in the bishops' hands while simultaneously limiting the opportunities for the bishops to make unnecessary exceptions. The bishops' powers were augmented by the introduction of a graduated scale of fines for clerical nonresidence: parish priests who were absent between three and six months without license forfeited one-third the annual value of their living: those absent six to eight months, one-half; and those over eight months, two-thirds. The fines were exacted in civil courts in Dublin. Further, cathedral dignitaries, who also held parishes with cure of souls, were required to reside on their benefices, the same as every other clergyman—with the exception that they could count up to four months of residence at the cathedral as time in residence, provided a curate was employed while the dignitary was engaged at the cathedral. The bishop maintained the right to license nonresidency in cases of illness, where there was no satisfactory residence for the benefice, and in the case of livings too small to support a full-time clergyman—provided the man holding the small living was engaged elsewhere as a curate or as an usher of a school. Significantly, for exceptions not falling into the preceding categories, the bishop had to obtain the approval of the archbishop of the province. Most important, each year the four archbishops were annually required to present a list of special exceptions to the Lord Lieutenant who then had the power to annul any licenses of which he disapproved.

Administratively, the effect of the 1824 residency act was to strengthen the bishops vis-à-vis the parish clergy, to strengthen the metropolitans vis-à-vis the suffragan bishops, and to strengthen the Irish administration vis-à-vis the archbishops. At all levels the amount of discretion on individual claims for non-residence was reduced. The overall impact of the act was greatly to diminish the opportunities for nonresidence.

As a result of the legislation of 1808 and 1824, the pattern of residence radically changed. This change is documented in table 32 which is prepared from parliamentary returns of 1806, 1819, and 1832. In order to keep the figures in perspective, one should remember that the graphic rise in the percentage of clergy residing in their benefices was largely a result of the residence acts of 1808 and 1824; but may also be partially ascribed to the augmentation of glebe houses, glebe lands, and church facilities effected by the Board of First Fruits. Also, one should note that in many of the livings where the incumbent was absent, a resident curate substituted for him; in other cases, divine service was conducted by an incumbent or a curate from an adjoining benefice. This fact should be recalled before jumping to unnecessarily harsh conclusions about the general residence practices before 1808 (even with this caution in mind, strongly negative judgments are dictated). The reader will notice that the returns for 1806 and for 1819 are somewhat different in form than those for 1832. This is because the two earlier studies collected information not only upon clerical residences within the boundaries of the benefices, but also on those clergymen who, although not resident within the legal limits of their living, resided sufficiently close to be able to perform duty regularly. Although comparable data are not available for 1832, the data for earlier years are presented

since they are of value in obtaining an accurate indication of the realities
of Irish church life.

Clergymen, Pluralities, and Unions

If we assume that the quality of the clergy remained at least steady during the first thirty years of the nineteenth century—from the evidence on
clerical residence, the augmentation of the number of glebe houses, and
the increases in the number of churches—we can draw the irrefutable conclusion that the church in the thirty years immediately after the Union was
considerably strengthened. (Further, as will be discussed later, the quality
of the clergy—meaning their devotion to religious duty—was rising during
this period.) Another index of the new vitality of the Church of Ireland is
found in the increase in the number of Irish clergy. In 1806 there were
1,253 members of the cloth in Ireland. This number had grown to 1,977
by 1826.[154]

On two other matters related to the church's administrative health—
pluralities and parochial unions—it is not possible to be as precise about
change over any given period of time as we have been on clerical residence
and on church and glebe house construction; but clearly the increase in the
number of benefices implies that both the number of unions and the number
of pluralities probably declined in the years under study. There are not,
however, sufficient data available to allow us to determine precisely how
much each declined. Therefore, we must be satisfied with a picture of the
number of unions and pluralities as they were revealed by the returns of
1819. Looking first at the number of unions, they were reported as follows:[155]

Armagh, 11; Clogher, 2; Derry, 2; Down and Connor, 26; Dromore,
1; Kilmore, 6; Meath, 42; Raphoe, 1. *Total: 91.*

Dublin, 28; Kildare, 19; Ferns and Leighlin, 45; Ossory, 22. *Total:
114.*

Cashel and Emly, 31; Cloyne, 27; Cork and Ross, 18; Killaloe and
Kilfenora, 36; Limerick, Ardfert, and Aghadoe, 39; Waterford and
Lismore, 27. *Total: 178.*

Tuam and Ardagh, 27; Clonfert and Kilmacduagh, 14; Elphin, 20;
Killala and Achonry, 14. *Total: 75.*

Nationally, therefore, 36.39 percent (458 of 1,263) of the benefices of the
Church of Ireland were unions of two or more parishes. Given the other
trends in the internal administration of the church one can expect this
number to have dropped with each passing year.

Table 32
Clerical Residence, 1806, 1819, 1832

Diocese	1806 Benefices	1806 Resident incumbents	1806 Percentage resident	1806 Resident near benefice	1819 Benefices	1819 Resident incumbents	1819 Percentage resident	1819 Resident near benefice	1832 Benefices	1832 Resident incumbents	1832 Percentage resident
Armagh	74	54	73.0%	4	78	71	91.0%	2	88	72	81.8%
Clogher	43	27	62.8	–	44	27	61.4	1	45	32	71.1
Derry	49	41	83.7	–	54	39	72.2	2	57	54	94.7
Down & Connor	64	43	67.2	4	79	61	77.2	–	83	70	84.3
Dromore	23	13	56.5	7	23	14	60.9	2	25	19	76.0
Kilmore	32	9	28.1	9	33	23	69.5	1	39	33	84.6
Meath	92	45	48.9	10	101	79	78.2	2	103	89	86.4
Raphoe	26	20	76.9	–	31	27	87.1	–	34	31	91.2
Provincial Total	403	252	62.5	34	443	341	77.0	10	474	400	84.4
Dublin	87	43	49.4	15	87	45	51.7	12	102	84	82.4
Kildare	41	15	36.6	3	43	16	37.2	5	47	31	66.0
Ferns & Leighlin	87	40	50.0	16	92	65	70.7	9	118	88	74.6
Ossory	62	18	29.0	7	59	35	59.3	1	59	38	64.4
Provincial Total	277	116	41.9	41	281	161	57.3	27	326	241	73.9
Cashel & Emly	53	18	34.0	7	57	38	66.7	5	60	37	61.7
Cloyne	74	24	32.4	9	77	44	57.1	2	89	54	60.7
Cork & Ross	62	32	51.6	4	77	40	51.9	3	85	63	74.1
Killaloe & Kilfenora	48	21	43.8	2	51	41	80.4	–	73	52	71.2
Limerick, Ardfert & Aghadoe	90	26	28.9	7	105	52	49.5	4	106	63	59.4
Waterford & Lismore	54	13	24.1	7	52	32	61.5	4	54	35	64.8
Provincial Total	381	134	35.2	36	419	247	58.9	18	467	304	65.1

Tuam & Ardagh	46	18	39.1	1	49	31	63.3	4	59	44	74.6
Clonfert & Kilmacduagh	14	5	35.7	2	14	10	71.4	1	15	12	80.0
Elphin	34	9	26.5	5	37	20	54.1	1	32	26	81.2
Killala & Achonry	20	11	55.0	1	20	14	70.0	–	22	16	72.7
Provincial Total	114	43	37.7	9	120	75	62.5	6	128	98	76.6
National Total	1,175	545	46.4	120	1,263	824	65.2	61	1,395	1,043	74.8

Note: The reader must be warned that these figures should be taken as indicative rather than definitive. The original material on the church in the years 1806 and 1819 was gathered at a time when the collection of data by the government was at best simplistic, often eccentric, and at worst haphazard. Neither the 1806 nor the 1819 returns were ever fully tabulated; many answers to governmental queries were obscure (probably by intention) and often the respondent refused to answer several of the government's questions. I have tabulated the returns for 1806 and 1819 myself, with attendant chances for interpretative error. In cases of obscure answers I have *not* included the individual in the tally of resident clergymen. (This on the assumption that if a clergyman were resident he would be apt to state the fact clearly, whereas if he were nonresident, he would tend to provide an opaque answer which would obscure his absence from the benefice.) Thus, my figures may tend somewhat to under-state the number of clergy resident in 1806 and 1819.

Sources: Papers Relating to the Established Church in Ireland, pp. 16–17, 24–25, 34–43, 76–77, 85, 102–373, H.C. 1807 (78), v; *Papers Relating to the State of the Established Church of Ireland,* pp. 20–21, 34–35, 50–51, 60, 66, 74, 96–97, 106, 108–359, H.C. 1820 (93), ix; *Third Report of His Majesty's Commissioners on Ecclesiastical Revenue in Ireland,* pp. 96, 146, 242, 282, 330, 354, 406, 436, 474, 502, 536, 560, 590, 612; *Fourth Report of His Majesty's Commissioners on Ecclesiastical Revenue and Patronage in Ireland,* pp. 100, 140, 234, 280, 316, 334, 346, 382, 430, 468, 516, 538, 604, 658, 668.

How many pluralists were there? In the early nineteenth century no one asked the question directly, so a straightforward answer is unavailable. We can, however, come close to an accurate answer by tabulating the number of clergymen in the 1819 returns who were reported to be "residing on other benefices":[156]

Armagh, 3; Clogher, 5; Derry, 3; Down and Connor, 8; Dromore, 3; Kilmore, 6; Meath, 10; Raphoe, 2. *Total: 40.*

Dublin, 17; Kildare, 10; Ferns and Leighlin, 10; Ossory, 13. *Total: 50.*

Cashel and Emly, 3; Cloyne, 15; Cork and Ross, 13; Killaloe and Kilfenora, 5; Limerick, Ardfert and Aghadoe, 14; Waterford and Lismore, 8. *Total: 58.*

Tuam and Ardagh, 8; Clonfert and Kilmacduagh, 3; Elphin, 1; Killala and Achonry, 3. *Total: 15.*

National Total: 163

It is clear that after Lord John Beresford became Archbishop of Armagh in mid-1822, he made great efforts to reduce the number of pluralists, especially in the late 1820s when he had become absolutely sure of his preeminence in the Irish church. The rule of his predecessors (only rarely violated) was that no man should be allowed to hold more than two benefices in the Church of Ireland, and that only in very exceptional cases could one of these benefices be an episcopal union. Beresford took up the enforcement with vigor and granted faculties only in the cases of single benefices and parliamentary unions, and refused to make any exceptions whatsoever in the case of episcopal unions of parishes. Under Beresford's administration, faculties for holding more than one benefice were, with minor exceptions, granted only to clerics with a master's degree who passed an examination by the Beresford chaplain; who promised to reside for a portion of each year in his benefice; and who promised to pay for a duly licensed curate when absent. Beresford refused to grant faculties for benefices more than thirty miles apart. The only relief from this austerity was Beresford's policy of allowing each bishop to give one faculty of his own choosing for a plurality to be held solely within that bishop's diocese. Below is the tally of faculties granted during 1820:

Year	Number of faculties granted to hold more than one benefice
1820	15
1821	18

	Number of faculties granted to hold more than
Year (cont.)	one benefice (cont.)
1822	9
1823	19
1824	10
1825	5
1826	10
1827	3
1828	4
1829	1

Clearly, in the matter of pluralities, the Church of Ireland was successfully dealing with its own shortcomings.[157]

Rural Deans

"Since I first became interested in our Church Establishment as a professional member of it," the Bishop of Clonfert and Kilmacduagh wrote the Archbishop of Cashel in 1814, "I have ever thought that for the temper of the age too much is left in its Discipline to the spontaneous and personal will of the Superior and of the subordinate." [158] One way to regularize relationships between the bishops and the parish clergy was to promote parliamentary statutes, such as the clergy residence acts which impinged on that relationship. Another way was to introduce a middle layer of clerical administrators between the parish and the episcopal level whose duty was to coordinate the two levels and see that necessary information was passed back and forth. This middle level of administration had been, during the eighteenth century, almost totally missing in the Church of Ireland. Archdeacons in the Irish church, in contrast to their English counterparts, did not have supervisory jurisdiction over the clergy, and the office of rural deans was almost extinct.

During the first two decades of the nineteenth century, however, the office of rural dean was revived. In tracing the genealogy of this revival one can go back almost as far as one wishes. Wililam Bedell, Bishop of Kilmore (1629–42) had created rural deans[159] but the chain of their succession was broken long before the nineteenth century. Anthony Dopping while Bishop of Meath (1682–97) contemplated establishing rural deanships[160] but nothing seems to have come of the idea. Actually, the effective touchstone is found in Bishop Berkeley's (Bishop of Cloyne 1734–53) revival of the institution of rural deans.[161] Charles Agar, who was Bishop of Cloyne, somewhat later (1768–79) was translated to Cashel and following the precedents of the Diocese of Cloyne, created rural deaneries in his new archdiocese. His example was followed by Archbishop Newcome of

Armagh and by Bishop O'Beirne of Ossory.[162] Other bishops followed suit and by 1820, sixteen of the twenty-two united dioceses had adopted the system of rural deans.[163] Often the rural deans were cathedral dignitaries, but in many other cases they were outstanding members of the parish clergy. The number per diocese varied but was usually about half a dozen. As a corollary of its other reforms, therefore, the Church of Ireland introduced a group of men whose duty it was to help coordinate religious policy and who could aid the bishop in making certain the level of parochial performance was satisfactory.

EVANGELICAL ANIMATION

When we turn from quantitative measures of church reform to qualitative indicators we are moving into an area which cannot be treated with statistical precision.[164] Nevertheless, it is clear that the attitudes and conduct of the churchmen associated with the Irish evangelical movement had a distinct impact upon the Church of Ireland. In the broadest terms, the evangelical served as an animating force within the church. It would, however, be a mistake to assume that the movement was a simple phenomenon. The movement was neither a unitary nor a unified one and there is no precise date on which the Church of Ireland became evangelical. Although the movement began in the eighteenth century and gathered force in the early nineteenth, it was not until mid-nineteenth century that the church could safely be described as predominantly evangelical, and it was only after disestablishment that it became overwhelmingly so. The movement did not take hold with equal rapidity on all levels of the church. At first, the evangelicals were found almost entirely among the laity and lower clergy. Later the movement spread upward to the archdiaconate; but not until the appointment of James O'Brien as Bishop of Ossory and Ferns in 1842, was an avowed evangelical raised to the bench. Indeed, it was not until disestablishment was well past, that the majority of the bishops would bear an evangelical label.

If one must select a specific year for the emergence of the evangelical party within the Church of Ireland as distinct from Methodist groups, then 1778 will serve well; in that year the Reverend Thomas Tighe, Rector of Drumgooland in County Down, began his ministry. Tighe had been a Fellow of Peterhouse College and was inspired by the evangelical principles of the Cambridge group. In the metropolis, the seedbed of Irish Anglican evangelicalism was for many years the Bethesda Chapel, Dublin. In 1805 B. Williams Mathias, one of the most fervent and famous of Irish preachers, was named to fill its pulpit. Another major apostle of the early period was the Reverend Peter Roe, who in 1800 founded the Ossory Clerical Association which has been described as an Irish equivalent to the Clapham set.

By 1810 the pioneering stages of the evangelical movement were over, and the succeeding years saw a period of steady growth in numbers and influence.[165]

The effect of a growing evangelical party upon the church's standards of conduct was important. Its influence on the church was three-fold: members raised the standard of the parish ministry, formed missionary agencies, and founded a large number of schools. At the parish level, an evangelical vicar was usually most attentive to his duties. This devotion was exemplified in the Kilkenney ministry of the famous Peter Roe who rigorously attended to the duties of catechizing, evangelical preaching, visitation of the laity, and the promotion of prayer meetings.[166] Naturally, when the individual evangelicals inched their way up the ecclesiastical pyramid, their influence grew as their authority increased. For example, the Reverend William Digby, Archdeacon of Elphin, was an exemplary evangelical clergyman. His bishop was Power Le Poer Trench, who, it will be recalled, was raised to the bench for political reasons at the age of thirty-two. Trench was a reasonably competent bishop but hardly a devout one until he came under Digby's influence. Though not a member of the evangelical party, Trench became convinced through Digby of the virtues of the evangelical position and sought to encourage the evangelical approach to parish duties among his clergy.[167] In the Province of Dublin in this period the Reverend Robert Daly was in the ascendant. A well-known evangelical who had held curacies in Ferns and in County Wicklow, Daly was promoted to the living of Powerscourt in 1814. This living was one of the most influential in the country, comprising a population of some 2,000 Protestants, a large portion of whom were landed gentry. Daly, therefore, had a superb base for his evangelical ministry. His influence grew continually and he was appointed Archbishop of Cashel in late 1842.[168] If it would not be accurate to conclude that the Church of Ireland was predominantly evangelical by 1830, undeniably it was tending more and more to evangelicalism with each passing year. As the evangelicals' influence grew, the devotion to religious duties increased among the parish clergy.[169]

Not only did the evangelicals animate the church in its ordinary functions, but they also created a band of special agencies to carry forward their purposes. These agencies aimed at the conversion of the Roman Catholic population to Protestantism. Whether the societies should be known as missionary societies (a phrase which implies that Ireland needed to be rescued from spiritual darkness), or proselytizing societies (a phrase which connotes a bigoted approach to soul-snatching), is irrelevant in a study of this sort. For the sake of neutrality, the agencies will be referred to as evangelical societies or agencies, and the reader left to his own moral judgments.

The most important characteristic of the evangelical societies was the simple fact that they were special-interest groups organized to promote a specific goal or a relatively narrow set of goals. Whereas the typical parish was a unit with generalized functions, ranging from public worship to making arrangements for marriages and provisions for burials, the evangelical societies usually concentrated on a single set of promotional activities. Paralleling the contrast between the general functions of the parish and the specialized functions of the societies was the contrast between the fixed geographic nature of the parish and the inter-diocesan character of most societies. Geographic boundaries, the very heart of the parochial system, were largely irrelevant to the evangelical agencies in their work. Representatives of the societies crossed parochial and diocesan boundaries at will. Further, instead of being under the control of the Irish prelates, each of the major societies was at least semi-autonomous. Each society's board of governors was composed partially of laymen. In some cases societies were under the control of a coalition of Dissenters and churchmen, and in still others lay Dissenters predominated. Even within the Church of Ireland, relations between evangelicals and other churchmen were tense; and when this tension was exacerbated by the presence of Dissenters on the governing boards of some of the societies, relations between the societies and the ecclesiastical authorities became unfriendly and, occasionally, openly hostile. The semi-autonomous characteristic of the evangelical agencies, combined with the refusal of the more enthusiastic evangelicals in the societies to accept the dictates of the Anglican prelates, meant that the societies always represented a potentially serious problem of control to the church. The relationship was a continually uneasy one, for the agencies animated the church and provided converts, while simultaneously presenting the possibility of schism within the Church of Ireland. For all their dangers, the societies, we can conjecture, were extremely useful in keeping the more enthusiastic evangelicals within the church. In many individual instances, the agencies must have served as a religious safety valve. The "second Reformation" movement in Ireland allowed the more zealous evangelicals to satisfy their urge to convert the Irish peasantry without having to become Dissenters to do so.

Analytically, the evangelical agencies can be divided into two categories: those that directly received government funds, and those which did not. Turning to the societies financed entirely by voluntary contributions, we will limit ourselves to three examples. The first is the Hibernian Bible Society which was founded in 1806. This was modeled on the British and Foreign Bible Society which had been established in 1804. To Irish evangelicals, the compelling argument for its formation was the report that in Ireland there were, with the exception of Dublin, only twelve towns in which Bibles and New Testaments could be purchased. The society set about rectifying this condition, and in its first twenty-three years distributed 209,000 Bibles.[170] From its formation until 1874, the Hibernian Bible Society issued 3,892,458 copies of the Scriptures in both Irish and English editions (what proportion of the Bibles was in Irish was not reported).[171] In its administrative set-up, the society was illustrative of the problem the specialized evangelical agencies created for the Church of Ireland: it was governed by a group of twenty-one persons of various denominations, including the Archbishops of Armagh and of Dublin. The churchmen on the executive committee were unable to control the society to their satisfaction. By the middle of 1821, the prelates on the committee were thoroughly disenchanted with what they believed was manipulation of the society by the Dissenters, and on 17 July 1821 the Archbishops of Dublin and of Armagh resigned from their positions in the society.[172] At their departure, the Bible agency was effectively liberated from episcopal control and became a free agent religiously—one which was still encouraged by the more evangelical Anglican clergy and laity but distrusted by the hierarchy.

If the conflict of the hierarchy with the Hibernian Bible Society illustrates the tensions between the multidenominational societies and the authorities of the Anglican Church, the relations of the church with the Sunday School Society for Ireland indicate that a successful accommodation was possible between the church and a multidenominational society. The board of governors of the Sunday School Society was multidenominational, but was dominated by strong upper-class and Anglican elements. Among the guardians were the Countesses of Kingston, Charleville, Meath, and Bandon; the Viscountess Powerscourt, Lady Norwood; Mrs. P. La Touche; the Earls of Meath and Bandon; the Count de Salis; Messrs. Peel, La Touche, and Parnell; the Bishop of Ferns.[173] Thus, although the society was not under the direct control of the Anglican prelates, it could be expected to work in concert with the Anglican Church in most of its activities. Equally conducive to harmony with the Established Church was the society's style of operation, which was one of minimal intervention in local Sunday schools. In its early years, the society operated under an agent system of paid operatives who were sent throughout the country to establish schools and make grants of Bibles, Testaments, and various other books.[174] At times the society made money grants to local schools, but in 1823 these were discontinued.[175] The society, therefore, became a coordinating agency which supplied advice, books, and a common title to what were essentially local religious activities. There is some indication that the society, being most tolerant of local desires, included, during its first decade and a half, some Roman Catholic schools in which the Roman Catholic cathechism was taught.[176] For a very limited expenditure the society created an impressive organization, at least on paper. From 2 schools and 87 scholars in 1810, the society had grown to 1,702 schools and 150,831 scholars in 1825.[177]

Our third example from among the voluntarily-financed societies is the Hibernian Church Missionary Society which was an exclusively Anglican organization. Modeled on the Church Missionary Society that had been founded in London in 1799, the Irish body was given an auspicious start in 1814 by the combined efforts of the leading Anglican evangelicals: B. W. Mathias, Robert Daly, William Shaw Mason, Robert Shaw, Arthur Guinness, David La Touche, and Major Sirr.[178] As an Anglican body whose focus was the evangelicalization of foreign lands, the society did not clash with the administrative practices of the Established Church.

From an administrative viewpoint, the societies which received a significant portion of their income from the government were considerably different from those which were financially independent. In the first instance, they differed because government grants were given on the assumption that most of the agencies receiving them would be more circumspect in their missionary activities than the independent ones. The government of Ireland was ostensibly the one for all the Irish people and the recipients of government funds could afford to offend the bulk of the people but not to inflame them. Second, the government-aided societies were more apt to be under the control of Anglicans than were the fully voluntary societies, since nearly all the major officials of Dublin Castle were Anglican. Unlike the financially independent societies, therefore, those with government subventions were unlikely to come into conflict with the Established Church. Another way in which the independent and the government-aided agencies differed was that the latter societies were invariably educational ones. The Irish officials had to justify a grant by declaring that the money was being spent for the general good. In the case of grants to societies which taught children to read and write, the argument was a plausible one; whereas, it would not be acceptable to argue publicly that the activities of itinerant preachers, for example, would be conducive to the general peace of the Irish countryside.

Unlike the independent societies which were products solely of the evangelical movement, the educational societies had historical antecedents which pre-dated the revival. These antecedents, to which we must now turn, involved a history of state legislation and financial provision in Irish education. The beginning of this tradition is found in the years immediately following the Reformation in the British Isles. In 1537 the Irish parliament passed a parish schools act (28 Henry VIII, c. 15). This act was a considered piece of governmental policy whose purpose was to assure civil order by weaning the Irish populace from its allegedly barbaric ways. To this end, Irish manner of dress and speech was discountenanced and parents were directed to have their children taught the English tongue. In order to effect the provision regarding the English language, spiritual promotion was, with certain exceptions, limited to those speaking English; all those taking holy orders were to swear to preach in English. Most important, each man taking holy orders was responsible for providing an English school within his vicarage or rectory. In theory, therefore, every benefice in the country was to have an elementary school. A sensible system in theory, but in practice the schools were slow to appear. Indeed, it is doubtful that any school was established in Henry VIII's reign; or even that any attempt was made to enforce the legislation until after the Restoration.[179] Hence, in 1695 the Irish parliament found it necessary to pass a statute again affirming that every incumbent should keep, or cause to be kept, an English school in his benefice (7 William III, c. 4). A later statute provided the legal facilities for the clergy and prelates to grant land and endow a resident Protestant schoolmaster (8 George I, c. 12) and another allowed similar facilities to certain laymen (5 George II, c. 4).

Now, the two salient characteristics of the parish school system were, first, that the government of Ireland from the sixteenth century onwards was committed to using legislative instrumentalities to establish and further the cause of Anglican educational agencies; and second, that the system was a failure. A survey of the schools made in 1788 revealed that of the 838 benefices reporting, only 361 contained operational parish schools, involving approximately 11,000 children.[180] In a return for 1810 covering 736 benefices, 549 parish schools with 23,000 students were reported. In less than half of the cases, however, were the schools sufficiently established to be conducted in a schoolhouse.[181] A third report of 1823 stated that there existed 782 parish schools in Ireland, with over 36,000 children in attendance, more than 15,000 of whom were Roman Catholics.[182] These numbers pale to insignificance when one realizes that the parish school system was intended to be a national system of education and that the Irish population in 1823 was probably well past the six million mark. Given, then, that there existed a long-standing inclination for the Irish government authorities to encourage Anglican schools and accepting the fact that this intervention was unsuccessful in terms of the government's desire for a nationwide school system, we can expect the government either to withdraw from the Anglican educational enterprise or to find other Anglican institutions upon which to use its legislative influence.

One potential alternative was for the government to greatly increase its aid to the Incorporated Society in Dublin for Promoting English Protestant Schools in Ireland, often referred to as the Charter School Society.[183] The society was the product of a series of ad hoc actions by Dublin clergy and laymen who, in the early years of the eighteenth century, created charity schools to teach elementary reading and the Anglican catechism to children of the lower classes. There were three such Protestant charity schools in Dublin in 1706 and fifteen in 1717. An early leader was Dr. Henry Maule, a zealous churchman who was later to become Bishop of Meath. Maule was, in 1717, the chief architect of the Dublin Society for Promoting Christian Knowledge; its purpose was the general establishment of charity schools. By 1725 the society was operating 163 schools containing 3,000 pupils. Financial problems slowed the society's growth, however, and it was only when Hugh Boulter, Archbishop of Armagh, took an interest that the agency's fortunes improved; for Boulter was largely responsible for a grant by the government in 1733 of a royal charter. A great boon to the society, the royal charter made it much easier to obtain subscriptions from the Irish gentry. Nevertheless, pious intentions outran funds, and in 1738 Boulter found it necessary again to petition the Crown for a grant. The king responded by subscribing £1,000 annually, a subvention which did not cease until 1794. Even with the royal grant, however, the society needed more funds. And in 1747, parliament was inveigled into setting an important precedent: the licensing duty on hawkers and peddlers was assigned to the society. In point of fact, this grant remained until the 1780s more important as a precedent than as revenue for until then it was almost wholly unproductive. Once the precedent had been set, however, it was but a small step for the government to make an outright grant to the society. Under pressure from the Duke of Dorset, Viceroy from 1751 through 1755, parliament granted a direct subvention to the Incorporated Society. In the first decade of parliamentary grants, from 1751 to 1760, the society received an average of £3,500 a year. By the last decade of the century the average was nearly £12,000 per annum, and in the first years of the nineteenth century, almost £20,000 each year. The grant reached its apogee in 1818 when £38,000 was given the Incorporated Society. Thereafter the grant declined sharply as other agencies became the chief recipients of parliamentary largess. Altogether it is estimated that a total of one and a quarter million pounds were voted the society between 1751 and 1831.[184]

Was the Incorporated Society viable as a permanent channel of educational funds to the Anglican establishment? The answer is apparently yes and actually no. At first glance, the Incorporated Society was an impressive organization. It boasted an executive committee around which revolved four satellite committees (accounts, law, teachers, and a standing committee); and on the local level, a committee in each district in which there was a Charter School. Behind this façade, however, bubbled administrative chaos; for despite the solar system of committees, the control of what went on in individual classrooms was left largely in the hands of individual teachers. The provision of standard textbooks and the rare inspections by members of the committee may have slightly moderated malfeasance by the Charter

School mentors—but only slightly. Investigators found that children in the schools were often underfed and underclothed. At Castle-Carberry School, for example, a visitor found in 1787 that there were fourteen boys and eighteen girls in the school but that the teachers could produce only twenty-four ragged shirts and shifts to clothe this group.[185] By and large, the schools appear to have taught only the three R's; and that, badly. Worse yet, the Incorporated Society's policy of separating Roman Catholic children from their parents often by "transplanting" them to distant areas from home resulted in the society's name becoming so smirched in the eyes of the Roman Catholic population that it could not adequately serve the purposes of the Dublin administration—which in the nineteenth century desired a school system that would be at once Anglican and acceptable to the Roman Catholics. The Incorporated Society's failure is best indicated by the fact that in 1830, after having received more than a million pounds in government subvention over the previous eight decades, it was schooling less than 900 children.[186]

If the parish school system and the Incorporated Society did not satisfy the government's desire for a national system of education compatible with the principles of the Established Church, a third option was available in the Association for Discountenancing Vice and Promoting the Knowledge and Practice of the Christian Religion,[187] founded in 1792 by three members of the Established Church. In the years 1792 to 1800, the association's income came wholly from voluntary subscriptions and totalled less than £2,000. This amount was spent chiefly on Bibles and Books of Common Prayer, on moral tracts, and on prizes for the promotion of catechismal examinationists. In 1800 the association was incorporated and successfully applied for a parliamentary grant, which began at £300 and was renewed annually until 1830. By 1823 it reached a peak of somewhat more than £9,000 and fluctuated considerably thereafter.

Parliamentary grants brought a marked change in this agency's style of operation. It ceased to be an association of obscure pamphleteers and became an organization of popular educators. Under the exclusive control of members of the Established Church, the association gave money towards the establishment of schools and towards the payment of teachers. As the closest approximation the church had to an official educational society, the APCK required that title to schools it aided be vested in the church wardens and in the Anglican minister of the parish in which it was located. The local Anglican priest was given sole power to appoint and dismiss the schoolmaster. School-teachers were required to be members of the Established Church, and the only catechism allowed was that of the Church of Ireland. Despite these religious rules the APCK attempted to attract children of all denominations to its schools and did not require children of non-Anglican faiths to attend catechismal instruction. Roman Catholic children were, however, required to read the Bible in the authorized version. And into the early 1820s the association was fairly successful in attracting Catholic children. Of the more than 8,000 youngsters in association schools in 1819, almost four and a half thousand were Roman Catholics.

Despite its attractions, the APCK could not serve as a mass educational agency acceptable to the government, attractive though that might have been to the authorities of the Anglican Church. The exclusively Anglican character of its management meant that the association was not completely trusted by the large Presbyterian population in the north of Ireland. A permanently acceptable agency of mass education needed to have Presbyterians represented in positions of authority. Further, as time passed, the Roman Catholics became increasingly suspicious of its activities. By the early 1820s the APCK had begun publishing avowedly anti-Catholic works and thus became marked as a proselytizing society. Moreover, from the government's viewpoint, the association's administrative network was probably too weak to bear the strain of large-scale education of the Irish populace, since it depended upon the presence of a resident Anglican minister for effective local operation—a prerequisite that was not fulfilled in a large number of Irish parishes in the early years of the nineteenth century.

In 1806, the government had appointed a commission to study Irish education. The commissioners worked from October of that year until October 1812, producing fourteen reports dealing in detail with specific institutions and societies and providing recommendations for further development. The commission was clearly under the hegemony of the Anglican hierarchy. The Archbishop of Armagh presided at most of the meetings, and when he was absent the Archbishop of Dublin or the Provost of Trinity took the chair. In their fourteenth summary report, the commissioners concluded that the opportunities for education among the Irish poor were insufficient and recommended the creation of a body or set of commissioners to administer parliamentary grants to establish schools and regulate popular education. Most important, the fourteenth report warned that no system of education in Ireland could be successful, unless it explicitly avowed as its leading principle that no attempt should be made to influence or disturb the position of any religious group.[188]

Thus, an Irish governmental commission was on record recommending massive state intervention in Irish education. This intervention was to be as neutral as possible between religious groups. For a time, the Irish authorities did not act upon this; the recommendation was only shelved, not forgotten. Although reluctant to create a set of educational commissioners who would administer a national system of elementary education, the Dublin Castle officials were willing to give money to a voluntary school society if it met the test of religious neutrality while being acceptable to the Anglican prelates. These governmental inclinations fit perfectly with the contours of another educational society that was just then coming to the fore. This one, the Society for Promoting the Education of the Poor in Ireland (usually known as the Kildare Place Society) was founded in 1811 by an interdenominational committee.[189] The Kildare Place Society's major precept was that its schools should be operated upon the most liberal principles and should be divested of all sectarian distinctions in Christianity. In practice, this meant that the Bible was to be read without comment and that doctrinal matters were not to be raised. These principles commended themselves to the government, and in 1816 a grant of £6,000 was voted the society. This grant rose greatly in subsequent years and in the year 1831 as high as £30,000.[190] The considerable magnitude of these parliamentary grants becomes obvious when one realizes that in the year 1833, when the British parliament began providing money for English elementary education, the first grant totaled £20,000. According to the society's thirty-fifth annual report, in 1830 there were 1,634 schools affiliated with the agency, educating 132,530 children.[191]

Although the Kildare Place Society was not under the control of the Anglican clerics in the same way the APCK was, the agency's operations were acceptable to Anglicans. Through the Kildare Place Society, local Anglican clergy and landowners received aid in founding schools which, while professing religious neutrality, inevitably had a strong Anglican flavor. The Kildare plan was therefore acceptable to the government. The Presbyterians in Ulster accepted the Kildare Place Society because what the Anglican clergy and gentry could do in areas they dominated, the Presbyterian clergy and their lay allies could do throughout much of Ulster. Significantly, the Roman Catholics gave the system a fair trial, and until 1820 there was considerable Roman Catholic adhesion to the Kildare Place schools. During the early 1820s, however, the Catholic laity under Daniel O'Connell (who had been one of the society's members) and the clergy under Bishop Doyle and the Reverend John MacHale, came to view the Kildare schools as proselytizing agencies. This view was at least partially correct; for, beginning in 1820, the society granted a portion of its income to schools associated with avowedly missionary societies such as the London Hibernian Society and the Baptist Society. For the time being, however, the parliamentary grants continued and the Kildare schools multiplied.

Now, if we combine the cases of the Incorporated Society, the APCK, and the Kildare Place Society, it becomes clear that in the years from 1800 to 1830 a large amount of government money found its way into the hands of Anglican clergy and laity—this money being spent on educational purposes. None of these three organizations was inconsonant with the administration of the Church of Ireland; and in the cases of the Incorporated Society and the APCK, the agencies were clearly under church control.

The considerable funds which went to the APCK and to the Anglican applicants for Kildare Place grants (unlike the moneys to the Incorporated Society) appear to have been efficiently used in the creation of a complex of Anglican elementary schools, which bolstered the tattered and tottering Anglican parish school system. Thus, the improvement in Anglican arrangements for elementary schooling may be seen as achieving in the field of education what the glebe house, church building, and residence legislation, did in the field of parish administration. All these developments were interrelated, and each of them represents a significant contribution to the administrative efficiency of the Church of Ireland. Simultaneous with these improvements in the administration of the church, which can be quantitatively determined, was a qualitative improvement in the performance of religious duties by the clergy. The keynote of the internal history of the Church of Ireland in the years from 1800 to 1830 is that the church was a much more efficient organization by the end of the period than it had been at the time of the Union.

THE CHANGING NATIONAL CONTEXT

The position of the church in Irish society was determined more by external factors than by matters of internal efficiency. The most important external factor was the church's relation to the Irish religious majority which was solidly Roman Catholic. Ironically, while the Church of Ireland was improving internally, it was losing ground externally; for the thirty years after the act of Union were the years in which the Roman Catholics of Ireland achieved cohesion as a religious and political group. As their identity crystallized, the Roman Catholics mobilized their resources not only to achieve their own political rights but to undercut the privileged position of the Established Church. The Protestant educational societies were the first agencies of the church to have their activities crimped by Roman Catholic objections, but all aspects of the church were increasingly open to public criticism and potential limitation. Churchmen were bewildered by this phenomenon for it seemed that the more they applied themselves to their religious duty, the more they were criticized. "It is an extraordinary fact," one clerical administrator wrote to Archbishop Beresford, "that the complaints against the non-residence of the Irish Clergy have increased in proportion as their residence and exertion have increased." [192]

During the first thirty years of the nineteenth century the Roman Catholic Church finished repairing the ravages of the penal times. The Catholic Church had suffered not only from the impoverishment of most of its constituents but from a shattering of ecclesiastical discipline. This discipline, of bishop over cleric, was reasserted only slowly during the second half of the eighteenth century and completely established only in the nineteenth. Over the same period of time the position in society of the Roman Catholic cleric changed considerably. From a humble social level, he rose by mid-nineteenth century to one close to that of the small gentry. The salary of a priest, which was returned at an average of £65 (exclusive of the expense of keeping a curate) in 1801, had risen to approximately £150 by 1825, with a few wealthy parishes yielding £500 a year. The total average income of a Catholic bishop in 1801 was a little more than £300 per annum. Twenty-five years later, Kildare and Leighlin, which yielded £450 to £500 a year, was considered one of the poorer dioceses. Although these sums did not rival the opulent rewards of the best paid Anglican clergy and bishops, it is clear that the Roman Catholic clergy and hierarchy were again obtaining a position of considerable social eminence in Irish society.[193] Unlike the Anglican Church in which a rise in clerical income was usually the result of legislative intervention, the rise in Roman Catholic clerical salaries served as an index of the changing position of the entire Roman Catholic population. Whereas the Church of Ireland was an established church, the Catholic Church was organized on an entirely voluntary basis, receiving no government funds for the support of its clergy or bishops. Hence, clerical incomes were a function of local giving and an index of local devotion and local economic conditions. Significantly, the voluntary system forged a "golden link" between the clergy and the people.[194] The Roman Catholic clergy and the Roman Catholic population of Ireland, therefore, rose or fell as a united body.

The crucial issue of the years 1800 to 1829 for the Roman Catholics was, of course, the drive for Catholic emancipation, a phrase denoting the right to sit in parliament but connoting the achievement of equality and dignity as well. The cause of the Catholic emancipation movement is too well known to need detailing here,[195] but one point is in order in reflecting on that movement: It should not be viewed simply as a political crusade, but as a part of a complex set of changes whereby the Catholics began to gain control over the centers of power within Ireland; and whereby the Roman Catholic Church achieved first organizational parity, and then superiority, over the Anglican Church. Catholic emancipation represents one aspect of the complex pattern of social and religious reorganization that is the chief theme of nineteenth-century Irish history.

In a narrow political sense, the issue of Catholic emancipation should have been settled soon after the Union. An implicit promise of the Union negotiators was that the Union would be followed swiftly by a Catholic emancipation measure. Pitt, the Prime Minister, however, was thwarted in his intentions by George III who refused to countenance emancipation. Consequently, in March 1801, Pitt and his ministers resigned in a gesture that to some historians smacks of hypocrisy and to others indicates a noble sacrifice of personal ambitions. The Roman Catholic leaders remained hopeful that when Pitt returned to office he would carry the measure. George III, however, again thwarted them, imposing as a precondition for Pitt's resuming office in 1804 that Pitt must pledge himself to resist all efforts at altering the constitution.[196] The effect of Pitt's failure to carry Catholic emancipation was enormous, for it determined the course of Roman Catholic history for at least the succeeding twenty-five years. Instead of being a boon granted gracefully by the government to the Roman Catholic prelates, Catholic emancipation became a prize to be wrenched from the government by the masses of Catholic laity under Daniel O'Connell. The Roman Catholic peasantry, therefore, became politicized and achieved an awareness of its power much sooner than would have been the case if Pitt's inclinations had been followed. Moreover, this politicalization process placed the newly organized Catholics on the side of the parliamentary opposition, and further, introduced them to extra-parliamentary methods of forcing parliamentary actions. In the longer run, the privileged position of the Anglican Church probably would have been left undisturbed much longer than it actually was if Catholic emancipation had been granted in 1801; for in having to fight for emancipation, the Roman Catholics achieved a political identity and momentum that was inevitably turned upon the Church of Ireland once the more pressing issue of emancipation was settled.

In the late 1820s, at the very time when the Roman Catholics were attaining political cohesion, the Church of Ireland's forces were fragmenting. Until the late 1820s, the church could count on a unified phalanx in parliament of unbending Tories and bishops of England and Ireland. The retirement of Lord Liverpool in 1827, however, left the various Tory factions fighting among themselves. Then, Lord John Russell's motion in 1828 to repeal the Test and Corporation Acts as they applied to Protestant Dissenters split a portion of the English bishops from some of their English fellows and from the Irish hierarchy. Peel was able to obtain the silent cooperation of the Archbishops of York and of Canterbury; and ultimately, thirteen of the twenty-one English bishops who voted cast their ballots for repeal of the statutes. The result of this liberalism on the part of the bishops was the alienation of the die-hard Tories from the church; and a further effect was to give a decided stimulus to agitation for Catholic emancipation.[197]

While the old Tory-Anglican alliance crumbled, the Irish bishops and clergy remained solidly against emancipation, a unified but politically ineffective cadre. Members of the bench, and especially Primate Beresford, did all they could to impede progress of the government's plans, but the ministry was no longer willing to pay attention to the prelates. Irish churchmen watched with a mixture of resignation and hysteria as parliament did the inevitable. "My ultimate reliance," the Bishop of Limerick wrote Sir Robert Peel, "is placed, where it cannot be shaken, in Divine Providence.

I trust that all will yet be right, but in the mean time, in defense of all that is dear to British Protestants, I am cheerfully prepared, if necessary, as others of my order have formerly done, to lay down life itself." [198] Catholic emancipation set in motion a trend towards rigid conservatism in the Church of Ireland at the very time the United Kingdom as a whole was experiencing a trend towards greater flexibility and liberalism. The new Roman Catholic M.P.s, together with the radicals and liberals in parliament, were the inevitable opponents of the Irish Anglican establishment.

We are now at a point where we can tie together the themes that run through the years 1800 to 1830. In essence, there were two currents of events. The first of these was the continual improvement in the efficiency of the Established Church in delivering pastoral services to the Irish Anglican population. On every quantitative index—residency, the number of benefices, the number of churches, the proportion of clergy resident on their benefices—the church improved. Qualitatively, the evangelical movement increased the assiduousness of the parish clergy in their work. Further, the church broadened its activities through the missionary agencies and through expanded educational involvement. The second current of events was the rise of the Roman Catholics in Ireland as a major power bloc, hostile to the privileged position of the Established Church. Whether or not the church had been able to strengthen itself sufficiently to enable it to ward off attacks from external foes was an issue that would be decided during the 1830s.

3 Reform by Critical Strangers, 1830–1867

INTRODUCTION

It is tempting to treat the great wave of reforms, that makes the 1830s such an attractive period for the British social historian, as being its own cause and effect. This is especially true for historians dealing with the secondary reforms of the period, for it is easy to treat them as almost inevitable concommitants of the greater improvements of the time—the electoral reforms and the revamping of the Poor Law. In the case of parliamentary reforms of the Church of Ireland effected during the 1830s, such an interpretation is especially misleading. The Anglican Church reforms were not postscripts to larger political events. The church reforms have a history and a logic of their own and were not merely a result of British political occurrences. Indeed, it is possible to argue that in all probability, the church reforms of the 'thirties would have occurred whether or not other contemporary governmental and social reforms had taken place. Unlike most English reform measures for which the reform bill of 1832 was a parliamentary battering ram, the changes in the Irish church were dependent only upon the Catholic emancipation measure of 1829. Once the Irish Catholics were represented in significant numbers by vocal spokesmen in the Commons, the latter's attention was inevitably called to the anomalies of the Protestant Church in Ireland. Further to argue the integrity of Irish church reform as an independent piece of political history, the crucial principle of church reform —that parliament could with propriety interfere with ecclesiastical property rights—had been established by the tithe reform measures of the 1820s. The precedents set in the 1820s and the energies released by Catholic emancipation worked themselves out in the 1830s in a predictable and logical pattern. To maintain that the reform of the Church of Ireland by parliamentary statesmen did not depend upon their being engaged in secular reform measures, is not to deny that the mentality with which those same statesmen approached secular affairs affected their approach to the church. Certainly, the moves toward reforms in municipal government, trade, and similar affairs advocated by Lord Liverpool, and his more enlightened Tory colleagues, reinforced their desire to improve gently the Anglican Church in Ireland. Likewise, the austere eyes of the reform-minded Whigs, sharpened by their investigations into the absurdities of electoral politics and municipal misgovernment, were apt to be double-quick in noticing the inefficiencies of a religious body. And to the acerbic tongues of the radicals, the Church of Ireland was an inviting target, for it was associated with Toryism and sufficiently archaic to be the target of any number of tracts and creeds. The Church of Ireland was not in itself an important object of reform. The Irish church matter, when compared to the electoral franchise, municipal government reform, and Poor Law reform was inconsequential; but the church became a symbol of a wide range of British institutions which needed revamping. Its reform, therefore, was something of a totemic ceremony. Indeed, it may well be argued that the reformers did to the Church of Ireland what they really would have liked to do to the Church of England, but which politics prevented their accomplishing. The Church of England in the 1830s was the focus of a hatred that was as surprising to churchmen as it was frightening; but, unlike the case of Ireland, the opponents of the Church of England were not able to affect reforms which would reduce the size of the religious establishment.

The changes which the Church of Ireland underwent after 1830 contrasted greatly with those which had occurred earlier. The reforms of the early nineteenth century (glebe house and clerical residence measures, increased church provision and educational subventions) were essentially affirmative measures. Although churchmen often worried about the various statutes, they were passed by men who generally believed in the usefulness to Irish society of the Church of Ireland; and the statutes were intended to enable the church to perform its job more effectively. In contrast to the affirmative tone of the earlier reforms, that of the 'thirties was essentially negative. The later reforms stemmed from a skepticism about the value of the Anglican Church in Ireland and from a belief that its resources should be reduced. A second difference between the reforms of the early century and those of the 1830s runs parallel to the differences in tone: the early reforms tended to augment the church establishment, while the actions of the 1830s diminished it. The earlier measures increased the revenues of the church and the strength of the establishment, but those of the 'thirties reduced its resources and suppressed a number of its bishoprics. Third, in contrast to earlier reforms, those of the 1830s altered the basic structural outlines of the church by rearranging dioceses and reducing the number of high offices in the establishment. Given the above contrasts between the earlier and later reforms, a fourth is implied: whereas most churchmen accepted the majority of church reforms of the early nineteenth century, those of the 'thirties were carried only over the indignant opposition of the majority of clergy and bishops of the Church of Ireland.

The reformers of the 1830s did not do their work for the convenience of the historian. A strictly chronological narrative of their activities would be confusing, for the church was knocked about like a shuttlecock from one issue to another. Basically, there were three major issues of the 1830s: tithes, the structure of the church as an organization, and the arrangement of the church finances. These issues often overlapped, and sometimes a single legislative measure treated all three. With minor exceptions, the central reforms were accomplished by the close of the year 1838. Thereafter, an uneasy quiet settled over the church. Whether churchmen realized it or not, the contractions forced upon the establishment in the 1830s were merely a prelude to the ultimate one, the disestablishment of the Church of Ireland in the late 1860s.

ONCE AGAIN THE TITHE QUESTION

Rural Agitation

On the thirteenth of December 1830 some cattle distrained for tithe arrears in the parish of Graiguenamanagh, County Kilkenny (Graig for short) were offered for sale, but there were no buyers, despite the large number of persons present. This marked the beginning of a series of passive resistance measures against tithe collection in Ireland. At Graig, collective action was involved; anyone bidding placed his life into danger. Moreover, a tax of one penny per acre was collected from the peasantry to pay for any legal expenses resulting from passive resistance and for the relief of distress caused by prosecutions. The instigators of the Graig resistance were not apprehended, although it is certain the local Roman Catholic priest, the Reverend Martin Doyle, was prominent in opposing tithes.[1] The method pioneered in Graig (essentially a non-violent approach), as well as more violent forms of agitation, spread quickly across Ireland in the years 1830 and 1831, bringing great distress to the Church of Ireland clergy and the fear of revolution to the Dublin Castle authorities.

Why the reoccurrence of widespread tithe agitation? One reason was clearly economic. The second half of the 1820s presented the spectacle of one long economic slide. If one sets the domestic and imported commodity price index at 100 for 1826, it was 95.3 for 1831 and 91.5 for 1832, a sure sign of economic recession and falling agricultural prices.[2] In addition, the harvest of 1829 was particularly bad, and it placed intensive economic pressure on a peasant population that was already living on the narrow margin of subsistence. At such a time, it was not surprising that the attention of the peasantry should be directed to the Anglican clergy's main source of income, the tithe charges. These charges were visible and painful to the peasantry and helped to support a relatively affluent class, whose very existence was opposed by the bulk of the peasantry.[3]

But to simply ascribe the new tithe agitation to economic causes is to fasten on too simple an explanation, for the situation was much more complicated than a plainly economic analysis might lead one to believe. For example, there is reasonable speculation that, following Catholic emancipation, the ultra-Protestants among the tithe owners became more rigorous in their collection of dues, and abolished the exemptions and customary reductions that had previously moderated the abrasiveness of tithes. In particular, it has been suggested that the custom of exempting the land of the Roman Catholic priests from tithes was abjured by the ultra-Protestants after emancipation.[4] If this was indeed a common movement, the inflamatory effects had national significance; once the tithe agitation received priestly backing, it could not be stopped by local authorities.

The support of local priests was greatly reinforced by the public statements of James Doyle, Roman Catholic Bishop of Kildare and Leighlin. Doyle, at once one of the most reasonable and most courageous of the Catholic prelates, published an open letter in 1831 to Thomas Spring-Rice, implicitly providing episcopal sanction for the tithe campaign. Doyle's views were that the law of tithes never had, either before or after the Reformation, the assent of the majority of the Irish population and as such was an imposition upon that population. Further, Doyle contended, the Anglican Church in Ireland was collecting tithes under false pretenses, because a quarter portion of the tithes was from time immemorial required to be set aside for the poor, an obligation which the Church of Ireland made no pretence of meeting. Doyle sanctified the entire tithe agitation by ascribing the Irishman's hatred of tithes to his innate love of justice; opposition to tithes being, therefore, an obligation to any man with a Christian sense of justice.[5]

While Doyle gave his episcopal blessing to the tithe agitation, Daniel O'Connell gave it his secular imprimatur. O'Connell, on this as on many other issues of the 1830s, seemed to walk both sides of the street at once. In a letter to his County Clare constituency in January 1830, he called for a petition from every parish in Ireland for the abolition of tithes. A little later in the same year, he declared at a public dinner that he would exert all his energies toward the abolition of tithes; and in his election manifesto of 1830 he pledged himself to working in the Commons for tithe abolition. On other occasions he used words similar to Doyle's, declaring the Church of Ireland, as established, to be unchristian. Yet, while seeming to encourage tithe agitation, O'Connell appeared to discountenance it as well. For example, in January 1831 he denounced an antitithe meeting in County Kilkenny as mischievous and contended that tithe abolition would naturally follow in the path of the repeal of the Union, the true goal to which Irishmen should turn their attention.[6] Whatever O'Connell's actual feelings on the tithe agitation, his ambiguous position allowed the populace the luxury of ignoring his negative statements on the agitation, while repeating his affirmative ones.

Simultaneously, in the metropolis the agitation was receiving the support of the scandalous and widely read antitithe newspaper *The Comet*. This weekly, which was published from 1 May 1831 to the end of December 1833 was produced by a group of young radicals. They advocated reform of the Irish Poor Law, Irish municipal reform, repeal of the Union, and abolition of tithes. Their best-known publication was *The Parson's Horn*

Book, an illustrated collection of verse and prose satire on the abuse and anomalies of the Irish Protestant Church establishment. The book was tasteless and vicious, but highly amusing and so popular that it quickly went through several editions. In May 1831, two of the society's leading young men, Messrs. Thomas Browne and John Sheehan, undertook to edit *The Comet,* which was then dealing with all forms of secular abuses but concentrating on the Church of Ireland and in particular on the tithe system. The silent financing for this venture came from two unnamed gentlemen: one, a Roman Catholic distiller from County Kildare, the other a Protestant country gentleman from the Queen's County. Eventually this popular antichurch publication failed, not for lack of readers, but because of a dispute between its two editors, Browne and Sheehan. After the split, Browne began an antichurch paper of his own, *The Buckthorn Comet,* which soon disappeared, whereupon his friends took up a collection and sent him to the United States of America where he "died prosperous and rich." His partner Sheehan was arrested and sentenced to three months in prison for a piece he had written about the Anglican bishops and clergy entitled, "The Blood Slugs." Lord Anglesey soon released him, however, and Sheehan decided to leave the antichurch cause to others.[7]

Amusing as were the antics of *The Comet,* and as relatively mild and high-minded as were the statements of Doyle and O'Connell, the warfare between the civil authorities and the tithe resisters in the countryside was anything but high-minded or amusing. By the winter of 1831, the peasantry in much of Leinster and Munster was refusing to pay tithes. There was, it is crucial to realize, no central anti-tithe organization, if for no other reason than that the eighteenth-century tithe statutes made associations to defraud clergymen of their tithes illegal. The agitation spread chiefly by social contagion. Often, repeal meetings dealt not only with repeal but with the injustices of the tithes, thus encouraging the peasant resistance.[8]

Simple refusal to pay tithes, followed by the tenants' preventing the sale of seized goods, as described in the Graig case, was a common non-violent means of frustrating the tithe proctors. But the peasants were unwilling to allow the bailiffs to seize their cattle without resistance, even if they were confident of preventing their alienation at the tithe sale. Here, they had an advantage over their opponents, for the machinery of tithe enforcement in secular courts was clumsy. A process had to be served, and a court decree obtained and executed, before the cattle could be seized for tithe arrears. Even then, the law allowed the enforcement officers only to seize cattle during daylight hours and outdoors; those under lock and key were safe.[9] The peasants relentlessly took advantage of these legal niceties. In the parish of Graig, which may be taken as typical, as soon as the enforcement officers approached, the peasants simply locked up all the livestock. As long as food could be provided, either by feeding the livestock in the buildings or by night grazing, the bailiffs were balked.[10] Even when cattle were successfully captured, the enforcing officers had a difficult job ahead of them. Because no one among the local inhabitants would buy the cattle, they had to be driven to the coast for export. In some cases, fodder for the cattle was refused to the drivers, and in one instance the cattle could not even be sold in Liverpool, since they were branded with the word "tithe." [11]

Behind these essentially nonviolent methods continually lurked the specter of violence. Some of the more desperate tenantry took to destroying property and to maiming animals which belonged to their opponents. Threats against human life became common; and the tithe collector, who was told that he had better collect his coffin before he began to collect the tithe,[12] was the recipient of attentions not unprecedented. Murder threats were often directed against the Church of Ireland incumbent, and in the case of Dr. Butler, a County Kilkenny clergyman, the threats were made good.[13] Riots between the authorities and resisters became common. In 1831 in Higginstown, Kilkenny, for example, the proctor and enforcement authorities were attacked. Eleven policemen, the process server, and sixteen resisters were wounded in the ensuing melee.[14]

To make the situation worse, the police seem to have been as much danger to the peace as were the tenantry. For example, at the fair of Castlepollard in County Westmeath, in May 1831, the police seized a tithe offender. A crowd attacked the police and carried off the offender. Then the police appear to have fired indiscriminately into the crowd, for nine or ten persons were killed by their gunfire.[15]

Were these isolated incidents? Clearly not. In the year 1831, a total of 1,148 court decrees were handed down for tithe recovery, the number rising to 1,821 in the succeeding year.[16]

The tithe agitation hit the Church of Ireland where it was most vulnerable, at the parish level. The income of the ordinary clergyman consisted chiefly of tithe payments, and without these payments he could not long remain in his parish. In addition, the agitation, when it took the form of threats or personal violence, was often directed at the local incumbent. Although the tithe agitation was not a united coherent one, its implicit strategy would have done credit to a political field marshal; for it was a strategy of attacking the opposition at its weak point, utilizing tactics well within the capabilities of the average rural peasant. Tabulated below are the amounts of tithe arrears in certain dioceses in the years 1829 through 1832.[17]

Armagh	£29,715
Clogher	20,654
Derry	15,232

Kildare	16,465
Ferns	40,777
Leighlin	34,986
Ossory	42,170
Cashel & Emly	42,517
Cork	29,825
Ross	44,737
Killaloe	15,618
Kilfenora	1,527
Limerick	6,121
Ardfert & Aghadoe	10,552
Tuam	4,027
Ardagh	11,473
Clonfert	1,600
Kilmacduagh	713
Elphin	4,036

Clearly outside of Connacht, the clergy were suffering a great deal financially. The Irish bishops did what they could to aid distressed clergy. John G. Beresford, Archbishop of Armagh, spent £1,000 of his own money to relieve the distress of clergy in the disturbed districts, subscribed £500 to relief funds, and spent £452 on his "own clergy" whose dues had not been paid, all this in the year 1832.[18] In January 1833 a committee was formed in London, pending government settlement of tithe difficulties, to relieve the distressed clergy and £50,000 was soon subscribed.[19] But charity was a stop-gap only, and eventually the government had to make a decisive attack on the Irish tithe question.

The Ministerial Solution

The government unfolded its legislative plan with deliberation, if not dignity. Predictably, the first ministerial step was to investigate the Irish tithe situation through parliamentary select committees, from which the first report appeared early in 1832. Next, in April of that year, an arrears measure was passed providing the clergy of the Church of Ireland with £60,000 to tide them over financially. Then, later in the summer, a major tithe composition measure was passed into law. Finally, in 1833 an additional one million pounds was voted to be used to clear up the tithe arrears. This money went to the distressed clergymen, but was effectively a gift to those who had refused to pay their tithes, for it obviated their obligation to pay tithe arrears.

The king's speech of 6 December had mentioned the subject of Irish tithes, and on 15 December 1831, the ministry moved simultaneously in both houses of parliament for select committees to inquire into Irish tithes. In the Commons, the move was guided by Edward Stanley, Chief Secretary for Ireland (commonly called Lord Stanley by contemporaries although in law he was not yet in possession of that title). Stanley attempted to coat the pill with sugar, continually emphasizing that the best interest of the Church of Ireland dictated that the method of collecting tithes be reformed. He made it clear that he believed tithes to be a form of clerical property, and avoided any hint of the radical notion that tithes were communal property. Surprisingly, Sir Robert Peel met the proposal for an inquiry with only mild disapproval. The motion for a committee of inquiry was agreed to, without division.[20]

In point of fact, the House of Commons select committee produced two reports, the first being completed in mid-February, 1832, the second in early June. The tone of the first report in its definition of the tithe problem was strongly biased against the tenantry, but the recommendations were generally towards an amelioration of the peasants' grievances. The committee reported what everyone already knew—that there was a widespread opposition to tithes in Ireland—and concluded, incorrectly, that the opposition was systematically organized. Besides producing civil disorder, the tithe opposition deprived "a highly respectable class of men," the Protestant clergy, of their legal incomes. In response, the committee recommended that the Irish administration vigorously employ its powers to put a stop to the tithe agitation. More constructively, the committee made the pivotal suggestion that any improvement in the tithe system "must involve a complete extinction of tithes, including those to Lay Impropriators, by commuting them for a charge upon Land, or an exchange for, or an investment of Land." The revenues of the church would thus be removed from all chances of pecuniary collision with the tenants of the land. And what about the clergy who had no incomes? For the present the committee recommended that the Lord Lieutenant and privy council be authorized to advance money to those clergymen who could establish that their income had been diminished by the tithe agitation.[21] When the report was presented to the House of Commons, Henry Grattan objected that "it was unjust, unsatisfactory, and premature." [22] The ministry felt otherwise, however, and the report became a touchstone in the drafting of its tithe bills. The second report of the Commons' tithe committee appeared after the ministry had already laid its plans and was totally irrelevant, both chronologically and substantively.[23]

Meanwhile, events in the House of Lords had been following a parallel path. On 15 December 1831 (the same day Stanley had moved in the Commons), Viscount Melbourne moved in the Lords for a select committee, of that house, on Irish tithes. This motion doubtless came as a disappointment to Lord John Beresford, for he feared the formation of such a group and was resolutely opposed to compulsory tithe composition, the remedy most apt to be recommended by such a select committee.[24] The conviction of the Archbishop of Canterbury—that the committee was a good idea[25]—scotched any hopes Beresford may have had of rallying the prelates of the united church in opposition to a tithe investigation. As had occurred in the Commons, the Lords agreed to a committee without division.[26] Just as the select committee of the House of Commons had produced two reports—one pertinent, the other irrelevant to later developments—so too, the Lords' select committee presented two reports. In words too close to those of the Commons' committee to be accidental, the Lords' group recommended in its first report that the government be empowered to grant financial relief to clergymen whose tithes were not being paid, and that a complete extinction of tithes was the only viable solution to the tithe problem. Those who lost their tithes were to be compensated by grants of land.[27] These recommendations were presented to the house in time to be a constituent part of the government tithe program.[28] But, like its counterpart in the lower house, the second report of the select committee[29] was irrelevant to later proceedings, being presented to the House of Lords in late June, long after the ministry had made up its mind about the direction it would follow.[30]

The Whig ministry continued its skillful coordination of events in the two houses after the reports appeared. On 8 March 1832, the Marquis of Lansdowne in the Lords and E. G. Stanley in the Commons each asked leave to move resolutions on the tithe measure. Lansdowne's resolutions were moved in the same speech in which the first report of the Lords' select committee was presented to the house. His five resolutions echoed the conclusions and the vocabulary of the select committees on tithes. The first defined the problem: a widespread and systematic opposition to tithes existed and many Anglican clergymen were reduced to pecuniary distress. Second, therefore, the Lord Lieutenant was to be authorized to issue moneys from the consolidated fund to relieve their distress. The third resolution provided that the Lord Lieutenant's grants should be apportioned on a sliding scale: amounts of individual grants would decrease as clerical income increased. To effect repayment of these sums under the terms of this third resolution, the government was, under the fourth one, allowed to collect for itself the arrears of the year 1831. Finally, Lord Lansdowne moved that Irish welfare dictated a permanent change in the tithe system and that such a change must involve a "complete extinction" of tithe through commutating tithes for land. Except for the demurrer of seven peers who objected to the last resolution, Lansdowne's program passed the Lords without formal division.[31]

Things went less smoothly for Stanley in the Commons, although he was eventually successful. Because he was submitting to the Commons the outlines of the government's tithe plan he wished to have his resolutions considered by a committee of the whole house; but when he moved that the speaker leave the chair and that the house resolve itself into a committee, he encountered unexpected opposition from the defenders of the Church of Ireland. As a maneuvering point, these defenders objected that it was improper to move on tithes until the complete reports of the Commons' select committee had been presented. The government steamrollered such opposition by the ridiculously large margin of 314 to 31, but had to put off the resolutions themselves until a subsequent sitting.[32] On the thirteenth of March, Stanley was able to introduce five resolutions which were identical in substance to the ones Lansdowne introduced into the Lords; with the exception that in resolution number three, Stanley set a limit of £60,000 to be allocated by the Lord Lieutenant to relieve clergy distress. Resolution by resolution, the ministry encountered and overcame opposition.[33] By the end of March 1832 therefore, both houses of the government were on record as in favor of a radical reworking of the Irish tithe system and desirous of measures for the relief of Irish parochial clergymen.

Having received a mandate from both houses, the ministry proceeded almost at once to introduce a clergy relief bill into the Commons, this being already through its second reading less than a week after the resolutions were passed.[34] The government bill followed the lines of the Commons' resolutions in proposing that the £60,000 to be placed at the Lord Lieutenant's disposal be advanced to distressed clergymen. This money was to be allocated to those whose tithes for 1831 were in arrears. The amount advanced to an individual clergyman was set at two thirds of the tithes due him (as calculated on his average annual receipts from 1828 through 1830), with a limit of £500 per applicant. In theory it was possible to view this grant as a complicated form of loan from the consolidated fund; for whenever the government provided a grant to a clergyman, the rights to his tithe arrears for 1831 would come under its jurisdiction. Presumably the government could recoup the money it advanced by collecting the tithes from the Irish tenantry. Much of the bill, therefore, was given over to detailing the rights of the government to the tithe arrears.[35]

The measure passed easily through the House of Commons, receiving its third reading in a small House by a vote of 52 to 7.[36] It passed unmaimed in both the Commons and the Lords, probably because it offered something to both extremes in the two houses. The radicals, while disapproving of funds allocated to Church of Ireland clergymen, were content to let the measure pass because it was part of a larger program that promised major revisions in the Irish tithe structure. To defenders of the church its virtues were obvious. "I am anxious to declare that I regard it as a seasonable, necessary, and I may add just measure of relief to the sufferings of an unoffending, meritorious and most loyal class of his Majesty's subjects," the Archbishop of Armagh declared in the House of Lords.[37]

The bill, which became law 1 June 1832, as 2 William IV, c. 41, was palliative and little more. One of its flaws was that it made the government the virtual tithe-holder-general for a large portion of the Irish clergy. It brought the Dublin administration into even more direct conflict with the Irish tenantry than it faced already, for now government law officers prosecuted peasants for the arrears of 1831 which fell due to the Crown. The Dublin authorities even went to the ridiculous length of using the military to lay siege to farm houses and mud cottages in order to distrain livestock from peasants for the tithes due the government. The government finally collected £12,000 at a cost of £28,000.[38] Moreover, besides exacerbating tensions in the countryside, the act did not even possess the virtue of adequately providing for the Anglican clergy. The £60,000 simply was not enough money. By May 1833, almost £50,000 had already been advanced,[39] and even before that date, careful observers realized that the statute was unsuccessful as a clergy relief measure.

Whatever its defects, the tithe arrears act temporarily took the clergy distress issue from before the public eye, thus allowing the government to concentrate on a major tithe reform bill. But having won time, the ministry, and especially Lord Stanley, lost nerve. Whereas the recommendations of the select committee of both houses and the resolutions of both called for a total extinction of tithes in Ireland, Stanley's bill was merely an extension of Goulburn's tithe composition measures of the 1820s. In place of tithe extinction, Stanley offered only compulsory composition. Apparently Stanley was frightened of establishing the principle that church revenues or property could be alienated. He feared the prospect of secularizing church revenues, an idea favored not only by the radicals but by some of Stanley's Whig colleagues as well.[40] The tithe measure was much more favorable to the Church of Ireland than its representatives had expected, and was therefore infuriating to the Irish Catholic members, to the radicals, and to the liberal reformers.

In structure, Stanley's bill, which was introduced on 5 July 1832 and received the Royal assent on 16 August (as 2 and 3 William IV, c. 119), was a bipartite measure, involving, as mentioned, an extension of Goulburn's tithe statutes and a plan to force payment of tithes upon landlords rather than upon tenants. The bill repealed those sections of earlier tithe composition acts which made composition conditional upon the joint consent of the incumbent and the parishioners. In its place was substituted a compulsory composition procedure whereby the Lord Lieutenant could force tithe composition—and it was clear that he was expected to do so—in any area where voluntary composition had not been effected. Whereas in the past, tithe compositions had been limited to twenty-one years, all past and future compositions were to be perpetual, unless changed by reevaluations which were to be conducted every seventh year. The second major set of provisions in the bill was more radical. Anyone who had a lease of less than three years was no longer liable to direct tithe payments. Ultimately the bill provided that tithes would be paid only by the land-owners themselves. Of course the landowner could turn about and raise the tenants' rent by the amount of tithe he was forced to assume, but at least the annual friction between the proctor and small tenant would be greatly reduced.[41]

At this point it is logical to ask, how did the measure work in actual practice? Fortunately a tithe commissioner, W. Daly, has left a memo-randum of his activities. In areas where no tithe composition existed, the first step under the act as passed was for the Lord Lieutenant to appoint a tithe commissioner. This appointee went to the parish involved and re-quired the churchwardens to convene a special vestry to take the sense of the parish *re* an agreement with the incumbent, or the tithe owner, for tithe composition. During the interval between the requisition for and the actual holding of a vestry meeting, usually about five weeks, the tithe commissioner visited the tithe owners to inquire what tithes were payable in the area. The commissioner then obtained an ordinance survey map and began a detailed survey of tithes due on each individual piece of land. In this part of the investigation, the commissioner often asked the tithe owner to produce his books, receipts, and copies of special agreements with indi-vidual tithe payers. When the special vestry met later, the commissioner attended the meeting; and if the tithe owner and the vestry could not agree to a composition, the commissioner himself set it at an average for the preceding seven years. The commissioner had discretionary power to add as much as one-fifth to the average if it appeared that tithe agitation or other circumstances indicated that the figure was artificially low (he rarely did so). Certificates were then made out and lodged with the registrar of the diocese indicating how much tithe was payable, to whom and by whom. The vestry, the incumbent, and the tithe owner had the right to appeal the commissioner's decision to the Lord Lieutenant within a month of its being promulgated.[42] By such procedure, the Whig ministry hoped to solve the Irish tithe problem. As will be discussed later, the measure was inadequate and ineffective. For the moment, however, the ministry was able to claim that it had done its best to effect tithe reform.

On a statistical level, the act appeared to be quite a success. In chapter 2 it was indicated that the annual value of tithes in Ireland in early 1832 was about £700,000; and that by February 1832, somewhat more than £442,000 was covered by the tithe composition acts of the 1820s. Table 33 indicates that by 1834 over £644,000 was covered by tithe compo-sitions. The additional increment of almost £200,000 in compositions may be attributed to the 1832 tithe measures.

But before the government could turn its back on the Irish tithe problem,

TABLE 33
LAY-ECCLESIASTICAL BREAKDOWN OF TITHE COMPOSITIONS, 1834
(In pounds)

Diocese	Lay impropriators	Ecclesiastics	Total
Armagh	3,295	33,458	36,753
Clogher	1,592	20,185	21,777
Derry	480	28,878	29,359
Down	3,480	13,087	16,568
Connor	3,915	16,855	20,770
Dromore	186	9,829	10,015
Kilmore	1,624	8,042	9,667
Meath	18,865	26,365	45,230
Raphoe	378	11,563	11,942
Dublin	2,795	28,588	31,384
Kildare	2,798	13,006	15,804
Ferns	6,171	24,558	30,729
Leighlin	4,919	22,578	27,497
Ossory	—[a]	—[a]	31,529
Cashel	4,229	22,353	26,583
Emly	2,952	7,471	10,424
Cloyne	12,217	43,030	55,248
Cork & Ross	5,259	38,691	43,950
Killaloe	3,785	22,889	26,674
Kilfenora	270	1,991	2,261
Limerick	5,882	19,423	25,306
Ardfert & Aghadoe	5,204	13,915	19,120
Waterford	566	3,392	3,958
Lismore	7,963	17,155	25,119
Tuam	622	16,659	17,282
Ardagh	3,147	8,923	12,071
Clonfert & Kilmacduagh	0	8,805	8,805
Elphin	4,123	9,061	13,184
Killala	1,458	6,640	8,099
Achonry	2,804	4,549	7,354
Totals	110,993	501,953	644,476

[a] Not determined.
Source: SCRO, D.260/M/OI, no. 1718.

the importunate Irish clergy appeared once more. The £60,000 provided under the tithe act of 1832 was inadequate to relieve clergy distress, and since the peasants continued to refuse to pay their tithes, those for 1832 were now largely unpaid. Therefore, in August 1833 the ministry introduced and passed a measure which was at once an extension of the 1832 arrears act and a public admission of the failure of the earlier statute. The 1832 arrears act had provided £60,000 to be granted the clergy— the amount in theory being recoverable from the tithe-owing peasantry; the new measure provided one million pounds (and hence was commonly known as the "Million Act") to be loaned to clergymen who were in distress because their tithes had not been paid in 1831, 1832, or 1833 through the tithe agitation. The loan was to be repaid by the individual clergymen in annual installments over a period of five years. Significantly, the ministry repealed the provisions of the 1832 tithe act under which the government collected the tithe arrears for 1831; all processes and decrees for the recovery of tithe by the government were stopped immediately. In other words, the £60,000 that had been advanced to pay tithe arrears in 1832 was now made a gift to those who had refused to pay their tithes, since the government now owned the arrears but was precluded by statute from collecting them.[43]

As events later worked out, the million pounds under the 1833 arrears act became a gift to the clergy just as the £60,000 under the 1832 arrears act became a gift to the tenantry. In September 1835, the Treasury was authorized to delay or suspend at its discretion enforcement of loan repayments due for 1834. Then, in August 1836, the Treasury was further permitted to defer requiring repayment until April 1837, with extension of these powers until April 1838. Finally, in 1838 the whole sum was simply written off, having thus been turned into a grant to the tithe owners.[44]

STRUCTURAL REORGANIZATION: THE CHURCH TEMPORALITIES ACT

Illumination with a Vengeance

The tithe measures with which the Whig government dallied were anything but thoroughgoing and significant measures of reform. At best, the tithe statutes of 1832–33 gave the ministry parliamentary breathing room by producing the impression that something was being done about agrarian chaos in Ireland. But the Whigs were faced with a more important issue. This was the major question of the proper position of the Church of Ireland in the governmental structure of the United Kingdom. After a good deal of hesitation, the Whigs effected in 1833 a reform in the Church of Ireland which included a pruning of its administrative machinery and a reduction of some of its resources. The parliamentary reorganization of the Church of Ireland which was accomplished in the first half of 1833, was closely related to a flood of information on the issue produced by parliamentary committees and by individual parliamentary returns. Every important detail of the revenues, organization, and administration of the Church of Ireland was investigated and publicly reported. Some of these investigations, such as the reports of the select committees on tithes, were instruments of specific legislative reforms; while other pieces of information were generally illuminating but not tied to a specific act. Not all of the reports mentioned below appeared before the Church Temporalities Act of 1833 was passed and therefore should not be thought of as contributory to that act. But reforms of the Church of Ireland continued throughout the 1830s; those returns and reports that did not shape the 1833 church temporalities measure contributed to the general body of knowledge and climate of opinion that produced the later statutes. For the sake of convenience all the major reports are mentioned below.

The flood of information began with a report on parochial unions published in 1831. Ever since Roman Catholic emancipation, the leaders of the Church of Ireland had suspected that they would be investigated. Archbishop Beresford had been told late in 1829 that the government had considered extending the powers of the royal commission on English ecclesiastical law to Ireland, but that this idea had been rejected.[45] Sir John Newport, the Church of Ireland's nemesis for twenty years, was once more in action, and it was he who initiated the first important Irish ecclesiastical inquiry of the 1830s. On 4 March 1830, Newport presented a four-part motion which was seconded by Thomas Spring-Rice. This motion proposed, in the first place, that a commission selected from the privy council for Ireland be appointed to inquire into the state of parish unions in Ireland; to investigate their value and other circumstances; and to decide which of the unions should be dissolved. Second, the commission was to determine from consultation with the Irish archbishops and bishops exactly how much curates were paid in Ireland; and, third, was to investigate the standards by which faculties for the holding of pluralities would be determined. Fourth, Newport proposed that while this investigation was in progress, the Crown suspend appointment to dignities and benefices within its gift, provision being made for the maintenance of divine service and the performance of religious duties by temporary personnel. The Tory government, while recognizing the expediency of permitting some investigation into parochial unions in Ireland, did everything it could to draw the venom from Newport's proposal. Lord Francis Leveson-Gower, Chief Secretary for Ireland, adroitly granted the principle of Newport's motion, while yet shaping the commission's operation to the ministry's inclinations. The Chief Secretary proposed an amendment to Sir John's resolution, under which a commission was granted to investigate parochial unions and curates' salaries and to report on faculties; any suspension of the government's right to appoint bishops, dignitaries, and parochial clergy to livings would not be involved in its gift. Newport, pleased to have been granted the commission, readily accepted Leveson-Gower's amendments.[46]

Irish churchmen, particularly Archbishop Beresford, were dismayed at the prospect of an inquiry and had to be handled gently by the government to avoid making a public outcry. Henry Goulburn, Chancellor of the Exchequer and close correspondent of Beresford, explained to the Lord Primate that he had been happily surprised to find Sir John's motion far less objectionable than those which he usually made, and that he, as chancellor, and his cabinet colleagues thought it best to adopt the agreeable portions of the motion. Goulburn agreed with Beresford that the result of such an inquiry would probably be injurious to the church since it would display to the public the few cases of abuse which still remained in the Church of Ireland.[47] Fortunately for Beresford's nerves, the Chief Secretary was a model of tact and subtlety in arranging the details of the ecclesiastical inquiry. Leveson-Gower made it clear to Beresford that the commission would be packed so as to provide the church with all the protection possible. Two days after the Commons had voted the inquiry, the Chief Secretary asked Beresford himself to preside and suggested that he include the Bishop of Cloyne, John Brinkley; Dr. John Radcliffe, who earned his livelihood practicing Irish ecclesiastical law; and Sir William McMahon, Master of the Rolls for Ireland.[48] Each of these appointments was bound to soothe Beresford; and just to be on the safe side, Leveson-Gower asked Beresford in the same letter for suggestions of additional members. Simultaneously, so as to be absolutely certain of Beresford's wishes, Goulburn asked Archdeacon Singleton to put himself in communication with the archbishop.[49] The three men originally suggested by the Chief Secretary served on the commission, as did two men added at the Lord Primate's suggestion: Richard Mant, Bishop of Down and Connor; and William Conyngham, Lord Plunket. The Chief Secretary later suggested the addition of Vesey Fitzgerald and John Henry North,[50] but only the latter actually served on the commission. Also, the Chief Secretary later tried to add the Duke of Leinster and Lord Donoughmore but the archbishop objected.[51] Ultimately, the Marquis of Downshire and the Marquis of Ormond were named as the noble ornamentation to the commission. The working secretary upon whom the actual organization of the investigation fell, was John C. Erck, a higher civil servant in the Board of First Fruits and the editor of the *Irish Ecclesiastical Register*. Perhaps the single person most knowledgeable about the operation of the Church of Ireland, Erck was dependent upon the good will of Irish churchmen for his livelihood. Beresford could rest assured, therefore, that no overly-zealous civil servant would upset the public sensibilities.[52]

The commission did not distort or suppress evidence, but its report was a model of blandness.[53] Although its terms of reference included all of Ireland, the report, which was signed 18 April 1831 and printed for the Commons on 13 July 1831, dealt only with the Province of Armagh in which there were 110 unions involving 346 parishes. The report received scant notice and caused the churchmen little harm.

But if the Church of Ireland's leaders were able to take the critical edge off the parochial unions inquiry, they were unable to blunt the thrust of the investigations that were to follow. The fall of the Tory ministry in November 1830 meant that future commissions would be instituted by a government which, if not hostile to the church, was at least willing to approach it with a critical spirit. This did not mean that the personnel or style of the investigatory commissions would change much, but rather that the ministry itself would be more willing than its Tory predecessor to use the official data as the basis for church reform measures.

In August 1832 the liberal government appointed a royal commission to report on ecclesiastical revenue and patronage in Ireland. This commission issued four reports in the years 1833 through 1837, documenting in detail the church's position in Ireland. The information provided in these reports, while not the cause of the church reforms of the 1830s, provided the ammunition whereby reformers established the need for change. The reports were especially important after the passage of the 1833 Church Temporalities Act (which the Whig government had decided upon even before the commission's data began to be assembled), when many liberals were inclined to feel that enough reforming had been done. They were convincingly contradicted by the succeeding volumes of the royal commission on the Irish church.

With ironic courtesy, the ministry allowed the Church of Ireland to be its own prosecutor. Except for John Henry North, the members of Beresford's earlier parish union commission served on the royal commission: Archbishop Beresford (chairman); Lords Ormonde, Downshire, and Plunket; Bishops Mant and Brinkley; Sir William McMahon, Dr. John Radcliff, with John Erck serving as secretary. To these names was added a number of new ecclesiastical members: Richard Whately, Archbishop of Dublin; Charles Lindsay, Bishop of Kildare; Richard Ponsonby, Bishop of Derry; Thomas Elrington, Bishop of Ferns and Leighlin; Edward Stopford, Archdeacon of Armagh and Beresford's chief ecclesiastical administrator; Thomas Burgh, Dean of Cloyne; Thomas Lefanu, Dean of Emly; and Richard Boyle Bernard, Dean of Leighlin. Bartholomew Lloyd, Provost of Trinity College, Dublin; and Francis Sadleir, Senior Fellow of Trinity College, Dublin (both of the latter in holy orders), were likewise named. Also appointed were Charles Kendal Bushe, Chief Justice of the Irish King's Bench; John Doherty, Chief Justice of Common Pleas in Ireland; Sir Henry Meredyth, Judge of the Irish High Court of Admiralty; and Sir Thomas Staples. Each of the above men was sympathetic to the clerical viewpoint, but four men were appointed whose presence must have made Beresford uneasy. One of these was the Duke of Leinster, whose name on the parochial unions commission Beresford had successfully blocked, but who was now appointed by the Whig government. The membership of Lord Stanley, Chief Secretary for Ireland, cannot have greatly pleased Beresford since the Archbishop knew that the Chief Secretary had plans for church reform. Two of the Church of Ireland's long-time critics were also appointed: Sir Henry Parnell and Sir John Newport.[54] Actually, Beresford need not have worried; for, of the non-clerical members, only Sir William McMahon and Sir Henry Meredyth regularly attended the commission meetings.[55]

Edward Stopford, as Archbishop Beresford's administrative right arm, had once written his superior, suggesting that in rebuilding Armagh cathedral Beresford content himself with a modest building so as "not to excite envy at the wealth of *"the richest Church in the world."* [56] Whether Stopford was being ironic or serious about the Church of Ireland's wealth, the commissioners' first report, dated 1 March 1833, seemed to indicate that the estimate might well be correct. Unfortunately for those who wished to camouflage the Irish church's vast holdings, the initial report dealt solely with the revenues of the archbishops and bishops. To tally the episcopal incomes first may have been necessary for accounting reasons; but from a public relations viewpoint it was counter-productive, for the British public learned of the great episcopal incomes before the information on the often miniscule incomes of local ministers appeared. The fact that the Archbishop of Armagh had an annual income of more than £17,000 a year and held more than 100,000 acres of land, was to many observers an indication that the Church of Ireland was anything but underendowed. The commission's second report, dealing with corporate revenues of cathedral chapters and individual incomes of the dignitaries, was completed in mid-April 1834.[57] The third report, dealing with patronage and income of parochial benefices in the Provinces of Armagh and Tuam, was printed for the Commons in May 1836;[58] and the fourth report, its counterpart for the Provinces of Dublin and Cashel, was printed in July 1837.[59] When the commission's work was done, there was little worth knowing about the patronage and revenues of the Church of Ireland that was not available in public print.

One important set of data that had never been accurately determined, however, was the actual religious make-up of the Irish population. The government met this inadequacy by appointing a commission under Lord Brougham to investigate public and religious instruction in Ireland. Although ostensibly an education body, the commission was empowered to gather details about the Established Church, such as the number of resident ministers, the benefices with glebe houses and churches, and in addition, to determine the religious composition of the Irish population. Hence, the religious enumeration of Ireland by Brougham's commission was the first reliable religious census Ireland ever had. It was accomplished by the intelligent expedient of referring the census returns of 1831 back to the original enumerators, in order that they might indicate the religious persuasion of the persons on their tally. The results are given in table 34 for each Church of Ireland diocese.

When juxtaposed with the information from Archbishop Beresford's commission on ecclesiastical revenues, the religious census led naturally to the conclusion that the Church of Ireland was a very expensive bauble, enjoyed only by a minority of the people and paid for by the tithes of the Roman Catholic majority. This point was underscored by a return requested by the House of Commons in July 1835, which enumerated the individual parishes in which there were less than fifty members of the Established Church. The tabulation also indicated which of these parishes had less than forty, thirty, twenty and ten members.[60] Other Commons' returns determined the precise number of resident and non-resident incumbents in Ireland and dealt with the arrangement for curates.[61] Daniel O'Connell obtained returns on the number of churches in Ireland and their relations to the parish structure.[62] Still another set of Commons' results made information available on the number of benefices in which divine service had not been performed for at least three full years.[63] Later, in 1837, a select committee investigated the ecclesiastical courts in Ireland, although it came to no formal conclusions.[64]

The results of all these commissions, committees and returns—which were supplemented by reports keyed to determining the effectiveness of specific pieces of ecclesiastical legislation, such as the tithe statutes—was that the British parliament was as well informed about the operation of the Irish church as it was about any institution in the whole empire. Without a doubt this flow of information facilitated the task of those who wished to reform the Irish church, and inhibited the activities of those who wished to preserve it untouched. To the detriment of those defending the Church of Ireland, the massive reports and returns produced only a static photograph of the church as it existed in the 1830s but did not give any indication of the improvement the church had undergone in the preceding three decades. Of course, it is open to question whether even a record of miraculous improvement would have been enough; for, whatever its virtues, the Church of Ireland remained a rich, intricate organization whose purpose was to purvey a religious delicacy to a small minority of the Irish people.

The Politics of Liberal Church Reform

Just before the Church of Ireland faced the problem of parliamentary alteration of its administrative structure, her second highest officer, Archbishop Magee of Dublin, died on 18 August 1831. Speculation on a successor, as on any major episcopal appointment, was endemic. The Home Secretary told the Lord Lieutenant that the Prime Minister had decided upon the appointment of William Bissett, Bishop of Raphoe, as the new

TABLE 34
IRISH RELIGIOUS DISTRIBUTIONS, 1834

Diocese	Anglican	%	Roman Catholic	%	Presby-terian	%	Other Protestant Dissenters	%	Total
Province of Armagh									
Armagh	103,012	21	309,447	62	84,837	17	3,340	1	500,636
Clogher	104,359	26	260,241	65	34,623	9	26	–	399,249
Derry	50,350	14	196,614	54	118,339	32	1,738	–	367,041
Down	27,662	15	58,405	31	98,961	52	3,530	2	188,558
Connor	66,888	18	95,545	26	193,261	53	5,924	2	361,618
Dromore	41,737	22	76,275	41	69,264	37	933	–	188,209
Kilmore	46,879	16	240,593	81	8,736	3	97	–	296,305
Meath	25,626	6	377,562	93	672	–	199	–	404,059
Raphoe	33,507	16	145,385	70	28,914	14	24	–	207,830
Total	500,020	17	1,760,067	60	637,607	22	15,811	1	2,913,505
Province of Dublin									
Dublin	106,599	21	391,006	78	2,290	–	2,082	–	501,977
Kildare	13,907	10	120,056	89	9	–	384	–	134,356
Ferns	24,672	12	172,789	87	19	–	300	–	197,780
Leighlin	20,391	11	169,982	89	191	–	288	–	190,852
Ossory	12,361	6	209,848	94	8	–	108	–	222,325
Total	177,930	14	1,063,681	85	2,517	–	3,162	–	1,247,290
Province of Cashel									
Cashel	6,178	3	196,256	97	62	–	26	–	202,522
Emly	1,246	1	97,115	99	1	–	1	–	98,363
Cloyne	13,866	4	328,402	96	14	–	195	–	342,477
Cork	35,220	10	303,984	89	510	–	871	–	340,594
Ross	5,988	6	102,308	94	–	–	2	–	108,298
Killaloe	19,149	5	359,585	95	16	–	326	–	379,076
Kilfenora	235	1	36,166	99	4	–	–	–	36,405
Limerick	11,122	4	246,302	96	85	–	191	–	257,700
Ardfert & Aghadoe	7,529	2	297,131	98	–	–	27	–	304,687
Waterford	5,301	11	43,371	88	110	–	433	1	49,215
Lismore	5,970	3	209,720	97	164	–	382	–	216,236
Total	111,813	5	2,220,340	95	966	–	2,454	–	2,335,573
Province of Tuam									
Tuam	9,619	2	467,970	98	367	–	65	–	478,021
Ardagh	17,702	8	195,056	91	466	–	12	–	213,236
Clonfert	4,761	4	119,082	96	2	–	3	–	123,848
Kilmacduagh	656	1	45,476	99	–	–	–	–	46,132
Elphin	16,417	5	310,822	95	250	–	135	–	327,624
Killala	7,729	5	136,383	95	38	–	139	–	144,289
Achonry	5,417	5	108,835	95	143	–	27	–	114,422
Total	62,301	4	1,383,624	96	1,266	–	381	–	1,437,572
National Total	852,064	11	6,427,712	81	642,356	8	21,808	–	7,943,940

Source: First Report of the Commissioners of Public Instruction, Ireland, pp. 9–45 [45], H.C. 1835, xxxiii. The commissioners were unable to determine the religion of 18,951 persons included in the 1831 census. No indication is given of how Jews and nonreligious persons were tallied, if at all. Percentages are rounded to the nearest percentum. "Church Methodists" were tallied as Anglican.

archbishop,[65] but Lord Grey, the Prime Minister, had others in mind. He offered the Dublin archbishopric to Henry Bathurst, Bishop of Norwich. Fortunately for the Irish church, Bathurst turned down the offer; he was already eighty-seven years of age and incapable of performing his duties in Norwich. Grey then turned to Henry Brougham, Lord Chancellor, for advice. Brougham suggested that Thomas Arnold of Rugby or Richard Whately of Oriel College be appointed. Although he had never heard of Whately before Brougham's suggestion, Grey decided upon him, thus providing the Archbishopric of Dublin with one of its most interesting incumbents.[66]

Whately was brilliant, mildly eccentric, politically liberal, and religiously tolerant. The youngest of nine children of a Surrey vicar, he had been privately schooled and had studied under Copleston at Oriel. Obtaining his B.A. in 1808, he was elected to an Oriel fellowship in 1811, a post which he kept until 1822 when he resigned to be married and to take a benefice in Suffolk. In 1825, he returned to Oxford as principal of Saint Alban's Hall (his vice-principal was John Henry Newman), a post he resigned a year later upon becoming a tutor in Oriel. There he remained until promoted by Earl Grey to the Protestant Archbishopric of Dublin.[67] While he was attached to Oriel it became clear that Whately was one of the two or three foremost logicians of his time. It also became clear that he was his own man. He scandalized the provost by throwing stones at the college birds and by playing ducks and drakes with the undergraduates. Whately's dog was trained to climb trees in the Christ Church meadow and drop from overhanging branches into the Cherwell.[68] Whately once preached a sermon with one leg dangling out of the pulpit, and, when visited by Bishop Bathurst, received him with feet on the table.[69]

Despite his eccentricity, Whately was a fortunate appointment for the Church of Ireland, for, unlike those "inside" the church, he had the gift of perspective about the external events which faced the Irish church. He described large districts of Ireland as similar, for the purpose of the Established Church, to parts of China or Turkey, with no places of worship, no congregation, and no payment for the clergy. Whately held the charitable but unrealistic belief that Roman Catholic priests ought to be paid by the state, and entertained the idea that this money should come from the revenue of the Established Church.[70] Obviously Whately was not a man to die on the ecclesiastical barricades, fighting against the inevitable progress of ecclesiastical reforms. Because of the recency of his appointment, he was not a major influence on the Church Temporalities Act of 1833. He was, however, crucial to the adjustment by the church to that act and to the tithe reforms which followed. Unlike many of the Irish prelates, he realized that the church must make accommodations with the government.

Turning now to the specific political events which led to the passage of the Church Temporalities Act, we should realize that the Whig government was in many ways ill-equipped to carry a measure of ecclesiastical reform. At the one extreme of the cabinet was the Marquis of Anglesey, Lord Lieutenant of Ireland, who was unsympathetic to the church and believed that the final solution to Irish civil disorder was the disestablishment of the Church of Ireland. He suggested that the state should confiscate Church of Ireland revenues, pay ministers with the funds, and use any surplus to aid the poor.[71] At the other extreme was Lord Stanley, Chief Secretary for Ireland, who, while favoring some measure of reform, was sympathetic to the Established Church and wished to strengthen rather than weaken it. He was opposed to the appropriation of any of the church revenues for non-Anglican uses, and especially feared secularization of this income.[72] Earl Grey was in the difficult position of holding his cabinet together on the church reform issue, while at the same time making sure that Stanley, to whom the task of drafting a measure fell, would frame an effective piece of legislation. As events developed, Grey was successful in keeping his cabinet together until after the Church Temporalities Act and an amending measure were passed. Then in May 1834, the long-suppressed differences on the subject of church revenues broke into the open and the cabinet split. (The public split, however, was in the distant future.)

In January 1831, the cabinet had contemplated the uniting of the Bishoprics of Cork and Cloyne, but decided against this bit of ad hoc episcopal reform;[73] so it was not until the summer of 1832, that the cabinet seriously began planning an Irish ecclesiastical reform measure. The division within the Whig cabinet was as follows: Lords Russell, Althorp, and Durham favored a scheme whereby the surplus left after the reorganization of the church's finances would be devoted to the education of the Irish population, without distinction of creed; whereas, Lords Grey and Stanley and a majority of the rest of the cabinet opposed the secularization of church revenues.[74] Stanley, in drafting the bill, acted superbly; for he not only produced a measure that the entire cabinet could back but gently gained the acquiescence of Lord John Beresford to the government's scheme.

Because Archbishop Beresford was opposed to any parliamentary reform of the Church of Ireland, the approach to Beresford was a most delicate business. Stanley, therefore, first worked through an intermediary (whether self-appointed or not is hard to say), a Reverend Christopher Darby. Sometime in the first half of September 1832, Darby wrote the Lord Primate a "strictly confidential" letter in which he said that "I have reason to know that unless Lord Stanley can obtain the confidence of the Primate, and the Heads of the Irish Church, our cause is lost." Stanley, the writer correctly noted, was in an uncomfortable position with the "ultra-Whig" administration. The church would have been lost but for his efforts, and unless the Chief Secretary met with reciprocal kindness and confidence from the heads of the church, he would resign his position in the government.[75] Beresford acknowledged Darby's letter, and the channels of communication between bench and cabinet were thereby opened.[76]

Stanley now decided that the time had arrived to write directly to Beresford. He moved quickly and presented the archbishop with the need to suppress a number of Irish bishoprics. Reluctantly, Beresford agreed and in doing so, provided both a plan of reduction and an insight into his own reasoning. If sees had to be reduced, Beresford suggested uniting Clonfert, Dromore, Raphoe, Cloyne, and Kildare to neighboring dioceses. He was inclined to think that the Archbishoprics of Cashel and of Tuam should be united to other dioceses, although in a postscript he added that he was no longer sure of the advisability of having Tuam suppressed. In accepting the unpalatable demands of the Whig ministry—that at least seven Irish bishoprics be suppressed—Beresford was moving chiefly from a conviction that suppression was inevitable and that the only realistic goal he could pursue was a prevention of the secularization of the income of the suppressed bishoprics:

> I do not hesitate to say, that a reduction in the number of the Sees and the appropriation of their income to the augmentation of the poorer livings, and the relief of the parochial Clergy . . . has been long thought by me to be a measure less objectionable than any of the schemes that have been submitted to the public notice.[77]

Now that Beresford was on record as approving the suppression of several bishoprics, Stanley simultaneously flattered the archbishop and pressed for further concessions. He informed Beresford in his next letter that the archbishop's letter of the twenty-second had been passed on to the Prime Minister and that Lord Grey had written "it has raised him [Beresford] very much in my estimation, and I not only approve, but think it necessary that you should continue your confidential communication with him; and you may, if you think it would be of any advantage state to him that it is with my entire and heart concurrence that you do so." Stanley, having let Beresford know that the archbishop's words were receiving their due attention at Westminster then indicated that he might himself suggest to the cabinet some measure of financial rationalization of the church. For example, the Chief Secretary favored the abolition of the parish cess and its replacement with a graduated tax upon all ecclesiastical benefices. This tax would replace both the church cess and the first fruits and, after defraying the expenses presently covered by the church rates, would be used for building glebe houses, augmenting poor livings, and similar religious projects. Stanley suggested that "a portion" of the revenues of the suppressed bishoprics be, upon the demise of their incumbent, paid into this fund. Stanley also felt that sinecures were a public disgrace to the Irish church and should be suppressed. Additionally, he suggested that the Lord Lieutenant and Irish Privy Council should be given increased powers to dissolve parochial unions; some of the expense incurred in these divisions would be paid from a fund to be raised by the graduated tax on Irish livings.[78]

The leader of the Church of Ireland accepted Stanley's proposal with remarkably little hesitation. His only major objection was to the idea that "a portion" of the revenues of the suppressed bishopric go to the general ecclesiastical fund that was to be created from the graduated tax on benefices. Not only was he willing to accept an increase in the privy council's power to dissolve unions, but he suggested that a statute be framed to make it easier to enforce residence by the clergy.[79] Stanley replied almost immediately in reassuring terms, explaining to the archbishop that when he said "a portion" of the revenues of the suppressed sees should be allocated to the ecclesiastical fund, he assumed that all the rest would go for church purposes as well.[80]

In the latter part of October 1832, the Whig cabinet began hammering out the final details of the plan for Irish church reform, and it became necessary for Stanley to wring further concessions from Beresford. This he did with consummate ease. He raised once again the specter of secularization of church revenues and then quickly assured Beresford that he was on his side, and that he would not give "any support to a *measure which should go to alienate the property of the Church, or convert it to secular purposes*" (the italics are Stanley's). To calm the archbishop, he stated that the cabinet had agreed that the income of the suppressed bishoprics would go into a fund to be used to augment poor livings and to build glebe houses and churches. This fund would also be sustained by a system of graduated taxation from 5 to 15 percent on all livings above £200 a year. The money thus derived would be placed in the hands of a board to consist solely of Anglicans, two thirds of whom would be ex officio (and presumably clerical) members. But then came the barb. The cabinet's opinion, Stanley stated, was that two of the archbishoprics, namely, Cashel and Tuam, should each be reduced to bishoprics and that the total number of these be then reduced to twelve. This meant that eight sees would have to be suppressed altogether, whereas Beresford had previously agreed to only six or seven being suppressed.[81]

Bending gracefully, Beresford agreed with the weak proviso that he did not approve if it meant any individual was required to make financial sacrifice.[82] So confident was Stanley of his hold over Archbishop Beresford that he did not even wait to receive the archbishop's acquiescence before suggesting that Beresford start contacting other churchmen about the reforms. Stanley went so far as to suggest that the churchmen themselves might submit to the government their opinions on which bishoprics and sinecures should be abolished.[83] Although this courtesy must, at best, have seemed of questionable value to the archbishop, Beresford agreed to communicate confidentially with some of his colleagues.[84]

One of Beresford's confidants was William Howley, Archbishop of Canterbury, and Beresford outlined the ministry's proposals to him. Interestingly, he admitted to the English Lord Primate that "I believe it will be admitted that a consolidation of seven or eight of the Irish sees might be made without inconvenience in the administration of church affairs, were that alone to be taken into consideration." He considered illusory, however, the idea that, aside from providing funds for augmenting poor livings and building churches and glebes, any great good would come from the scheme. Nevertheless, he was willing to support the government and even considered anticipating the program by introducing some reform measure into the House of Lords.[85] The Archbishop of Canterbury, while agreeing with most of Beresford's views, effectively scotched Beresford's idea of the Church of Ireland's producing its own reform plan: "In my judgment it would be better to accede to Mr. Stanley's proposal, than to anticipate them by the offer of voluntary concessions." [86]

The Archbishop of Canterbury was one of the few members of the English or Irish bench who showed any sympathy with Beresford's position. Beresford's Irish colleagues were opposed to the abolition of the church cess and equally opposed to a taxation on benefices. Most Irish bishops believed Beresford to be too conciliatory in his relations with Stanley.[87] The archbishop was unable to keep his troops in line; in mid-January 1833, he had the embarrassing task of telling the Chief Secretary that a petition in opposition to church reform was circulating among the clergy of the other dioceses of Ireland.[88] Even less pleasant was a revolt of the Irish bishops against Beresford in March 1833 while the bill was before parliament.[89] In the face of this storm Beresford was grateful that the Archbishops of Cashel and Dublin had remained loyal to him as well as the Archbishop of Canterbury.[90]

Despite the potential division in the Irish church, Beresford continued to work with the Whig ministry. In mid-January, Stanley informed Beresford that while the principle of non-secularization of church revenues would be maintained, it might be necessary to reduce even further the number of Irish bishoprics.[91] In response to Beresford's anguished protest,[92] Stanley offered him a token concession, namely, that the tax on the clergy be assessed on the basis of their income after necessary religious expenses, such as curate salaries, had been deducted.[93] Beresford wanted a good deal more in financial concessions than that; but there was little more he could do than state that the removal of such resident gentlemen as the bishops from the countryside was, even from a secular point of view, bound to operate disadvantageously to the public.[94]

After all this, Lord Stanley still had to obtain one more concession from Beresford. In December, Stanley had agreed under pressure within the cabinet to an appropriation of some of the revenue arising from the sale of church lands.[95] This proposal was tied to the equally radical suggestion that a government board be given power to suspend appointment to benefices of the Crown's or church's gift, where no divine service had been held for three years prior to the passage of the church reform bill. The proceeds from livings thus suppressed would be given to ecclesiastical commissioners to augment benefices and build glebe houses and churches.[96] After having told Stanley in letter after letter that he was opposed to any secularization of ecclesiastical revenues, Beresford could not accept the proposal to do so. As for the plan to allow the government to suppress benefices, he viewed it as a preliminary step to the setting aside of the Establishment and its replacement by the Roman Catholic Church.[97] But it was now too late for Beresford to call a halt to the proceedings. He had negotiated with the government for too many months to be able to convincingly repudiate the government bill. It was introduced on the twelfth of February, and on that date Beresford's objections became merely academic.

Just before the church bill was introduced, Lord Stanley was transferred to the post of Secretary of State for War and the Colonies, and responsibility for guiding the bill's passage fell to Lord Althorp. The proposal (which in the tradition of Irish reform legislation was passed in tandem with a coercion measure) deserves close attention, for it determined the administrative outlines of the Church of Ireland for almost four decades.[98] For our purposes, the bill may be divided into six parts: the suppression of bishoprics and the arrangement of dioceses; abolition of the church cess; establishment of the Ecclesiastical Commissioners; revenue of the commissioners; use of the resulting income by the commissioners; and the Ecclesiastical Commissioners' powers regarding parochial arrangements. Turning first to the matter of bishoprics, the bill dealt with them as one would expect, given our knowledge of Beresford-Stanley exchanges. Upon their next voidance, the Archbishoprics of Tuam and Cashel were to be reduced to bishoprics. The archepiscopal jurisdiction of Tuam was to be transferred to the Archbishop of Armagh and that of Cashel to the Archbishop of Dublin. The bishops of Tuam and Cashel were to become suffragan bishops in no way different in rank or privilege from the other suffragans of their respective provinces. The bill, therefore, proposed to radically alter the centuries-old provincial structure of the Church of Ireland, replacing the ancient four provinces with two. In the case of Tuam, the change was to be doubly severe, because the Diocese of Ardagh, which had been customarily held in modern times with Tuam, was now to be disassociated from Tuam and to be united with Kilmore. In addition to the reduction of the archbishoprics as soon as they became vacant, ten unions of sees were to be effected. This would drastically reduce the number of bishops in the Irish church: Dromore to be united to Down and Connor; Raphoe to Derry; Clogher to Armagh; Elphin to Kilmore; Killala and Achonry to Tuam; Clonfert and Kilmacduagh to Killaloe and Kilfenora; Kildare to Dublin; Ossory to Ferns and Leighlin; Waterford and Lismore to Cashel and Emly; Cork and Ross to Cloyne. The bishops of the sees to which the suppressed dioceses were united were to assume all the episcopal responsibilities of the additional see but none of the revenues.

Next, the Whigs proposed to revoke the rights of churchwardens to levy the church cess. It will be recalled that the right of the Irish parishes to levy rates for secular purposes had been abolished in the preceding decade, so the church cess clauses reduced the legal taxation powers of the parishes to nil. Effectively, the bill proposed to abolish the Irish parish system as a religio-political network. Whereas in England, the parish continued to be both a civil and religious unit, the Church of Ireland parish was now solely a religious unit. As a legal unit, its continued existence was not threatened, but it no longer had any civil functions or the power to exact anything but voluntary contributions. With the benefit of hindsight we can see that this usually neglected feature of the Church Temporalities Bill was a portent of the future, for the disestablishment of the parish in 1833 was an analog to the disestablishment of the entire Church thirty-six years later.

Fortunately for the Church of Ireland, the Whigs were not merely bent on pruning the administration of the church, but were also intent on creating new mechanisms that would use the church's resources more efficiently. Therefore, a new body, the Ecclesiastical Commissioners for Ireland, was to be formed. This would consist of the Archbishop of Armagh, the Lord Chancellor of Ireland, the Lord Chief Justice of Ireland; and three of the archbishops and bishops of Ireland plus three lay members of the Church, all to be appointed by the Lord Lieutenant. This commission would be staffed by civil servants, including a secretary, treasurer, and other subordinate officers.

Now, if the Ecclesiastical Commissioners were to effect improvements in the Church of Ireland, they clearly had to have money at their disposal. Here the Church Temporalities Bill was most generous. The incomes of the suppressed bishoprics including all tithes, rents, and other emoluments were to be transferred to the Ecclesiastical Commissioners as soon as the sees became vacant. Further, the revenues of Armagh and of Derry, which greatly exceeded those of all other Irish dioceses, would be reduced. Although the original bill left the matter open, during the course of debate it was decided that when the See of Armagh became vacant, Beresford's successors should be required to pay annually £4,500 to the Ecclesiastical Commissioners. In the case of Derry, the incumbent, Richard Ponsonby, agreed to pay £4,160 per year beginning with the passage of the bill. A third source of income for the commissioners was to come from the remaining funds of the Board of First Fruits. This was a minor source of income, and with the bill's passage the practice of levying first fruits was to cease. More important was a fourth proposed source of income: the graduated tax upon ecclesiastical livings. In structure the proposed tax was similar to that of the modern income tax. Under the original scheme, those clergymen earning under £200 a year were exempted and those with livings worth £200 would be taxed at the rate of 5 percent a year, with the percentage rising to 15 percent on livings worth over £1,200 a year. Bishoprics were to be taxed at 5 percent for those under £4,000, graduating to 15 percent on those over £10,000.

The bill made complex provision for episcopal lands. These arrangements appear to the modern eye to be baroque in their complexity, but their principle was simple. Whereas it had previously been the custom for individual bishops to rent out their lands on any terms that suited themselves—subject only to the restriction on alienation of the land from the church—the new arrangements were to rationalize and standardize this part of the church's financial organization. Hence, in place of the chaotic system of uncontrolled rental practice, the bill proposed that the primary tenants of all archbishoprics and bishoprics (not merely of the suppressed sees) were to have the right to purchase in fee-simple the land which they rented, subject to annual perpetual rents as well as a purchase sum. The purchase price was to be set by the Ecclesiastical Commissioners, not by the prelates, and to be calculated according to the rental value of the property. When the former tenant paid for the property in perpetuity, the money was to go to the Ecclesiastical Commissioners. From this revenue and the perpetual annual rents, the commissioners were to pay the respective bishops a sum equal to the former annual rent plus the average renewal fine of the piece of ground. The surplus of the money received by the commissioners, over that paid to the bishops, was to be placed at the commissioners' discretion. Not only did the proposed arrangement promise a good deal of money for the coffers of the Ecclesiastical Commissioners, but the plan represented a basic change in church finance. No longer did all the prelates' money stem directly from lands, and no longer did the prelates completely control their own investments. Gradually, amateur investment by individual bishops was to be replaced by national, professional financial administration. Gradually the bishops, who had once been landed magnates, were to become salaried civil servants.

A final source of income proposed for the Ecclesiastical Commissioners involved their discretionary administrative jurisdiction. In the cases of beneficies under the patronage of the Crown, or of an archbishop, bishop, or other dignitary, or any ecclesiastical corporation (in other words, in all benefices except those under lay patronage) in which divine service had not been celebrated for three years prior to its becoming vacant, the commissioners were to have the right to suspend the appointment for as long as they thought necessary and to apply the revenues of the benefice to their own account. This provision was directed at the non-cures in the Irish church; and under its terms, all but the non-cures which were in the gift of laymen would be abolished. This abolition would be a gentle, rather than a wholesale, reform and would leave the present holder of the non-cure undisturbed.

Given all these sources of income—the suppressed bishoprics, the reduction of the revenues of Armagh and Derry, the remaining revenue of the Board of First Fruits, the tax on benefices, the surplus from the sale of land perpetuities to episcopal tenants, and the money from suspended benefices—how much annual income would the Ecclesiastical Commissioners receive? The proceeds of the income tax were projected at approximately £60,000 a year,[99] and the total annual income of the Ecclesiastical Commissioners predicted to be £150,000.[100] These estimates proved to be reasonably accurate. In 1834 the Ecclesiastical Commissioners actually received £68,728; in 1835, £168,027; and in 1836, £181,845. Their income did not remain permanently at such a high plateau; but nevertheless, by 1861, approximately three million pounds had passed into the commissioners' treasury.[101]

The demands against these sums were as follows: the commissioners were to continue the activities of the now-suppressed Board of First Fruits, namely, building and repairing churches purchasing glebe lands, constructing glebe houses, and augmenting small livings. Additionally, the commissioners were to assume the expenses that had previously been paid out of the parochial cess. These included the payment of the parish clerks and expenses involved in the performance of divine service. With the centralization of these financial matters, the Church of Ireland came increasingly to resemble a branch of the civil service.

Among the discretionary powers which the bill proposed to grant the Ecclesiastical Commissioners, was the right to divide united benefices and overly large individual parishes. To effect such a division, the commissioners would be required to have the approval of the Lord Lieutenant and the Irish Privy Council, plus the certified consent of the patron of the living. Glebe lands in such cases could also be divided. Obviously, it was probable here that the revenues of the old parish would be insufficient to support two new parish units unless augmented, or that an additional church or glebe house might be needed; so, the exercise of power to divide parishes implied in most cases an expenditure on the part of the Ecclesiastical Commissioners.

In concluding our discussion of the Whig church bill, one clause deserves special attention. This was clause 147, the notorious appropriations clause, which was apparently added to the bill as something of an afterthought. (The clause is not found in the first printing of the bill.)[102] It provided that if there was any surplus left to the Ecclesiastical Commissioners after they had carried out their responsibilities, the surplus was to "be applied to such purposes as Parliament shall hereafter appoint and direct." The meaning of this phrase was muddled. How would parliament know when a surplus existed? The commissioners had an almost limitless number of projects to spend the money on; additional churches, glebe houses, and glebe lands could always be purchased, thereby preventing any surplus from accruing. But meaningless or not, the phrase caused great consternation in the ranks of churchmen and of political conservatives, for it raised the possibility of Established Church funds being used for secular purposes, such as the education of Roman Catholic children.

The passage of the bill through parliament was too complicated and drawn out an affair to merit retelling in detail;[103] but the fate of the appropriation clause should be followed, for it was the bill's most inflammatory feature. The Whig majority in the House of Commons was large enough to allow it to pass any measure it wished, but the House of Lords was another matter. Almost certainly the Lords would remove clause 147 and perhaps would reject the entire bill if it included the offending statement. Stanley, who himself had never been at ease about the clause, convinced the Prime Minister that the surplus money was apt to be small and therefore the issue was not worth the trouble it was bound to cause the ministry. Having convinced Grey, Stanley canvassed the other members of the cabinet and obtained the support of the majority of his colleagues. Thereupon Grey went to see the king to propose dropping the clause. The king agreed, and on 21 June, Stanley was able to announce to the Commons the elimination of the clause. The radicals were outraged, because the nationalization of surplus church revenues had been the most radical principle in the bill. The O'Connellite M.P.'s felt betrayed and lost all interest in the measure now that it no longer held any hope of revenues beneficial to the general welfare of the Irish people.[104]

There was still some question as to how the Lords as a group would act. In essence, the question really was what position the Duke of Wellington would take; for without his support, no effort to confront the Commons had the slightest chance of success. The Duke was inclined at first to give battle. If he did fight and if he won, the ministry was determined to resign.[105] Wellington, however, realized that his party could not maintain for long a ministry of its own, and that the Whigs would in all probability return stronger than ever and bent on revenge. Hence, Wellington decided against confronting the government and carried enough of his colleagues with him to ensure passage of the bill with only minor amendments.

Poor Archbishop Beresford came through the process like a bedraggled spaniel. Having been enticed step by step onward by Lord Stanley, he had been betrayed at the last moment by the government's introduction of a bill more radical than he had envisaged. He was chaffed by his fellow bishops for having sold his principles to the great detriment of their church. "I am fully aware," he complained to his friend Henry Goulburn, "that the sanction which I am supposed to have given the Irish Church Bill, has exposed me to much misrepresentation on the part of those who found their accusation upon mere hearsay." Beresford weakly pleaded, "It is but fair, however, that should my name be quoted in the house as an advocate of the measure in all its parts, or even in many of its principal bearings, no greater share of responsibility should be attached to me than I can justly be said to have incurred." [106] However Beresford felt about the measure and his participation in its creation, the bill passed quickly into law, the Commons accepting the Lords' amendments and the royal assent being given 14 August 1833.

Except for the deletion of clause 147, the final statute did not differ significantly from the bill as first introduced into the Commons.[107] Whereas the original bill had provided that three prelates in addition to the Archbishop of Armagh be appointed Ecclesiastical Commissioners, the final statute specified four bishops and added the Archbishop of Dublin as well. Another minor concession to the churchmen was the raising of the exemption from the clerical income tax from £200 to £300. Concerning the Bishopric of Kildare, which was scheduled to be united to Dublin, one significant change was made during the bill's passage. The Deanery of Christ Church Cathedral, Dublin, which was customarily held *in commendam* with the Bishopric of Kildare, had not been mentioned in the original bill. In the final statute, the Deanery of Christ Church was separated from Kildare and united to the Deanery of Saint Patrick's Cathedral, Dublin; all the patronage of the Deanery of Christ Church was transferred to the Archbishop of Dublin. Another alteration in passage was the stiffening of the provision for non-cure benefices. The bill had provided that when a benefice, outside of lay patronage in which divine service had not been celebrated for three years prior to the voidance became vacant, that the commissioners had the right to suspend appointment altogether. In the final version, the commissioners were given power to suspend the benefice upon voidance, if divine service had not been performed three years previous to 1 February 1833. This meant that a non-cure holder had no chance to quickly perform religious service in order to perpetuate the office, and that the Ecclesiastical Commissioners could draw up a list in advance of benefices which they would suppress as soon as they fell vacant. From an administrative viewpoint, the most important addition to the bill was the provision that archdeacons in Ireland were to have the same powers and jurisdiction as archdeacons in England. Thus, the crucial middle rank of administrative officers between the bishop and the parochial clergy was greatly strengthened.

The Act's Importance

In a sense, the remainder of this chapter is chiefly about the influence of the Church Temporalities Act upon the Church of Ireland, but at this point a focused summary is appropriate. Administratively, the most visible change in the church was the reconstitution of its diocesan structure. This was no minor reform. The diocesan changes are indicated in table 35. The dates in parenthesis indicate the year in which the voidance of the minor bishopric occurred, thereby making its union with another diocese possible.

If the Church Temporalities Act greatly altered the top of the administrative pyramid at the bottom, the parish level, it had a significant impact as well. Whereas the Irish parish had been a statutory body with legal powers to tax the entire population for Anglican religious purposes, after passage of the act, it became solely a religious unit with no levying power whatsoever. In a sense therefore, the parish was disestablished.

It was, however, on the level of what would today be called "middle management" that the Church Temporalities Act wrought its greatest change in the administration of the church. Although certain middle level personnel were ignored by the act, most notably the rural deans and dignitaries of cathedral chapters (Christ Church, Dublin, and Saint Patrick's being the only ones affected by the measure), the archdeacons and the Ecclesiastical Commissioners received considerable attention. By granting Irish archdeacons the same powers and jurisdiction as their English counterparts, the act standardized a much-needed liaison between the bishops and the priests. This development was propitious, for with the reduction of the number of Irish bishoprics it became increasingly difficult for a bishop to keep in close personal touch with each parish. Most important, the Ecclesiastical Commissioners were introduced as a central body of middle level administrators to coordinate many church investments, to oversee parish operations, and to improve parochial efficiency. Thus, in contrast to the episcopal and the parochial levels, the administrative powers and personnel of middle level administrations were actually augmented.

Turning from the structural to the dynamic effects of the Church Temporalities Act, it is clear that the behavior of the church as an organization was changed. First, the act made the church's operation much more professional than it had been previously. For example, whereas before the

TABLE 35
IRISH DIOCESAN REORGANIZATION

Diocesan arrangement prior to 1833 Church Temporalities Act	*Irish Diocesan arrangements under 1833 Church Temporalities Act*
Archbishop of Armagh	Archbishop of Armagh (archdiocese) &
Bishop of Clogher	Clogher
Bishop of Derry	Bishop of Derry & Raphoe (1834)
Bishop of Down & Connor	Bishop of Down, Connor, & Dro-
Bishop of Dromore	more (1842)
Bishop of Kilmore	Bishop of Kilmore, Elphin (1841), &
Bishop of Meath	Ardagh (1839)
Bishop of Raphoe	Bishop of Meath
	Bishop of Tuam, Killala, & Achonry
Archbishop of Tuam (archdiocese) &	(1834)[a]
Ardagh	
Bishop of Clonfert & Kilmacduagh	Archbishop of Dublin (archdiocese) &
Bishop of Elphin	Kildare (1846)
Bishop of Killala & Achonry	Bishop of Cashel, Emly, Waterford, &
	Lismore (1833)[b]
Archbishop of Dublin	Bishop of Cloyne, Cork, & Ross
Bishop of Kildare	(1835)
Bishop of Ferns & Leighlin	Bishop of Ferns, Leighlin, & Ossory
Bishop of Ossory	(1835)
	Bishop of Killaloe, Kilfenora, Clon-
Archbishop of Cashel (archdiocese) &	fert, & Kilmacduagh (1834)
Emly	Bishop of Limerick, Ardfert & Agha-
Bishop of Cloyne	doe
Bishop of Cork & Ross	
Bishop of Killaloe & Kilfenora	
Bishop of Limerick, Ardfert & Agha-	
doe	
Bishop of Waterford & Lismore	

[a] Until 1839 Tuam remained an archdiocese with Ardagh, Killala, and Achonry attached. With the death of Archbishop Trench in that year, it ceased to be an archdiocese and Ardagh was separated.

[b] Until 1838 Cashel remained an archdiocese, with Emly, Waterford and Lismore attached. With the death of Archbishop Laurence in that year, it ceased to be an archdiocese.

Source: Powicke and Fryde, pp. 352–79.

act the Irish bishop had served the dual roles of bishop and landed magnate, under the statute his lands were gradually reduced and he became increasingly dependent upon central authorities for income. From the role of both bishop and magnate he was reduced gradually to becoming solely a bishop, which in any case was his primary professional obligation.

Similarly, the financial managements of the church became much more professional. No longer did individual bishops, men who were at best gifted amateurs and often less than gifted, completely determine the investment procedures for the episcopal lands.

A second characteristic of the newly reformed church in contrast to the church of the early nineteenth century, was an increasingly centralized organization. The Ecclesiastical Commissioners, for instance, enforced the same standards of residence and religious observance throughout the country. No longer could unobservant bishops allow the perpetuation of non-cures, for the commissioners abolished such livings whenever they fell vacant. Increased centralization was also the natural result of reshaping the ecclesiastical map from four provinces to two. The reduction of the bishoprics reinforced this trend. With centralization came a third new characteristic, namely, standardization. Ecclesiastical anomalies were greatly reduced. The archdiaconate, a rank which previously had carried no responsibilities in some dioceses and heavy duties in others, was established throughout the kingdom on a uniform basis.

It is undeniable that the impact of increased professionalization, centralization, and standardization upon the church as an organization was that it became considerably more efficient. Its financial resources were more intelligently managed and investments produced a greater yield than previously. Purely parasitic offices which produced emoluments and involved no responsibilities were greatly reduced. Moreover, the abolition of the parish cess, while financially painful, reduced considerably the friction at the local level between Anglican priests and churchwardens and the Roman Catholic majority. This is not to say that life under the Church Temporalities Act was idyllic for Irish churchmen. Far from it; for the policy of suppressing bishoprics and non-cure benefices only when they became vacant meant that the church was in a continual administrative flux for three decades after the passage of the statute. Nevertheless, when considered in purely administrative terms one must conclude that the Church Temporalities Act, far from being destructive of the Church of Ireland, contributed considerably to its well-being.

If we ask what the act meant to the church politically, the answer is less clear. By making the Church of Ireland a subject of parliamentary debate, the Whig ministry set a precedent that was potentially dangerous to the organization's survival (although undoubtedly an imperative as far as Irish social justice was concerned). Lord Stanley had been solicitous of the church's well-being and convinced that he was performing a service to the institution; there was no guarantee that the next set of reformers would be as sympathetic.

TITHES AGAIN

Renewed Agitation, 1833–1838

Having reorganized the Irish church structure and modified the Irish tithe system, the Whig politicians thought they had bought peace in Ireland. They could not have been more wrong, for it became clear that the Irish peasantry still nursed grievances. Although the process of compulsory tithe composition proceeded apace, the peasantry was far from satisfied. The most obvious grievance was that although the 1832 tithe act had reduced tithes and made their incidence more predictable through compulsory composition, tithes still existed. Moreover, the process of composition often caused friction where none had previously existed. The applotment process, for example, might aggravate the tithe payers; or the reluctance of the clergyman to accept a voluntary composition would force recourse to compulsory machinery and perhaps stimulate the peasants to new agitation.[108] These reasons, combined with economic factors, spurred the tenantry in many parts of Ireland to renewed tithe opposition. Three representative cases will illustrate the style and temper of this renewed opposition and the government response. The first is a series of events which took place in the Parishes of Glanntane and Kilshannick in County Cork. The rector of the parish was the Reverend John Lombard who had been there fifty-one years, nineteen years as curate and thirty-two years as rector. During this latter period, the Reverend Mr. Lombard claimed to have been on good terms with the populace, and in later evidence it was pointed out that until the year 1832 when £12 remained unpaid, no arrears had ever occurred. Because of those arrears in 1832, a horse was seized. When the sale of the horse was about to begin, a band of more than one hundred peasants collected and assaulted with stones and pistols the son of the rector and two men who were in the rector's employ. Four men were apprehended for this deed, and the aged rector, now in a state of dudgeon, began taking to law peasants only three and four pounds in arrears. Eventually seventy-one dragoons and twenty-one police officers were needed to seize twenty cows, three horses and one goat.[109] This case is useful for it points out, first, that even the "better" sort of resident rector of the Church of Ireland was vulnerable to agitation, and second, that the number of military and police needed to enforce tithe decrees made the wholesale support of the tithe system by the government prohibitively expensive.

A second case, from the parish of Newcastle in the county of Limerick indicates the violence latent in confrontations between the peasants and the tithe enforcers. The rector, the Reverend Thomas Locke, had not taken advantage of the Million Act and had arrears to collect. Thirty bailiffs, thirty rank and file dragoons, and a number of policemen were dispatched to the parish in April 1834 to distrain livestock of those in default. Having seized ten pigs, two carts, and two cows, the government party was confronted with a mob of angry locals. Stones began to fly and the peasants fired some shots. Thereupon the military and police replied with gunfire. One peasant was certainly killed and another was found lying "apparently dead." Nevertheless, arrears remained unpaid; and in May and June the troops had to be called out on several occasions to implement the seizure of livestock for arrears. Finally, Dublin Castle tired of the entire business (military and police having been employed for a total of seventy days on this matter) and refused to permit any further dispatch of troops or police, and the peasants were left the apparent victors.[110]

The third case, from County Armagh, illustrates the way in which tithe enforcement procedures could be stacked against the peasant. In early December 1834, a force was dispatched in response to the application of the Reverend James Blacker who wished assistance in destraining livestock for payment of tithe arrears. The force assembled, seized some animals, and was confronted by a band of angry peasants. A fight followed in which one countryman was killed and others wounded. Now, the interesting point about this case is that whenever a military force was dispatched to aid tithe enforcement, a local magistrate was required to be present to see that civil justice was done; and in this instance, the magistrate present was the Reverend James Blacker, the man who had brought the original complaint. In explanation, the Reverend Mr. Blacker claimed that the other two magistrates of the district had refused to take part.[111] Whatever the reasons, the resentment of the Irish peasant, when his prosecutor and his guarantor of justice were found to be one and the same person, was clearly justified.

Despite the tithe legislation, in the years from January 1833 through November 1837, writs and processes totaling 31,624 were issued by the courts of Ireland for the recovery of tithes. In the same period, 769 persons were committed to prison in consequence of proceedings connected with the recovery of tithes.[112]

If the obvious injustices of the Irish tithe system make most modern observers sympathetic with the plight of the peasantry, the plight of the parish clergy demands understanding as well. The Irish clergy were once again in general distress. As in the past, clergy relief societies were formed but they were just as inadequate as they had been earlier.[113] In desperation the clergy were encouraged to band together to underwrite their legal expenses and to proceed for recovery of their dues in civil courts. This mass recourse to civil justice was the final admission that the ecclesiastical courts had no effective jurisdiction over laymen. "I have advised them to adopt this course for many reasons," rationalized Archbishop Beresford, "and among others because I do not see why they are to be the only men in the country who are treated as outlaws and deprived of the protection it is professed the law holds out to all." [114]

The Whigs Collapse

The Whig ministry had passed, in 1832 and 1833, both tithe reform and church temporalities measures and had done so despite serious differences within the cabinet between the liberal reformers and the more conservative members of the cabinet. These differences were soon to scuttle the ministry. To understand the complex snarl of events impinging on the Church of Ireland in 1834 it is important not to view them as a logical narrative. Too many things were happening simultaneously, and the motivations of those involved were too diverse to allow linear depiction. One strand of events was the amending of the Church Temporalities Act of 1833. Although generally successful, it suffered from a handful of technical flaws. The act made it possible for the Ecclesiastical Commissioners to abolish non-cure benefices, but not to abolish sinecure benefices (admittedly few existed) or sinecure dignities. This latter category was an important omission for there were in Ireland ten deaneries, ten precentorships, five chancellorships, five treasurerships, forty-six prebends, and two vicar choralships without any cure of souls, parochial duties, or spiritual functions attached.[115] Another flaw in the 1833 act was that its passage had taken longer than expected, and therefore the Easter vestry cess had become due before enactment. A clause should have been inserted which would have given the Ecclesiastical Commissioners retroactive power to pay this cess even though it fell due before the bill was actually passed. For this and other purposes, the Ecclesiastical Commissioners needed an additional £100,000.[116] Another flaw in the original Church Temporalities Act was that it had not provided for the case in which the chief tenant of a bishop or archbishop did not wish to purchase his land in perpetuity, but in which a sub-tenant did wish to do so. These faults in the Church Temporalities Act the ministry proposed to mend in a Church Temporalities Amendment Bill introduced in the late spring of 1834. Despite one set of ministerial resignations in June and the creation of a totally new Whig ministry in July, the bill found its way onto the statute books without undue difficulty.[117]

The second important strand of events was not so simple. Late in 1833 the ministry began reconsidering tithe reform. In the ministry's analysis there were two options: either it could replace tithes with a land tax, or it could replace them with a Crown rent. The first alternative was tied to the idea of paying the Roman Catholic clergy from the collected taxes. The Catholic clergy, however, were determined not to share a land tax with the Protestant Church, and the ministry therefore abandoned that idea. By the end of December 1833, E. J. Littleton, the Chief Secretary for Ireland, was confidently expecting that a Crown rent would be imposed which would be redeemable by land or by money. The Crown rents not redeemed after five years' time would become a permanent charge upon the man who owned the ground. Hence, at the end of five years the tithe problem would largely have disappeared and the government would have to deal only with those who had not exercised their option.[118]

However convincing this plan was to the Chief Secretary, when the time came to prepare a bill, the Cabinet decided upon a land tax solution to the tithe problem.[119] Under a bill introduced in late February 1834, the cabinet proposed that, as of the first of November 1834, payments for tithe composition should be abolished. A land tax would be substituted, payable to the government and by the same person and in the same amount as in tithe compositions. The land tax would be under the jurisdiction of the Commissioners of His Majesty's Woods, Forests, Land, Revenues, Works and Buildings. The land tax revenues would be passed on to those to whom tithe and tithe compositions had previously been due. Provisions were detailed allowing those upon whom the new land tax fell to redeem the tax.[120]

As the tithe bill proceeded through the Commons under Littleton's charge, observers gained the impression that the ministry really did not know what it was doing. This impression was confirmed when Henry Ward, liberal M.P. for St. Albans, split the ministry by introducing a resolution about the Irish church on 27 May 1834. This resolution, a distillate of ten others Ward had previously intended to bring forth, raised the very questions that the Whig ministry had heretofore successfully avoided. Ward moved:

> That the Protestant Episcopal Establishment in Ireland exceeds the spiritual wants of the Protestant population; and that, it being the right of the State to regulate the distribution of Church property, in such manner as Parliament may determine, it is the opinion of this House, that the temporal possessions of the Church of Ireland as now established by law, ought to be reduced.[121]

Here was the central issue of all church reform: Was property in general, and church property in particular, untouchable? The church stalwarts viewed her property as inalienable and saw appropriation as dangerous. "The friends of the Church of England, and of every valuable and venerable institution," editorialized the conservative *Christian Observer,* "are beginning to awake to a sense of their common danger, well-knowing that the work of injustice and spoliation having commended its ravages on the Established Church will spread to everything else." [122] On a higher philosophic plane, the *Edinburgh Review* stated that either there was an essential difference between ecclesiastical and private property, or in sanctioning an appropriation of the former the existence of the latter came into jeopardy.[123]

Lord Althorp, the leader of the House of Commons, realized that the Whig ministry would not answer the church property question in unison, so when Ward moved his resolution, Althorp asked for an adjournment. The cabinet met, and it became clear that while a majority approved in principle the appropriation of ecclesiastical property, a minority adamantly opposed it. This minority had no choice but to resign, and the list is as follows: Lord Stanley, Secretary for the Colonies; Sir James Graham, First Lord of the Admiralty; the Duke of Richmond, Postmaster General; and the Earl of Ripon, Lord Privy Seal. They were replaced, respectively, by Thomas-Spring Rice, Lord Auckland, the Marquis of Conyngham (without a cabinet seat), and the Earl of Carlisle. The newly constituted cabinet then proposed to strike a bargain with Ward: the ministry, having decided to issue a commission to investigate the religious make-up of the Irish population and the adequacy of Irish popular educational institutions, asked Ward to withdraw his resolution. Since the commission had already been issued, Ward had nothing to gain by withdrawing his motion, and therefore refused. The ministry, while probably agreeing in principle with Ward's resolution, could not for obvious political reasons allow passage since it was a challenge to the government and therefore rejected it by 396 to 120 votes.[124]

The fuss over Ward's motion delayed the progress of the tithe bill, and before the cabinet could secure its passage another crisis intervened. The Irish coercion bill was in need of immediate renewal. Littleton, Chief Secretary, was hesitant to renew coercion, since it might well cause a reaction in Ireland that would impede passage of the tithe bill. Therefore, Littleton, with the agreement of Lord Wellesley, the Lord Lieutenant, enlisted Lord Brougham in opposition to renewal of the coercion act. Lord Wellesley decided that he could govern Ireland without the meeting clauses of the coercion act and so indicated to Francis Blackburne, the Irish Attorney General. Meanwhile Littleton had informed Lords Melbourne and Althorp of the secret decision made by Wellesley, and though not pleased with secrecy within the cabinet, Althorp approved Littleton's secret negotiations with O'Connell. Littleton and O'Connell agreed that if the meeting clauses of the coercion act were not renewed, O'Connell would not oppose the tithe bill. But then, a portion of the intrigue became known, namely, the secret opposition of Brougham, Wellesley, and Littleton to renewed coercion; the dealings with O'Connell still remained secret. In view of past public remarks by Lord Wellesley who favored maintaining the meeting clauses, the cabinet decided that the clauses should be renewed. This unwittingly broke Littleton's promise to O'Connell; and when on 30 June, Littleton was forced to inform O'Connell of the government's decision, O'Connell was outraged and laid bare the secret negotiations before the Commons. Littleton offered to resign and was dissuaded; but Lord Grey, feeling he had been betrayed, resigned and in early July 1834 Lord Melbourne was called upon to form a government.[125]

Two successive cabinets having split on Irish religious measures, the remaining part of the farce was the suffocation of Littleton's tithe bill. The measure emerged in early August after its recommitment to the Commons as a badly battered measure. In the process, the land tax system was abandoned and rent charges were substituted as the instrument for replacing tithe compositions; the right to all arrears was to be extinguished. Whatever the merits of the amended bill might have been, the Lords refused to pass the measure and when Sir Robert Peel formed his government in December 1834, he was faced with the same problems that had plagued the Whigs.[126]

The Liberals Frustrated, 1835–1837

Peel's ministry took office as a minority government. As he explained to Archbishop Beresford, the ministry was under the "absolute necessity of promising to parliament some immediate, practical solution" of the Irish tithe problem if it wished to stay in office.[127] Unlike the Whigs, however, the Tories planned to promote reform only with the cooperation of the church. Peel, therefore, asked Beresford to send the archbishop's chief administrative aide, Archdeacon Stopford, to London to help the government in drafting the tithe bill.[128] The actual preparation and presentation of the bill was left in the hands of Sir Henry Hardinge, Chief Secretary for Ireland. Hardinge's bill, presented on 20 March 1835, was, to the churchmen's surprise, little different from Littleton's bill of the previous year. Whereas the Whigs had proposed to abolish tithe compositions and reduce the tithe owner's revenue to an equivalent of 80 percent of the composition, the Tory bill offered the church only 75 percent. The Tories, however, omitted anything that could be interpreted as an appropriation clause.[129]

Hardinge's bill is more important for the chain of reaction it elicited than for its content. The liberals and radicals were outraged by the bill, for it seemed to consolidate the church's hold on its ecclesiastical property. While others were sputtering, Lord John Russell coolly appraised the situation and calculated how and when to make his move. Russell had for years been an advocate of the secularization of a portion of the Church of Ireland's revenues and had been one of the chief figures responsible for the split in Grey's cabinet on the appropriation issue. As an ambitious politician, Russell not only wished to work church reform but to oust the Tory government as well. Therefore, on 30 March 1835, when the Commons was in committee on Hardinge's bill, Russell electrified the house by moving the following resolution:

> That the house resolve itself into a committee of the whole house to consider the temporalities of the Church of Ireland and that it is the opinion of this committee that any surplus which may remain after fully providing for the spiritual instruction of the members of the Established Church in Ireland, ought to be applied locally to the general education of all classes of Christians.[130]

Here again was the heart issue of all Irish church reform: the question of appropriation. Debate raged for days, and only on the seventh of April was it possible to bring the resolution to a vote. The decision was 285 in favor of Russell's resolution, 258 opposed.[131] In a single brilliant maneuver Russell had destroyed the Tory ministry (it resigned soon thereafter) and had guaranteed that the new liberal ministry would have to embody an appropriation clause in any tithe reform bill it presented. Simultaneously, Russell effected a minor revolution in English party politics, for Lord Stanley and his followers, the old-line Whigs, voted against the resolution and found themselves in the Tory camp.

It was, of course, one thing to topple the Tories and quite another to pass a tithe bill embodying the principle of appropriation. Lord Melbourne's new government immediately set about shaping an Irish tithe measure. Lord Mulgrave was named Lord Lieutenant, and Lord Morpeth Chief Secretary. The liberal ministry, before framing its church reform measure, made sure it had control of the Commons. In particular, it needed the Irish members on its side: for any tithe bill could not be convincing if it gained the disapproval of both the Anglican Church and the O'Connellites. O'Connell's support was obtained in what is usually known as the "Lichfield House Compact," under which O'Connell undertook not to press for disestablishment of the church, repeal of the Union, or parliamentary reform in return for the reduction of tithes (including an appropriation clause), municipal reform in Ireland, and the appointment of men of popular sympathies to Irish public office posts.[132]

Having at least the tacit support of the Irish nationalist members, the ministry brought forward its tithe bill on 6 July 1835.[133] The bill as presented by Lord Morpeth was everything the church had feared. Where tithes were concerned, Morpeth's bill followed the precedents of Littleton's and Hardinge's bills of earlier sessions. Tithes and tithe composition were to be abolished and replaced by Crown land rents, payable by the owner and to be collected by the Commissioners of Land Revenues. As in earlier bills, the Crown rents were to be set at rates lower than the tithes and tithe composition previously payable—in this case 70 percent of the former amounts. After paying a small percentage for collection fees, the tithe owners would therefore receive slightly less than seven tenths of the tithe compositions due to them. Although these provisions, in theory, would have reduced the income of the clergy of the Established Church, the clergy were at that time having such difficulty collecting tithes that, had this bill passed and the peasantry accepted it, the clergy's actual income probably would have risen.

The tithe clauses somewhat irritated but did not appall the Tories. It was Morpeth's church reform clauses that left them aghast. Morpeth proposed to abolish, upon their becoming vacant, all benefices in Ireland in which there were fewer than fifty members of the Established Church. Such livings were to come under the care of neighboring pastors and their glebe lands, houses, and all sources of income were to be sequestered. These monies were to be accumulated by the Ecclesiastical Commissioners in a separate reserve fund. Further, when a benefice with more than fifty souls and more than £300 annual income became vacant, the Lord Lieutenant in Council was, on the advice of the Ecclesiastical Commissioners, to reduce the income to a point at which he felt the spiritual duties should be commensurate with income. The only limit was that they could not reduce the income to below £300 a year. Since 860 of Ireland's approximately 2400 benefices had fewer than fifty souls,[134] this meant that more than one third of the parishes in Ireland would be ripe for abolition, that a goodly portion of the remainder would be eligible for reduction under the £300 clause, and that all incumbents would—in theory at least—have their income reduced by the amount the Crown rent fell short of the former tithe compositions. Scant wonder churchmen panicked.

The surplus taken from the suppressed benefices was to be applied to the moral and religious education of the Irish people, without distinction of religious persuasion. This was an almost exact statement of the principle upon which the Irish national system of education, founded by Lord Stanley in 1831, was based. The bill of appropriation was, therefore, doubly bitter to most churchmen, for it involved not only appropriation of the church's revenues but allocation of those revenues to a school system of which a majority of Anglican clergymen thoroughly disapproved.

While most conservatives raged, Sir Robert Peel remained cool and analytic. To his mind the problem with Morpeth's bill was that it was really two bills, a tithe reform measure and a church reform measure. In general he approved of the former and strongly disapproved of the latter. His plan, therefore, was to convince the Commons to divide the bill into its two segments and proceed individually with each.[135] After several days of acrimonious debate filled with statistics of clerical anomalies and an inordinate number of long speeches, Peel's amendment was turned down by a vote of

319 to 282.[136] The same coalition of liberals, radicals, and Irish members that killed Peel's amendment pushed Morpeth's bill through the Commons, granting only token amendments.

The House of Lords received the bill in mid-August. Although willing to accept most of the tithe reform provisions, the majority of the Lords refused to countenance appropriation of church revenues for secular purposes. Faced with the Lords' rejection of the appropriation clauses, the cabinet had either to press the issue and somehow override the upper house, or to drop the bill entirely. The ministry decided on the latter course and Morpeth's imaginative measure was extinguished. Significantly, in blocking Morpeth's bill, the House of Lords entered into a relationship with the Church of Ireland that was to continue until disestablishment. Henceforth, Irish churchmen would trust their defense not to political parties in the Commons, but to the corporate strength of the House of Lords, which, Tory or old-line Whig almost to a man, could be depended upon to defend the Irish religious establishment.

Frustrated by the Lords in 1835, the liberals tried again in 1836. The invective on both sides was as sharp as ever; but this time it seemed as if the liberals had read the scenario already and were less than totally enthusiastic about a course of action which they knew could only end by their again being stymied by the House of Lords. Morpeth's second church bill was, in its tithe features, almost identical to that of 1835. In the church reform segments, however, it was somewhat milder than its predecessor, although maintaining the principle of appropriation of church surpluses for educational purposes. A new body, the Ecclesiastical Committee of the Privy Council of Ireland, was proposed. Essentially it was to be a sub-committee of the privy council that would exercise the ecclesiastical functions of the Lord Lieutenant in Council without diminishing the powers of the Ecclesiastical Commissioners. In contrast to its predecessor, Morpeth's 1836 bill did not flatly state that, in the normal case, parishes with less than fifty souls should be abolished. Rather, it stated that benefices (in contradistinction to parishes) with less than fifty souls should not yield the incumbent more than £100 annually. A salary schedule, proportional to the number of parishioners was presented. (For example, benefices with 50 to 500 parishioners were to yield £100 to £200 a year, and for those with 500 to 1,000 souls, a salary range of £200 to £300 was prescribed). Whereas Morpeth's earlier bill had sought to jar loose surplus revenue chiefly through suppressing small parishes, this bill was intended to do so by regimentation and limitation of all clergy salaries.[137]

Whatever the method, the principle was the same: Church of Ireland revenue was to be appropriated and used for secular purposes. This principle being anathema to the peers, they efficiently eviscerated the bill which the Commons sent them. As had occurred in the previous session, the tithe portions of the bill were only slightly modified. Clergy income was to be reduced to 75 (not 70) percent of tithe compositions as the Commons had specified; but the clauses that would have led to a surplus available for appropriation (the limitation of clergy income clauses) were totally removed. Indeed, the bill, as it returned to the Commons from the Lords was only half the size of the original, so vigorous had their lordships been with the amending scissors.[138] Knowing it was beaten, the liberal ministry dropped the matter. Only slight consolation could be found in the passage of a non-controversial statute to facilitate the purchase of episcopal perpetuities by episcopal tenants.[139]

The principle of appropriation of church revenues, to which the liberals were wedded, was increasingly a liability. The liberals had the choice of either abandoning this widely proclaimed principle or failing to effect any measure of tithe reform. Still, the liberals did not fully realize their dilemma, and in 1837 Lord Morpeth trotted out yet another tithe reform appropriation bill. Predictably, the tithe provision differed only slightly from those of his two preceding bills. The appropriation sections, however, were gentler than in the past. Although the Ecclesiastical Commissioners and Lord Lieutenant in council were to have the power to reduce clerical income, these powers were much less extensive as proposed in this bill than in Morpeth's two previous efforts. The principle of appropriation was, instead, embodied in the provision of taxing all benefices, dignities and bishoprics which would become vacant after the bill's passage, at a rate of 10 percent of their annual income. This money was then to be applied to the education of the Irish people, irrespective of their religious persuasion.[140] If the bill had passed the Commons, another frustration by the Lords was inevitable; but this time the confrontation was avoided, because the king died before the bill passed, and a dissolution followed.

Russell's Solution

Gradually the liberals realized that it was useless to adhere to the principle of appropriation if it prevented their accomplishing any practical change in the tithe system. After the general election they returned chastened, with a considerably diminished majority. The cabinet was now convinced that tithe reform was necessary even if appropriation had to be jettisoned, and Lord John Russell, ever quick on his political feet, agreed. Having been supposedly the implacable foe of the Church of Ireland, Russell now attempted to present himself as a moderate religious reformer. Part of his new image involved contacting the church leaders before introducing any legislative measure.

Accordingly, in the middle of March he approached the Archbishop of Canterbury with an outline of some tithe proposals which he wished forwarded to Archbishop Beresford.[141] Beresford refused to comment.[142] Simultaneously Russell approached Frederick Shaw, M.P. for the University of Dublin, and confidant of the Irish prelates. At the end of an evening's sitting in mid-March, Russell invited Shaw into his private room and explained that the ministry was anxious to proceed with a tithe bill, but it was also anxious to know if the bill would be favorably received by the friends of the Church of Ireland. Russell gave Shaw copies of two documents on tithes. After consulting Sir Robert Peel, Shaw returned the documents to Russell with his refusal to comment. Having taken this apparently honourable course, Shaw proceeded to inform Archbishop Beresford of the substance of the documents (which Russell may have wished him to do anyway), at the same time enjoining Beresford to secrecy. Shaw's analysis of Russell's maneuvering was that he might well be trying to ensnare the church leaders by showing them certain proposals, for the ministry would then be able to say either that the church had rejected these, or that the church had assented to the principle of certain ones. In either case, the ministry's hand against the church would have been strengthened.[143] Beresford was not surprised, therefore, when he heard from his regular parliamentary informant, Henry Goulburn, that Russell was intending to move a set of resolutions in the Commons at the end of April covering the government's intentions on Irish tithes.[144] The most important of the resolutions are summarized below. Russell moved that:

1. Tithe composition in Ireland should be commuted into a rent charge payable by the owner of the land, and that the charge should be seven-tenths of the existing tithe or tithe composition. (This represented a 30 percent drop, at least in theory, in income of the parochial clergymen.)

2. At the "expiration of existing interests," the seven-tenths rent charge was to be "purchased" by the state at the rate of sixteen years' purchase of the original tithe composition (i.e. £1,600 for each £70 of tithe rent charge, equalling twenty-two and a half years purchase of the 70 percent charge).

3. When the state extinguished rent charges (which themselves replaced tithes and tithe compositions) this sixteen years' purchase money was to be paid to the Ecclesiastical Commissioners for Ireland. The Ecclesiastical Commissioners would be free to invest the purchase money as they pleased, either in land or stocks, and presumably would return the interest on the investment to the incumbent from whose tithe the principal of the investment originated. Hence, tithes would disappear and the clergy's income would come from investments under full control of the Ecclesiastical Commissioners.

4. The state, having purchased the rent charge, would have the right to continue to levy that charge (or tax), but would use the resulting revenues to underwrite education and to defray certain local expenses

previously defrayed by the Consolidated Fund. Any surplus was to be added to this fund.

5. Further provision should be made to regulate ecclesiastical duties and better distribute ecclesiastical revenues in Ireland.[145]

Now, behind Russell's nearly opaque phraseology, the alert contemporary observer could detect that a retreat from the principle of appropriation was being carried out. Henry Goulburn correctly noted that between resolution number five, as enumerated above, and the paying of rent charges into the Consolidated Fund, there was no necessary connection at all. No money was to be taken from the church, so no question of appropriation was involved.[146] What Russell was actually proposing was a two-fold scheme: first, that the money Irish peasants paid in tithes be converted into a tax (and simultaneously reduced) that would be paid to the government for education and other local benefits; and, second, that the parochial clergy of the Church of Ireland be endowed by tax revenues raised throughout the British Isles which would be paid to the Ecclesiastical Commissioners, and would yield roughly 70 percent of their former tithe revenues.

Hidden behind hostile rhetoric was an extraordinarily generous plan. Unhappily, Archbishop Beresford could only see the 30 percent reduction in clergy incomes and not the freedom the new state endowments would provide. Beresford responded to Russell's resolutions by placing them before a large meeting of his clergy where the plan was unanimously declared utterly destructive to their interest and to the stability of the church. A committee was appointed to prepare a petition against it. Beresford argued that Russell really was appropriating church money since he was not giving the clergy full value for their tithes by replacing them for a rent charge or for purchase. Somehow Beresford missed the fact that although the income of the clergy was reduced, there was no usage of religious money for secular purposes. Indeed, Beresford even opposed the provision for state purchase of the rent charge (actually a form of church endowment). He wanted this to remain payable to the clergy,[147] although it would seem obvious that it would thereby be identified as a Protestant tax and opposed by the peasantry.

If Beresford did not understand the government's resolutions he might perhaps be excused, for finance was never his strong suit, but his chief administrator, Archdeacon Stopford, cannot be excused so easily. Stopford was long experienced in church finance and had worked out for himself an elaborate calculation of the church's financial position. But instead of explaining to Beresford that no appropriation was involved, Stopford ranted about the need to baffle the dishonest scheme of the government ministers and about the need to make a resolute stand against diverting the rent charges from the church.[148] The church's leaders, therefore, had misunderstood what was actually being proposed, and their actions in the weeks to follow had little touch with reality.

Mild as Russell's resolutions were, the conservatives, to whom parliamentary momentum was gradually swinging, came surprisingly close to defeating them. On the fourteenth of May, Russell moved that the Commons resolve itself into a committee to consider his resolutions. Sir Thomas Acland countered with a resolution that the Commons rescind those of 7 and 8 April 1835, which had affirmed the principle of appropriation and had postulated that no tithe reform could be achieved without such appropriation.[149] This was politics with a vengeance. The Commons knew that Russell was retreating from his original adherence to appropriation, and the conservatives wished to make this retreat as obvious and humiliating as possible. Debate continued on Acland's motion for two nights, and the ministry was finally able to defeat it by the uncomfortably narrow margin of 317 to 298.[150] Russell, stunned by this close call, announced three days later that his ten resolutions would be replaced by a single one, merely affirming that the tithes and the compositions should be replaced by a rent charge.[151] In point of fact, he never introduced the resolution but allowed the bill to be presented without prelude.

In contrast to the tithe bills of preceding sessions, Russell's bill passed relatively smoothly through both houses because it involved no major controversial principle. It received the royal assent on 15 August 1838.[152] Under Russell's measure tithes and tithe compositions were abolished and replaced by a rent charge equal to 75 percent of the nominal value of the tithes. Responsibility for payment of this fee rested with the landlord, not the tenant. Further, arrears of tithes on the part of the peasant were erased from the books. In a parallel move beneficial to the clergy, the £640,000 lent them under the Million Act was converted into an outright grant and the £360,000 still available under its provision was allocated to clergymen to whom the peasants owed arrears. Moreover, any clergyman who still owed money that had been loaned by the now defunct Board of First Fruits had his debt reduced so that he only had to pay £3 for every £100 that remained unpaid.

The passage of Russell's tithe act was a double irony. On one count, its content was ironic when contrasted with that of his original ten resolutions, for these resolutions had actually offered a more generous solution to the church than was embodied in the final act. Originally, Russell had proposed to endow the clergy of the Church of Ireland by compensating the church with large amounts of capital in exchange for extinguishing her right to levy tithes. This original solution would have left the church much more secure financially and no longer directly dependent upon agricultural taxation for its parochial revenues. Strangely, the leaders of the church did not perceive the advantages of Russell's original plan, and in the face of strong conservative opposition, Russell simply retreated to replacement of tithes with land rents, a much less secure form of income. The second irony is that Russell's bill, coming as it did after three years of embittered debate about Irish tithes, contained little, if anything, that Sir Robert Peel would not have approved of in 1835. All the rhetoric, invective and frustration of the intervening years had been in vain.

Undeniably, the 1838 tithe act was a success. By making the rent charges (which replaced tithes) a primary expense to the landowners, one of the most objectionable features of the old system—that it fell chiefly upon small tenants—was eliminated. Although landlords undoubtedly forced a portion of the burden of the new rent charge downward onto the peasantry (through raising rents), the final incidence fell at least partially—and probably mostly—upon the landlord rather than the tenant. Admittedly, the new rent charges were simply the old tithes renamed and reduced, but the former were never to have the visibility or inflammatory power of the tithes. Especially fortunate was the extinction of the tithe proctors, since landlords now paid the tithes directly. Therefore, because the new arrangements were less irritating to the Irish peasantry and because the landlords were more apt to pay the rent charges than the peasants had been to pay the tithes, the Church of Ireland benefited.

And why then had the churchmen, especially Archbishop Beresford, been so opposed to tithe reform? There is no simple answer. Partially, one might conjecture, because they had been under pressure so long that they could not view any reform measure with objective eyes. Partially, too, one might add, because they constantly looked at the wrong set of financial calculations. Beresford and his colleagues focused their attention upon the reduction of the nominal income of the clergy by 25 percent. At no time did they calculate precisely what the change would mean in actual incomes; they continually refused to admit that only a handful of Irish clergymen ever received the complete nominal value of their tithes; and that in many instances, the new arrangements, while reducing the theoretical value of clergy incomes, would raise the actual income. A third reason the clerics opposed tithe reform was simply that in principle, they opposed any reduction—theoretical or actual—in the Irish religious structure. Always in the back of their minds was the fear that once parliament began pruning the Irish church, it would continue to do so until the church was weakened or destroyed.

Perhaps the only losers in the 1838 tithe settlement were the Irish landlords. By having to incorporate the church tithes in their rents they came to be the unenviable focus of peasant resentment. Previously, the church had served with the landlords as a focus of peasant discontent. Now, to its own benefit and the landlords' discomfort, the church ceased to be a major peasant grievance (although still a complaint of a less pressing order). But if their landed parishioners were perhaps badly served by the legislation, the clergymen of the Church of Ireland could breathe a sigh of relief. They had weathered eight years of criticism, attack, reform, and reorganization. If weaker politically in 1838 than it had been in 1830, the church itself was more efficiently organized and more reliably financed.

THE LATER YEARS OF THE ESTABLISHMENT

The Ecclesiastical Commissioners at Work

The work of the Ecclesiastical Commissioners, like that of most middle-level managers, was undramatic but essential. Their duties were threefold. First, they were money managers. Their revenue came from the suppressed bishoprics, from suppressed benefices, from the tax on the Bishopric of Derry (and eventually the Archbishopric of Armagh), from the sale of episcopal perpetuities, and from the income tax on benefices valued at £300 or more annually. The money was collected by the commissioners and eventually disbursed. Any surplus of income over expenditure was invested according to the commissioners' best judgment. A second managerial responsibility of the commissioners was that, collectively, they acted much like today's purchasing agent. Within a given set of revenues, the commissioners created an order of priorities for the numerous demands on their resources. These calls ranged from requests for stoves to heat drafty churches to petitions for construction of new church buildings. Third, by acting both as money managers and as purchasing agents, the commissioners implicitly served to standardize practice and facilities in the Church of Ireland. In some cases, such as the suppression of sinecure benefices, the commissioners acted openly and explicitly as arbitrators of ecclesiastical standards. In other cases, such as when they decided to improve a small rural church, or when they refused to enlarge an opulent Dublin parish church, their standardizing influence was less obvious but real nonetheless.

Two paradoxes characterized the operations and behavior of the Ecclesiastical Commissioners. The first was that although the commissioners did not consider that they and their staff comprised a government department,[153] they possessed most of the characteristics of one. The commission as a body was a creation of parliament. Its powers were established and limited by statute law. Its membership was defined by statute. Its staff came under Treasury scrutiny. Annual reports had to be made to the Lord Lieutenant. And certain of its actions, such as suppressing benefices, had to receive viceregal sanction. Thus, the Ecclesiastical Commissioners as a corporate group differed only slightly from the "official" branches of the Irish civil service. But unlike most of the employees of the civil service the majority of the commissioners were essentially amateurs, serving without pay (this characteristic the Ecclesiastical Commissioners shared with the Commissioners of National Education in Ireland). And, although under the jurisdiction of statute law and under the eye of the Treasury and the Lord Lieutenant, the Ecclesiastical Commissioners experienced much less interference in their day-to-day affairs than most government departments.

The second paradox associated with the Ecclesiastical Commissioners is that, through their behavior, they reversed the connotations of the word "Erastian." In the eighteenth century the Irish church had been undeniably Erastian, and in that period the relationship to the state had implied corruption, incompetence, and inefficiency in the church's administration. Undeniably, the creation of the Ecclesiastical Commissioners made the Church of Ireland more Erastian than ever, for the church's middle level administration was now largely in the hands of a quasi-government board which operated according to the procedure and standards of the British civil service. That civil service, if not yet given completely to utilitarian calculations of the most efficient mode of operation, was at least much more efficient and rational in its administration than the Church of Ireland had ever been. The performance of the Ecclesiastical Commissioners therefore established that Erastianism could produce an improvement in the administrative efficiency of a religious organization.

At the top of the organizational ladder were the commissioners themselves. They were divided into two groups according to appointment, those who were not paid for their work as ecclesiastical commissioners and those who were paid. In the former category were the Archbishops of Armagh and of Dublin, the Chancellor of Ireland, and the Chief Justice of Ireland, each of whom served ex officio. In addition, four other bishops were commissioners without salary. Three paid members were also installed, two of these being named by the government, the third jointly by the two archbishops. On the first board, Francis Sadleir, John Caillard Erck, and William C. Quinn served as the professional commissioners. Quinn was the joint selection of Beresford and Whately; Erck was the longtime secretary to the Board of First Fruits and to the parliamentary commissioners on the Irish church, while Sadleir was a Senior Fellow of Trinity College, Dublin. Since the board was an amalgam of unpaid prelates and ex officio officials and professionals, it is logical to ask if the professionals and the amateurs behaved alike in their attention to duty. The answer is no. As one might expect, the professionals, being essentially civil servants, were regular in attending the formal meetings of the commissioners, while the others, the bishops and law officers, had pressing obligations on other fronts. Hence, in examining the attendance figures at board meetings for the years 1838 through 1840, one finds that the three paid commissioners were almost always in attendance (business was transacted almost daily), whereas only one or two of the unpaid members were present except on special occasions.[154] Operationally, therefore, the daily affairs of the Ecclesiastical Commissioners devolved upon the professional nucleus of paid commissioners.

The commissioners' office establishment grew quickly. By 1837, there were in addition to the three paid commissioners each earning £1,000 a year: a secretary at £600, a treasurer at £500, twenty-seven clerks earning from somewhat above £20 to £220 a year, seven architects with salaries ranging from £500 (plus four percent of the outlay on buildings they supervised) to £516 (plus an outlay commission). This was in addition to agents for episcopal estates and suppressed benefices who were employed on a commission basis.[155] The size of the staff remained relatively stable for the next three decades, consisting in the later 1860s of the commissioners, a secretary, treasurer, traveling agent, two architects, and twenty-five clerks, plus agents on commission.[156] At that time the salaries of the paid commissioners and staff totaled slightly more than £8,000 each year.[157] Although the commissioners insisted they were not a government department, an outside observer would have been hard pressed to explain how this official establishment differed from other government agencies.

How efficient were the Ecclesiastical Commissioners? To a modern observer the ratio of appropriation for staff salaries to total revenue seems reasonable. For example in the year 1852–53, the salaries of commissioners and officials were somewhat over £5,500, as compared to total revenue of more than £122,000.[158] Certainly a salary charge of less than 5 percent of total revenue for permanent officers is hardly excessive; nor can the roughly £1,500 for postage, printing, and miscellaneous expenses be called outrageous. Nevertheless, the royal commission of the late 1860s, while commending the Ecclesiastical Commissioners' financial accounting methods, stated that the costs of administration were too high. In particular the practice of paying of up to 10 percent to local managers of former episcopal lands and suppressed benefices was judged as excessive.[159] But because this royal commission was basically hostile in its outlook to the Church of Ireland, its judgment should be treated skeptically. It is hard to believe that a 5 to 10 percent commission was excessive for collecting rents from the disaffected, hostile, and occasionally violent Irish peasantry.

The day-to-day activity of the commissioners was a series of small decisions. Matters of principle rarely arose. In addition to collecting their revenues, the commission's responsibilities were as follows. In the first place, they investigated the expenses necessary for maintaining divine service in each parish and underwrote those expenses. These charges ranged from the payment of sextons' salaries to the buying of elements for Holy Communion; to the provision of fonts, stoves, and church bells. Second, the commissioners had to examine and pay the claims outstanding on the vestry cess before it was abolished. These claims were completely extinguished within a few years. A third task was the most onerous and important one, the examination of the estimates of the provincial architects for repair or construction of Anglican Churches. Each individual estimate had to be scrutinized in detail and, further, a set of priorities established among the competing projects. The commissioners' other main task was the suspension of appointments of clergy to non-cure and sinecure benefices and dignities. Additionally, there were minor duties such as the augmentation of small benefices, the terminating of the few remaining obligations of the defunct Board of First Fruits, and the administration of some minor charities.[160]

Business was usually transacted smoothly, but there were exceptions. For instance, in 1847 the commissioners suspended the Rectory of Killeshin in the Diocese of Leighlin. The vicar of the parish, however, claimed that the entire revenue of the parish was rightfully his, even if the rectorial arrangements were suspended. A hassle ensued and the commissioners, having great difficulty in establishing title to the rectorial portion of the rent charge, turned to the Attorney General for Ireland for help. That law officer, however, decided that the commissioners did not have sufficient grounds to win their point, and they could only plead with the Lord Lieutenant for his support.[161] Such cases were rare, if for no other reason than that only about half a dozen benifices came up for suspension each year.

If on occasion, the commissioners could be balked by intransigent local clergy or others, the commissioners, for their part, could be arbitrary and high-handed. The case of the Church of Saint Nicholas Within is a case in point. The Dean and Chapter of Saint Patrick's, Dublin, possessed the rectorial rights to the church and claimed ownership of the institution and property. In the mid-1830s, the Ecclesiastical Commissioners directed that the church be razed without informing the dean and chapter, who did not learn about the levelling until after it had been completed (whether through indifference or inefficiency on their part is uncertain, probably both). Upon hearing of the commissioners' action, the dean and chapter protested vigorously, primarily because they claimed the pews had been bought by the owner of a public house who was using them to accommodate his customers and the communion table, altarpiece, and windows were sold to the new Roman Catholic chapel in Baldoyle. The commissioners replied that the church had been about to fall down, that they had given due notice of their intentions; they flatly refused to answer the chapter's question about whence their statutable rights to destroy the building arose. Probably, the commissioners were within their legal rights, but certainly they engendered little good will within the church by their tactless and high-handed treatment of the Dean and Chapter of Saint Patrick's.[162]

And occasionally the commissioners could be embarrassed by administrative oversight. The comic opera case of the parish clerk's signature is such an instance. In 1852, a Reverend Robert Browne assumed a benefice in the Diocese of Tuam and found that his predecessor's appointee as parish clerk had been totally unqualified for the job, being neither able to read nor write his own name. Actually this man had served only as sexton, but the receipts for income from the Ecclesiastical Commissioners were signed in his name. The Reverend Mr. Browne pointed this out to his diocesan who had the matter investigated and regularized. There the matter should have dropped, for it was hardly important. But the Reverend Mr. Browne came into conflict in 1855 with the Ecclesiastical Commissioners about the withdrawal of the augmentation grant from his previous benefice. He wrote letters to the Lord Lieutenant and to Lord Palmerston resurrecting the parish clerk issue and, by implication, suggested incompetence upon the part of the commissioners in allowing such an abuse to occur. The unfortunate harassed commissioners then had to placate the Dublin Castle authorities by convincing them that no administrative bungling was involved.[163]

These three cases—the Killeshin case, the Saint Nicholas Church issue, and the parish clerk affair—are fair examples of the everyday work of the commissioners, being essentially trivial, graceless, and undramatic in themselves. Small decision by small decision, the commissioners did their job; and by 1865, they had built 90 new churches and rebuilt 198, in addition to the completed buildings or renovations that had been begun by the former Board of First Fruits or by local parishioners.[164]

How much money did the commissioners have at their disposal? Naturally, not as much as they wanted, but a goodly sum nevertheless. Yearly revenues were normally well over £100,000 a year and in exceptional years, over £200,000. In the beginning, the commissioners' sources of revenues were a bit shaky. The income tax on benefices was at first small, since it became due only upon new appointments to benefices. It was therefore a continually growing income source but a small one at first. The income from suppressed bishoprics and benefices was similarly slow in materializing, as was income from the sale of episcopal perpetuities. Faced with obligations, but short of income, the commissioners were empowered by 4 and 5 William IV, c. 90, s. 45, to borrow up to £100,000 from the Board of Works. This the commissioners did, with £46,000 of roughly £176,000 income for the first year of their operation on loan from the Board of Works. Once the funds from the sale of perpetuities had materialized, the Ecclesiastical Commissioners repaid the loan.[165]

When the Church Temporalities Bill had been introduced into parliament, some observers suggested that the idea of appropriating surplus revenue of the Ecclesiastical Commissioners (an idea which subsequently was dropped) was superfluous, because there would never be a surplus. In reality they were right, although their implication, that the absence of a surplus would be owing to the commissioners' spendthrift habits, was incorrect. The annual reports of the commissioners to the Lord Lieutenant and the surviving letterbooks indicate that these administrators did not have enough resources to do everything they would have liked in the basic area of church construction and rebuilding. Further, although the Church Temporalities Act of 1833 had provided that, if a surplus of income ever developed the commission could spend it on grants for the building of glebe houses (sections 77 and 92), no such grants were ever made because no surplus accrued.[166] Now since the Church Temporalities Act had provided that any surplus over the expenses of church construction, divine service, and so forth, could be allocated in grants for other church purposes, there was no motivation for the commissioners to be prodigal in their use of resources— as there would have been had the appropriation clause passed. And, assuming that the commissioners spent their money as effectively as possible and still were pressed for funds, we can conclude that under the Church Temporalities Act of 1833 the Ecclesiastical Commissioners were not over-endowed but may well have been under-endowed.

Although the government interfered only rarely with the work of the Ecclesiastical Commissioners, on three occasions governmental and parliamentary actions complicated the commissioners' financial affairs. The first occasion was the intervention in September 1844 by Lord Heytesbury, the newly arrived Lord Lieutenant. Heytesbury objected to the commissioners' use of the money from perpetuities (the "perpetuity purchase fund") for repairing and building churches. In the Lord Lieutenant's view, the money from the sale of perpetuities was properly to be maintained as capital, not to be used as a source of annual expenditure. The commissioners replied that although they had been unwilling to do so, the pressing demands upon them had forced them to use the perpetuities money. Tactfully, they reminded the Lord Lieutenant that, by law, the money was available to them to use as part of their annual income if they so desired. The commissioners firmly disagreed with Heytesbury's opinion that the need to dip into the principal of the perpetuity fund had now passed.[167] Heytesbury was unimpressed, and informed the commissioners that they should frame their estimates in the future without using the capital of the perpetuity purchase fund. To this the commissioners grudgingly agreed, although they would not promise, should a future emergency arise, to leave permanently the fund untouched or to invest it all in government stock as the Lord Lieutenant desired.[168] Although the commissioners' freedom of financial action was thus limited, they were more inconvenienced than hobbled, for the commissioners often sold their government stocks, thereby making a fiction of their obedience to the government's orders.

More painful was the reduction (in 1854) and the abolition (in 1857) of the Ministers' Money, a tax which had been created by an act of the pre-revolution Irish parliament (17 and 18 Charles II, c. 7). By that statute the householders of certain cities were taxed for the payment of Anglican ministers. This tax was not to exceed twelve pence for each pound of yearly assessed value of the house, and for the purposes of the act no house was to be valued above £60. The tax was collected by the churchwardens and paid to the incumbents. The cities and boroughs of Dublin, Cork, Limerick, Waterford, Drogheda, Kilkenny, Clonmel, and Kinsale came under the act. Altogether about £15,000 a year was levied. The flaws of such an act were obvious. First, the law was objected to because it was badly administered. Once a house was rated, the assessment continued even though the house was reduced by dilapidation. On the other hand the £60 valuation limit meant that a house could be worth several times this valuation and still be liable for only the assessment based on the limitation figure. In the second place, it will be noticed that none of the towns mentioned lie in the north of Ireland. The Presbyterians of the north, therefore, were exempted from the tax while the Catholics of the south were not. The third, and by far the most important objection to the tax, however, was that it was largely borne by non-Anglicans. When the Church Temporalities Act had abolished vestry cess in rural areas, the Ministers' Money, a counterpart in the cities and boroughs, was forgotten. It was a grievance whose alleviation the Irish Catholics justly desired.[169]

In the mid-1840s the question of Ministers' Money was raised in the Commons and eventually a select committee was appointed. That committee, reporting in late July 1848, recommended that the charge for the Ministers' Money be taken from the rate payers and transferred to the Ecclesiastical Commissioners.[170] Although no immediate action was taken, in 1854 a statute was passed which modified the collection and distribution of the Ministers' Money. Under the modifying statute, the amount payable to clergy from the Ministers' Money was cut by 25 percent. This amount was no longer collected by the churchwardens and paid to the ministers; instead it was paid to the ministers by the Ecclesiastical Commissioners. The commissioners were not expected to pay this amount from their own funds; rather they were to recoup the expenses from the various local government corporations whose responsibility it now became to assess the money (according to a newly rationalized tax schedule).[171]

This act satisfied nobody, although it probably displeased the clergy the least, for they now had a trustworthy paymaster in the Ecclesiastical Commisioners and were relieved from any direct relationship with the collection of an unpleasant tax. The Ecclesiastical Commissioners fared badly, however, for although they were in theory to be reimbursed by the municipalities, the latter lagged far behind in their payments. Hence, in the year 1855–56, the commissioners paid out over £12,000 in Ministers' Money, but received less than £5,000 from the municipalities.[172] At the same time the Roman Catholic rate payers were still vexed, because a statute requiring them to pay taxes for the support of Protestant clergy remained on the books.

The obvious solution was to make the whole amount a charge on the Ecclesiastical Commissioners, with local taxation to be totally abolished. A bill embodying this suggestion was proposed in 1857 by a private member, William Fagan, M.P. for Cork City.[173] The liberals concurred with the measure, the conservatives opposed, and the bill became law.[174] The immediate impact of such a statute—throwing the complete burden for paying the Ministers' Money on the Ecclesiastical Commissioners—was that the commissioners were able in the fiscal year 1856–57 to make grants for the building of only two new churches.[175] In later years the commissioners rearranged their finances to allow continued church building, but there is no doubt that the new burden significantly reduced their freedom of financial action.

The abolition of the Ministers' Money, as a charge on the municipalities, marked the completion of a set of financial developments that had moved the Church of Ireland from a financial system similar to that of the Church of England to a new position unprecedented in the British Isles. Whereas before the reforms of the 1830s, the Church of Ireland, like the Church of England, had been organized financially around a series of small, direct transactions between clergymen and tithe payers, between bishops and lease holders, and between urban rate payers and churchwardens, by 1857 most direct contracts between individual churchmen and the bulk of the Irish population had ceased. Tithes were replaced with a rent charge payable by landlords. One by one, episcopal estates came under the control of the Ecclesiastical Commissioners or, at minimum, had most of their leases converted to perpetuities, and finally, the Ministers' Money was no longer collected by local churchwardens from urban rate payers, but was supplied directly by the Ecclesiastical Commissioners. As the financial tendrils of the Irish church were shorn, the interpenetration of the church and Irish society lessened, and chances for conflict with the society seemingly were reduced.

The Church and Popular Education

In 1831 the Church of Ireland underwent a disquieting prelude to the religious reforms of the thirties when the grants to the Protestant educational societies were terminated and replaced by a state system of elementary education.[176] The Anglican Church had previously been aided directly in its educational ventures by immediate grants to the Association for the Promotion of Christian Knowledge and to the Incorporated Society. Indirectly, the Anglicans had been aided by government grants to the Kildare Place Society. During the 1820s it became clear, however, that these arrangements were unacceptable to the Roman Catholics who composed the great majority of the population. The result was that, in 1831, the government terminated all grants to religious societies and established a state system of elementary education which had the following characteristics:

It was a system in which denominational religious instruction was separated from literary and general moral instruction. All children in the schools were compelled to attend literary instruction, but no child was compelled to attend denominational teachings of a faith other than his own. In return for its financial assistance, the state secured control of the texts and curricula employed in the Irish national schools for general instruction, but not control over denominational instruction. Although nondenominational in the sense that every national school was open to any child regardless of his religious upbringing another characteristic of the national school system undercut the theory of non-denominationalism. On the local level the schools were usually managed by the local Anglican clergyman or gentleman, the Presbyterian minister, or the Roman Catholic priest. Any given national school was usually populated overwhelmingly with children of the same denomination as the school manager.

To a modern observer, what this system should have meant to the Anglican clergy seems obvious. A local Anglican clergyman could become manager of a school and receive a generous government grant, then appoint an Anglican teacher, and run a school composed almost entirely of Anglican children. In that school, the Anglican teacher could have interpreted the moral material inherent in the general literary texts in terms consistent with Anglican attitudes; and in the time set aside for religious instruction at day's end, the minister himself, or a deputy, could come into the school and catechize the children in Anglican doctrine. All this seems clear to us but, for inexplicable reasons, the bulk of the clergy of the Church of Ireland refused to have anything to do with the national system of education. Indeed, they treated it as a product of the devil rather than as a convenient source of government funds. Great friction arose in the Church of Ireland between those who opposed the national system and the minority who accepted it, and eventually a large amount of money was lost through the church's unsuccessful efforts to operate its own school system.

When the system was announced, Richard Whately, Archbishop of Dublin, agreed to serve as one of the commissioners; but that did not gain the churchmen's adherence, for Whately was a newly arrived Englishman appointed by a Whig government. Actually, it is questionable if anyone could have effected the adhesion of the majority of the Anglican clergymen in Ireland to any government system of education. A considerable segment of the Anglican clergy still maintained that it was the right of the Established Church to control any system of education the state might frame. Others, while granting supervisory powers to the state, disliked the provisions in the regulations of the national system giving local clergymen of any denomination a right to visit any local national school. The Commissioners of National Education were mistrusted by some clergymen, for the presence of Presbyterians and Roman Catholics meant that non-Anglicans would have the right to participate in decisions about Anglican schools which joined the system. Reinforcing the tendency to reject the national system, because it was not under complete Anglican hegemony, were assorted theological objections. Some Anglican churchmen denounced the dichotomy which, in theory at least, was drawn in national schools between moral and literary training and religious instruction. The viewpoint of such critics was that all proper education was religious and that non-religious education was not education. A second theological objection was that the regulations of the national system of education banned (an inaccurate allegation) or limited (a correct one) the use of the Bible in the schools. Granted, the Bible could not be used except during the last hour of the day when doctrinal religious instruction was permitted. But this objection seems a trifle academic because in real life it is hard to see how an average child could profitably absorb more than one hour of Bible instruction each day and still learn to read, write, and cipher.

Much of the Anglican opposition to the national system of education has to be ascribed to the pathological fear and hatred of the Roman Catholic Church which the Church of Ireland evinced during this era. By the 1830s a large group of Anglican clergymen were evangelical in outlook and were thus in extreme theological opposition to the Catholic Church. Further, the achievement of Catholic emancipation combined with the Catholic support for the Whig reforms of the Church of Ireland's constitution, left many churchmen in a blind fury whenever the words Catholic or Whig were mentioned. The national system of education, being the child of a Whig ministry and acceptable to the Roman Catholic priesthood was not, therefore, a system that could be rationally contemplated by many Irish Anglicans.

Archbishop Whately was the only Anglican clergyman of eminence to support the national system during its early years. Even as late as mid-century it was estimated that, at most, one quarter of the Anglican clergy favored the church's having anything to do with it. Significantly the Anglicans in finding fault with the national system of education did not, like the Presbyterians and the Roman Catholics, try to bend it to their own will. Rather, they trusted their case to parliament, hoping that when the Tories returned to office they would abandon the national system or at least provide funds so the Church of Ireland could operate its own schools. Churchmen and laity flooded parliament with petitions, mass meetings occurred, the most colorful of which were held in the evangelical temple, Exeter Hall, trumpeting the churchmen's rage. It all added up to nothing, however, for when Sir Robert Peel came to office in late 1834 he showed no inclination to meet the church's demands.

Having failed to influence parliament, the Anglican opponents of the system turned to creating their own educational one. At first, the Church Education Society, founded in 1839, was a considerable success. The presidents were the Archbishop of Armagh and eleven other prelates; the vice presidents, a galaxy of nobility and gentry, twenty-one deans, and twenty-eight archdeacons. The large number of bishops, deans, and archdeacons confirm that the great majority of those in high church offices supported the Church Education Society rather than the national system of education. A managing committee of laymen and clerics conducted central operations in Dublin, but the real power base of the system was the group of local educational societies organized for each diocese. In its first decade, the Church Education Society was well supported by voluntary subscriptions. The income of the central organization of the Church Education Society (which represented about one seventh of the total income of all branches of the society) rose from £1,854 in 1839 to nearly £6,000 in 1849. By mid-century, therefore, the Church of Ireland was probably spending between £50,000 and £60,000 annually on primary schooling. In 1849, the society claimed 1,868 schools with about 112,000 children on the rolls.

But things were not as rosy as they might at first appear. The landlord class in Ireland was in serious financial trouble after the famine and £50,000 a year in voluntary philanthropy could not be kept up indefinitely. Just how large was this amount becomes clear when one recalls that, during the same period, the average annual income of the Ecclesiastical Commissioners, with their massive endowments, was only about £150,000 annually. The leaders of the church knew that the Church Education Society needed money or it could not continue indefinitely. For a moment in the 1840s, during Peel's administration, it appeared that they might obtain an outright grant from the government. Under the influence of Archbishop Beresford, Peel's Lord Lieutenant, Earl DeGrey, proposed that the government give up supporting the national system, and Peel was receptive to the idea. Lord Eliot, the Chief Secretary, however, argued against any change and Peel eventually came to accept his view. With Peel's decision, the Anglican leaders lost their last chance to have the national system of education replaced with a denominational one.

During the 1850s the minority which favored joining the national system grew. The arguments for this view were first, that the clergy of the Established Church had a duty to educate the masses; and, second, that the rules of the national system could actually be squared with Anglican views concerning religious instruction. Most compelling, however, was the argument from expediency. The Church of Ireland was increasingly short of funds and any connection with the national system would provide large amounts of money for schools managed by Anglican clergymen and lay leaders. Even the most ardent supporters of the Church Education Society recognized the potence of the financial argument. Throughout the 1850s, churchmen constantly petitioned parliament for a separate grant to their society, but the government refused to budge. In the face of the government's unwavering refusal to grant aid to the Church Education Society and recognizing the pressing need for additional educational funds, the more moderate Church Education Society supporters wavered. By the late 1850s, it was clear that the majority in opposition to a connection with the national system of education was declining. Although the income of the society stayed roughly level during the decade, in 1855 a decline began in the number of shools and children in the Anglican system.

Finally, early in the year 1860, the Anglican leaders surrendered to reality. Archbishop Beresford, who was still serving as one of the presidents of the Church Education Society, addressed a circular to the patrons of schools in connection with the Clogher Diocesan Church Education Society. In the circular, he pointed out that many of the diocesan society's schools were in poor condition, that salaries were too small to obtain proper teachers, and that books and other school requisites were in short supply. Reluctantly, therefore, he advised the patrons to seek aid from the Commissioners of National Education, rather than allow the children of the Church of Ireland to grow up in a state of ignorance. Beresford himself, it is important to note, was not abandoning the principle of the Church Education Society. He was suggesting, however, that the society was a luxury that should be supported if the parish could afford it; but if not, local patrons should place their schools under the national system rather than suffer local children to receive inadequate schooling.

Certain of the Church Education Society's vice-presidents—notably the Lord Chancellor, the Dean of Emly, and the society's honorary secretary, the Reverend Hamilton Verschoyle (soon to become Bishop of Kilmore, Elphin, and Ardagh)—adopted Beresford's views. In response, a fanatical defense of the society was raised by its enthusiasts during which Beresford was compared to Judas Iscariot. But the anti-Beresford forces were fighting a losing battle. In 1860 the Commissioners of National Education introduced special regulations for Protestant schools which allowed them to receive grants with fewer children on the rolls than was required for other denominations. This tempted many patrons with small schools away from the Church Education Society. Despite the trumpets of the society's defenders, the Church Education Society faltered. By 1863, the society had been reduced to approximately 1,500 schools and 70,000 scholars and was down to 1,200 schools and 52,000 pupils in 1870. Gradually, piecemeal, the schools of the Church Education Society came under the aegis of the Commissioners of National Education.

The Church of Ireland's reaction to the creation of the national system of education can only have been harmful to the church's long range stability. The violence of the division between supporters of the national system and advocates of the Church Education Society was certainly dysfunctional. Equally important, the church was inevitably damaged financially. Because the bulk of the Irish clergy were not sufficiently perspicacious to recognize that the operation of the national system of education could be reconciled with Anglican educational principles, the church spent hundreds of thousands of pounds on its own educational network when it should have been receiving the bulk of that money from the Irish administration. When it is recalled that in the mid-1850s the money given in voluntary subscriptions for church education was equal to roughly one third of the income of the Ecclesiastical Commissioners, and when one also recalls that the Ecclesiastical Commissioners were short of resources for church building and repair, it is obvious that the church education funds could have been used well elsewhere. If the church's leaders had accepted the government connections from the beginning, instead of going through decades of impoverishing private education endeavor, thousands of pounds each year would have been liberated and could have been solicited directly for religious purposes.

If the Church of Ireland's position on popular education indicated a lack of touch with fiscal reality, its negotiations with the government indicated a failure to recognize political reality. Churchmen continually pressed the government for a separate grant to underwrite their denominational schools without ever reflecting that money is a medium of exchange. The Church Education Society adherents failed to recognize that they had nothing to promise the government that would convince the state to grant aid. The national system of education operated perfectly well without the Church Education Society's schools being in association, so that was no compelling educational argument for the government's giving the Anglican system a separate grant. Further, as the power of the Roman Catholic Irish grew in political circles, there was no compelling political reason for a ministry to court the Anglican churchmen's favor, since more Catholic votes would probably be lost than Protestant votes gained. The leading prelates, clergy, and laity of the Church of Ireland had, it appears, failed to recognize that the church to which they gave allegiance had become unimportant to men in the center of national power.

Upon reflection, the activities of the Ecclesiastical Commissioners in the nineteenth century's middle decades, and the reactions of the Anglican authorities to the national system of education, appear as balancing episodes. The former episode was characterized by a keen sense of financial and political reality and an efficient use of religious resources, the latter by a refusal to deal with the financial and political world as it actually existed and by a squandering of the church's limited funds.

Lost Illusions

In England, the middle years of the nineteenth century witnessed the simultaneous phenomena of evangelical piety and ritualist romanticism. In contrast, Ireland was untouched by the Oxford Movement and the evangelicals were uncontested. By mid-century, evangelicalism was the dominant theme in Irish Anglicanism.[177] The evangelical clergymen were assiduous in performing their religious duties and in trying to extend the church's influence. Although the missionary-proselytizing agencies had lost most of their momentum by mid-century, the evangelicals found alternate outlets for their energies.

One such outlet was the Achill mission experiment. Achill Island, lying off the coast of Mayo, is sixteen miles long and seven wide. The religious census of 1834 reported that of the 5,000–6,000 inhabitants only 76— mostly coast guardsmen, their families, and persons connected with relief committees—were Protestant. The Achill peasants lived chiefly by fishing, neglecting the good tillage land that existed on the island, and in 1831 suffered from famine. In that year the Reverend Edward Nangle, an Anglican priest, visited the island and conceived the idea of a mission. He convinced the island's major landlord to lease him more than one hundred acres at a nominal rent upon which he founded his missionary establishment. A steward was engaged to superintend the farm and the reclamation of waste land. A schoolmaster and then a scripture reader were hired, and in 1834 the Reverend Mr. Nangle and his family took up permanent residence. The mission prospered, and Nangle erected mission schools throughout the island. Additional scripture readers and missionaries came to aid Nangle; and by 1852, twenty-seven schools were in operation and a Protestant population of nearly 700 was claimed.[178]

An evangelical with zeal equal to the Reverend Mr. Nangle was the Reverend Alexander Dallas, who had started his professional life as a British army officer but turned to the cloth and subsequently became rector of an English parish. For some reason he became interested in the conversion of the Irish Roman Catholics and concocted the novel (if questionable) scheme of sending on the same day, 16 January 1846, a packet of religious tracts to 20,000 leading Irish Catholic citizens. On the following Saint Patrick's Day, every Roman Catholic priest in Ireland received a letter urging him to head a movement to lead forth the people to light and liberty. In 1847, the Reverend Mr. Dallas inaugurated a special fund for converting Irish Roman Catholics and collected £10,000 within two years. Dallas himself chose County Galway as the field of his own missionary activities. Not surprisingly, given Dallas's propensity for religious promotions, a society was founded in 1849 to press his design, the society being named the Irish Church Mission to the Roman Catholics. For the remainder of his life,

Dallas directed this organization and upon his death in 1869, it was reported that his Irish Church Mission Society had erected twenty-one churches, forty-nine schoolhouses, twelve parsonages and four orphanages.[179]

In turn, the Irish Church Mission Society fostered yet another organization, this one bearing the grandiose title, The Society for Protecting the Rights of Conscience in Ireland. The group was formed to protect converts to the Church of Ireland, who allegedly were oppressed and persecuted by the Roman Catholic peasantry and priesthood upon their changing faiths. The society's sponsorship was not limited to evangelicals; Richard Whately, Archbishop of Dublin, had a share in its formation.[180] What significant effects, if any at all, the new societies had upon the membership of the Church of Ireland, is hard to determine. As we will note later, the 1861 census was to dispell any claims they made to mass conversion of the peasantry.

A less quixotic and more productive society than any of those mentioned above was the Church Extension Society for Belfast. Despite Belfast's having an Anglican population in 1861 of over 30,000, there were only eight parish churches. Formed in 1862 the extension society successfully remedied this failing and the Church of Ireland proportion of the population gradually increased.[181]

The crowning point of the evangelicals' efforts during the nineteenth century was the revival of 1859, a phenomenon which affected the entire British Isles. In Ireland, the revival affected most of the country but was most intense in the Protestant areas of the north. Significantly, the revival was supported by Protestants of all denominations, with the exception of the Unitarians. The clergy of the Established Church were in general favorable to it, although they often deplored its excesses. At its worst, the revival was nothing more than an emotional outlet for hysterical women and overwrought men and children. Cases of men and women seized by fits and groanings were common, but the more common experience was an intensification of religious devotion which strengthened, rather than disrupted, church discipline. Within the Church of Ireland, the most important administrative effect was the strengthening of the position of laymen. Under the influence of revivalism, laymen became more fervid and more confident of their spiritual powers. Further, laymen often took upon themselves the formation of prayer meetings, Bible classes, and similar extra-liturgical activities. Indirectly, therefore, the revival strengthened the position of the laity in the Church of Ireland over and against the clergy.[182] This development was to have important implications a decade later when the Church of Ireland was seperated from the state, for one of the first reactions of the laity at that time would be an attempt to overthrow the clergy and to seize control of the church.

In 1861, the first census of religion since 1834 was taken. When it was published two years later, the results, while permitting various interpretations, stilled forever any hopes churchmen may have had for the conversion of Ireland to Anglicanism. The results of that census are summarized in table 36.

The first reaction to these figures was the recognition that the Church of Ireland had lost somewhat less than one fifth of its number in less than three decades, a loss the thin lines of the Irish Anglicans could ill afford. An absolute loss in population occurred in twenty-seven of the thirty-two dioceses, and increases occurred only in five: Connor, Down, Dromore, Emly, and Kilfenora. In those twenty-seven dioceses which lost members, the decline was from 715,029 in 1834 to 538,225 in 1861—a diminution of 176,804, or about 25 percent of their original numbers. The greatest absolute loss occurred in the Diocese of Clogher where church members declined by 39,164, dropping it from the second most populous diocese to fourth. In percentage terms, the Dioceses of Clonfert and Ferns suffered most, losing nearly one-half their numbers. Among the five dioceses which gained in members, the Diocese of Connor must have been most consoling to disturbed churchmen, for the growth came chiefly in the town of Belfast; and inadequate as church sittings were in Belfast, it was obviously a fertile field for church extension.[183]

But if the Church of Ireland lost in absolute numbers its leaders at least possessed the slight comfort that it had gained relatively. Between the census of 1834 and that of 1861, lay nearly three decades of famine, high death rates, and emigration. As a result, the Irish population had signally decreased from 7,954,100 to 5,798,967. The famine and its aftermath fell hardest on the poorest sections of the population which were predominantly Roman Catholic. The result was that vis-à-vis the Roman Catholic Church, the Church of Ireland experienced considerable gains. In 1834 the Roman Catholics represented 80.9 percent of the population, their proportion having dropped to 77.7 percent in 1861. Whereas in 1834 there were 13.25 members of the Established Church to every 100 Roman Catholics, in 1861 there were 15.35 to each 100. Nevertheless, this was hardly a victory, for in every one of the Irish dioceses the Catholics outnumbered the Anglicans. In only three dioceses did the Protestants as a group outnumber the Catholics: Connor and Down, where the Presbyterians were in an absolute majority; and Dromore where the Anglicans and Presbyterians together outnumbered the Catholics.[184] The optimists within the Church of Ireland had good reason to be abashed by the 1861 census, for it invalidated any claims they may have wished to make about a massive renaissance in Irish Anglicanism. No amount of harping upon the increase in numbers relative to the Roman Catholics could obscure the sepulchral tones of the census data.

The census of 1861 should not be taken as a solitary turning point in the

TABLE 36
IRISH RELIGIOUS DISTRIBUTIONS, 1834 AND 1861

	Anglicans		Anglicans as % of total population	
Diocese	1834	1861	1834	1861
Province of Armagh				
Armagh	103,012	85,583	20.6%	22.2%
Clogher	104,359	65,195	26.1	24.8
Derry	50,350	43,738	13.7	14.9
Raphoe	33,507	22,213	16.1	13.0
Down	28,025	28,868	14.8	17.6
Connor	66,888	80,125	18.5	20.8
Dromore	41,737	44,474	22.2	25.8
Kilmore	46,879	31,646	15.8	15.1
Elphin	16,465	10,506	5.1	5.2
Ardagh	17,702	11,044	8.3	8.1
Meath	25,626	16,289	6.3	6.4
Tuam	9,619	9,041	2.0	2.9
Killala	7,729	4,724	5.4	5.4
Achonry	5,417	3,392	4.7	3.1
Province of Dublin				
Dublin	106,599	100,267	21.2	19.4
Kildare	13,907	12,499	10.3	12.7
Cashel	6,790	4,721	3.3	3.9
Emly	1,246	1,414	1.3	2.3
Waterford	5,301	2,943	10.8	6.8
Lismore	5,970	4,775	2.8	3.3
Cloyne	13,866	11,746	4.0	5.5
Cork	35,229	26,736	10.4	11.2
Ross	6,061	4,746	5.3	6.8
Ferns	24,672	14,383	12.5	9.5
Leighlin	20,391	13,022	10.7	10.4
Ossory	12,361	8,258	5.6	5.9
Killaloe	19,149	12,700	5.0	5.6
Kilfenora	235	251	.7	1.1
Clonfert	4,761	2,521	3.9	3.9
Kilmacduagh	656	434	1.4	1.8
Limerick	11,122	8,679	4.3	5.0
Ardfert & Aghadoe	7,529	6,424	2.5	2.9
National Total	853,160	693,357	10.7	11.9

Note: The reader will notice that in four instances (Down, Elphin, Cashel, and Ross) the 1834 census figures as corrected and published in 1863 differ slightly from those figures as originally published. Compare tables 34 and 36. The differences are so small as to be insignificant.

Source: The Census of Ireland for the Year 1861, Part IV, Report and Tables Relating to Religious Professions, Education and Occupation of the People, vol. 1, pp. 30–31, 33 [3204-III], H.C. 1863, lix.

history of the Church of Ireland. Although the feverish activity of the evangelicals had set the tone for much of the church's attitudes during the middle third of the nineteenth century, a countertheme of retreat had always been present. This countertheme was indicated by a series of minor threats, frustrations, and the diminution of prerogatives which the church suffered in the middle years of the century. For example, in 1847 the Irish bishops, headed by Archbishop Whately, made a visionary attempt to promote the revival of suppressed bishoprics. The bill, as introduced into the House of Lords, was permissive rather than normative. It permitted the Lord Lieutenant to fill any see which had been suppressed under the Church Temporalities Act of 1833, and to disunite the see from its associated part immediately upon its being presented with an ordinary. Neither the financial provisions of the 1833 act, nor the provision reducing the number of Irish bishops in the House of Lords, was to be affected.[185] In explaining why the measure was necessary, Whately made the infelicitous statement that the Church of Ireland might be considered as an English colony; and though its members might be comparatively few and scattered, it was incumbent upon the legislature to provide them with pastoral superintendence. In his own jurisdiction, for instance, Whately felt that a suffragan bishop for Kildare was necessary. Lord Lansdowne tactfully pointed out that the provision for archdeacons in the Church Temporalities Act met the needs for ecclesiastical supervision. Thereupon Whately withdrew the bill without attempting a second reading.[186]

Being balked by parliament was painful, but actually losing previously-held prerogatives was humiliating. Although the parliamentary franchises were open to all denominations, and although the vestries had lost their power, there remained one area where the *ancien regime* still triumphed, and that was the municipal corporations. The sixty-eight Irish corporations were legally open to Roman Catholics, but power in all but two was in Protestant hands. This anomaly, combined with the obviously corrupt nature of the corporations, made them natural targets for the reformers of the 1830s. From 1835 onwards, the reformers pressed their cause, but the House of Lords insisted on modifying bill after bill in a manner unacceptable to the Commons. Only in 1840 was an Irish municipal reform bill passed. Fifty-eight of the sixty-eight corporations were abolished and their functions transferred to the counties. In the ten remaining municipalities, the old closed corporations were replaced by elected councils. The result was that the Roman Catholics took charge of a number of large town governments, and became influential in all of them. The election of Daniel O'Connell as Lord Mayor of Dublin in 1841 was symbolic of the deposition of the Anglicans in the municipalities. To complete the process of de-Anglicanizing the cities, the Town Improvement Act of 1849 removed

the few governmental functions (lighting, fire fighting, etc.) that had ad-
hered to municipal vestries, even after the great majority of these had been
converted into purely ecclesiastical units. Finally, in 1856 the jurisdiction
of the Archbishop of Dublin over the Liberty of Saint Sepulchre's was
abrogated. With that final step, the Anglican Church was completely disestablished at the local government level.[187]

Undoubtedly, the most portentous change in Irish life, which bore upon
the Church of Ireland during the middle decades of the nineteenth century,
was the rapidity with which the Roman Catholic Church gained political
influence. As indicated in the last chapter, the hierarchy of the Roman
Catholic Church in Ireland had gradually reasserted its authority and
standardized its discipline during the first three decades of the nineteenth
century. By 1830 the Roman Catholic priest was no longer able to play
the game of ecclesiastical politics against his superiors, and for this reason
he took up the game of secular politics. At the local level, therefore, the
Roman Catholic priest became a political figure to rival the previously
unchallenged Protestant landlord.[188]

Despite the interest of the Catholic clergy in politics, the Catholic Church
as an institution was not notably troublesome to either the British government or to the Established Church in Ireland during the 1830s and the
first half of the 1840s. The reason for this relative quiescence was that the
Catholic Church was in tight financial straits. The population of the country was growing rapidly, and this was chiefly a burden on the Catholic
ecclesiastical organization. The Catholic Church not only had to provide
religious facilities for the increasing numbers of the faithful but had to
provide charities and relief services as well. The demands upon the Catholic
Church for capital needs, such as new church buildings, were prodigious.
At the same time, the resources of the Catholic middle classes were
strained to the utmost, and the church could not expect anything but
modest increments of income to meet the large increase in the demands
placed upon it. The result, therefore, was that the Catholic Church could
not afford to be overly truculent in its attitude towards Dublin Castle, for
it needed every financial bone it could scrounge. Hence, for example, the
majority of the Catholic priesthood chose to accept state aid through the
Commissioners of National Education, even though this implied certain
minor limitations upon their powers as educators.[189]

The Irish famine, while nationally a disaster, was a great blessing to the
Roman Catholic Church. The famine reversed the course of Irish social
history and thereby transformed the Catholic Church's financial position.
After the famine, the pattern of increasing division of farm land was reversed. Whereas Catholic landholdings had previously been subdivided,
they now were passed on intact from father to son. The Encumbered
Estates Act brought the Catholic small landowner into his own. Emigration

removed hundreds of thousands of abject poverty cases. The Catholic middle classes began to prosper. And, all the time, the population dropped. As a result, the demands upon the church for capital expenditure for church buildings and similar purposes dropped, as did demands upon the church as a dispenser of relief. Simultaneously the classes upon which the Catholic Church depended for voluntary contributions had more discretionary income to give to the church. For the first time, the Catholic Church could afford to be finicky about the money offered to it by the government, confident in the knowledge of its increased prosperity and security in Irish society.[190]

The point which adds irony and vigor to this process is that the famine, while ultimately a blessing to the Roman Catholic Church, was simultaneously harmful to the Established Church. The landlords, whose estates passed to the new Catholic owners under the Encumbered Estates Act, had been Protestant gentry who had been the local bulwarks of the Anglican Church. Moreover, during the worst years of the famine, the rent charges, which were the chief source of income of local incumbents, often went unpaid or were paid only in part, thus further injuring the Established Church.

Moreover, certain events in the mid-1840s predisposed the Catholic Church to be less trusting of the British government than it had previously been, and more inclined to prosecute its own ends through political negotiation. Specifically, during the 1840s a series of events occurred that raised the Catholic bishops' hackles. These included Peel's reformation of the Charitable Bequests Board in a manner unacceptable to most Catholic bishops and his founding of the secular Queen's Colleges to extend the provision for higher education in Ireland. Then, in 1848, Lord John Russell raised the possibility of the government in some way endowing the Catholic clergy, an idea which was viewed by the Catholic authorities as an attempt to subvert their church. The result was that by the late 1840s, the Catholic bishops as a group had become prickly, highly defensive, and wary of anything the government proposed.

Now, just at the point when the Catholic Church was entering a period of relative financial prosperity, and at a time when its bishops were vexed and irritated, a man came on stage whose personality and principles greatly reinforced the Catholic Church's tendencies to aggressive action. This man was Paul Cullen, appointed Roman Catholic Archbishop of Armagh in 1849 and translated to the Archbishopric of Dublin in 1852. Cullen had spent most of his clerical career in Rome and had become the essence of the ultra-montane mentality. He quickly assumed control of appointment of Irish bishops.[191] This power, when combined with his authoritarian methods, meant that Cullen controlled the Irish Catholic Church with a rigor not seen for several preceding centuries—if ever. Cul-

len's second characteristic was his continual prosecution of what he felt to
be the Catholic Church's religious grievances. Since he was thoroughly
Romanized, he had a contempt for the secular government and a distrust
of anything resembling religious neutrality. In the early 1850s, Cullen
dabbled openly in electoral politics. After the demise of the Independent
Irish Party, the Catholic hierarchy and priesthood were, it is claimed, the
chief political outlets for the Irish populace.[192] The Roman Catholic
Church's goals were anti-government in one sense and anti-Established
Church in every sense; but this should not be confused with nationalism.
Cullen, having experienced the Italian troubles of 1848, was thoroughly
distrustful of all nationalists, including Irish nationalists; he managed the
difficult juggling act of being simultaneously opposed to the British government and to the Irish nationalists.

In any case, Cullen's and the Roman Catholic Church's political goals
in the 1860s were three-fold: equitable land legislation, state-financed
denominational education at all levels, and the disestablishment of the
Protestant Church in Ireland. This latter idea, disestablishment, had received little attention in the previous twenty years; for after the church
reforms of the 1830s, anti-Establishment agitation had been remarkably
scarce. In 1844, Henry Ward, liberal member for Sheffield, had moved that
the Commons resolve itself into a committee on the state of church temporalities in Ireland, his clear intention being to proceed then to disestablishment. The Commons scouted the motion by a vote of 274 to 179.[193]
A similar motion was proposed in 1849 by a member named Osborne, but
it lost by a majority of 67 votes.[194] When a select committee on Irish
ecclesiastical revenues was proposed in 1853, the motion went down to
even more decisive defeat, 260 to 98.[195] Three years later, a motion to
resolve the Commons into a committee to consider Irish temporalities lost
by 70 of the 256 votes cast.[196] Another attempt to force a select committee
on the Irish church was blocked in 1863.[197] Archbishop Cullen set out to
reverse this string of defeats. In 1864 he was instrumental in forming the
National Association. The goal of the association was the manipulation of
public opinion to bring pressure upon political candidates to support the
demands of the Catholic Church. When combined with the efforts of other
Irish politicians and English voluntaryists, the activities of this association
would eventually be successful as regards the Established Church. These
activities will be discussed in the next chapter.

At this point it suffices to note that the Anglican Church was faced in
the 1860s with a formidable opponent in the Roman Catholic Church
which was becoming richer each year and hence freer to press its own ends
without fear of the financial consequences. At the head of the Catholic
Church in Ireland was Archbishop Cullen, a stern, truculent, single-minded
man, whose tight control of the Catholic organization made that organiza-

tion an efficient engine for battering down the walls of the Church Establishment. Cullen's shrewd association of the cause of disestablishment with the cause of land reform meant that his program was an attractive political package, both to the Irish voters and to the politicians who sought their votes. In the face of this program the Established Church was vulnerable. The revenues of the Ecclesiastical Commissioners were increasingly inadequate to their purposes. Protestant landlords as a class were yearly in a more precarious position. The value of the Established Church as a bastion of civil order in Ireland was now almost totally discounted by British politicians. The humiliation of disestablishment and the necessity for drastic ecclesiastical reorganization were imminent.[198]

A Final Profile of the Established Church

How was the Church of Ireland constituted on the eve of its disestablishment? To answer the question we must look at several facets of the church: its laity, the arrangement of benefices, its clergy and bishops, and its aggregate income. Turning first to the Anglican laity, we find that the impression that the average Anglican was on the upper rung of the economic ladder was vividly confirmed by the census of 1861. In nineteenth-century Ireland, certain professions were Protestant and others Catholic. The occupational ladder shown in table 37 indicates that the Protestants were more apt to be found in the skilled trades, in professions, and in positions of power than were the Catholics. The table groups all Protestants together, the majority of Protestants in Ireland being Anglican. In surveying the pyramid, it is well to remember that Protestants made up approximately 23 percent of the population in 1861.

The last thing one could legitimately argue is that we know precisely what the status hierarchy of nineteenth-century Irish occupations was. But without undue argument, we can accept the idea that Protestants were found in the more desirable occupations, as viewed by contemporary Irishmen. While by no means a precise sociological tool the ladder as presented in table 37 is useful, for it graphically presents the fact that there was a direct correlation between being a Protestant and having a high status occupation. Whether Protestants were in the more lucrative and prestigious occupations in numbers greater than their proportion of the total population because there was a strong Protestant bias in the occupational structure, or because the Protestants were more willing to sacrifice to reach those positions, is an argument best pursued in a monograph on historical sociology. The central point is that the constituency of the Protestant denominations, and by implication, the constituency of the Church of Ireland, was made up of the more wealthy and influential Irishmen. The wealth meant that, when disestablishment took place, the church would have considerable voluntary resources to call upon. Simultaneously, the laity's holding posi-

TABLE 37
OCCUPATIONS GROUPED BY PERCENTAGE OF PROTESTANTS
AND CATHOLICS EMPLOYED

% Protestant		% Catholic
100		0
	needle makers, linen thread makers, damask designers, artisans in pearl	
90		10
	nobles, barons, knights, baronets, cotton weavers, army surgeons, flax yarn makers	
80		20
	land agents, teachers of Irish, bankers, insurance agents, photographers, army officers, druggists, factory overseers, surgeons, authors, barristers	
70		30
	house agents, judges, physicians, linen and damask weavers, attorneys and solicitors, engravers, saddlers, merchants	
60		40
	watch makers, landed proprietors, portrait painters, artists, gunsmiths, weavers, poor-law clerks, coast guards, mill workers, prison officers, apothecaries	
50		50
	embroiderers, excise officers, rent collectors, postmasters, engineers, hotel keepers, clerks, drapers, flax dressers, grocers, parish clerks, factory workers	
40		60
	milliners, shirt makers, pawnbrokers, leather dealers, sculptors, pensioners, painters, glassers and decorators, constabulary and metropolitan police, saddlers and harness makers, process servers	
30		70
	gate keepers, letter carriers, stewards, dressmakers, shopkeepers, skilled weavers, coat makers, carpenters, farmers, loaders, housekeepers	
23		77
	brick layers, rope and twine makers, carters, seamstresses	
20		80
	flax spinners, tanners, bootbinders, musicians, publicans, bakers, blacksmiths, tailors, knitters, stablemen, domestic, servants, prostitutes, waiters, butchers, thatchers, basketmakers, slaters, charwomen, farm laborers, fishermen	
10		90
	tobacconists, peddlers, cattle dealers, wool weavers, masons, chimney sweeps, old clothes dealers, carriage brokers, brogue makers	
0		100

Source: Adapted from A. Hume, *Results of the Irish Census of 1861*, p. 51.

tions of influence in the community meant that it was used to exercising authority; and thus the laity would be inclined to seek influence and power in the affairs of the church.

If the Irish Anglican layman was apt to be higher on the occupational ladder than his average countryman, he was also apt to be better educated. Given below are the percentages of persons of various faiths, five years old and above, who were neither able to read nor write at the taking of the 1861 census:[199]

Established Church	16.0%
Roman Catholic	46.8
Presbyterians	11.1
All Protestants	13.7
National Average	38.7

The members of the Anglican Church, therefore, were much more apt to possess the requisites for basic literacy than were most Irishmen but were less likely to be literate than was the average Protestant. The comparison of the Presbyterians and the Church of Ireland constituency is instructive, for the Presbyterians had embraced the national system of education, while the Anglicans had stumbled along for years with their own inadequate independent system.

One further characteristic of the Anglican population: it was more apt to be found in towns and cities than was the general population. The following figures indicate this phenomenon:[200]

Established Church members:
    11.9 percent of total population
    16.6 percent of population living in parliamentary boroughs

Roman Catholics:
    77.7 percent of total population
    74.4 percent of population living in parliamentary boroughs

Presbyterians:
    9.0 percent of total population
    6.8 percent of population living in parliamentary boroughs

Turning from the lay population to the organization of the church on the local level, one finds that the number of benefices in Ireland had been continually increasing since the late eighteenth century when the first accurate returns are available. It will be recalled that in 1787 there were 1,120 benefices in Ireland, and that the corresponding number for 1832 was 1,395. In 1867 the Church of Ireland had 1,518 benefices. Largely through the exertions of the Ecclesiastical Commissioners, the church thus had a more comprehensive local organization than it had possessed anytime during the previous eighty years. Despite whatever vicissitudes the Church of Ireland had suffered from external forces, its efficiency in delivering religious services on the local level had increased. The benefices were divided among the united dioceses as follows:[201]

United Diocese	Number of Benefices
Armagh and Clogher	170
Meath	105
Tuam, Killala, and Achonry	77
Down, Connor, and Dromore	150
Derry and Raphoe	112
Kilmore, Elphin, and Ardagh	118
Dublin and Kildare	154
Ossory, Ferns, and Leighlin	171
Cashel, Emly, Waterford, and Lismore	104
Limerick, Ardfert and Aghadoe	95
Killaloe, Kilfenora, Clonfert, and Kilmacduagh	89
Cork, Cloyne, and Ross	170
Exempt Jurisdiction of Newry and Mourne	3
	1,518

Table 38 indicates the distribution of church population among the various dioceses and benefices. At a time when the Church of Ireland population was declining in absolute numbers, the large number of small benefices must have been a concern for church authorities. Nearly one third of the church's benefices contained one hundred or fewer Anglicans. This was a most precarious situation, for even a slight population shift in any local area would have had a major impact upon these small benefices.

If Ireland was better served with Anglican benefices in 1867 than it had been thirty and sixty years earlier, was it also better served with churches? The answer is yes. Earlier we found that there were 1,001 churches and chapels of ease in Ireland in 1787, and 1,293 in 1832. By 1864 the number of churches had risen to 1,579. In this matter, as on the matter of benefices, the Church of Ireland was in a stronger position in 1867 than it had been anytime during the preceding century.[202]

Granted that the Church of Ireland was more efficient in providing religious services to its constituency in 1867 than it had been at any time during the preceding century, had the position of the average clergyman improved in commensurate fashion? Table 39 provides an indication of the net incomes of the Irish clergy in 1867. This table should be compared with table 22 in the preceding chapter which indicates the situation in 1832,

TABLE 38
IRISH BENEFICES ACCORDING TO CHURCH POPULATION, 1867

Diocese	5,000 or more	2,000 to 4,999	1,000 to 1,999	750 to 999	500 to 749	200 to 499	100 to 199	40 to 99	30 to 39	20 to 29	Under 20
Armagh	–	7	24	19	12	15	9	8	3	–	5
Clogher	–	8	15	10	8	17	2	2	–	–	–
Meath	–	–	–	–	5	20	29	35	9	–	7
Derry	–	1	10	14	15	20	5	4	–	–	–
Raphoe	–	–	7	4	7	15	5	–	–	–	–
Down	–	3	2	5	7	16	8	4	1	–	–
Connor	–	18	10	7	13	15	9	2	–	–	–
Dromore	1	8	4	3	5	8	–	–	–	–	–
Exempt jurisdiction of Newry and Mourne	–	2	–	–	–	–	–	–	–	–	–
Kilmore	–	–	9	10	8	16	6	1	–	–	–
Elphin	–	–	2	2	3	6	13	4	3	1	3
Ardagh	–	–	3	2	1	13	8	3	–	–	–
Tuam	–	–	–	–	5	11	10	17	2	3	2
Killala	–	–	–	1	2	6	6	–	–	–	–
Achonry	–	–	–	–	3	3	1	4	1	–	–
Dublin	3	9	14	6	11	29	13	11	–	5	3
Kildare	–	1	2	2	1	7	9	7	1	1	2
Ossory	–	–	–	3	–	9	13	14	4	8	7
Ferns	–	–	3	1	1	19	15	18	1	1	–
Leighlin	–	–	1	4	1	16	12	15	2	–	6
Cashel	–	–	1	–	–	6	8	11	1	2	4
Emly	–	–	–	–	–	1	3	7	2	1	6
Waterford	–	–	1	1	–	1	3	1	–	–	2
Lismore	–	–	1	–	1	2	3	13	5	5	11
Cork	–	2	4	2	6	15	10	16	5	3	3
Cloyne	–	1	1	1	2	6	13	27	6	8	13
Ross	–	–	–	–	1	8	6	5	1	2	1
Killaloe	–	1	–	1	3	17	9	21	2	3	4
Kilfenora	–	–	–	–	–	–	1	2	–	1	–
Clonfert & Kilmacduagh	–	–	1	–	–	2	7	5	1	–	1
Limerick	–	2	–	–	1	10	10	12	5	3	10
Ardfert & Aghadoe	–	–	–	2	–	7	8	18	4	1	2
Total	4	63	115	100	122	336	254	287	59	48	92

Source: Report of Her Majesty's Commissioners on the Revenues and Condition of the Established Church (Ireland), p. xxxi. A small number of benefices upon which information was unavailable is excluded from the table.

bearing in mind that between 1832 and 1867 an inflation of somewhat less than 10 percent had occurred.[203] The comparison reveals that although the modal income of the clergy remained the same (£100 to £200 a year), the number of clergymen receiving incomes over £400 annually had dropped considerably. Moreover, whereas sixty benefices in 1832 had yields over £1,000 per annum, only seven benefices yielded above that figure in 1867. In addition, no benefice in 1867 was worth above £1,100 a year, whereas in 1832 three benefices were valued above £2,000. Hence, the Church of Ireland clergy, as a group, were worse off in terms of sterling income in 1867 than they had been thirty-five years earlier. To some extent, however, this decline in real income in sterling was offset by a growth in the number of benefices with glebe houses, housing represented a form of implicit income.

A comparison on the other hand of table 40 with table 17 in the first chapter indicates that the patronage of benefices in the Church of Ireland had not changed significantly since Beaufort's enumeration of 1787. In contrast to the Established Church in England, ecclesiastics (mostly bishops) of the Established Church in Ireland controlled most of the patronage. Laymen controlled relatively little of the patronage. This concentration in episcopal hands was probably useful as long as the Church of Ireland was established by law, for it meant that the authority of the bishop was considerably strengthened. On the eve of disestablishment, though, we can see with the aid of hindsight that it was a potential liability as well. After disestablishment all patronage of parish livings was to cease. The Irish arrangement was, therefore, potentially divisive; for disestablishment would automatically undercut the position of the bishops who themselves had previously controlled the majority of clerical appointments and simultaneously would admit laymen to a share in the selection process— the laity as a group being notably inexperienced in choosing clerical incumbents. This observation is not merely a theoretical comment; for in point of fact, one of the greatest difficulties the disestablished church as an organization would encounter was discovering a process whereby bishops and laymen together could amicably select the incumbents of the vacant benefices.

The Irish bishops had once flaunted incomes greater than those of most of their English counterparts, but the bishops, much more than the clergy, were reduced financially in the middle decades of the nineteenth century. Table 41 contrasts the data presented on episcopal incomes in the last chapter with the income as reported in 1867. The reader should bear in mind that not only were the bishops rewarded less in monetary terms for their services, but that many bishops were now the overseers of two, three, and four united dioceses.

TABLE 39
IRISH BENEFICES ACCORDING TO NET REVENUES, 1867
(In pounds)

Diocese	1,000 to 1,100	900 to 999	800 to 899	700 to 799	600 to 699	500 to 599	400 to 499	300 to 399	200 to 299	100 to 199	Under 100
Armagh	3	–	4	5	3	7	10	5	19	28	21
Clogher	–	1	–	3	1	4	7	8	9	16	16
Meath	1	–	–	–	1	–	5	13	35	33	17
Derry	–	2	3	3	4	5	4	19	10	11	12
Raphoe	1	–	1	–	–	2	2	7	9	6	11
Down	–	–	–	–	1	2	1	5	14	16	8
Connor	–	–	–	–	1	–	2	9	15	29	18
Dromore	–	–	–	1	–	2	2	6	7	8	3
Newry & Mourne, exempt jurisdiction	–	–	–	–	–	1	–	–	1	1	–
Kilmore	–	–	–	1	2	2	8	10	7	7	14
Elphin	–	–	–	–	–	–	–	3	7	17	10
Ardagh	–	–	–	–	1	–	4	7	6	10	2
Tuam	–	–	–	–	–	2	3	8	10	9	18
Killala	–	–	–	–	–	–	1	–	5	6	3
Achonry	–	–	–	–	–	–	2	1	4	2	3
Dublin	1	–	–	–	1	3	6	13	30	31	34
Kildare	–	–	–	–	–	1	2	6	6	17	3
Ossory	1	–	–	–	1	1	4	9	19	14	6
Ferns	–	–	–	–	2	2	7	10	13	14	11
Leighlin	–	–	–	1	–	–	4	5	17	18	12
Cashel	–	–	–	2	–	5	4	7	6	8	1
Waterford	–	–	–	–	–	–	–	1	4	2	2
Emly	–	–	–	–	–	–	4	3	6	3	4
Lismore	–	–	–	–	–	–	4	4	8	16	10
Cork	–	–	–	–	2	5	5	12	16	18	10
Cloyne	–	–	1	–	2	2	13	22	16	15	7
Ross	–	–	–	–	–	–	1	2	10	6	5
Killaloe	–	–	–	–	–	3	–	11	16	26	11
Kilfenora	–	–	–	–	–	–	–	1	–	3	1
Clonfert & Kilmacduagh	–	–	–	–	–	–	1	6	5	1	4
Limerick	–	–	–	1	1	4	–	5	15	15	12
Ardfert & Aghadoe	–	–	–	–	–	–	1	7	11	15	8
Total	7	3	9	17	23	53	107	225	356	421	297

Source: Same as for table 38, p. xxxii. Benefices for which information was unavailable are excluded from the table.

TABLE 40

PATRONAGE OF IRISH BENEFICES, 1867

Diocese	In royal patron-age	Royal and ecclesi-astical patron-age in turns	Royal and lay patron-age in turns	Royal, lay and ecclesi-astical in turns	Lay includ-ing trustees and Trinity College	Lay and ecclesi-astical in turns	Ecclesi-astical (chiefly Epis-copal)
Armagh	4	1	–	–	16	3	81
Clogher	1	–	–	–	11	–	53
Meath	31	10	5	1	24	1	33
Derry	2	–	–	–	19	1	51
Raphoe	5	–	–	–	12	–	22
Down	6	2	–	–	20	–	19
Connor	6	–	–	–	25	–	43
Dromore	–	6	–	–	2	–	21
Newry & Mourne, exempt jurisdic-tion	–	–	–	–	3	–	–
Kilmore	1	5	–	–	5	–	40
Elphin	1	2	–	–	5	–	29
Ardagh	1	–	–	–	5	1	23
Tuam	1	1	–	–	6	–	41
Killala	1	–	–	–	1	–	13
Achonry	1	–	–	–	1	–	10
Dublin	7	–	–	–	28	4	80
Kildare	10	3	–	–	8	3	11
Ossory	9	2	–	–	8	1	35
Ferns	1	2	–	–	7	2	47
Leighlin	3	9	–	–	12	–	33
Cashel	3	1	–	–	1	–	28
Emly	3	–	–	–	–	–	17
Waterford	4	–	–	–	–	–	5
Lismore	11	–	–	–	20	–	11
Cork	2	–	–	–	18	–	48
Cloyne	11	–	–	–	5	1	60
Ross	–	–	–	–	2	–	22
Killaloe	1	1	–	–	5	–	60
Kilfenora	1	–	–	–	1	–	3
Clonfert & Kilmacduagh	1	1	–	–	6	3	6
Limerick	9	–	–	–	15	–	29
Ardfert & Aghadoe	9	1	–	–	18	–	14
Total	146	47	5	1	309	20	988

Source: Same as for table 38, p. xxxii. Benefices for which information was unavailable are excluded from the table.

TABLE 41
NET INCOME OF IRISH BISHOPS, 1831 AND 1867
(In pounds)

Diocese	1867	1831	Comments
Armagh & Clogher	8,882	14,494	Armagh formerly a single archdiocese
Dublin & Kildare	7,261	7,786	Dublin formerly a single archdiocese
Derry & Raphoe	5,680	12,159	Formerly Derry only
Kilmore, Elphin, & Ardagh	4,781	6,225	Formerly Kilmore only
Tuam, Killala, & Achonry	4,311	6,996	Formerly Tuam & Ardagh
Cashel, Emly, Waterford, & Lismore	3,923	6,308	Formerly Cashel & Emly
Limerick, Ardfert & Aghadoe	3,812	4,973	
Ferns, Leighlin, & Ossory	3,424	5,730	Formerly Ferns & Leighlin
Meath	3,502	4,068	
Down, Connor, & Dromore	3,724	4,204	Formerly Down & Connor
Killaloe, Kilfenora, Clonfert, & Kilmacduagh	2,910	3,966	Formerly Killaloe & Kilfenora
Cloyne, Cork, & Ross	2,106	4,091	Formerly Cloyne only

Total episcopal net income, 1867: £54,319
Total episcopal net income, 1831 (including suppressed sees not mentioned above): £128,808

Note: Amounts less than £1 are ignored in the individual returns but included in the grand total. The amount subtracted from gross income to yield net income includes the taxes paid to the Ecclesiastical Commissioners.
Source: Same as for table 38, pp. xxv and xxx.

Turning finally to the financial structure of the Church of Ireland as a whole, one finds that the church's balance sheet changed considerably between 1832 and 1867. Although the financial reports of the royal commission of 1867 must be treated with caution, its work remains the best information we have on the church just before disestablishment.[204] The church's annual revenues (excluding implicit income) in 1867 was as follows:[205]

Land rental	£204,932	19s	7d
Tithe rent charge	364,224	16	11
Other sources	15,530	6	1
Total Net Revenue	£584,688	2s	7d

Rearranging this annual revenue by category of person or organization to which it was paid we derive the following results:[206]

Archbishops and bishops	£54,319
Deans, chapters, cathedral dignitaries and minor corporations	31,572
Beneficed clergy	398,035
Ecclesiastical Commissioners	100,762
	£584,688

We can now compare these figures to those presented in the last chapter for the year 1832:

Archbishops and bishops	£128,808
Deans, chapters, cathedral dignitaries, and minor corporations	52,541
Beneficed clergy	520,063
	£701,412

If one can accept the accuracy of the figures for the two years involved, then the Church of Ireland had suffered a serious diminution of income during the middle decades of the nineteenth century.[207] The other major financial developments of the period 1830–37 were the creation of the Ecclesiastical Commissioners, the replacing of tithes with the tithe rent charge, the abolition of the vestry cess, and the rearrangement of episcopal finances. Nevertheless, despite these important changes, the Church of Ireland in 1867 still depended for its revenues chiefly upon land rents and revenues whose origin was the modified tithe system. Despite the changes in this period, the Church of Ireland remained dependent on the same generic forms of income in 1867 that it had depended upon in 1767. Reforms had occurred, but revolution awaited.

In the years 1833–67 the Church of Ireland had undergone several shocks to its organizational life. Its administrative structure had been reorganized by parliamentary decrees and its finances reformed, if not revolutionalized. The church was increasingly an entity in a world unsympathetic to its very existence. Yet, it is possible to argue reasonably that from an administrative viewpoint the church was as strong in 1867 as it had been in 1830. The number of benefices had increased as had the number of churches. Although less well-off financially than it had been earlier, its revenues were close to adequate for its need. Moreover, if one wished to calculate religious efficiency in the same way as calculating production efficiency of a factory, the church was producing more religious service for less money in 1867 than it had earlier. It was, in that sense, therefore, a more efficient organization on the eve of disestablishment than it probably had been for centuries. But that was irrelevant. Pressure outside the church turned the attention of parliament not to the question of the church's efficiency but to the major issue of whether the Church of Ireland as a state church should exist at all. The following chapter narrates parliament's decision on that question.

4   The Intricacies of Disestablishment, 1868–1869

The Attack

The disestablishment of the Church of Ireland had little to do with political philosophy, even though the disestablishment question produced a welter of pamphlets, tracts, and books, arguing the question from a philosophical or moral viewpoint. This pamphlet literature is fascinating in itself, but almost totally irrelevant to the actual course of events. To understand what actually happened we must concentrate not on a philosophic analysis of the arguments of the pro- and anti-disestablishment literature, but on the actions of the men who wielded influence and held power.

Operationally, there were only two stages in the disestablishment sequence. The first of these evolved when the Irish Catholic Church made it clear to British liberal politicians that Ireland would not be tranquil until the Established Church of Ireland was removed as a grievance. This point was spelled out in heavy letters by Archbishop Cullen's National Association in the years 1864 to 1868. The second stage was William Ewart Gladstone's framing and passing of the actual disestablishment statute. Once Gladstone had become convinced of the necessity of disestablishment, the course of events was set. Like some great juggernaut, he could be influenced to change his direction a few degrees one way or another, but never to reverse course. Following the introduction of his disestablishment resolution in March 1868, events can be understood only with Gladstone as the focus of attention.

Turning first to Cullen's role, his position was articulated through the National Association founded in Dublin in 1864.[1] This society, which worked closely with English political liberals, sought the disestablishment of the Church of Ireland, the redistribution of land in Ireland, and state aid to denominational schools, with the church issue having priority. The National Association had the support of the Roman Catholic bishops, and of prominent liberal laymen, such as Peter MacSwiney, the Lord Mayor of Dublin, John Dillon of Young Ireland fame, W. J. O'Neill Daunt, formerly one of Daniel O'Connell's lieutenants, and Sir John Gray, proprietor of the *Freeman's Journal*. The association was an avowed political pressure group, aiming at molding public opinion and influencing members and candidates for parliament.

Because of the centrality of the disestablishment demands to the National Association's program, the association forged a seemingly strange alliance. It worked in tandem with English and Scottish Dissenters who also desired the disestablishment of the Church of Ireland—in their case a first step to disestablishing the Church of England. The British Nonconformists operated under the banner of the Society for the Liberation of the Church from State Patronage and Control (usually known as the Liberation Society). This group had been founded in London in 1853 by Dissenters, almost entirely of the liberal political party. O'Neill Daunt served as the link between the National Association and the Liberation Society; and the combined efforts of the two groups ensured that during the second half of the 1860s, the Irish Church question would be canvassed throughout the British Isles.

Significantly and ironically, the National Association, as the voice of the Roman Catholic Church in Ireland, came to demand a solution to the church question which was in conflict with Catholic dogma. According to Paley's majority principle, which was sanctioned as the official Roman position, the Irish bishops under Cullen should have been pressing for the replacement of the Anglican Church as the Established Church by the Roman Catholic Church. Instead, the Irish Catholic hierarchy almost to a man preferred a situation of religious voluntaryism, in which no state religion whatsoever was to exist. Theologically, this position implied that the state had no conscience, since if it did, morality impelled a religious establishment. This voluntarist position, despite its being theologically heterodox, was taken by the bishops for practical reasons: it made an alliance with the British liberals possible, and allowed the presentation of a political package to the British electorate which any hint at Roman Catholic establishment would have spoiled. In the end, Rome approved Ireland's theological pragmatism.

During the late 1860s certain words which bear notice flew around the voluntarist camp. Although the overwhelming majority of the Catholic hierarchy favored voluntarism, a minority of laymen with some episcopal sympathy desired "concurrent endowment" under which the Anglican Church would no longer be the state church, but in which all denominations would receive funds from its former revenues. To some extent, concurrent endowment already existed in Ireland, since the Maynooth Seminary for Catholics and the *Regium donum* for Presbyterians were provided by the British government. Concurrent endowment after disestablishing the Anglicans would have greatly augmented the income of the Roman Catholics and the Presbyterians, but most of the Catholic clergy were reluctant to accept large-scale government grants. Assuming that the Anglican Church in Ireland were disestablished, another word in use by the Catholics and the Dissenters was their demand that the Church of Ireland be "disendowed" as well as disestablished. This word implied that all of its funds and resources would be taken from the Anglican Church and that none would be granted by the state to replace them. A third term often used was "secularization" referring to the Anglican Church's revenues. This denoted the application of the funds taken from the Church of Ireland to general measures of social welfare, such as education, to be distributed by the state without distinction of religious creed.

Early in 1868 appeared the report of a self-appointed body, the *"Free-man's Journal* Church Commission" which was a lengthy and detailed investigation of the facilities, membership, and practices of the Anglican Establishment in each of the Irish dioceses.[2] This report brought matters to a head and made it clear to liberal politicians, especially Gladstone, that the Irish church question had to be solved with dispatch. But in granting that Cullen's agitation, when combined with that of the Liberation Society, influenced Gladstone to take up quickly the Irish church question, three qualifications must immediately be made. First, the National Association's activities merely accelerated Gladstone's raising the issue; his conviction that the issue was a matter of moral justice and political necessity was reached after several years of independent personal reflection on his part. Second, the real import of the antichurch agitation, therefore, was facilitative rather than causal in the Church of Ireland's disestablishment. Although the anti-Church of Ireland movement should not be credited with converting Gladstone, it should be credited with converting the majority of liberal party members of parliament and the majority of the United Kingdom's electorate. Hence, when Gladstone began his own campaign, he was sowing seeds on ground that had already been broken by the Catholic and Dissenting workers. Third, once having decided to pursue disestablishment, Gladstone was not thereafter significantly influenced by the spokesmen of the Roman Catholic Church. With the exception of minor details related to Maynooth, Gladstone did not work closely with the Roman Catholics. Cullen and his allies were left with no option but to accept the details of Gladstone's measure whether they approved of them or not.

The Defensive Reaction

Of course, almost all Irish churchmen fought vociferously against any diminution of the Irish religious establishment. Keeping that reaction in mind as their most characteristic response, we should note that the Irish bishops were not, in the first years of the agitation, the unthinking die-hards they are often depicted to have been. In the early days of the anti-establishment agitation, the Church of Ireland bishops confidentially submitted to the government a draft of a church reform bill which they wished it to undertake. The bishops' bill was designed to answer two criticisms of the Established Church: the first was that the church was overloaded with cathedrals and cathedral dignities; and the second, that the material rewards of many parishes were not proportioned to the religious duty involved—some rich parishes having few members while some large parishes yielded inadequate incomes to the incumbents. In response to the first criticism, the bishops suggested that seventeen of the thirty Irish cathedrals and chapters be abolished, and that nineteen of the thirty-two deanships be suppressed upon their becoming vacant. The cathedral chapters and associated dignities would be abolished at once, not upon vacancy. This was strong-minded reform sentiment indeed, and the bishops were equally firm on provisions in the draft bill for the income of benefices. They suggested that the parish unions be rearranged so as to provide more equal distribution of duties and that any income accruing to a benefice above a £500 net income ceiling should be paid to the Ecclesiastical Commissioners. The commissioners would be empowered to augment Irish benefices so that every one would be worth at least £300 annually and, if a curate were needed, worth a minimum of £400 per annum. Thus, both the cathedral network and the parochial structure were to be rationalized.[3]

Nothing, however, came of this flexible and intelligent response by the Church of Ireland bishops to criticism, but this was not their fault. The bishops submitted their proposal to Lord Palmerston's government and the ministry informed them in April 1864 that the government would not be a party to introducing the bill to parliament—or even commit itself to supporting the bill if the bishops themselves introduced it. In the face of government inertia it was hopeless for the bishops to proceed. Unhappily, they did not even have the bill laid on the table of the House of Lords, which would have manifested their desire to remedy defects in the Church of Ireland. The decision not to publicize the bill was made because a general election was expected and the prelates were afraid of the church's becoming involved in party warfare.[4] Later events made it clear that neither the liberal party nor the Irish nation would accept anything less than complete disestablishment, but it is fair to note that if reform, not ecclesiastical revolution, were desired, the Anglican bishops in Ireland were willing to cooperate.

The leaders of the conservative political party were, like the bishops, ready to accept reform of the Church of Ireland. In June 1867, Earl Russell moved the conservative party off dead center on the church question. Although himself a liberal, Russell held a view of the Irish church similar in many regards to that of most conservatives. Having been the scourge of the Irish church in his younger days, Russell was now sympathetic and desired its reform rather than its disestablishment. Therefore, he moved in the Lords that the Crown be petitioned to appoint a royal commission to investigate the "Nature and Amount of the Property and Revenues of the Established Church in Ireland, with a view to their more productive Management, and to their more equitable application for the Benefit of the Irish People."[5] The members of the conservative party in the Lords, led by Lords Derby and Cairns, were in accord with Russell's desire to save the Anglican Church by removing its remaining anomalies and were therefore agreeable to the commission. The only difference between liberals and conservatives was the conservatives' objection to the phrase "and to their more equitable application for the Benefit of the Irish People," which implied that church revenues might possibly be used for non-Anglican purposes. The phrase opened the door to secularization, but this was not what Russell really had in mind. Russell, the old man, rejected the idea of secularization which had been so useful to young Russell the politician. What he had in mind, rather, was the possibility of concurrent endowment—that is, a defense of the Church of Ireland by allowing a portion of its revenues to be used to endow all Irish denominations.[6] The Bishop of Ferns, Leighlin, and Ossory, James T. O'Brien, moved that the offending phrase be struck and the following words inserted: "and also as to the Means by which they may be made best to promote the Efficiency of the Established Church in Ireland," a clause which precluded the royal commission's considering either secularization of the church's funds, or concurrent endowment. After profitless debate and one division, a compromise was agreed upon whereby a full stop was inserted after the word "management" with nothing following. Compromise achieved, the resolution passed without division.[7]

Although Lord Russell had introduced the motion, it was the conservatives who were now responsible for effecting an investigation of the church, and presumably, introducing moderate reforms based on the investigation. From the beginning, the conservatives' efforts were ill-fated. For one thing, there was little enthusiasm among able parliamentarians for serving on such a commission. Originally Derby desired two members, Lords Buccleuch (chairman) and Dufferin, and one of the following: Lords Carnarvon, DeVesci, Romney, Stanhope (plus one illegible name), in addition to five or six other commissioners of whom Sir Robert Peel, Edward Howes, and Thomas Ball were the best known.[8] Not all the members of the proposed cast were willing to join the production, and in mid-August the government had to admit that the Chief Secretary had contacted a number of individuals, but that he had received a "great many answers declining the request that the writers should serve on the Commission." [9] Even those who agreed to serve often did so reluctantly. Lord Stanhope consistently refused government pleas to assume the chairmanship, although he, unlike Lord Buccleuch, agreed to serve on the commission. But so unenthusiastic was Stanhope about the task, that he later tried to resign altogether when he learned that, contrary to his previous expectations, some of the commissioners' meetings were to be held in Ireland! [10] Lord DeVesci, a Church of Ireland stalwart, tried to withdraw his name on the grounds that he was a member of the Church Defense Society and was only prevented from doing so by the information that the list of members had already been submitted to the Queen.[11] In the end, the commission was composed as follows: Lords Meath (chairman), Stanhope, and DeVesci; Sir Joseph Napier, Col. Robert Adair, and Messrs. John Ball, Evelyn Shirley, George Clive, and Edward Howes.[12] Obviously, this was not a collection of the best-known names in British politics. Significantly, and intentionally, no ecclesiastics were included.

Ill-starred in its personnel, the commission did a hurry-up job, which, as noted in the previous chapter, was far from perfect methodologically. Nevertheless, hurry as it might, the course of events outran the commission whose report was not signed until 27 July 1869. Before then, Gladstone's famous resolutions of March 1868 had changed the entire grounds of debate; for these made disestablishment, not reform, the focus of discussion. Nevertheless, with full knowledge of Gladstone's resolutions, the commissioners put forward their report. This document is worth brief attention because it represents the only viable alternative to disestablishment; and had it garnered sufficient support, the report, rather than Gladstone's plan, would have shaped the Irish church.

In essence, the recommendations were to extend the church reforms of the 1830s, consolidating and reducing the church's organization to a size commensurate with the number of Anglican worshippers. Hence, the report's keynote was reduction. The Irish church, it suggested, needed only one archbishop, and that should be the Archbishop of Armagh. Further, it had too many bishops and dioceses. It was suggested that dioceses should be united as follows: Meath united to the united dioceses of Dublin and Kildare; Killaloe and Kilfenora united to Limerick; Clonfert and Kilmacduagh and Elphin and Ardagh to the united diocese of Tuam, Killala, and Achonry; Cashel and Emly to Limerick; Waterford and Lismore to the united diocese of Ferns, Leighlin, and Ossory; Kilmore to the united diocese of Armagh and Clogher; Ardfert and Aghadoe to the united diocese of Cloyne, Cork, and Ross. Even though the workload of the individual bishops would increase as sees were suppressed, the commission suggested rigid limits to episcopal incomes. The Archbishop of Armagh was to be limited to £6,000 a year, and £4,500 for the other bishops. (This income was not to be subject to ecclesiastical taxation.) All episcopal lands, it was suggested, should be placed in the hands of the Ecclesiastical Commissioners. Since the bishoprics would be reduced, the commissioners suggested that only eight cathedral chapters should continue and that the chapters and dignities of the other cathedrals should be suppressed. Similarly, the number of archdeacons (thirty-three) was to be reduced, in this instance to two per united diocese for a total of sixteen. To raise further the standards of religious performance, the Ecclesiastical Commissioners were to be given powers to suppress benefices where divine service had not been performed for twelve months, instead of three years as stipulated in the

1833 Church Temporalities Act. Powers were to be granted to suppress livings with fewer than forty members. Further, livings worth above £300 per annum and with fewer than one hundred members were to be specially taxed. To these major recommendations, the commission added several dozen minor suggestions for improving the daily administration of the church.[13]

Conceivably the royal commission's report could have become the rallying point for the defenders of the Church of Ireland and could have been presented as an alternative to disestablishment. But here again the report was ill-starred: Irish churchmen refused to accept it. This is somewhat surprising because except for the reduction of the bishoprics, the royal commission's major recommendations had been presaged by the abortive bishops' bill of 1864. Richard Chenevix Trench, Archbishop of Dublin, was on a visitation to Cork when the royal commission's report appeared. Trench interpreted the report not as a viable defense against disestablishment, but as a humiliating curtailment of the church's privileges. Therefore, in his charge to the clergy of the diocese he denounced the report, and the majority of the Irish episcopate joined his repudiation.

Whatever the moral probity of the churchmen's decision, they made a disastrous mistake in tactics. Disraeli, now leader of the conservatives, would have been willing to join the Irish bishops in fighting disestablishment if they had accepted the royal commission's recommendation. Once the bishops had rejected the report, the position of Disraeli and all church sympathizers became impossible, for there was now no convincing alternative to disestablishment to present to the electorate and to parliament. The Irish bishops had played into their opponents' hands by leaving the electorate and parliament with the choice of either disestablishing the Church of Ireland, or doing nothing whatsoever about it.[14]

GLADSTONE'S ATTITUDE

The Colossus Ponders

"It is a matter of congratulation that the Irish Church question should at last have passed out of the region of statistics," the *British Quarterly Review* reported in April 1868 (p. 487). A month earlier, Gladstone had introduced his church resolutions and the course of disestablishment had begun. He had been anything but precipitate in his decision; and if British journalists had been bored by the six-year battle of statistical pamphlets that had preceded his motion, they would have been somnambulized by the thirty-years' thought and internal dialogue Gladstone had given to church matters.

As is well known, Gladstone began as an earnest defender of the Anglican Church. The baseline for charting his changing religious opinions is his ponderous two-volume work, *The State in Its Relations with the Church* (London, 1838). The book reads like a Gladstone speech, and is apt to make anyone with even a distant affection for the English language somewhat uncomfortable. In essence, Gladstone sketched an idealized portrait of the medieval Catholic Church. His position was simple: first, the church possessed truth, and second, the state was not morally neutral. Therefore, it followed that the state had the duty to pursue moral good as revealed by the church, and that an Established Church was a necessary essential of the national government. In practice, this meant that moral imperatives necessitated that the Church of Ireland and the Church of England be legally established as national churches. In the case of Ireland, the fact that the majority was alienated from the Anglican Church was irrelevant, for the possession of truth, not popular approbation, was the justification for a religious establishment.

Gladstone's religious work was hardly a literary success and was a black mark against his name in political circles. Almost as soon as it was published, he realized that it had been a mistake, and he soon abandoned for all practical purposes the opinions he had recently annunciated. Yet, he did not publicly repudiate his book. When in 1844 Peel decided to raise the grant to Maynooth Seminary, Gladstone as President of the Board of Trade was in an embarrassing position because his book had denounced the grant to the Roman Catholics. Most young politicians would probably and simply have admitted that their ideas had changed and remained in the cabinet, but not Gladstone. In a gesture that he himself later was to view as absurd, Gladstone resigned from the cabinet and then proceeded to vote in favor of the augmented Maynooth grant.[15] All of this was very confusing, but the Maynooth affair had a strangely liberating effect on Gladstone. Having played sacrificial lamb to his former high Anglican principles, he then felt free to continue his migration from a lofty theological view of the Irish establishment to a pragmatic political outlook. More than twenty years later he told John Bright that, once he had left office on the Maynooth affair, he had become free with respect to all Irish ecclesiastical questions. Consequently, when standing for Oxford in 1847, he declined to pledge himself in principle to the defense of the Irish Established Church.[16]

Probably because no politic occasion arose upon which he could express his new religious views, Gladstone did not publicize them until 1865, although his change of opinion was known to his friends and colleagues. Early in 1865, he had written to Robert Phillimore that he was not loyal to the Irish church "as an establishment." But he went on to add that, "I will never be a party, knowingly, to what I may call frivolous acts of disturbance, nor to the premature production of schemes of change." [17] In other words, he favored disestablishment, but only when politically propitious. On 28 March 1865, Gladstone shied at an opportunity to make his position clear when he spoke on a private member's motion that the present state of the Irish church was unsatisfactory. Although publicly admitting that he was no longer committed to defending the Irish church establishment he did not pronounce unequivocally for disestablishment.[18] Undoubtedly, some of Gladstone's hesitation in declaring for disestablishment stemmed from his apprehension about the general election which was at hand, an election in which he would again face the conservative voters of the University of Oxford. Hence, when questioned by his friend, the Reverend John Hannah, about his views,[19] he made an ambiguous reply that "the question is remote and apparently out of all bearing on the practical politics of the day. I think it would be for me worse than superfluous to determine upon any scheme or basis of a scheme with respect to it." The remainder of the letter was so ambiguous that the reader could draw any interpretation he liked.[20]

The Oxford electors did not permit Gladstone to obfuscate his failure to defend the Church of Ireland, and he subsequently lost his seat. This loss, like his resignation during the Maynooth affair, was less of a failure than a gift of freedom. Upon hearing of his Oxford defeat, Gladstone sped north and managed to win a seat for South Lancashire. Having previously sat for a pocket borough (Newark) and for the University of Oxford, he was immersed for the first time in popular electoral politics. His words in Manchester indicated his new sense of freedom: "At last, my friends, I am come among you. And I come . . . unmuzzled." [21] Gladstone kept quiet about the Church of Ireland, however, until December 1867. Why was the time now ripe for moving on the church question? Three reasons: First, Lord Palmerston, the greatest single roadblock to reform legislation, died in October 1865. Second, Lord Russell handed over the liberal party leadership to Gladstone on Christmas Day 1867 (that power would be transferred to Gladstone had become clear weeks earlier). Third, the liberals had fought among themselves on electoral reform, and Disraeli had dished them by passing an electoral reform law. Gladstone needed to find an issue that would unite the liberal party and, once reunited, they could sweep the minority conservative government from office. By mid-December 1867, Gladstone had decided that disestablishment of the Church of Ireland was that issue. On the ninth of December, John Bright sent Gladstone a copy of a plan Bright had devised in 1852, the essence of which was the severance of all connection between parliament and Irish religious bodies, with compensation to each for its loss of income.[22] Gladstone agreed with Bright that the principle of state establishment of religion in Ireland should be destroyed, and said that the basis of Bright's plans was the best he had seen, although he differed on points of detail.[23] At last Gladstone publicly announced his intention of reforming the Church of Ireland in a speech at Southport on 19 December 1867.[24]

The Colossus Thunders

Having made his decision, Gladstone eschewed subtlety and made a frontal assault on the church. On 23 March 1868, he moved three aggressive resolutions concerning the Church of Ireland. The first of these stated that it was the opinion of the House of Commons that the Established Church of Ireland should cease to exist as an establishment, with due regard to all personal interests and all individual rights of property. Second, Gladstone moved that, facilitatory to disestablishment, no new personal interests should be created by public patronage and that the Ecclesiastical Commissioners for Ireland were to confine their operation to matters of immediate administrative necessity. The third resolution asked the Queen to place at parliament's disposal her interest in the temporalities of the Church of Ireland.[25] The conservative government's response was to try to forestall the Commons' going into committee on Gladstone's resolutions. Accordingly, after Gladstone had moved that the house resolve itself into a committee, young Lord Stanley moved an amendment that precluded a committee and substituted an affirmation that the Commons, "while admitting that considerable modifications in the temporalities of the United Church in Ireland may, after the pending inquiry, appear to be expedient, is of opinion that any proposition tending to the disestablishment or disendowment of that Church ought to be reserved for the decision of a new Parliament." [26] So intense was feeling on the issue that only after several nights of acrid debate did the Commons finally vote whether or not to go into committee. Gladstone won the battle by 60 votes (330 to 270) and was well on the way to winning his holy war.[27]

Disraeli and the conservative party were now in an embarrassing position. The cabinet was divided on how firm a resistance to make to the attack on the Church of Ireland. A High Church group headed by Lord Derby and by Gathorne Hardy favored all-out resistance. But the Church of Ireland was hardly a popular cause, and others—notably, Stanley and Pakington—favored giving in on disestablishment and concentrating on obtaining the best possible terms for the disestablished church. Lord Cairns opposed disestablishment from a Low Church point of view, while Disraeli himself was partial to concurrent endowment.[28] Despite their internal problems and in spite of their initial defeat by Gladstone, the conservatives fought doggedly against his resolutions. Eleven nights of debate in committee were necessary before a division could be taken on the first resolution. That division Gladstone carried by a majority of 65 (330 to 265) thus sealing the fate of the Church of Ireland.[29] Gladstone was greatly relieved. "This," he said to the Duchess of Sutherland, "is a day of excitement—almost of exultation. We have made a step, nay a stride, and this stride is on the pathway of justice, and of peace, and of national honour and renown." [30] Disraeli was as disappointed as Gladstone was exalted. He immediately announced that the vote had altered the relations between the ministry and the House of Commons, and asked for an adjournment to consider the position.[31] Disraeli advised the Queen to dissolve parliament as soon as the new election registers under the recent electoral reform act were prepared (they were to be ready in November). It was decided that the conservative ministry would stay in office until then.[32]

The passage of the remainder of Gladstone's resolutions was now a foregone conclusion. His second and third resolutions were agreed to without a division because the conservatives realized that opposition was futile. In addition to the original three resolutions, a fourth was passed— stating that when disestablishment was effected, the grants to Maynooth Seminary and the grants to Presbyterian ministers would cease, due regard being had for personal interests.[33]

Even though he had passed his resolutions and forced a general election, Gladstone was not yet content. He continued to force the pace by introducing a bill to legally prohibit the filling of any archbishopric, bishopric, dignity, or benefice in Ireland in Crown or ecclesiastical patronage; and to transfer the revenues of benefices left vacant to the Ecclesiastical Commissioners. Further, the commissioners were to be legally prohibited from making any new grant for building or remodeling churches or glebe houses, for the augmentation of benefices, or for the purchase of glebe houses and glebe lands. The proposed statute was to take effect immediately and remain in force until 1 August 1869, by which time, presumably, the work of disestablishment would be completed.[34] The bill met little difficulty in the Commons. The committee stage lasted less than one hour, and the only change made was the addition of an extra clause that the right of any person to a share in the future Maynooth Grant or *Regium donum* should be subject to the pleasure of parliament. The House of Lords, however, rejected it by a vote of 192 to 97.[35]

This was only a minor setback, however, and Gladstone approached the November elections with gusto. In common-sense terms, the liberal party platform as understood by party members was to disestablish the church but to "give back to the Church (besides all recent endowments) the Churches, parsonages and glebes . . . [and] to give the same or an equivalent, once for all, to the Roman Catholics and Presbyterians." [36] On the hustings, the oratory was often less commonsensical, however. Gladstone, at Wigan on 22 October, made an anti-Church of Ireland speech in which he likened the Protestant ascendancy to "some tall tree of noxious growth, lifting its head to Heaven and poisoning the atmosphere of the land so far as its shadow can extend. It is still there, gentlemen, but now at last the day has come when, as we hope, the axe as been laid to the root." [37] Not surprisingly, the Anglican loyalists were inflamed. One Sussex farmer re-fused to vote for the local liberal candidate because "Gladstone wanted to bring over the Pope," and one orator, after stating to the electors that Gladstone was a Roman Catholic, produced the following couplet:

> For what does Gladstone want, I say,
> But book, and mass, and Peter's pay? [38]

In general, however, it appears that the liberals behind the oratory of Glad-stone and John Bright conducted a more vigorous campaign on the dis-establishment issue than did the conservatives. Whereas Gladstone stumped the English countryside, Disraeli was content to write an address to the electors of Buckinghamshire and to make a single speech.[39]

During the campaign, there appeared another book by Gladstone on the church question (the official publication date was 23 November 1868)[40] entitled, *A Chapter of Autobiography* (London: J. Murray). It was the reverse of the book he had written in 1838, although, thankfully, much shorter. Unlike its predecessor, this small volume did not become mired in theology, but was chiefly an explanation of Gladstone's political develop-ment and action on the Irish church question. In essence, it was a tract by the older, liberal Gladstone, repudiating the writings of the young, con-servative Gladstone. Ironically, at the very time Gladstone was dispatching his earlier arguments, these were being assumed by the conservatives. One observer, noting the irony that Disraeli (who had flirted with disestablish-ment in his High Wycombe campaign of 1835) was now using Gladstone's old propositions, likened the contest between Disraeli and Gladstone to the fencing match between Hamlet and Laertes, in which the combatants change weapons during the struggle.[41]

When the returns were tallied the liberals had a majority of 112 seats. Disraeli resigned and Gladstone became Prime Minister. Gladstone's major-ity in the Commons was large enough to allow him to approach disestablish-ment of the Irish church any way he desired.

FRAMING THE DISESTABLISHMENT BILL

The Church of Ireland's Defenders

Clearly, the Church of Ireland had little chance of a sympathetic hearing in the liberal House of Commons and scant chance of influencing any bill as it passed through the lower house. The church's defense therefore rested on the collective actions of the peers in the House of Lords and on the ability of the Church of Ireland's leaders to negotiate private concessions from the liberal ministry before the disestablishment bill was made public. The House of Lords will be considered later; at this point, our central concern is with the character of the church's leaders and their attitude towards negotiating concessions.

Unhappily for the Church of Ireland, Richard Chenevix Trench, Archbishop of Dublin, and Marcus Gervais Beresford, Archbishop of Armagh, were incapable of meeting the challenge thrust upon them. Trench was a saintly, uncompromising, gentle man, but the Church of Ireland in its trouble needed a rugged, truculent negotiator.[42] Trench was one of the most gifted and sophisticated men of his time in the humane studies, and was one of the early practitioners of the scientific study of philology. It was he who suggested the development of the *Oxford English Dictionary*. During his lifetime he published nearly three dozen volumes of poetry, history, theology, and philology. He was, however, not equipped for the rough-and-tumble realities of religious politics as played by W. E. Gladstone. The commitment to truth that Trench developed in his humane studies became merely an unbending failure to accept reality when he was thrust into the political arena. Not only did Trench refuse to negotiate with Gladstone, but he also turned his back on those conservatives who wished to defend the church from disestablishment by reducing the establishment:

> If you ask the policy which recommends itself here to the best and most earnest Churchmen, it is, first, to fight for everything which we possess, as believing it rightfully ours; recognizing of course the right of Parliament to re-distribute *within the Church* its revenues according to the changed necessities of the present time. If this battle is lost, then, totally rejecting the process of gradual starvation to which Disraeli would submit us, to go in for instant death at the hands of Gladstone. . . .[43]

Trench's counterpart, the Archbishop of Armagh (Marcus Gervais Beresford), was simply a cipher.[44] Beresford was the son of the late George de la Poer Beresford, Bishop of Kilmore and Ardagh and the grandson of the Right Honorable John Beresford who had been the head of the Revenue Board in pre-Union Ireland and the chief controller of Irish patronage. He was also related to the Marquis of Waterford and to the late Archbishop of Tuam. Having been advanced to the Bishopric of Kilmore, Elphin, and Ardagh in 1854, Marcus Beresford was chosen to succeed his cousin as Lord Primate of All Ireland in 1862. Marcus Beresford, unlike his cousin, did not distinguish himself during the early years of his primacy. He had almost no influence on the course of disestablishment legislation, although he later was a significant contributor to reshaping the disestablished church. In the late 1860s, however, the Church of Ireland was without effective leadership. No member of the hierarchy stepped forward to fill the gap at the negotiating table left by the absence of the two primates; and what little leverage the church obtained on Gladstone's legislation was to be achieved, as will be discussed later, chiefly through the voluntary activity of a single archdeacon.

Strangely indisposed as they were to compromise, the only show of concerted opposition to the government made by the Irish churchmen was the almost pathetic performance of the Church Congress of September 1868. Irish churchmen invited the congress to meet in Dublin for the express purpose of mustering as many friends of the church as possible. The keynote sermon was preached by the Very Reverend William Connor Magee, Dean of Cork and soon to be Bishop of Peterborough, on the text (Luke v:7) "And they beckoned unto their partners, which were in the other ship, that they should come and help them." The Dean of Cashel, the Very Reverend John C. MacDonnell, lectured on the fallacy that the Church of Ireland was the church of the rich. He admitted that the majority of landowners were members of the communion, but argued that the rich landowners were nonresident and those who were resident were not rich. The Reverend Alexander Irwin detailed the progress in churches and clergy that the Church of Ireland had made in the preceding sixty years.[45] These and the other speeches and sermons of the congress were no doubt comforting to the Church of Ireland leaders, but they were a needless self-indulgence. The speakers were preaching to the converted. Instead of listening to orators restating views identical with their own, the Anglican hierarchy should have been preparing to negotiate with unsympathetic politicians. The bishops, however, lacked the resolution to face the unpleasant task of dickering with the cabinet in order to protect their religious interests.

Gladstone's Early Inclinations

Everything was now in Gladstone's hands. To a remarkable degree he himself kept control of every detail of the bill's drafting. It is clear that Gladstone personally collected and analyzed the technical data about the Church of Ireland from which liberal policy was shaped.[46] He began work in December, immediately after taking office as Prime Minister. On the twenty-third one of his colleagues reported, "We have now had two Cabinets, and they have been wonderfully harmonious. Gladstone is quite an altered man; real responsibility makes him calm and his power of work is prodigious." [47]

Naturally outsiders tried to influence Gladstone's outlook. For example, Samuel Hinds, who had resigned as Bishop of Norwich in 1857, sent Gladstone a long letter dealing with the proper mode of treating property alienated from the church. Hinds assumed that the Church of Ireland was to be left with its churches, schoolhouses, clerical residences, and some of the bishops' lands, and that the bulk of alienated property would therefore consist of rent charges. Hinds' idea was that the rent charges should be held in trust by the state and only the annual proceeds expended. And who should control how they were spent? A commissioner responsible to parliament was the owner. On what was the money to be spent? Primarily, the retired bishop postulated, on the building of residences for clergymen without distinction of religious persuasion, and on pensions for disabled clergymen—again, without religious distinction.[48] Hinds was here suggesting a form of concurrent endowment without using that term. Gladstone ignored the suggestions and suggested that Hinds, a former intimate of the late Richard Whately, use his influence with the Irish clergy to obtain their consent to Gladstone's projected church bill.[49]

Instead of soliciting ideas from others, Gladstone sat down and drafted a bill himself. Logically, the first problem of attack, assuming disestablishment, was to decide how the Church of Ireland was to be transposed from an established church to a voluntary one. In Gladstone's analysis, there were three options. The first of these was that the bishops and clergy could be treated like the civil servants of an abolished department: all obligations to the church could be abrogated and they could be given pensions without duty. A second option was to allow the present ecclesiastical law of Ireland, insofar as it related to the present bishops and clergy, to continue while making all new appointments under voluntary contract. This method, Gladstone felt, had the advantage of disturbing the Church of Ireland as little as possible but the great disadvantage of involved and very complicated arrangements in ecclesiastical courts, because two classes of clerics would inevitably be created. Third, Gladstone suggested the church could be immediately and totally disestablished and the ecclesiastical courts and laws as civil statutes abolished—but with the added provision that the ecclesiastical arrangements and existing laws should be held as contracts between the bishops, clergy and laity of the disestablished church until the newly disestablished church decided to alter them.[50] Gladstone eventually opted for the third alternative because it provided both immediate disestablishment while making the reorganization task of the leaders of the disestablished church as easy as possible.

What resources did Gladstone intend to leave the disestablished church? In the case of the religious professionals in the church (bishops, dignitaries and clergy) he proposed to continue their salaries as long as they continued their present duties. Their income would be paid from an endowment representing the capitalized value of their incomes. Owners of advowsons were to be compensated, although just how, Gladstone had not decided in December 1868. Students of divinity were to receive stipends for their training according to an arrangement to be defined in detail later. Another category of grant was to be made to the Church of Ireland as a corporate body. This was to consist of all functioning churches, all glebe houses, and all graveyards. Private endowments and property given outright were to remain in the hands of the church. Endowments or property given only in part by private philanthropy were to be the subject of an option to the church: it could either receive the value of the private gift or receive the value and also purchase the residue on favorable terms. Obviously, neither the compensation of private individuals nor the transfer of graveyards, churches, and residences from the Established Church to the disestablished Church of Ireland required any intermediate agency; it could be easily accomplished by a single statute. In the case of endowments which Gladstone proposed to give the disestablished church to compensate for loss of the tithe rent charge, a body had to be created to manage the money until the church itself could effectively take over. This body would also take charge temporarily of whatever episcopal estates and glebe lands remained to the church. Already, the Church of Ireland possessed such a body—the Ecclesiastical Commissioners for Ireland—but Gladstone felt its membership, being partially made up of Irish bishops, was not suitable. Hence, he planned to create a new set of lay church commissioners to manage the church's resources in the transitional stage and to extinguish the state's last obligations to the formerly Established Church of Ireland.[51]

These half-defined ideas were hammered into a draft bill before the end of December. On the twenty-sixth, Gladstone dispatched the heads of a disestablishment bill to his Irish confidant.[52] Significantly, that confidant was not the Lord Lieutenant, Lord Spencer, but the Chief Secretary, Chichester Fortescue. Gladstone had specifically requested that Fortescue stay on in Dublin and act as his confidential agent because both the Lord Lieutenant and the Under-Secretary for Ireland were new and inexperienced.[53] Working in tandem with Fortescue was the Irish Attorney General, Edward Sullivan. On the first of January 1869 Gladstone informed Sullivan that he was just at the point of having the bill drafted. He added that the Lord Lieutenant was to pass a night at Hawarden. "I will then let him into the secret. We will otherwise remain restricted as now until we reach a further stage." [54]

Gladstone's penchant for secrecy and preference for personal management of the disestablishment measure did not mean that he did not want contact with interested parties. Indeed, he strongly desired much greater communication with the leaders of the Church of Ireland than they were willing to enter into. Not that Gladstone was very much interested in the opinions of Irish churchmen, but if at all possible he wished to convince his opponents that it was desirable for them to surrender quietly rather than fight publicly. The churchmen bridled, however, at the thought of dealing with their executioner. The acknowledged leader of the Church of Ireland at this time was Archbishop Trench of Dublin, and it was to Trench that Gladstone turned with the hope of initiating discussions. The Prime Minister informed the archbishop that "it will ever be my wish to have as much and as free communication with your Grace, in relation to our modes of procedure, as you may think fit to encourage . . . and in the second place, all views and wishes which may be entertained by the Primate and the Irish Bishops, and by other leading clergy in general, will at all times have my most respectful attention." This sounded generous enough, but Gladstone added in a paragraph noteworthy both for its tactlessness and awkwardness:

> I must not assume anything, yet I cannot exclude from view the possibility that the time may come, if it has not arrived, when the authorities of the Irish Church may desire to consider not so much whether the transition is to be effected, as the manner and conditions of it, and the point of arrival for which we are to make.[55]

In other words, Gladstone was prepared to talk with the Irish clergy about the details of disestablishment, but any discussion implied the acceptance of disestablishment on their part.

From a tactical viewpoint, Archbishop Trench would have done well to enter into negotiations, for disestablishment was inevitable. Understandably perhaps, he chose to abstain in principle from the humiliating bargaining with the government. Trench replied to Gladstone with a graceful, nearly meaningless letter, in which he recognized Gladstone's desire to hurt the Church of Ireland as little as possible, while carrying disestablishment and stating that all communication from himself or from the Archbishop of Armagh would be conducted in the spirit of that conviction.[56] This reply was much more important for what it did not say than for what it did. Trench had failed to raise either substantive points or to suggest a further personal meeting with Gladstone. Although polite enough in tone, he had administered a snub to the Prime Minister of the United Kingdom at the very moment the Prime Minister was contemplating the Irish church bill. Indeed, Trench decided that he could not conscientiously enter into negotiations, either directly or indirectly with Gladstone, a resolution which he maintained even when he visited England in February to meet with various English and Irish bishops.[57]

Gladstone's reaction was precisely what one would expect from a practical politician: irritation with those who refused to accept political reality. "The prelates and leaders of the Irish Church have at present a great and probably last opportunity of acting effectually upon the manner of proposals we shall have to make in the points that have not been publicly and authoritatively defined," Gladstone wrote to Sir William Heathcote. He added, ominously, "A garrison does not commonly, even if it may in rare cases, mend its terms by prolonging resistance when the end is, humanly speaking, certain." [58] Petulantly he told another correspondent, "the policy of silence on which the Irish prelates, or most of them, have resolved, leaves the Government to construct its own measure, without being able to say to its friends or to Parliament this is what the Irish Church desires. . . ." [59]

Whether Trench, as leader of the Church of Ireland, was right in snubbing the Prime Minister depends on whether one views the church matter as a question of politics or of religious principle. If one feels, as Trench apparently did, that consorting with the government about the disestablishment of the church was to immerse oneself in evil, then Trench's path was the correct one. If, in contrast, one views the disestablishment as a question of politics in which it behooved the church to protect its interests as best it could, then Trench and his fellows failed miserably. From a purely administrative point of view, it is undeniable that an organization is more apt to survive when its leaders are close to the center of power where vital decisions are made. Trench's policy barred the Irish bishops from the corridors of power.

The Convocation Issue

Not only did Gladstone and the Church of Ireland prelates fail to have fruitful discussions, they collided on a side issue—the question of convocation. In early January 1869, the Irish bishops and clergy forwarded a memorial to Gladstone asking for permission to meet in convocation for the purpose of discussing disestablishment. On the surface, the issue was a simple one requiring the Prime Minister to say either yes or no according to his political inclinations. Upon investigation, however, the issue was a complicated one that had a history independent of the disestablishment negotiations.

In order to understand the situation, we must step back and survey a set of events which began in the early 1860s. In 1861 the Irish bishops petitioned the Crown to convene the Irish convocation, a body which had not met since 1711. The petition was forwarded because of events in England. From 1717 to 1847 the Convocation of Canterbury had met only as a formality. It assembled every few months and was then prorogued to a date a few months later when its sole business was again to be prorogued for a few months. From the early 1830s onwards there was growing sentiment favoring reviving the English convocations as representative bodies of the Church of England. Gradually, in the late 1840s and 1850s, the convocation of Canterbury began to conduct minor debates and to receive petitions. In 1855, the convocation sat for more than one day for the first time in well over a century. Finally, in 1860, the government gave permission for the Convocation of Canterbury to meet to frame a new canon—to allow a parent to be a godparent. Then in March 1861, the Convocation of York was revived by the new archbishop, Charles Longley (his predecessor, Archbishop Thomson, had been opposed in principle to the Convocation of York's meeting and had refused to convene it). In 1860, therefore, the Irish prelates had the example of two English convocations to emulate.[60]

Substantive issues as well as emulation of the English were involved. When the English convocations changed the canon relating to sponsors at baptism, the Irish prelates, ever conscious of their being part of the United Church of England and Ireland, wished to meet to pass a similar canon. The Act of Union had made the liturgy and discipline of the two churches identical and this was the first potential divergence from that unity. If the Irish convocation could not meet the canons would not be identical; but if the changed canon was assimilated by the Church of Ireland de facto, without the sanction of the Irish convocation, the Church of Ireland would be tacitly surrendering its power of self-regulation. The upper house of the Convocation of Canterbury communicated directly with the Irish prelates asking for the advice and concurrence of the Church of Ireland on all matters of common interest. Further, the upper house of the Convocation of York expressly recognized the right of the Irish branch of the united church to share in any deliberation that required assembling in convocation.[61]

Consequently, Irish churchmen could not avoid the convocation issue. The Diocesan Conference Committee of Down and Connor presented the Archbishop of Armagh, Lord John Beresford, with a petition that he and the Archbishop of Dublin take steps to secure "that the voice of the Irish provinces of the United Church should be heard in Convocation." [62] Even without this stimulus, the Irish prelates would probably have acted, and on 20 July 1861 Beresford transmitted a memorial to the Queen—which is to say, to Lord Palmerston's government, asking to be allowed to meet in combined convocation with the Convocations of York and Canterbury. The prelates received a curt reply from Sir George Grey refusing royal permission for a general synod of the United Church of England and Ireland.[63]

Having failed to obtain a general synod of the entire Irish and English church, Archbishop John Beresford, in March 1862, turned to request permission for a convocation of the Church of Ireland. Beresford's personal appeal to Palmerston was then reinforced in November by a memorial of the Irish bishops again asking permission. The government simply ignored the request.[64] Frustrated in their petitioning, the Irish prelates turned to historical argument. In March 1863, Marcus Beresford, newly appointed Archbishop of Armagh, sent the government a long memorandum detailing the history of Irish convocation and arguing for its continuance. The central point of the historical argument was that Irish convocations had met regularly, both before and after the Reformation, and thus had the sanction of history similar to the ancient precedents of common law. Although the Irish convocation had last met in 1711, it could not, it was argued, have been extinguished; since after 1717, the Convocation of Canterbury did not meet to do any business until the mid-nineteenth century. Yet it still existed.[65] The historical approach producing no response, Beresford, acting for his own province of Armagh, turned to legal counsel. In so doing, he implicitly surrendered on the question of a convocation for the entire Church of Ireland and concentrated on the question of whether or not he, as Archbishop of Armagh, could summon a synod of the bishops and clergy of the united Provinces of Armagh and Tuam. The case was somewhat complicated, for in the Province of Dublin (comprising the former Provinces of Cashel and Dublin) the Archbishop of Dublin, as metropolitan, convened every third year a synod of the bishops, dignitaries and clergy under his jurisdiction. This practice, while well-established in the south, had long been allowed to lapse in the northern province; and Marcus Beresford was worried that he, as archbishop, no longer possessed the right to convene his bishops and clergy. Legal counsel replied that he did indeed have the power to convene his bishops and clergy in provincial synod as often as he wished, and that authorization from the sovereign was not necessary.[66]

Beresford did not have the courage of his legal convictions, however. In February 1864, he satisfied himself with sending the legal opinion about provincial synods to the government together with yet another request for permission for the Irish convocation to meet;[67] he did not actually assemble his provincial synod. When in 1865 the English canon on clerical subscription was changed, the Irish archbishops again asked to be allowed to meet in convocation and this time were informed that they were mistaken in supposing that the Irish church had any convocation; that, in fact, such a body did not exist.[68]

Although provincial synods were held at triennial intervals in Dublin, they were not called, it appears, to meet specific crises. Therefore, in 1867, John C. MacDonnell, Dean of Cashel, and William Connor Magee, Dean of Cork and soon to be Bishop of Peterborough, began agitating for the assemblage of provincial synods of the Church of Ireland. The opening volley was fired on 28 October 1867, when MacDonnell preached a sermon in Belfast on the corporate life of the church in which he strongly recommended the necessity of restoring diocesan and provincial synods or the revival of convocation. This marked an important turning point in the course of events; for heretofore, the Archbishop of Armagh had been clearly in charge of developments and had been satisfied to merely petition the government about convocation or about the northern provincial synod. A muddled set of church negotiations followed which are not worth detailing, but which may be summarized as follows: a strong group of clergy and dignities, led by MacDonnell, Magee, and Edward Stopford, pressed for the revival of convocation and for the meeting of both provincial synods to discuss the impending church crisis; distrust developed between some of the bishops and the activist clergy. The clergy claimed that the "episcopal caucus" was not qualified to represent the church during such important events, the bishops being jealous of the clergy's prerogatives and not willing to share power with them. The archbishops stalled by submitting the question of the legality of provincial synods to legal counsel again. In September 1868, the archbishops, however, did begin drafting a petition to the government for the revival of convocation. Some dignitaries were very mistrustful of the archbishops' intentions—especially Beresford's—believing that it was all a game, the next step of which was the government's refusal of the right to meet, followed by civil regrets from Beresford in public and chuckling in private; then, the fall of the curtain and the clergy go home to bed.[69]

What can we make of all this? First, it is clear that at the very time when the church needed to stand united, jealousy and mistrust separated the archbishops and a group of the more important dignitaries in the Church of Ireland. The gulf was partially a result of the dignitaries' refusal to accept the bishops as sole representatives of the church in a critical period, and partially a result of a contest for power between the episcopate and the higher clergy. Second, it becomes clear that the archbishops' desire for a revival of convocation was much less intense than it might at first appear. While wishing to revive convocation as the representative body of the Church of Ireland, the archbishops appear to have recognized that its actual meeting might, at best, be a mixed blessing because of the antics of the lower house. Therefore, Beresford, at least, appears to have been effectively neutral on the question, willing to petition for convocation's revival but quite as satisfied if the petition were denied as if the petition were granted. Possibly the archbishops' failure to summon provincial synods and their prolonged petitioning on convocation could have been helpful to the church's survival as an organization if the archbishops had quietly taken upon themselves the role of negotiators with the government. This they did not do, however, and thus left the clergy without a sanctioned means of self-expression and the government without an official source of advice on the church's viewpoint.

When Gladstone received the memorial on convocation, he considered it a "good sign." With a grasp of cold political realities he added, "They can never dream we shall let them meet except to consider terms and mode of transmission" (transmission here meant the process of disestablishment).[70] Lord Granville, Secretary for the Colonies, doubted whether it was possible for the Irish prelates to agree to conditions of surrender before the assembling of convocation, and also doubted whether it was necessary to impose surrender conditions,[71] but the Prime Minister had no such scruples. In his reply to the Irish memorial he predicted that the cabinet would follow the precedent of Lord Palmerston's government and refuse to allow the Irish convocation to meet. Gladstone predicated this answer on the reasonable assumption that the Irish convocation would assemble to oppose disestablishment. He added, however, that it was a totally distinct question what view the cabinet would take, if the intentions of the Irish prelates were simply to consider the establishment of the new church order. If this were the case, the government, it was strongly implied, would allow writs to be issued and the assembled prelates and clergy to issue a general reservation or protest before proceeding to a discussion of the details of the disestablished church.[72] The prelates would not accept Gladstone's "monstrous proposal that we may meet to do *his* work, but shall not meet if we intend to do our own." [73] And there the convocation issue finally died.

Establishing Ecclesiastical Contacts

With each passing day it became increasingly obvious that the Irish prelates were failing to deal realistically with the government, and the dignitaries and clergy of weight became increasingly uneasy. One of them, Archdeacon Edward Stopford, took it upon himself to become the unofficial representative of the Church of Ireland to the liberal government. On 22 December 1868 Stopford wrote to Gladstone from the archdeaconry at Kells stating:

> Opposed as I am on principle to the disestablishment of the Church in Ireland, to which I can be no party, I yet desire now to reconcile those who agree with me on that question, to accept the inevitable, and at once to withdraw the Church in Ireland from the arena of party conflict, by accepting a measure of disestablishment in this session of Parliament.

He continued:

> I believe that by a measure wisely drawn in a liberal spirit, this result could be obtained. I believe also that a measure improperly or unwisely drawn, will throw us back on a traditional system of church defence which I have long disapproved, and which I wish now to terminate.

Stopford deprecated Gladstone's listening to those few within the church who advocated disestablishment and instead offered his own services as a consultant:

> I have been long engaged in Ecclesiastical affairs and am familiar with all details. I believe I have the confidence of clergy and laity. I am one of the founders of a "Lay and Clerical Association," which promises to become at once influential. I am in constant communication with many influential clergymen and laymen. . . .[74]

What motivated this extraordinary offer? We can accept at face value the statement that Stopford was at least partially concerned with the Church of Ireland's welfare. Stopford, a clerical administrator of wide experience and diverse contacts, was part of the middle level cabal of dignitaries that strongly disapproved of the prelates' handling of affairs. As an administrator he must have been greatly pained to see the church's leaders fumbling incompetently in their relations with Gladstone. Having granted Stopford his sincere concern for the church welfare, it is fair to note that, as his letter makes obvious, he was a man full of his own importance who obviously desired to be at the center of power. And what headier post could such a man find than in becoming unofficial ambassador of the Church of Ireland to the Prime Minister of the British Empire? Finally, it is fair to note that one of his chief colleagues in the anti-episcopal cabal in Ireland (William Connor Magee) had been nominated by the conservatives to the See of Peterborough in England, and Stopford may have entertained visions of winning a similar honor from the liberals for himself.

Gladstone's reply was cool, but interested. He asked Stopford if he were working alone or speaking for others.[75] Stopford answered that he was not authorized at the present to speak on the part of anyone but himself, but that he had held sessions with many influential persons favorable to his views. He added that he, Dean MacDonnell of Cashel, and Bishop Magee of Peterborough (the original nucleus of the Irish anti-episcopal caucus) were on the verge of founding an association to promote their views. Significantly, Stopford made it clear (to the modern reader if not to Gladstone) that he was intentionally moving against the Church of Ireland prelates; for he asked Gladstone to allow a lay and clerical synod to be held in Ireland as in Canada and Australia, but without power to make legally binding canons.[76] This suggestion was made at the very time the Irish bishops were known to be drafting their memorial on convocation, a petition which would almost inevitably be refused.

After consulting the Attorney General for Ireland, Gladstone decided not to encourage a church meeting as suggested by Stopford,[77] but he welcomed assistance by the Irish churchman on technical questions. With a measure of relief and of skepticism he noted, "Archdeacon Stopford unequivocally offers his co-operation. He evidently thinks himself a considerable person as a man of business." [78] Later, he described Stopford's position in relation to the government as "cooperation under protest." [79] Eventually, as the following statement indicates, Gladstone came to view Stopford as the representative of the entire Irish church:

As long as they [the Irish prelates] stand, following up the resistance of last year, with the sullen silence they now maintain, like Ajax before Ulysses in the underworld, it is not in my power, whatever may be in my will, to go any pledge whatever, except that I shall act for the best and so will the Govt.

Archdeacon Stopford has manfully stepped into the breach; and if a certain number, even of those around him and above him, on that side of the water, . . . would do the like, it would be of great service to the Irish Church in the hour of need.[80]

Gladstone invited Stopford to visit Hawarden to discuss the Church of Ireland bill. Stopford arrived on 14 or 15 January 1869.[81] Before Stopford's visit, Gladstone remained uncommitted, determined to guide the discussions according to what he saw in Stopford,[82] but Stopford's personality soon overcame the Prime Minister's hesitation. "The mists of the I.C. Question seem melting away," Gladstone wrote to the Chief Secretary for Ireland after his meeting with Stopford.[83]

Unfortunately, no direct record of the Gladstone-Stopford conversations is available. Gladstone informed Bishop Wilberforce that the discussion had turned in part upon the main points which a disestablishment bill would have to deal with and that in this regard they were "satisfactory." The second part of the discussions centered on the present and probable future attitude of the Church of Ireland's leaders to the government measure and the effect that attitude would in turn have on the ministry and on important provisions of the bill. Stopford's opinion was that the bishops of the Church of Ireland would remain universally silent until after the second reading of the bill. It was difficult, Stopford reported to Gladstone, for only one or two of the bishops to step out of line, and also difficult for members of the next order of clergy—some of whom were extremely well disposed to work with the government—to come out without episcopal sanction. Gladstone suggested that if some episcopal support were given from England, the three leading churchmen in favor of dealing with the government (probably meaning Stopford, Bishop Knox of Down, Connor, and Dromore, and Dean MacDonnell of Cashel) could then operate publicly as a nucleus in Ireland, pressing for adjustment and accommodation. Stopford accepted this suggestion and agreed to act upon it, with the aid of the Bishop of Peterborough, William Connor Magee, former Dean of Cork.[84]

While employing Archdeacon Stopford, Gladstone was simultaneously raising a coterie of English bishops who were willing to cooperate, albeit reluctantly, with his Irish church policy. The majority of English bishops would not collaborate with Gladstone, and most felt it their duty to defend the Church of Ireland, although it is far from clear that their defense was heartfelt. In the mid-1860s a shrewd and cynical Irish churchman had likened the relations of the Church of England and the Church of Ireland to that of Louis XI of France and the astrologer Martius Galeotti. As related by Scott, when the king had resolved to put the astrologer to death and had given secret orders to the royal attendants to execute him the minute he left the royal presence, he paused to ask him to divine the hour of his own death. The astrologer replied that this would take place exactly twenty-four hours before that of the king. Naturally, the superstitious monarch countermanded the order of execution and watched carefully from

then on over the astrologer's health. In the same way, the leaders of the
Church of England protected the Church of Ireland, not from conviction
or with enthusiasm, but from the fear that the dismemberment of the
Church of Ireland would be a portent of their own destruction.[85]

A minority of the English bishops, however, were willing to work with
the government. The chief of these was Samuel Wilberforce, Bishop of
Oxford. Wilberforce was the English bishop one would most have expected to find so engaged: he had a thorough knowledge of how non-dis-
establishment Anglican communions operated,[86] and was an intuitively
political person and a political realist. Of his own volition Wilberforce
wrote to Archbishop Trench as soon as the results for the general election
of 1868 were clear, suggesting that the time had come when the leaders
of the Church of Ireland had to consider whether any compromise was
possible and, if so, on what matters. He argued that the government had
a strong enough majority to make it impossible for the church to win a
reversal of its sentence, and that attempts to delay the measure by churchmen might produce an extremist reaction from the church's opponents.
Therefore, he argued, much more could be gained by compromise than
by resistance.[87] Almost needless to say, Trench rebutted the argument.[88]

Obviously Wilberforce needed only slight encouragement by Gladstone
to become a valuable government ally. Gladstone first made contact with
him on 11 December when both were guests of Lord Salisbury at Hatfield.
Gladstone charmed Wilberforce, and the bishop obviously came under the
politician's spell.[89] During their conversations at Hatfield, Gladstone became convinced that Wilberforce's position was in substance that of Stopford; namely, willingness to cooperate under protest.[90] Cagily, Gladstone
did not directly pursue Wilberforce, but had two (unnamed) friends write
to him without using Gladstone's name, and by early January he was able
to report, "I think we have got the Bishop of Oxford right on the Irish
Ch[urch]." [91] Actually, he need not have been so devious, for on the
thirtieth of December 1868, Wilberforce had written a semi-public letter
to Archbishop Trench forcefully arguing the need to compromise.[92] Gladstone opened direct discussion with Wilberforce in mid-January in a letter
in which he described Archdeacon Stopford's activities and pointed out
that some help from the English side of the water would strengthen the
hand of the moderates with the Church of Ireland.[93] Wilberforce agreed to
work with the government—albeit like Stopford, under protest—and
promised to contact the Bishops of Peterborough and Chester.[94] Gladstone
obliquely encouraged Wilberforce to action: "Now for every practical purpose all those who have opposed it [the church measure] are opponents
until they signify, as emphatically as they spoke or acted before, that with
the change of the scales their opinion as to the right mode of action has
changed. Those who *act* like Archdeacon Stopford become our practical

supporters, and have a right to be considered. . . ." [95] As if there were any doubt about Wilberforce's being on Gladstone's side, the bishop sent the Prime Minister a copy of a pamphlet he was writing on the church question—a proof copy of which he had sent to Archbishop Trench, the Bishop of Limerick, Archdeacon Stopford and Lord Plunket. [96]

After Wilberforce, the prelate one would most have expected to join the pro-compromise coalition was William Connor Magee who had been appointed to Bishop of Peterborough shortly before Disraeli left office. He was the first Irish churchman since the Reformation to be appointed to an English bishopric. Disraeli's first choice for Peterborough had been Canon Champneys, a Low Churchman, to whom the Queen had objected. Instead, she suggested Magee, then Dean of Cork, who was a moderate evangelical and one of the greatest preachers of the day. [97] Magee had been, along with Archdeacon Stopford and John MacDonnell, the Dean of Cashel, the leader of the antiepiscopal caucus which had opposed the Irish prelates noncompromise policy. Hence, even before Archdeacon Stopford met with Gladstone, Stopford had conferred with Bishop Magee. [98] Magee assured Stopford that he was willing to do all he could to bring about a desirable settlement. [99] Magee's willingness to work with Gladstone stemmed from his belief that "the Government wants to deal generously, if they dare or can; and want help against their own extreme men." He was worried, however: "We are in the position of a part of a garrison besieged by an army, half regular, half savages. Is Gladstone strong enough to keep his savages from scalping us, if we once lay down our arms?" [100]

The web binding the pro-compromise ecclesiasticals was strengthened when Wilberforce wrote Magee two letters outlining his own position and enclosed a copy of the letter to Lord Lyttelton, which Wilberforce intended to publish. Magee agreed to cooperate with the Bishop of Oxford since their views on the future of the Church of Ireland were identical. [101] Bishop Magee, although concurring with the sentiments of Wilberforce's pamphlet, would have preferred it not to be published. (When Archbishop Trench protested, Wilberforce decided, on the basis of his longtime friendship with Trench, not to have it published.) [102] Eventually, Magee would become disgruntled when, in his view, the ministry did not go far enough to meet the demands for concessions to the Church of Ireland; and he would speak eloquently against the second reading of the disestablishment bill. For the time being, however, he was one of Gladstone's ecclesiastical supporters.

Three other English bishops were on the periphery of Gladstone's clique. The Bishop of Chester, William Jacobson, worked fairly closely with Wilberforce, and on at least one occasion joined Wilberforce in visiting Gladstone to discuss the Irish church question. [103] The Bishop of Saint David's, Wales, Connop Thirlwall, was disposed to work with Wilberforce and Jacobson.[104] The Bishop of Gloucester, Charles Ellicott, while opposing disestablishment, was pleased that Gladstone, rather than an enemy of the church, was in charge, and hoped for the bill's passage in the present session.[105]

Given Gladstone's tactical assumption that the best way to draw out latent Irish support for a compromise with the government was to have a nucleus of English bishops endorse a transaction with the liberal ministry, how successful was he? On the second of February, he optimistically spoke of the Bishops of Meath, Limerick, Derry, Killaloe, and Down as being among the "more favourable" Irish bishops.[106] On 3 February, however, the Irish bishops met; only Bishop Knox of Down, Connor, and Dromore spoke out against the intransigent attitude of the Irish hierarchy.[107] The adhesion of Bishop Knox can hardly have been a great comfort, for Gladstone earlier had been informed by Wilberforce that the Bishop of Down "is worse than nobody." [108] Hence, as judged by its effect upon the attitudes of the Irish hierarchy, Gladstone's dealings with the British bishops and with Stopford were far from successful.

On 10 February 1869, a group of English and Irish bishops assembled. Those present were: the Archbishops of Canterbury, York, Armagh, and Dublin; the Bishops of London, Durham, Saint David's, Oxford, Llandaff, Bangor, Norwich, Gloucester, Bristol, Ely, Chester, Rochester, Lichfield, Hereford, Peterborough, Meath, Limerick, and Derry. In essence, there were three groups present: the leading Irish prelates, the English bishops from Gladstone's pro-compromise caucus, and other assorted, influential English prelates. The meeting accomplished little, although it did allow Gladstone's friends to present their case. The Irish bishops repeated their refusal to negotiate and most of the English bishops present remained unenthusiastic about any one course of action.[109]

Benefits to the Church

To note that Gladstone's negotiations with the English bishops brought him little direct political gain is not to conclude that the work of Stopford, Wilberforce, and company was wasted; for the negotiations considerably benefited the Church of Ireland, obtaining for the church concessions that would not otherwise have been granted. Before turning to details of specific issues, we must first ask, what, in general, did the Church of Ireland leaders want, assuming they recognized the inevitability of disestablishment. For an answer we can turn to Archbishop Trench who, while refusing to negotiate directly with Gladstone, came over to England and made contacts in moderate circles. In particular, he worked with Lord Carnarvon, Sir William Heathcote, and Sir Roundell Palmer. After a dinner with Trench and Carnarvon on the eleventh of February, Palmer (a liberal who had refused a place in Gladstone's cabinet because he opposed church disestablishment) sent Gladstone a list of suggestions which, if adopted by the government, would probably result in an influential portion of the Irish bench advising their people to acquiesce to the measure. One can safely assume that these suggestions embody Trench's ideas and indeed, may well have been sent to Gladstone with Trench's knowledge and approval. The suggestions were as follows:

1. The Church of Ireland to retain all churches and glebe houses "with whatever property appertains to them," (probably meaning glebe lands and grave yards) and all endowments of private gift
2. All parochial endowments left to the church since the reformation to be guaranteed
3. The life interests of present incumbents to be preserved
4. A reasonable interval of time to be allowed before the disestablishment becomes effective
5. The Church of Ireland to be free to assemble national synods or any other appropriate body to frame new arrangements for its administration
6. When the new church system is adopted, the church to be completely free from state intervention[110]

Significantly, only four days after Palmer's letter Bishop Wilberforce, who had been contacting various prelates on Gladstone's behalf, wrote to Gladstone asking to be empowered to offer certain concessions which would be "of weight enough to tear the heart out of the opposition" and would draw the majority of English and Irish prelates, under protest, behind Gladstone's church policy. Those conditions were strikingly similar to the ones relayed by Palmer to Gladstone after meeting with Trench. As stated by Wilberforce they were:

1. The disestablished church to be totally free of state interference
2. All existing life interests to be preserved and capitalized
3. The Church of Ireland to maintain possession of all churches, glebe houses, post-Reformation endowment and private benefactions
4. The church to be given sufficient time to make new arrangements before the act became effective[111]

Clearly, the close similarity between the guarantees asked in the Palmer and the Wilberforce letters to Gladstone as the price for the Irish bishops' compliance was not accidental. Both Palmer and Wilberforce were in contact with men on the highest echelon of the Church of Ireland, and their letters represent an indirect communication of terms from the Irish prelates to the Prime Minister.

On 10 February Gladstone, in an interview with Bishop Magee, stated that he would leave the Church the following:

1. All life interests to be capitalized in a lump sum for a church trust fund
2. Incumbents to be allowed composition of their life interests
3. The Church of Ireland to decide for itself whether or not state patronage of Crown livings would continue
4. Two years of grace to be allowed before the church act could become operative
5. All churches to be turned over to the Church of Ireland provided it undertook to keep them up
6. The life value of glebe houses to be given to the Church of Ireland[112]

The difference between Gladstone's position and the church's was, in the first instance, that whereas the church leaders wished to be given glebe houses and glebe lands outright, the Prime Minister was willing to turn over only the value of life interests. A second difference was that the churchmen wanted to maintain all post-Reformation endowments, a boon which Gladstone was not willing to promise. The third difference was not made clear in the correspondence, but there was some difference between the way the church wanted life interests of the clergy treated and Gladstone's inclinations. In the course of events the glebe problem was a subject of prolonged negotiation betwen Gladstone, the Irish bishops, the Irish Presbyterians, and the Roman Catholics in Ireland. The post-Reformation endowments question received comparatively little attention in negotiation and was eventually determined primarily by Gladstone himself. The matter of life interests of the clergy was the subject of secondary bargaining.

Turning then to the specific negotiations about glebe houses and glebe lands, it is well to recall that Gladstone's original instinct, as expressed in December 1868, was to allow the church to keep all its glebe houses and its glebe lands up to a certain limit. By early January 1869, however, the Prime Minister was under pressure to be less generous. John Bright, one of his confidants at this stage in the proceedings, advised him to leave the church only its buildings and parsonages, and no glebe lands whatsoever.[113] Gladstone replied that he proposed to treat the church liberally on the matter but acknowledged that "the glebe houses are undoubtedly the toughest nut we have got to crack." He continued: "It is probable that the Presbyterians may play a rather important part in the matter. This peculiar cross between Scotchman and Irishman has undoubtedly a very good nose for catching any scent of public money." [114] Presumably, for every concession granted the Church of Ireland in lands and houses, the Presbyterians would demand a corresponding bounty, an escalation of expense the economy-minded Prime Minister would not countenance.

The Presbyterian pressure against generosity to the Church of Ireland was reinforced by the Irish Roman Catholics. Gladstone corresponded with Sir John Gray, the proprietor of the *Freeman's Journal*, who was his tie-line to the Roman Catholic hierarchy. In mid-January, Gray reported that Cardinal Paul Cullen, Roman Catholic Archbishop of Dublin, and his "ecclesiastical counselors" (meaning the Irish Catholic bishops) had met and were of the strong opinion that Gladstone's proposals would not result in complete disendowment of the Church of Ireland or in perfect religious equality. In particular, if the glebe houses and lands occupied by the Anglican churchmen were handed over to the Church of Ireland, the Catholic hierarchy would oppose this course on the grounds that Gladstone proposed not a complete disendowment of the Church of Ireland, but merely a partial disendowment. Such a course, the Catholic prelates believed, would merely substitute "an unassailable for an assailable unequality [sic]." The Catholic prelates were willing to give the Church of Ireland options to purchase the glebe lands and glebe houses at market prices and to have a loan fund set up to advance money for that purpose. This fund, the Catholic prelates felt, should advance money for the building of Roman Catholic churches as well as for the repurchase of Protestant glebe houses and lands.[115]

Archdeacon Stopford tried to argue the case for the Church of Ireland. Stopford sent Gladstone a memorandum on the glebe question which Gladstone read carefully and circulated to his colleagues as an able statement of the church's viewpoint.[116] Stopford also met directly with the Chief Secretary for Ireland, Chichester Fortescue. In reply to Fortescue's argument that most of the glebe houses had been built from public rather than private endowments (and hence should not be turned over to the Church of Ireland after disestablishment), Stopford argued that nevertheless, the glebe houses, having been almost all built since the reign of William III, were identified with Protestantism and were regarded with feelings not very unlike those associated with the churches. Stopford pointed out that ever since Gladstone had introduced his resolutions in March 1868, churchmen and the general public had expected that the houses would be treated like churches, since very little distinction had been drawn at that time by Gladstone between the two. If the glebe houses were not left as a gift to the disestablished church, it would be generally considered an act of excessive severity. Stopford's final argument was that of the sum of £1,167,000 which had been recorded (during an unspecified time span) in building and restoring the 936 Irish glebe houses, more than 50 percent (£618,000) had been paid personally by the incumbents.[117]

Fortescue was impressed by Stopford's arguments and communicated them to Gladstone with some additional reflections of his own. The Chief Secretary reported to the Prime Minister that his researches in Irish ecclesiastical law revealed that there was no trace of any power in ecclesiastical law to compel an incumbent to build a glebe house beyond the discretionary power of a bishop to oblige a clergyman (where the net revenue for the benefice exceeded £100 a year) to lay out two years' income on a house. In point of fact, many glebe houses in the past had been built voluntarily by the incumbent for his own advantage and that of the Church of Ireland. Many of these houses, Fortescue argued, would not have been built if it had been known that on a certain date the Church of Ireland would lose the residence undertaken by the sacrifice of the incumbent. To deprive the church of the houses, therefore, was to break faith. A second major argument in the church's favor put forward by Fortescue was that the houses were of little value to the state, but of great value to the church. Hence, by implication the general welfare would be increased by leaving them in church hands.[118] These arguments led Fortescue to propose a plan under which the disestablished Church of Ireland would be given the right to buy back limited quantities of glebe land and all the glebe houses. The latter would be included in the purchase, but listed at no value, or at a very moderate value.[119] A fortnight later, he modified his scheme to give one half of the value of the glebe houses free to the church, with the balance to be purchased by the church. The reasoning behind this division was that approximately half of the value of the Irish glebe houses represented private expenditure, the other half public expense.[120]

Gladstone did not see the virtue in Fortescue's plan,[121] and in the bill he eventually introduced, the church was given the option of purchasing its glebe houses from the state at the rate of twelve times the annual value of the building. Thus, in a period of less than three months, from mid-December to early March, Gladstone moved away from an inclination to give the church the glebe houses, and some glebe lands, to a determination to give it no lands and only a first option on the purchase of the residences. One wonders if this trend in the Prime Minister's thinking could have been stopped, or reversed, if the Irish bishops had agreed to negotiate directly with him.

Besides the glebes, a second specific issue of negotiation was the question of how to treat the interests of the Church of Ireland clergy who were serving at the time of disestablishment. These men had become clergymen with the expectation that their salaries would be paid for life under a state-church arrangement, and justice dictated that they be compensated for the state's breaking the implicit contract it had with them. Gladstone clearly recognized this obligation, and, further, was disposed to compensate these interests by capitalizing them in a manner to be of greatest possible service to the disestablished church as well as to individual clergymen.[122] Hence, the difference between the churchmen's desires and the liberal ministry's inclinations was much less than on the glebe question.

Archdeacon Stopford drafted a clergy compensation plan worthy of our attention because it established the vocabulary employed in subsequent discussion. The first principle of Stopford's plan was that all clergy, dignitaries, and bishops had a right to an annuity from the government yielding a continuation of the cleric's annual income for the rest of his life. Second, Stopford suggested the principle of "voluntary commutation," under which clergymen could capitalize the value of their annuity and hand it over to the authorities of the Church of Ireland. This would be an act of faith on the clergymen's part, for they would undertake commutation on trust that the church authorities would invest the money prudently and thus be able to pay them undiminished salaries for the rest of their lives. The value to the church authorities of this plan was that if they invested the money shrewdly, the authorities could reap a return on the clergymen's capital greater than the salary they had to pay to him. A third aspect of Stopford's plan was the idea of "compounding," under which a clergyman could quit the Irish ministry and Ireland altogether if he wished and receive a sum to compensate him for his loss of prospects. Stopford suggested that this sum should be one-half the capitalized sum of the clergyman's life interests. Quite openly, it was a compensation for those clergymen who could not tolerate the idea of continuing in a non-established church.[123]

It soon became clear that Gladstone would accept the principle of Stopford's plan; although he questioned Stopford's additional suggestion that some kind of bonus be employed to induce clergymen to commutate and also wondered if it were right, in the case of the compounders, to give a man a capital sum equal to one-half his life interest and then allow him to simply disappear.[124] Here Gladstone's perspective and that of Stopford differed, for Gladstone was concerned about the effect that compounding and retirement from the Church of Ireland by clergy would have upon the congregations, while Stopford was worried about preserving the rights and interests of the clergy, irrespective of what this did to individual congregations. Stopford, who was not taken into the cabinet's confidence during the actual drafting of the bill, became worried that the measure would include the principle of voluntary commutation without the addition of the bonus and inducements necessary to make it work.[125] He need not have fretted, for with the addition of some stipulations about the payment of curates (negotiated by Edward Sullivan, the Attorney General; Chichester Fortescue, the Chief Secretary; and John MacDonnell, the Dean of Cashel),[126] Gladstone's bill when it appeared was patterned, in its provisions for clergy interest, on Stopford's plan.

Why was Gladstone so much more willing to meet the church's requests concerning life interests than he had been concerning glebes and glebe lands? The answer appears to be that, on the life interests issue, the church's desires followed the lines of a precedent with which Gladstone was acquainted and of which he approved, namely, that of Canada. During the second half of the eighteenth century, lands in Canada known as the "clergy reserve lands" had been granted to endow the Anglican clergy. At first the revenue from the lands was allotted solely to Anglican clergymen, but later Presbyterians came to share in the bounty. During the nineteenth century, however, the Roman Catholics and the Free Church party among the Presbyterians agitated against the reserved land system; and in 1853, an act was passed by the Canadian legislature asking the British government to completely secularize the lands. In turn, the British government gave the Canadian legislature power to deal with the matter itself; but by the time the matter came up, the Anglican clergy had garnered enough support to block complete secularization. Therefore, instead of complete secularization, the bill provided that the life interests of the clergymen should be bought out by the immediate payment of a lump sum. The churchmen of Canada then created an arrangement whereby a clergyman could commute his life interest and turn it over to the Incorporated Church Society, which would invest it and pay his lifetime salary. The scheme was a great success, for the church authorities invested the money so well that they had a surplus left after paying out lifetime salaries.[127] Gladstone was aware of the Canadian events and had watched them with interest. Moreover, Canadian churchmen had publicized the success of their arrangement so that the scheme was reasonably well known by those politicians and clergy seriously interested in church reform (Stopford in his original plan had referred to the "Canadian precedent"). Therefore, when Stopford let it be known he was asking on behalf of the church for a settlement on the Canadian model, he was making a move predestined to be successful. Gladstone also viewed the plan within the framework of the Canadian experience, and in discussing the final proposals in the Commons, made it clear that they were merely an adaptation.[128]

If Gladstone and the churchmen made at least indirect contact on both the issue of glebe houses and lands, and the question of life interests, they made no significant contact on the general question of church endowments. The differences in outlook on this question were too great for any negotiation. The church would have liked to have kept all its endowments. Gladstone, however, refused to permit retention of any which stemmed from the state. Quite correctly, Bishop Magee concluded, "This reduces the question now to one of good terms on details." [129]

The Presbyterians and the Roman Catholics

Naturally, the most important and complicated negotiations Gladstone conducted were centered on the Church of Ireland, but he also had to conduct tertiary bargaining with the Presbyterians and with the Roman Catholics. In the second half of December 1868, Gladstone received a statement of Presbyterian claims and asked the Chief Secretary for Ireland to determine whether the statement represented the official claims of the Presbyterian Church, or merely individual viewpoints.[130] The Prime Minister followed this with a direct request to the Moderator of the Presbyterian Church in Ireland, asking him to put forward in writing their claims that should be compensated in the disestablishment bill.[131]

The Presbyterians assumed that they would lose all government grants which they presently received, but expected compensation similar to that being given to the Anglican Church. The most important of these government subventions was the *Regium donum* which had been provided since the early eighteenth century. This was essentially an augmentation of the salaries of the Presbyterian ministers. The Presbyterian clergy, therefore, had a just claim to have their life interests from this source guaranteed, just as the clergymen of the Established Church had such a claim for their entire salaries. A second claim was made, that the assistant ministers in the Presbyterian Church deserved some compensation, for they had entered the ministry with the expectation that at some time in the future they would be eligible for a grant from the *Regium donum,* an expectation which was now being extinguished. Third, the government had given a small amount to the Presbyterian Clergy Widows Fund. More important was a fourth government subvention that was now to be lost: the government paid the salaries of £250 a year to professors at the General Assembly's college in Belfast, plus £250 for general college expenses. These subventions would now cease and therefore had to be compensated.[132]

In view of the compensation needed for the *Regium donum* and for the theological professors, the Presbyterians asked for the same rights of commutation that were to be granted the Church of Ireland. In the bill as finally drafted, Gladstone granted this request. He was also disposed to grant compensation for the Presbyterian assistant ministers and for the Belfast College building grants, although he felt the claims were not, in strict justice, a clear-cut right of the Presbyterians.[133] The real issue at hand, therefore, became not whether the state would grant compensation under each head, but how much it would grant. Leaders of the Presbyterian Church argued that their rate of compensation should be higher than that of the Anglicans. The reasoning behind this claim was that the Church of Ireland population in Ireland was roughly equal to the Presbyterian population, yet the Church of Ireland had about 2,000 ministers and the Presbyterian Church only 500. Clearly, the logic went, the Church of Ireland was overstaffed and less efficient than the Presbyterian Church. Hence, the rate of compensation for the Presbyterian ministers should be greater than for Anglican priests.[134] Gladstone was not to be swayed from the principle of treating all denominations alike and he suggested that fourteen years' purchase (that is, multiplying the annual amount payable by fourteen) was a reasonable minimum to compensate all of those with vested interests,[135] and this rate was eventually proposed in his draft bill. By and large, the Presbyterian leaders were satisfied.

A similar set of negotiations took place with the Roman Catholics. In these dealings, Gladstone was essentially trying to determine what a just course of action was, not what a politically expedient course would be, for he knew that the Roman Catholics in Ireland would support almost any measure disestablishing the Anglican Church. In Gladstone's thinking, the Presbyterian College in Belfast and the Maynooth Seminary were tandem cases and must have identical solutions. Since they were religious institutions, they could no longer receive state money; and since they had received state money in the past, they each deserved to be compensated. The principle of religious equality dictated that the compensation for Maynooth be the same as that for the Presbyterian College and for Anglican interests. Hence, the Roman Catholics were to receive a capital sum equal to fourteen times the seminary's annual grant, just as the Presbyterian College was to receive fourteen times its yearly state grant.[136] Gladstone arrived at this conclusion of his own volition without any political pressuring, and the Catholic authorities intelligently recognized that they had no alternative but to accept his solution.

The only point, other than Maynooth, about which the Roman Catholics and the government had dealings was on the Rock of Cashel. The rock belonged to the Established Church, but was not maintained. Near the end of January 1869, Archbishop Leahy sent Gladstone a memorial asking that in the church disestablishment bill he would somehow provide, by purchase or other means, that the Rock of Cashel be turned over to the Roman Catholic Church. These claims were repeated by both Bishop Moriarty and Archbishop Cullen. Gladstone did not wish to become involved in a dangerous side issue. Since the original memorialists had insisted that they sought the site not as Roman Catholics, but merely as Irishmen wishing to prevent the ruin of an historic site, Gladstone employed the convenient expedient of taking them at their word. In the bill, he provided that unused places of worship, of historical value, were to be vested in the Commissioner of Public Works to be maintained as national monuments.[137]

By the end of February 1869, Gladstone had completed his own study of the Irish religious situation, had communicated directly with the Roman Catholic and Presbyterian Churches, and indirectly with the Church of Ireland (through Stopford and the English bishops). All this time he was drafting, and having others draft, various portions of the bill. On the first of March the long awaited measure was introduced.

THE CHURCH BILL FROM INTRODUCTION TO ROYAL ASSENT

The Contents of Gladstone's Bill

Gladstone's Irish church bill was logical in its construction and rigorous in its completeness.[138] Its purposes were fourfold. First, the severing of all official relations between the Irish religious denominations and the state; second, the creation of an interim agency to facilitate the transition between the eras of establishment and disestablishment; third, the creation of a body to continue the religious work of the Church of Ireland; and fourth, the sequestration of surplus church revenues and their application to the general welfare.

The first clause of Gladstone's bill proclaimed that the union of churches of England and Ireland, which had been formed in the Act of Union of Great Britain and Ireland, would be dissolved; and that the Church of Ireland, now separated from its sister church, would cease to be established by law. The date for the disestablishment was 1 January 1871.

This drastic surgery accomplished, the remainder of the bill dealt with the means of moving gracefully from the days of an Anglican state church in Ireland to a totally voluntary religious situation. For the future of the church, no section was more important than the set of clauses which defined the powers of the newly disestablished Church of Ireland (clauses 19 through 22). The government operated on the principle of providing the church with the maximum freedom to guide its own future, short of ecclesiastical chaos. Hence, all laws restricting the Irish church's meeting in assembly, synod, or convocation, were to be repealed. Once having met and agreed among themselves what future religious structures and practices they wished to adopt, the representatives of the Church of Ireland were to be granted a charter under the title of "Representative Body of the Church of Ireland." As a legal unit, this group could hold property and would be the legal embodiment of the Church of Ireland. Significantly, in order to avoid ecclesiastical anarchy, Gladstone's bill provided that the ecclesiastical law of Ireland, the existing articles of doctrine, and the established modes of discipline would continue to be binding upon the church until of its own free will, the church chose to alter them. The effect of this provision was to give the leaders of the Church of Ireland full freedom to modify their doctrine and practice if they wished, while simultaneously guaranteeing that religious practice and order would be maintained until they explicitly undertook to do so. Simultaneously, all ecclesiastical courts and ecclesiastical laws in Ireland—a legal embodiment of the principle of establishment—were, with the exception of matrimonial ones, to cease to exist as statute laws. In the future, the ecclesiastical laws adopted by the Church of Ireland would be regulations for the internal operation of the organization and would not have the status of government law.

While providing for the formation of the Representative Church Body for the disestablished church, Gladstone's bill also formed another corporate entity: the Commissioners of Church Temporalities in Ireland (clauses 3 through 13). The body was essentially a central clearing house for settling all the financial details of disestablishment. In a sense, the Temporalities

Commissioners were successors to the Ecclesiastical Commissioners, reconstituted and given expanded powers. Unlike the Ecclesiastical Commissioners who were to be dissolved as a body when the act became effective, the Church Temporalities Commission was to be a professional body with no unpaid members, such as bishops, included. Moreover, unlike the Ecclesiastical Commissioners, the Temporalities Commissioners unquestionably would be civil servants—not half civil servant, half independent as their predecessors had been.

The powers of the Church Temporalities Commissioners were to be considerable; for in theory all church property and all life interests were to be confiscated, and then those whose interests were damaged would necessitate compensation by the commissioners. And what compensations were the commissioners to make? One category of claims was to consist of individuals whose professional future was damaged by the Irish church bill (clauses 10 to 17, 41, 43, 44). For example, all the beneficed clergy, dignitaries, bishops, and archbishops, had assumed their positions with the understanding that they were entering into the stable and secure employment of a government-financed venture. Gladstone's bill, therefore, honored these expectations by providing that the Church Temporalities Commissioners would issue each of these office holders an annuity equal to the amount of his yearly salary (less the expense of maintaining a permanent curate and a diocesan schoolmaster if the incumbent had regularly employed them). This annuity was to last for life, or until the office holder ceased to discharge his religious duties. Permanent curates were to be compensated with a lifetime annuity equal to their salary. This was to be voided, however, if the annuitant left the curacy for which the annuity was given. This provision was potentially harmful to the Church of Ireland, for it would have made it difficult to induce an able permanent curate to take up a full incumbency in his own right, since he would be compromising his own financial security to do so. Temporary curates were to receive up to £200 in a single gratuity; diocesan schoolmasters and parish clerks were to receive lifetime annuities as long as they performed their duties in the same school or church for which their annuity was granted. Interestingly—in an obvious instance of social class bias—Gladstone's bill provided that organists, vergers, and other minor functionaries were to receive not a lifetime annuity, but a gratuity of up to one year's salary as compensation. The two Ecclesiastical Commissioners who had been salaried, and those members of their staff who would not be needed by the Church Temporalities Commissioners, were to be paid an unspecified amount annually and set jointly by the Treasury and the Ecclesiastical Commissioners before their final dissolution. The vicars-general and other officials of the church courts, who would suffer by dissolution of those courts, were to be paid a lifetime annuity in amounts at the discretion of the Church Temporalities Commissioners.

A second, minor category of persons deserving compensation were those individuals or corporate bodies who owned the right of presentation to benefice or cathedral dignities. The amount of this compensation was to be set by the Church Temporalities Commissioners on principles undefined in Gladstone's bill (clause 18).

More important was the third set of claims, namely, those of the Church of Ireland as a body to endowments, buildings, and revenues (clauses 25–30). Here Gladstone was far from generous. The Church Temporalities Commissioners were to entertain and, it was assumed, grant applications from the Representative Church Body for title to all churches actually in use as Anglican houses of worship; burial grounds annexed to the churches were to be included in the conveyance. The provisions for glebe houses were less benevolent. The church was allowed to buy back the see and glebe houses for a moderate price (twelve times the annual value if no building charge was outstanding). Additional land, up to ten acres for a glebe house and thirty acres for a see house, could also be re-purchased by the church on terms to be negotiated between the Church Temporalities Commissioners and the Representative Church Body. Perhaps most controversial were the provisions for endowments. Gladstone stoutly refused to allow the church to keep any endowments that came from the state. This left the church with only private benefactions, and even these were limited to ones acquired after 1660 (in theory the Presbyterian congregations were considered as part of the church until after the Restoration).

Following the Canadian precedent, as interpreted by Archdeacon Stopford, Gladstone's bill gave the clergymen, dignitaries, and bishops of the church an opportunity to use their annuities to aid the church (clauses 23 and 24). The annuities could be converted into a capital sum and turned over to the Representative Church Body for its management. The church body would pay the annuitants a salary and absorb any loss or assume any profits its management of the money yielded. This was not the same thing as reendowment of the church; rather, it was the grant of a license to the church authorities to speculate with its clergy's money, if the clergy approved.

In order to meet their fiscal obligations the Church Temporalities Commissioners were, with certain restrictions, empowered to sell the property vested in them which was not claimed or repurchased by the Representative Church Body (clause 33). When the commissioners had fulfilled all their obligations under the measure, the surplus money remaining was to be expended by the government in the promotion of assorted Irish social welfare services: infirmaries, hospitals, lunatic asylums, industrial and reformatory schools; education for the deaf, blind, and mentally retarded (clause 59). Presumably the principle behind these arrangements was that the majority of the church's endowments came from the state originally, and hence from taxation of people of all denominations; and that as many of these bequests as possible should be returned for the benefit of the entire nation.

One of the misconceptions often entertained about Gladstone's church bill is that it was a boon to the peasantry because it relieved them of tithe rent charges. Actually, all that happened was that the tithes that were formerly paid to the church were to be turned over to the government in the personages of the Church Temporalities Commissioners. Doubtless this new arrangement was more palatable to the majority of Irishmen since it was well known that the revenues so raised would eventually go for social welfare services, not for the support of the Protestant Church; but from an economic point of view, the incidence of the tax on the Irish population remained unchanged. The only major difference was the provision that the person liable to the tax could redeem it for twenty-two-and-a-half times the amount he paid annually, and could pay this redemption in equal installments over a period of forty-five years (clause 32).

As was to be expected, given a knowledge of Gladstone's communications with Presbyterian and Roman Catholic authorities, those denominations were equally compensated for their losses (clauses 36 through 40). Those ministers receiving the *Regium donum* were, like Anglican clergymen, to have the right to a lifetime annuity equal to the amount they formerly received. The same held for the professors at the General Assembly's College in Belfast. Assistant ministers were to be compensated for their loss of prospects by a lifetime annuity, the amount to be determined by the Church Temporalities Commissioners. Ministers and professors were to have the same rights of commutation as that possessed by the Anglican priests. Both the Presbyterian College and Maynooth Seminary were to be compensated for their loss of government revenues by capital grants equal to fourteen times the former annual grants. Similarly, a fourteen-fold grant was to be made to the Presbyterian Clergy Widows Fund. Finally, any debts the trustees of Maynooth owed to the Commissioners of Public Works were cancelled.

Although the convenience of the Maynooth and Presbyterian provisions in Gladstone's Irish church bill was compelling—since it allowed Gladstone to sever all state-religious financial ties in one fell swoop—it is worth noting, that in one sense, the provisions were in violation of the internal logic of his bill. Unlike all the other expenses and interests which were compensated by the Church Temporalities Commissioners, the Presbyterian and Roman Catholic interests had not previously been a charge on the Established Church, but had been paid directly by the exchequer of the United

Kingdom. Therefore, the compensation money was not properly a charge on the funds of the Established Church, but on the exchequer. Of course, in reality the source of the compensation made little difference, because the excess resources of the Church Temporalities Commissioners were eventually to be confiscated by the state for social welfare services; in effect, the money was simply being subtracted in advance from Irish social service funds.

Viewed solely as an exercise in legislative draftsmanship Gladstone's Irish church bill was an impressive, polished document. The bill was logical, coherent, and self-consistent. It provided strong guidelines for action, but left both major parties, the Church Temporalities Commissioners and the Representative Church Body, a good deal of freedom to perform their tasks as they saw fit. The measure was doubtless painful to the church, but at least it was intended to shorten the pain by taking effect quickly. Gladstone made certain that the measure was even handed out among religious denominations. He was scrupulous and humane in protecting the pecuniary interests of all individuals concerned. The only nagging doubt was whether or not the bill provided the church as an organization with all the endowments to which it was entitled. But this was more a moral than a political question, and Gladstone and the leaders of the Church of Ireland profoundly differed on the answer.

The Commons: Minor Alterations

After all the planning, drafting, and negotiating on the Irish church bill, its passage through the House of Commons was a mixture of verbiage and anti-climax. The long speeches in debate appear to have been made not to the members of parliament but to the public outside its walls. No real conflict occurred during passage, and to describe the set speeches of the opposition as grand tactics would be trumpery. The plain fact was that Gladstone had such a large majority in the Commons that the conservative speeches were more in the nature of a ritual than of practical politics. Some amendments were passed, but these alterations had the liberals' approval. Hence, rather than dwelling unnecessarily on the details of debate, one can simply establish the following chronology of events during 1869.

1 March, bill read the first time after debate (bill 27)

18 March, second reading moved and debated

19 and 22 March, second reading debated

23 March, question put. Ayes 368, Noes 250. Bill read a second time

15 April, Commons resolves itself into committee by vote of 335 to 229

16, 19, 22, 23, 26, 29 April; 3, 4, 6, 7 May, bill considered in committee

7 May, bill reported (now bill 112)
13 May, bill, as amended, considered
28 May, bill recommitted and considered (now bill 123)
31 May, bill read a third time. Ayes 361, Noes 247

The majority of Irish churchmen remained unalterably opposed to the bill and would not countenance its passage in any form. Frustrated in the Commons, the churchmen had recourse to an expedient that was novel in the history of the Church of Ireland: they convened an assembly of the entire church, north and south, attended by both clerical and lay delegates. This conference, held in Dublin on 13 and 14 April, was a no-surrender circus. The Archbishop of Armagh, Marcus Gervais Beresford, opened the proceedings with a bitter denunciation of Gladstone's bill: "We are not come here to amend Mr. Gladstone's Bill, or to throw out any suggestions respecting it. We condemn it utterly, from first to last, in principle. We look upon it as confiscation." The Dean of Clonfert, James Byrne, complained that, "The modern history of Ireland is mainly a record of alternate rebellion and confiscation; but this is the first time in our annals that rebellion has been followed *by the confiscation of the property of the loyal.*" The Reverend Dr. Traill, a Fellow of Trinity College, Dublin, thundered, "I hope, my Lord, that this day Mr. Gladstone will receive such an answer from our Church throughout the length and breadth of the land; that he will hear such a response from the Giant's Causeway to Cape Clear, such a reverberation from Macgillicuddy's Reeks to the Mountains of Mourne, as will convince him that all-powerful though he be with his giant majority in the House of Commons, that . . . he will still find that the Protestants of Ireland will not endeavour to smooth the rugged path upon which he has chosen to enter. . . ." The speeches rang on and on, bitter, pompous, frustrated, and anguished. None of them had the slightest effect upon the events taking place in Westminster.[139]

Given the fact that there were no effective political pressures impinging on the passage of Gladstone's bill (the conservative party was numerically weak, the Anglican churchmen ineffective, the Presbyterians and Roman Catholics satisfied), one would expect, correctly, that the changes in the bill would be minor. What were they? [140] The significant ones were as follows: The amended bill actually named the three men who would be Church Temporalities Commissioners: James Anthony Lawson, one of the Justices of the Court of Common Pleas in Ireland; Viscount Monck; and George Alexander Hamilton, conservative politician and privy counselor. The salaries of the commissioners which had been left blank in the original bill were set at a maximum of £2,000 a year. Although all cathedrals were to be dissolved as legal bodies, a new amendment provided that every dean and archdeacon was to maintain his title and precedence for life. The amended bill made it clear that any clergyman or bishop who was eligible for an annuity on the basis of his maintaining his position in the church, could move, with the approval of the Representative Church Body, to other benefices or bishoprics within the Church of Ireland, and still maintain his right to the government annuity. This addition greatly improved the bill by facilitating clerical mobility and allowing outstanding clergy to be promoted without compromising their financial position. The bill as it finally passed the Commons protected the annuitant rights of clergymen who were prevented by age or disability from staying at their posts. Also, the maximum total gratuity to those deserving curates, who did not legally qualify as permanent ones, was raised from two hundred to six hundred pounds, to be calculated at the maximum rate of £25 for each year of service.

The Church of Ireland was given a financial boon when the price of rebuying the glebe houses was reduced from twelve years annual rental value to ten. New provisions were introduced to assure that the Church of Ireland retained plate, furniture, and moveable chattels belonging to the churches. The amended bill tightened the accounting procedures for the Church Temporalities Commissioners and brought their accounts within the mold prescribed by the Exchequer and Audit Departments Act of 1866. The amount of compensation to the Presbyterian College in Belfast was limited to £15,000, and provision was made for compensation to the theological professor of the nonsubscribing association of Presbyterians to whom the government had made grants in the past. A new clause was introduced directing the Church Temporalities Commissioners to ascertain whether the chancellor and prebendaries of Christ Church, Dublin, were entitled to the right of succession to certain benefices; and if so entitled, to compensate them adequately. The amended bill stipulated that whenever capital sums were paid in lieu of annuities (as in commutation by clergymen) this sum was to be calculated at the rate of 3.25 percent per annum. The figure was generous because reasonably safe investment policies at that time were producing over 4 percent a year. The Church Temporalities Commissioners were empowered to borrow money from the Treasury, if necessary. In addition to the alterations enumerated above, dozens of small changes were made in the bill by the House of Commons.

While the Commons was tinkering with Gladstone's bill, important Irish and English bishops assembled on 6 May 1869 to decide what to do when the measure reached the House of Lords. Present were the Archbishops of Canterbury, York, Armagh and Dublin; and the Bishops of London, Durham, Saint David's, Oxford, Llandaff, Norwich, Gloucester, Bristol, Ely, Chester, Rochester, Lichfield, Hereford, Peterborough, Limerick, and Derry —all of whom had been present at the February bishops' caucus—with the addition of the following who had not previously caucused, the Bishops of Ripon, Worcester, Lincoln, and Tuam. Predictably, such a diverse body of prelates did not come to any conclusion on how to proceed; but, significantly, the Irish bishops made it clear that they would fight uncompromisingly against the bill's second reading in the House of Lords and have amendments ready for the committee stage.[141] The battle in the Lords, therefore, promised to be a good deal more interesting than the puppet show in the Commons.

The Lords: Serious Bargaining

"The Irish deputation have been and done it!" the Bishop of Peterborough wrote exultantly to a friend, "The Lords will throw out the Bill. Cairns and Derby evidently see that to pass it would estrange all their Irish and many of their English supporters." [142] The bishop's jubilation was unfounded, however, for the peers of the realm were anything but firm in their resolve to vote against the bill. The Queen was averse to any course of action that would bring the two houses of parliament into conflict; and even the leaders of the Church of England were not certain of the wisdom of blocking passage. Archibald Campbell Tait, Archbishop of Canterbury, was convinced that a rejection of the second reading, especially if it were by a small minority of bishops' votes, would be far more dangerous to the Church of Ireland than would its passage. He wrote to Lord Cairns, the Ulster barrister who was the unofficial commander of the Church of Ireland's defenses, that it would be best to devote opposition efforts to securing amendments in the later stages of debate.[143] Even before the second reading, Lord Granville, Secretary of State for the Colonies, was contacted by the Archbishops of Canterbury and of York who wished information on amendments that might be acceptable to the liberal ministry.[144] Archbishop Tait also corresponded directly with Gladstone, but to no avail.[145] The Irish bishops did little in debate to stiffen the peers' backbone. ("The Archbishop of Dublin made a melancholy and almost inaudible 'keen' for the Irish Church. No one listened to him.")[146] The second reading passed on 18 June by a vote of 179 to 146. Nearly forty conservative peers voted with the majority, and three liberal peers with the minority. Bishop Thirlwall of Saint David's was the only bishop to vote for the second reading, and sixteen English and Irish bishops voted against it. The two English archbishops and ten English bishops abstained.[147]

After the second reading, the Lords went to work for eight nights and had produced sixty-two amendments to the bill by the time it was read for the third time on 12 July. Most of the sixty-two amendments were minor, but a goodly number of them were of signal importance. The description of the amendments is best presented in two parts: first those amendments of significance which the Commons was willing to accept; and second, those it refused.[148]

The Lords suggested, and the Commons (meaning the Prime Minister) agreed, that the Church Temporalities Commissioners should be required to be members of either the Church of England or of Ireland; that the commissioners should reimburse each claimant for all reasonable expenses incurred by him in establishing his claims to compensation under the measure; that the rules of procedure by the Church Temporalities Commissioners should be subject to Irish privy council approval; that Roman Catholics who, but for the provisions of ancient statutes would have possessed advowsons, should be compensated.

These were significant, but secondary changes. Much more important was the amendment to which the Commons agreed, dealing with private endowments. Instead of the complicated business of compensating the Representative Church Body for all private endowments given the church since 1660, the Church of Ireland was to receive £500,000 as a lump sum settlement. This solution had the beauty of simplicity and doubtless saved a good deal of litigation. Also of prime importance was the agreed addition that the clergy of the Church of Ireland who took up their appointment before the passage of the act were not bound by any alteration in articles, doctrine, or rites of the church, so long as they made known their dissent within six months after the alteration. Further, such dissent was not to deprive the clergy of their annuities or compensations under the act. The significance of this provision only became clear after disestablishment, when the laity and the more evangelical clergy tried to alter the doctrine and ritual of the Church of Ireland. The Lords' amendments provided those holding more traditional Anglican views with security, and thus reinforced their position in the liturgical-theological battles that ensued.

The Commons' agreement to these amendments was forwarded to the Lords on the sixteenth of July. But in the same message, the Commons also refused to accept a goodly number of the Lords' modifications. For example, the Commons refused to accept the Lords' amendment postponing the effective date of the act to 1 May 1871 and instead insisted on 1 January 1871. More important, a major clash between the two houses came on the clause which dealt with glebe houses. In place of the Commons' provisions for the Church of Ireland's purchasing the glebes at ten times their annual value, the Lords inserted a scheme of concurrent endowment of Irish religion. The Lords' plan was to remove the provisions requiring the church to pay for each glebe house, and to substitute a free gift of glebe houses to the Church of Ireland. In addition, annexed glebe lands of ten acres were to be allowed free to each clergyman and thirty acres free to each bishop. Further, the Lords proposed in cases where an Anglican, Roman Catholic, or Presbyterian minister or bishop lacked a residence, that housing and annexed lands should be provided free of charge by the Church Temporalities Commissioners out of the funds of the former Established Church.[149]

This was obviously an endowment of religion, and was in direct opposition to Gladstone's principle of severing all relations between the state and Irish religious denominations. Gladstone was not even tempted to accept the idea of concurrent endowment of the Irish denominations; but even if he had been willing, political factors would have militated against his supporting it. Archdeacon Stopford informed him that "I can find no support for it in Ireland." [150] Cardinal Cullen informed Cardinal Manning (who passed the letter on to Gladstone) that the Irish Roman Catholic bishops did not want government money, and that in his opinion, the concurrent endowment scheme was a device to renew the endowment of the Church of Ireland while silencing the Catholics with mere crumbs.[151] Writing to Gladstone directly, Cullen said that in his opinion, the bill as modified in Lords would do no good in Ireland, because it failed to satisfy the Protestants and the Catholics looked on it as a measure for strengthening the Protestant church. The Catholics, Cullen noted, would look on the granting of glebes to Catholic bishops and clergy as an insult rather than as a step towards religious equality.[152] As if the political realities were not convincing enough, the financial realities underscored the lesson. Gladstone estimated that the concurrent endowment plan granted about £1,100,000 in glebe houses and lands to the Church of Ireland, an expense that Gladstone, ever financially stringent, would not tolerate.[153]

Another point of contention was the Lords' proposal that the amount of commutation for bishops and clergymen, who commutated and had the money paid to the Representative Church Body, be calculated at fourteen times their yearly income. The Commons replied by suggesting a capital sum sufficient to provide their annual income (certainly less than the fourteen years' purchase) plus a 7 percent bonus to the Church of Ireland and to the Presbyterian Church if four-fifths of the ecclesiastical members decided to commutate. On this point, unlike that of concurrent endowment, a matter of bargaining, not principle, was involved. Some minor bargaining was also dictated on the question of how much to pay for curates' compensation.

The two remaining matters on which the houses clashed were related. The Commons wished to specify that the residue, left over after the Church Temporalities Commissioners had done their work, would be applicable only to certain specific purposes. The Lords wished to leave the residue to be distributed at the discretion of a future parliament. Related to this difference was the conflict on the preamble of the bill. The Commons' version specified that the surplus funds be used for the general advantage of the Irish people and not for the maintenance of religion. The Lord's version left the uses unspecified.

These issues then—glebe houses, commutation bonus arrangements, curates' salaries, and allocation of the surplus—split the two houses. Gladstone was not willing to consider giving way on the glebe houses because the Lords' amendment involved concurrent endowment, an arrangement inimical to the principle of his bill; but he was willing to modify his stance on the three other topics. After the Commons had sent its response to the Lords' amendments to the upper house, Gladstone met with his cabinet to decide terms for negotiations. He and the cabinet agreed that they would be willing to barter on the residue (or surplus) clauses, leaving to a future parliament the decision of what to do with surplus church property. The liberal government was also inclined to make further slight improvement in the terms of curates' annuities and to grant some further pecuniary concession to the church as a whole, though not a very large amount.[154]

Having determined the boundaries of negotiation, Gladstone, at first, shrewdly avoided a direct approach to his opponents, but went instead to the Queen. Victoria, while unwilling to endorse any particular proposal, approved Gladstone's inclination to reestablish contact with the Archbishop of Canterbury, Archibald Campbell Tait. Cannily, Gladstone asked the Queen's permission to employ Gerald Wellesley, Dean of Windsor, as an intermediary between himself and the archbishop. Wellesley was one of the Queen's closest ecclesiastical advisors and Gladstone well knew that his usefulness would not be limited to acting as message-carrier between the Prime Minister and the Lord Primate. Indeed as events worked out, Wellesley became not only an intermediary link between Gladstone and the English bishops, but an intermediary link in a chain to the Irish bishops: Gladstone to Wellesley to Bishop Magee of Peterborough to the Irish prelates.[155]

In any case, the Dean of Windsor's first job was to contact Archbishop Tait. The message Gladstone wished communicated was that, under no circumstances, would the cabinet accept the idea of concurrent endowment. He argued that postponing the allocation of the surplus to a later parliament was unnecessary to the Church of Ireland's interests, since in any case the surplus could not be used for religious purposes (he made this argument while, as we know, being willing to give way on the point). Gladstone also communicated to Tait through Wellesley, that the ministry was prepared to make finance concessions to the curates, and to stimulate commutation worth £170,000 to £180,000.[156]

On 18 July, Disraeli entered the stage; Lord Bessborough served as his messenger. Disraeli wrote that he was willing to give in to Gladstone and allow the present parliament to specify the manner in which the residue, left in the hands of the Church Temporalities Commissioners, would be spent. But he demanded pecuniary concession to the Church of Ireland in the form of commutation bonuses and curates' allowances costing, Gladstone had estimated, an additional £900,000 to £1,000,000. Gladstone himself was now willing to concede, at most, an additional £250,000, although some members of the cabinet were inclined to give up to £500,000.

Disraeli's terms were therefore refused but in such a way as to leave the door open to further bargaining.[157]

On Monday the nineteenth, it was the turn of the Archbishop of Canterbury to meet with Gladstone; and on the twentieth, the Archbishop gave Gladstone a memorandum from yet another interested party, Lord Cairns. Since Cairns was the Church of Ireland's unofficial spokesman, it was natural that he would want larger concessions for the church than would Disraeli, whose interest in the church was less than wholehearted. It was tactically stupid, however, for Cairns to follow the course he now chose; he demanded concessions worth an estimated £1,119,000. This was considerably more than Disraeli had asked, and the demand irritated Gladstone a good deal. Simultaneously, while making Gladstone angry, Cairns implicitly let Gladstone know that the opposition was far from united on the Irish church bill, and that Gladstone could therefore proceed more firmly than if he faced a cohesive band of opponents. Even the Archbishop of Canterbury was surprised at Cairns's demands and told Gladstone that he personally had not meant to back any demand for more money than Disraeli had claimed. Gladstone told the archbishop that the government would concede an additional £300,000 and no more.[158]

Tuesday night the Cairns phalanx in the House of Lords raised its demands for financial concessions to an estimated £1,400,000. The cabinet met at 11:00 the next morning to determine its response to this financial escalation. The cabinet considered four courses of action: to wash its hands of the Irish church bill altogether; to go through all the amendments and revise them again, and then if the Lords still would not agree, to refuse any further responsibilty for the measure; to go through only the endowment amendments and, if the Lords still were unreasonable, abandon responsibility for the measure; to send the bill back to the Commons with the intention of having the Commons adhere to its amendments as last adjusted. The cabinet chose the third course, which is to say it chose to continue negotiation.[159]

Gladstone now turned to exploiting certain pressure points. First, on Wednesday, 21 July, he wrote the Queen soon after the cabinet meeting, explaining the cabinet's position. This meant that the Dean of Windsor and the Archbishop of Canterbury would soon be in the proceedings, undoubtedly pressing for concessions from the opposition. Second, he let Sir Roundell Palmer know the government's intentions, and Palmer became convinced that the opposition should concede to the government. Palmer was useful because he had excellent contacts among higher churchmen and among conservative leaders. In particular, Gladstone used him as a bridge to Lord Salisbury.[160] Third, and most important, Gladstone deputized Lord Granville to deal with Lord Cairns. Since Gladstone was ill on Thursday,

22 July, the conclusive negotiations of that day fell almost completely on Granville's shoulders. Granville and Cairns negotiated for most of the day. In the morning Cairns held out for concessions worth £850,000. After the morning meeting there was a second conversation between Granville and Cairns. A third meeting was scheduled for 4:00 in the afternoon. Cairns went off to see Lord Salisbury and Archbishop Tait. He returned for the afternoon meeting and met with Granville and with the Irish Attorney General, Edward Sullivan. To Granville's surprise, Cairns agreed to an arrangement which actually yielded less than the £300,000 the liberals had been willing to give the church. Between 5:00 and 6:00 Gladstone was able to telegraph the Queen and followed with a letter at 7:00 which informed her that the Lords had accepted the bargain and that general satisfaction prevailed.[161]

What was the bargain? First, the Lords gave up the idea of concurrent endowment, an amendment which Gladstone opposed on principle, and on which he would not waver. Second, the government gave in to the Lords on the issue of the residue; they left to a later parliament the application of the surplus in the hands of the Church Temporalities Commissioners when their work could be completed. Third, in the case of the Anglican and Presbyterian denominations, it was provided that if three-quarters of those of each denomination eligible for annuities decided to commutate by 1 January 1873, the respective denominations were to receive a 12 percent bonus. This was strong encouragement to commutation. Whether the bonus may be looked on as a partial reendowment of religion is hard to say, but Gladstone clearly did not view it as a violation of his principle of religious neutrality. Fourth, the highly technical arrangements for compensation for curates were made slightly more generous.[162]

Why the Lords had given way so quickly was a mystery to Gladstone. "The proceedings upon the other side which ended so favourably are almost inexplicable," he told Lord Clarendon.[163] They are not explicable to a modern observer either, unless one is willing to accept the speculation that the reason the Lords crumbled is because the conservative opposition to the bill was disunified. Cairns and Disraeli differed on terms, Archbishop Tait pressed for moderation, and Lord Salisbury's opinions were molded by the moderate Sir Roundell Palmer. Clearly, on the afternoon of 24 July, Cairns was told by Salisbury and by Archbishop Tait that they would not fight for the £850,000 demand he had made that morning, much less for the £1,400,000 involved in the Lords' amendments over and beyond the concurrent endowment scheme. Cairns's retreat was probably the action of a man who had just lost his allies.

The bill received the royal assent on 26 July, and, save for a few details, that was the end of the matter.

A CONCLUDING VIGNETTE

William Alexander, Bishop of Derry and Raphoe, wrote the following:

I can never forget the summer night just after the division when I reeled out into the cool air almost hearing the crash of a great building.

A kindly touch was laid upon my arm. I turned, and saw a Roman Catholic Bishop of my acquaintance who had obtained a place to listen to the debate.

"I cannot pretend not to be pleased," he said, "though personally I am sorry for you and others."

Then he patted my arm again, and added—

"Now, my dear Lord, you see what these English are!" [164]

5 Completing an Administrative Revolution, 1870–1885

INTERPRETATIONS OF THE NEW AGE

The views of two anonymous essayists:

> The abolition of the Irish Establishment is in some respects the most remarkable event connected with the ecclesiastical history of these kingdoms which has occurred since the days of the Reformation.[1]
>
> It may be remembered that the mover of the [disestablishment] bill, in his celebrated speech of the 1st of March, compared the Irish church to Gloucester in "King Lear." The change to be effected, he said, was imagined to be a "leap over a precipice 'ten masts high,'" but was really only the fall of a few feet." There are senses, indeed, in which the leap of the Church of Ireland may be as dangerous as Gloucester supposed . . . but . . . these results may be to a considerable extent arrested as we will presently show, by the wisdom and liberality of Irish churchmen themselves.[2]

A member of an influential Irish religious family wrote:

> It [the Church of Ireland] is not in the position of a Church which has never had an establishment. It is like a child who has been only lately set to walk on its legs. It has the double disadvantage of having to learn and unlearn.[3]

And William Connor Magee, Bishop of Peterborough and an acute observer of the Irish ecclesiastical scene, told an Irish dignitary:

> Your three rocks are coming over the surface already.
> 1. Liturgical revision,
> 2. Lay tyranny, and
> 3. Schism between north and south.
> Still, I think you will weather them; but the second is your greatest danger.[4]

REORGANIZING THE CHURCH

Jockeying for Position

The clergy and laity of the Church of Ireland had approximately a year and a half after the passage of the church disestablishment act to organize for the future. A great deal of work had to be done. The entire structure of the church had to be revamped, and the financial underpinnings of the organization had to be totally remade. Churchmen also had to wrestle with questions of doctrine, because disestablishment made manifest some doctrinal fissures within the church which had previously been latent and invisible. All this restructuring had to be accomplished by clergy and laity who were inexperienced in the workings of a voluntary church. Reorganization therefore, was an architectural experiment and a hazardous one at that. In carpentering their new structure the churchmen could not afford to fail, for if the walls of the newly formed Church of Ireland crumbled they probably would never be rebuilt.

Reorganization was immensely difficult because it involved the redistribution of power within the Church of Ireland. Clearly, it was necessary for the role of the laity to be redefined and upgraded. Whereas in the old days of the Established Church they had been the bottom of the ecclesiastical pyramid, the laity as a collective group now assumed a dual role: they continued in theology to be the bottom of the church pyramid, but in practice were now elevated to a new position of power. Admittedly, before disestablishment the members of Parliament had possessed great influence on the church's activities; but this was a very different situation than occurred after 1869, when laymen as a group acquired large-scale powers in the Church of Ireland. The laity's new-found powers arose because they were now expected to pay more of the church's expenses than they had in the past. In return for their financial aid they expected increased control over the church. The aggressive spirit of the laity was reinforced by their tendency to be more evangelical theologically than the majority of clergymen. Hence, they demanded greater power not only because it was now paying for the religious tune, but because the tune played by the clergy often offended the more evangelical laity.

If the increased importance of the laity implied that the reorganized Church of Ireland would have to come to terms with the principle of religious democracy, there was a pre-existent principle that also had to be considered. That was the principle of religious aristocracy, or religious hierarchy, implied in the division of the church into laity, lower clergy, dignitaries, and bishops. Inevitably, the independence and authority of the ecclesiastics had to be lowered if the position of the laity were to be raised. The delicate task for the Church of Ireland as a collective body was to find a way to merge the principles of religious democracy and religious hierarchy without lowering the prestige of the clergy to the point that large-scale defections and resignations would occur. The process of negotiation between the professionally religious and the laity was a necessarily unpleasant business. To the Church of Ireland's great good fortune and considerable credit, it weathered the years of reorganization, and did not allow internal friction to produce a permanent schism.

The reorganization process began soon after Gladstone's statute was on the books. In April 1869, there had been a general convention of the laity, clergy, and prelates of the Church of Ireland to protest against the course of the disestablishment legislation. After disestablishment it would perhaps have been natural to simply reconvene that body. To do so, however, would have implied granting the laity equal rights with the clergy in the reconstruction process. Hence, instead of recalling the national convention, the bishops tried to protect their prerogatives; on 18 August 1869 the Archbishops of Armagh and Dublin each called for their respective provincial synods (groups which did not include laymen) to meet in Saint Patrick's Cathedral, Dublin, in mid-September. The synods punctiliously observed ecclesiastical protocol. The Archbishop of Dublin and his suffragan bishops invited the Provincial Synod of Armagh and Tuam to sit jointly with the Provincial Synod of Dublin and Cashel. The northern synod met on the tenth of September, and accepted the invitation, thus making it possible for the joint synods to begin meeting in united session on 14 September. Operationally, the united provincial synods were simply the old Irish convocation, revived under a new name. Like convocations of old, the united synods were composed of two houses. Twelve members—two archbishops, and ten bishops— formed the upper house, with Archbishop Beresford in the chair. The lower house was composed of representatives of the lower clergy and dignitaries. The Very Reverend John West, Dean of Saint Patrick's, was selected as the prolocutor of the lower house.[5]

When the united synods began to deliberate, it became clear that two sets of tensions hampered their work. The first of these arose from anxiety about what was the proper relationship between the laity and the clergy. Friction mounted even though the laity were not even present. One group in the lower house wished it made clear that when the laity were eventually convened with the clergy, the right to legislate concerning doctrine and church discipline was to be left solely to the clergy. This was a minority viewpoint, however. A related issue which arose in the lower house was whether or not there would be "voting by orders." This phrase, which acquired unfortunate overtones in subsequent meetings of the Church Convention, simply meant that each category of persons (bishops, clergymen, or laymen) who would sit at the eventual Church Convention would vote with those of his category, and that a majority of each category would be needed to pass any piece of church legislation. Obviously, such an arrangement gave any one group veto power over the other. At this stage no clear majority could be obtained on the matter and it was dropped, to be settled later when the power and disposition of the laity would be easier to assess. Similarly, there was a good deal of nervousness about whether or not deans, archdeacons, and certain other dignitaries should have an ex officio right to sit in the lower house. The "liberal" party, led by Dean MacDonnell of Cashel, successfully sought the elimination of ex officio representation, over the protests of those who were afraid of anything that smacked of the diminution of clerical prestige.[6]

A second, less explosive, set of tensions involved the abrasions of the lower house and the upper. Hard feelings between the bishops and certain of the higher clergy had been smouldering since the beginning of the liberal party's disestablishment campaign, and there was, in addition, the natural jealousy of one order against the other. Many of the clergy would have liked to have seen a resolution passed stating that the parochial clergy were not sufficiently represented in the synods as presently constituted and that the parochial representation should be increased. This resolution did not pass, but it revealed that some of the clergy felt aggrieved vis-à-vis their ecclesiastical superiors.[7]

The resolutions finally agreed upon by the united synods may be summarized as follows:

1. The united synods bravely proclaimed that they were not now originating a constitution for a new religious communion but repairing a sudden breach in one of the most ancient churches in Christendom. To heal this breach, the cooperation of the faithful laity was more than ever desirable.

2. The representatives of the clergy elected to the general assembly, or convention, of the Church of Ireland that was soon to be convened, were to be elected by diocesan synods.

3. Diocesan synods were to be composed of all the licensed clergy of the diocese, provided they had been in holy orders for five years.

4. The number of men to be selected as representatives by each diocese was to consist of one representative for each ten clergymen entitled to vote.[8]

These resolutions on the part of the bishops and clergy seem smooth and reasonable enough, but they hid a potentially nasty division between the laity and the professionally religious. After the two archbishops had summoned the provincial synods to meet, the leading lay representatives—fearing the ecclesiastics would steal a march on them—convened a meeting of their own. This meeting actually preceded that of the united ecclesiastical synods, being held on 31 August 1869 at Molesworth Hall, Dublin. The laymen were miffed to begin with, because the bishops had refused the request of the executive committee of the April 1869 clergy-laity protest meeting to allow that church conference to meet once again; and they had instead convened an exclusively ecclesiastical assembly, namely, the united synods.[9] So disgruntled were some of the laymen, that at their Molesworth Hall meeting there was some talk of replacing the Archbishops of Armagh and Dublin as heads of the church with the Dukes of Leinster and Abercorn.[10] Cooler minds prevailed, however, and the laymen, under the gavel of the Earl of Meath, turned to petitioning the Archbishops of Armagh and of Dublin for permission to meet in a lay conference. To this end, the archbishops were asked to take steps to secure the election of lay delegates from each of the Irish dioceses.[11]

Wisely, the archbishops granted this request and 417 laymen were selected to represent the church population of Ireland. These laymen assembled on 12 October, in the Ancient Concert Rooms, Great Brunswick Street, Dublin. At the opening of the meeting the two archbishops jointly presided, thus symbolically invoking their continuing authority. One of the most important actions of the lay convention was to partially conciliate the bishops by passing the Duke of Abercorn's motion. This affirmed that in the General Convention of clergy and laity which would eventually be called to shape the church's new constitution, voting by orders would be the rule when controversial issues were included.[12] Abercorn's willingness to concede voting by orders to the clergy and bishops was crucial to the reconstruction progress, for Archbishop Trench himself had stated that he would refuse to have anything further to do with reorganization unless the three orders method was made fundamental to the new structure.[13]

While the affirmation of voting by orders pleased the clergy and bishops, a second decision did not. Sir Joseph Napier moved that the lay convention go on record as preferring an equal number of lay and clerical delegates at the actual church convention. William Johnston, M.P., moved an amendment, however, that there be two lay delegates for every clerical delegate; this motion passed.[14] When Archbishop Trench had first heard the suggestion of two lay delegates to each clerical delegate, he expressed what must have been the opinion of many clergymen and bishops: "The suggestion . . . is a very nasty one, as indicating the desire of a petty triumph." [15] Nevertheless, Trench correctly noted, as long as voting by orders was maintained, the actual number of members of each order was irrelevant, for what was involved was a matter of symbolism, not substance.

Having sat in silence during the debates on ratio of laymen to clergymen in the General Convention, the archbishops decided that it would be best if a layman assumed the chair for the remainder of the lay convention, and the Duke of Abercorn was selected. For a moment it seemed as if the laymen were going to throw over the traces, for it was proposed that, when the General Convention of the Church of Ireland was called the convener of elections for laymen would be the Duke of Abercorn. Had this motion been adopted, it would have symbolically affirmed that the laity, not the bishops, were at the head of the church. Fortunately for the unity of the church as an organization, the motion was amended to state that the respective bishops would initiate the election process for lay delegates.[16]

At the close of their meeting the laymen submitted their resolutions to the Archbishops of Armagh and of Dublin. In addition to the resolutions concerning the General Assembly of the Church of Ireland, the laymen asked that a committee be created, consisting of two lay and two clerical delegates from each united diocese to meet in Dublin to prepare a draft of a constitution to be submitted to the Church Convention. The archbishops agreed to this suggestion, and in January 1870 the drafting of the new Church of Ireland constitution began in earnest.[17]

The Draft Constitution

The framers of the church's new constitution were under considerable pressure. Financial reconstruction could not begin until the new constitution was formed. In addition, the drafting committee was under the great strain of knowing that it had to provide a workable organizational plan which would please the bishops, clergy, and laity—none of whose interests necessarily coincided. The drafting committee held its first meeting on Wednesday, 5 January 1870, and continued its work until the constitution was completed on Friday, 28 January.[18] (The bishops scheduled a caucus of their own two days before the committee as a whole met,[19] a good indication of distrust between the laity and the prelates.) The drafting committee consisted of the two archbishops and ten bishops and of four representatives from each of the twelve united dioceses—two of whom were clergymen, two of whom were lay. To this group were added by invitation thirteen "learned persons," mostly lawyers and persons versed in ecclesiastical law. Four honorary secretaries served the drafting committee.[20] This aggregate of bishops, clergy, lawyers, squires, and burgers appeared to be an ungainly and unmanageable group, having little in common. "There seems to me hardly a hope that the Committee will ever be able to produce a joint report, or even two reports, which express all the dissimilarity of our minds on points [that are] most important," the melancholy Archbishop of Dublin whined before the committee met.[21] Yet, after the committee's first meeting, Trench was hopefully reporting that "we all behaved as prettily as possible; indeed, I hope that there was something more than prettiness of behaviour among us, and that the end will not put our very friendly beginning to shame." [22] The archbishop was not to be disappointed, for the committee produced an excellent document in a very short period of time.[23]

The draft constitution was completed in late January 1870. Sensibly, the committee prefaced the draft with a set of procedural ground rules governing debate in the General Convention of the Church of Ireland where the draft would be accepted, rejected, or amended. These general standing orders, as they were called, do not warrant much scrutiny except insofar as they indicate the power balance within the drafting committee. Significantly, even in considering the draft constitution, the bishops were to vote separately from the other two orders, the clergy and laity. Moreover, if any three members of the laity or clergy demanded that they themselves should vote separately, then the two lower orders' votes, which otherwise were to be aggregated, were to be divided. In the case of a vote by orders, a majority of each order voting was necessary to pass any measure. Therefore, to be effective in shaping the constitution of the Church of Ireland in the General

Convention, any one order had a veto right over the actions of the other two. The continuing power of the prelates was indicated by the standing order that placed the Lord Primate of All Ireland in the chair, and in his absence the prelate next in order of precedence.[24]

The body of the draft constitution consisted of suggestions arranged under five major heads, the first three of which concern us here (the other two topics will be discussed later in this chapter): the general constitution of the Church of Ireland, the structure of the Representative Church Body, the nature of ecclesiastical law and church tribunals, the election of bishops and clergy, and specific questions of church finance. Turning first to the new framework of the Church of Ireland, the basic problem to be solved was the merging of the principle of religious democracy and lay power with apostolic hierarchy and clerical prestige. To satisfy both the clerical and the lay interests, the drafting committee presented an ingenious pyramid of synods and committees which ranged from the local select vestry to diocesan synods to the General Synod of the Church of Ireland. On each of these levels considerable power was to be granted to the laity, while various ex officio and veto powers were to be granted to the clergy and prelates. The ascending arrangement of synods resembled those of the Presbyterian and other Dissenting Churches, while the arrangement of the clergy and bishops remained that of the historic Catholic Church. By allowing the two systems of hierarchy and synodical democracy to coexist and commingle, the drafting committee effectively merged the principle of congregationalism and episcopacy—a stroke of administrative brilliance, if, perhaps, of theological expediency.

Beginning at the top of the pyramid, the drafting committee sketched plans for the General Synod of the Church of Ireland which would be the church's highest deliberative body.[25] As one might expect, the General Synod was to consist of three distinct orders, bishops, clergy and laity—the assent of each of which was necessary to make an act of the synod binding. Confusingly, although there were to be three orders in the General Synod, there were to be only two houses: the upper, the House of Bishops; the lower, the House of Representatives consisting of both the lower clergy, and the laity. Moreover, except for the consideration of formal bills, the two houses normally were to sit together for the purpose of debate, although the bishops would always vote separately. The proposed merger of the lower clergy and laity in a legislative group which debated together but which voted in two sections, was somewhat awkward. On most issues the members of the lower house would vote without distinction between clergy and laity; but if six individuals of either order so requested, votes would have to be tallied separately for each order. It seemed almost as if the drafting committee had tried to squeeze the laity into the old two-house system which had prevailed under the antique Irish convocation arrangements. In any case, the two-house system served to set off the bishops from the representatives of the rest of the Church of Ireland. Doubtless this isolation emphasized the bishops' prestige and gratified their sense of position, but it meant that the bishops could easily become labelled as obstructionists by those laymen who opposed the principle of episcopacy. One lay delegate, whose ignorance equalled his prejudice, was convinced that voting by orders meant voting by orders of the archbishop.[26] Although each order was to have the right to block the actions of the others, this arrangement quickly became known as "the bishops' veto." Some historians have deplored this label as misleading,[27] but it is actually an accurate appellation. The bishops alone among the three orders were a small, cohesive set of men, with nearly identical interests and prejudices, and they alone could be expected to employ the veto provisions; any measure repugnant to the majority of either of the two lower orders would probably be repugnant to the church as a whole, and therefore, no veto would be necessary.

How was the lower house to be composed? The drafting committee suggested that it be composed of 100 representatives of the clergy, and 150 representatives of the laity. This was clearly a compromise suggestion, since the bishops and clergy preferred numerical parity, while the laymen desired (as indicated by their resolutions of the October lay conference) a 2 to 1 majority over the clergy. The ratio of 1.5 to 1 was a halfway measure. In any case, the actual numbers were of minor significance, since voting by orders would prevent the laity from bulldozing the clergy. And how were the clerical and lay representatives to be selected? By diocesan synods was the drafting committee's answer. Each united diocese meeting in synod (the details of which will be described later) was to elect a certain number of laymen, ranging from ten to sixteen, depending on the circumstances of the united diocese, and six to ten clergymen. Every cleric in priest's orders was to be eligible for election as was every layman over twenty-one years of age who was a communicant. A declaration by a layman that he was a member and a communicant of the Church of Ireland was the only evidence of his qualification to be required.

Significantly, the Archbishop of Armagh and the Archbishop of Dublin were to be the official conveners of elections for the General Synod, which was to be summoned every third year, and for special meetings upon the petition of one third of the members of any one order. When the delegates eventually met in General Synod, their legislative actions were to resemble those of the Houses of Commons and Lords. Bills were to pass through either house in three readings and be accepted, rejected, or amended by the other house, with differences ironed out in conference. When legislating, the General Synod was to have powers over the doctrine, discipline, and diocesan arrangement of the Church of Ireland, restricted only by procedural limitations embodied in the constitution and the need to receive consent of the diocesan synods involved when any realignment of dioceses was contemplated.

Below the General Synod of the Church of Ireland, the drafting committee proposed twelve diocesan synods (for the sake of convenience synods of united dioceses were referred to as diocesan synods) each of which was to be a replica of the General Synod.[28] This was sound administrative architecture, for the similarity between the diocesan synods and the General Synod made administration smoother and made it easier for everyone concerned to understand exactly how the church now functioned. Each diocesan synod, it was suggested, should consist of a bishop, of all the clergy and priests of the united diocese, and laymen in number ranging from one to two for each clergyman in attendance—the precise number to be set by the diocesan synod itself. Should the provision allowing a greater number of lay than clerical synod men on the diocesan level be interpreted—as in the case of the General Synod of the whole church—as a symbolic slap at the clergy by the laity? No, for in this case, unlike the case of the General Synod, there was a sound functional reason for having more than one lay synodsman from each parish. The reason was simply that, given the realities of the Irish social structure, the local squire would almost inevitably be returned as the first of the local synodsmen, and only by allowing the presence of a second representative would the small farmers as a class be represented.[29] In any event, on controversial issues, voting by orders was to be resorted to, a practice which would prevent the laity from gaining control through their numerical strength.

Although the diocesan synods were unicameral, the upper house–lower house distinction in the General Synod, between the bishops and the clergy and laity, was to be replicated on the diocesan level by giving the individual bishops power to veto any act of the diocesan synod. This veto was to be subject, however, to review by the bench of bishops. In effect, therefore, the bishop was to become a one-man upper house representing the episcopal estate on the diocesan level in the same way the House of Bishops represented it on the national level. Doubtless the individual bishops would have to be most careful about using the power of veto, for its careless employment would totally alienate the laity. Nevertheless, the point remains that the drafting committee, while permitting religious democracy in the form of diocesan synods, was simultaneously preserving religious aristocracy by giving the bishops a right to negate the proceedings of the clergy and representative laity.

The lay diocesan synodsmen were to be chosen by election by the general vestry of the local parish. This would tie the system of diocesan synods to the system of parish government.[30] To become a member of the general vestry, a male, who was resident or owned property in the parish, and who was twenty-one years of age or above had merely to sign an affidavit of membership in the Church of Ireland. In addition to the general vestry, which was essentially a male membership list, each parish was to have a select vestry to overlook local religious affairs. This select vestry was to consist of the incumbent and his curates, two churchwardens, and three to ten lay communicants to be annually elected by the general vestry. Significantly, of the two churchwardens one was to be elected by the vestrymen, the other appointed by the incumbent. Thus, even on the local level, an attempt was made to strike a balance between the interests of the laity and of the professionally religious.

This, then, was the new organization proposed by the constitutional drafting committee. We can discern that the new structure was to be founded on three principles. The first of these was that the operations of the various levels of the new church organization, from parish level to diocesan level to national synod, should be as similar as possible. Hence, the diocesan synods were a replication of the General Synod, and the local select vestries similar, although not congruent, exercises in representative government. The principle of administrative similarity meant that the workings of the General Synod of the church would be comprehensible to any churchman who had even a modest idea of how his own parish and diocese operated. The second principle underlying the proposed constitution was equally intelligent from the viewpoint of administrative efficiency: the three levels of administration were to be not only similar in operation, but were to be directly interrelated in function. Communication and cooperation between levels was guaranteed by the system of elections under which the local general vestries elected the diocesan synodsmen, and the diocesan synods elected national synodsmen. Since each incumbent was invited to the diocesan synod, as well as at least one representative layman from each parish, there would be a minimum of two individuals from each parish directly involved with church policies at the diocesan level. Further, the selection of clerical and lay representatives to the General Synod from among the clergy and lay members of the diocesan synod meant that a local parish often had one of its representatives, lay or clerical, involved in religious decisions made at the national level. Even parishes without such representation were only one step away from the national level, since their diocesan synodsmen and incumbents could be expected to be in contact with their colleagues in the diocesan synods who were elected to the General Synod. The third principle underpinning the draft constitution was the belief that on every level an explicit recognition had to be made both of the rights of the clergy and of the laity. On each therefore, the laity had electoral rights. Similarly, on each level, the religious professionals were deferred to: the House of Bishops voted separately, the individual bishop had temporary veto power in his diocesan synod, and the local incumbent had exclusive patronage of one of the two churchwardenships. The drafting committee had produced an intelligent and ingenious scheme, but whether or not the Church Convention would accept the plan remained to be seen.

If the primary problem facing the drafting committee was to beget a viable constitution for the Church of Ireland, its second most pressing task was to establish the outlines of the Representative Body of the Church of Ireland. This Representative Church Body was not controversial, but speed was of the essence, because the church would not obtain title to its compensation and property until the body was operational. The drafting committee suggested that the Representative Church Body, which was to hold legal title to all the church's property and endowments, should consist of forty-eight members. These members were to include the twelve archbishops and bishops; two elected members—one lay, the other clerical—from each united diocese; and twelve members to be co-opted by the bishops and elected members. In order to assure continuity, one third of the elected members and one third of the co-opted members were to retire each year. The first task of the Representative Church Body would be to apply to the queen for a charter of incorporation.[31]

Closely related to the establishing of a new general constitution for the Church of Ireland, was the drafting committee's third task, the framing of arrangements for the maintenance of ecclesiastical discipline.[32] The drafting committee took the existing ecclesiastical law as given, and did not consider the modification of that law to be within its province. Instead, the committee concentrated on reorganizing the courts through which the ecclesiastical law was enforced. Because the ecclesiastical courts dealt almost entirely with the religious actions of the clergy, the nature of the new court system was of more pressing concern to the clergy and bishops than to the laity. In December 1869, the ever-worried Archbishop of Dublin had written:

> I see that one of the points which we shall have to fight, and a most important one, will be to resist the setting up of Diocesan Church Courts, for the more prompt and easy worrying of clergy with ritualistic or Puseyite proclivities. I propose to stand, and, as at present advised, will consent to nothing else, to the maintenance of the Bishop's Court, as it now stands, with him and the Chancellor, his legal assessor, the sole judge in the Court, with, of course, a Court of Final Appeal to which causes might be carried.[33]

The bishops carried their case successfully in the drafting committee. The final draft suggested that an ecclesiastical court be formed in every united diocese (referred to for convenience as a "diocesan" court even when more than a single diocese was under its jurisdiction) and that a high court, the Court of the General Synod, be formed for appeal purposes. Diocesan courts were to be presided over by the bishops of the diocese and by a chancellor of the bishop's choosing. The chancellor was to be a barrister of ten years' standing. To help these two judges, a diocesan registrar was to be appointed. In order to prevent the clergy and lay officials of the Church of Ireland from being unnecessarily harassed by the more fractious laity, a charge against anyone involving a matter of doctrine was not to be heard (except if pressed by a bishop) unless brought forward by at least four male communicants of legal age. In addition, in such cases the persons preferring the charge were to post a sum to be set by the registrar or chancellor (not exceeding £50) as security for the payment of costs if such were awarded in the course of the action.

On the national level the Court of the General Synod was to be constituted so as to minimize lay interference. Any plaintiff or defendant who was not satisfied with the justice of the diocesan court could appeal his case to the higher court. The Court of the General Synod was to consist of the Archbishops of Armagh and of Dublin, together with the bishop first in order of precedence, and three laymen. The three laymen were to vary from case to case, but were to be chosen in each instance from a slate of six to ten laymen put forward by the General Synod. To be eligible to serve, they were required to hold, or to have held, high judicial office such as probate, equity, or common law in judgeships (obviously the drafting committee was confident that Anglican laymen would continue to dominate the secular legal system or it could not have demanded such high qualifications). Certainly at the high court level, the laity would seem to have a somewhat larger voice than at the diocesan level; the slate of lay judges, unlike the lay chancellor in the diocesan courts, was not to be picked directly by the prelates. Even so, the bishops would be in a position to dominate the high courts, since the registrar of the high court, who was the registrar of the Diocese of Dublin, was under the patronage of the Archbishop of Dublin and if necessary could be influenced quite easily by the bishops in the selection of laymen from the slate to serve on any individual case. Whether or not the bishops would ever need to use their considerable powers to control the diocesan courts and the high court against the laity remained to be seen, but clearly the constitution put forward by the drafting committee gave them nearly complete control of the system of church courts. In 1872, even after the General Convention had strengthened the laity's hands, a democratically inclined observer was to complain that "the different church courts are, in regard to their constitution, characterised by a common defect—*apparent* power is granted to the people, and of *real* power they have none." [34]

The Church Convention Deliberates

Having produced the blueprints for the new system of governing the Church of Ireland, for the Representative Church Body, and for the reconstructed system of ecclesiastical courts, the drafting committee turned matters over to the General Convention of the Church of Ireland, a body established for the sole purpose of passing on plans for the future organization of the church. Originally, Archbishop Trench had wished to merely reassemble jointly the Irish convocation and the lay conference and proceed from there. Ecclesiastical lawyers, however, advised him that the Irish Church Act required that the members of the General Convention be selected in an election conducted specifically for that convention, so that Trench's dream of maintaining historical continuity with the convocation of the old Church of Ireland was dashed.[35] In any case, the General Convention assembled in Saint Patrick's Cathedral, Dublin, on 15 February 1870 and, after service, adjourned to the Ancient Concert Rooms, Great Brunswick Street, for the afternoon's business.

A contemporary observer could well have gauged the testy temper of some of the lay delegates by noting their indignation when the lesson for the day—the story of Korah, Dathan and Abiram, and their opposition to Moses and Aaron—was read. It was the proper lesson for the service, but the parallels seemed to fit a trifle too closely.[36] Indeed, it was not until the fifth day of activity that the standing orders under which the convention was to be conducted were approved.[37]

Turning to substantive issues, the convention moved reasonably quickly through the preamble of the draft constitution, with Archdeacon Stopford's amendment—affirming the Church of Ireland's continuance in communion with the Church of England—the only major addition to the draft. More important was the amendment, adopted without division, which changed the relation between laymen and clergymen in the future General Synod of the Church of Ireland from the 1.5 to 1 ratio, suggested by the drafting committee, to 2 to 1. In its original form, the motion was presented by Professor Galbraith of Trinity College, with the support of the Dean of Ardagh, A. W. West. Although accepted without division, the measure must have been mildly painful to the bishops and the more hierarchically-minded clergy. The drafting committee had tried to effect an obvious compromise between double representation and equal representation by suggesting a layman/clergyman ratio of 1.5 to 1, but this was now overthrown. Nevertheless, the move was more symbolic than structural, because the provision for voting by separate orders in the future General Synod was accepted. A complementary change was made in the draft constitution by changing ordinary meetings of the General Synod from triennial assemblies to annual meetings. This, to some extent, strengthened the hands of the laymen and clergy against the bishops.[38]

On 24 February, the General Convention came upon its first really divisive question: should the General Synod of the reorganized Church of Ireland allow the bishops to have a veto right? The draft constitution provided that the House of Bishops in the General Synod would vote separately from the House of Representatives (clergy and laity), and that no measure was to be passed unless a majority of both the House of Representatives and the House of Bishops approved. F. G. Bloomfield, a lay delegate from the Diocese of Ossory, moved that the bishops' veto be overridden in cases in which two thirds of both lay and clerical orders repassed a measure vetoed by the bishops. The Bloomfield amendment was lost but by a vote which revealed deep division within the General Convention: ayes, 43 clergymen and 172 laymen; noes 146 clergymen and 155 laymen. In other words, the laity was about evenly divided, with a small majority favoring abolition of the bishops' veto, while the great majority of the clergy viewed the bishops' veto as an important defense against excessive democracy in the church. Fortunately, this potentially explosive situation was calmed by the intervention of the Duke of Abercorn, one of the Church of Ireland's leading laymen. He introduced a compromise amendment providing that the bishops' veto could be overridden if clergy and laity each repassed the previously-rejected measure by a two-thirds vote, and if less than two thirds of the bishops again negated the measure. This compromise left the bishops with an absolute veto right, but raised the number of bishops needed to exercise that right from a simple majority to a two-thirds majority. At the same time, the House of Representatives was given a method of challenging the bishops, which, at a minimum, would call the serious dissatisfaction of the lower house to the bishops' attention. On this crucial amendment, the churchmen decisively indicated that in the main they preferred compromise to party strife. The Abercorn compromise passed by a majority of 281 votes.[39]

In its version of the constitution, the drafting committee had suggested that when bills were introduced either in the House of Representatives or the House of Bishops, they be considered according to the same principles and procedures as bills passing through the Houses of Commons and Lords. As soon as the veto power of the House of Bishops was redefined by the Abercorn amendment, however, the procedures for three readings, according to parliamentary principles in the House of Bishops, became largely superfluous. Hence, the General Convention cleared away several procedural complications by providing that it would be the usual procedure for the two houses to sit together in deliberation; and that, if the bishops wished to discuss or vote on a bill, they could withdraw to do so separately. These provisions were simple, and avoided the time-consuming complication of forcing the House of Bishops to go through the motions of acting as an ecclesiastical analog to the House of Lords.[40]

A good deal of minor haggling occurred on the sections of the constitution establishing diocesan synods of which two changes were of some moment. One change was in the normal expectation as to membership in diocesan synods. It now became the general expectation that there would be two lay synodsmen for each clergyman, although a lesser number could be adopted if the diocese preferred. The original draft had suggested one synodsman per clergyman as the usual ratio, although a ratio of up to 2 to 1 had been permitted; the change, therefore, was not in the range of permissible arrangements but in which arrangements were to be considered customary. The second change was in appeal procedures, when a diocesan bishop exercised his veto power. The draft constitution had provided that if two-thirds of the lay synodsmen and two-thirds of the clergy in the diocese objected to the bishop's vetoing the measure in question, it would be submitted to the House of Bishops for their decision. The appeal to this body disquieted some of the laity. The Earl of Meath, therefore, brought in an amendment to have the appeal sent not to the House of Bishops but to the General Synod. This amendment lost on a vote in which voting by orders was called for by ten clergymen. The vote was, laymen: ayes 95, noes 21; clergy: ayes 46, noes 47. Having lost by a single clergyman's vote, the earl decided to press the laity's cause, and when the question was again raised, he won his amendment by a goodly margin.[41]

When the General Convention adjourned on 2 April 1870, it had laid most of the foundation for the Church of Ireland as a voluntary denomination. Since the provision for the Representative Church Body and its charter had been handled with relatively little difficulty, the remaining important problem to be considered was the matter of ecclesiastical courts. Therefore, when the General Convention reassembled in mid-October 1870 it discussed these courts. After considerable wrangling, a partial victory was won by the forces of democracy. The draft constitution had provided that each bishop would rule his own court in conjunction with a chancellor of his own choosing. However, the General Convention decided diocesan courts should consist of the bishop as judge, the chancellor (who was to act as judge if the bishop was the person pressing charges), and one clergyman and one layman. Further, whereas the draft constitution had provided that the high court—the Court of the General Synod—was to consist of three prelates and three laymen, the final version provided for a high court composed of two prelates and three laymen. The General Convention, therefore, had reduced somewhat the control of the bishops over the ecclesiastical courts.[42]

The changes made in the draft constitution by the assembled delegates of the General Convention steered almost completely in the direction of strengthening the popular element in the Church of Ireland and weakening the episcopal element. Having said this, the changes were as important for what they did not accomplish as for what they did. While moving in the direction of increased popular control of the church, the General Convention did not abandon the hierarchical element it had inherited from the past. The bishops were still allowed to vote separately and maintained absolute veto power over church legislation if two-thirds of their number agreed to the veto. The bishops remained the chief officers of the ecclesiastical courts even though they did not have the iron-like control envisaged in the draft constitution. Despite the preponderance of laymen in the synods, the provision for voting by orders meant that the position of the clergy in diocesan synods and in the General Synod would remain secure. The delegates to the Church of Ireland's constitutional convention had acted with moderation. Despite wide divergences of opinion the convention had not been rent by extremest elements. A middle ground between congregationalism and hierarchical authoritarianism had been found.

Appointments and Promotions

We must now turn to the topic which logically follows a discussion of the realignment of the Church of Ireland's new organizational structure, namely, the new arrangements for the appointment of professional religious personnel. The appointment process in the former Established Church had been a relatively simple one: anyone wishing to be a bishop was dependent upon the patronage of highly placed politicians; and anyone wishing a dignity or benefice was dependent upon the good will of a bishop or an owner of an advowson. These relationships were to change dramatically when the Church of Ireland was disestablished. The power of presentation to benefices was taken from the bishops, laymen, and corporate patrons and given to a mixed board of clergy and laity. The selection of an incumbent was now accomplished through a complicated mechanism involving laymen, clergymen, and the diocesan bishop. Instead of being dependent upon a member of the hierarchy for appointment to a benefice, the Anglican clergyman now became dependent upon the good will of a committee, most of whose members were laymen. Similarly, aspirants to the prelacy now depended upon the good will of laity, clergy, and bishops. Naturally, men formerly appointed as bishops by English politicians differed greatly from the sort of men picked by an internal committee of laymen, clergy, and prelates. Similarly, the man who would satisfy a wide range of lay selectors on the parish level was often a very different sort of person from the man chosen under the bishops' patronage in the old days.

The touchstone in the evolution of the church's appointment and promotional methods was the draft constitution of January 1870. The first issue was how to select the beneficed clergy. The drafting committee suggested that each diocesan synod should elect a committee of patronage to consist of three laymen and three clerics. Similarly, each parish was to elect three "nominators." When a vacancy occurred in a parish, the three parochial nominators for the parish concerned and the committee of patronage for the diocese were to meet together to form a board of nomination. The board of nomination was to put forward the names of three persons in priest's orders suitable for undertaking the cure and submit them to the bishop of the diocese, who would normally choose one of them to fill the vacancy. The bishop could, however, refuse to institute any of the three, at which point a two-thirds majority of the board of nomination (providing it included two of the three parochial nominators) could appeal the matter to the college of bishops. Three points are worth noting about this suggested arrangement. First, the board of nomination was constituted so that laymen had a two-thirds majority. Second, the suggested arrangements emphasized the diocesan point of view over the parochial, giving the diocesan representative two thirds of the votes on the board of nomination. Third, the bishop was to retain some semblance of power, having the right of selection among candidates and the power of rejecting all three candidates.[43]

Although the draft constitution's recommendations on the selection of parochial clergy seemed a reasonable compromise between lay and episcopal powers and between diocesan and parochial interests, the General Convention modified the arrangements considerably in the direction of lay and parochial control. Instead of the six-member synodical committee of patronage suggested by the drafting committee, the General Convention settled on a committee of patronage to consist of the bishop, one clergyman, and two laymen. This group was to meet together with the three nominators elected from among the laymen of the vacant parish to form a selection committee. This change reduced the proportion of diocesan members on the selection committee from six-ninths to four-sevenths and reduced the power of those holding a diocesan viewpoint vis-à-vis those with solely parochial interests. More important, whereas the drafting committee recommended that the board of nomination present the bishop with the names of three clergymen for his choice, the final version provided for the selection of only a single candidate. The bishop could refuse to accept the nominee; but in that case, a majority (not two-thirds as originally stipulated) of the board of nomination could appeal to a tribunal of the General Synod for redress (not to the College of Bishops as originally proposed). Obviously, these modifications considerably lessened the power of the bishops, reducing each diocesan to a near-cipher in the selection process. Thus, a marked contrast evolved between the Church of Ireland as an established and as a disestablished body; in the former days the bishops, more than anyone else, had influence over patronage appointments, but in the new era the bishops' powers were slight, and the laity's preponderant.[44]

A similar tendency to undercut the patronage of the bishops was shown in the way the General Synod treated the matter of appointments to deaneries and cathedral offices. The drafting committee had proposed that the bishops be given the power in their own diocese of appointing all deans, dignitaries, archdeacons, and other cathedral officers. The General Convention, much less convinced of the value of the cathedral chapters and much less in sympathy with episcopal prestige, decided that for the present the bishops should maintain only the patronage of the archdeaconries. No appointment was to be made to any deanery, dignity, or prebendal office, pending a study by the General Synod on the financial resources of the church and a consideration of what would be the best way to select such office holders.[45]

The bishops themselves were to be chosen under the following arrangements. When a vacancy occurred in a bishopric (other than an archbishopric) the diocesan synod was to be convened. The clerical members of the synod were to select three clergymen for nomination, of whom one, at least, would not belong to the diocese involved. These three names were then to be submitted to the lay members of the diocesan synod for the acceptance and rejection of the three names, or of any one or two of them, by majority vote. In the case of rejection by the laymen, replacements were to be chosen by the clergymen and submitted to the lay members of the diocesan synod as before. Next, the three approved nominees were to be sent to the College of Bishops who would select the man to become next bishop of the vacant see. The process as suggested by the drafting committee, then, gave the power of primary selection of candidates to the local diocesan clergy, and power of final selection to the assembled bishops—with the laymen of the diocesan conference possessing only a veto right over candidates chosen by the clergy of the diocese.[46]

From the knowledge of the General Convention's modification in the draft constitution in earlier cases, one would expect the convention to augment the power of the laity in the episcopal election process and diminish that of the clergy and bishops. This is exactly what happened. As finally enacted, the Church of Ireland's constitution provided that bishops would be elected by a process beginning at the diocesan level, but with both laity and clergy, not merely clergy, voting for candidates. Once assembled, each lay and clerical member of the diocesan synod was to nominate one, two, or three persons for consideration. From these names, a select list of the leading candidates was to be compiled (the details of compilation need not detain us). Balloting between the leading candidates was to proceed by a complicated process under which the diocesan synod was to continue voting (one vote per member) until one candidate had a majority. If that majority was a two-thirds majority of each order, the candidate was declared elected as bishop. If the majority were a simple majority, then the synod was to continue voting until a second person received a majority of votes, whereupon the two names were to be sent to the House of Bishops where the final decision would then be made.[47]

This left only the selection process for the Archbishops of Dublin and Armagh to be determined. Here the drafting committee became a trifle confused. It agreed that when an archbishopric became vacant, the clergy of the diocese should send the names of three persons (two of whom were already bishops) to the College of Bishops where a final decision would be made. From then on, the constitutional drafting committee was uncertain what to do in the likely event that another see would become vacant by the promotion of a suffragan bishop to one of the archepiscopal sees; or, in the case of the election of the Archbishop of Dublin to the Archbishopric of Armagh, which would probably set off a chain reaction forcing the filling of Dublin, and perhaps another see as well, if someone already on the bench were named to Dublin.

When the General Convention convened it moved purposefully toward a solution of the issue which the drafting committee had not met, and did so with reasonable simplicity. Instead of setting up complicated rules for Armagh and for Dublin, the General Convention realized that the major problem was deciding how to elect the Primate of All Ireland, the Archbishop of Armagh, and that any consequential effects on the Archbishopric of Dublin could be treated like those on any other see. When Armagh became vacant, the clerical and lay members of the diocesan synod were to meet together and present four names of men, already bishops, to the bench of bishops, and these in turn would select one of the four to be Archbishop of Armagh. The vacancy in the diocese, from which the new Primate of All Ireland came, was to be filled by the assembled bishops also. The bishops were to choose between a clergyman selected by the Armagh diocesan synod and one chosen by the synod of the diocese with the vacant bishopric. Thus, by filling the highest appointment in the church—the Archbishopric of Armagh—the preponderant voice went to the bishops who composed the roster of potential candidates and also made the final decision.[48]

After our description of these complicated arrangements for selecting and promoting Irish clergymen, it is logical to ask, How well did they work? At a rather high level of abstraction we can conclude that they worked satisfactorily; because, when put to the test, they were accepted by the laity and by the professionally religious, and through these arrangements the churchmen successfully filled the slots which became vacant from time to time in the Irish church. No widespread revolt against the arrangements occurred at any level. But this abstract recognition of success, while valid, ignores the complications, injustices, and bitterness which occurred in individual cases. For instance, turning first to the arrangements for filling bishoprics (the Lord Primacy of all Ireland did not fall vacant until late 1885 and was not filled until 1886, and is thus outside the time boundary of this study), two contrasting elections in the Diocese of Meath indicate how the system could work at its best, and at less than its best. The first instance occurred in October 1876 when an election was called to replace Bishop Butcher who had died unexpectedly. The diocesan synod assembled and proceeded to nominate five candidates. Aware of the danger of splitting the synod into factions, the supporters of the three lower candidates transferred their votes to the first two, Lord Plunket and Dean Duant. On the second vote

Plunket received a majority, but not the required two-thirds majority of the votes. Sensibly, on the third ballot most of the supporters of Dean Duant gracefully gave over their votes to Plunket and thereby settled the election without hard feeling or factional strife.[49]

Now, the 1876 Meath episcopal election was very civilized and flawlessly conducted. Yet, in 1885, following Plunket's elevation to the Archbishopric of Dublin, the diocesan synod fell into an unproductive and undignified wrangle about his successor. Three candidates were named on the select list from which the new bishop was to be chosen: Charles Reichel, Dean of Clonmacnoise; Joseph S. Bell, Rector of Kells; and Canon Wynne, incumbent of Saint Matthias's Church in Dublin. In the subsequent balloting, Reichel and Bell received the largest number of votes, but neither of them was able to obtain the two-thirds majority necessary for election. Accordingly, matters were sent to the College of Bishops for a choice between the two. Before the bishops could convene, however, the followers of Canon Wynne objected that the proceedings were invalid, on the grounds that a vote should have been taken in the Meath diocesan synod on whether or not his name should be included in the list sent to the bishops. The objection was referred to the Court of the General Synod, where it was subsequently upheld. Therefore, the diocesan synod had to meet again and begin the selection process anew. On the second election attempt only two names, those of Reichel and Bell, were placed on the select list, but neither of them could obtain a two-thirds majority. Finally, the matter was sent to the bench of bishops, who selected Reichel. The entire affair, while not significant in itself, clearly indicates that the machinery for electing bishops was far from perfect.[50]

Listed below are the names and previous appointments of the bishops of the Church of Ireland elected under the diocesan electoral system up to 1885:[51]

Date	Name	Diocese	Previous appointment
1872	Maurice F. Day	Cashel	Dean of Limerick
1874	John R. Darley	Kilmore	Archdeacon of Ardagh
1875	Robert S. Gregg	Ossory	Dean of Cork
1876	Lord Plunket	Meath	Precentor of St. Patrick's
1878	William P. Walsh	Ossory	Dean of Cashel
1878	Robert S. Gregg	Cork	Bishop of Ossory
1884	William B. Chester	Killaloe	Archdeacon of Killaloe
1884	Samuel Shone	Kilmore	Archdeacon of Kilmore
1885	Lord Plunket	Dublin	Bishop of Meath
1885	Charles Reichel	Meath	Dean of Clonmacnoise

From this admittedly limited number of cases, what can we conclude regarding the appointment of Irish bishops under the new system? In the first place, it is clear that appointments to bishoprics in the Church of Ireland had become an internal matter. Previously, outsiders—usually English-men—often were introduced to the bench without their having had any experience in the Irish church. Second, the policy of promotion from within the Church of Ireland extinguished the last vestiges of the English-Irish jealousies which had once flawed the unity of the hierarchy and embittered the Irish clergy. Third, it is clear that those men elected bishops were experienced in middle level church administration; having been deans, archdeacons, or cathedral dignitaries before becoming bishops. This guaran-teed that they would be conversant with the administrative needs of the church and knowledgeable about the duties of an ecclesiastical administra-tor.

These three conclusions all point to ways in which the elective system of choosing bishops facilitated the efficient administration of the church. There was, however, a fourth characteristic which was less functional: the diocesan synods tended to elect clergymen from among their own number. In four of the ten elections held between 1872 and 1885 the man named as bishop was already a major administrator of the diocese for which he was elected bishop. In the case of Robert Gregg's translation from Ossory to Cork, he merely returned home to a diocese where he had been previously dean and succeeded his own father as bishop. Lord Plunket's translation from Meath to Dublin returned him to a city where he was already well known as a former cathedral dignitary. All this is not to say that the Church of Ireland suddenly became inbred in its choice of bishops to a dysfunctional degree, but simply that a narrow outlook by members of the diocesan synod in choosing bishops was always a potential danger.

Turning from the episcopal to the parish level, we find that the arrange-ments were sufficiently satisfactory to prevent any widespread disaffection on the part of those concerned, but that there were serious drawbacks none-theless. One great flaw was that in actual practice it appears that the parish viewpoint usually prevailed over the diocesan. The board of nomination consisted of the bishops, three diocesan nominators, and three parochial nominators; but the parish nominators, it is reported, usually acted as if the choice was theirs alone, and the diocesan nominators and bishops seldom summoned nerve enough to resist.[52] Charles Reichel, while yet a parish clergyman, had been instrumental in convincing the General Convention of the Church of Ireland to modify the draft constitution of the church so as to increase the power of the parish elements vis-à-vis the diocesan elements in selecting local incumbents. Later, however, when serving as Bishop of Meath, even he became disenchanted with the system, concluding that it inadequately protected the interests of the diocese.[53]

The trend towards excessive localism in the election of incumbents was reinforced by the tendency of some parishes to reverse the elections made by the board of nomination. Although in church law they did not have a right to do so, some congregations operated on the principle that they not only had the power to choose deputies to sit on the board of nomination, but that they could veto the choice of that board, if they wished. Since they had no formal power to veto the choice the means of veto had to be ad hoc. One newly elected vicar, for instance, when taking his stand at the reading desk was met with cries of "down with Mr. ——." [54]

This increased jealousy by local congregations of their rights and alleged rights in the election of clergymen was part of a larger change which came over the church after disestablishment. In the days of the Established Church, the incumbent was largely independent of his congregation. His appointment was usually made by the bishop and chances of promotion were mostly dependent upon pleasing the bishop or impressing the patron of a desirable living. The clergyman's income was paid in tithe rent charges and was often augmented by grants from the Ecclesiastical Commissioners. Now, all that was changed. The newly-appointed clergyman (a man chosen before disestablishment had his lifetime annuity) was dependent upon his congregation for a significant portion of his livelihood. This obvious financial dependence quickly changed the attitude of the laymen towards their minister. Often the attitude became, according to one keen observer, "We pay. He is our hired man." [55]

The most telling evidence of the changed dependency relationship between clergymen and congregations is found in the new practice of clergymen touting for jobs. The diocesan bishop, the diocesan nominators, and the parish nominators were all figures to impress if one wanted an incumbency. The ambitious young clergyman had to become a huckster of his own talent. "I am extremely popular in my Parish," a candidate for promotion wrote to William Alexander, *and a good preacher.* Alexander's unsent reply was, "I am glad to hear that you are a good preacher, but sorry that you think so." [56] The same prelate was of the opinion that the dependent position many clergy occupied after disestablishment was a result of the undignified custom of canvassing for parochial support, which placed the clergyman in a sycophant's role even before he assumed office. [57]

And what a job it must have been to line up parish support and then, after being appointed, to keep everyone happy! A typical parish might have a militia captain who remembered the brevity of the chaplain of the forces and was disposed to grumble over the length of the sermon. The principal grocer, perhaps an ultra-Calvinist, would criticize the sermons for underplaying the idea of predestination; while the baker, a man of marked Wesleyan tendencies, would be disquieted when the pastor mentioned the doctrine of election. Meanwhile, the local squire, a liberal in politics with an eye to a seat for the county, would oppose on political grounds any allusion to the papacy, while the local colonel, a man with strong ties in the north, might admire the anti-Catholic parts of the incumbent's sermons! [58]

Scant wonder, therefore, that the clergymen of the disestablished Church of Ireland were sometimes dissatisfied with their lot. It is noteworthy that in 1871 there were 2,221 clergymen in the service of the Church of Ireland, and only ten years later there were 1,828.[59] Admittedly, the number of men in Anglican orders in Ireland may have been unnaturally swollen just before disestablishment because of the financial advantages offered to a parson under Gladstone's church act, and the financial pinch of disestablishment undoubtedly dictated reducing the number of benefices. But a shrinkage of nearly four hundred clergymen in a ten-year period seems abnormally large. Fortunately, we need not merely speculate about the possibility and extent of clergy dissatisfaction. In 1878, the Supply of Clergy Committee, reacting to the increasing shortage of qualified clergymen, sent a questionnaire to each clergyman asking him a series of questions about the impediments to attracting men to take up the ministry in the Church of Ireland. The answers to these questions were, of course, largely an expression of the things with which the clergyman answering the questionnaire was himself dissatisfied. The answers of those clergymen responding to the question about impediments to attracting men to the clergy may be classified as follows:[60]

Responses indicating dissatisfaction with low, uncertain, or "dead level" salaries	149
Responses indicating resentment of the excessive power of the laity	141
Responses indicating the church's clerical training facilities were too expensive or theologically inadequate	59
Responses indicating disapproval of too many men of low birth entering the Irish church	12

Accepting the fact that there was considerable dissatisfaction among the Irish clergy about the post-disestablishment arrangements, and accepting the suggestion that this dissatisfaction was partially responsible for reducing the number of clergy serving the Church of Ireland, we should ask the following question: Did any change occur in the sort of person who became an Irish clergyman? Apparently the answer is yes, although this cannot be documented statistically. No less an observer of social distinctions than J. P. Mahaffy noted, "that by abolishing the glebes and rectories it [the Irish Church Act] tended inevitably to abolish the only resident gentry in the wilder parts of Ireland. . . . Now this class has almost disappeared. The present clergy, with all their virtues and their self-denial, cannot hope to replace it socially. Their means are too straitened, their traditions are rarely those of country gentlemen." [61] Another observer wrote:

Time was when the sons of noblemen and large landed proprietors worked their way as Fellow-Commoners through Trinity College and when "Hon. and Rev." was not a very rare designation of a country parson. . . . The cutting off of this class of candidates from the ministry of the Church is to be lamented.

Somewhat cattily, he continued:

> We have . . . witnessed the anomaly of a curate in sole charge of a somewhat aristocratic parish, who being but lately promoted from the position of a Scripture-reader to poor Romanists, possessed qualification which, while sure to gain him a hearing from the cattle-drivers at Ballinasloe fair, were little likely to recommend the Gospel to the young ladies in the Squire's pew.[62]

Coincident with the apparent change in the social class origin of the men who entered the Church of Ireland ministry, there appears to have been some lowering of the educational and intellectual standards as well. Archbishop Trench in his charge of October 1875 felt it necessary to speak out against the temptation to fill the church's ranks with Scripture readers, schoolmasters, and others of high characters but limited education. In his own diocese, Trench promised to continue demanding a university degree and a divinity testimonium of all candidates for orders.[63] Trench's brave intentions were not, however, equalled by those of his colleagues. In 1880, the Archbishop of Armagh stated in a visitation charge that the education of candidates for ordination was generally below the required standard and that the requirement of a university degree had been dispensed with in many cases. In 1881, the Bishop of Derry and Raphoe reported that of the forty-six clergy ordained by him in the previous ten years, only twenty-five had taken university degrees, and eleven had not attended university at all.[64] Neither the apparent lowering of the social status of aspirants to the cloth, nor the apparent decline in educational attainments was disasterous to the Church of Ireland; for, obviously, the church continued to operate. Indeed, in some cases, the changes in class origins and in education may have benefited the church, for clergymen were increasingly men with limited social and intellectual tastes who were willing to accept the comparatively austere style of life required of a clergyman after disestablishment.

The Cathedral Network

The Irish cathedral chapters were very much the poor sisters in the arrangements for the reorganization of the Church of Ireland. As a group, the leaders of the Church of Ireland, especially the laymen, showed limited enthusiasm for the cathedral system. This lack of enthusiasm in a time of organizational crisis was only natural, for the cathedrals were far from essential to the church's continuous functioning. Consideration of the cathedral system was shunted aside until matters of general finances of parish and episcopal organization had been settled. When the cathedral network was reworked, it underwent a reduction greater than any other branch of the church's organization. The cathedral reforms and diminutions were all the more drastic because the cathedral network, unlike the episcopal arrangements, had been almost completely untouched by the ecclesiastical reform acts of the 1830s.

Gladstone's disestablishment act dealt with the cathedral system chiefly in a negative manner. As of 1 January 1871 all cathedral corporations, both sole and aggregate, were dissolved. This did not mean that the deans, dignitaries, and prebendaries were suddenly tossed from their stalls but that, as a legal body, they ceased to have any existence. Hence, the former corporations could no longer sue or be sued as corporate entities, or enter into contracts, or buy and sell property. All contracts made on behalf of the former legal corporations now had to be entered into by an individual designated by the chapter, who would himself be responsible in law for seeing that the contractual obligations were fulfilled. When dissolving the cathedral chapters as legal corporations, the government refused to compensate these bodies for their loss of privileges; Gladstone's act provided only for compensation for the life interests of the deans and chapter members as individuals. These provisions did not in any way prevent the reorganized Church of Ireland from deciding to maintain cathedral chapters, but it meant if it did so that the chapters would be solely an internal grouping of the professionally religious with no more claim to secular legal status than the church courts.[65]

As mentioned in an earlier section, the draft constitution contained provisions allowing the bishops of the respective dioceses to appoint deans, dignitaries, and all subordinate officers of the chapter—a provision which implied that the cathedrals would continue to function as previously. The General Convention, however, suspended all new cathedral appointments until the General Synod had time to consider the matter at a future date. Eventually, in 1872, the General Synod framed new rules for the cathedral system—rules which were somewhat modified when the church's new constitution was codified in 1879. The most important change made in the Irish cathedral system after disestablishment was that with the exception of the deans, membership in the chapters now became honorific rather than remunerative and was limited to clergymen already holding benefices in the given diocese. The chapter of each cathedral (with the exception of Saint Patrick's, Dublin) was named by the bishop of the diocese, a small crumb of patronage which by no means made up for the immense parochial patronage taken from the bishops after disestablishment. The bishop's right to name all cathedral officers was a small privilege, since the men selected (after 1870) by the bishops had to be clergymen previously elected to a local benefice by the diocesan board of nomination, a body usually dominated by the lay parochial nominators. Before the Church of Ireland was disestablished, most of the prebends had been tied to specific individual parishes. The post-disestablishment arrangement dissolved these relationships and allowed the holder of any incumbency in the diocese to be named to any dignity or prebend. Thus, from being a system of chapters each of whose members were recruited without geographic discrimination, but whose cathedral offices after appointment were often tied to specific incumbencies and whose cathedral appointments were often financially lucrative, the cathedral system was transformed into a means of rewarding good performance by clergymen already within the diocese, regardless of which parish within that diocese they held. Almost paradoxically, the cathedral system became simultaneously more diocesan in its orientation and less limited by ancient parish associations.[66]

Since there were no longer any direct ties between specific prebends and individual parishes, some chapters ceased using the title of prebend and simply called all men below the rank of dignity, "canon." Others maintained some or all of the titles of prebend along with the ancient name of the office (e.g., Prebend of Saint Michael's) but merely as a means of keeping a historical tradition intact, since, under the new arrangements, the holder of the prebend in question might well be the incumbent of a totally different parish.[67]

At the same time that the old direct ties of specific parishes with specific prebends were disappearing most of the cathedral churches were becoming identified as both a cathedral and a local parish church. It became the usual practice, although not a required one, for the dean of the cathedral to also be the incumbent of the cathedral parish. This merging of roles of vicar and dean in one person was a natural working out of Irish ecclesiastical traditions and of the pressures of forced reorganization. Historically, the Irish cathedrals had usually been closer to the parochial framework than had the cathedral in England. Disestablishment reinforced this relationship by making it necessary for the Church of Ireland to cover the country with parish churches as cheaply as possible. Understandably, therefore, most cathedrals were forced to double as parish units, while simultaneously maintaining their cathedral characteristics.[68]

The dual nature of the majority of Irish cathedrals necessitated a complicated, hermaphroditic set of governing arrangements. In the case of the parish cathedrals—all the Irish ones except Armagh, Christ Church, Dublin, Saint Patrick's, Dublin, and Downpatrick—general vestries were formed just as in parish churches. The general vestry elected a cathedral select vestry to oversee the cathedral portion of the operation jointly with the dean and chapter, and a parish select vestry to oversee jointly with the incumbent of the parish the parochial work. Since the usual practice was for the bishop to name the man selected as incumbent of the cathedral parish as dean, the two bodies—the select cathedral vestry and the select parish vestry—usually had the same presiding officer and often had individual laymen in common membership on both boards. In the non-parochial cathedrals of Belfast, Armagh, and Dublin, special arrangements were made to insure lay participation in their management. This was done through the creation of cathedral boards which served as the counterpart of the cathedral select vestries of the parochial cathedrals.[69]

Mention of the two Dublin cathedrals calls to notice the special arrangements necessary for their operation. Previous to the Church Temporalities Act of 1833, the two cathedrals had operated separately, with the Dean of Christ Church serving simultaneously as Bishop of Kildare. The 1833 reforms separated the Christ Church Deanship from the Kildare Bishopric and amalgamated the Deanship of Saint Patrick's with the Deanship of Christ Church. In 1872 the General Synod of the Church of Ireland dissolved this union. Christ Church became the cathedral church of the Archdiocese of Dublin (until 1887 the deanship was held by the Archbishop of Dublin). At the same time Saint Patrick's became a national cathedral, serving not one diocese or province but the whole Church of Ireland. In its chapter was at least one representative of each of the dioceses. Unlike the other deanships which were collative by the various bishops, the Dean of Saint Patrick's was now chosen by members of the chapter from among their own number.[70]

If the General Synod of the Church of Ireland considered the cathedral system a topic of secondary importance in the early days of reorganization, by the mid-1880s, churchmen were taking a more appreciative view. In 1882, the church's cathedral committee recommended that certain cathedrals should be financially assisted because they had insufficient resources. The finance committee did not at that time have any funds available for such a proposal, but in 1886 the Representative Church Body was able to divide a bequest of £10,000 between various cathedrals and deaneries.[71] In addition, the restoration or expansion of cathedral buildings somewhat counteracted the neglect shown the cathedral system by many churchmen.[72] Nevertheless, it is impossible to gainsay the fact that the cathedral system of the Established Church of Ireland was a luxury the church, as a voluntary denomination, was unable to afford. The old cathedral network had been a curious middle level between the lower clergy and the bishops but had not functioned effectively as an intermediary of administration or communication. Because the archdeacons and rural deans performed the roles of middle-level administration reasonably well, the framers of the new church organization had two options: either abolish the cathedral network or redefine it so that it produced an adequate result for the money invested in it. The churchmen chose the second option. They decided that all but the four major cathedral churches would serve double duty as parish churches; and, more important, that a stall in a cathedral chapter was a non-financial recognition of service by meritorious local incumbents. From an administrative viewpoint, the new arrangements meant that the cathedrals were now a useful adjunct to the parish system and therefore merited continued support.

THE REVISION CONTROVERSY

During the 1870s the Church of Ireland experienced several theological disputes which provide us with an indication of the tensions and hatreds within the church. Emphatically, we are not here interested in the subtleties of the theological arguments. Fascinating as the arguments are from the viewpoint of an intellectual historian (hopefully they will soon be adequately treated by a scholar of the history of ideas) their merit in logic is irrelevant to our purpose. Instead, the opposing groups on doctrinal matters are viewed as separate power blocs, groups which attempted to work their own will through internal political maneuvering. Essentially, the two opposing sides were the extreme evangelicals and the traditional Anglicans. The evangelicals desired to modify the doctrine and liturgy of the Church of Ireland in order to remove the vestiges of "popery" or, if one prefers, to reduce the "Catholic" element in the Irish church. They comprised a strong band of laymen, plus the more evangelical wing of the clergy. Opposed to the evangelicals were those who wished the church to retain its liturgy and doctrine as inherited from the United Church of England and Ireland. This group consisted of all the bishops, about half of the clergy, and also a strong bloc of laymen. Now, it will be noticed that the divergences in theological questions approximately paralleled those differences which we observed on organizational questions earlier. Those who favored retaining the church's old doctrinal formularies tended to be men who also were convinced of the need to maintain the prestige and power of the bench of bishops and to protect the integrity of the parish incumbents. Conversely, those who tended to push for congregationalism and lay control in church government were apt to be simultaneously involved in attempts to mold the church's doctrine along evangelical or Dissenting lines.

Theological controversy had been smoldering within the Irish church about Prayer Book revision ever since Gladstone's church act was passed. In order to comprehend fully this explosive situation one must realize that the question of Prayer Book revision was not solely an Irish matter, but part of a larger religious controversy which involved the Church of England as well as the Church of Ireland. Increasingly, the English clergy were divided into two camps, ritualist and anti-ritualist. In 1867 a royal commission had been appointed to inquire into variations in religious ceremony in the English church. Four reports were issued between 1867 and 1870. Coincident with the liturgical conflict in England was a general agitation for revision of the Book of Common Prayer, which was especially strong among evangelicals. Basically, this group was reacting to the threat of the Oxford Movement, and wished to purge from the Prayer Book all traces of sacerdotalism and "Romanism." As if the atmosphere of the Anglican Church in the British Isles were not already tense enough, the dogma of papal infallibility was announced in mid-1870. The impact such an event would have on a religious community already uneasy about the "Catholic" nature of some of its own religious practices is obvious.[73]

Even before the Church of Ireland was separated from the Church of England and disestablished, divine service in Ireland was conducted along slightly different lines than in England. For instance, during prayers the Irish clergymen stood with their backs to the altar, instead of kneeling. In Ireland the old custom of a weekly offertory continued, while in England it was often dropped. In Ireland it was usual for the congregation to sit during the reading of the Gospel, whereas most persons in England customarily stood.[74] But these were small differences. The pressures of anti-Roman Catholicism, fear of growing ritualism, the background of the English revision controversy, and the evangelical temper of the Irish laity meant that most Irish churchmen would not be satisfied with small divergences from English customs. Instead, it became clear that a majority of the members of the Church of Ireland would not be satisfied with less than a major revision of the Prayer Book.[75]

When, therefore, the General Convention of the Church of Ireland reassembled in October 1870, it soon became enmeshed in the revision question. In the abstract the opposing positions were clear. At one extreme (if "extreme" is a proper word for a desire to preserve the status quo) were those who wished nothing done to the Prayer Book. This wing was led by the archbishops and bishops. At the other extreme were those demanding extensive revision of the Book of Common Prayer, mostly laymen. An anonymous lay pamphleteer provided the following sample of revisionism at its most aggressive pitch:

> The Ritualistic and pro-Popish party in our Church, shelter themselves under *antiquity*. . . . These men rely more on the Prayer Book than on the Bible and this fact of itself should excite our suspicions. . . . The Prayer Book was compiled from the Romish Breviary, Missal, and Ritual. The common prayers were taken from the Breviary; the administration of the sacraments, burial, matrimony, and visitation of the sick, from the Ritual; and the consecration of the Lord's Supper, Collects, Gospels, and Epistles from the Mass Book. . . .[76]

The changes demanded by this revisionist pamphleteer may be summarized as follows: (1) the restoration of the Lord's Supper "to its original mode of celebration" and the purification of the Communion service, presumably from Catholic overtones; (2) the abolition of priestly absolution in the visitation of the sick; (3) the abolition of the declaration of regeneration in the baptismal service; (4) the removal of the lessons from the Apocrypha from the burial service and substitution of lessons from the Book of Revelation; (5) the removal of the lessons and collects for Saints Days.[77]

The leading revisionist was William Brooke, Master of the Court of Chancery and a pronounced evangelical who was widely respected throughout the church. Originally, during the meetings of the constitutional drafting committee Brooke had opposed touching the Prayer Book.[78] Something, however, changed his mind, and it was he who set off the revision controversy in the General Convention when, on 19 October 1870, he gave notice that he intended to move for a committee of the General Convention, comprised of twelve laymen and twelve bishops and clergymen, to revise the Prayer Book. Brooke explained the need for revision in a memorial which preceded his proposed motion: a few passages had been made the pretext, in his view, for the introduction of doctrines and practices at variance with the overall tenor of the Prayer Book—practices repugnant to the scriptures and opposed to the principles of the reformed church. In other words, the Book of Common Prayer was not Protestant enough for his tastes. Fortunately for church unity, Brooke's resolution was considerably toned down by an amendment of the Duke of Abercorn, which stated that the revision committee's purpose would be to suggest changes that would check the introduction and spread of novel doctrines and practices opposed to the principle of the reformed church, but that such changes were not to involve or imply any change in the church's doctrines.

Nevertheless, when the revision committee's twenty-six members were appointed (instead of twenty-four as originally proposed) a major division in the church became apparent. The thirteen members that were to be chosen from among the clergy and bishops were composed solely of members of the clergy. The bishops refused to have anything to do with Brooke's committee. Indeed, the Archbishop of Armagh read a formal statement to the convention annunciating the bishops' unanimous disapproval of the appointment of Master Brooke's committee. They unanimously refused to serve on the committee, stating that since it would be their duty to give a united and unprejudiced consideration to the eventual report of Master Brooke's committee, it was not expedient for any of their number to take part in its proceedings.[79]

Undeterred by the dangerous division within the church, Master Brooke's committee went into the wilderness to deliberate and returned with a report for the 1871 General Synod of the Church of Ireland.[80] The committee's recommendations, all of which were strongly evangelical and anti-Catholic in tone, were of four sorts. The first category consisted solely of one proposed addition to the catechism:

Q. How are the Body and Blood of Christ taken and received in the Lord's Supper?

A. Only after a Heavenly and spiritual manner; and the mean whereby they are taken and received is Faith.

Second, Brooke's committee suggested three major changes in the substance of various divine services. From a doctrinal viewpoint, the most important of these amendments was a proposed addition to the declaration at the end of the Communion service declaring that no adoration was being done to any presence of Christ—which some persons mistakenly supposed to be in the elements by virtue of their consecration (five members of Brooke's committee objected to this recommendation). The committee suggested (with one member dissenting) that the absolution in the office for the visitation of the sick be omitted. On a split vote (seven in opposition) Brooke's committee proposed that the words in the ordination service which implied that the priest acquired power to forgive sins, should be replaced. A third major category of proposed changes consisted of miscellaneous alterations in parts of the Prayer Book not tied to any specific service. The old ornaments rubric was to be replaced by more austere and definitive canons, the word "priest" when found in the Prayer Book was to be understood as a synonym for "presbyter," and most saints' days were to be removed from the church calendar. Finally, Master Brooke's committee recommended a thorough, anti-Catholic revision of the ecclesiastical canons, the details of which will be mentioned later.[81]

A disastrous split within the Church of Ireland was now possible. A committee which the prelates unanimously opposed had tampered with a central document of the Anglican faith, and was now presenting its alterations to the General Synod for approval. It was certain that the vast majority of laymen and a small majority of the clergy were in favor of the proposed changes, and it was equally certain that the bishops would stand obdurate. As pressures reached the danger point, moderate men worked hard to prevent an explosion. Chief among these was the Reverend Dr. George Salmon, who had served on Master Brooke's committee, thus winning the confidence of the lay revisionists. Simultaneously, as Regius Professor of Divinity in Trinity College and as the author of some noted theological works, he enjoyed the respect of the bench of bishops. Happily Salmon was able to frame a compromise solution which allowed both sides to save face. This compromise was to have consideration of the most controversial elements of Brooke's report postponed (including issues such as the Communion rubric) and in its stead a new committee appointed with the approval and cooperation of the bishops. This new committee was not limited to consideration of the means alone of preventing new doctrinal innovations as Brooke's had been, but would consider complete revision of the formularies of the Church of Ireland. Fortunately for the church's organizational well-being, both Brooke and the bishops were willing to compromise. Brooke met with representatives of the bishops and promised that if they consented to the new revision committee's appointment, he would do everything in his power to induce the synod to allow him to withdraw all his recommendations and to resist all discussion of doctrine during the April 1871 session of the General Synod. The bishops, faced with the options of opposing all revision, or compromising in order to keep the church intact, chose the latter alternative. Accordingly, the bishops as a group agreed to form part of a revision committee, serving together with two-score clergymen and laymen from the General Synod, the revision committee being charged to report to the synod at its 1872 session.[82]

Despite the bishops' desire that anything touching on doctrinal matters be held in abeyance, the General Synod in its 1871 session did revise the ecclesiastical canons governing public worship.[83] In one sense, this was a form of Prayer Book revision, for no Irish Book of Common Prayer was printed without the canons being included. These changes in the canons were based on the recommendation of Brooke's committee. The important revisions in the canons were of a decidedly Protestant, Puritan, or evangelical nature, whichever term one prefers. For example, the fourth canon prescribed that every priest (actually the word "priest" was not used, "presbyter" and "deacon" being employed with "minister" being used as the generic term for presbyter and deacon) should conduct divine service only in a plain white surplice, or, if he preferred, a plain black gown when preaching. Without a doubt, the clarity of this regulation was a vast improvement of the incomprehensible ornaments rubric which had been inserted in the Prayer Book in 1559, and never interpreted to any-one's satisfaction thereafter.[84] Equally without doubt, the Irish canon effectively precluded the use in Ireland of the fancy dress so popular with the Anglo-Catholic party in England. The fifth Irish canon as adopted by the General Synod dictated that the celebrant of Holy Communion read the prayer of consecration while standing at the north side of the Communion table. Standing on the north side was in contrast to the Anglo-Catholic practice of kneeling facing the altar. The same canon forbade the minister or any other person to make the sign of the cross during religious service, except when indicated in the rubric. Further, no one was to bow or in any other way make obeisance to the Lord's table. Bells were not to be rung during divine service. Except to the dangerously ill, the administration of Holy Communion in private houses was forbidden (canon 16). The Communion table itself was to be a simple, moveable table, made of wood (canon 34). No lighted lamps or candles were to be allowed in any Irish church during the services except when necessary for the purpose of giving light (canon 35). Crosses of any sort were banned from the Communion table and from the wall behind the table (canon 36). During the administration of Communion the minister was prohibited from elevating the paten or the chalice, and from mixing water with the wine, or using wafer bread (canon 37). Incense was not allowed in any place where public worship was held (canon 38). Processions were banned, and it was unlawful to carry any cross, banner, or picture in any religious service or ceremony (canon 39).

Significantly, the General Synod decided to reprint at the end of the canons the thirtieth canon from the English canons of 1604. This canon, dealing with the public baptism of infants, was not usually printed in English Books of Common Prayer. The canon's purpose was to explain the making of the sign of the cross by the minister in the baptism of infants. The Church of England, the canon explained, maintained the sign of the cross in the service because it was a very ancient custom. But since the custom was liable to misinterpretation, it was necessary to explain that the sign of the cross when used in baptism was no part of the substance of the sacrament of baptism. When the minister used water and pronounced the words, "I baptize thee in the name of the Father, and of the Son, and of the Holy Ghost," the infant was fully and perfectly baptized. The sign of the cross made afterwards added nothing to the sacrament and was simply an outward ceremony symbolizing the dedication of the infant to Christ who died upon the cross.

Obviously, the passage of a canonical code so strongly anti-Catholic in tone indicates something significant about the relative strength and position of the two groups within the Church of Ireland vying for power at this time. Although in a technical sense not involving a revision of church doctrine, there is no question that the revised canons represented a victory for those who preferred to see the Church of Ireland purged of anything that might be confused with Roman Catholic theology or practice. Undoubtedly, the preponderance of power within the Church of Ireland was in the hands of the revisionists. Short of intransigence (and the potential rupture of the church body) on the part of the bishops, there was now little the conservatives could do to stop the revisionists except appeal to their sense of tolerance and fair play. It will be recalled that under Gladstone's church act a clergyman who had taken his office before the act was not bound by any new practice or formulary of the disestablished church, so long as he signified his dissent in writing within a month after the alteration was made. A good indication of the opinion of a large minority of clergymen about the revisionist steamroller is found in the fact that 350 clergymen, including one bishop, recorded their dissent from the canons passed by the General Synod.[85]

Rather than enmeshing ourselves in the details of the Prayer Book revi-

sion controversy which was not concluded until 1878,[86] we can profitably
pass on to the question, What changes were effected after the second revision committee reported to the General Synod, and what conclusions
about the church as an organization can be drawn from those changes?
First the changes. The Prayer Book as finally published in 1878 included
the Brooke committee's catechismal addition, that the Lord's Supper was
taken only in a heavenly and spiritual manner, through faith. Also, as
originally recommended by Brooke's group, the names of all saints, except
those for whose feasts services were specially appointed, were erased from
the church calendar. In the office for the visitation of the sick, the absolution
which had so offended the ardent revisionists was changed to the form of
absolution included in the Communion service. During the course of the
proceedings, there was long debate about the need to add further sentences
to the Communion rubric (the so-called Black Rubric), but a compromise
was reached whereby there was no major change in the rubric for the
service, but under which two explanatory paragraphs were added to the
preface of the Prayer Book to satisfy the more enthusiastic members of the
revisionist party. A similar expedient was invoked when dealing with the
baptismal service in which the phrase, "This child is regenerate" offended
the more severely Protestant members of the General Synod. The defenders
of the Prayer Book maintained their position against modification and
against the addition of a new baptismal rubric but allowed a paragraph to
be added to the preface explaining the service more fully. In the same way,
modification of the service for the ordination of priests was prevented, but
the revisionists were solaced with a paragraph in the preface. Probably the
most illusive problem the General Synod faced was what to do about the
Athanasian creed. The revisionists would have liked to change some of its
wording, or required the reading of a portion only. No agreeable modification was found; but the simple compromise of making its use permissive
was adopted, thus maintaining the creed intact but forcing no one to use it
against his conscience.

From our brief survey of the revision controversy, we can conclude that
a serious rift in the Church of Ireland existed between the overwhelming
majority of the laity and a moiety of the clergy on the one hand, and
about half of the clergy and the bishops on the other. First, this split was
on doctrine and liturgy, issues so explosive that there was a real possibility
of an organizational schism. Second, the revisions made actually represented a successful response to the threat of division. The viability of the
Church of Ireland as a voluntary religious body was firmly established by
a successful weathering of the revision crisis. Third, it is clear that the
compromise which guaranteed the church's survival was won at the expense of the bench of bishops. It will be recalled that the bishops at first
tried to hold a no-revision position but they were manifestly unsuccessful.

If one compares the final alterations in the Prayer Book with those recommended by Master Brooke's committee, of whose existence the bishops disapproved and whose recommendation they vigorously opposed, it becomes clear that the revisionists of Brooke's stripe had won the day. The changes in the ecclesiastical canons were effected along the lines detailed in the Brooke committee report. The church calendar, the cathechism, and the office for the visitation of the sick, were also revised along lines desired by Brooke's group. The opponents of revision were generally successful in holding the line on revision of the Communion service, the ordinal, and baptismal service, but at the price of accepting a preface which was written to satisfy the revisionists. On matters of central importance—such as those of liturgy and doctrine—it was implicitly established that, in the face of strong lay and clerical pressure, the bishops would not dare to exercise their veto powers because of the permanent rupture in the church that might result. On matters of central importance, democracy not hierarchy was established as the dominant principle.

REFINANCING THE CHURCH

Planning and Preparation

While the viability of the Church of Ireland as a voluntary religious organization was established by the awkward, yet successful, handling of the Prayer Book revision crisis, the financial survival of the organization was secured by monetary planning and investment policies which were almost breathtakingly adept.[87] The planning for refinancing the church began early and undramatically with the constitutional drafting committee's recommendations for future fiscal arrangements. The Church of Ireland, it will be recalled, was awarded compensation in property and sterling under Gladstone's church act. It was to receive: £500,000 in lieu of private endowments; the churches and schoolhouses in actual use; an option to buy the glebe houses and part of the glebe lands on favorable terms; and the right to speculate with the clergy's annuity money, if the clergy as a group agreed to commute their annuities.

The drafting committee's recommendations about use of these resources were presented to the General Convention of the Church of Ireland in late March 1870. Since the Representative Church Body, the legal embodiment of the Church of Ireland, had been chosen earlier in the month, the draft scheme was essentially a detailed plan of finance for the Representative Church Body to follow. The committee divided its suggestions into three heads: the sustentation fund, church property, and commutation. According to the draft committee the average life expectation of the Irish clergy who had been employed before disestablishment was approximately fifteen years. In guaranteeing their life income, the government was essentially giving the church fifteen years notice of the day when it would have to pay for its own clergy. Therefore, churchmen had to start at once to raise a fund, to be known as the sustenation fund, that would be large enough in fifteen years to support the Irish clergy. Taking compound interest into account, it was estimated that it was necessary for each member of the church to subscribe at least 2 percent of his annual income to achieve the desired end. The committee recommended that a campaign be initiated to raise these funds, and an elaborate fund-raising organization was outlined. The second major issue was church property, which included the churches, glebe houses, and the £500,000 compensation for private endowment. The drafting committee urged moving quickly to reclaim the parish churches for the Church of Ireland and to repurchase the glebe houses. No recommendation was made, however, about the disposal of the one-half million pounds.[88]

When it came to the subject of commutation, the drafting committee was at pains to disabuse the General Convention of the notion that the bulk sum paid to the church for the clergy's commutation of their lifetime government annuities represented a re-endowment of the church. Most of the money from commutation, the committee noted, would have to be paid out to clergy for salaries, although almost certainly a surplus would remain to the church's favor. Since the church would make a percentage of profit on each clergyman who commutated, it was necessary to stimulate the clergy to commutate by making the process as attractive as possible. This was all the more important, because the church act stipulated that, in dioceses where three fourths of the clergy commutated, the church would receive a 12 percent bonus. Every effort would be made, therefore, to assure that clergymen who were considering commutation were offered maximum safety. This would be accomplished by making clerical salaries a first liability, after the repurchase of church property, on the Representative Church Body. Further, to assure safety for the clergy, a Guarantee Fund would be established to back the church's obligations to commutating clergy. The committee also recommended that an arrangement be made for those clergymen who wished to leave the church. Such clergymen, the committee suggested, should be treated as follows: They should be allowed to commutate (thus assuring the 12 percent commutation bonus to the church) and then be allowed to draw one-third to two-thirds of the value of their life interests (depending on age, and other factors) in a lump sum and, if they wished, to retire. (The clergyman's drawing of the lump sum was called "compounding.")

Overall, the advantages to the Church of Ireland of the plan of commutation and compounding were:

1. The church received the bonus of 12 percent on the life interests of commutating clergy.

2. The church received profit accruing from investment of the commutation capital. The commutation money from the government was awarded on the basis of a 3.5 percent interest rate, but most investments paid more than 3.5 percent.

3. The church retained the residue left in each case of a clergyman's compounding.

4. When combined with the efforts to raise the sustenation fund, the commutation plan offered an opportunity for a substantial re-endowment of the clergy of the Church of Ireland.[89]

The General Convention quickly endorsed the principles of the drafting committee's financial suggestions, although it did ask that details of commutation and compounding be elucidated in the future. These details were provided by the Representative Church Body (which had assumed responsibility for financial-legal transactions) when the General Convention assembled in October 1870 and was approved in a slightly modified form by the convention.[90]

Commutation, Compounding, and Capital Advances

The most immediate goal for the Representative Church Body was to effect the swift commutation of as many Irish clergymen as possible. Operationally, the commutation procedure was divided into three steps: the determination by the Church Temporalities Commissioners, representing the government, of the amount of annuity due each claimant; the payment of a lump sum according to the number of annuitants who commuted by the Church Temporalities Commissioners to the Representative Church Body; and the management of the commutation capital by the Representative Body. The Church Temporalities Commissioners framed the regulations in October 1869 and sent a copy to every incumbent and every other known claimant in Ireland. The claimants were asked to complete a questionnaire giving details of their situation and providing other information which was to be the basis for adjudicating claims.[91]

New Year's Day, 1871, was the date on which annuitants could effect the commutation of their life income. The following alternatives were open to any individual clergyman: He could decide to keep accepting his government annuity for life, which would come to him directly from the Church Temporalities Commissioners. If he chose this path, he continued to occupy his glebe house and glebe lands and was, therefore, in the same financial position as he was before disestablishment. Second, a cleric could choose to commutate his annuity and his life interests in the glebe house and lands and could elect to be paid by the Representative Church Body. In such case, his cash income would be larger than previously because of his commutation of the life interest in the house and lands. Probably the Representative Church Body would buy back his glebe house and a portion of his former glebe lands and let him occupy them for life, but usually the lands would be less than he previously held. Third, the clergyman could decide to commutate his lifetime annuity but not to commute his life interests in the glebe house and lands. In that case he would be in the same position, in terms of annual cash income and life interests in glebe house and lands, as the clergyman in the first example who did not commutate at all. The only difference would be that in the first case, the clergyman's paymaster would be the government, and in this case, the Church of Ireland.[92]

There was, as might be expected, considerable implicit pressure on the individual clergyman to follow either of the latter two courses described above, each of which involved commutation of his interests and payment of their value to the Representative Church Body. One such pressure was the knowledge that simply by commutating, a clergyman could provide his church with a 12 percent bonus on his capitalized life interests without diminishing his own income. (Of course, this step involved his having faith that the church would continue to pay his income.) Local pressures must have borne heavily on individual clergymen in this regard. Further, self-interest came into the calculation. The clergyman knew that the church act required that before he could leave his present parish for another one he must, whether he had commutated or not, receive the permission of the Representative Church Body. That body made it clear that it would not accept transfers unless the clergyman had made a satisfactory arrangement for the financial security of his previous parish. A clergyman could do this, if he were an annuitant who did not commutate, by endowing his parish successors through heavily insuring his own life. Clearly, however, it was easier to make satisfactory arrangements if the clergyman had the commutation capital to rely on. For an ambitious clergyman, desirous of another parish, therefore, there was considerable implicit pressure upon him to commutate. Further, the commutation arrangements offered certain benefits to a clergyman irrespective of his desires for election to another incumbency. For instance, if he commutated, his income was paid in quarterly rather than semi-annual installments. Favorable terms for loans from the Representative Church Body were available to him if he had life insurance as security. He also had the option of surrendering a portion of his lifetime income and receiving from the Representative Church Body a capital sum. In the case of a clergyman who needed capital for the purchase of a small estate, for example, or of a clergyman who was promoted to a living at a higher stipend so that he no longer needed all his annuity salary—these possibilities under the commutation plan were attractive.[93]

The combination of tacit coercion with the attractive features of the commutation plan made it an instant success. The Representative Church

Body noted in its report for 1872 that of the 2,157 ecclesiastical persons entitled to government annuities, 1,837 had already commutated, and each united diocese in Ireland was well over the three-quarter mark required to earn the 12 percent bonus for the church.[94] A year later the list of those clergy eligible for commutation who had not done so comprised only 108 names, and 19 of those persons were dead![95] Altogether, by 1874, only 423 of the 5,721 persons of all sorts (including sextons, schoolmasters, and parish clerks) to whom government annuities were awarded, refused to commutate.[96] The capitalized value of the annuities of the commutating clergy which were placed in the church's hands was £596,913. With the 12 percent bonus, the amount handed over to the church by the state was £7,581,075.[97] From this money, the church had to pay the lifetime salaries of all those who were in employment before disestablishment. Nevertheless, the Church of Ireland clearly had gained a good deal of room for financial maneuver.[98]

Under the church's arrangements, a minister who commutated had the additional right to compound. This meant he could elect to take a sum, usually ranging from one third to two thirds of his commutation money (which was the capitalized value of the government annuity he was surrendering). This transaction simultaneously freed him from any further obligation to the Church of Ireland. Now, the crucial point is that the authorities of the Church of Ireland encouraged compounding. Why? First, because when a man compounded, he extinguished a liability upon the commutation fund which no longer had to underwrite his salary. The church's financial advisers desired the removal of all liabilities from the fund as soon as possible, because then they could invest the residue in a completely unfettered manner. Second, in certain cases, such as those of bishops and high-income clergymen, the church was saved from a high-risk situation whenever one of these men compounded; the risk was that several of these highly paid men would live an inordinately long time and thus seriously deplete the commutation fund by drawing large annual salaries for several years. Third, the church had an opportunity to make a profit on the compounding transaction. Every time a man compounded he left behind in church hands an average of approximately half his capitalized life interests. Not all of the residue left behind was profit, for usually the church had to hire a replacement. If, however, the replacement was paid less than the predecessor's annual annuity value, then the church had made a net profit on the transaction. This profit was very large in instances where a man compounded and retired from the ministry and was not replaced at all.

In a case somewhat similar to compounding, the church's financial managers also encouraged men who did not compound to consider taking lump sum advances on their commutation capital in return for drawing smaller annual salaries for the rest of their lives. By so doing, the clergymen reduced the long-term liabilities against the commutation capital.

A good deal of scorn in church circles was reserved for clergymen who practiced the "three C's": "commutated, compounded and cut." Actually, many of those who compounded chose to become stipendiary clergy and continued to do duty while receiving the ordinary income paid to men appointed after disestablishment, minus a certain deduction on account of the capital sum they had received.[99]

The compounding and advances scheme was a considerable success. Although only one bishop agreed to compound (Bishop Alexander of Derry who compounded on terms so unfavorable to himself that he was able to endow the Bishopric of Derry with an income of £2,000 a year), all of the other bishops who had commutated consented to take large advances of capital. From 1871 to 1874, 753 of the 2,059 ecclesiastical persons who had commutated also compounded. The compounders consisted of one bishop, 452 incumbents and 300 curates. The 753 compounders received £1,169,650 from the Representative Church Body out of the commutation fund. These payments to ecclesiastical persons were equal to roughly half of their capitalized life interests, and therefore set free for church purposes a large capital sum, namely £1,108,955. This money the Representative Church Body was now free to spend as it saw fit. The annual value of the life annuities which were extinguished by the compounders would have required an annual payment by the Representative Church Body of £172,764. By 1879 compounding had occurred to the extent of £1,290,202, with an additional £989,861 advanced to the bishops and clergy who wished not to compound the full value of their life expectations. Ultimately, the total number of clergymen that compounded was 1,102. The total amount paid to church personnel in composition and advances was £2,494,409. A total of £1,651,097, the residue of capitalized life interests, was left in church hands, an amount freed through the compositions scheme for any use the Representative Church Body wished, certainly a successful piece of financing.[100]

Other Financial Transactions

The Representative Church Body as the legal embodiment of the Church of Ireland assumed possession from the Church Temporalities Commissioners of the churches and graveyards in actual use, a simple set of transactions over which we need not linger. More complex were the provisions for the church's repurchase of glebe houses and see houses. The ecclesiastical residences, it will be recalled, could be repurchased by the church at ten times their annual value or for an amount equal to the building charge, whichever was less. It was universally recognized by contemporaries that this was a bargain price and that the houses were worth a great deal more. Hence, when the Representative Church Body repurchased a residence it was taking a small step towards reendowing the Church of Ireland, for through the transaction the church acquired property worth more than the capital spent in its acquisition.[101]

Unlike the arrangements for the purchase of houses, those for purchase of glebe lands and see lands involved the purchase of the property at fair market prices. The Representative Church Body, although not making a profit on the transactions, bought as much land as possible to go with the houses, and in most cases the Church Temporalities Commissioners allowed them to purchase more than the suggested limit, of ten acres to accompany a glebe house, and thirty acres to go with a see house.[102] By the end of the year 1878, the Representative Church Body had repurchased 831 of the estimated 930 glebe houses in Ireland.[103]

When the transactions were finally completed, 935 glebe and see houses were repurchased from the state, which is to say, almost all of the ecclesiastical residences in Ireland eventually were returned to the Church of Ireland. For these residences the Representative Church Body paid £117,134 and, for the attached lands, £392,125—making a total expenditure of £509,259. Whenever possible, the Representative Church Body encouraged local parishes to assist with the purchase of the local glebe houses, and eventually the parishes assumed £420,703 of the cost.[104] The Representative Church Body, then, by combining less than £90,000 of its own resources with an appeal to local charity was able to secure for the Church of Ireland a complete set of ecclesiastical residences and lands worth considerably more than the approximately half-million pounds the church paid for it.

The collection of the £500,000 which the church received as compensation for all its private endowments was a routine matter. The complicated part came later when the Representative Church Body had to compensate those who had previously drawn upon their private endowments (such as incumbents whose benefices were endowed). After meeting all the claims for such compensation, the Representative Church Body had a surplus of £150,000. This money was invested in American bonds and used to endow poor parishes, to cover the expenses of the General Synod, and to endow certain bishoprics and the Deanery of Saint Patrick's, Dublin.[105]

The Representative Church Body managed its investments very well. A useful baseline for judging its success is the figure used by the government to establish the commutation of annuities, namely, an expectation of 3.5 percent annually as a reasonable return on a safe investment. Actually the church did much better than this in obtaining about 4.5 percent each year on its investments. In the early 1870s, about £1,500,000 was invested in land mortgages and an equal amount in railway debentures and blue-chip stocks. The income on the investments was 4.8 percent for many years, but then fell slightly as mortgages became a less attractive investment because of the Irish land acts. When this occurred, mortgages were largely dropped from the portfolio. The Church of Ireland was fortunate indeed that her laymen included some of the ablest financial names in Ireland—names such as Cairns, La Touche, Mulholland, and Carson. These men served on the Representative Church Body and were the most faithful of financial stewards. Without their shrewd investment policies, the Church of Ireland as an institution would have had a difficult time surviving.[106]

Private Philanthropy

Whatever the Representative Church Body received from the government as compensation for lost interests, and however well it managed its resources, the Church of Ireland as an institution desperately needed to receive a large influx of new private gifts in the years immediately following disestablishment. The financial problem was a simple one: the bulk of the money which the church received from the government, most of which was commutation capital, would inevitably decrease year after year as clerical annuities were paid. Therefore, to prevent the church being virtually unendowed when the last of the payments was made, voluntary funds had to be raised to replace the outgoings. To this end, the constitutional drafting committee suggested to the General Convention that a "sustention fund" be established immediately. The plan was an intelligent blend of central direction and local incentives. A central committee was to be appointed by the General Convention and an analogous committee was to be formed in each diocese. Every member of the Church of Ireland was to be invited to subscribe to the sustention fund, hopefully at an average rate of 2 percent of his annual income. The cunning part of the arrangement was the suggestion that, in subscribing to the sustention fund, each subscriber be at liberty to allocate his subscription to a particular parish or diocese. The subscription would be funneled into the hands of the treasurer of the central committee, thus guaranteeing national coordination, and would be credited to the account of the individual parish or diocese designated by the subscriber. (Non-designated funds were to be under the full control of the Representative Church Body.)[107]

The General Convention moved swiftly, and a sustention appeal, based on the constitutional drafting committee's guidelines, was framed and published by late April 1870. It was estimated that £230,000 a year was necessary from private gifts to secure successfully the re-endowment of the Church of Ireland's clergy.[108] Given below are the annual total contributions to the sustention fund from 1870 to 1885:[109]

1870	£229,753
1871	214,709
1872	248,445
1873	230,179
1874	257,021
1875	218,499
1876	212,095
1877	197,739
1878	174,403
1879	165,007
1880	147,768
1881	153,818
1882	154,486
1883	178,444
1884	190,611
1885	137,117

The results of the sustenation appeal, then, were substantial but not overwhelming. If somewhat below expectation, the laity's response nevertheless made it clear that the laymen were still strongly inclined to support their church.

The declining contributions to the sustenation fund over a period of time may in all probability be ascribed to three causes. The first is the simple one of diminishing returns, so common to most human activities. In the case of the Anglican laity who were asked year after year to dig deeply into their resources to support their church's reendowment, it is hardly surprising to find them responding with a little less enthusiasm as the years passed. Second, it is clear that gradually the social class upon which the Anglican Church in Ireland depended for its larger contributions, was losing ground in Irish society. Increasingly the landlords were coming under economic stress and political duress. The Land Act of 1881 was a sign of the downward slide of the Anglican gentry. Third, one should remember that the population of Ireland was continually declining during the second half of the nineteenth century, and although the Church of Ireland's number declined a trace more slowly than the Irish population as a whole, its numbers decreased nevertheless. The number of Anglicans in Ireland in the years 1861, 1871, and 1881, with the Anglican proportion of the total population was as follows: 693,357 (12 percent); 667,998 (12.3 percent); 639,574 (12.3 percent).[110] With fewer church adherents and less wealth among them, it was only natural that the sustenation appeals would generate a diminishing response.

To return to the financial arrangements: Although the investment of funds of the entire church was handled centrally by the Representative Church Body, the funds for each diocese were maintained as a separate accounting entity; each diocese was responsible for creating its own scheme for the levy and expenditure of its share of the general fund. This arrangement may at first glance seem a trifle awkward, but it is really a very common one in the modern institutional world, especially the academic sphere. It is quite common for modern universities to have a central agency for investing the funds of the various schools and colleges of the university, while allowing the colleges and schools to balance their individual budgets as they see fit. Such a scheme avoids the pitfalls of excessive "congregationalism" on the part of local units and provides for expert, professional investment of the funds through the central treasury. At the same time the participation of the constituent units in the fund-raising is guaranteed, and the partial independence of the smaller units is preserved. To make such a system work, it is essential that guidelines be established by the central authorities (or by a consensus of the constituent units) about the practices of the smaller units. The Church of Ireland achieved working consensus by allowing each diocese to devise its own scheme, but on accounting principles standard throughout the church. Also, organizational outlines were required to be similar for each diocese and each diocesan scheme had to provide for the participation of individual parishes, so that local initiative was preserved.[111]

Admittedly, the scheme had certain drawbacks. For one thing it froze large amounts of capital in a specific parish or diocese. This meant that when future changes in the distribution of the church population occurred, it would be difficult to realign the diocesan endowments to fit the new population patterns.[112] Also, in the cases of the poorer dioceses, such as Tuam, Killaloe, and Limerick, the scheme did not provide enough endowment to weather times of financial hardship. Hence, in the later 1880s it was necessary for the churches of Dublin and of the northern Diocese of Down, Connor, and Dromore to come to the aid of the poorer western dioceses.[113] While noting the awkwardness of the diocesan financial arrangements, the fact remains that such local arrangements were probably necessary to provide incentive for local giving; and that possessing endowments of limited application was preferable to having no endowments at all.

A Financial Summary

The refinancing of the Church of Ireland was undoubtedly the most successful of the steps taken in reorganization of the church after disestablishment.[114] Unlike the questions of church policy and religious doctrine, financial matters were non-controversial. Everyone wanted the church as well endowed as possible, and almost everyone was willing to accept the prescriptions of the financial experts in effecting the re-endowment. If we examine the invested assets of the Church of Ireland at the termination date of this study, 1885, we find that it had £6,475,005 in capital, which came from the following sources:

From government for the compensation of private endowments	£ 500,000
Commutation money saved through composition	1,561,032
Commutation capital still liable to annuities	2,230,496
From private subscriptions	2,183,477
Total	£6,475,005

Hence, within fifteen years after disestablishment, approximately one third of the church's capital stemmed from the private philanthropy of the faithful.[115]

We can gain a clearer view of the impact of the financial arrangements framed after disestablishment if we step past our 1885 time barrier for the moment and examine the situation on the eve of the Irish revolution. In the years 1870 to 1916 the Church of Ireland received £8,008,329 from private benefactions.[116] The total amount of compensation paid to all church interests by the government was £10,208,988.[117] In 1916, the Church of Ireland had in its coffers £9,321,354, plus title to its churches and almost all of its glebe and see houses with accompanying lands.[118] Therefore, out of a cash flow of somewhat over 18 million pounds, the church had been able to retain slightly more than half, a feat of financial wizardry.

Most of the other half was paid in the form of annual salaries or of lump capital payments to bishops and clergy who had manned the church before disestablishment. As the pre-disestablishment clergy retired or died, their places were taken by men whose annual stipends had to be entirely paid by the church, with no government money to back the church's liability. The major portions of the £500,000 handed to the church in compensation of private endowments had to be passed on to those whose expectations were hurt by the termination of the endowments. Also, about half a million pounds were spent repurchasing residences and lands for the bishops and clergy.

The vital point which the church had to reach was the stage where annual liabilities against commutation capital could be met entirely out of interest on the remaining capital. As each year passed this situation came closer, for fewer and fewer predisestablishment clergy were alive to draw from the source, and the investment profits accrued each year. Finally, in 1893 the interest was large enough to bear the liabilities and therefore the commutation capital ceased to shrink.[119] At that point the church was in the happy position of knowing that its assets were totally free from obligations to the past. The 1916 accounting of the way in which the commutation capital had been used is given below:

Total paid to Representative Church Body on account of commutation by Irish clergy	£7,581,075
Paid to annuitants as equivalent of their former salaries	1,553,814
Paid in lump sums to those who compounded or requested advances	2,494,409
Composition balances left to the church after composition and advances effected	1,651,097
Profits made by investments	1,881,753

The latter two items on the accounting sheet were available for whatever purpose the Representative Church Body wished to pursue. It chose to divert most of the money (nearly £2.7 million) to the investment account which underwrote the stipends of the Irish clergy.[120]

In 1905 there was over £5.2 million in the fund which endowed the income of the Irish clergy. This was not enough to pay a full salary for each cleric, and it was assumed that the interest from this capital would be equalled in each parish by an annual subscription by the parishioners towards the minister's salary. If this were the case, the average stipend of the Irish clergyman in 1905 would have been slightly less than £216 a year.[121] Now, when it is recalled that the modal income for an Irish clergyman on the eve of disestablishment was between £100 and £200 a year, it becomes clear that the average clergyman did not suffer very much financially by disestablishment. Granted, the church tended to cut down the larger parochial incomes to a level of rough equality throughout the country, but this did not affect the majority of the clergy.

The group whose financial position was most hurt by disestablishment was the body of prelates (the bishops on the bench when disestablishment occurred were, of course, not affected but their successors were). Contrasted in table 42 are the annual incomes of the bishops in 1867, as presented in chapter 3, and the bishops' salaries in 1919.

Besides losing a large portion of its income, the bench of bishops lost the right for any of its members to sit in the House of Lords, and further, most episcopal lands were considerably diminished. The bishops of the Church of Ireland were reduced from being rather wealthy landed magnates with aristocratic associations, to being merely well paid gentlemen of the cloth.

With the exception of the bishops, no group in the Church of Ireland suffered very much financially from disestablishment. Admittedly, the laity was called upon for the first time to underwrite a major portion of the expenses of the Anglican religion in Ireland, but it can well be argued that

TABLE 42
ANNUAL INCOME OF IRISH BISHOPS, 1867 AND 1919
(In pounds)

	1867	1919
Armagh & Clogher[a]	8,882	2,500
Dublin & Kildare	7,261	2,500
Derry & Raphoe	5,680	2,000
Down, Connor, & Dromore	3,724	1,752
Cloyne, Cork, & Ross	2,106	1,703
Cashel, Emly, Waterford, & Lismore	3,923	1,549
Kilmore, Elphin, & Ardagh	4,781	1,542
Ferns, Leighlin, & Ossory	3,424	1,535
Meath	3,502	1,500
Killaloe, Kilfenora, Clonfert, & Kilmacduagh	2,910	1,500
Tuam, Killala, & Achonry	4,311	1,493
Clogher[a]	–	1,442
Limerick, Ardfert & Aghadoe	3,812	1,408
Total episcopal income	54,319	22,424

[a] Clogher was disunited from Armagh in 1886.

Source: The 1919 salaries are from the *Irish Times*, 26 July 1929.

its contributions were long overdue anyway. The contributions of the laity, when combined with the expertise of the Representative Church Body, insured that the Church of Ireland would enter the twentieth century, if no longer a wealthy church, indisputably a financially healthy church.

6 Conclusion

The title of this book includes two words which are fashionable today and hence are often used indiscriminately: *reform* and *revolution*. The best way to draw together the conclusions of this study is to ask whether the use of these two words is justified. *Reform,* much the less divisive of the two words, means to improve something without destroying its basic framework. *Revolution* on the other hand denotes a complete turnabout in relationships, or the replacing of one structure with another one; it usually connotes a swift change as well as a radical one. This study has indicated that reform, but not revolution, occurred in the following four areas: diocesan and provincial arrangements, parochial facilities and organization, middle-level managerial structure, and the cathedral system.[1]

In the eighteenth century the Church of Ireland was organized on a geographic basis. The country was divided into provinces and the provinces into dioceses. The same geographic principle of organization was operant in 1885. Modifications, however, had been made. Whereas the church in the second half of the eighteenth century had been organized into four provinces, each with its own archbishop, and into a total of twenty-two archbishoprics and bishoprics, the Church Temporalities Act of 1833 reduced the number of provinces and archbishops to two and the total number of archbishoprics and bishoprics to twelve. This was reform, certainly, but hardly revolution.

The arrangements for the provision of pastoral services on the local level underwent somewhat more radical changes than did the diocesan system. These alterations were directly keyed to improving the delivery of religious service to the Anglican population. Although in theory the basic unit of organization in the Church of Ireland was the parish, in practice it was the benefice (usually composed of more than one parish) served by a single clergyman. In the late 1780s there were 1,120 benefices in Ireland. By 1832 this number had risen to 1,395, and by 1867 to 1,518. In effect, the increase in the number of benefices meant that extra strands were being added to the Church of Ireland's network of local religious units. Consequently the delivery of pastoral services to the laity by religious professionals became more regular with each passing year. Also, as the number of benefices rose the number of parish unions declined, which is to be expected since normally the two figures vary inversely.

A related problem of parochial organization, the holding of several benefices simultaneously by a single cleric, was a great hindrance to the Church of Ireland's efficient operation during the eighteenth century. The rules on pluralities were murky at best. The practice was for the Archbishop of

Armagh to allow pluralities if the benefices involved were within thirty miles of each other (exceptions to these limits were sometimes granted). If, however, a man held a position without cure of souls he could hold his sinecure office (or offices) in addition to his benefices with cure of souls. Occasionally a pluralist was able to assemble an annual income well over £1,000, much of it for sinecure benefices, and the rest from benefices with cure of souls which he farmed out to curates at £75 a year or less. Eighteenth and early nineteenth-century statistics being almost non-existent, the earliest reliable estimate of the number of Irish clergy holding two or more benefices with cure of souls is for the year 1819 when 163 clergymen were returned as "residing on other benefices," a clear indication of pluralism. After Lord John Beresford became Archbishop of Armagh, the number of pluralists dropped because of his refusal to grant faculties except in exceptional cases. Even when granting a faculty for a plurality he exacted a promise from the cleric to live a portion of each year on each benefice and to pay for a licensed curate when absent. The final solution of the problem of pluralities came soon after disestablishment when the Church of Ireland did away with pluralities except in the case of adjoining benefices, and such cases were more an informal union of parishes than pluralism in the eighteenth-century sense of the term.

In the eighteenth century, the Church of Ireland's parish operations were hobbled by noncure benefices and by sinecure benefices and dignities. Although technically different, all these positions had one glaring common flaw: they paid clergymen for doing nothing. Reform began with the Church Temporalities Act of 1833, which allowed the Ecclesiastical Commissioners to move against the noncures by providing that, in the case of those benefices not under lay patronage in which divine service had not been celebrated for three years prior to the passage of the act, the commissioners could suspend the appointment and apply the revenue to the general good of the church. The amending act of 1834, which slightly modified the previous year's legislation, made it possible for the Ecclesiastical Commissioners to abolish sinecure benefices and dignities as well as noncures. Even before disestablishment, therefore, most of the nonproductive offices in the Church of Ireland had been reformed out of existence.

Another aspect of the eighteenth-century parochial structure which needed improvement was the supply of churches. There were only 1,001 churches in Ireland in 1787, a figure well below half the number of parishes and, indeed, 119 below the number of benefices. This meant that the Anglican laity was poorly provided with places for worship, and that some clergymen were appointed to benefices which had no facilities for divine worship. The number of parish churches had risen to 1,182 by 1832 and, when chapels of ease are counted, to 1,293. During the remainder of the years under study the church moved regularly towards the goal of having one church in every benefice.

While the number of churches was augmented because they were obviously necessary to the provision of religious services, the number of glebe houses was augmented, because the houses indirectly facilitated the provision of local pastoral services by making it convenient for the incumbent to reside in his benifice (or, alternatively, inconvenient for him to obtain permission not to reside!). According to Beaufort's estimates, there were only 354 glebe houses in all of Ireland in 1787, a figure which means that less than one third of the Irish clergy had a place to live if they wished to reside. During the twenty-three latter years of the eighteenth century, the Board of First Fruits was able to obtain a series of annual grants of £5,000 a year from the Irish parliament which enabled the board to provide grants toward the building of glebe houses. Grants to begin 116 houses were made before the Union. After the Union, the board received a windfall in the form of compensation money for the ecclesiastical boroughs. In addition the board obtained a continuing grant from the parliament of the United Kingdom which rose suddenly in 1810 to £60,000, a level at which it remained until 1817 when it began declining until it ceased altogether in 1823. These funds made it possible for the board to lend and grant money generously for the provision of glebe houses. The policy of stimulating glebe house construction was continued by the successors of the Board of First Fruits, the Ecclesiastical Commissioners for Ireland, although under less generous terms. The result was that when the time came for the disestablished Church of Ireland to repurchase the glebe houses necessary for its continued operation, the Representative Church Body obtained more than nine hundred glebe houses.

Turning to the third of the four areas in which major reforms were effected, we should recall that, in the eighteenth century, the Church of Ireland lacked an efficient middle level of administration capable of tying together the diocesan and the parish strata. The Church of Ireland, in contrast to the Church of England, did not regularly employ archdeacons as communicating officers between the bishop and the clergy. Neither was the office of rural dean employed to any significant extent. The only ties between the episcopal and clerical levels were the deans and chapters of the various cathedrals, and they were an undependable and idiosyncratic collection at best. This situation changed in the late eighteenth and early nineteenth century. Bishop Berkeley revived the office of rural dean in the Diocese of Cloyne during the mid-eighteenth century and the Archbishops of Cashel and of Armagh later followed suit. By 1820 sixteen of the twenty-two archbishops and bishops were employing the system. The rural deans were regular parish clergymen who were responsible for communicating the bishops' policies to the dioceses' other clergymen. They also were responsible for communicating basic intelligence on the state of the benefices to the bishops. In dioceses where the system was introduced, the bishop divided the entire diocese into rural deaneries, thus providing a consistent pattern of middle level administration and communication.

Another major reform in the middle level administration of the Church of Ireland came with the passage of the Church Temporalities Act of 1833 which gave archdeacons in Ireland the same authority and duties as they held in England. The same act introduced yet another development in the intermediate administration by creating the Ecclesiastical Commissioners for Ireland. This group was an assortment of archbishops, bishops, legal figures, civil servants, and laymen. Collectively it served as a dispenser of money for church building and glebe construction, and as a standardizer of financial practices and of certain ecclesiastical practices. The commissioners did not, by any stretch of the imagination, have the prestige of the bench of bishops. They performed the technical administrative tasks which needed to be standardized throughout the church. Major policy issues were left to the bishops.

The reforms in the middle level of the church—the reintroduction of rural deans, the empowering of archdeacons on English lines, and the formation of the Ecclesiastical Commissioners—were most propitious, for they occurred during the same broad time span when the Church Temporalities Act was reducing the number of bishops and thus making it increasingly difficult for an individual bishop to keep close watch over each incumbent. Ironically, while the top echelon of the church was being reformed by reduction, the middle level was being reformed by augmentation.

The cathedral system, the fourth major reform area, was the last to be revised. Until disestablishment, the Irish cathedral system was a jumble of peculiarities. In the eighteenth century, every bishopric except Kilmore and Meath had at least one cathedral and chapter under its aegis; and after the rearrangement of bishoprics in 1833 only Meath lacked a cathedral and chapter (however, the Deanery of Clonmacnoise, without chapter, was within its bounds). Historically, the cathedrals were the mother church of the diocese and in theory, service was conducted regularly in each of them. The actual practice varied widely and in most rural cathedrals religious practice was limited by the chapter's being non-residential. Many of the cathedral offices were sinecures. Others were tied to the cure of souls in specific parishes. In the former case the incumbent was not apt to take part in any but rare ceremonial functions, and in the latter, the parochial duty often prevented the officeholder from carrying out cathedral duties. Each chapter, whatever its peculiar composition, was a legally incorporated body and most of the individual officers were corporations sole.

All this changed not, as one might expect, in 1833, for the Church Temporalities Act almost totally ignored the cathedrals, but in the early

1870s. Under the financial strain of disestablishment it became very important that the church not waste its resources. Therefore, the cathedral system was made more functional than it had ever been in the past. The responsibilities of all but four of the cathedral churches were redefined so that they served simultaneously as parish churches and as cathedral churches. Similarly, the pressures of disestablishment meant that the cathedral chapters became much less opulent bodies than they had been in the past. Most of the sinecures had been abolished already by the Ecclesiastical Commissioners before disestablishment and the last disappeared after disestablishment. Now, the cathedral offices which often previously had borne large emoluments and which usually were attached to specific parishes, became (with the exception of the deanship) honorific offices which could be held by any clergyman incumbent in the diocese. Gladstone's church act dissolved all cathedral corporations, both sole and aggregate, thus removing that legal privilege from the chapters, dignitaries, and deans. The General Synod of the Church of Ireland erased the eccentric arrangements which had previously governed the conduct of cathedral matters and in their place decreed standard procedures for the management of the cathedrals. These arrangements, in line with other post-disestablishment reforms, introduced a strong lay element into the management of cathedral affairs.

These reforms in the cathedral system bordered on the revolutionary and bring us to those changes in the Church of Ireland for which we can unhesitatingly use the word revolutionary. The reader will have noticed that the majority (but certainly not all) of the developments in the four major areas of reform—diocesan and provincial arrangements, parochial facilities and organization, middle level managerial structure, and the cathedral system—were made before disestablishment. By contrast, in the areas of revolution, none of the changes was completed until after 1869, although the groundwork was laid before that year. When viewing these turnabouts in the church which are summarized below, the critical reader may well agree that they are indeed reversals of practices and relationships, but may still disagree that the changes merit the word *revolutionary* since that word usually connotes swiftness as well as denotes a reversal. To this, one can reply that the proper perspective for judging whether or not a series of events in the Church of Ireland in the eighteenth and nineteenth centuries was revolutionary is not the perspective of the mid-twentieth century, but the perspective of the church in Ireland since Norman times. Using this perspective, it becomes clear how little the church had changed since the diocesan framework was firmly established. The Protestant Reformation, although of massive political, theological, and social significance, had changed the church very little organizationally. The Reformed Church of Ireland clung to the same basic administrative framework—a hierarchical structure divided into geographical units—that it had embraced before the Reformation. Therefore, in talking about changes that occurred within the time boundaries of this study, 1800–1885, changes which wildly bent the old hierarchical framework, we are discussing events that legitimately are labelled "revolutionary."

The common theme underlying most of the reversals in the practice of the Church of Ireland during the period 1800–1885 was the replacement of the principle of hierarchical ecclesiastical government by the simultaneous invocation of the principles of democracy and of hierarchy. The most telling indicator of the emergence of the idea of democratic ecclesiastical administration is found in the radically changed position of the laity in the Church of Ireland. In the eighteenth century the laymen were the lowest stratum of the administrative pyramid. Granted, certain gentry and nobility had considerable power in the church through owning advowsons, through having influence over the tenantry, or through political contacts. However, these laymen, most often politicians or noblemen, wielded their power in the church because they were powerful individuals and not because the laity as such was expected to have any influence. When the eighteenth-century situation is compared to the circumstances of the Church of Ireland after disestablishment, the contrast is formidable. After disestablishment the selection of local incumbents was no longer in the hands of the bishops, but under the control of committees made up of the local bishop plus diocesan clergymen and laymen, and the decision-making process was usually dominated by laymen. Whereas before disestablishment an aspiring incumbent had to seek the favor of the patron of the benefice he desired, usually the diocesan bishop, afterward he had to canvass for the votes of laymen.

Now, at this point a critic might object that the change in the position of the laity actually was not great because the House of Commons was a committee of laymen which had possessed control over the Irish church. The leaders of that committee, the Prime Minister and cabinet, it might be argued, controlled the highest ecclesiastical appointments; so in reality, little had changed except that after disestablishment one group of laymen was replaced by another in church affairs. There were, however, several differences of capital importance. In the first instance, the pre-disestablishment politicians did not have power over the church because they were laymen but because they were politicians advisory to the monarch. Only after disestablishment did laymen *qua* laymen have a place in the government of the church. Further, after 1869 the clergy and bishops of the church were responsible to a specific constituency of laymen (their own parishioners) in a direct and functional manner quite without parallel in the era of the establishment. Third, the post-disestablishment laity, to which the clergy and bishops were responsible, was concerned chiefly with seeing that the religious professionals maintained a high level of performance in their religious duties; in contrast the politicians of the pre-disestablishment years had viewed the church chiefly (but not entirely) as a patronage resource and had showed relatively little concern for standards of pastoral devotion. Fourth, related to the preceding point is the fact that after disestablishment, the laity who held authority in church matters consisted entirely of Irish citizens who were adherents of the church. Previously, the laymen in parliament who had influenced the church were mostly non-Irish and a number of them were Roman Catholics and Dissenters. There is a great difference between occasional interference in religious affairs by outsiders and continuing control by concerned adherents. Hence, both in theory and in practice, the position of the laity in the church structure truly had undergone a revolutionary change.

Focusing our attention on the bishops of the Church of Ireland we can notice in detail additional facets of the revolutionary process. Irish bishops before disestablishment were appointed by the Crown, which is to say by the English Prime Minister. The Crown had free rein to appoint any clergyman of the Anglican persuasion to the post irrespective of his national background or previous ecclesiastical experience. Manipulation of the appointments to the Irish bench to serve English political purposes meant that during the eighteenth century there was a decided division in the bench between English and Irish bishops. The worst factionalism was over by mid-eighteenth century, however, and the two nationalities, if still not socially merged, at least ceased feuding publicly. Nevertheless, throughout the nineteenth century the common practice of appointing Englishmen with no experience in the Church of Ireland to Irish bishoprics continued, and continued to be resented. The last two holders of the Archbishopric of Dublin before disestablishment, Richard Whately and Richard Chevenix Trench, were Englishmen whose appointments aroused animosity in the church, especially since each of them had literary and intellectual pretensions beyond the taste of most Irish clergymen. After disestablishment every man raised to the bench was a clergyman of the Church of Ireland and it was common for new bishops to have had experience previously as administrators within the church. Hence, the ecclesiastical revolution that was church disestablishment ended both outside appointments and the possibility of national divisions among the bishops.

One of the great problems of the eighteenth-century episcopate was that the bishops were expected to be political as well as religious officials. Political duties were especially heavy in the first third of the eighteenth century when the small membership of the Irish temporal peerage meant that the bishops had considerable political leverage and that the government depended upon them to ensure control of the Irish House of Lords. From the middle third of the century onward, however, the addition of new temporal peers meant that the bishops' political importance declined, and that the average bishop could spend less time in parliament than previously. The major reduction in this position of the bishops came in 1800 when the Act of Union limited the Irish bench to four seats in the House of Lords of the United Kingdom. After 1800, the Irish bishops were politically of negligible importance to the government, although the three bishops and one archbishop sitting at any one time continued to have major political duties as representatives of the church's interests; if the Church of Ireland was unimportant to the politics of Westminster, the politics of Westminster were very important to the Church of Ireland. Even these four lobbyists for the church's interests were abolished by Gladstone's church act. The situations in the eighteenth century and in the last three decades of the nineteenth were, therefore, diametrically opposite: in the eighteenth the church had played a major government role and politics had been an important part of the bishops' work; in the late nineteenth the church was politically of no importance and politics formed no part of the bishops' work.

In the eighteenth century it was thought notable if a bishop resided regularly in his diocese and supervised its religious welfare. It was the general practice for individual prelates to have large houses in Dublin which they occupied for the parliamentary session and social season, and it seems to have been the usual practice for the Irish bishops to spend a portion of each year travelling to England or the continent. In the early nineteenth century, under the twin influences of evangelicalism and parliamentary investigation, the Irish bishops spent more time in Ireland than they had previously. Once the Irish parliament had been abolished, the bishops had less excuse than previously to linger in Dublin; and after the number of bishoprics was reduced in 1833, their added individual responsibilities gave them reason to spend more time in their dioceses. Disestablishment put an end forever to the last traces of extended episcopal absenteeism. The men who became bishops after disestablishment were remarkably devoted to duty, and, in any case, the laymen of the now-voluntary church made a point of keeping their prelates up to the mark.

One aspect of the bishops' circumstances that was turned nearly upside down in the years under study was the bishops' financial condition. In the eighteenth century, the richest Irish bishops were nearly ecclesiastical princes and even the poorest was an ecclesiastical nobleman. In the last quarter of the eighteenth century, the Archbishop of Armagh was receiving about £8,000 annually, which was approximately equal to the income of the Archbishop of Canterbury; even the poorest of Irish bishops received £2,000, which was certainly more than was derived from several of the English bishoprics. The net income of the Lord Primate of All Ireland was well over £14,000 in 1830 and the poorest bishop netted nearly £4,000.

But soon thereafter the bishops' position began to change. The church temporalities and tithe reform acts of the 1830s reduced the prelates' financial rewards so that the Archbishop of Armagh's net income in 1867 was under £9,000 and the poorest bishopric about £2,100. The income of the bishops appointed after disestablishment was shockingly low in comparison to the above figures; the Archbishop of Armagh received an income of £2,500 in 1919, while the least well-remunerated bishop earned slightly over £1,400. The Irish prelates had declined from being ecclesiastical princes and nobility to mere middling gentry.

Simultaneously, a revolution occurred in regard to the privileges the bishops were able to confer upon their subordinates. Beaufort's survey of 1787 revealed that more than half the parishes in the Church of Ireland were under the patronage of Irish bishops. This patronage gave the Irish bishops much greater powers of reward and control over the clergy than their English counterparts possessed. The Irish bishops kept these powers until disestablishment, but when the new church order was framed in 1870, they suddenly ceased to have the power to name incumbents to benefices. Instead of having sole control over the majority of Irish benefices, the bishops were now members of selection committees composed of clergy and laity. The only crumb of patronage left in their hands was the right to name cathedral officers; but this right was circumscribed by the requirement that the cathedral officers be incumbents of the dioceses. Thus the bishops were transformed from patrons of their dioceses to being merely supervisors and coordinators of clerical behavior.

Behind many of the reversals in the position of the officers of the Church of Ireland lies a major revolution in the relationship between church and state. This change is obvious but should not be ignored. Before 1869 the Church of Ireland was an open organizational system. Parliament could meddle at will with its structure, finances, and theology. Successive ministries used major church appointments as patronage rewards for the politically faithful. At the same time, the threat of royal commissioners and parliamentary inquiries continually made the prelates uneasy. Suddenly, with disestablishment, the Church of Ireland became a closed system as far as the government was concerned. Except for the Church Temporalities Commissioners, whose job it was to terminate equitably the remaining government-church relationships, the church leaders now had nothing to do with the state. This meant that the church was free to determine its own dogma, liturgy, organization, and financial policies without reference to anyone but its own membership.

While the reversal of the church's position vis-à-vis the state, from an open system to a closed one, was a phenomenon occurring suddenly in 1869, the position of the church as a servant of the civil order began to change long before disestablishment. The Archbishop of Dublin, for example, had once possessed responsibility for governing the Liberty of Saint Sepulchre's in Dublin; and the Dean and Chapter of Saint Patrick's, Dublin, were in charge of the Liberty of Saint Patrick's. In both these jurisdictions, the ecclesiastics controlled the courts, markets, and matters of everyday civil government. The municipal reforms of the nineteenth century removed these areas from the jurisdiction of the Archbishop, Dean, and Chapter.

Similarly, the Irish parish in the eighteenth century was both an ecclesiastical and a civil unit. The Irish parish had fewer civil responsibilities than did its English counterpart because Irish local government was mainly the concern of the county grand juries. Nevertheless, in the eighteenth and early nineteenth centuries, the Irish vestries had the power to collect small taxes for the maintenance of the local church and for minor civil services such as roads and sanitary services. In Dublin some parishes provided police services and fire patrols. During the 1820s the right of the Irish Anglican parishes to levy rates for secular purposes was abolished, and the reformers of the 1830s took away the vestries' right to levy the church cess. Hence, three decades before disestablishment, the Irish parish had already been transformed from a religio-political unit into a specialized ecclesiastical body.

One of the most interesting aspects of the Irish ecclesiastical revolution was the change in the system for the discipline of the professionally religious. Before disestablishment the control system was woefully inadequate. For example, assuming a bishop avoided major scandal and heresy, there was no way to make him perform his religious duties. He held appointment for life and was dependent upon no one for the continuation of his income or for the preservation of his position. He could, as the case of Frederick Hervey, Bishop of Derry, indicates, dabble in politics, absent himself from his diocese, and gadfly about Europe without limitation. Only if a bishop was desirous of being promoted was it possible to control his behavior somewhat, for in that case he had to please the civil authorities and the Crown with his probity and political reliability. The weakness of the control system was a result of the church's curious one-way dependency relationship, in which a man was dependent upon the civil authorities for promotion but not for maintenance of position. After disestablishment bishops continued to hold appointment for life, but they were much less willing to incur the wrath of the laity than their predecessors had been to offend the Dublin Castle authorities. The reason for this was partially that the laity, unlike the civil authorities before disestablishment, had the power to invoke negative sanctions. The laity could vote no-confidence in a bishop through refusing to cooperate in diocesan fund drives; and laymen could raise embarrassing questions at diocesan synods and could manipulate the local press and public opinion in ways the British cabinet never could have done.

Parallel changes occurred in the control system governing local incumbents. Barring heresy and gross misconduct, before disestablishment local incumbents were in office for life, and like the prelates could do as they pleased if they were willing to give up their prospects of advancement. In the early years of the nineteenth century, the most irritating problem for a conscientious bishop was the near impossibility of forcing his clergy to reside in their benefice even though they were canonically required to do so. The bishop had no effective sanction available short of deprivation and this weapon was too powerful and too complicated to invoke in most cases. During the early nineteenth century, conscientious bishops tried to invoke canon law to force residence and found that the cost was prohibitive, being several hundred pounds in each case. Canon law on clerical residency being unenforceable, secular law was therefore required. A residency act of 1808 gave the bishops sanctions to use against the clergy who refused to reside, including sequestration of the profits of their benefices and, ultimately, deprivation of appointment. Regulations were further tightened in 1824.

These changes were important, but dealt only with residency. A truly revolutionary development occurred after disestablishment when the clergy, appointed under the new arrangments, found their every act under critical scrutiny of their parishioners. The parishioners now had the power to punish the clergy for any dereliction of duty by a most direct and unmistakeable means: withholding of contributions towards the clergyman's stipend. Since roughly one half of most nonannuitant clergymen's salaries came from annual gifts of the parishioners, a minister who failed to attend to his duties could be effectively fined up to half of his annual livelihood by the church people. The control of clerical behavior by the laity would have been called Jacobinical by eighteenth century Irish clergymen and pointed to as a sure proof of ecclesiastical revolution.

The Irish ecclesiastical courts, while manifestly of secondary importance in the ecclesiastical control system, are of interest because of the turnabout in their status after 1869. In the eighteenth century, the courts handled a good deal of business that may be labelled civil in nature and, because the courts were an arm of an Established Church, they had a status in public law. Under the court's purview came decisions relating to marriage and to last wills and testaments. The courts also had powers relating to the collection of tithes, and could punish laymen for refusal to pay. Naturally the ecclesiastical courts also handled all ecclesiastical cases. The courts were too slow and expensive for the effective prosecution of most clerical cases. As far as enforcing the payment of tithes by laymen, by the early nineteenth century the courts had become almost totally impotent and the clergy had to have recourse to the secular ones. Then, after disestablishment the ecclesiastical law was reduced to a set of private rules for the internal government of the Church of Ireland, and the ecclesiastical judges, as part of the control system of the Church of Ireland, were transformed from public arbiters to private umpires.

No change in the Church of Ireland was more revolutionary than the revision of its financial system after disestablishment. Before the Irish Church Act became effective, the Church of Ireland was relatively rich: it had a collective annual income well over £500,000. The church relied upon land rental and tithe rent charges as the chief source of revenue, drawing a relatively small income from voluntary contributions. There was no central machinery for the management of church financial resources. When the church was thrust upon its own resource by Gladstone's church act, everything changed. The church ceased to depend upon land rentals and tithes (tithes ceased being paid to the church and most church lands were confiscated) and came to rely instead upon two new sources for its annual income: returns from investments managed by the Representative Church Body and the voluntary subscriptions of the laity. The financial stress of disestablishment meant that the church's treasury had to come under a single central authority and that control of church resources was infinitely better managed than it had been previously. The church was much less endowed financially after disestablishment than it had been before: the return on the roughly £9,000,000 the church held in 1916 would not have produced the approximately £585,000 the church was receiving each year before disestablishment and, in addition, the value of money had deteriorated considerably. Nevertheless, despite the financial revolution, the Church of Ireland continued to be a fiscally sound organization even after it ceased to be a state church.

All these changes in the Church of Ireland in the period 1800 to 1885 were greater than those it had undergone since reorganization on the basis of the territorial diocese shortly before the Norman conquest of Ireland. Administratively the changes were far more dramatic than those engendered by the Protestant reformation. The ability of the Church of Ireland to survive such an aggregation of changes, especially those following disestablishment, was an indication of the extraordinary viability of the church as an organization. The survival of that organization after 1869 is notable enough, but the style and good grace of most of the bishops and clergy in adapting to the changed circumstances of their calling were almost supererogatory. Perhaps even the gentlemanly clergy and aristocratic bishops of the eighteenth century would have been impressed.

Reference Matter

Abbreviations Used in the Notes

APL	Armagh Public Library
BM	British Museum, London
DCL	Dublin City Library
NLI	National Library of Ireland, Dublin
PROB	Public Record Office of Northern Ireland, Belfast
PROD	Public Record Office, Republic of Ireland, Dublin
QUB	Library of Queen's University, Belfast
RCB	Library of the Representative Church Body, Dublin
SCRO	County Record Office, Stafford
TCD	Library of Trinity College, Dublin

Notes

1 Although the term "Church of Ireland" did not become the sole official title of the Irish Anglicans until after the disestablishment act of 1869, it is a much less cumbersome title than any of the alternatives and will therefore be used throughout this study to denominate the Anglican communion in Ireland. Prior to 1800 "Church of Ireland" and "Established Church" were used in official documents and government statutes. From 1800 until disestablishment the official title was "The United Church of England and Ireland."

2 For an excellent summary of classical bureaucratic theory see Peter M. Blau, *Bureaucracy in Modern Society.*

3 For a discussion of the theoretical problems involved in separating formal and informal systems see Chris Argyris, *Integrating the Individual and the Organization,* pp. 7–12.

4 Douglas McGregor, *The Human Side of Enterprise,* passim.

5 For readable modern histories of the Church of Ireland see Thomas J. Johnston, John L. Robinson, and Robert Wyse Jackson, *A History of the Church of Ireland,* and Walter A. Phillips, ed., *History of the Church of Ireland from the Earliest Times to the Present Day.*

6 See Wilhelm Pauck, "The Nature of Protestantism," *Church History* 6 (March 1937):3–23.

7 In this study, "suffragan" is used to denote a bishop who was under the jurisdiction of an archbishop, or metropolitan, and not to mean "assistant bishop." The office of suffragan bishop in the second sense did not exist in the Church of Ireland.

    Although the number of metropolitans and suffragans remained constant throughout the eighteenth century, there were minor changes in diocesan relations. In 1741 Ardagh, which had been united to Kilmore, was separated therefrom and annexed to Tuam. Hence, throughout the study, Ardagh will be treated as if it were in the Province of Tuam.

    In 1741, Kilfenora was separated from Tuam and held *in commendam* (as an additional personal office, without permanent annexation) by the Bishop of Clonfert. In 1752, when the Bishop of Clonfert, John Whitcombe, was translated from Clonfert to Down and Connor, Kilfenora was formally united with Killaloe. See D. A. Chart, "The Broadening of the Church," in Phillips, 3:275, and Richard Mant, *History of the Church of Ireland,* 2:765–66.

8 See T. W. Freeman, *Ireland: A General and Regional Geography,* pp. 111–17, and F. Maurice Powicke and E. B. Fryde, eds., *Handbook of British Chronology,* pp. 351–79.

    Several comments are in order: first, the ranking archbishop was the Archbishop of Armagh, who was to the Church of Ireland what the Archbishop of Canterbury was to the Church of England. He was the metropolitan of Ireland and was titled "Lord Primate of all Ireland." The second ranking archbishopric was Dublin, the possessor of which was "Lord Primate of Ireland." The Archbishops of Cashel and of Tuam were, respectively, Primates of Munster and of Connacht. Second, the anomalous position of the Diocese of Ardagh bears notice. Although located in the Province of Armagh, it was annexed to the Archdiocese of Tuam. Third, although the table of dioceses omits mention of them, ancient dioceses were joined to many of the eighteenth-century dioceses. (For example, in 1569 the Diocese of Clonmacnoise had been united to Meath.) These ancient dioceses are not mentioned, for they had ceased to have any reality as administrative units and in general usage were not employed as part of the formal title of the dioceses. Fourth, certain other dioceses, although united to a second see, continued to exist as recognizable units, either because of their having administrative implications (for instance, through possession of a cathedral chapter) or through their name being kept alive in general ecclesiastical usage. Thus, Connor which was united to Down in 1441 continued as a recognizable entity within the united diocese and is so recognized in the table of dioceses. Fifth, having recognized that in certain diocesan unions both dioceses kept in some measure their own identity, the fact remains that it is often inconvenient to give the whole title of a united see. This becomes especially true after the reforms of the 1830s when, to be fully proper, it would be necessary to refer to the "Bishop of Killaloe, Kilfenora, Clonfert, and Kilmacduagh," hardly a convenient label. In later chapters, therefore, for the sake of convenience, a bishop will often be referred to by the name of his primary see, with the assumption that the reader will realize that he is often also bishop of one or more secondary sees united to the chief diocese. (A reference table for the nineteenth century similar to table 1 is provided in table 35 in chapter 3.) Sixth, unlike the other bishoprics, the rank of Bishop of Kildare was not an independent office. Because of the smallness of the diocesan revenue, the bishop was always simultaneously Dean of Christ Church Cathedral, Dublin. The Bishop of Kildare had no residence in the diocese and always lived in Dublin (Beaufort, p. 119; Mant, 2:169).

9   The only exceptions to this statement were the lordship of Newry and Mourne in the Diocese of Dromore and the wardenship of Galway in the Diocese of Tuam. The lordship of Newry maintained an exemption from ecclesiastical jurisdiction that it had held from pre-Reformation times when it was a monastic exemption. The lay lord of the district exercised jurisdiction in the granting of marriage licenses and probating of wills and in ecclesiastical matters which usually came under ecclesiastical auspices. Geographically, the exempt jurisdiction was quite extensive, encompassing about 100,000 statute acres and several thousand Protestants. In contrast, the wardenship involved only a single benefice governed by the college and lay corporation of Galway. See *Report of Her Majesty's Commissioners on the Revenues and Condition of the Established Church (Ireland)*, pp. 113–14 [4082], H.C. 1867–68, xxiv; *Third Report of Her Majesty's Commissioners on Ecclesiastical Revenue and Patronage in Ireland*, p. 9, H.C. 1836 (246), xxiv.

10 This is in contrast to the Roman Catholic parishes which were reorganized in the eighteenth century and diverged considerably from medieval arrangements. A. J. Otway-Ruthven, *A History of Medieval Ireland*, p. 118.

11 Son of a French refugee who became Rector of Navan and Provost of Tuam; born 1 October 1739; B.A. Trinity College Dublin, 1759; LL.D. (*hon. causa*), 1789. Succeeded his father as Rector of Navan. His ecclesi-

astical survey was compiled under the auspices of the Marquis of Buckingham, Lord Lieutenant (see James Leslie, *Armagh Clergy and Parishes,*
p. 201). The manuscript notes for Beaufort's survey are preserved in the
library of the Representative Church Body. In these notes are found data
on individual parishes which were not published in the final version of
the survey. This material should be of use to parish and to local historians (see Representative Church Body, MS. O, 11–12).

12   J. C. Beckett, "Anglo-Irish Constitutional Relations in the Later Eight-
eenth Century," *Irish Historical Studies* 14 (March 1964):20–28; J. C.
Beckett, "Swift as an Ecclesiastical Statesman," in H. A. Crone, T. W.
Moody, and D. B. Quinn, eds., *Essays in British and Irish History in
Honour of James Eadie Todd,* p. 138; F. W. Buckler, "The Establishment
of the Church of England: Its Constitutional and Legal Significance,"
Church History 10 (March 1941): 299–346; Stephen Neill, *Anglicanism,*
pp. 435–40; (extract) Richard Robinson to Marquis of Buckingham, 18
September 1788, NLI MS. 8893 (6).

13   See John Henning, "The Anglican Church in Ireland: Prayers against
Irish Rebels," *Irish Ecclesiastical Record,* 5th ser., 64 (October 1944):
247–54.

14   Lewis P. Curtis, *Chichester Towers,* p. 1.

15   Derived from Mant, 2:781–91.

16   Ibid.

17   "The Church of Ireland," *Church Quarterly Review* 29 (January 1885):
454.

18   The Countess of Moira to the Earl of Huntingdon, 26 January 1765, in
Historical Manuscripts Commission, *Report on the Manuscripts of the
late Reginald Rawdon Hastings, Esq., of the Manor House, Ashby de la
Zouch,* 3:144.

19   Hugh Boulter to Duke of Newcastle, 4 March 1725, *Boulter Letters,*
1:12, quoted in Mant, 2:420.

20   John L. McCracken, "Central and local administration in Ireland under
George II" (Ph.D. thesis), p. 73. Of the fifty-seven spiritual peers who
sat on the bench in the reign of George II, twenty-eight were English
(p. 72).

21   Robert Fowler to Lord George Germain, 16 August 1780, in Historical
Manuscripts Commission, *Report on the Manuscripts of Mrs. Stopford-
Sackville, of Drayton House, Northamptonshire,* 1:271 (hereafter cited
as *MSS Stopford-Sackville*).

22   Boswell, *Life of Johnson,* 14 April 1775, quoted in Norman Sykes,
Church and State in England in the XVIIIth Century, p. 41.

23   J. H. Plumb, *England in the Eighteenth Century* (Baltimore: Penguin
Books, 1950), p. 181.

24   Duke of Newcastle to Duke of Dorset, 25 January 1752, *MSS Stopford-
Sackville,* 1:179.

25   Lord Buckinghamshire to Lord George Germain, 28 October 1779,
MSS Stopford-Sackville, 1:259.

26   Sir Thomas Butler to Lord Townshend, 21 January 1772. RCB MS. A3.

27   Jemmett Browne to Lord Townshend, 12 February 1770. RCB MS. A3.

28   Powicke and Fryde, p. 370.

29   Duke of Newcastle to Duke of Dorset, 31 January 1752, *MSS Stopford-
Sackville,* 1:181.

30   Sykes, pp. 96–146.
31   William Stuart to Charles Brodrick, 1 August 1811. NLI MS. 8886.
32   Beaufort, p. 105.
33   John Healy, *History of the Diocese of Meath,* 2:99.
34   For a codification of a bishop's powers see John C. Erck, *The Ecclesiastical Register,* pp. xvii–xxiii.
35   Erck, p. xvii.
36   C. H. Davis, "The Irish Convocation," *Church of England Magazine* 55 (25 July 1863): 49–52; "Synods of the Church in Ireland," *Literary Churchman* 2 (30 December 1865): 549–53.
37   (Extract) Richard Robinson to Marquis of Buckingham 18 September 1788. NLI MS. 8893 (6).
38   For a list of the archbishops' powers see Erck, pp. xiv–xvi.
39   Kenneth Milne, *The Church of Ireland: A History,* p. 48.
40   Ibid., p. 49.
41   Mant, 2:767–68.
42   John Hotham to Viscount Sackville, 9 July 1782, in *MSS Stopford-Sackville,* 1:279.
43   See Erck, p. xxiii; Raymond Kennedy, "The Administration of the Diocese of Dublin and Glendalough in the Eighteenth Century" (Ph.D. thesis), p. 61.
       In theory the courts also had the right to prosecute certain offenses, such as simony and nonresidence among the clergy and defamation either against clergy or laity; in addition to the already mentioned ecclesiastical causes, the consistorial court had jurisdiction over laymen in prosecuting blasphemy, perjury, drunkenness, heresy, schism, sacrilege, and usury. This entire skein becomes laughable, however, when one realizes that, by the early nineteenth century, the church had given up prosecuting these matters because the spiritual courts had the power neither to fine nor to imprison (see Erck, p. xxiii).
44   For a revealing discussion of the problem of nonresidence, see (a copy) Marquis of Buckingham to John Cradock, 10 April 1788. NLI MS. 5022.
45   McCracken, pp. 73–74.
46   DCL, Gilbert Collection, MS. 94, pp. 346–47.
47   J. T. Ball, *The Reformed Church of Ireland (1537–1889),* p. 216.
48   Valentine Cloncurry, *Personal Recollections of the Life and Times, with Extracts from the Correspondence of Valentine Lord Cloncurry,* p. 191.
49   W. D. Killen, *The Ecclesiastical History of Ireland,* 2:319.
50   See William S. Childe-Pemberton, *The Earl Bishop, The Life of Frederick Hervey, Bishop of Derry, Earl of Bristol.*
51   Earl of Buckinghamshire to [Richard Woodward] Bishop of Cloyne, 5 October 1783, in Historical Manuscripts Commission, *Report on the Manuscripts of the Marquess of Lothian preserved at Blickling Hall, Norfolk,* p. 420.
52   Earl of Northington to Duke of Rutland, 27 February 1784, in Historical Manuscripts Commission, *The Manuscripts of His Grace the Duke of Rutland, K.G. preserved in Belvoir Castle,* 3:76.
53   Kenneth Milne, "The Irish Corporations in the Eighteenth Century" (Ph.D. thesis), pp. 7–8.
54   Ibid., pp. 49–55.
55   Thomas Percy to Reverend E. Hudson, 22 December 1794, in Historical

Manuscripts Commission, *The Manuscripts and Correspondence of James, First Earl of Charlemont*, 2:256–57.

56   James Leslie to Lord Townsend, 22 December 1769, RCB MS. A3.
57   John Oswald to Lord Townshend, 15 April 1768, RCB MS. A3.
58   Mant, 2:569–70.
59   John Hotham to Viscount Sackville, 9 July 1782, in *MSS Stopford-Sackville*, 1:280.
60   Richard Marlay to Lord Charlemont, 18 October 1794, in Historical Manuscripts Commission, *The Manuscripts and Correspondence of James, First Earl of Charlemont*, 2:250.
61   Mant, 2:659–60.
62   Derived from DCL, Gilbert Collection, MS. 94, pp. 321–59.
63   Sykes, p. 61.
64   John D'Alton, *The Memoirs of the Archbishops of Dublin*, p. 343.
65   The statement was made by Theophilus Bolton, Archbishop of Cashel from 1729 to 1744, and was reported by Swift. Mant, 2:581.
66   See Constantia Maxwell, *Dublin under the Georges, 1714–1830*, pp. 101–02.
67   Joseph Stock to Henry F. Stock, 21 March 1810; 7 April 1810; 24 January 1811; 9 May 1811; 13 May 1811; 18 May 1811. TCD MS. N. 5.8.
68   Frederick Hervey to Lord Townshend, 26 January 1768; Joseph Bourke to Lord Townshend, 3 October 1772. RCB MS. A3.
69   See, e.g., Denison Cumberland to Lord Townshend, 14 September 1772; William Gore to Lord Townshend, 12 November 1772. RCB MS. A3.
70   The most useful collection of material on Irish cathedrals is Hugh A. Boyd's "The Cathedral System in the Church of Ireland Since the Disestablishment" (B.Litt. thesis).
71   Ibid., pp. 25–29.
72   See F. R. Bolton, *The Caroline Tradition of the Church of Ireland, with Particular Reference to Bishop Jeremy Taylor*, pp. 171–82.
73   Ibid., pp. 182–97.
74   Boyd, passim.
75   Erck, pp. xxiv–xxxiii.
76   Ibid., p. xxxiii.
77   Boyd, p. 39.
78   Chart, in Phillips, 3:235–36.
79   Erck, p. xxvii.
80   Boyd, p. 84.
81   Ibid., p. 47.
82   Boyd, pp. 53–54; Erck, p. xxix.
83   *Second Report of His Majesty's Commissioners on Ecclesiastical Revenue and Patronage, Ireland*, p. 12, H.C. 1834 (523), xxiii.
84   Erck, pp. xxv–xxvi.
85   *Second Report of His Majesty's Commissioners on Ecclesiastical Revenue and Patronage, Ireland*, pp. 8–9.
86   Ibid., pp. 13–14; Boyd, p. 56. The position at Limerick, which possessed such revenue at one time, is unclear.
87   Again, nineteenth-century information has been used because of the inadequacy of eighteenth-century sources. *Second Report of His Majesty's Commissioners on Ecclesiastical Revenue and Patronage, Ireland*, pp. 14–15.
88   Erck, p. xxx.

89   Bolton, p. 188; *Second Report of His Majesty's Commissioners on Ecclesiastical Revenue and Patronage, Ireland,* p. 10. The case of Kildare Cathedral is difficult. Beaufort (p. 119) reports that the Kildare canons were indeed minor canons, while the later parliamentary report (p. 10) maintains that they were not minor canons but full canons of the cathedral. As will be discussed later, the Kildare situation was unique, the canons sharing all the usual cathedral chapter functions, plus having an endowment of their own, of the sort usually reserved for subsidiary foundations.

90   *Second Report of His Majesty's Commissioners on Ecclesiastical Revenue and Patronage, Ireland,* p. 11.

91   Boyd, p. 290.

92   Beaufort, p. 119; Boyd, p. 40; *Second Report of His Majesty's Commissioners on Ecclesiastical Revenue and Patronage, Ireland,* p. 11.

93   Beaufort, p. 118; Boyd, p. 40; *Second Report of His Majesty's Commissioners on Ecclesiastical Revenue and Patronage, Ireland,* p. 11.

94   Mant, 2:169–73, 400–06.

95   Erck, p. xxv.

96   *The Rights of the Clergy of Ireland Candidly Considered by a Friend of the Constitution,* p. 11.

97   TCD MS, Registry of the Archbishop of Dublin, Box XII.

98   Milne, "The Irish Corporations in the Eighteenth Century," pp. 49–61.

99   Boyd, p. 25; Erck, pp. xxv–xxx; *Second Report of His Majesty's Commissioners on Ecclesiastical Revenue and Patronage, Ireland,* p. 15.

100 Bolton, pp. 171–97.

101 [Mrs] Finian Fields, "Origins of Local Government in Ireland," *Eire-Ireland* 1 (Winter 1966): 69–79; McCracken, pp. 125–39.

102 Edward P. Brynn, "A Political History of the Church of Ireland, 1800–1841" (M.Litt. thesis), pp. 46–48.

103 Ibid., pp. 48–52.

104 John L. Spence, "Life in Early Eighteenth Century Rural Ulster as reflected in a Parish Record Book," *Ulster Journal of Archaeology,* 3d ser., 6 (1943): 35–48.

105 E. J. Young, "St. Michan's Parish in the Eighteenth Century," *Dublin Historical Record* 3 (Sept.–Nov. 1940): 1–7.

106 See Erck, pp. xxiv–xlvi.

107 Mant, 2:574.

108 Ibid., 2:575.

109 Ibid., 2:343–44.

110 Enclosure by Edward Stopford, in Edward Stopford to Lord John Beresford, 22 February 1830. APL, Beresford Papers, 11.

111 (Copy) Rules of Irish Privy Council on Unions, 1726, NLI MS. 8893 (6).

112 Under the common law, a bishop had the right to make perpetual unions. Actually, there is no record of this having been done in modern times. For a more detailed chronology of seventeenth- and eighteenth-century legislation on the subject, see *Report of His Majesty's Commissioners of Ecclesiastical Inquiry, Ireland,* pp. 5–9, H.C. 1831 (93), ix.

113 Chart, in Phillips, 3:217–18.

114 Marquis of Buckingham to John Cradock, 10 April 1788. NLI MS. 5022.

115 St. John D. Seymour, *The Diocese of Emly,* p. 253.

116 D. A. Chart, "The Close Alliance of Church and State," in Phillips, 3: 202; Buckingham to Cradock, 10 April 1788. NLI MS. 5022; R. H. Murray, "The Church of the Restoration," in Phillips, 3:143; Sykes, p. 217.
117 Mant, 2:776–77.
118 William King to William Wake, July 1722, reproduced in Mant, 2:380–81.
119 Buckingham to Cradock, 10 April 1788. NLI MS. 5022.
120 (Copy) John Pelissier to Earl of Abercorn, 20 July 1753. PROB, D. 623 IA 1/2–155.
121 (Copy) John Hamilton to Abercorn, 20 June 1755. PROB, D. 623 IA 1/3–94.
122 (Copy) John McClintock to Abercorn, 5 June 1747. PROB, D. 623 IA 1/1c.
123 Mant, 2:777–78; [Richard Woodward] *The Present State of the Church of Ireland,* pp. 41–47.
 Like most eighteenth-century statistics, Woodward's should be treated most tentatively. He does not mention whether curates are included in his tabulation of the number of clergymen (probably they are not, but this is not certain). Whether the figures are in Irish or English money is not stated. The figures evidently do not include implicit income, such as lodging in glebe houses. Clonfert and Kilmacduagh were treated differently from the other dioceses, the large number of small sinecures and dignities therein not being included. Worst of all from a statistical point of view, Woodword determined his overall average by adding together the diocesan averages and dividing by the number of dioceses. Obviously a weighted average was necessary, since the number of clergymen in each diocese was not identical. Having said all this, Woodward remains the most useful reporter on eighteenth-century clergy salaries.
124 Erck, p. xlvi.
125 H. I. De Salis to Lord Dacre, 17 August 1784, in Historical Manuscripts Commission, *The Manuscripts of Rye and Hereford Corporations; Capt. Loder-Symonds, Mr. E. R. Wodehouse, M.P., and others,* p. 376.
126 George Howse to Lord George Germain, 14 August 1780, in *MSS Stopford-Sackville,* 1:271.
127 Lord Strangford to Earl of Abercorn, 11 September 1755. PROB, D. 623 IA 1/3–105.
128 Lord Chief Baron Forster to Lord Townshend, 19 December 1771. Endorsed "most certainly" by Townshend. RCB MS. A3.
129 Charles Bingham to Lord Townshend, 3 December 1770. RCB MS. A3.
130 Charles [Moss] to Lord Townshend, 20 May 1770. RCB MS. A3.
131 John Butler to Lord Townshend, 28 September 1768. RCB MS. A3.
132 For an indication of the material lost, see Terence P. Cunningham, "The 1766 Religious Census, Kilmore and Ardagh," *Breifne* 1 (1961):357–62.
133 Murray in Phillips, 3:161, with arithmetical corrections. The problems of establishing population patterns from figures for houses liable to a tax are obvious. Hence Murray's population estimates must be treated with caution.
134 The discussion of the Presbyterians in the eighteenth century is based upon J. C. Beckett's excellent *Protestant Dissent in Ireland, 1687—1780,* passim.

135   On the penal code, see Robert E. Burns, "The Irish Penal Code and Some
      of Its Historians," *Review of Politics* 21 (January 1959): 276–99;
      Robert E. Burns, "The Irish Popery Laws: A Study of Eighteenth Cen-
      tury Legislation and Behavior," *Review of Politics* 24 (October 1962):
      485–508; Lecky, 1:145–71; Henry Parnell, *A History of the Penal Laws
      against the Irish Catholics; from the Treaty of Limerick to the Union,*
      passim; J. G. Simms, "Irish Catholics and the Parliamentary Franchise,
      1692–1728," *Irish Historical Studies* 12 (March 1960): 28–37.
136   For useful studies see Maureen McGeehin [Wall], "The Catholics of the
      Towns and the Quarterage Dispute in Eighteenth Century Ireland," *Irish
      Historical Studies* 7 (September 1952): 91–114; Maureen Wall, *The Penal
      Laws, 1691–1760.*

CHAPTER 2

1   Charles Broderick to William Bennet, 9 September 1802. NLI MS. 8892.
2   The proper title for the new church became "The United Church of
    England and Ireland." In this study "Church of Ireland" will be retained
    for purposes of consistency and convenience.
3   For an excellent recent account, see G. C. Bolton, *The Passing of the
    Irish Act of Union: A Study in Parliamentary Politics.*
4   The act of Union is most conveniently available in *Certain Acts relating
    to the Parliament of Ireland,* H.C. 1886 (124), lii.
5   One of the most striking characteristics of the Union was the almost negli-
    gent ease with which ecclesiastical matters were decided. The union of
    the two churches was carried out by enactment of the British and the
    Irish parliaments, without the summoning of a convocation or synod of
    either church. With one major exception, little thought was given to pos-
    sible improvements in the proposed arrangements. This exception was
    the plan of Thomas O'Beirne, Bishop of Meath. O'Beirne proposed that
    the union of the churches be more than merely nominal. He argued that
    when the state, in all its parts became one, the church should become one
    also. Specifically, he desired a complete merger of the two churches under
    the government of the See of Canterbury. The new church would be
    known simply as the Church of England, with no reference to Ireland's
    previous ecclesiastical independence. The jurisdiction of the Irish arch-
    bishops, O'Beirne maintained, should be continued but under the primacy
    of the Archbishop of Canterbury. This radical plan failed to stir either
    ecclesiastical or governmental interest and was quietly ignored. See
    Thomas O'Beirne to Lord Castlereagh, 13 November 1799, and enclosed
    memorandum, reproduced in Charles Vane, *Memoirs and Correspon-
    dence of Viscount Castlereagh, Second Marquess of Londonderry,* 3:2–8.
6   In addition to the clauses quoted above, the draft of the Union bill had
    contained a clause providing that "whenever his Majesty shall summon a
    Convocation of the Clergy, the Archbishops, Bishops, Priests, and Clergy
    of the several provinces in England and Ireland shall be respectively sum-
    moned to and sit in the respective convocation of the several provinces
    of the United Church, in like manner and subject to the same regulations
    as are at present by law established with respect to the convocations of
    the Church of England." The clause was dropped as unnecessary and
    likely to raise objections. Lord Auckland to Lord Castlereagh, 1 May

1800, reproduced in Vane, 3:293–95; J. T. Ball, *The Reformed Church of Ireland (1537–1889)*, p. 237.

7   Edward P. Brynn, "A Political History of the Church of Ireland, 1800–1841" (M.Litt. thesis), pp. 67–68; John R. Garstin, *Historical Notices of the Anglican Archbishops of Armagh, Primates of All Ireland, during the nineteenth century,* pp. 3–6.

Since this study was written I have received from *Church History* for evaluation for publication an article by Edward Brynn entitled "Some Repercussions of the Act of Union on the Church of Ireland, 1801–1820." It is a very good piece and I strongly recommended it for publication. Despite the article's excellence I have made no changes in my own study. This for two reasons: first, because the article's discussion of the Union engagements is a précis and stylistic revision of his earlier, comprehensive thesis; second, because in the statistical section of his article Brynn uses categories of quantitative analysis appropriate to his study but not to mine. Thus, references to work by Brynn in the notes that follow are references to his M.Litt. thesis.

8   Brynn, pp. 66–67.

9   Michael MacDonagh, *The Viceroy's Post-Bag. Correspondence hitherto unpublished of the Earl of Hardwicke, First Lord Lieutenant of Ireland after the Union,* pp. 43–46.

10   Marquis of Buckingham to Lord Grenville, 20 January 1800, reproduced in Historical Manuscripts Commission, *The Manuscripts of J. B. Fortescue, Esq., preserved at Dropmore,* 6:106–07 (hereafter cited as *MSS Fortescue*); Brynn, pp. 64–65; F. Maurice Powicke and E. B. Fryde, eds., *Handbook of British Chronology,* p. 370.

11   Lord Hardwicke to Lord Pelham, 2 October 1801, quoted in MacDonagh, pp. 95–96. Most of the correspondence that follows is found in Mac-Donagh, pp. 95–119, but without citation. The bulk of the material is now in the British Museum. I have supplied BM references wherever possible.

12   Lord Pelham to Lord Hardwicke, 27 October 1801, cited in MacDonagh, p. 96.

13   Hon. John Beresford to Lord Hardwicke, 30 October 1801. BM Add MS. 35,731, fols. 157–58.

14   MacDonagh, p. 97. No reference or citation is given.

15   (Copy) William Stuart to Henry Addington, 27 November 1801, BM Add MS. 35,771, fols. 152–53; MacDonagh, pp. 98–100.

16   MacDonagh, p. 98.

17   (Copy) Henry Addington to Lord Hardwicke, 19 December 1801. BM Add MS. 35,771, fol. 153; MacDonagh, p. 100.

18   (Copy) Lord Hardwicke to Henry Addington, 22 December 1801. BM Add MS. 35,771, fol. 154; MacDonagh, pp. 100–01.

19   (Copy) Charles Abbot to William Stuart, 23 December 1801. BM Add MS. 35,771, fols. 155–57; MacDonagh, pp. 101–04.

20   William Stuart to Charles Abbot, 27 December 1801. BM Add MS. 35,771, fols. 157–61; MacDonagh, pp. 105–07.

21   (Copy) Lord Hardwicke to Henry Addington, 28 December 1801. BM Add MS. 35,771, fols. 163–64; MacDonagh, pp. 107–09.

22   (Copy) Lord Hardwicke to William Stuart, 29 December 1801. BM Add MS. 35,771, fol. 165; MacDonagh, p. 109.

23 Henry Addington to Lord Hardwicke, 2 January 1802, in MacDonagh, pp. 110–11.
24 (Copy) William Stuart to Lord Hardwicke, 31 December 1801. BM Add MS. 35,771, fol. 168; MacDonagh, pp. 111–12.
25 Lord Hardwicke to Henry Addington, 5 January 1802. BM Add MS. 35, 771, fols. 168–69; MacDonagh, p. 112.
26 Powicke and Fryde, p. 377.
27 MacDonagh, p. 120; Powicke and Fryde, p. 369.
28 MacDonagh, pp. 123–25; Powicke and Fryde, p. 357.
29 Powicke and Fryde, p. 367.
30 MacDonagh, pp. 122–23.
31 Henry Addington to Lord Hardwicke, 9 January 1803, cited in MacDonagh, pp. 121–22.
32 MacDonagh, p. 126.
33 Lord Waterford to Lord Hardwicke, 23 December 1803, reproduced in MacDonagh, pp. 126–27. See also (Copy) Lord Hardwicke to Lord Waterford, 27 December 1803. BM Add MS. 35,745, fols. 12–13; also reproduced in MacDonagh, pp. 127–29. See also Lord Waterford to Lord Hardwicke, 29 December 1803. BM Add MS. 35,745, fols. 34–35.
34 Lord Hardwicke to Henry Addington, 13 January 1804, cited in MacDonagh, p. 130.
35 MacDonagh, p. 132.
36 Lord Waterford to Lord Hardwicke, 26 June 1804, reproduced in MacDonagh, pp. 145–46; Lord Hardwicke to Lord Waterford, 10 July 1804, quoted in MacDonagh, pp. 145–46.
37 Lord Ely to Lord Hardwicke, 11 May 1804, reproduced in MacDonagh, p. 133.
38 Henry Addington to Lord Hardwicke, 14 May 1804, quoted in MacDonagh, p. 135.
39 Lord Hawkesbury to Lord Hardwicke, 20 May 1804, quoted in MacDonagh, p. 136.
40 Lord Hardwicke to Lord Hawkesbury, 24 May 1804, quoted in MacDonagh, pp. 137–39; Lord Hardwicke to Lord Hawkesbury, 25 May 1804 (enclosure) quoted in MacDonagh, pp. 139–42.
41 Lord Hardwicke to William Stuart, [?] September 1804, quoted in MacDonagh, p. 146.
42 William Stuart to Lord Hardwicke, 28 September 1804, quoted in MacDonagh, p. 147.
43 MacDonagh, p. 147; Powicke and Fryde, p. 367.
44 MacDonagh, pp. 149–50; Powicke and Fryde, pp. 353, 362, 365, 370.
45 Brynn, p. 81; Powicke and Fryde, p. 368.
46 For an illuminating discussion of the financial responsibility of the Anglican bishops, see Charles W. Coolidge, "The Finances of the Church of England, 1830–1880," (Ph.D. thesis), pp. 31–74. Coolidge's study deals with Church of England bishops, but is, with small modification, applicable to the Church of Ireland prelates as well.
47 Cf. Coolidge, p. 41, with *First Report of Her Majesty's Commissioners on Ecclesiastical Revenue and Patronage, Ireland*, p. 7, H.C. 1833 (762), xxi.
48 *First Report of His Majesty's Commissioners on Ecclesiastical Revenue and Patronage, Ireland*, pp. 7–8.

49 Compiled from ibid., pp. 214–15. A small number of eccentric leases are excluded.
50 Compiled from Coolidge, pp. 238–46.
51 *Second Report of His Majesty's Commissioners on Ecclesiastical Revenue and Patronage, Ireland*, p. 13, H.C. 1834 (523), xxiii.
52 Brynn, pp. 126–29; 1 Hansard 14:630–32, 19 May 1809.
53 [Thomas L. O'Beirne], *A Letter from an Irish Dignitary to an English Clergyman on the Subject of Tithes in Ireland, written during the Administration of the Duke of Bedford*, pp. 18–20; 1 Hansard 14:626, 19 May 1809; 2 Hansard 7:597, 15 May 1822; 3 Hansard 2:907, 22 February 1831; "Memorandum on Tithes, October 1807," BM Add MS. 44, 221, fols. 1–10; John Reade, *Observations upon Tythes and Rents addressed to the Clergy and Impropriators of Ireland*, pp. 1–2, 34–37.
54 *Parliamentary Register*, 9:444, 8 May 1789.
55 1 Hansard 14:626, 19 May 1809. Unhappily, Parnell did not note which system (English or Irish) of currency or of acreage he was using.
56 PROB, D. 175.
57 See *The Oxford Dictionary of the Christian Church*.
58 For a discussion of the history of appropriations and impropriations, see *Report of His Majesty's Commissioners of Ecclesiastical Inquiry, Ireland*, pp. 6–9, H.C. 1831 (93), ix.
59 See Daniel A. Beaufort, *Memoir of a Map of Ireland*, p. 137.
60 D. A. Chart, "Close Alliance of Church and State," in Walter A. Phillips, ed., *History of the Church of Ireland from the earliest times to the present day*, 3:218; Louis A. Landa, *Swift and the Church of Ireland*, pp. 135–36; William E. H. Lecky, *A History of Ireland in the Eighteenth Century*, 1:201.
61 Landa, p. 136.
62 The entire report is reproduced in John Finlay, *A Treatise on the Law of Tithes in Ireland, and Ecclesiastical Law connected therewith*, pp. 91–103.
63 Lecky, 1:201–02.
64 Portions quoted in Finlay, p. 107. The act exempted from its operation any parish in which tithe of agistment had been paid within the previous ten years, but this was a mere formality as the tithes had almost universally lapsed. (I am grateful to Professor J. C. Beckett for calling this point to my attention.)
65 Duke of Rutland to Thomas Orde, 23 May 1786, in Historical Manuscripts Commission, *The Manuscripts of His Grace the Duke of Rutland, K.G., preserved at Belvoir Castle*, 3:302.
66 Richard Woodward to William Preston, 25 June 1786, in ibid., 3:315.
67 Thomas Orde to Duke of Portland, 25 June 1786, in ibid., 3:312–14. Orde repeated his warning about the necessity of obtaining the warm concurrence of the clergy in a later letter. Thomas Orde to Duke of Rutland, 24 October 1786, in ibid., 3:350–51.
68 *Parliamentary Register*, 7:12, 18 January 1787.
69 Lord Tyrone to John Beresford, 13 September 1786, reproduced in William Beresford, ed., *The Correspondence of the Right Hon. John Beresford, illustrative of the Last Thirty Years of the Irish Parliament*, 1:310.
70 Mant, 2:712–13.

71   Orde to Hutchinson, 9 April 1787, in Historical Manuscripts Commis-
     sion, *The Manuscripts of the Duke of Beaufort, K.G., the Earl of
     Donoughmore and others,* 1:310.
72   Hutchinson to George Rose, 19 June 1788, in ibid., pp. 322–23; Mant,
     2:713–14.
73   Notes by Thomas Spring-Rice on Grattan's plan of 1780. NLI MS.
     13,385 (2).
74   *Parliamentary Register,* 7:336–60, 13 March 1787.
75   *Parliamentary Register,* 8:191–237, 14 February 1788.
76   *Parliamentary Register,* 9:442–64, 8 May 1789.
77   For the sake of completeness three minor tithe measures of the eighteenth
     century should be mentioned. "An Act to encourage the Improvement of
     barren and waste Land and Bogs" (5 Geo. II, c.9) removed all hemp,
     flax, and rape tithes from reclaimed wastelands for five years after their
     reclamation. A second measure (33 Geo. II, c.25) exempted reclaimed
     land from all tithes for seven years after its improvement. Third, in
     1788, "An Act for the better ascertaining the Tithe of Hemp," limited
     hemp tithes to 5s. an acre. Finlay, *Treatise,* pp. 106–07, 112–14, 127.
78   Finlay, *Treatise,* pp. 128–35.
79   See Vane, 3:161–74.
80   2 Hansard 9:374, 16 May 1823.
81   Lord Castlereagh to Lord Grenville, 18 September 1800, *MSS Fortescue,*
     6:323.
82   Memorandum on Tithes, reproduced in Vane, 4:193–205. It is not
     altogether certain, although it is highly probable, that this memorandum
     was a direct response to Grenville's letter. The dating of the memo,
     "September, 1800" (p. 198) is strongly suggestive that the memo was
     produced for Grenville's benefit, and the comments of the 18 September
     1800 letter to Grenville imply that a memo on tithe and rent is enclosed.
     The HMC version of the letter, however, makes no mention of an
     attached memorandum.
83   Lord Buckingham to Lord Grenville, 17 September 1800, *MSS Fortescue,*
     6:319–20.
84   Lord Buckingham to Lord Grenville, 11 December 1806, *MSS Fortescue,*
     8:463–67.
85   Duke of Bedford to Lord Grenville, 14 January 1807, in *MSS Fortescue,*
     9:9–14. Bedford used the word *"modus"* to refer to the process of
     establishing long-term tithe rates in money terms. Although *"modus"*
     was sometimes employed in this sense in contemporary usage, it will not
     be so used in this study, for as indicated above (p. 99) the word has a
     strict meaning in legal terminology, namely, *a modus decimandi* referring
     to a set of immemorial local customs for unusual arrangements for tithe
     payment.
86   Duke of Bedford to Lord Spencer, 14 March 1807, in ibid., 9:82–97.
87   Lord Grenville to Duke of Bedford, 11 March 1807, in ibid., 6:68–72.
88   1 Hansard 11:79, 27 April 1808.
89   1 Hansard 14:625–48, 19 May 1809.
90   1 Hansard 16:658–89, 13 April 1810.
91   1 Hansard 20: 588, 11 June 1811.
92   Kingston, it was alleged, had canvassed his tenants and incited them to
     resist payment of tithes. Robert Disney to Charles Brodrick, 23 January
     1816 and 7 May 1816. NLI MS. 8861 (8), cited in Brynn, p. 222.

93 1 Hansard 34:480–82, 13 May 1816.

94 2 Hansard 2:221–23, 5 July 1820.

95 See B. R. Mitchell with Phyllis Deane, *Abstract of British Historical Statistics,* p. 488, and D. G. Chaytor, *The Law and Practice relating to the Variation of Tithe Rent-Charges in Ireland,* pp. 67–68.

96 James Kidney to T. B. Clarke, 8 September 1823. PROB, D. 1108/B–#83.

97 Ibid., 6 November 1823. PROB, D. 1108/B–#84.

98 (Copy) Lord Liverpool to William Stuart, 24 February 1822. BM Add MS. 37,300, fols. 291–97.

99 Brynn, pp. 231–32.

100 Ibid., p. 233.

101 2 Hansard 7:1029–45, 13 June 1822.

102 Brynn, p. 237.

103 (Copy) Lord John Beresford to Lord Wellesley, 13 February 1823. RCB MS. A2 and NLI MS. 4838.

104 (Copy) Lord John Beresford to Lord Liverpool, 15 February 1823. BM Add MS. 37,300, fols. 298–304 and RCB MS. A2.

105 This assertion is somewhat questionable in view of a Beresford letter to Lord Liverpool, dated 23 March 1822, promising cooperation "in any wise legislation for the church" (APL, Beresford Papers, 2). Further, Beresford worked for the passage of the tithe leasing bill.

106 (Copy) Lord John Beresford to William Howley, 17 February 1823. NLI MS. 4838 and RCB MS. A2.

107 Richard Laurence to Sir Robert Peel, 24 April 1823. BM Add MS. 40,355, fols. 341–42.

108 BM Add MS. 37,300, fols. 325–26. The memorial was signed by the Archbishops of Dublin and of Tuam and by the Bishops of Kildare, Kilmore, Down and Connor, Clonfert and Kilmacduagh, Cork and Ross, Killala and Achonry, Elphin, Ossory, Waterford and Lismore, Dromore, Killaloe and Kilfenora, Ferns and Leighlin, Raphoe and Limerick, Ardfert and Aghadoe.

109 2 Hansard 8:367–416, 4 March 1823; see also "View of Public Affairs," *Christian Observer* 23 (March 1823): 195.

110 Henry Goulburn to Lord Hardwicke, 5 March 1823. BM Add MS. 37,300, fols. 316–17.

111 *A Bill to make provision for facilitating the Commutation of Tithes in Ireland, by Ecclesiastical Persons and others entitled thereto,* H.C. 1823 (170), ii.

112 *Journal of the House of Commons,* 78, pp. 96, 149, 252, 254, 414.

113 *A Bill to provide for the establishing of Compositions for Tithes in Ireland, for a time to be limited,* H.C. 1823 (152), ii; 2 Hansard 8:494–501.

114 Henry Goulburn to Lord Wellesley, 8 March 1823. BM Add MS. 37,300, fols. 331–33.

115 *A Bill (as Amended by the Committee) To provide for the establishing of Compositions for Tithes in Ireland, for a time to be limited,* H.C. 1823 (363), ii; *A Bill (as Amended on Recommitment) To provide for the establishing of Compositions for Tithes in Ireland, for a time to be limited,* H.C. 1823 (480), ii; 2 Hansard 9:366–76 (16 May 1823), 602–09 (30 May 1828), 802–10 (6 June 1828), 989–93 (16 June 1828); *Journals of the House of Commons* 78: 96, 135, 251, 321, 373, 414, 435, 455, 480, 481, 485.

116   *A Return of the Number of Applications for Special Vestries, under the
       Tithe Composition Act etc.,* H.C. 1824 (178), xxi.
117   5 Geo. IV, c. 63.
118   To complete the picture, one set of financial developments peripheral to
       the main line of financial reforms should be mentioned. This is the 1826
       Vestry Act (7 Geo. IV, c. 72). It will be recalled that the vestries had
       power to strike two sorts of rates: those for church building and main-
       tenance and those for general welfare. In the face of mounting radical
       and nationalist criticism, Goulburn and Peel introduced a measure which
       was almost bizarre in nature. It removed the vestry's right to tax the
       parish for social welfare measures, such as the support of orphans, while
       reaffirming the vestry's right to levy a cess for church purposes. This
       incredibly insensitive move meant that the Catholics, as they pushed
       their cause, could unhesitatingly list the parochial system as one of their
       legitimate grievances. The act probably sounded the death knell for the
       old system of parish government, since it now had few functions and in
       its remaining functions it was unacceptable to the Roman Catholics. Not
       surprisingly, in 1833 the old parish system was to be reformed out of
       existence. See Brynn, pp. 263–68; *A Bill to consolidate and Amend the
       laws which regulate the levy and application of Church Rates in Ireland,*
       H.C. 1826 (115), ii; *A Bill (as Amended by the Committee) to consoli-
       date and Amend the laws which regulate the levy and application of
       Church Rates in Ireland,* H.C. 1826 (256), ii.
119   Emmet Larkin, "Economic Growth, Capital Investment, and the Roman
       Catholic Church in Nineteenth-Century Ireland," *American Historical
       Review* 72 (April 1967): 856–57. The article does not define the phrase
       "maintenance of the clergy" with sufficient precision to indicate if the
       bishops, monks, and nuns are included as well as secular priests.
120   Larkin (p. 880) estimates that Irish national income in 1831 was
       £41,000,000. Unfortunately there are no estimates of Irish national
       income by professional economists. Larkin's estimate, therefore, must be
       employed with caution, especially in view of the intuitive methods he
       employed.
121   On the varying size of individual glebe lands, see Erck, passim.
122   *Copies of the Case and Opinions of the Law Officers of the Crown in
       Ireland, on the subject of the Re-evaluation of the Benefices to the First
       Fruits Fund, as taken on an Address to His Majesty of the 14th of March
       last,* pp. 1–3, H.C. 1831 (195), xv; *Oxford Dictionary of the Christian
       Church.*
123   *Copies of the Case and Opinions of the Law Officers of the Crown in
       Ireland, on the subject of the Re-evaluation of the Benefices to the First
       Fruits Fund, as taken on an Address to His Majesty of the 14th of
       March last,* p. 3; E. Curtis, J. C. Beckett, and J. B. Leslie, "Address of
       the Bishop and Clergy of Cloyne to the Queen, 1711," *Journal of the
       Cork Historical and Archaeological Society,* 2d ser., 46 (July–December
       1941): 138–39; Mant, 2:434.
124   [Edward Stopford], "Statement of First Fruits Fund, 1823–4." APL,
       Beresford papers, 1.
125   James Godkin, *Ireland and Her Churches,* p. xviii.
126   [Edward Stopford], "Statement of First Fruits Fund, 1823–4;" Enclosure
       in Edward Stopford to Lord John Beresford, 22 February 1830. APL,
       Beresford Papers, 11.

127 William Stuart to Charles Brodrick, 7 February 1802. NLI MS. 8869 (8).
128 *Accounts Relating to the Church Establishment of Ireland,* p. 34, H.C. 1823 (135), xvi.
129 See William Knox to Lord Hardwicke, 13 October 1802. BM Add MS. 35,736, fols. 260–63; Knox to Hardwicke, 26 October 1802. BM Add MS. 35,736, fols. 258–59; William Stuart to Hardwicke, 30 October 1802. BM Add MS. 35,736, fols. 274–75; Hardwicke to Stuart, 8 November 1802. BM Add MS. 35,736, fol. 276; Stuart to Charles Brodrick, 11 November 1802. NLI MS. 8869 (1); Brodrick to Stuart, 25 November 1802. NLI MS. 8869 (1).
130 1 Hansard 9:497, 20 April 1807; see also the list of Board of First Fruit expenditures in *Accounts Relating to the Church Establishment of Ireland,* pp. 10–25.
131 *Accounts Relating to the Church Establishment of Ireland,* pp. 3–4; Edward Stopford to Lord John Beresford, 22 February 1830; [Edward Stopford], "Statement of First Fruits Fund, 1823–4."
132 *Accounts Relating to the Church Establishment of Ireland,* pp. 5–16; Edward Stopford to Lord John Beresford, 27 February 1830; *Third Report of His Majesty's Commissioners on Ecclesiastical Revenue and Patronage in Ireland,* pp. 12–14, H.C. 1836 (246), xxv.
133 *Accounts Relating to the Church Establishment of Ireland,* p. 4.
134 Ibid., p. 33. Amounts of less than £1 are ignored.
135 Edward Stopford to Lord John Beresford, 27 February 1830.
136 Chapels of ease are included in the tally of churches. For information on individual dioceses see Beaufort, p. 137; *Third Report of His Majesty's Commissioners on Ecclesiastical Revenue and Patronage in Ireland,* pp. 96–97, 146–47, 242–43, 282–83, 330–31, 354–55, 406–07, 436–37, 474–75, 502–03, 536–37, 560–61, 612–13; *Fourth Report of His Majesty's Commissioners on Ecclesiastical Revenue and Patronage in Ireland,* pp. 100–01, 140–41, 234–35, 280–81, 316–17, 334–35, 346–47, 382–83, 430–31, 468–69, 516–17, 538–39, 604–05, 658–59, 668–69, H.C. 1837 (500), xx.
137 Charles Lindsay to Lord Hardwicke, 13 October 1805. BM Add MS. 35,762, fols. 237–38.
138 William Stuart to Charles Brodrick, 24 March 1806, NLI MS. 8869 (5).
139 William Stuart to William Elliott, 8 April 1806, *MSS Fortescue,* 8:90.
140 Brynn, p. 104.
141 The Archbishop of Armagh reported that Duigenan "brings it forward partly to give the Bishops more power, of which they certainly stand much in need, and partly to stay the progress of Sir John Newport" (William Stuart to Charles Brodrick, 2 March 1806. NLI MS. 8869 [4]).
142 1 Hansard 6:429, 13 March 1806.
143 Ibid., col. 428.
144 William Stuart to Charles Brodrick, 24 March 1806.
145 William Stuart to William Elliot, 8 April 1806.
146 William Elliot to Lord Grenville, 6 April 1806, in *MSS Fortescue,* 8:82.
147 Lord Grenville to Duke of Bedford, 18 April 1806, in ibid., p. 105.
148 William Stuart to Charles Brodrick, 24 April 1806. NLI MS. 8869 (4).
149 William Stuart to Duke of Bedford, 27 April 1806, in *MSS Fortescue,* 8:130–31.
150 Duke of Bedford to Lord Grenville, 2 May 1806, in ibid., pp. 128–30.

151 Lord Grenville to Duke of Bedford, 6 May 1806, in ibid., p. 135.
152 *Papers Relating to the Established Church in Ireland,* H.C. 1807 (78), v.
153 Brynn, p. 115.
154 Alfred T. Lee, *The Irish Church, Its Present Condition: Its Future Prospects,* p. 71.
155 Compiled from *Papers Relating to the State of the Established Church of Ireland,* pp. 20, 34, 44, 60, 66, 74, 96, 106, 108–49, 178, 236.
156 Ibid.
157 On policy matters see Edward Stopford to Lord John Beresford, 6 July 1828. APL, Beresford Papers, 1; Circular of Lord John Beresford to Irish bishops, 1823. APL, Beresford Papers, 2. For specific figures see *An Account of the Number of Faculties or Dispensations which have in each of the last Ten Years been granted in Ireland, for the purpose of enabling Ecclesiastical Persons to hold more than one Benefice, and of the Rules and Regulations under which such Faculties are now granted,* p. 1, H.C. 1830 (279), xix.
158 Christopher Butson to Charles Brodrick, 21 March 1814. NLI MS. 8872 (2).
159 W. D. Killen, *The Ecclesiastical History of Ireland,* 2:353.
160 John Healy, *History of the Diocese of Meath,* 2:353.
161 Chart, in Phillips, 3:213.
162 Ibid., p. 269; Mant, 2:738–39.
163 See Erck, pp. 5–128.
164 The reader should be warned at once against placing much reliance on the best-known account of Irish evangelicalism, Richard S. Brooke's *Recollections of the Irish Church.* This is a highly readable but lamentably partisan memoir. The general tenor of Brooke's outlook can be gained from his witty sexual slur: "about this time [the 1840s] Kingstown received a visit from the Rev. Dr. Pusey. I believe he came upon a mission of health, as some of his young people were delicate" (p. 101).
165 Alan R. Acheson, "The Evangelicals in the Church of Ireland, 1784–1859" (Ph.D. thesis), pp. 1–76; Thomas J. Johnston, John L. Robinson, and Robert Wyse Jackson, *A History of the Church of Ireland,* pp. 250–52; Killen, 2:382–89.
166 R. B. McDowell, *Public Opinion and Government Policy in Ireland, 1801–1846,* p. 26.
167 Acheson, p. 88; Killen, 2:390.
168 Acheson, p. 90; Powicke and Fryde, p. 363.
169 Of course the examples cited here are not intended to be taken as proof that the evangelicals raised the standards of the parish ministry. For a conclusive argument of this point, Acheson's thesis should be read in its entirety.
170 McDowell, p. 30.
171 Killen, 2:390.
172 Acheson, p. 152; Killen, 2:390.
173 "Hibernian Sunday School Society," *Christian Observer* 13 (December 1814): 845.
174 J. G. McWalter, *The Irish Reformation Movement, in Its Religious, Social and Political Aspects,* p. 146.
175 *First Report of the Commissioners of Irish Education Inquiry,* p. 61, H.C. 1825 (400), xii.
176 See the testimony of J. D. La Touche, in *Appendix to the First Report of*

the Commissioners of Irish Education Inquiry, p. 669, H.C. 1825 (400), xii.

177   First Report of the Commissioners of Irish Education Inquiry, p. 63.

178   Johnston et al., p. 253.

179   R. Barry O'Brien, Fifty Years of Concessions to Ireland, 1831–1881, 1:16.

180   Reports from the Commissioners of the Board of Education in Ireland. Eleventh Report on Parish Schools, p. 273, H.C. 1810–11 (107), vi.

181   Ibid., pp. 273, 277.

182   Appendix to the First Report of the Commissioners of Irish Education Inquiry, pp. 14–15.

183   The standard history of the charity school movement in the British Isles, including Ireland, is M. G. Jones, The Charity School Movement: A Study of Eighteenth Century Puritanism in Action. See also Reports from the Commissioners of the Board of Education in Ireland. Third on Protestant Charter Schools, H.C. 1809 (142), vii.

184   On the grants, see Donald H. Akenson, The Irish Education Experiment: The National System of Education in the Nineteenth Century, p. 32.

185   First Report of the Commissioners of Irish Education Inquiry, p. 7.

186   Akenson, p. 36.

187   On the APCK see Akenson, pp. 80–83, and Chart, in Phillips, 3:259–61.

188   Reports from the Commissioners of the Board of Education in Ireland. Fourteenth, View of the Chief Foundations with some general remarks, p. 2, H.C. 1821 (744), xi, originally printed H.C. 1812–13 (21), vi.

189   The standard history of the Kildare Place Society is H. Kingsmill Moore, An Unwritten Chapter in the History of Education, being the History of the Society for the Education of the Poor in Ireland, generally known as the Kildare Place Society, 1811–1831.

190   Report from the Select Committee on Foundation Schools and Education in Ireland, p. 11, H.C. 1837–38 (701), vii.

191   Quoted in George L. Smyth, Ireland: Historical and Statistical (London: 1844), 3:232.

192   Edward Stopford to Lord John Beresford, 27 February 1830.

193   J. A. Murphy, "The Support of the Catholic Clergy in Ireland, 1750–1850," in J. L. McCracken, ed., Historical Studies 5 (London: Bowes and Bowes, 1965): 112–13.

194   Ibid., p. 119.

195   For detailed treatment see, James A. Reynolds, The Catholic Emancipation Crisis in Ireland, 1823–1829.

196   Donald H. McDougall, "George III, Pitt and the Irish Catholics, 1801–1825," Catholic Historical Review 31 (October 1945): 255–81.

197   Clyde J. Lewis, "The Disintegration of the Tory-Anglican Alliance in the Struggle for Catholic Emancipation," Church History 29 (March 1960): 25–43.

198   John Jebb to Sir Robert Peel, 11 February 1829. BM Add MS. 40,398, fols. 233–34.

CHAPTER 3

1   Patrick O'Donoghue, "Opposition to Tithe Payments in 1830–31," Studia Hibernica, no. 6 (1966), pp. 69–70.

2   B. R. Mitchell, with Phyllis Deane, *Abstract of British Historical Statistics,* p. 470.
3   See Patrick O'Donoghue, "Causes of the Opposition to Tithes, 1830–38," *Studia Hibernica,* no. 5 (1965), pp. 9–10.
4   Edward P. Brynn, "A Political History of the Church of Ireland, 1800–1841" (M.Litt. thesis), p. 305.
5   O'Donoghue, "Opposition to Tithe Payments in 1830–31," p. 76.
6   Ibid., p. 76.
7   For a MS history of *The Comet* see NLI MS. 3517.
8   O'Donoghue, "Opposition to Tithe Payments in 1830–31," pp. 79–83.
9   R. B. McDowell, *Public Opinion and Government Policy in Ireland, 1801–1846,* p. 144.
10 O'Donoghue, "Opposition to Tithe Payments in 1830–31," p. 71.
11 Ibid., p. 72.
12 Thomas Thackeray to Lord John Beresford, 20 January 1832, APL, Beresford Papers, 8.
13 G. Locker Lampson, *A Consideration of the State of Ireland in the Nineteenth Century,* p. 153.
14 Ibid., pp. 153–54.
15 John Healy, *History of the Diocese of Meath,* 2:168.
16 *Tithes, Ireland. Returns of Orders of the Honourable The House of Commons dated 21 April and 1 December 1837,* p. 1, H.C. 1837–38 (253), xxxviii.
17 *A Return of the Arrears of Tithes due in the several Dioceses of Ireland from the 1st May 1829,* pp. 2–19, H.C. 1833 (509), xxvii. Because of the fragmented nature of the returns, not all dioceses are included in the table. Although the table does not differentiate, one can safely assume that the great bulk of the tithes in arrears was owed to the clergy, rather than lay impropriators, simply because the clergy owned rights to most Irish tithes. Some of the returns did not even include lay impropriators' arrears. Amounts of less than £1 are ignored.
18 Lord John Beresford to Charles J. Blomfield, 24 January 1833. RCB MS. A2.
19 "View of Public Affairs," *Christian Observer,* no. 408 (December 1835), p. 822.
20 3 Hansard 9:259–96.
21 *Report from the Select Committee on Tithes in Ireland,* pp. 3–5, H.C. 1831–32 (177), xxi.
22 3 Hansard 10:525–26, 20 February 1832.
23 *Second Report from the Select Committee on Tithes in Ireland,* H.C. 1831–32 (508), xxi.
24 Brynn, p. 307.
25 William Howley to Lord John Beresford, 22 December 1831. RCB MS. A2.
26 3 Hansard 9:230–51.
27 *Minutes of Evidence taken before the Select Committee of the House of Lords appointed to inquire into the Collection and Payment of Tithes in Ireland, and the State of the Laws relating thereto,* pp. 3–4, H.C. 1831–32 (271), xxii.
28 3 Hansard 10:1269–82, 8 March 1832.
29 *Second Report from the Select Committee of the House of Lords ap-*

pointed to inquire into the Collection and Payment of Tithes in Ireland, and the State of the Laws relating thereto, H.C. 1831–32 (663), xxii.

30   3 Hansard 13:1080, 28 June 1832.
31   3 Hansard 10:1281–82, 1305.
32   3 Hansard 10:1374.
33   3 Hansard 11:134–202, 13 March 1832; 3 Hansard 11:970–1012, 27 March 1832; 3 Hansard 11:1042–76, 28 March 1832; 3 Hansard 11:1113–56, 30 March 1832; 3 Hansard 11:1234–44, 2 April 1832.
34   3 Hansard 11:1402, 6 April 1832.
35   *A Bill to facilitate the Recovery of Tithes in certain cases in Ireland, and for Relief of the Clergy of the Established Church,* H.C. 1831–32 (346), iv.
36   3 Hansard 12:591, 16 April 1832.
37   3 Hansard 12:745, 8 May 1832.
38   Thomas Daly, *Outline of a Plan for the Abolition of Tithes and for making a Provision for the Ministers of the Protestant, Established and Roman Catholic Church in Ireland,* pp. 3–4.
39   *Tithes (Ireland) Act. Extracts from Returns to several Orders of the Honourable House of Commons, dated 24 May 1833,* p. 5, H.C. 1833 (480), xxvii.
40   Brynn, pp. 315–16.
41   *A Bill to amend Three Acts passed respectively in the Fourth, Fifth and in the Seventh and Eighth Years of the Reign of his late Majesty King George the Fourth, providing for the establishing of Compositions for Tithes in Ireland; and to make such Compositions permanent,* H.C. 1831–32 (599), iv.
42   W. Daly, c. 1833, SCRO, D. 260/M/OI–1895.
43   *A Bill for the Relief of the Owners of the Tithes in Ireland and for the Amendment of an Act passed in the last Session of Parliament entitled "An Act to amend Three Acts passed respectively in the Fourth, Fifth, and Seventh and Eighth years of the reign of His late Majesty King George the Fourth, providing for the establishing of Compositions for Tithes in Ireland, and to make such Compositions permanent,* H.C. 1833 (641), iv; *A Bill (as amended by the Committee) For the Relief of the Owners of Tithes in Ireland and for the Amendment of an Act passed in the last Session of Parliament entitled "An Act to amend Three Acts passed respectively in the Fourth, Fifth, and Seventh and Eighth years of the reign of His late Majesty King George the Fourth, providing for the establishing of Compositions for Tithes in Ireland, and to make such Compositions permanent,* H.C. 1833 (665), iv. The measure received the royal assent on 29 August 1833, as 3 & 4 William IV, c. 100. The measure was shaped as much as possible to the convenience of the Irish churchmen. Richard Whately, Archbishop of Dublin, worked closely in Whitehall with the draftsmen of the bill. See Richard Whateley to Lord John Beresford, c. 15 August 1833. RCB MS. A2.
44   *Essays on the Irish Church by Clergymen of the Established Church in Ireland,* p. 133; Memorandum by [Thomas] O'Hagan in Thomas Spring-Rice papers, dated 29 June 1838. NLI MS. 13,385 (2).
45   Henry Goulburn to Lord John Beresford, 16 December 1829. PROB, D. 664/A–123.
46   2 Hansard 22:1273–74; 2 Hansard 22:1279, 1291.

47 Henry Goulburn to Lord John Beresford, 5 March 1831. PROB, D. 664/A–131. Goulburn's political relationship to Beresford was extremely close and warrants further study. When elected M.P. for the City of Armagh, Beresford informed Goulburn, "I am very pleased that you have been elected not only because of 'private friendship' but because I think you will continue to bestow upon the Irish Church those advantages which she may expect to derive from your talents, your knowledge of business and your official situation which has been my chief motive in recommending you for the representation of the City of Armagh" (Copy, Lord John Beresford to Henry Goulburn, 11 August 1830. PROB, D. 664/A–207). Goulburn replied that he would do all he could to promote the interests of the Irish Church (Goulburn to John G. Beresford, 15 August 1830. PROB, D. 664/A–208).

48 (Copy) Lord Francis Leveson-Gower to Lord John Beresford, 6 March 1830. PROD, IA–41–133, Leveson-Gower letterbooks, vol. 3.

49 (Copy) Lord Francis Leveson-Gower to Archdeacon Singleton, 6 March 1830. PROD, IA–41–133, Leveson-Gower letterbooks, vol. 3.

50 (Copy) Lord Francis Leveson-Gower to Archdeacon Singleton, 16 March 1830. PROD, IA–41–133, Leveson-Gower letterbooks, vol. 3.

51 (Copy) Lord Francis Leveson-Gower to Archdeacon Singleton, 5 April 1830. PROD, IA–41–133, Leveson-Gower letterbooks, vol. 3.

52 For the membership see *Report of His Majesty's Commissioners of Ecclesiastical Inquiry, Ireland,* pp. 1–2, H.C. 1831 (93), ix.

53 Some of the minutes of the meetings of the ecclesiastical commissioners are found in APL, Beresford papers, 4.

54 *First Report of His Majesty's Commissioners on Ecclesiastical Revenue and Patronage, Ireland,* p. 3, H.C. 1833 (762), xxi.

55 Memorandum by John Erck, 26 December 1833. SCRO, D. 260/M/OI–1916.

56 Edward Stopford to Lord John Beresford 17 May 1830. APL, Beresford papers, 5. The inner quotation marks and italics are Stopford's.

57 *Second Report of His Majesty's Commissioners on Ecclesiastical Revenue and Patronage, Ireland,* H.C. 1834 (523), xxiii.

58 *Third Report of His Majesty's Commissioners on Ecclesiastical Revenue and Patronage in Ireland,* H.C. 1836 (246), xxv.

59 *Fourth Report of His Majesty's Commissioners on Ecclesiastical Revenue and Patronage in Ireland,* H.C. 1837 (500), xxi.

60 *Parochial Benefices (Ireland),* H.C. 1835 (388), xlvii.

61 *Clergy Residence. Ordered by the House of Commons to be Printed 28 February 1833,* H.C. 1833 (35), xxvii; *Curates, Ireland,* H.C. 1833 (721), xxvii; *Clergy Residence (Ireland),* H.C. 1835 (81), xlvii.

62 *A Return of all the Number of Churches in each Benefice or Union in Ireland; Specifying the Number of Parishes, if more than one, in each such Benefice; and also, in each case of more Parishes than one, stating the Distance from the nearest Boundary of any Parish not having a Church in itself, to the Church; and also stating the Distance from the most remote Boundary of every such Parish to the Church,* H.C. 1833 (400), xxvii.

63 *An Account of all Benefices in Ireland in which Divine Service according to the Forms of the United Church of England and Ireland has not been celebrated within the Three Years ending 12th February 1833,* H.C. 1833 (399), xxvii; *An Account of all Benefices in which Divine Service*

according to the Forms of the United Church of England and Ireland has not been celebrated within the Three Years ending 12th February 1833, H.C. 1833 (491), xxvii.

64 *Report from the Select Committee appointed to inquire into the State of the Prerogative and Ecclesiastical Courts in Ireland,* H.C. 1837 (412), vi.

65 Lord Melbourne to Lord Anglesey, 6 Sept. 1831. PROB, D. 619, carton VI–41.

66 Owen Chadwick, *The Victorian Church,* part I, p. 53.

67 Whately, like his counterpart Beresford, suffers from the lack of a modern biographer. A good deal of light (much of it probably unintentional) is shed on his character by his daughter's collection of his papers. See E. Jane Whately, *Life and Correspondence of Richard Whately, D.D., Late Archbishop of Dublin.* See also "Life and Correspondence of Archbishop Whately," *Christian Observer,* n.s., no. 350 (February 1867), pp. 88–105; "Richard Whately," *Dublin Review,* n.s. 8 (January 1867): 1–25.

68 A. Dwight Culler, *The Imperial Intellect. A Study of Newman's Educational Ideal,* p. 38.

69 Chadwick, p. 53.

70 Ibid., p. 54.

71 Ibid., p. 51.

72 Brynn, pp. 299, 310, 315.

73 Lord Melbourne to Lord Anglesey, 22 January 1831. PROB, D. 619, carton VI–7; Lord Melbourne to Lord Anglesey, 22 January 1831. PROB, D. 619, carton IV–18; Lord Melbourne to Lord Anglesey, 30 January 1831. PROB, D. 619, carton VI–22.

74 Brynn, pp. 324–25.

75 Christopher Darby to Lord John Beresford, c. September 1832. RCB MS. A2.

76 The answer is referred to in Christopher Darby to Lord John Beresford, 13 September 1832. RCB MS. A2.

77 (Copy) Lord John Beresford to Lord Stanley, 22 September 1832. RCB MS. A2.

78 Lord Stanley to Lord John Beresford, 30 September 1832. RCB MS. A2.

79 (Copy) Lord John Beresford to Lord Stanley, 4 October 1832. RCB MS. A2.

80 Lord Stanley to Lord John Beresford, 5 October 1832. RCB MS. A2.

81 Lord Stanley to Lord John Beresford, 30 October 1832. RCB MS. A2.

82 (Copy) Lord John Beresford to Lord Stanley, 1 November 1832. RCB MS. A2.

83 Lord Stanley to Lord John Beresford, 1 November 1832. RCB MS. A2.

84 (Copy) Lord John Beresford to Lord Stanley, 2 November 1832. RCB MS. A2.

85 (Copy) Lord John Beresford to William Howley, 7 November 1832. RCB MS. A2.

86 William Howley to Lord John Beresford, 17 November 1832. RCB MS. A2.

87 Brynn, pp. 333–34.

88 (Copy) Lord John Beresford to Lord Stanley, 12 January 1833. RCB MS. A2.

89 (Copy) Lord John Beresford to William Howley, 16 March 1833. RCB MS. A2.

90   Brynn, p. 346; (copy) Lord John Beresford to William Howley, 21 March 1833. RCB MS. A2.
91   Lord Stanley to Lord John Beresford, 16 January 1833. RCB MS. A2.
92   (Copy) Lord John Beresford to Lord Stanley, 21 January 1833. RCB MS. A2.
93   Lord Stanley to Lord John Beresford, 28 January 1833. RCB MS. A2.
94   (Copy) Lord John Beresford to Lord Stanley, 2 February 1833. RCB MS. A2.
95   Brynn, pp. 336–37.
96   Lord Stanley to Lord John Beresford, 9 February 1833. RCB MS. A2.
97   (Copy) Lord John Beresford to Lord Stanley, 14 February 1833. RCB MS. A2; (copy) Beresford to Stanley, 23 February 1833. RCB MS. A2.
98   *A Bill to alter and amend the Laws relating to the Temporalities of the Church in Ireland,* H.C. 1833 (59), i.
99   William L. Mathieson, *English Church Reform, 1815–1840,* p. 77.
100 Chadwick, p. 57.
101 N. D. Emerson, "The Last Phase of Establishment," in Walter A. Phillips, ed., *History of the Church of Ireland from the Earliest Times to the Present Day,* 3:305.
102 Cf. the first printed version of the bill, H.C. 1833 (59), i, with the slightly later version actually introduced by Althorp: H.C. 1833 (210), i.
103 For a useful summary of the bill's course through parliament, see Olive J. Brose, *Church and Parliament. The Reshaping of the Church of England, 1828–1860,* pp. 46–50.
104 Chadwick, pp. 57–59.
105 Edward J. Littleton to Lord Anglesey, 13 July 1833. PROB, D. 619, carton VII–#24.
106 (Copy) Beresford to Goulburn, 20 March 1833. RCB MS. A2.
107 Cf. the bill as originally introduced with the bill as amended by Commons committee, H.C. 1833 (431), i, and with the final statute, 3 and 4 Will. IV, c. 37. Note also the Lords amendments, H.C. 1833 (594), i.
108 See Patrick O'Donoghue, "Causes of the Opposition to Tithes, 1830–38." His comments on the irritating aspects of composition appertain specifically to the 1823 act, but are applicable to the 1832 act as well.
109 *A Copy of the Correspondence between the Irish Government and Magistrates of the Parishes of Glanntane and Kilshannick, previously to a Police Force being appointed in the present Year, for the protection of Persons employed in the Collection of Tithe in the above Parishes; Also a Copy of the Memorial of the Rev. Mr. O'Keefe upon the Subject, and a Copy of Mr. Littleton's Answer thereto,* H.C. 1834 (109), xliii.
110 *Copy of the Correspondence between the Reverend Thomas Locke, Rector of Newcastle, in the county of Limerick, and the Chief or Under Secretary for Ireland, from the Month of February, 1834 to the present time, relative to the Collection of Tithes payable to Mr. Locke; and also of any Correspondence on that subject during the same period between the Chief Secretary or Under Secretary for Ireland and the Commander of the Forces, or any Magistrate or Officers of Police in the Limerick District,* H.C. 1835 (119), xlvii.
111 *Copy of the Proceedings of an Investigation held at Armagh, of the Transactions which took place in the Neighborhood of Keady, between the Police and Country People, on collecting an arrear of Tithe due to the Reverend James Blacker, wherein one man was killed and several*

wounded; with a Copy of the Inquest and all other Documents connected with that Transaction, H.C. 1835 (179), xlvii.

112 *Tithes, Ireland. Returns to Orders of the Honourable The House of Commons dated 21 April and 1 December 1837,* H.C. 1837–38 (253), xxxviii.

113 John Pratt to E. J. Littleton, 19 September 1834. SCRO, D. 260/M/OI–343.

114 (Copy) Lord John Beresford to Duke of Wellington, 3 October 1835. RCB MS. A2.

115 Memorandum of John Erck prepared for the Lord Lieutenant, c. January 1834. SCRO, D. 260/M/OI–309.

116 3 Hansard 23:422–23, 2 May 1834.

117 The bill received the royal assent on 15 August 1832, as 4 and 5 Will. IV, c. 90. For the bill in passage see, *A Bill to amend an Act made in the Third and Fourth year of the Reign of His present Majesty entitled, "An Act to alter and amend the Laws relating to the Temporalities of the Church of Ireland,"* H.C. 1834 (308), i. The Bill as amended by the Commons committee is found in H.C. 1834 (496), i.

118 E. J. Littleton to Sir John Newport, 31 December 1833. NLI MS. 796. The difference between a land tax and a Crown rent was that a land tax would fall on all those presently liable for tithes, while a Crown rent would fall only on those actually owning the land.

119 Early in the year Lord Cloncurry had submitted a plan for the replacement of tithes with a land tax. He was convinced that Lord Wellesley had given the proposal his full sanction. Whether or not this claim is accurate, and whether the Cloncurry proposal was determinative in the ministry's choice of a land tax over Crown rents, is impossible to determine. See Valentine Cloncurry, *Personal Recollections of the Life and Times, with Extracts from the Correspondence of Valentine Lord Cloncurry,* pp. 355, 359.

120 *A Bill to Abolish Compositions for Tithes in Ireland, and to substitute in lieu thereof a Land Tax, and to provide for the Redemption of the same,* H.C. 1834 (60), iv.

121 3 Hansard 23:1395. The ten resolutions which Ward had originally planned to introduce are found in H.C. 1834 (35), xliii.

122 "View of Public Affairs," *Christian Observer* 34 (June 1834): 446.

123 "Appropriation of Church Property," *Edinburgh Review* (American edition) 60 (January 1835): 253.

124 3 Hansard 24:10–87, 2 June 1834.

125 Locker Lampson, pp. 163–64.

126 *A Bill (as Amended on Re-commitment) to Abolish Compositions for Tithes in Ireland, and to substitute in lieu thereof a Land Tax, and to provide for the Redemption of the same,* H.C. 1834 (545), iv; Memorandum by [Thomas] O'Hagan to Thomas Spring-Rice, 29 June 1838. NLI MS. 13,385 (2).

127 Sir Robert Peel to Lord John Beresford, 14 February 1835. BM Add MS. 40,414, fols. 9–10.

128 Sir Robert Peel to Lord John Beresford, 14 February 1835. BM Add MS. 40,414, fols. 9–10.

129 Brynn, pp. 371–72.

130 3 Hansard 27:373–74.

131 3 Hansard 27:969–74.

132 Emerson in Phillips, 3:299
133 *A Bill For the better Regulation of Ecclesiastical Revenues, and the promotion of Religious and Moral Instruction in Ireland,* H.C. 1835 (360), ii.
134 3 Hansard 29:808, 21 July 1835.
135 3 Hansard 29:288, 7 July 1835.
136 3 Hansard 29:1067–72, 23 July 1835.
137 *A Bill For the better Regulation of Ecclesiastical Revenues and the Promotion of Religious and Moral Instruction in Ireland,* H.C. 1836 (218), i.
138 *A Bill (as amended by the Lords), intitled An Act for the Better Regulation of Ecclesiastical Revenues in Ireland,* H.C. 1836 (498), i.
139 6 and 7 Will. IV, c. 99.
140 *A Bill For the better Regulation of Ecclesiastical Revenues, and the Promotion of Religious and Moral Instruction in Ireland,* H.C. 1837 (283), i.
141 (Copy) Lord John Russell to William Howley, 15 March 1838. PROB, D. 664/A–353.
142 (Copy) Lord John Beresford to William Howley, 20 March 1838. PROB, D. 664/A–355.
143 Frederick Shaw to Lord John Beresford, 17 March 1838. PROB, D. 664/A–351.
144 Henry Goulburn to Lord John Beresford, 2 April 1838. PROB, D. 664/A–358.
145 As formulated by Russell ten resolutions were presented. The arrangement and editing of minor details is mine. See *Tithes in Ireland. Resolutions intended to be Proposed by Lord John Russell,* H.C. 1837–38 (73), xxxviii.
146 Henry Goulburn to Lord John Beresford, 2 April 1838.
147 (Copy) Lord John Beresford to Henry Goulburn, 6 April 1838. PROB, D. 664/A–359.
148 Edward Stopford to Lord John Beresford, 20 April 1838. PROB, D. 664/A–361.
149 3 Hansard 42:1203–13.
150 3 Hansard 42:1353–58, 15 May 1838.
151 3 Hansard 42:1363, 18 May 1838.
152 1 and 2 Victoria, c. 109. To determine the changes in passage compare the statute to *A Bill to abolish Compositions for Tithes in Ireland, and to substitute Rent-charges in lieu thereof,* H.L. 1838 (305), iv. Few significant changes were made. The conversion rate for tithe compositions was raised from seventy per cent to seventy-five per cent. Arrears of most of the tithes then due were, at O'Connell's suggestion, remitted, and the £640,000 that had been voted to the clergy under the Million Act was forgiven and the remaining £360,000 applied to compensating the clergy for arrears.
153 R. B. McDowell, *The Irish Administration, 1801–1914,* p. 14.
154 *A Return of the Names of the Ecclesiastical Commissioners for Ireland, which have attended each of the Meetings of the Board held during the Years 1838, 1839, and 1840, respectively, distinguishing the Unpaid from the Paid Commissioners,* H.C. 1840 (591), xxxix.
155 *Ecclesiastical Commission (Ireland). Return to an Order of the Honourable The House of Commons dated 25 January, 1838,* H.C. 1837–38 (142), xxxviii.
156 *Report of Her Majesty's Commissioners on the Revenues and Condition*

of the Established Church (Ireland), p. xviii [4082], H.C. 1867–68, xxiv.

157 *Report and Account of the Ecclesiastical Commissioners for Ireland, for the Year ended the 1st day of August 1867*, p. 9, H.C. 1867–68 (379), xxiii.

158 *Report and Account of the Ecclesiastical Commissioners for Ireland, for the Year ended the 1st day of August 1852*, p. 7, H.C. 1852–53 (3), xli.

159 *Report of Her Majesty's Commissioners on the Revenue and Condition of the Established Church (Ireland)*, p. xvii.

160 *Report of the Ecclesiastical Commissioners for Ireland, for the Year ending 1 August 1835*, pp. 1–3, H.C. 1836 (130), xxv.

161 *The Report of the Ecclesiastical Commissioners for Ireland, for the Year ending the 1st day of August 1853*, p. 3, H.C. 1854 (31), xx.

162 *St. Nicholas' Church (Dublin)*, H.C. 1844 (59), xliii.

163 (Copy) Ecclesiastical Commissioners to Thomas Larcom, 27 October 1855; (copy) Robert Plunket and Mark Perrin to Thomas Plunket, 20 April 1852. Letterbook of the Ecclesiastical Commissioners for Ireland, vol. 8, PROD, IA-15-89.

164 *Churches etc. (Ireland). Return to Two Orders of the Honourable The House of Commons, dated 2 March and 27 June 1867*, pp. 2–6, H.C. 1867 (476), liv.

165 *Ecclesiastical Commission, Ireland. Return to several Orders of the Honourable the House of Commons dated 31 July 1835*, p. 2, H.C. 1835 (460), xlvii; *Report of Her Majesty's Commissioners on the Revenues and Condition of the Established Church (Ireland)*, p. xvi.

166 (Copy) R. H. Franks to C. P. Fortescue, 29 January 1869. Letterbook of the Ecclesiastical Commissioners for Ireland, vol. 12, PROD, IA-15-91.

167 *Copy of the Correspondence between the Lord Lieutenant and the Irish Ecclesiastical Commissioners in reference to the Application of a Portion of the Perpetuity Fund to the Building and Repairing of Churches in Ireland*, H.C. 1845 (621), xlv.

168 *Copy of the Correspondence between the Lord Lieutenant of Ireland and the Irish Ecclesiastical Commissioners, in reference to the Application of a Portion of the Perpetuity Fund to the Building and Repairing of Churches in Ireland*, H.C. 1846 (484), xlii.

169 *Report from the Select Committee on Ministers' Money (Ireland)*, pp. iii–iv, H.C. 1847–48 (559), xxxiii.

170 Ibid., pp. vi–vii.

171 17 Victoria c. 11.

172 *Annual Report and Account of the Ecclesiastical Commissioners for Ireland, for the Year ending the 1st day of August 1856*, p. 3, H.C. 1857 (13), iv.

173 3 Hansard 145:282, 14 May 1857.

174 20 and 21 Victoria c. 8.

175 *Annual Report and Account of the Ecclesiastical Commissioners for Ireland, for the Year ending the 1st day of August 1857*, p. 2, H.C. 1857–58 (10), xxvi.

176 For documentation and for an extended discussion of the material in this section see Donald H. Akenson, *The Irish Education Experiment: The National System of Education in the Nineteenth Century*. At present there is in preparation a Ph.D. thesis in University College, Dublin, by Stanley Horrall on the Church of Ireland and primary education, 1831–69. Its completion should shed new light on the subject.

177   See Alan R. Acheson, "The Evangelicals in the Church of Ireland, 1784–1859" (Ph.D. thesis), pp. 157–61.
      Because the church was still under governmental patronage at the episcopal level, the number of evangelicals on the bench remained small until the early 1860s. One can conjecture that the government's reluctance to promote Irish evangelicals to the bench was partially a result of the traditional governmental distrust of anything but broad churchmanship and partially a result of the adherence of most evangelicals to the Church Education Society, a body whose propaganda constantly harassed the Dublin administration. The major breakthrough for the evangelicals came in 1862 with the appointment of John Gregg to the See of Cork, Cloyne, and Ross, and the elevation of Hamilton Verschoyle to the Bishopric of Kilmore, Elphin, and Ardagh. They joined three evangelicals already on the bench: Robert Daly (Cashel, Emly, Waterford, and Lismore), James O'Brien (Ferns, Leighlin, and Ossory), and Joseph Singer (Meath).

178   Killen, 2:498–500. This fascinating piece of domestic religious colonialism has received little modern attention. Certainly it merits a scholarly article.

179   Ibid., 2:502–05.

180   Ibid., 2:504–05.

181   J. C. Beckett, "Ulster Protestantism," in T. W. Moody and J. C. Beckett, eds., *Ulster since 1800, a Social Survey*, pp. 165–66.

182   "The Religious Movement in Ireland," *Church of England Magazine* 47 (3 December 1859): 365–67; Alfred R. Scott, "The Ulster Revival of 1859" (Ph.D. thesis), passim.

183   *The Census of Ireland for the Year 1861, Part IV, Report and Tables Relating to Religious Professions, Education and Occupation of the People*, vol. 1, p. 29, [3204–III], H.C. 1863, lix.

184   Ibid., vol. 1, pp. 31–33; *Roman Catholics and Members of Established Church (Ireland)*, H.C. 1863 (289), 1.

185   *A Bill entitled An Act to alter and amend several Acts relating to the Temporalities of the Church in Ireland*, H.L. 1847 (193), iii.

186   3 Hansard 93:753–55, 21 June 1847.

187   J. C. Beckett, *The Making of Modern Ireland, 1603–1923*, pp. 321–22; Raymond Kennedy, "The Administration of the Diocese of Dublin and Glendalough in the Eighteenth Century" (Ph.D. thesis), p. 197; H. A. Wheeler, "St. Michael's Parish," *Dublin Historical Record* (January 1960): 100.

188   Emmet Larkin, "Church and State in Ireland in the Nineteenth Century," *Church History* 31 (September 1962): 301–02.

189   Ibid., p. 303; Emmet Larkin, "Economic Growth, Capital Investment, and the Roman Catholic Church in Nineteenth-Century Ireland," *American Historical Review* 72 (April 1967): 859–62.

190   Larkin, "Economic Growth," pp. 862–66.

191   John H. Whyte, "The Appointment of Catholic Bishops in Nineteenth Century Ireland," *Catholic Historical Review* 48 (April 1962): 23–29.

192   E. R. Norman, *The Catholic Church and Irish Politics in the Eighteen Sixties*, p. 3. On the Independent Irish Party see J. H. Whyte's excellent, *The Independent Irish Party, 1850–9*.

193   3 Hansard 75:534–671, 10 and 11 June 1844.

194   3 Hansard 107:107–74, 10 July 1849.

195   3 Hansard 127:862–955, 31 May 1853.
196   3 Hansard 142:712–72, 27 May 1856.
197   3 Hansard 170:1988–2020, 19 May 1863; 3 Hansard 171:1560–1717, 26 June and 29 June 1863.
198   For a thorough history of the Catholic Church's political activities in this period see E. R. Norman, *The Catholic Church and Ireland in the Age of Rebellion, 1859–1873*.
199   *The Census of Ireland for the Year 1861, Part IV, Report and Tables relating to Religious Professions, Education, and Occupation of the People*, vol. 1, pp. 39, 41.
200   Ibid., pp. 20, 33.
201   *Report of Her Majesty's Commissioners on the Revenues and Condition of the Established Church (Ireland)*, p. xxx.
202   *Established Church etc. (Ireland) Return to an Order of the Honourable The House of Commons dated 9 February 1864*, H.C. 1864 (267), xliv; Alfred T. Lee, *The Irish Church. Its Present Condition: Its Future Prospects*, p. 71.
203   B. R. Mitchell with Phyllis Deane, *Abstract of British Historical Statistics*, pp. 471–72.
204   For an excellent discussion of the limitations of the 1867 commission's data, see Hugh Shearman, "The Economic Results of the Disestablishment of the Irish Church" (Ph.D. thesis), pp. 148–54. The report was hastily prepared and the data probably somewhat underestimate actual revenue.
205   Ibid., pp. 152–53; *Report of Her Majesty's Commissioners on the Revenues and Condition of the Established Church (Ireland)*, pp. i, 249.
206   Derived from *Report of Her Majesty's Commissioners on the Revenues and Condition of the Established Church (Ireland)*, pp. xxii, xxv, 249; Shearman, pp. 152–53. Amounts less than £1 are ignored. In addition to corrections in the royal commissioners' accounts specified by Shearman, I have completed the transfer of taxes on episcopal incomes from the bishops to the Ecclesiastical Commissioners, an accounting operation which the Royal Commissioners failed to perform.
207   Accepting the figures is of course the problem. "Stackpoole's Return" of 1864 had estimated the net revenue of the church at £448,943 (*Established Church, etc. [Ireland], Return to an Order of the Honourable The House of Commons, dated 9 February 1864*, p. 111). This would indicate that the commissioners of 1867 erred on the side of overestimation. On the other hand, after disestablishment it was found that whereas the 1867 commissioners had reported £364,224 in the tithe rent charge, the actual figure was £409,689. Similarly, instead of £204,932 in land rents, the figure later established was £225,622 (Shearman, p. 159). Actually neither set of figures—those given before disestablishment to the royal commission and those given shortly after by clergymen to the Church Temporalities Commissioners after the disestablishment—is necessarily accurate. In the former instance, the clergy may well have understated their income in the face of inevitable criticism of the wealthy minority position they occupied. In the latter case they were attempting to establish their salaries for the future, so may well have been motivated to exaggerate their income. In the face of conflicting and insufficient evidence, the issue cannot be resolved.

CHAPTER 4

1   The description of the National Association's activities is based on E. R.
    Norman's *The Catholic Church and Ireland in the Age of Rebellion,
    1859–1873,* passim. For a convenient précis of that work, see Norman's
    The Catholic Church and Irish Politics in the Eighteen Sixties.
       Since this book was written a number of attractive studies of the
    Church of Ireland in the disestablishment era have appeared. R. H. A.
    Eames's *The Quiet Revolution: The Disestablishment of the Church of
    Ireland* (privately printed, 1970), and W. G. Wilson's *The Church of
    Ireland—Why Conservative? A Brief Review of Disestablishment and
    Some of Its Effects* (Dublin: APCK, 1970) are readable popular pam-
    phlets. Hugh Shearman's booklet *How the Church of Ireland Was Dis-
    established* (Dublin: Church of Ireland Disestablishment Centenary Com-
    mittee, 1970), deals almost entirely with the years after disestablishment.
    Kevin B. Nowlan contributes a graceful sketch, "Disestablishment: 1800–
    1869," to *Irish Anglicanism, 1869–1969,* ed. Michael Hurley (Dublin:
    Allen Figgis Ltd., 1970), pp. 1–22.
       By far the most significant of the newly available studies is P. M. H.
    Bell's *Disestablishment in Ireland and Wales* (London: SPCK, 1969).
    Although Bell and I differ slightly on points of detail and somewhat more
    on points of emphasis, I have not seen the need to make any changes in
    the present study. Bell's book is especially illuminating on the attitudes
    of conservative politicians toward the Church of Ireland.
2   *The Church Establishment in Ireland. The Freeman's Journal Church
    Commission.* The reader will notice that in this chapter, as well as the
    preceding one, I have intentionally avoided the mire of controversial
    tracts which were published during the period. On the pro-church side
    there was one work which in its wealth of data and argument ranks with
    the *Freeman's Journal* report, namely, Alfred T. Lee's, *The Irish Church.
    Its Present Condition: Its Future Prospects.*
       The sources from which much of the period's polemical flac was drawn
    were the census of 1861 and the parliamentary returns of 1864. Later,
    the royal commissions' report of 1868 was gleaned by the pamphleteers.
    Anyone studying the Church of Ireland at this time would do well to use
    the parliamentary information directly, and not use propagandistic
    sources.
3   Enclosure in Lord Cairns to Lord Mayo, 22 July 1867. NLI MS. 11,216
    (2).
4   Marcus Beresford to Lord Mayo, 2 June 1867. NLI MS. 11,216 (1). The
    Irish landlords were reported to be in violent opposition to the bill.
    (Copy) Richard C. Trench to Stephen Spring-Rice, 21 June 1864. NLI
    MS. 4457.
5   3 Hansard 188:367, 24 June 1867.
6   See "The Irish Church Question," *British Quarterly Review* 47 (April
    1868): 497–505.
7   3 Hansard 188:393–423, 24 June 1867.
8   Lord Derby to Lord Mayo, 14 July 1867. NLI MS. 11,216 (2).
9   3 Hansard 189:1610, 16 August 1867.
10 Lord Stanhope to Lord Mayo, 20 October 1867. NLI MS. 11,216 (5).
11 Lord DeVesci to Lord Mayo, 21 October 1867. NLI MS. 11,216 (3);

(copy) Lord Mayo to Lord DeVesci, 24 October 1867. NLI MS. 11,216 (3).

12 *Report of Her Majesty's Commissioners on the Revenues and Conditions of the Established Church (Ireland)*, p. iii [4082], H.C. 1867–68, xxiv.

13 Ibid., pp. vii–xix.

14 Henry E. Patton, *Fifty Years of Disestablishment*, pp. 6–8.

15 Philip Magnus, *Gladstone: A Biography*, pp. 42, 68–70.

16 (Copy) W. E. Gladstone to John Bright, 10 December 1867. BM Add MS. 44,112 fols. 65–66.

17 Gladstone to Robert Phillimore, 13 February 1865, quoted in Vincent A. McClelland, *Cardinal Manning: His Public Life and Influence, 1865–1892*, p. 171.

18 For the debate see 3 Hansard 178:385 ff.

19 John Hannah to W. E. Gladstone, 8 June 1865. BM Add MS. 44,406, fols. 272–74.

20 (Copy) W. E. Gladstone to John Hannah, 8 June 1865. BM Add MS. 44,406, fols. 276–77.

21 Magnus, p. 172.

22 John Bright to W. E. Gladstone, 9 December 1867. BM Add MS. 44,112, fols. 63–64; J. F. M. D. Stephen, "Gladstone and the Anglican Church in Ireland and England, 1868–1874" (M.Litt. thesis), p. 70.

23 (Copy) W. E. Gladstone to John Bright, 10 December 1867. BM Add MS. 44,112, fols. 65–66.

24 Magnus, p. 191.

25 3 Hansard 191:32–33.

26 3 Hansard 191:507, 30 March 1868.

27 3 Hansard 191:941, 3 April 1868.

28 Robert Blake, *Disraeli*, p. 479.

29 3 Hansard 191:1678, 30 April 1868.

30 Magnus, p. 192.

31 3 Hansard 191:1675, 30 April 1868.

32 See 3 Hansard 191:1686, 4 May 1868; Magnus, p. 192.

33 3 Hansard 191: 1886, 7 May 1868.

34 *A Bill to Prevent for a limited time, new Appointments in the Church of Ireland, and to restrain, for the same period, in certain cases, the Proceedings of the Ecclesiastical Commissioners for Ireland*, H.C. 1867–68 (117), ii.

35 3 Hansard 193:298, 29 June 1868.

36 Lord Granville to W. E. Gladstone, 29 August 1868. BM Add MS. 44,165, fols. 174–77.

37 Magnus, p. 193.

38 "The Ministry and the Irish Church," *Fraser's Magazine* 79 (January 1869):113.

39 Llewellyn Wodward, *The Age of Reform, 1815–1870*, p. 190. On the elections in Ireland, see David Thornley, *Isaac Butt and Home Rule*, pp. 25–61.

40 Stephen, p. 88.

41 "The Irish Church Bill," *Fraser's Magazine* 80 (August 1864): 257, 261.

42 For biographical details, see *DNB* and J. Bromley's *The Man of Ten Talents: A Portrait of Richard Chenevix Trench, 1807–86, Philologist, Poet, Theologian, Archbishop*. Bromley's otherwise sound biography suffers from a failure to recognize adequately that (as will be established

later) Trench's inability to negotiate was strongly detrimental to the
Church of Ireland's position.

43   R. C. Trench to Samuel Wilberforce, 18 April 1868, quoted in Bromley,
     pp. 171–72. The italics are Trench's.

44   For biographical details, see *DNB* and John R. Garstin, *Historical Notices
     of the Anglican Archbishops of Armagh, Primates of All Ireland, during
     the Nineteenth Century,* pp. 9–11.

45   John C. MacDonnell, *The Life and Correspondence of William Connor
     Magee, Archbishop of York,* pp. 162–63; Henry Seddall, *The Church of
     Ireland: A Historical Sketch,* pp. 168–74.

46   Stephen, p. 150.

47   Lord Clarendon to John Delane, 23 December 1868, quoted in Stephen,
     p. 150.

48   Samuel Hinds to W. E. Gladstone, 14 December 1868. BM Add MS.
     44,417, fols. 122–23.

49   (Copy) W. E. Gladstone to Samuel Hinds, 30 December 1868. BM Add
     MS. 44,417, fols. 287–88.

50   "As to the mode of transition from the Established to the non-Established
     Status in Ireland," [—December 1868]. BM Add MS. 44,756, fols. 134–
     35.

51   "Memo of December 17 and December 18/68;" "Property to vest in
     Commissioners on trusts to be declared on January 1, 1871;" "Proposed
     to be given to the Church." BM Add MSS. 44,756, fols. 136–42.

52   (Copy) W. E. Gladstone to Chichester Fortescue, 26 December 1868.
     BM Add MS. 44,121, fols. 81–82.

53   (Copy) W. E. Gladstone to Chichester Fortescue, 24 December 1868.
     BM Add MS. 44,121, fols. 79–80.

54   (Copy) W. E. Gladstone to Edward Sullivan, 1 January 1869. BM Add
     MS. 44,418, fols. 4–5. Unfortunately, the heads of Gladstone's bill are
     not available. A jumbled, fragmented, partially legible early draft is
     found in the BM Add MS. 44,756, fols. 146 ff.

55   (Copy) W. E. Gladstone to Richard C. Trench, 14 December 1868.
     BM Add MS. 44,417, fols. 138–42. Also reproduced in [Maria M.
     Trench], *Richard Chenevix Trench, Archbishop: Letters and Memorials,*
     2:65–66.

56   Richard C. Trench to W. E. Gladstone, 22 December 1868. BM Add MS.
     44,417, fols. 238–39.

57   Sir William Heathcote to Sir Roundell Palmer, 8 February 1869, repro-
     duced in Trench, 2:76–77.

58   W. E. Gladstone to Sir William Heathcote, 31 December 1868, repro-
     duced in Trench, 2:71.

59   (Copy) W. E. Gladstone to William Jacobson, 19 January 1869. BM Add
     MS. 44,418, fol. 171.

60   Owen Chadwick, *The Victorian Church,* pt. I, pp. 309–24.

61   Bishop Reeves's bound collection of notes on the Irish Convocation.
     TCD, MS. 1062.

62   "Synods of the Church of Ireland," *Literary Churchman* 2 (30 December
     1865): 552.

63   *Convocation (Ireland). Return to an Address of the Honourable the
     House of Commons, dated 21 July 1864,* p. 1, H.C. 1864 (562), xliv;
     *A Copy of Any Memorials to Her Majesty from the Irish Prelates,
     presented during 1861 and 1862, relating to Synodical Action in Ireland;*

and Copy or Extracts of Correspondence relating thereto, pp. 1–2, H.C. 1863 (258), xlvi.

64 *Convocation (Ireland). Return to an Address of the Honourable the House of Commons, dated 21 July 1864, p. 1; A Copy of any Memorials to Her Majesty from the Irish prelates, presented during 1861 and 1862, relating to Synodical Action in Ireland; and Copy or Extracts of Correspondence relating thereto,* pp. 3–5.

65 *Convocation (Ireland). Return to an Address of the Honourable the House of Commons, dated 21 July 1864,* pp. 7–12; Bishop Reeves's notes on the Irish convocation.

66 *Convocation (Ireland) Return to an Address of the Honourable the House of Commons, dated 21 July 1864,* pp. 2–19. The opinion was rendered by A. J. Stephens, Q.C.

67 Ibid., pp. 1–2.

68 "Synods of the Church in Ireland," pp. 552–53.

69 See MacDonnell, 1:163–64, 177–93.

70 (Copy) W. E. Gladstone to Edward Sullivan, 7 January 1869. BM Add MS. 44,418, fol. 78.

71 Lord Granville to W. E. Gladstone, 7 January [1869]. BM Add MS. 44,166, fols. 5–6.

72 (Copy) W. E. Gladstone to Richard Trench, 4 January 1869. BM Add MS. 44,418, fol. 149; also reproduced in Trench, 2:73–74.

73 Richard C. Trench to Marcus G. Beresford, 15 January 1869, reproduced in Trench, 2:74.

74 Edward A. Stopford to W. E. Gladstone, 22 December 1868. BM Add MS. 44,417, fols. 233–34.

75 (Copy) W. E. Gladstone to Edward A. Stopford, 24 December 1868. BM Add MS. 44,417, fol. 246.

76 Edward A. Stopford to W. E. Gladstone, 24 December 1868. BM Add MS. 44,417, fols. 257–60.

77 (Copy) W. E. Gladstone to Edward Sullivan, 7 January 1869. BM Add MS. 44,418, fol. 78.

78 (Copy) W. E. Gladstone to Edward Sullivan, 1 January 1869. BM Add MS. 44,418, fols. 4–5.

79 (Copy) W. E. Gladstone to Samuel Wilberforce, 17 January 1869. BM Add MS. 44,345, fols. 54–55.

80 (Copy) W. E. Gladstone to Dr. Monsell, 28 January 1869. BM Add MS. 44,418, fol. 207.

81 Whether the date of Stopford's arrival was 14 or 15 January is uncertain. Compare Stephen, pp. 80–81, with calendar for 1869 and with the following letters: (copy) W. E. Gladstone to Edward A. Stopford, 11 January 1869. BM Add MS. 44,418, fol. 124; (copy) W. E. Gladstone to Edward Sullivan, 11 January 1869. BM Add MS. 44,418, fol. 127.

82 W. E. Gladstone to Edward Sullivan, 7 January 1869.

83 (Copy) W. E. Gladstone to Chichester Fortescue, 19 January 1869. BM Add MS. 44,536, fol. 102.

84 (Copy) W. E. Gladstone to Samuel Wilberforce, 17 January 1869. BM Add MS. 44,345, fols. 54–55.

85 John C. MacDonnell, "Irish Church Politics and Church History," *Contemporary Review* 3 (1866): 392–93.

86 See his *A History of the Protestant Episcopal Church in America* (New York: Stanford and Swords, 1849).

87   Samuel Wilberforce to Richard C. Trench, 20 November 1868, quoted in Reginald Wilberforce, *Life of the Right Reverend Samuel Wilberforce, D.D.,* 3:276.
88   Richard C. Trench to Samuel Wilberforce, 21 November 1868, reproduced in Trench, 2:62–63.
89   See R. Wilberforce, 3:271–72.
90   (Copy) W. E. Gladstone to Samuel Wilberforce, 17 January 1869. BM Add MS. 44,345, fols. 54–55.
91   (Copy) W. E. Gladstone to Lord Granville, 6 January 1869. BM Add MS. 44,166, fol. 4.
92   Reproduced in R Wilberforce, 3:277–80.
93   W. E. Gladstone to Samuel Wilberforce, 17 January 1869.
94   Samuel Wilberforce to W. E. Gladstone, 20 January 1869. BM Add MS. 44,345, fols. 56–61.
95   (Copy) W. E. Gladstone to Samuel Wilberforce, 21 January 1869. BM Add MS. 44,345, fol. 62.
96   Samuel Wilberforce to W. E. Gladstone, 29 January 1869. BM Add MS. 44,345, fols. 63–64.
     The pamphlet was an amplification of the arguments put forward in his 30 December 1868 letter to Trench. It was in the form of a letter to Lord Lyttelton, entitled, *Answer of the Constituencies.* R. Wilberforce, 3:282. Technically, it was printed but not published.
97   Blake, p. 489.
98   See W. E. Gladstone to Edward Sullivan, 7 January 1869.
99   William Magee to Edward A. Stopford, 23 January 1869. BM Add MS. 44,418, fols. 203–06.
100 William Magee to John MacDonnell, 22 January 1869, reproduced in MacDonnell, 1:212–13.
101 William Magee to John MacDonnell, 29 January 1869, reproduced in MacDonnell, 1:213–14.
102 R. Wilberforce, 3:283.
103 William Magee to John MacDonnell, 10 February 1869, reproduced in MacDonnell, 1:214.
104 (Copy) W. E. Gladstone to Chichester Fortescue, 2 February 1869. BM Add MS. 44,121, fols. 95–96.
105 Charles Ellicott to W. E. Gladstone, 8 March 1869. BM Add MS. 44,419, fols. 179–83.
     Stopford had suggested Ellicott to Gladstone as an ally. Edward A. Stopford to W. E. Gladstone, 6 February 1869. BM Add MS. 44,419, fols. 29–33.
106 W. E. Gladstone to Chichester Fortescue, 2 February 1869.
107 Samuel Hinds to W. E. Gladstone, 6 February 1869. BM Add MS. 44,419, fols. 21–22.
108 Samuel Wilberforce to W. E. Gladstone, 20 January 1869.
109 R. Wilberforce, 3:284–86; see also, William Magee to John MacDonnell, 10 February 1869, reproduced in MacDonnell, 1:214–18.
     During the second half of January 1869 Gladstone was dealing with Queen Victoria about the Irish Church question. These negotiations were irrelevant to the substance of the bill because the Queen was deeply concerned only about preserving the rights of the Crown. Of course, once it had been decided to convert the Irish Established Church into a voluntary church, there was no place for royal patronage. See J. C. Beckett,

"Gladstone, Queen Victoria, and the Disestablishment of the Irish Church, 1869," *Irish Historical Studies* 13 (March 1962):38–47.

110 Memorandum of Sir Roundell Palmer to W. E. Gladstone, 12 February 1869, reproduced in Trench, 2:80–82.

111 Samuel Wilberforce to W. E. Gladstone, 16 February 1869. BM Add MS. 44,345, fols. 65–66.

112 William C. Magee to John C. MacDonnell, 10 February 1869, reproduced in MacDonnell, 1:215.

113 John Bright to W. E. Gladstone, 9 January 1869. BM Add MS. 44,112, fols. 74–75.

114 (Copy) W. E. Gladstone to John Bright, 11 January 1869. BM Add MS. 44,112, fol. 76.

115 John Gray to W. E. Gladstone, 11 January 1869. BM Add MS. 44,418, fols. 116–19.

116 (Copy) W. E. Gladstone to Edward A. Stopford, 3 February 1869. BM Add MS. 44,419, fol. 9; (copy) W. E. Gladstone to Edward Sullivan, 3 February 1869. BM Add MS. 44,419, fols. 10–12.

117 Chichester Fortescue to W. E. Gladstone, 8 February 1869. BM Add MS. 44,121, fols. 97–103.

118 Memorandum of Chichester Fortescue to W. E. Gladstone, 8 February 1869. BM Add MS. 44,121, fols. 104–15.

119 Ibid.

120 Chichester Fortescue to W. E. Gladstone, 22 February 1869. BM Add MS. 44,121, fols. 118–27.

121 (Copy) W. E. Gladstone to Chichester Fortescue, 22 February 1869. BM Add MS. 44,121, fol. 128.

122 (Copy) W. E. Gladstone to Dr. Monzell, 28 January 1869. BM Add MS. 44,418, fol. 207.

123 Enclosure in Edward A. Stopford to W. E. Gladstone, 6 February 1869. BM Add MS. 44,419, fols. 31–36.

124 (Copy) W. E. Gladstone to Edward A. Stopford, 8 February 1869. BM Add MS. 44,419, fol. 48.

125 Edward A. Stopford to W. E. Gladstone, 27 February 1869. BM Add MS. 44,419, fol. 94.

126 Chichester Fortescue to W. E. Gladstone, 23 February 1869. BM Add MS. 44,121, fols. 129–34.

127 Hugh Shearman, "The Economic Results of the Disestablishment of the Irish Church" (Ph.D. thesis), pp. 233–36.

128 Ibid., pp. 234, 237–38.

129 William C. Magee to John C. MacDonnell, 18 February 1869, reproduced in MacDonnell, 1:219.

130 (Copy) W. E. Gladstone to Chichester Fortesque, 23 December 1868. BM Add MS. 44,121, fol. 78.

131 (Copy) W. E. Gladstone to C. L. Morell, 5 January 1869. BM Add MS. 44,418, fols. 23–24.

132 (Copy) W. E. Gladstone to Chichester Fortesque, 22 February 1869. BM Add MS. 44,121, fol. 128; Robert Allen, *The Presbyterian College, Belfast, 1853–1953,* pp. 120–21.

133 (Copy) W. E. Gladstone to John Bright, 15 February 1869. BM Add MS. 44,536, fol. 115.

134 John Bright to W. E. Gladstone, 14 February 1869. BM Add MS. 44,112, fols. 83–86.

135 (Copy) W. E. Gladstone to Chichester Fortescue, 22 February 1869.
136 Ibid.
137 E. R. Norman, *The Catholic Church in Ireland in the Age of Rebellion, 1859–1873*, pp. 361–62.
138 *A Bill to put an end to the Establishment of the Church of Ireland, and to make Provision in respect of the Temporalities thereof, and in respect of the Royal College of Maynooth*, H.C. 1868–69 (27), iii.
139 The quotations and summary of proceedings are from Henry Seddall's, *The Church of Ireland: A Historical Sketch*, pp. 188–95.
140 For the changes in passage through the Commons, see the bill as amended in committee—H.C. 1868–69 (112), iii—and as modified on recommitment—H.C. 1868–69 (123), iii.
141 R. Wilberforce, 3:283–86.
142 William C. Magee to John C. MacDonnell, 7 June 1869, reproduced in MacDonnell, 1:226–27.
143 Bromley, p. 187.
144 Lord Granville to W. E. Gladstone, 4 August 1869. BM Add MS. 44,166, fols. 111–17.
145 P. T. Marsh, *The Victorian Church in Decline*, pp. 34–35.
146 William C. Magee to John C. MacDonnell, 16 June 1869, reproduced in MacDonnell, 1:228.
147 3 Hansard 197:305–06; Seddall, p. 197.
148 To determine which of the Lords' amendments the Commons accepted and which it did not, compare the following: *A Bill (as Amended by the Lords) entitled An Act to put an end to the Establishment of the Church of Ireland, and to make Provision in respect of the Temporalities thereof, and in respect of the Royal College of Maynooth*, H.C. 1868–69 (209), iii; *Irish Church Bill. Commons Amendments to Lords Amendments and the Reasons for disagreeing to several of the Lords Amendments*, H.C. 1868–69 (232), iii.
149 To determine on which of their amendments the Lords allowed themselves to be overridden, and on which they held their ground, compare the Commons amendments to the Lords' with *Irish Church Bill. Lords Amendments to Commons Amendments to Lords Amendments, and reasons assigned to the Lords for insisting on certain of their Amendments*, H.C. 1868–69 (231), iii.
150 Edward A. Stopford to W. E. Gladstone, 26 June 1869. BM Add MS. 44,421, fols. 67–68.
151 Paul Cullen to Henry Manning, 13 July 1869. BM Add MS. 44,249, fols. 90–91.
152 Paul Cullen to W. E. Gladstone, 14 July 1869. BM Add MS. 44,421, fols. 150–51.
153 Gladstone's memo on Irish Church problem. BM Add MS. 44,758, fols. 1–14, entry for 18 July 1869.
154 Ibid., entry for 17 July 1869.
155 Ibid., entry for 17 July 1869; Bromley, pp. 188–89; William C. Magee to John C. MacDonnell, 21 July 1869, reproduced in MacDonnell, 1: 233–34.
156 Gladstone's memo on Irish Church problem, entry for 17 July 1968.
157 Ibid., entries for 18 and 19 July 1869; (copy) W. E. Gladstone to Lord Granville, 18 July 1869. BM Add MS. 44,166, fols. 101–02.

158 Gladstone's memo on Irish church problem, entries for 19 and 20 July 1869.

159 Ibid., entry for 21 July 1869; (copy) W. E. Gladstone to Lord Clarendon, 24 July 1869. BM Add MS. 44,537, fol. 13.

160 Gladstone's memo on Irish church problem, entry for 21 July 1869; (copy) W. E. Gladstone to Edward Cardwell, 19 July 1869. BM Add MS. 44,537, fol. 11.

161 Gladstone's memo on Irish church problem, entry for 22 July 1869; W. E. Gladstone to Lord Clarendon, 24 July 1869. BM Add MS. 44,537, fol. 13; Lord Granville to W. E. Gladstone, 4 August 1869. BM Add MS. 44,166, fols. 111–17.

162 Compare the Lords amendments to the final statute, 32 and 33 Victoria, c. 42.

163 W. E. Gladstone to Lord Clarendon, 24 July 1869.

164 Eleanor Alexander, *Primate Alexander, Archbishop of Armagh,* p. 173.

CHAPTER 5

1 "Results of Disestablishment in Ireland," *British Quarterly Review* 56 (July 1872): 195.

2 "The Irish Church Act, 1869," *London Quarterly Review* 127 (July–October 1869, American edition):262.

3 E. W. Whately, "The Constitution of the Church of Ireland," *The Churchman* 1 (October 1879):124.

4 William C. Magee to John C. MacDonnell, 23 September 1869, reproduced in John C. MacDonnell, *The Life and Correspondence of William Connor Magee, Archbishop of York,* 1:236–37.

5 *The National Synod of the Church of Ireland. The Synods of Armagh and Dublin in September 1869, together with the Journal of the Lower House of the United Synods,* pp. 1–10.

6 Ibid., pp. 12–20.

7 Ibid., p. 15.

8 Ibid., pp. 22–24.

9 Richard C. Trench to Thomas C. Trench, 6 August 1869, reproduced in [Maria M. Trench], *Richard Chenevix Trench, Archbishop, Letters and Memorials,* 2:105–06.

10 Eleanor Alexander, *Primate Alexander, Archbishop of Armagh,* p. 175.

11 Alfred T. Lee, ed., *Journal of the General Convention of the Church of Ireland, First Session, 1870; with the Statutes passed and an Appendix containing the Division Lists, etc.,* p. vii (hereafter cited as *JGC/First*).

12 "Reconstruction of the Irish Church," *London Quarterly Review* 33 (January 1870, American edition): 409–10.

13 Richard C. Trench to Thomas C. Trench, 22 September 1869, reproduced in Trench, 2:106.

14 "Reconstruction of the Irish Church," p. 410.

15 Richard C. Trench to Thomas C. Trench, 22 September 1869.

16 "Reconstruction of the Irish Church," p. 411.

17 Lee, *JGC/First,* pp. viii–ix.

18 Ibid., p. ix.

19 Richard C. Trench to Thomas C. Trench, 27 December 1869, reproduced in Trench, 2:116.

20 *Draft of an Act of Constitution, with Standing Orders and a Finance Report, prepared by the committee appointed in conformity with the Recommendation of the Lay Conference, to be submitted to the General Convention of the Church of Ireland,* pp. 3–4.
21 Richard C. Trench to Thomas C. Trench, 27 December 1869.
22 Richard C. Trench to Mrs. R. C. Trench, 5 January 1870, quoted in Trench, 2:117.
23 One probable reason for the committee's being able to work smoothly and rapidly was that the members had a good deal of information on Anglican churches elsewhere in the world. Basically, there were two sorts of precedents among the churches of the Anglican world as to the forming of new constitutions. One of these, exemplified by Victoria and Tasmania, involved the petitioning of the legislature for permission to effect constitutional revision, and was thus not directly applicable to the Irish situation where the ties between state and church were totally severed. Under the other precedent, embodied in the cases of New Zealand and South Australia, the churches formed their constitutional assemblies without consulting outside authorities. Their constitutions, therefore, were documents agreed to by "consensual compact" of those within the church. During the 1850s the constitution of the church in New Zealand was redrawn upon the lines of the Episcopal Church in the United States. In 1868 the Reverend W. Sherlock, Perpetual Curate of Bray, compiled an edition of the constitutions of the Episcopal Church of America and of the Church in New Zealand, with related material from the Lambeth Conference. This collection was intended specifically for the guidance of those who would be involved in the reconstruction of the Church of Ireland. In addition, Archbishop Trench had Sherlock draw up a book entitled, *Suggestions towards the Organization of the Church of Ireland based on that of the Reformed Episcopal Churches Abroad.* This document was in the hands of the drafting committee and the Church Convention as those bodies proceeded with reconstruction. See C. A. Webster, "The Reconstruction of the Church," in Walter A. Phillips, ed., *History of the Church of Ireland from the earliest times to the present day,* 3:363–64.
24 *Draft of an Act of Constitution,* pp. 5–11.
25 See ibid., pp. 12–25.
26 J. Bromley, *The Man of Ten Talents: A Portrait of Richard Chenevix Trench, 1807–86, Philologist, Poet, Theologian, Archbishop,* p. 194.
27 Ibid., p. 195; Trench, 2:119.
28 See *Draft of an Act of Constitution,* pp. 25–32.
29 George A. Chadwick, "The Disestablished Church of Ireland—II. The Constitution," *The Churchman* 3 (November 1880): 84.
30 See *Draft of An Act of Constitution,* pp. 33–37.
31 Ibid., pp. 38–43.
32 Ibid., pp. 57–75.
33 Richard C. Trench to Thomas C. Trench, 8 December 1869, reproduced in Trench, 2:115.
34 "The Disestablished Church in Ireland," *Fraser's Magazine,* n.s. 6 (August 1872):137.
35 Richard C. Trench to Earl of Courtown, 27 October 1869, reproduced in Trench, 2:108–09.
36 Bromley, p. 195.

37 Lee, *JGC/First,* pp. 6–18.
38 Ibid., pp. 21–36, 187–88.
39 Ibid., pp. 37–40.
40 Ibid., pp. 42–44, 189–90.
41 Ibid., pp. 67, 73, 97–98.
42 R. Babington, *The Irish Churchman's "Vade Mecum," or, A.B.C. of the Statutes and Canons of the Church of Ireland and of the Diocesan Rules of the Dioceses of Derry and Raphoe,* pp. 31–32; Alfred T. Lee, ed., *Journal of the General Convention of the Church of Ireland, Second Session, 1870,* pp. 23 ff; Robert R. Warren, *The Law of the Church of Ireland: An Essay,* pp. 20–85.
43 *Draft of an Act of Constitution,* pp. 44–50.
44 Lee, *JGC/First,* pp. 201–04.
45 Ibid., p. 207; *Draft of an Act of Constitution,* p. 55.
46 *Draft of an Act of Constitution,* pp. 50–53.
47 Lee, *JGC/First,* pp. 204–06.
48 Ibid., pp. 206–07; *Draft of an Act of Constitution,* pp. 53–55.
49 John Healy, *A History of the Diocese of Meath,* 2:219–21.
50 Ibid., 2:228–29.
51 Compiled from F. Maurice Powicke and E. B. Fryde, eds., *Handbook of British Chronology,* pp. 352–79; Healy, 2:228; Henry E. Patton, *Fifty Years of Disestablishment,* pp. 74–88; Henry Seddall, *The Church of Ireland: A Historical Sketch,* pp. 364–66.
52 "The Church of Ireland," *Church Quarterly Review* 29 (January 1885): 476.
53 Healy, 2:206.
54 "Four Years' Experience of Disestablishment—Part III," *Christian Observer and Advocate,* n.s., no. 3 (March 1875), p. 221.
55 Alexander, p. 290.
56 Ibid., p. 33.
57 Ibid., p. 290.
58 J. Duncan Craig, *Real Pictures of Clerical Life in Ireland,* pp. 463–64.
59 Patton, p. 93.
60 The bale of questionnaires is found in the RCB, MS. A14. The replies listed above are those with the largest number of answers. Five hundred and sixteen reply sheets are extant. A large number of respondents did not answer the query about impediments to attracting candidates to the Irish ministry. A scattering of miscellaneous answers was also given.
61 J. P. Mahaffy, "The Romanisation of Ireland," *Nineteenth Century* 50 (July 1901):33.
62 "Four Years' Experience of Disestablishment—Part III," pp. 215–16.
63 Bromley, p. 213.
64 Robert Allen, *The Presbyterian College, Belfast, 1853–1953,* pp. 140–41.
65 32 and 33 Victoria, c. 42; Hugh A. Boyd, "The Cathedral System in the Church of Ireland since the Disestablishment" (B.Litt. thesis), pp. 142–44.
66 Boyd, p. 203; *Weekly Telegraph,* 10 March 1906.
67 Boyd, p. 57.
68 Ibid., pp. 51–52, 213–14.
69 Ibid., pp. 196, 223–28.
70 Ibid., pp. 196, 201–03; *Weekly Telegraph,* 10 March 1906.
71 Boyd, p. 202.

72 Saint Finbar's Cork, consecrated in 1870, was completed by the addition of spires in 1878. The restoration of Christ Church, Dublin, was completed in 1878. Saint Mary's, Tuam, was reopened in the same year after restoration which had begun in 1860. The restoration of Saint Brigid's, Kildare, was begun in 1871, but not completed until 1896. In 1887 Saint Columb's, Derry, and Saint Flannan's, Killaloe, were reopened after restoration. The rebuilding of Armagh cathedral was completed in 1888. Slightly later, Saint Canice's, Kilkenny, underwent renovation.

73 Desmond Bowen, *The Idea of the Victorian Church. A Study of the Church of England, 1833–1889,* p. 121; A. Elliott Peaston, *The Prayer Book Revisions of the Victorian Evangelicals,* passim; C. A. Webster, "The Reconstruction of the Church," in Phillips, 3:381.

74 "Review of Irish Episcopal Charges," *Christian Observer,* n.s., no. 69 (September 1843), pp. 616–17

75 Patton, pp. 27–28.

76 "McV," *The Advantages of Disestablishment by a Lay Delegate,* pp. 5–6.

77 Ibid., p. 20.

78 Richard C. Trench to Mrs. Richard C. Trench, 5 January 1870, quoted in Trench, 2:117.

79 Lee, *Journal of the General Convention of the Church of Ireland, Second Session, 1870,* pp. 14–15, 39, 41, 51–52.

80 This is not the place to go into the details of the committee's deliberations. The committee's printed private papers and are found under the title *Master Brooke's Committee* in the National Library of Ireland (I274108 b2). The material would form the basis of a useful scholarly article on Irish liturgical development.

81 *Report of the Committee appointed by the General Convention of the Church of Ireland on October 31, 1870, pursuant to the motion of the Duke of Abercorn* (Dublin: Hodges, Foster and Co., 1871), pp. 64–88.

82 See Alfred T. Lee, ed., *Journal of the General Synod of the Church of Ireland, First Special Meeting and Session of 1871,* especially pp. 40–55.

83 *Constitutions and Canons Ecclesiastical Agreed to and Decreed by the Archbishops, Bishops, and the Representatives of the Clergy and Laity, of the Church of Ireland at a General Synod held in Dublin in the Year of Our Lord 1871* (Dublin: Hodges, Foster and Co., 1871), passim.

84 See *The Oxford Dictionary of the Christian Church.*

85 *Trench,* 2:142. The fact that some of these dissenting protests were not registered within the one month time limit does not detract from their value as an indication of clerical opinions on the revision controversy.

86 For the bound collection of the private, printed papers of the revision committee (untitled), see the NLI, I26403 c3. For debates in the General Synod on revision, see the debates for 1872–74 (edited by Robert S. Gregg), and for 1875–78 (edited by Morgan W. Jellett).

87 Attention should at once be called to the work of Hugh Shearman, "The Economic Results of the Disestablishment of the Irish Church" (Ph.D. thesis). This is a thorough, scholarly work to which I am very much indebted for details of financial reconstruction.

     A recently published booklet of Shearman's, *How the Church of Ireland Was Disestablished* (Dublin: Church of Ireland Disestablishment Centenary Committee, 1970), is a précis of his doctoral thesis. Although certainly readable and useful, this booklet is too brief to reflect fully the rigorous scholarship of the doctoral work.

Two articles of Shearman's dealing with aspects of the financial reconstruction of the Church of Ireland also have been published: "Irish Church Finances after the Disestablishment," in H. A. Crone et al., eds., *Essays in British and Irish History in Honour of James Eadie Todd*, pp. 278–302; "State-aided Land Purchase under the Disestablishment Act of 1869," *Irish Historical Studies* 4 (March 1944):58–80.

Hereafter when Shearman is cited, the reference is to the unpublished thesis. References to the published articles will give the article's title.

88 *Draft of an Act of Constitution*, pp. 76–84.

89 Ibid., pp. 84–96. A complicated, not entirely competent plan of clergy insurance was also included.

90 Lee, *JGC/First*, pp. 170, 173–74, 176; Shearman, p. 388.

91 Shearman, pp. 302–21; *Weekly Telegraph*, 30 December 1905.

92 Shearman, pp. 269–73.

93 Ibid., pp. 270–73; *Weekly Telegraph*, 30 December 1905.

94 Representative Church Body, *Report of the Proceedings laid before the General Synod of the Church of Ireland at its Second Ordinary Session, 1872*, p. 7.

95 Representative Church Body, *Report of the Proceedings of the Representative Church Body laid before the General Synod of the Church of Ireland at its Third Ordinary Session, 1873*, p. 6.

96 Shearman, pp. 306–07.

97 W. R. Moore, "The Financial System of the Church of Ireland since Disestablishment," in Patton, p. 316; *Weekly Telegraph*, 13 January 1906.

98 At this point a note is in order about the vexed matter of curate annuities and commutation. The church act provided that it was possible in some cases for a man to be appointed a curate up to 1 January 1871, and still be eligible for an annuity, subject to the approval of the Church Temporalities Commissioners. The wording of the act underemphasized the discretionary powers of the Church Temporalities Commissioners, and also made it appear as if an incumbent could simply appoint a curate and have the government support him for life. The result was an increase in the number of curates in the church. Presbyterian critics of the church disestablishment arrangements claimed that four hundred new curates were aded by the church in a vast grab for undeserved government funds (Seddall, pp. 320–21; Shearman, p. 335).

Apparently there was a great curates' scramble, although not to the degree suggested by the more acerbic critics. Shearman's examination of the advertisements in the *Irish Ecclesiastical Gazette* indicates a sharp rise in the advertisements for curates soon after the church act was passed. In some cases curacies were offered to divinity students (Shearman, pp. 337–39). One observer noted the case of a curate appointed "on spec." The terms were that if the Church Temporalities Commissioners granted him an annuity he would have it and stay, otherwise he would be paid nothing and go away (W. Bence Jones, *What Has Been Done in the Irish Church since Disestablishment*, pp. 8–9).

On the eve of the passage of the church act there were 720 curates in the Irish church (including 157 part-time curates and those holding suspended benefices). This number had risen to 921 by 1 January 1871. The figure 921 was the number finally approved as legitimate. In addition, 310 claims for annuities as permanent curates were disallowed (William L. Bernard, *Decisions under the Irish Church Act, 1869*, p. iv). Now, we have no way of knowing precisely how many of those 310 denied claims represented attempts to gain an annuity for a man newly named to a curacy, but a reasonable speculation is that most of them were probably for newly appointed curates. Hence, it appears that the church successfully received annuities for an increment of 201 permanent curates appointed after the passage of Gladstone's church act, and tried, unsuccessfully, to gain annuities for at least as many more new curates.

Did the 201 new permanent curates granted annuities by the Church Temporalities Commissioners represent successful jobbery by the church? No. The Church of Ireland before the disestablishment was probably understaffed in curates. The church had undergone nearly a decade of uncertainty, and local rectors had often been hesitant to hire curates. The best estimate is that the church was probably about 200 curates below its normal complement (Shearman, p. 341; the estimate is based on the situation in the mid-1830s). Hence, the new appointments recognized by the Church Temporalities Commissioners merely replenished this cohort. The Church Temporalities Commissioners were most rigorous in examining each individual claim. Their rejection of roughly a quarter of the claims made is a good indication of their determination to prevent jobbery.

And what about the 310 rejected claims? Were they conscious attempts to defraud the government? Certainly not all of them. A goodly number were a result of the church act's being somewhat unclear. It was easy to misinterpret the act as meaning that any incumbent could gain a government-paid curate simply by appointing him, so many incumbents appointed a curate without realizing that the Church Temporalities Commissioners would critically scrutinize the necessity of the appointment (Shearman, pp. 336–37). Having said this, the fact remains that many clergymen were probably consciously attempting to take advantage of the government, and were willing to come quite close to intentional fraud in their efforts.

99   See Healy, 2:215.
100 Moore in Patton, p. 317; Shearman, pp. 405–11; *Weekly Telegraph,* 3 February 1906.
101 Shearman, pp. 264–65, 351.
102 Ibid., pp. 348–49, 354.
103 Representative Church Body, *Report of the Proceedings of the Representative Church Body laid before the General Synod of the Church of Ireland at its Ninth Ordinary Session, 1879,* p. 9.
104 J. A. Maconchy, "Glebes," in Patton, p. 331.
105 Shearman, p. 402.
106 "Church of Ireland Finance," *Church Quarterly Review* 60 (July 1905): 306–07; Shearman, pp. 419–20.
107 *Draft of an Act of Constitution,* pp. 78–82.
108 Lee, *JGC/First,* Appendix, pp. 57–63. The appeal was (perhaps intentionally) unclear about how many successive years it would be necessary to raise £230,000. Presumably the committee meant that this amount would have to be raised each year until the remaining annuities which had to be paid could be paid out of the interest on the commutation money. In reality, this situation was not reached until the 1890s.
109 Shearman, p. 415.
110 *Census of Ireland, 1881, Part II, General Report,* p. 54 [C. 3365], H.C. 1882, lxxvi.

111 "Four Years Experience of Disestablishment—Part II," *Christian Observer and Advocate*, n.s., no. 2 (February 1875), 117–20; Representative Church Body, *Report of the Proceedings laid before the General Synod of the Church of Ireland at its Second Ordinary Session*, pp. 11–13; Shearman, pp. 403–04, 429–31.

112 Shearman, pp. 432–33.

113 Patton, pp. 87–88.

114 The reader will note that I have (intentionally) omitted discussion of two topics associated with the disestablishment of the Church of Ireland, but not germane to an internal administrative study of this sort. The first of these is the activities of the Church Temporalities Commissioners who were the government's agents in closing out the Established Church. The second topic is the effect of disestablishment upon the Irish economy. Both of these topics are exhaustively treated in Shearman's thesis, and the second is also discussed in considerable detail in his article on state aided land purchase under the Irish Church Act (*Irish Historical Studies*, March 1944).

115 Shearman, pp. 424–25.

116 Moore in Patton, p. 320.

117 Shearman, "Irish Church Finances after the Disestablishment," p. 283.

118 Moore in Patton, p. 320.

119 "Church of Ireland Finance," *Church Quarterly Review* 60 (July 1905): 308.

120 Moore in Patton, pp. 317–18. Amounts less than £1 are ignored.

121 "Church of Ireland Finance," p. 309.

CHAPTER 6

1 The data referred to in this chapter have been presented earlier, with full citation. Hence, notes are here dispensed with.

Bibliography

The preparation of this preface to the formal bibliography reminds me once again how pleasant and rewarding it is to pursue scholarly work concerning the Church of Ireland. The reasons for these positive feelings are fourfold: first, there exist two excellent studies of the church which provide necessary background; second, there is a mass of reasonably reliable—if not always coherently organized—material about the Church of Ireland in the parliamentary papers of the British government; third, the present-day authorities of the Church of Ireland have followed an enlightened policy of maintaining the church's archives in excellent order and of welcoming researchers into those archives; fourth, there are a number of helpful specialist studies of various aspects of the church in thesis form which Irish and English university libraries have generously made available.

The first point above of course refers to the study written by Richard Mant and that edited by Walter A. Phillips. Mant's volume, *History of the Church of Ireland* (1840), is a constant reminder that nineteenth-century scholarship at its best set standards which twentieth-century scholars often fail to achieve. Phillips's three-volume *History of the Church of Ireland from the Earliest Times to the Present Day* (1933) is a composite work, but is so skillfully edited that the three volumes seem to flow from a single hand.

The parliamentary papers provide a mine of information. The researcher must be constantly alert, however, to the attitudes which underlie each report and must be careful to check the statistical procedures and methods of data collection employed; nineteenth-century arithmetic is often more obscure than nineteenth-century prose. The first important public investigations of the Church of Ireland were those published in 1807 and 1820 (items here referred to are listed below, under "Parliamentary Papers," in chronological order). For most students, study of the nineteenth-century church will begin with a mastery of the four reports of the Royal Commissioners on Ecclesiastical Revenue and Patronage, published in 1833, 1834, 1836, and 1837. The findings of the Royal Commission of the 1830s can profitably be compared to the report of the Royal Commission on the Revenues and Conditions of the Established Church in Ireland, which is found in the parliamentary papers for 1867–68. The results of this latter investigation must be read skeptically and in full: the report was a rush-job and corrections to statements made in the body of the report are found in appendixes.

The Church of Ireland maintains two excellent repositories of records. The library of the Representative Church Body in Dublin operates as a full-time library, with professional staff. The Armagh Public Library—which despite its name is not a governmentally operated library—operates on a part-time basis, with special arrangements for visiting scholars being easily concluded. Each library has an excellent and well-cared-for manuscript collection. The Beresford papers, the single most valuable collection for the history of the Church of Ireland in the nineteenth century, are found in the original at Armagh and in copy in Dublin. The other major collection of papers for this period is the British Museum's assemblage of the Gladstone papers.

Of the unpublished theses listed below I would call special attention to Boyd's on the cathedral system, Brynn's on the political history of the Church of Ireland in the first four decades of the nineteenth century, Shearman's on the finances of disestablishment, and Stephen's on Gladstone's church policies.

There is one category of material of which the reader should be very chary. This is the mass of pamphlet literature which begins in the late eighteenth century and which by disestablishment seemed to have become one of Ireland's staple commodities. The value of these pamphlets as sources of raw data is limited since most were written with the idea of promoting a specific controversial viewpoint. Further, simply paraphrasing their contents—to indicate "attitudes" or whatever—is not a profitable exercise. Perhaps the techniques of content-analysis (which have yet to be applied by Irish historians) will someday be applied to this huge body of material; certainly an analytic study that would replace the impressionistic discussions presently available would help clarify our knowledge of nineteenth-century Irish religious behavior.

With the exception of some important items, only works cited directly in the text are included in the bibliography that follows.

MANUSCRIPT MATERIAL

The following archives have provided useful manuscript material (the specific citation of individual articles is given in the text):
Armagh Public Library
British Museum, London
Dublin City Library
National Library of Ireland, Dublin
Public Record Office of Northern Ireland, Belfast
Public Record Office, Republic of Ireland, Dublin
Library of Queen's University, Belfast
Library of the Representative Church Body, Dublin
County Record Office, Stafford
Library of Trinity College, Dublin

Unpublished Theses

Acheson, Alan R. "The Evangelicals in the Church of Ireland, 1784–1859." Ph.D. thesis, Queen's University, Belfast, 1967.

Binns, June R. "A History of Methodism in Ireland from Wesley's Death in 1791 to the Re-Union of Primitives and Wesleyans in 1878." M.A. thesis, Queen's University, Belfast, 1960.

Boyd, Hugh A. "The Cathedral System in the Church of Ireland since the Disestablishment." B.Litt. thesis, Trinity College, Dublin, 1950.

Brynn, Edward P. "A Political History of the Church of Ireland, 1800–1841." M.Litt. thesis, Trinity College, Dublin, 1968.

Coolidge, Charles W. "The Finance of the Church of England, 1830–1880." Ph.D. thesis, Trinity College, Dublin, 1958.

Kennedy, Raymond. "The Administration of the Diocese of Dublin and Glendalough in the Eighteenth Century." Ph.D. thesis, Trinity College, Dublin, 1968.

Lundeen, Thomas B. "The Bench of Bishops: A Study of the Secular Activities of the Bishops of the Church of England and of Ireland, 1801–1871." Ph.D. thesis, University of Iowa, 1963.

McCracken, John L. "Central and Local Administration in Ireland under George II." Ph.D. thesis, Queen's University, Belfast, 1948.

Milne, Kenneth. "The Irish Corporations in the Eighteenth Century." Ph.D. thesis, Trinity College, Dublin, 1962.

Patterson, Robert L. "The Crisis of the Unreformed Church of England, 1828–1833." Ph.D. thesis, Yale University, 1960.

Scott, Alfred R. "The Ulster Revival of 1859." Ph.D. thesis, Trinity College, Dublin, 1962.

Shearman, Hugh. "The Economic Results of the Disestablishment of the Irish Church." Ph.D. thesis, Trinity College, Dublin, 1944.

Stephen, J. F. M. D. "Gladstone and the Anglican Church in Ireland and England, 1868–1874." M.Litt. thesis, Cambridge University, 1955.

Parliamentary Papers

(The order of listing is chronological.)

Papers relating to the Established Church in Ireland, H.C. 1807 (78), v.

Reports from the Commissioners of the Board of Education in Ireland.

First, on Free Schools of Royal Foundation, H.C. 1809 (142), vii.

Second, on Schools of Private Foundation, H.C. 1809 (142), vii.

Third, on Protestant Charter Schools, H.C. 1809 (142), vii.

Fourth, on Diocesan Free Schools, H.C. 1810 (174), x.

Fifth, on Wilson's Hospital, H.C. 1810 (175), x.

Sixth, on the Blue Coat Hospital, H.C. 1810 (176), x.

Seventh, on the Hibernian School, H.C. 1810 (177), x.

Eighth, on the Foundling Hospital, H.C. 1810 (193), x.

Ninth, on Schools founded by Erasmus Smith, Esq., H.C. 1810 (194), x.

Tenth, on the Hibernian Marine School, H.C. 1810 (243), x.

Eleventh, on Parish Schools, 1810–11 (107), vi.

Twelfth, on Classical Schools of Private Foundation, H.C. 1812 (218), v.

Thirteenth, on English Schools of Private Foundation, H.C. 1812 (219), v.

Fourteenth, View of the Chief Foundations, with some general Remarks, H.C. 1812–13 (21), vi. The fourteen reports reprinted, H.C. 1813–14 (47), v.

A Bill for explaining and clearing up certain Doubts respecting the Scites of Parish Churches within Ireland, H.C. 1812–13 (157), i.

A Bill to amend and explain an Act passed in the Parliament of Ireland, in the 39th year of his late Majesty, to enable certain Persons to recover a just Compensation for the Tithes withheld from them in the years 1797 and 1798, H.C. 1820 (145), i.

Papers relating to the State of the Established Church of Ireland, H.C. 1820 (93), ix.

Estimate of the Expense of Building Churches and Glebe Houses and for Purchasing Glebes in Ireland, for One Year, Ending the 5th January 1821, H.C. 1820 (207), ix.

A Bill to amend the Laws for collecting Church Rates and Money, advanced by the Trustees and Commissioners of the First Fruits of Ecclesiastical Benefices in Ireland, H.C. 1823 (87), i.

A Bill to make provision for the facilitating the Commutation of Tithes in Ireland, by Ecclesiastical Persons and others entitled thereto, H.C. 1823 (170), ii.

A Bill to provide for the establishing of Compositions for Tithes in Ireland, for a time to be limited, H.C. 1823 (152), ii.

A Bill (as Amended by the Committee) to provide for the establishing of Compositions for Tithes in Ireland, for a time to be limited, H.C. 1823 (363), ii.

A Bill (as Amended on Recommitment) to provide for the establishing of Compositions for Tithes in Ireland, for a time to be limited, H.C. 1823 (480), ii.

A Bill for uniting the Parishes of Kilternan and Kilgobban, situated in the Barony of Rathdown, and County of Dublin, in Ireland, H.C. 1823 (490), ii.

Accounts relating to the Church Establishment of Ireland, H.C. 1823 (135), xvi.

Accounts relating to the Church Establishment of Ireland, H.C. 1823 (241), xvi.

A Return of the Number of Applications for Special Vestries, under the Tithe Composition Act; with the Number of Cases in which Commissioners have been appointed, and the Number in which the Vestries have adjourned sine die, H.C. 1824 (19), xxi.

An Account of the Names and Description of all Parishes in Ireland, from which Memorials have been forwarded to the Lord Lieutenant, separately, for holding Vestries or taking any other Proceedings under the Tithe Composition Act of last Session, etc., H.C. 1824 (173), xxi.

A Return of the Number of Applications for Special Vestries under the Tithe Composition Act, etc., H.C. 1824 (178), xxi.

Returns of any Instances which may have occurred, wherein the Archbishops or Bishops have refused their Assent to the Agreements entered into between the Incumbents and Parishioners in Vestry assembled, under the Tithe Composition Act, H.C. 1824 (284), xxi.

Statement of the Number of Acres belonging to the Church of Ireland; Distinguishing such as form part of Glebe Lands, and distinguishing such as are Uncultivated, H.C. 1824 (402), xxi.

A List of the Parishes in Ireland, with the names of their respective Incumbents; and distinguishing those Parishes in which the Incumbent is not resident; also a Statement of the number of Acres belonging to the Church in Ireland, distinguishing such as form part of Glebe Lands, and distinguishing such as are Uncultivated, H.C. 1824 (436), xxi.

A Return of the Number of Parishes, and of the Number of Benefices, in each Diocese in Ireland; stating, the Number of Benefices in the gift or patronage of the Archbishop or Bishop of each Diocese; the Number in the gift of the Crown, the Number in the gift of the Universities, the Number in the gift of Lay Proprietors, and the Number Impropriate, or without Churches or Incumbents, H.C. 1824 (438), xxi.

Statement of the Number of Acres belonging to the Church in Ireland; distinguishing such as form part of Glebe Lands, and distinguishing such as are Uncultivated, H.C. 1824 (462), xxi.

A Return of the Number of Parishes and of the Number of Benefices, in each Diocese in Ireland; stating, the Number of Benefices in the gift or patronage of the Archbishop or Bishop of each Diocese; the Number in the gift of the Crown, the Number in the gift of the Universities, the Number in the gift of Lay Proprietors, and the Number Impropriate or without Churches or Incumbents, H.C. 1824 (463), xxi.

A Bill to alter and amend the law relating to Church Rates, Ireland, and to regulate the same, H.C. 1825 (79), iii.

First Report of the Commissioners of Irish Education Inquiry, H.C. 1825 (400), xii.

A Bill to consolidate and Amend the laws which regulate the levy and application of Church Rates in Ireland, H.C. 1826 (115), ii.

A Bill (as Amended by the Committee) to consolidate and Amend the laws which regulate the levy and application of Church Rates in Ireland, H.C. 1826 (256), ii.

An Account of the Number of Faculties or Dispensations which have in each of the last Ten Years been granted in Ireland, for the purpose of enabling Ecclesiastical Persons to hold more than one Benefice, and of the Rules and Regulations under which such Faculties are now granted, H.C. 1830 (279), xix.

Report of His Majesty's Commissioners of Ecclesiastical Inquiry, Ireland, H.C. 1831 (93), ix.

Copies of the Case and Opinions of the Law Officers of the Crown in Ireland, on the subject of Re-valuation of the Benefices to the First Fruits Fund, as taken on an Address to His Majesty of the 14th of March last, H.C. 1831 (195), xv.

A Bill to facilitate the Recovery of Tithes in certain cases in Ireland, and for Relief of the Clergy of the Established Church, H.C. 1831–32 (346), iv.

A Bill to amend an Act of the Seventh and Eighth years of the reign of His late Majesty King George the Fourth, relating to the Union of Parishes in Ireland, H.C. 1831–32 (532), iv.

A Bill to amend Three Acts passed respectively in the Fourth, Fifth and in the Seventh and Eighth Years of the Reign of his late Majesty King George the Fourth, providing for the establishing of Compositions for Tithes in Ireland; and to make such Compositions permanent, H.C. 1831–32 (599), iv.

Report from the Select Committee on Tithes in Ireland, H.C. 1831–32 (177), xxi.

Second Report from the Select Committee on Tithes in Ireland, H.C. 1831–32 (508), xxi.

Minutes of Evidence taken before the Select Committee of the House of Lords appointed to inquire into the Collection and Payment of Tithes in Ireland, and the State of the Laws relating thereto, H.C. 1831–32 (271), xxii.

Second Report from the Select Committee of the House of Lords appointed to inquire into the Collection and Payment of Tithes in Ireland, and the State of the Laws relating thereto, H.C. 1831–32 (663), xxii.

Church Temporalities (Ireland) Bill. Schedule (A), H.C. 1833 (57), i.

A Bill to alter and amend the Laws relating to the Temporalities of the Church in Ireland, H.C. 1833 (59), i.

A Bill to alter and amend the Laws relating to the Temporalities of the Church in Ireland, H.C. 1833 (210), i.

A Bill (as Amended by the Committee) to alter and amend the Laws relating to the Temporalities of the Church in Ireland, H.C. 1833 (431), i.

Amendments Made by the Lords to the Bill, intitled, an Act to alter and amend the Laws relating to the Temporalities of the Church in Ireland, H.C. 1833 (594), i.

A Bill for the Relief of the Owners of Tithes in Ireland, and for the Amendment of an Act passed in the last Session of Parliament intitled, "An Act to amend Three Acts passed respectively in the Fourth, Fifth, and Seventh and Eighth years of the reign of His late Majesty King George the Fourth, providing for the establishing of Compositions for Tithes in Ireland, and to make such Compositions permanent," H.C. 1833 (641), iv.

A Bill (as Amended by the Committee) for the Relief of the Owners of Tithes in Ireland, and for the Amendment of an Act passed in the last Session of Parliament intitled, "An Act to amend Three Acts passed respectively in the Fourth, Fifth, and Seventh and Eighth years of the reign of His late Majesty King George the Fourth, providing for the establishing of Compositions for Tithes in Ireland, and to make such Compositions permanent," H.C. 1833 (665), iv.

First Report of His Majesty's Commissioners on Ecclesiastical Revenue and Patronage, Ireland, H.C. 1833 (762), xxi.

Church of Ireland. Resolutions to be proposed by Lord Viscount Althorp, H.C. 1833 (31), xxvii.

Clergy Residence. Ordered by the House of Commons to be Printed 28 February 1833, H.C. 1833 (35), xxvii.

Church Temporalities, Ireland. Resolutions intended to be moved by Mr. Halcomb before going into Committee, H.C. 1833 (64), xxvii.

An Account of the Respective Values of the Several Benefices in the Different Dioceses in Ireland, H.C. 1833 (265), xxvii.

A Return of the present Rates of Renewal Fines on Bishops' Leases in the several Dioceses in the Kingdom of Ireland; specifying in each Diocese the Principle upon which the Calculation of the Renewal Fine is founded; also, stating the Number of Leases in each Diocese which have Expired from 1st January 1800 to 1st January 1833, H.C. 1833 (381), xxvii.

Church Rates, Youghal, H.C. 1833 (383), xxvii.

An Account of all Benefices in Ireland in which Divine Service, according to the Forms of the United Church of England and Ireland has not been celebrated within the Three Years ending 12th February 1833, H.C. 1833 (399), xxvii.

A Return of all the Number of Churches in each Benefice or Union in Ireland; specifying the Number of Parishes, if more than one, in each such Benefice; and also, in each case of more Parishes than one, stating the Distance from the nearest Boundary of any Parish not having a Church in itself to the Church; and also stating the Distance from the most remote Boundary of every such Parish to the Church, H.C. 1833 (400), xxvii.

Tithes, Ireland, H.C. 1833 (441), xxvii.

Tithes, Cork, H.C. 1833 (471), xxvii.

Tithes (Ireland) Act. Extracts from Returns to several Orders of the Honourable House of Commons, dated 13 February and 24 May 1833, H.C. 1833 (479), xxvii.

Tithes (Ireland) Act. Extracts from Returns to several Orders of the Honourable House of Commons, dated 24 May 1833, H.C. 1833 (480), xxvii.

An Account of all Benefices in Ireland in which Divine Service, according to the Forms of the United Church of England and Ireland, has not been celebrated, within the Three Years ending 12th February 1833, H.C. 1833 (491), xxvii.

A Return of the Arrears of Tithes due in the several Dioceses of Ireland, from 1st May 1829, H.C. 1833 (509), xxvii.

Tithes, Ireland. Return to an Order of the Honourable House of Commons, dated 21 May 1833, H.C. 1833 (511), xxvii.

A Return of the Numbers of Churches in each Benefice or Union in Ireland; specifying the Number of Parishes, if more than one, in each such Benefice; and also, in each case of more Parishes than one, stating the Distance from the nearest Boundary of any Parish not having a Church in itself to the Church, and also stating the Distance from the most remote boundary of every such Parish to the Church—so far as relates to the Diocese of Limerick, Ardfert and Aghadoe, and Kildare, H.C. 1833 (521), xxvii.

An Account of the Advances made from the Consolidated Fund in Ireland for paying the Commissioners appointed on behalf of the Incumbents and Parishes for establishing a Composition for Tithes, and also the Repayments into the exchequer on account of said Advances, pursuant to 4 Geo. IV. c. 99 (in British Currency), H.C. 1833 (523), xxvii.

An Abstract of the Amounts of Gross and Net Incomes of Parochial Benefices in Ireland, taken from the Returns made to His Majesty's Commissioners for inquiring into Ecclesiastical Revenues and Patronage, H.C. 1833 (651), xxvii.

Curates, Ireland, H.C. 1833 (721), xxvii.

A Bill to amend an Act made in the Third and Fourth year of the Reign of His present Majesty intitled, "An Act to alter and amend the Laws relating to the Temporalities of the Church of Ireland," H.C. 1834 (308), i.

A Bill (as Amended by the Committee) to amend an Act made in the Third and Fourth year of the Reign of His present Majesty, intitled, "An

Act to alter and amend the Laws relating to the Temporalities of the Church of Ireland," H.C. 1834 (496), i.

Irish Tithe Bill. Clauses intended to be proposed in the Committee by Mr. Littleton, H.C. 1834 (57), iv.

A Bill to abolish compositions for Tithes in Ireland, and to substitute in lieu thereof a Land Tax, and to provide for the Redemption of the same, H.C. 1834 (60), iv.

Irish Tithe Bill. Clauses intended to be substituted in the committee for Clause 122, H.C. 1834 (69), iv.

A Bill (as Amended by the Committee) to abolish Compositions for Tithes in Ireland, and to substitute in lieu thereof a Land Tax, and to provide for the Redemption of the same, H.C. 1834 (286), iv.

A Bill (as Amended on Re-commitment) to abolish Compositions for Tithes in Ireland, and to substitute in lieu thereof a Land Tax, and to provide for the Redemption of the same, H.C. 1834 (545), iv.

Second Report from His Majesty's Commissioners for inquiring into the Unions of Parochial Benefices in Ireland, H.C. 1834 (406), xxiii.

Second Report of His Majesty's Commissioners on Ecclesiastical Revenue and Patronage, Ireland, H.C. 1834 (523), xxiii.

Resolutions respecting the Irish Church to be Proposed by Mr. Ward, on Tuesday, 27 May 1834, H.C. 1834 (35), xliii.

A Copy of the Correspondence between the Irish Government and Magistrates of the Parishes of Glanntane and Kilshannick, previously to a Police Force being appointed in the present Year, for the protection of Persons employed in the Collection of Tithe in the above Parishes; Also a Copy of the Memorial of the Rev. Mr. O'Keeffe upon the Subject, and a Copy of Mr. Littleton's Answer thereto, H.C. 1834 (109), xliii.

Tithe Compositions, Ireland, H.C. 1834 (309), xliii.

Irish Church Bill. Clauses and Amendments to be proposed by Mr. Bingham Baring in the Committee, H.C. 1835 (84), ii.

Church of Ireland Bill. Clauses 9, 10, 11, 12, 13, and 14, As proposed to be amended, H.C. 1835 (86), ii.

A Bill for the better Regulation of Ecclesiastical Revenues, and the promotion of Religious and Moral Instruction in Ireland, H.C. 1835 (360), ii.

First Report of the Ecclesiastical Commissioners under the Act 3 & 4 Wm. IV, relating to the Temporalities of the Church in Ireland, dated 9th August 1834, H.C. 1835 (113), xxii.

Clergy Residence (Ireland), H.C. 1835 (81), xlvii.

A Return of all the Clergymen now in the Commission of the Peace in Ireland; distinguishing those belonging to the Established Church, the Catholic Church, and the various Congregations of Dissenters, H.C. 1835 (102), xlvii.

Copy of the Correspondence between the Reverend Thomas Locke, Rector of Newcastle, in the County of Limerick, and the Chief or Under Secretary for Ireland, from the Month of February, 1834 to the present time, relative to the Collection of Tithes payable to Mr. Locke; and also of any Correspondence on that subject during the same period between the Chief or Under Secretary for Ireland and the Commander of the Forces, or any Magistrate or Officers of Police in the Limerick District, H.C. 1835 (119), xlvii.

Church Temporalities (Ireland) Act. Return to an Order of the Honourable House of Commons, dated 25 March 1835, H.C. 1835 (169), xlvii.

Copy of the Proceedings of an Investigation held at Armagh, of the Transactions which took place in the Neighborhood of Keady, between the Police and Country People, on collecting an arrear of Tithe due to the Reverend James Blacker, wherein one Man was killed and several wounded; with a Copy of the Inquest, and all other Documents connected with that Transaction, H.C. 1835 (179), xlvii.

Suspended Benefices (Ireland), H.C. 1835 (382), xlvii.

Parochial Benefices (Ireland), H.C. 1835 (388), xlvii.

Tithe Composition, Ireland. Returns to an Order of the Honourable the House of Commons, dated 7 April 1835, H.C. 1835 (405), xlvii.

Ecclesiastical Commission, Ireland. Return to several Orders of the Honourable the House of Commons, dated 31 July 1835, H.C. 1835 (460), xlvii.

A Calculation of the Incomes of the Archbishops, Bishops, Dignitaries, and Parochial Clergy of Ireland, before the Church Temporalities Act, under the Church Temporalities Act, and under the proposed Bill for the better regulation of Ecclesiastical Revenues, and the promotion of Religious and Moral Instruction in Ireland, H.C. 1835 (461), xlvii.

A Bill for the better Regulation of Ecclesiastical Revenues, and the Promotion of Religious and Moral Instruction in Ireland, H.C. 1836 (218), i.

A Bill (as Amended on the Report) for the better Regulation of Ecclesiastical Revenues, and the Promotion of Religious and Moral Instruction in Ireland, H.C. 1836 (432), i.

A Bill to amend two Acts, passed respectively in the third and fourth and in the fourth and fifth Years of His present Majesty, for altering and amending the Laws relating to the Temporalities of the Church of Ireland, H.C. 1836 (466), i.

A Bill (as Amended by the Lords) intitled An Act for the better Regulation of Ecclesiastical Revenues in Ireland, H.C. 1836 (498), i.

A Bill (as Amended by the Lords) intitled, An Act to amend two Acts, passed respectively in the third and fourth, and in the fourth and fifth Years of His present Majesty, for altering and amending the Laws re-

lating to the Temporalities of the Church of Ireland, H.C. 1836 (578), i.

Report of the Ecclesiastical Commissioners for Ireland, for the Year ending 1 August 1835, H.C. 1836 (130), xxv.

Third Report of His Majesty's Commissioners on Ecclesiastical Revenue and Patronage in Ireland, H.C. 1836 (246), xxv.

Tithes Composition (Ireland), H.C. 1836 (5), xl.

Clergy (Ireland). Return to an Order of the Honourable The House of Commons, dated 24 March 1835, H.C. 1836 (355), xl.

Tithes, Ireland. Return to an Order of the Honourable The House of Commons, dated 18 February 1836, H.C. 1836 (420), xl.

Ecclesiastical Commission (Ireland). Return to an Order of the Honourable The House of Commons, dated 16 May 1836, H.C. 1836 (485), xl.

A Bill for the better Regulation of Ecclesiastical Revenues, and the Promotion of Religious and Moral Instruction in Ireland, H.C. 1837 (283), i.

Report from the Select Committee appointed to inquire into the State of the Prerogative and Ecclesiastical Courts in Ireland, H.C. 1837 (412), vi.

Copy of the Report of the Ecclesiastical Commissioners of Ireland, to His Excellency the Lord Lieutenant, dated 8 August 1836, H.C. 1837 (100), xxi.

Fourth Report of His Majesty's Commissioners on Ecclesiastical Revenue and Patronage in Ireland, H.C. 1837 (500), xxi.

Churches, Ireland, H.C. 1837 (306), xli.

A Bill to amend an Act passed in the Parliament of Ireland in the Tenth and Eleventh Years of His Majesty King Charles the First, for the Preservation of the Inheritance, Rights and Profits of Lands belonging to the Church and Persons Ecclesiastical, H.C. 1837–38 (41), i.

A Bill to consolidate the Jurisdiction of the several Ecclesiastical Courts in Ireland into One Court, and to enlarge the Powers and Authorities of such Courts; and to alter and amend the Law in certain Matters Ecclesiastical, H.C. 1837–38 (227), iii.

A Bill to encourage and facilitate the Purchase of Perpetuities by the Leasees of Church Lands in Ireland, H.C. 1837–38 (595), v.

Report from the Select Committee on Foundation Schools and Education in Ireland, H.C. 1837–38 (701), vii.

Tithes in Ireland. Resolutions intended to be Proposed by Lord John Russell, H.C. 1837–38 (73), xxxviii.

Ecclesiastical Commission (Ireland). Return to an Order of the Honourable The House of Commons, dated 25 January 1838, H.C. 1837–38 (142), xxxviii.

Tithes, Ireland. Returns to Orders of the Honourable The House of Commons dated 21 April and 1 December 1837, H.C. 1837–38 (253), xxxviii.

Dublin Curates, H.C. 1837–38 (582), xxxviii.

Ministers' Money (Ireland), H.C. 1837–38 (730), xxxviii.

A Bill to abolish Compositions for Tithes in Ireland, and to substitute Rent-charges in lieu thereof, H.L. 1838 (305), iv.

A Bill to consolidate the Jurisdiction of the several Ecclesiastical Courts in Ireland into one Court, and to enlarge the Powers and Authorities of such Court, and to alter and amend the Law in certain matters Ecclesiastical, H.C. 1839 (343), iii.

The Annual Report of the Ecclesiastical Commissioners of Ireland, to the Lord Lieutenant, dated 13 August, 1838, H.C. 1839 (196), xvi.

A Bill to amend Three Acts of the Reign of his late Majesty for altering and amending the Laws relating to the Temporalities of the Church in Ireland, H.C. 1840 (492), i.

A Bill to alter and amend the Law regarding Process upon Contempts in the Courts Ecclesiastical in England and Ireland, and to facilitate the Discharge of Persons who now are or hereafter may be in Custody for Contempts of any such Courts, H.C. 1840 (569), ii.

A Bill to amend an Act of the First and Second Years of the Reign of Her present Majesty, to abolish Compositions for Tithes in Ireland, and to substitute rent-charges in lieu thereof, H.C. 1840 (139), iii.

The Annual Report of the Ecclesiastical Commissioners of Ireland, to the Lord Lieutenant, dated 12 August 1839, H.C. 1840 (111), xxviii.

A Return of the Names of the Ecclesiastical Commissioners for Ireland, who have attended each of the Meetings of the Board held during the Years 1838, 1839 and 1840 respectively; distinguishing the Unpaid from the Paid Commissioners, H.C. 1840 (591), xxxix.

A Bill to facilitate the Recovery of Arrears of Tithe Compositions in Ireland, vested in Her Majesty, under the Provisions of an Act of the First and Second Years of Her present Majesty, for abolishing Compositions for Tithes in Ireland, and for substituting Rent-charges in lieu thereof, H.C. 1841 (27), iii.

A Bill for the more easy Recovery of Arrears of Compositions for tithes from Persons of the Persuasion of the People called Quakers in Ireland, H.C. 1841 (355), iii.

The Annual Report of the Ecclesiastical Commissioners of Ireland to the Lord Lieutenant, dated 15 August 1842, H.C. 1843 (137), xxviii.

A Return of the Manner in which the Sum of £6,313, expended as Salaries to Commissioners and Officers of the Ecclesiastical Commissioners of Ireland, in the Year ended the 1st day of August 1842, was expended stating the Names of the Commissioners, and the Amount paid as Salary to each of them, and to each of the Officers of the Commission, H.C. 1843 (204), l.

St. Nicholas' Church (Dublin), H.C. 1844 (59), xliii.

Churches and Chapels (Ireland), H.C. 1844 (190), xliii.

Tithes (Ireland). Return to the Order of the Honourable The House of Commons, dated 27 March 1844, H.C. 1844 (305), xliii.

Copy of the Correspondence between the Lord Lieutenant and the Irish Ecclesiastical Commissioners, in reference to the Application of a Portion of the Perpetuity Fund to the Building and Repairing of Churches in Ireland, H.C. 1845 (621), xlv.

Copy of the Correspondence between the Lord Lieutenant of Ireland and the Irish Ecclesiastical Commissioners, in reference to the Application of a Portion of the Perpetuity Fund to the Building and Repairing of Churches in Ireland, H.C. 1846 (484), xlii.

A Bill intitled An Act to alter and amend several Acts relating to the Temporalities of the Church in Ireland, H.L. 1847 (193), iii.

A Bill intitled An Act to amend the Laws relating to the Ecclesiastical Unions and Divisions of Parishes in Ireland, H.L. 1847–48 (163), iv.

A Bill (as Amended in Committee) intitled An Act to amend the Laws relating to the Ecclesiastical Unions and Divisions of Parishes in Ireland, H.L. 1847–48 (196), iv.

Ecclesiastical Unions and Divisions of Parishes (Ireland). Clause proposed to be added on Report. Suggested by Archdeacon Beresford, H.L. 1847–48 (196a), iv.

A Bill intitled An Act to enable Archbishops and Bishops and other Persons in Ireland to compromise Suits touching their Rights of Patronage as to Ecclesiastical Benefices, in certain Cases, H.L. 1847–48 (216), iv.

Report from the Select Committee on Ministers' Money (Ireland), H.C. 1847–48 (559), xxiii.

Ecclesiastical Courts (Ireland), H.C. 1850 (642), li.

A Bill intitled An Act to consolidate and Amend the Laws relating to the Erection and Endowment of Churches and Chapels and Perpetual Curacies in Ireland, H.L. 1851 (218), iii.

A Bill (with Amendments made in Committee) intitled An Act to consolidate and amend the Laws relating to the Erection and Endowment of Churches and Chapels and Perpetual Curacies in Ireland, H.L. 1851 (274), iii.

A Bill intitled An Act to amend an Act of the Eleventh and Twelfth Years of Her Majesty, relating to Poor Rate Poundage and the Valuation of Ecclesiastical Property in Ireland; and to provide for the Renewal of Leases of Lands disappropriated from Bishoprics, H.L. 1851 (201), iv.

A Bill intitled An Act to consolidate and amend the Laws relating to Ecclesiastical Residences in Ireland, H.L. 1851 (217), iv.

A Bill (with the Amendments made in Committee) intitled An Act to consolidate and amend the Laws relating to Ecclesiastical Residences in Ireland, H.L. 1851 (275), iv.

A Bill intitled An Act to repeal certain Statutes relating to the Irish Branch of the United Church of England and Ireland, H.L. 1851 (219), vi.

The Report of the Ecclesiastical Commissioners for Ireland, for the Year ending the 1st day of August 1851, H.C. 1852 (23), xviii.

The Report of the Ecclesiastical Commissioners for Ireland, for the Year ending the 1st day of August 1852, H.C. 1852–53 (3), xli.

A Bill to Alter and improve the Mode of taking Evidence in the Ecclesiastical Courts of England and Ireland, H.C. 1854 (105), ii.

The Report of the Ecclesiastical Commissioners for Ireland, for the Year ending the 1st day of August 1853, H.C. 1854 (31), xx.

A Return for all Lands and Houses belonging to the Established Church in Ireland, setting forth the Name of each Diocese, the Situation and Extent of all such Lands and Houses, Rents payable out of same, whether held by Incumbents or leased to others, H.C. 1854 (499), lviii.

A Bill to Provide that the Property or Income Tax payable in respect of the Income from Ecclesiastical Property in Ireland shall be a Deduction in estimating the Value of such Property for the Purpose of Taxation by the Ecclesiastical Commissioners, H.C. 1854–55 (48), ii.

The Report of the Ecclesiastical Commissioners for Ireland, for the Year ending the 1st day of August 1854, H.C. 1854–55 (9), xvi.

The Report of the Ecclesiastical Commissioners for Ireland, for the Year ending the 1st day of August 1855, H.C. 1856 (50), xix.

Annual Report and Account of the Ecclesiastical Commissioners for Ireland, for the Year ending the 1st day of August 1856, H.C. 1857 (13), iv.

A Bill further To amend the Law relating to the Erection and Endowment of Churches, Chapels, and Perpetual Curacies in Ireland, H.C. 1857–58 (17), i.

A Bill further to Amend the Law relating to Ecclesiastical Residences in Ireland, H.C. 1857–58 (16), ii.

A Bill (as Amended in Committee) further To amend the Law relating to Ecclesiastical Residences in Ireland, H.C. 1857–58 (78), ii.

Annual Report and Account of the Ecclesiastical Commissioners for Ireland, for the Year ending the 1st day of August 1857, H.C. 1857–58 (10), xxvi.

Annual Report and Account of the Ecclesiastical Commissioners for Ireland, for the Year ending the 1st day of August 1858, H.C. 1859 (18), xii.

A Bill intitled An Act further to amend certain Acts relating to the Temporalities of the Church in Ireland, H.C. 1860 (227), ii.

Annual Report and Account of the Ecclesiastical Commissioners for Ireland, for the Year ending the 1st day of August 1859, H.C. 1860 (22), xxxi.

Annual Report and Account of the Ecclesiastical Commissioners for Ireland, for the Year ending the 1st day of August 1860, H.C. 1861 (4), xviii.

Annual Report and Account of the Ecclesiastical Commissioners for Ireland, for the Year ending the 1st day of August 1861, H.C. 1862 (228), xix.

A Bill to Amend the Law relating to District Parochial Churches in Ireland, H.C. 1863 (122), ii.

Lords Amendments to the District Parochial Churches (Ireland) Bill, H.C. 1863 (249), ii.

Annual Report and Account of the Ecclesiastical Commissioners for Ireland, for the Year ended the 1st day of August 1862, H.C. 1863 (167), xv.

A Return showing the Number of Members of the Established Church in each Diocese in Ireland, in the Years 1834 and 1861 respectively; together with the present Amount of the Revenues of the Established Church in each such Diocese, including the Sums paid on its Account during the Year 1861, out of the Funds administered by the Irish Ecclesiastical Commissioners, H.C. 1863 (204), xlvi.

A Copy of any Memorials to Her Majesty from the Irish Prelates presented during 1861 and 1862, relating to Synodical Action in Ireland; and Copy or Extracts or Correspondence relating thereto, H.C. 1863 (258), xlvi.

Roman Catholics and Members of Established Church (Ireland), H.C. 1863 (289), l.

The Census of Ireland for the Year 1861, Part IV, Report and Tables Relating to Religious Professions, Education and Occupation of the People, vol. I [3204–III], H.C. 1863, lix.

Annual Report and Account of the Ecclesiastical Commissioners for Ireland, for the Year ended the 1st day of August 1863, H.C. 1864 (334), xviii.

Established Church, etc. (Ireland). Returns to an Order of the Honourable The House of Commons, dated 5 May 1863, H.C. 1864 (56), xliv.

Established Church, etc. (Ireland). Return to an Order of the Honourable The House of Commons, dated 9 February 1864, H.C. 1864 (267), xliv.

A Return from the Ecclesiastical Commissioners of Ireland of the Number of Benefices of the Established Church in which the Emolument exceeds £200 per Annum, but does not exceed £250, £300, and £400 per Annum respectively, H.C. 1864 (273), xliv.

Convocation (Ireland). Return to an Address of the Honourable The House of Commons, dated 21 July 1864, H.C. 1864 (562), xliv.

Annual Report and Account of the Ecclesiastical Commissioners for Ire-

land, for the Year ended the 1st day of August 1864, H.C. 1865 (268), xv.

Clonpriest, etc. Benefices. Return to an Order of the Honourable The House of Commons, dated 14 February 1865, H.C. 1865 (117), xli.

A Bill to Validate certain Orders made by the Lord Lieutenant in Council under the Church Temporalities Acts in Ireland, H.C. 1866 (134), i.

Annual Report and Account of the Ecclesiastical Commissioners for Ireland, for the Year ended the 1st day of August 1865, H.C. 1866 (347), xxiii.

A Bill to Amend the Law which regulates the Burials of Persons in Ireland not belonging to the Established Church, H.C. 1867 (109), i.

A Bill to Validate certain Orders made by the Lord Lieutenant in Council under the Church Temporalities Acts in Ireland, and to increase the Stipends payable by the Ecclesiastical Commissioners for Ireland to certain Incumbents in Ireland, H.C. 1867 (267), i.

Churches, etc. (Ireland). Return to Two Orders of the Honourable The House of Commons, dated 20 March and 27 June 1867, H.C. 1867 (476), liv.

Annual Report and Account of the Ecclesiastical Commissioners for Ireland for the Year ended the 1st day of August 1866, H.C. 1867 (371), xx.

A Bill to Amend the Law which regulates the Burials of Persons in Ireland not belonging to the Established Church, H.C. 1867–68 (5), i.

Lords Amendments to the Burial (Ireland) Bill, H.C. 1867–68 (251), i.

A Bill (as Amended in Committee), to Amend the Law which regulates the Burials of Persons in Ireland not belonging to the Established Church, H.C. 1867–68 (294), i.

A Bill to Prevent, for a limited Time, new Appointments in the Church of Ireland, and to restrain, for the same Period, in certain respects, the Proceedings of the Ecclesiastical Commissioners for Ireland, H.C. 1867–68 (117), ii.

Annual Report and Account of the Ecclesiastical Commissioners for Ireland, for the Year ended the 1st day of August 1867, H.C. 1867–68 (379), xxiii.

A Copy of the Commission issued by Her Majesty under the Great Seal for Inquiring into the Revenues and Other Matters relating to the Established Church in Ireland, [3956], H.C. 1867–68, xxiv.

Report of Her Majesty's Commissioners on the Revenues and Condition of the Established Church (Ireland), [4082], H.C. 1867–68, xxiv.

Copy of the Declaration of the Roman Catholic Laity of Ireland sent by the Earl of Fingall to the Chief Secretary for Ireland, H.C. 1867–68 (161), liii.

Copy of Observations on Dr. Maziere Brady's letter to "The Times," of the 26th day of March 1866 by the Irish Ecclesiastical Commissioners, together with any Replies to the Observations addressed to the Ecclesiastical Commissioners by Dr. Maziere Brady, H.C. 1867–68 (274), liii.

Burials in Churchyard (Ireland), H.C. 1867–68 (370), liii.

Irish Church Bill. Lords Amendments to Commons Amendments to Lords Amendments, and Reasons assigned by the Lords for insisting on certain of their Amendments, H.C. 1868–69 (23), iii.

A Bill to Put an end to the Establishment of the Church of Ireland, and to make Provision in respect of the Temporalities thereof, and in respect of the Royal College of Maynooth, H.C. 1868–69 (27), iii.

A Bill (as Amended in Committee) to Put an end to the Establishment of the Church of Ireland, and to make Provision in respect of the Temporalities thereof, and in respect of the Royal College of Maynooth, H.C. 1868–69 (112), iii.

A Bill (as Amended in Committee and on Consideration as Amended) to Put an end to the Establishment of the Church of Ireland, and to make Provision in respect of the Temporalities thereof, and in respect of the Royal College of Maynooth, H.C. 1868–69 (123), iii.

A Bill (as Amended by the Lords) intitled An Act to put an end to the Establishment of the Church of Ireland, and to make Provision in respect of the Temporalities thereof, and in respect of the Royal College of Maynooth, H.C. 1868–69 (209), iii.

Irish Church Bill. Lords Amendments to Commons Amendments to Lords Amendments, and reasons assigned by the Lords for insisting on certain of their Amendments, H.C. 1868–69 (231), iii.

Irish Church Bill. Commons Amendments to the Lords Amendments, and the Reasons for disagreeing to several of the Lords Amendments, H.C. 1868–69 (232), iii.

Annual Report and Account of the Ecclesiastical Commissioners for Ireland for the Year ended the 1st day of August 1868, H.C. 1868–69 (328), xix.

A Bill to Amend the Thirty-second Section of the Irish Church Act, 1869, H.C. 1871 (244), ii.

Account of the Commissioners of Church Temporalities in Ireland, For the Period from 26 July 1869 to 31 December 1870; together with the Report of the Comptroller and Auditor General thereon, H.C. 1871 (264), lv.

Irish Church Act (Curates' Income), H.C. 1871 (493), lv.

A Bill intitled An Act to amend the Irish Church Act, 1869, so far as respects a Vacancy in the office of Commissioner of Church Temporalities in Ireland, H.C. 1872 (87), ii.

A Bill intitled An Act to amend The Irish Church Act, 1869, H.C. 1872 (284), ii.

Accounts of the Commissioners of Church Temporalities in Ireland, For the Year ended 31st December 1871, from 26 July 1869 (the Commencement of the Commission) to 31st December 1871; together with the Report of the Comptroller and Auditor General thereon, H.C. 1872 (373), xlvi.

Irish Church Act (1869) (Commutation of Tithe Rent Charge). Return to an Order of the Honourable The House of Commons dated 6 June 1873, H.C. 1873 (264), lii.

Irish Church Act (Commutation). Return, H.C. 1875 (52), lvii.

A Bill to Amend the Irish Church Act of 1869, by extending to Lessees and Tenants holding under the Irish Church Act Temporalities Commissioners the right of purchasing the Fee Simple of their Holdings, subject to the Conditions allowed by section seventy of the Act of the thirty-fifth and thirty-sixth years of Victoria, chapter ninety, to purchasers of Tithe Rent-charge, H.C. 1876 (103), iii.

A Bill to Further amend the Irish Church Act Amendment Act, H.C. 1877 (48), ii.

Returns of the Officers and Persons in the Employment of the Commissioners of the Irish Church Temporalities, with a Statement of the Salary, Duties and Date of Appointment of Each; And of the Days in the Year 1876 in which the Court of Appeal Sat and the Number of Appeals Disposed of, H.C. 1877 (122), lxvi.

Returns as to each Diocese, separately, and also of the Totals as to all Ireland, of the Aggregate Amount of the Annual Income now vested in the Commissioners of Irish Church Temporalities, etc., H.C. 1877 (235), lxvi.

A Bill to Amend the Glebe Loan (Ireland) Amendment Act, 1875, H.C. 1878 (9), iii.

A Bill to Amend The Irish Church Act, 1869, and to provide further compensation to certain Persons being Priests and Deacons of the late Established Church of Ireland, H.C. 1880 (sess. 2), (179), iii.

Report of the Comptroller and Auditor General upon the Account of the Commissioners of Church Temporalities in Ireland, For the Year ended 31st December 1880, together with the Account for the above Period, and that from 26th July 1869 (the Commencement of the Commission), to 31st December 1880, H.C. 1881 (268), xxviii.

Return showing the Financial Position of the Irish Church Temporalities Commission, now represented by the Irish Land Commission, H.C. 1882 (153), l.

Statement of the Number of items payable to the Irish Church Temporalities Funds, classified according to their Amount, H.C. 1882 (345), l.

Report of the Comptroller and Auditor General upon the Account of the Irish Land Commission, on Account of Church Temporalities in Ireland,

For the Period from 1st January 1881 to 31st March 1882, together with the Account for the above Period, and that from 26th July 1869 (the Date of the Irish Church Act), to the 31st March 1882, H.C. 1882 (394), l.

Census of Ireland, 1888, Part II, General Report, [C. 3365], H.C. 1882, lxxvi.

Report of the Comptroller and Auditor General upon the Account of the Irish Land Commission, on Account of Church Temporalities in Ireland, For the Year ended 31st March 1883, together with the Account for the above Period, and that from 26th July 1869 (the Date of the Irish Church Act) to the 31st March 1883, H.C. 1884 (54), xxii.

Report of the Comptroller and Auditor General upon the Account of the Irish Land Commission, on Account of Church Temporalities in Ireland, For the Year ended 31st March 1885, together with the Account for the above Period, and that from 26th July 1869 (the Date of the Irish Church Act) to the 31st March 1885, H.C. 1886 (53), xx.

Certain Acts relating to the Parliament of Ireland, H.C. 1886 (124), lii.

BOOKS AND PAMPHLETS

Abbey, Charles J., and Overton, J. H. *The English Church in the Eighteenth Century.* 2 vols. London: Longmans, Green and Co., 1878.

Akenson, Donald H. *The Irish Education Experiment: The National System of Education in the Nineteenth Century.* London: Routledge and Kegan Paul, 1970.

Alexander, Eleanor. *Primate Alexander, Archbishop of Armagh.* London: Edward Arnold, 1913.

Allen, Robert. *The Presbyterian College, Belfast, 1853–1953.* Belfast: William Mullan and Son, Ltd., 1954.

Argyris, Chris. *Integrating the Individual and the Organization.* London: John Wiley and Sons, Inc., 1964.

Babington, R. *The Irish Churchman's "Vade Mecum," or A.B.C. of the Statutes and Canons of the Church of Ireland and of the Diocesan Rules of the Dioceses of Derry and Raphoe.* Londonderry: Londonderry Sentinel Office, 1876.

Ball, J. T. *The Reformed Church of Ireland (1537–1889).* London: Longmans, Green and Co., 1890. Dublin: Hodges, Figgis and Co., 1890.

Barkley, John M. *A Short History of the Presbyterian Church in Ireland.* Belfast: Publications Board, Presbyterian Church in Ireland, 1959.

Beaufort, Daniel A. *Memoir of a Map of Ireland.* London: W. Faden and James Edwards, 1792.

Beckett, J. C. *The Making of Modern Ireland, 1603–1923.* London: Faber and Faber, Ltd., 1966.

————. *Protestant Dissent in Ireland, 1687–1780.* London: Faber and Faber, Ltd., 1948.

Beresford, William, ed. *The Correspondence of the Right Hon. John Beresford, illustrative of the Last Thirty Years of the Irish Parliament.* 2 vols. London: Woodfall and Kinder, 1854.

Bernard, William L. *Decisions under the Irish Church Act, 1869.* 2d ed. Dublin: Alexander Thom, 1871.

Blake, Robert. *Disraeli.* Garden City, New York: Anchor Books, 1968.

Blau, Peter M. *Bureaucracy in Modern Society.* New York: Random House, 1956.

Bolton, F. R. *The Caroline Tradition of the Church of Ireland, with particular reference to Bishop Jeremy Taylor.* London: SPCK, 1958.

Bolton, G. C. *The Passing of the Irish Act of Union: A Study in Parliamentary Politics.* London: Oxford University Press, 1966.

Bowen, Desmond. *The Idea of the Victorian Church. A Study of the Church of England, 1833–1889.* Montreal: McGill University Press, 1968.

Bromley, J. *The Man of Ten Talents: A Portrait of Richard Chenevix Trench, 1807–86, Philologist, Poet, Theologian, Archbishop.* London: SPCK, 1959.

Brooke, Richard S. *Recollections of the Irish Church.* London: MacMillan and Co., 1877.

Brose, Olive J. *Church and Parliament: The Reshaping of the Church of England, 1828–1860.* Stanford: Stanford University Press, 1959.

[Browne, Thomas, et al.] *The Parson's Horn-Book.* 2d ed. Dublin: Browne and Sheehan, 1831.

Chadwick, Owen. *The Victorian Church.* London: Adam and Charles Black, 1966. Part I.

Chaytor, D. G. *The Law and Practice Relating to the Variation of Tithe Rent-Charges in Ireland.* Dublin: William McGee, 1897.

Childe-Pemberton, William S. *The Earl Bishop: The Life of Frederick Hervey, Bishop of Derry, Earl of Bristol.* 2 vols. New York: E. P. Dutton and Co., 1924.

The Church Establishment in Ireland. The Freeman's Journal Church Commission. Dublin: James Duffy, 1868.

Cloncurry, Valentine. *Personal Recollections of the Life and Times, with Extracts from the Correspondence of Valentine Lord Cloncurry.* Dublin: James McGlashan, 1849.

Constitutions and Canons Ecclesiastical, Agreed to and Decreed by the Archbishops, Bishops, and the Representatives of the Clergy and Laity, of the Church of Ireland at a General Synod held in Dublin in the Year of Our Lord, 1871. Dublin: Hodges, Foster and Co., 1871.

Craig, J. Duncan. *Real Pictures of Clerical Life in Ireland*. London: James Nisbet and Co., 1875.

Crone, H. A.; Moody, T. W.; and Quinn, D. B., eds. *Essays in British and Irish History in Honour of James Eadie Todd*. London: Frederick Muller, Ltd., 1949.

Crookshank, C. H. *History of Methodism in Ireland*. 3 vols. Belfast: R. S. Allen; London: T. Woolmer, 1885–88.

Culler, A. Dwight. *The Imperial Intellect: A Study of Newman's Educational Ideal*. New Haven: Yale University Press, 1955.

Curtis, Lewis P. *Chichester Towers*. New Haven: Yale University Press, 1966.

D'Alton, John. *The History of Tithes, Church Lands, and Other Ecclesiastical Benefices, with a Plan for the Abolition of the Former and the Better Distribution of the Latter*. Dublin: Richard Coyne, 1832.

––––––. *The Memoirs of the Archbishops of Dublin*. Dublin: Hodges and Smith, 1838.

Daly, Thomas. *Outline of a Plan for the Abolition of Tithes, and for making a Provision for the Ministers of the Protestant, Established, and Roman Catholic Churches in Ireland*. Dublin: William Wakeman, 1834.

Draft of an Act of Constitution, with Standing Orders and a Finance Report, prepared by the Committee appointed in conformity with the Recommendation of the Lay Conference, to be submitted to the General Convention of the Church of Ireland. Dublin: Hodges, Foster and Co., 1870.

Erck, John C. *The Ecclesiastical Register*. Dublin: J. J. Nolan, 1820.

Essays on the Irish Church by Clergymen of the Established Church in Ireland. 2d ed. Oxford and London: James Parker and Co., 1868.

Fallon, Maura. *Church of Ireland Diocesan Libraries*. Dublin: Library Association of Ireland, 1959.

Finlay, John. *The Office and Duty of Church-Warden and Parish Office in Ireland*. Dublin: John Cumming, 1827.

––––––. *A Treatise on the Law of Tithes in Ireland and Ecclesiastical Law connected therewith*. Dublin: John Cumming, 1828.

Freeman, T. W. *Ireland: A General and Regional Geography*. 3d ed. London: Methuen and Co. Ltd., 1965.

Garstin, John R. *Historical Notices of the Anglican Archbishops of Armagh, Primates of All Ireland, during the nineteenth century*. Dundalk: William Tempest, 1900.

General Convention of the Church of Ireland, Resolutions and Amendments upon which divisions were taken: The Votes of the Delegates; and Tables of Attendance. Dublin: John Robertson and Co., 1870.

Gladstone, William E. *A Chapter of Autobiography*. London: J. Murray, 1868.

————. *The State in Its Relations with the Church*. 2 vols. 4th ed. London: John Murray, 1841.

Godkin, James. *Ireland and Her Churches*. London: Chapman and Hall, 1867.

Gregg, Robert S., ed. *Journal of the General Synod of the Church of Ireland, Second Session, 1872*. Dublin: George Herbert, 1872. *N.B.* The annual journals for 1873 and 1874 were compiled by the same editor and issued by the same publisher.

Hammond, J. L. *Gladstone and the Irish Nation*. London: Longmans, Green and Co. Ltd., 1938. Reprint ed. London: Frank Cass and Co. Ltd., 1964.

Healy, John. *History of the Diocese of Meath*. 2 vols. Dublin: APCK, 1908.

Historical Manuscripts Commission. *The Manuscripts and Correspondence of James, First Earl of Charlemont*, vol. 2. London: HMSO, 1894.

————. *The Manuscripts of the Duke of Beaufort, K.G., the Earl of Donoughmore and others*. London: HMSO, 1891.

————. *The Manuscripts of the Earl of Buckinghamshire, the Earl of Lindsey, the Earl of Onslow, Lord Emly, Theodore J. Hare Esq., and James Round, Esq., M.P.* London: HMSO, 1895.

————. *The Manuscripts of Rye and Hereford Corporations; Capt. Loder-Symonds, Mr. E. R. Wodehouse, M.P., and others*. London: HMSO, 1892.

————. *The Manuscripts of His Grace the Duke of Rutland, K.G., preserved at Belvoir Castle*, vol. 3. London: HMSO, 1894.

————. *The Manuscripts of J. B. Fortescue, Esq., preserved at Dropmore*, vols. 1, 4, 6, 8, 9, 10. London: HMSO, respectively, 1892, 1905, 1908, 1912, 1915, 1927.

————. *The Manuscripts of the Right Honourable F. J. Savile Foljambe, of Osberton*. London: HMSO, 1897.

————. *Reports on the Manuscripts of the Earl of Eglington, Sir J. Stirling Maxwell, Bart., C.S.H. Drummond Moray Esq., C. G. Weston Underwood Esq., and G. Wingfield Digby Esq.* London: HMSO, 1885.

————. *Report on the Manuscripts of the late Reginald Rawdon Hastings, Esq., of the Manor House, Ashby de la Zouche*, vol. 3. London: HMSO, 1934.

————. *Report on the Manuscripts of the Marquess of Lothian preserved at Blickling Hall, Norfolk*. London: HMSO, 1905.

————. *Report on the Manuscripts of Mrs. Stopford-Sackville, of Drayton House, Northamptonshire*, vol. 1. London: HMSO, 1904.

Hume, A. *Results of the Irish Census of 1861, with a special reference to the condition of the Church in Ireland*. London: Rivingtons, 1864.

Jellett, Morgan W. ed. *Journal of the Session of the General Synod of the*

Church of Ireland. Dublin: Hodges, Foster and Co., 1875. *N.B.* The annual journals for 1876 through 1884 were compiled by the same editor and issued by the same publisher.

Johnston, Edith M. *Great Britain and Ireland, 1760–1800: A Study in Political Administration.* Edinburgh: Published for the University Court of the University of St. Andrews, by Oliver and Boyd, 1963.

Johnston, Thomas J.; Robinson, John L.; and Jackson, Robert Wyse. *A History of the Church of Ireland.* Dublin: APCK, 1953.

Jones, M. G. *The Charity School Movement: A Study of Eighteenth Century Puritanism in Action.* Cambridge University Press, 1938. Reprint ed. London: Frank Cass and Co. Ltd., 1964.

Jones, W. Bence. *What Has Been Done in the Irish Church since Disestablishment.* Dublin: Ponsonby, 1875.

Killen, W. D. *The Ecclesiastical History of Ireland.* 2 vols. London: MacMillan and Co., 1875.

Lampson, G. Locker. *A Consideration of the State of Ireland in the Nineteenth Century.* London: Archibald Constable and Co. Ltd., 1907.

Landa, Louis A. *Swift and the Church of Ireland.* Oxford: Clarendon Press, 1954.

Lecky, William E. H. *A History of Ireland in the Eighteenth Century.* 5 vols. New ed. London: Longmans, Green and Co., 1892.

Lee, Alfred T. *The Irish Church Establishment: The Statements of Sir John Gray, M.P., in His Speech Delivered in the House of Commons, April 10, 1866, Examined.* London: Rivington's, 1866.

––––––. *The Irish Church: Its Present Condition, Its Future Prospects.* London: William Skeffington, 1866.

––––––, ed. *Journal of the General Convention of the Church of Ireland, First Session, 1870; with the Statutes passed and an appendix containing the Division Lists, etc.* Dublin: Hodges, Foster and Co., 1870.

––––––. *Journal of the General Convention of the Church of Ireland, Second Session, 1870.* Dublin: Hodges, Foster and Co., 1871.

––––––. *Journal of the General Synod of the Church of Ireland, First Special Meeting and Session of 1871.* Dublin: Edward Purdon, 1872.

Leslie, James. *Armagh Clergy and Parishes.* Dundalk: William Tempest, 1911.

––––––. *Ferns Clergy and Parishes.* Dublin: Church of Ireland Printing and Publishing Co. Ltd., 1936.

McClelland, Vincent A. *Cardinal Manning: His Public Life and Influence, 1865–1892.* London: Oxford University Press, 1962.

MacDonagh, Michael. *The Viceroy's Post-Bag. Correspondence Hitherto Unpublished of the Earl of Hardwicke, First Lord Lieutenant of Ireland after the Union.* London: John Murray, 1904.

MacDonnell, John C. *The Life and Correspondence of William Connor*

Magee, Archbishop of York. 2 vols. London: Isbister and Co. Ltd., 1896.

McDowell, R. B. *The Irish Administration, 1801–1914.* London: Routledge and Kegan Paul, 1964.

———. *Irish Public Opinion, 1750–1800.* London: Faber and Faber Ltd., 1944.

———. *Public Opinion and Government Policy in Ireland, 1801–1846.* London: Faber and Faber Ltd., 1952.

McGregor, Douglas. *The Human Side of Enterprise.* New York: McGraw-Hill Book Co. Inc., 1960.

"McV." *The Advantages of Disestablishment by a Lay Delegate.* Dublin: John Robertson, 1869.

McWalter, J. G. *The Irish Reformation Movement, in Its Religious, Social, and Political Aspects.* Dublin: George Herbert, 1852.

Magnus, Philip. *Gladstone: A Biography.* Paperback ed. London: John Murray, 1963.

Mant, Richard. *History of the Church of Ireland.* 2 vols. London: John W. Parker, 1840.

Marsh, P. T. *The Victorian Church in Decline.* London: Routledge and Kegan Paul, 1969.

Master Brooke's Committee. Papers printed for private circulation. Dublin, 1870.

Mathieson, William L. *English Church Reform, 1815–1840.* London: Longmans, Green and Co., 1923.

Maxwell, Constantia. *Dublin under the Georges, 1714–1830.* 2d rev. ed. London: Faber and Faber Ltd., 1956.

Milne, Kenneth. *The Church of Ireland: A History.* Dublin: APCK, 1966.

Mitchell, B. R., with Deane, Phyllis. *Abstract of British Historical Statistics.* Cambridge: Cambridge University Press, 1962.

Moody, T. W., and Beckett, J. C., eds. *Ulster since 1800: A Social Survey.* London: British Broadcasting Co., 1957.

Moore, H. Kingsmill. *An Unwritten Chapter in the History of Education, being the History of the Society for the Education of the Poor of Ireland, generally known as the Kildare Place Society, 1811–1831.* London: MacMillan and Co., 1904.

The National Synod of the Church of Ireland. The Synods of Armagh and Dublin September, 1869, together with the Journal of the Lower House of the United Synods. Dublin: Hodges, Foster and Co., 1869.

Neill, Stephen. *Anglicanism.* 3d ed. Harmondsworth, Middlesex: Penguin Books Ltd., 1963.

Norman, E. R. *The Catholic Church and Ireland in the Age of Rebellion, 1859–1873.* London: Longmans, Green and Co. Ltd., 1965.

———. *The Catholic Church and Irish Politics in the Eighteen Sixties.*

Dundalk: For the Dublin Historical Association by Dundalgan Press, 1965.

Nowlan, Kevin B. *The Politics of Repeal: A Study in the Relations between Great Britain and Ireland, 1841–50.* London: Routledge and Kegan Paul, 1965.

[O'Beirne, Thomas L.] *A Letter from an Irish Dignitary to an English Clergyman, on the Subject of Tithes in Ireland, written during the Administration of the Duke of Bedford.* Dublin: Richard Milliken, 1822.

O'Brien, R. Barry. *Fifty Years of Concessions to Ireland, 1831–1881,* vol. 1. London: Sampson Law and Co., 1885.

Orders and Regulations agreed upon by the Trustees and Commissioners of the First Fruits Payable out of Ecclesiastical Benefices in Ireland. Origin unspecified, 1811.

Otway-Ruthven, A. J. *A History of Medieval Ireland.* London: Ernest Benn Ltd., 1968.

Parnell, Henry. *A History of the Penal Laws against the Irish Catholics; from the Treaty of Limerick to the Union.* London: J. Harding, 1808.

Patton, Henry E. *Fifty Years of Disestablishment.* Dublin: APCK, 1922.

———. *History of the Church of Ireland, for use in schools.* 7th ed. Dublin: APCK, 1961.

Peaston, A. Elliott. *The Prayer Book Revisions of the Victorian Evangelicals.* Dublin: APCK, 1963.

Phillips, Walter A., ed. *History of the Church of Ireland from the earliest times to the present day.* 3 vols. London: Oxford University Press, 1933.

Powicke, F. Maurice, and Fryde, E. B., eds. *Handbook of British Chronology.* 2d ed. London: Royal Historical Society, 1961.

Proposed Amended Draft of an Act of Constitution, to be submitted to the General Convention of the Church of Ireland. Belfast: William and George Baird, 1870.

Reade, John. *Observations upon Tythes and Rents addressed to the Clergy and Impropriators of Ireland.* 2d ed. Dublin: C. P. Archer, 1818.

Representative Church Body. *Report on Commutation.* Dublin: Hodges, Foster and Co., 1870.

———. *Report of the Proceedings laid before the General Synod of the Church of Ireland at its Second Ordinary Session, 1872.* Dublin: Hodges, Foster and Co., 1872. *N.B.* The annual reports 1873 through 1884 were by the same publisher.

———. *Report of the Representative Church Body of the Church of Ireland.* Dublin: Edward Purdon, 1871.

———. *Resolutions in connection with Commutation and Compounding.* Dublin: Representative Church Body, 1870.

Reynolds, James A. *The Catholic Emancipation Crisis in Ireland, 1823–1829.* New Haven: Yale University Press, 1954.

The Rights of the Clergy of Ireland Candidly Considered by a Friend of the Constitution. Dublin: G. Faulkner, 1767.

Seddall, Henry. *The Church of Ireland: A Historical Sketch.* Dublin: Hodges, Figgis and Co., 1886.

Seymour, St. John D. *The Diocese of Emly.* Dublin: Church of Ireland Printing and Publishing Co. Ltd., 1913.

Sherlock, W. *Suggestions toward the Organization of the Church of Ireland, based on that of the Reformed Episcopal Churches Abroad.* Dublin: Hodges, Foster and Co., 1869.

Smyth, George L. *Ireland: Historical and Statistical.* 3 vols. London, 1844.

Sources for the Study of Local History in Northern Ireland. Belfast: Northern Ireland Public Record Office, 1968.

Statutes passed at the First Session of the General Convention, 1870. Dublin: Hodges, Foster and Co., 1870.

Stopford, Edward A. *A Hand-Book of Ecclesiastical Law and Duty for the Use of the Irish Clergy.* Dublin: Hodges, Smith and Co., 1861.

Sykes, Norman. *Church and State in England in the XVIIIth Century.* Cambridge University Press, 1934. Reprint ed. Hamden, Conn.: Archon Books, 1962.

Thornley, David. *Isaac Butt and Home Rule.* London: MacGibbon and Kee, 1964.

[Trench, Maria M.] *Richard Chenevix Trench, Archbishop, Letters and Memorials.* 2 vols. London: Kegan Paul, Trench and Co., 1888.

[Untitled]. Bound Collection of private, printed papers of the Prayer Book Revision Committee, n.d., found in National Library of Ireland.

[Untitled]. Memorandum on the Established Church. Printed, origin unspecified, c. 1865, found in National Library of Ireland.

Vane, Charles. *Memoirs and Correspondence of Viscount Castlereagh, Second Marquess of Londonderry,* vol. 3. London: Henry Colburn, 1849.

Wade, John. *The Extraordinary Black Book, etc.* London: Effingham Wilson, 1831.

Wall, Maureen. *The Penal Laws, 1691–1760.* 2d ed. Dundalk: Dundalgan Press Ltd., 1967.

Warren, Robert R. *The Law of the Church of Ireland.* Dublin: William McGee, 1895.

Whately, E. Jane. *Life and Correspondence of Richard Whately, D.D., Late Archbishop of Dublin.* 2 vols. London: Longmans, Green and Co., 1866.

[Whately, Richard]. *Letter from the Archbishop of Dublin to His Excellency the Lord Lieutenant of Ireland relative to the Re-Establishment of the Bishoprick of Kildare, in Union with that of Leighlin.* London: Printed for private circulation, by John W. Parker, 1842.

Whyte, J. H. *The Independent Irish Party, 1850–9.* London: Oxford University Press, 1958.

Wilberforce, Reginald G. *Life of the Right Reverend Samuel Wilberforce, D.D.,* vol. 3. London: John Murray, 1887.

Wilberforce, Samuel. *A History of the Protestant Episcopal Church in America.* New York: Stanford and Swords, 1849.

Williams, Basil. *The Whig Supremacy, 1714–1760.* Oxford: Clarendon Press, 1939.

Woodward, Llewellyn. *The Age of Reform, 1815–1870.* 2d ed. Oxford: Clarendon Press, 1962.

[Woodward, Richard]. *The Present State of the Church of Ireland.* 7th ed. Dublin: W. Sleater, 1787.

ARTICLES

"Appropriation of Church Property." *Edinburgh Review* (American edition) 60 (January 1835):251–72.

Beckett, J. C. "Anglo-Irish Constitutional Relations in the Later Eighteenth Century." *Irish Historical Studies* 14 (March 1964):20–38.

————. "Gladstone, Queen Victoria, and the Disestablishment of the Irish Church, 1868–9." *Irish Historical Studies* 13 (March 1962):38–47.

————. "The Government and the Church of Ireland under William III and Anne." *Irish Historical Studies* 2 (March 1941):280–302.

————. "William King's Administration of the Diocese of Derry, 1691–1703." *Irish Historical Studies* 4 (September 1944):164–80.

Brose, Olive J. "The Irish Precedent for English Church Reform: The Church Temporalities Act of 1833." *Journal of Ecclesiastical History* 7 (October 1956):204–25.

Buckler, F. W. "The Establishment of the Church of England: Its Constitutional and Legal Significance." *Church History* 10 (March 1941):299–346.

Burns, Robert E. "The Irish Penal Code and Some of Its Historians." *Review of Politics* 21 (January 1959):276–99.

————. "The Irish Popery Laws: A Study of Eighteenth-Century Legislation and Behavior." *Review of Politics* 24 (October 1962):485–508.

Chadwick, George A. "The Disestablished Church of Ireland—I. Finance." *The Churchman* 3 (October 1880):1–12.

————. "The Disestablished Church of Ireland—II. The Constitution." *The Churchman* 3 (November 1880):81–88.

————. "The Disestablished Church of Ireland—III. Revision." *The Churchman* 3 (December 1880):161–73.

"The Church of Ireland." *Church Quarterly Review* 29 (January 1885):447–80.

"Church of Ireland Finance." *Church Quarterly Review* 60 (July 1905): 302–16.

Davis, C. H. "The Irish Convocation." *Church of England Magazine* 55 (25 July 1863):49–52.

"The Disestablished Church in Ireland." *Fraser's Magazine,* n.s. 6 (August 1872):135–49.

[Mrs.] Finian Fields. "Origins of Local Government in Ireland." *Eire-Ireland* 1 (Winter 1966):69–79.

"Four Years' Experience of Disestablishment—Part I." *Christian Observer and Advocate,* n.s. 1 (January 1875):25–40.

"Four Years' Experience of Disestablishment—Part II." *Christian Observer and Advocate,* n.s. 2 (February 1875):113–22.

"Four Years' Experience of Disestablishment—Part III." *Christian Observer and Advocate,* n.s., no. 3 (March 1875):215–26.

Henning, John. "The Anglican Church in Ireland: Prayers against Irish Rebels." *Irish Ecclesiastical Record,* 5 ser., 64 (October 1944):247–54.

"Hibernian Sunday School Society." *Christian Observer* 13 (December 1814):845–49.

"The Irish Church Act, 1869." *London Quarterly Review* (American edition), 127 (July–October 1869):259–70.

"The Irish Church Bill." *Fraser's Magazine* 80 (August 1869):257–72.

"Irish Church Bill." *London Quarterly Review* (American edition), 126 (April 1868):291–306.

"The Irish Church Question." *British Quarterly Review* 47 (April 1868): 487–505.

Larkin, Emmet. "Church and State in Ireland in the Nineteenth Century." *Church History* 31 (September 1962):294–306.

————. "Economic Growth, Capital Investment, and the Roman Catholic Church in Nineteenth-Century Ireland." *American Historical Review* 72 (April 1967):852–84.

Lewis, Clyde J. "The Disintegration of the Tory-Anglican Alliance in the Struggle for Catholic Emancipation." *Church History* 29 (March 1960): 25–43.

"Life and Correspondence of Archbishop Whately." *Christian Observer,* n.s., no. 350 (February 1867):88–105.

McCracken, J. L. "The Conflict between the Irish Administration and Parliament, 1753–6." *Irish Historical Studies* 3 (September 1942):159–79.

MacDonnell, John C. "Irish Church Politics and Church History." *Contemporary Review* 3 (1866):392–409.

McDougall, Donald J. "George III, Pitt, and the Irish Catholics, 1801–1805." *Catholic Historical Review* 31 (October 1945):255–81.

Mahaffy, J. P. "The Romanisation of Ireland." *Nineteenth Century* 50 (July 1901):30–43.

"The Ministry and the Irish Church." *Fraser's Magazine* 79 (January 1869):113–34.

Murphy, J. A. "The support of the Catholic Clergy in Ireland, 1750–1850." In J. L. McCracken, ed. *Historical Studies,* vol. 5 (London: Bowes and Bowes, 1965), pp. 103–21.

Nowlan, Kevin B. "The Relations between Church and State in the Age of Emancipation." *Proceedings of the Irish Catholic Historical Committee, 1961* (Dublin: M. H. Gill and Son Ltd., 1960), pp. 25–31.

O'Donoghue, Patrick. "Causes of the Opposition to Tithes, 1830–38." *Studia Hibernica,* no. 5 (1965), pp. 7–28.

———. "Opposition to Tithe Payments in 1830–31." *Studia Hibernica,* no. 6 (1966), pp. 69–98.

Pauck, Wilhelm. "The Nature of Protestantism," *Church History* 6 (March 1937):3–23.

"Prayer-Book Revision in the Church of Ireland." *Christian Observer,* n.s., no. 8 (August 1877), pp. 681–95.

"Reconstruction of the Irish Church." *London Quarterly Review* (American edition) 33 (January 1870):397–417.

"The Religious Movement in Ireland." *Church of England Magazine* 47 (3 December 1859):365–67.

"Results of Disestablishment in Ireland." *British Quarterly Review* 56 (July 1872):195–232.

"Review of Irish Episcopal Charges." *Christian Observer,* n.s., no. 69 (September 1843), pp. 614–30.

Roche, Kennedy F. "The Relations of the Catholic Church and the State in England and Ireland, 1800–1852." In James Hogan, ed., *Historical Studies,* vol. 3 (London: Bowes and Bowes; Cork: Cork University Press, 1961), pp. 9–24.

Shearman, Hugh. "State-aided Land Purchase under the Disestablishment Act of 1869." *Irish Historical Studies* 4 (March 1944):58–80.

Simms, J. G. "Irish Catholics and the Parliamentary Franchise, 1692–1728." *Irish Historical Studies* 12 (March 1960):28–37.

Spence, John L. "Life in Early Eighteenth Century Rural Ulster as reflected in a Parish Record Book." *Ulster Journal of Archaeology,* 3 ser., 6 (1943):35–38.

Stephen, M. D. "Liberty, Church and State: Gladstone's Relations with Manning and Acton, 1832–70." *Journal of Religious History* 1 (December 1961):217–32.

"Synods of the Church in Ireland." *Literary Churchman* 11 (30 December 1865):549–53.

"View of Public Affairs." *Christian Observer,* no. 390 (June 1834), pp. 445–49.

"View of Public Affairs." *Christian Observer,* no. 408 (December 1835): pp. 819–24.

[Wall], Maureen McGeehin. "The Catholics of the Towns and the Quarterage Dispute in Eighteenth-Century Ireland." *Irish Historical Studies* 7 (September 1952):91–114.

Whately, E. W. "The Constitution of the Church of Ireland." *The Churchman* 1 (October 1879):123–27.

"Richard Whately." *Dublin Review,* n.s. 8 (January 1867):1–25.

Wheeler, H. A. "St. Michael's Parish." *Dublin Historical Record* 15 (January 1960):97–104.

Whyte, John H. "The Appointment of Catholic Bishops in Nineteenth-Century Ireland." *Catholic Historical Review* 48 (April 1962):12–32.

———. "Bishop Moriarty on Disestablishment and the Union, 1868." *Irish Historical Studies* 10 (September 1956):193–99.

Young, E. J. "St. Michan's Parish in the Eighteenth Century." *Dublin Historical Record* 3 (September–November 1940):1–7.

Index